MOON HANDBOOKS
VIRGINIA

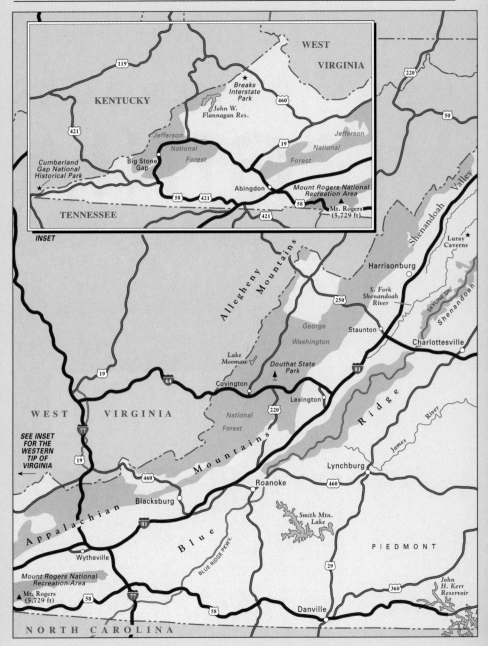

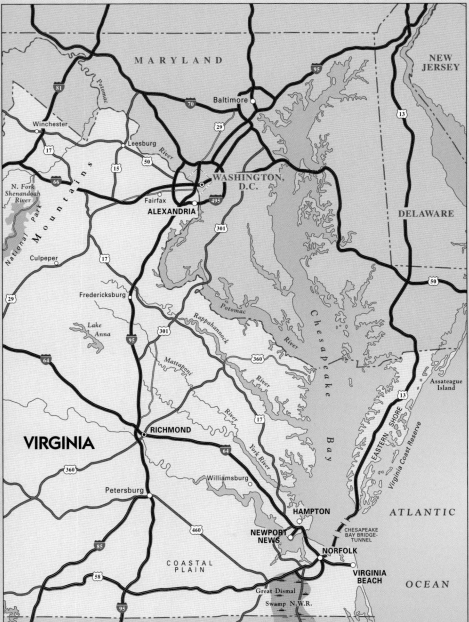

reconstructed settlers' ships,
Jamestown settlement

MOON HANDBOOKS

VIRGINIA

INCLUDING WASHINGTON, D.C.

SECOND EDITION

JULIAN SMITH

AVALON
TRAVEL

Moon Handbooks: Virginia
Including Washington, D.C.
Second Edition

Julian Smith

Published by
Avalon Travel Publishing
5855 Beaudry Street
Emeryville, CA 94608, USA

Printing History
First edition—1999
Second edition—April 2002
5 4 3 2 1

Please send all comments, corrections,
additions, amendments, and critiques to:

Moon Handbooks: Virginia
AVALON TRAVEL PUBLISHING
5855 BEAUDRY ST.
EMERYVILLE, CA 94608, USA
email: atpfeedback@avalonpub.com
website: www.moon.com

ISBN: 1-56691-394-2
ISSN: 1537-5803

Editor: Kevin McLain
Series Manager: Erin Van Rheenen
Copy Editor: Ginjer Clarke
Graphics: Melissa Sherowski, Erika Howsare
Production: Amber Pirker
Map Editors: Naomi Adler Dancis, Olivia Solis
Cartography: Mike Morgenfeld, Suzanne Service, Chris Folks, Kat Kalamaras
Index: Vera Gross

Front cover photo: © James Lemass

Distributed by Publishers Group West

Printed in the United States by R.R. Donnelley

ABOUT THE AUTHOR
Julian Smith

I travel a lot; I hate having my life disrupted by routine.

—Caskie Stinnett

Born and raised in New York State, Julian Smith has been writing since he could read, and traveling since his first family vacation. His affection for Virginia developed during four years at the state's university, where he wrote for local publications, played in a few bands, explored the Blue Ridge, and managed to wrangle a B.A. from the Biology Department.

He gained valuable travel writing experience with a self-publishing venture that nine months later resulted in the one-pound, eight-ounce *On Your Own in El Salvador*, the first in-depth travel guide to the country. His *Moon Handbooks: Ecuador* came two years later.

Thinking it might be fun to write a guidebook to a place where he spoke the language at above a third-grade level, Julian returned to Virginia, where everyone kept saying the same thing: "Oh, you're still here?" And there was much rejoicing. Since then he has contributed to *Road Trip USA, Road Trip USA: California and the Southwest*, and others.

As far as other jobs for travel writers go, Julian has done pretty well. He's worked as a National Park ranger, guided tourists through the Central American rainforest, and tried (futilely) to protect the organic vegetable garden of one of the richest men in the world from marauding rodents.

Along the way he's found himself freezing atop Kilimanjaro, meditating in a Japanese Zen temple, doused with rum in a Cuban santería ceremony, and fleeing from pygmies in Uganda, through no fault of his own—honestly.

Snowboarding, mountain biking, and rock climbing keep things interesting (and orthopedists in business) out West, where he recently completed a master's degree in Wildlife Ecology in the mountains of northern Utah. Who knows where he'll be by the time you read this, but wherever it is, three things are guaranteed—Little Debbie Swiss Rolls, funky music, and *The Simpsons*.

Contents

INTRODUCTION **1**

THE LAND **2**
Natural History, The Mountains; Central Virginia; The Coast; Climate; Conservation

HISTORY **9**
Precolonial Era; The Colonial Period; The Revolutionary War; Between the Wars;
The Civil War; 20th Century

ECONOMY AND GOVERNMENT **25**
Economy; Government

THE PEOPLE **26**
Settlement; Current Statistics; Attitudes

SPECIAL TOPICS

Best Virginia Town Names *2*	*Captain John Smith* *12*
Conservation Organizations	*Virginia's Eight Presidents* *17*
and State Agencies *6*	*Soldiers and Politicians* *20*
Virginia's Tribes Today...................*11*	*Key Dates in Virginia History* *24*

ON THE ROAD **29**

OUTDOOR RECREATION **29**
General Resources; Hiking and Camping; Bicycling; Horseback Riding;
Climbing; Rafting, Kayaking, and Canoeing; Boating; Surfing; Fishing; Hunting;
Birdwatching; Caves and Caverns; Skiing; Golf; More Outdoor Recreation

CIVIL WAR–RELATED ACTIVITIES **40**
Reenactments; Civil War Trails

ORGANIZED TOURS **41**
Bus Tours; Outdoor Tours

HOLIDAYS AND FESTIVALS **42**

SHOPPING **44**
Crafts; Antiques; Local Specialties; Taxes

ACCOMMODATIONS **45**
Price Ranges; Hotels and Motels; More Personal; Camping; Youth Hostels; Home
Stays; Home Exchanges; Traveling with Pets

FOOD **48**
Classic Country Cuisine (a.k.a. Home Cookin'); Seafood; Virginia Wine

TRANSPORTATION **51**
By Car; By Bus; By Train; By Air

INFORMATION AND SERVICES **55**
When to Go; Health and Safety; Maps; Information; Money; Student Travel; Gay
and Lesbian Travelers; Travelers With Disabilities; Traveling With Children;
Senior Travelers; Travel Insurance; Time Zones; Business Hours; Tipping

SPECIAL TOPICS

Dirt Rules 31
Virginia Cycling Clubs 32
One Nation, Underground 36
Fly the Friendly Skies 39
Virginia's Offbeat Best 42
Virginia's Best Music Events 43
Virginia Hotel Chains 46

Virginia's Best Romantic Getaways 47
Crab Lingo 49
Resources for Drivers 51
Major Car Rental Companies 52
Travel Insurance Companies 53
Amtrak Virginia Lines 54
Major Airlines Serving Virginia 54

CENTRAL VIRGINIA 60
Highlights; Access

RICHMOND AND VICINITY 62
History; Orientation; Safety; Central Richmond; Jackson Ward; The Fan; South
of the Fan; Carytown; Riverfront; Shockoe Slip; Shockoe Bottom; Church Hill;
Other Sights; Accommodations; Food; Nightlife; The Arts; Shopping; Recreation;
Events; Transportation; Information; Near Richmond

PETERSBURG AND VICINITY 88
History; Sights; Accommodations; Food; Entertainment and Recreation; Events;
Transportation; Information

FREDERICKSBURG AND VICINITY 93
History; Sights; Accommodations; Food; Entertainment and Recreation; Events;
Transportation; Information; Across the River; Fredericksburg and Spotsylvania
National Military Park

CHARLOTTESVILLE 102
History; Orientation; Sights; Accommodations; Food; Entertainment; Recreation;
Shopping; Events; Transportation; Information

CHARLOTTESVILLE VICINITY 112
North of Charlottesville; West of Charlottesville; South of Charlottesville

LYNCHBURG AND VICINITY 119
History; Sights; Accommodations; Food; Entertainment; Shopping; Events;
Transportation; Information; Thomas Jefferson's Poplar Forest; Bedford;
Appomattox Court House National Historic Park; Yogaville; Smith Mountain
Lake; Booker T. Washington National Monument

DANVILLE 130
History; Orientation; Sights; Accommodations; Food; Events; Information

SPECIAL TOPICS

Fighting for Richmond 67
Central Virginia Wineries 80
African American History in Petersburg 89
George's Lie 90
The Crater Fiasco 91
Food and Fun in Emporia 92
The Virginia Statute of Religious Freedom 93

The Inn at Little Washington 113
Thomas Jefferson 116
The Virginia Garlic Festival 118
The Beale Treasure .122
Luckless Wilmer Mclean 127
The Wreck of the Old 97 131

THE COAST **134**
Highlights; Access
NORTHERN NECK 135
George Washington Birthplace National Monument; Westmoreland State Park;
Stratford Hall Plantation; Reedville; Irvington and Vicinity
MIDDLE NECK 140
Urbanna; Indian Reservations
COLONIAL WILLIAMSBURG 141
History; Visiting Colonial Williamsburg; Historical Sights; Other Sights;
Accommodations; Food; Recreation; Events; Transportation; Information; Near
Williamsburg; Jamestown; Yorktown; James River Plantations
NORTHERN HAMPTON ROADS 162
Newport News; Hampton
NORFOLK AND VICINITY 170
History; Sights; Accommodations; Food; Entertainment and Recreation; Events;
Transportation; Information; Portsmouth; Great Dismal Swamp National
Wildlife Refuge
VIRGINIA BEACH AND VICINITY 183
Sights; Accommodations; Food; Water Sports; Other Activities; Entertainment;
Shopping; Events; Transportation; Information; Back Bay National Wildlife
Refuge; False Cape State Park
THE EASTERN SHORE 196
Eastern Shore of Virginia National Wildlife Refuge; Kiptopeke State Park; Cape
Charles; Eastville; Wachapreague; Onancock; Onancock to Chincoteague;
Chincoteague; Assateague Island and Chincoteague National Wildlife Refuge;
Tangier Island

SPECIAL TOPICS
Westmoreland Berry Farm and Orchard 138   Bonny Barbara Allen 186
Coast Area Wineries 144   The Chesapeake Bay Bridge-Tunnel 199
You Can't Drive the Hampton Roads.......163   Offshore Eden 201
Naturally Yours Tour 165   The Town That Turned
Rockin' Roads 166   Paul Newman Down.................210

SOUTHWEST VIRGINIA **213**
Highlights; Access; Resources
ROANOKE AND VICINITY 215
History; Orientation; Sights; Accommodations; Food; Shopping; Entertainment;
Events; Transportation; Information; Near Roanoke
BLACKSBURG AND VICINITY 226
History; Virginia Tech; Accommodations; Food; Entertainment and Recreation;
Transportation; Information; Mountain Lake and Vicinity
NEW RIVER VALLEY 231
Wytheville; Galax; New River Trail State Park; Mt. Rogers National Recreation Area

ABINGDON **237**
History; Sights; Accommodations; Food; Entertainment and Recreation; Events;
Shopping; Information and Transportation

FAR SOUTHWEST **242**
Tazewell and Vicinity; Breaks Interstate Park; Big Stone Gap; Natural Tunnel
State Park; Cumberland Gap National Historical Park

SPECIAL TOPICS

Southwestern Virginia Wineries *221*	*The Saltville Massacre* *237*
The Electronic Village *227*	*King Coal* *244*
The Great Frontier Escape *229*	*Burke's Garden* *246*
The Birthplace of Mountain Dew & Dr. Pepper 232	*Country Music's Legendary Carter Family* . . .*248*

THE SHENANDOAH **250**
Highlights; Access; Resources

WINCHESTER AND VICINITY **254**
History; Sights; Accommodations; Food; Entertainment; Events; Shopping;
Information; Near Winchester

THE NORTHERN VALLEY **261**
Front Royal; Strasburg; West of the Interstate; New Market and Vicinity; Luray

SHENANDOAH NATIONAL PARK **269**
History; Habitats; Access; Hiking; Other Recreation; Accommodations,
Camping, and Services; Information

HARRISONBURG AND VICINITY **276**
History; Sights; Accommodations; Food; Entertainment; Shopping; Events;
Information; Near Harrisonburg

STAUNTON AND VICINITY **281**
History; Sights; Accommodations; Food; Entertainment and Tours; Events;
Shopping; Information and Transportation; Waynesboro

ALLEGHENY HIGHLANDS **287**
Outdoor Recreation; Access; Monterey; Ramsey's Draft Wilderness Area; Warm
Springs; On the Road to Hot Springs; Hot Springs; Douthat State Park

LEXINGTON **293**
Sights; Accommodations; Food; Entertainment and Recreation; Events;
Shopping; Information and Transportation

SOUTH OF LEXINGTON **301**
Natural Bridge; Blue Ridge Parkway

SPECIAL TOPICS

Civil War in the Shenandoah *252*	*"Mad Ann" Bailey* *281*
Patsy Cline Chronology *256*	*Frontier Culture Museum* *283*
Mata Hari of the Confederacy *261*	*The Great Oil Hoax of 1895* *287*
Shenandoah Area Wineries *267*	*Humpback Covered Bridge* *288*
The Appalachian Trail *270*	*Stonewall Jackson* *296*
Ghosts of Harrisonburg *278*	*The Devil's Marbleyard* *303*

NORTHERN VIRGINIA **305**

Highlights; Arriving and Getting Around

ARLINGTON COUNTY AND VICINITY 308

History; Arlington National Cemetery; Near Arlington National Cemetery; Accommodations; Food; Entertainment and Recreation; Events; Information

OLD TOWN ALEXANDRIA 317

History; Orientation; Sights; Accommodations; Food; Entertainment and Recreation; Events; Shopping; Transportation; Information

NEAR THE BELTWAY 326

McLean; Great Falls Park; Riverbend Park; Great Falls Town; Wolf Trap Farm Park

HUNT COUNTRY 329

Manassas National Battlefield Park; Bull Run Regional Park; Leesburg; Vicinity of Leesburg; Middleburg and Vicinity; Sky Meadows State Park

DOWN THE POTOMAC 340

Huntley Meadows Park; Mount Vernon; Woodlawn Plantation; Mason Neck; Prince William Forest Park

SPECIAL TOPICS

D.C.'s Missing Piece *309*	*A Man's Home Is. . .*	
Sprawl *314*	*Something Else Entirely* *331*	
Washington & Old Dominion Trail *324*	*Northern Virginia Wineries*..............*332*	
Hunt Country Fun *329*	*The Gray Ghost of Loudoun County* *338*	

SIDE TRIP TO D.C. **344**

HISTORY 344

THE MALL SIGHTS 346

Smithsonian Institution

MORE CAPITAL SIGHTS 353

Tidal Basin; Capitol Hill; The White House; Old Downtown and the Federal Triangle; Adams-Morgan; Upper Northwest; Georgetown; East of the Capitol

ACCOMMODATIONS 366

Under $50; $50–100; $100–150; $150–250; Over $250

FOOD 370

Politically Correct; Expensive; Fun

ENTERTAINMENT AND NIGHTLIFE 372

Clubs; Theater and Concerts; Comedy; More Events and Entertainment

TRANSPORTATION 375

Getting There; Getting Around

SPECIAL TOPICS

Using the Metro in D.C. *348*	*the Life Span of Money* *356*

RESOURCES 377
SUGGESTED READING 378
INTERNET RESOURCES 382
INDEX...384

Keeping Current

Writing a guidebook is a never-ending process—the printed page is only a snapshot of the constant flux of prices, recipes, operating hours, openings, and closings. We welcome your comments, corrections, even the occasional polite rant—anything that will make the next edition of *Moon Handbooks: Virginia* better, or at least more fun to read. Thanks ahead of time, and send it all to:

Moon Handbooks: Virginia
Avalon Travel Publishing
5855 Beaudry Street
Emeryville, CA 94608
email: atpfeedback@avalonpub.com

Abbreviations

AAA—American Automobile Association
AT—Appalachian Trail
AYH—American Youth Hostels
DCR—Virginia Department of Conservation and Recreation
d—double occupancy

HI—Hostelling International
mph—miles per hour
pp—per person
Rt.—Route
s—single occupancy
VTC—Virginia Tourism Corporation

Maps

Virginia .ii–iii

INTRODUCTION

The Civil War in Virginia 18–19

ON THE ROAD

Driving Distances 53

CENTRAL VIRGINIA

Central Virginia 64–65
Richmond and Petersburg Vicinity 66
Downtown Richmond 70–71
Fredericksburg 94
Downtown Fredericksburg 95
Charlottesville 103
Downtown Mall Area 106
Lynchburg .120
Downtown Lynchburg 121

THE COAST

The Coast 136–137
Williamsburg 142–143
James River Plantations 160
Newport News and Hampton 164
Norfolk and Vicinity 171
Downtown Norfolk 172
Virginia Beach 184
The Eastern Shore 197

SOUTHWEST VIRGINIA

Southwest Virginia 214–215
Roanoke Valley 216
Downtown Roanoke 218
Abingdon .238

THE SHENANDOAH

The Shenandoah 251
Civil War in the Shenandoah 253
Winchester 255
The Appalachian Trail 270
Harrisonburg 277
Staunton 282
Lexington .294

NORTHERN VIRGINIA

Northern Virginia 306–307
Arlington County and Vicinity . . .310–311
Old Town Alexandria 318
Leesburg 334

SIDETRIP TO D.C.

Washington, D.C. and Vicinity 345
The Mall 346–347
The Metro .349
Central Washington, D.C. 354–355

═══ Divided Highway	⊛ National Capital	☛	National Battlefield Park
═══ Primary Road	◉ State Capital		
─── Secondary Road	○ City	⚑	State Park
▪▪▪▪ Tunnel	○ Town	ᴧ	Campground
┄┄┄ Trail	★ Point of Interest	⛷	Ski Area
⬯ U.S. Interstate	• Accommodation	├───┤	Railroad
⬯ U.S. Highway	▾ Restaurant/Bar	⋯⋯	Ferry
◯ State Highway	▪ Other Location	Ⓜ	Metro Station
▢ County Road	✶ International Airport	▲	Mountain
	✗ Airfield/Airstrip	⚓	Swamp

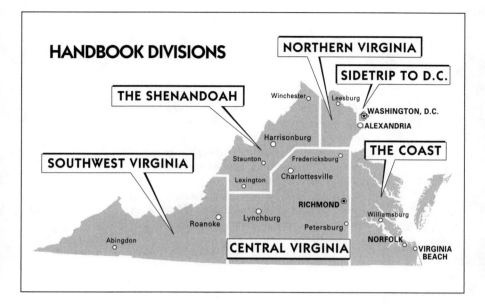

HANDBOOK DIVISIONS

NORTHERN VIRGINIA

SIDETRIP TO D.C.

THE SHENANDOAH

Winchester

Leesburg

WASHINGTON, D.C.
ALEXANDRIA

Harrisonburg

Staunton

Fredericksburg

THE COAST

SOUTHWEST VIRGINIA

Charlottesville

Lexington

RICHMOND

Williamsburg

Roanoke

Lynchburg

Petersburg

Abingdon

CENTRAL VIRGINIA

NORFOLK

VIRGINIA BEACH

I saw in their eyes something I was to see over and over in every part of the nation—a burning desire to go, to move, to get under way, anyplace, away from any Here. They spoke quietly of how they wanted to go someday, to move about, free and unanchored, not toward something but away from something. I saw this look and heard this yearning everywhere in every state I visited. Nearly every American hungers to move.

John Steinbeck, *Travels With Charley*

Introduction

President John F. Kennedy once described Washington, D.C., as a city of "northern charm and southern efficiency." Just across the Potomac spreads a state that's pretty much the opposite, and proud of it. From the banking towers of Richmond to the most remote Blue Ridge farm, Virginia embodies the best of the two worlds it bridges and the result is one of the most fascinating and endearing states in the country.

Any American who's sat through the seventh grade knows Virginia oozes history from every pore like few other states in the Union. Virginia's story is really the story of the United States itself. The American Revolution ended a few miles away from Jamestown, where the first European settlers in the New World landed in 1607. The Civil War began and ended here, and more battles raged in Virginia than anywhere else.

Virginia's gorgeous scenery is one reason the state has always been such a magnetic lure, first for settlers and now for visitors. To the west, the sublime Shenandoah Valley borders the Blue Ridge Mountains, which tumble eastward into the patrician pasturage of the Piedmont and Tidewater. Virginia's coast is a world in itself, embracing vistas of open ocean, windswept islands, and the moody waters of one of the largest bays in the world.

All around the state lies an abundance of antique stores, plantation homes, B&Bs, historic monuments, and world-class museums. Cities of all sizes host concerts, fairs, and festivals throughout the year, while the buds of spring and the fiery autumn colors set their own calendar. Lovers of the outdoors are drawn to mountain biking, river rafting, fishing, skiing, and hiking galore from one end to the other.

Best of all, though, in this state of 40-cent soda machines and billion-dollar aircraft carriers, urban sprawl and

Bull Run Castle

wild ponies, are the Virginians themselves. Any visitor who ventures beyond the interstates and must-see hordes will quickly discover Virginia's true treasure: her inhabitants, who embody the best of Kennedy's two criteria—southern warmth, northern know-how—along with a generous helping of that unique ingredient summed up in the popular quotation:

To be a Virginian, either by birth,
marriage, or adoption,
Or even on one's mother's side
Is an introduction to any state in
the union,
A passport to any foreign country,
And a benediction from Almighty God.

The Land

Heaven and Earth never agreed to frame a better place for man's habitation. Here are mountains, hills, plaines, valleyes, rivers, and brookes, all running into a faire Bay, compassed but for the mouth, with fruitful and delightsome land.
—Captain John Smith, 1607

Virginia stretches from the Appalachian Mountains to the Atlantic Ocean, encompassing the three distinct physical regions of the Mid-Atlantic. The state's 40,767 square miles start in rugged **mountains** in the west, then spread across a flat, fertile **central region** known as the Piedmont. A defined drop-off, about even with Richmond, marks the beginning of the **coastal plain** or Tidewater, drained by rivers flowing into Chesapeake Bay. Across the bay the southernmost splinter of the peninsula that protects the Chesapeake Bay—Virginia's Eastern Shore—faces the open Atlantic.

More than anything, Virginia's landscape is defined by water. Natural waterways attracted the first colonizers to sheltered harbors and lured

explorers upriver into the heart of the country. Four major rivers—the Potomac, York, Rappahannock, and James—reach as far as the West Virginia border for their headwaters. Incredibly fertile soil provided the early colonists with productive farmland. The serpentine rivers carried flatboats laden with cotton and tobacco downriver on their first step to the warehouses of Europe. And always the mountains stood to the west, a dramatic backdrop where life changes little as the years roll by.

NATURAL HISTORY

During the Paleozoic Era (620–230 million years ago), all of Virginia west of the Blue Ridge and part of the Piedmont lay under a great inland sea. Geologic upheavals thrust beds of sediment to mountainous heights. Today we can see evidence of those upheavals in marine fossils embedded in limestone hillsides. The Appalachian Mountains began to rise in the Mesozoic Era (230–70 million years ago), only to be gradually worn down by wind and water into their present rounded contours. Debris washed down from the eastern slopes created the deltas and floodplains of ocean-bound rivers, creating rich farmland all the way to the coast.

Reaching into two geographic provinces, Virginia hosts both northern and southern species of flora and fauna at the extremes of their natural ranges. Visitors can see two seasons in a day simply by driving from the base of the Blue Ridge, where spring buds are blooming, to the top, where bare trees of winter remain. It's also possible to see northern tree species such as fir and

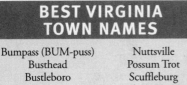

BEST VIRGINIA TOWN NAMES

Bumpass (BUM-puss)	Nuttsville
Busthead	Possum Trot
Bustleboro	Scuffleburg
Lively	Short Pump
Hurt	Simplicity
Modest Town	Village
Mollusk	

© JULIAN SMITH

idyllic rural Virginia

palachians, soaring from the nearly flat farmland of the central part of the state. West of the Blue Ridge the **Allegheny Mountains** undulate into West Virginia like waves of stone, separated by rivers flowing in long, narrow valleys. Almost all of Virginia's southwestern tip is higher than 1,600 feet in elevation, ranging as high as 3,000 feet on the Cumberland and Kanawha plateaus that extend into Kentucky.

Between the Blue Ridge and the Alleghenies stretches the **Shenandoah River,** sharing its name with a valley and a way of life. Stretching from Staunton, Virginia, to Harper's Ferry, West Virginia, the fruitful river basin produces apples, chickens, corn, and cattle in such profusion that it was nearly contested to death during the Civil War. Down the middle runs thin Massanutten Mountain, splitting the North and South Forks of the Shenandoah River for 50 miles before they join at Front Royal and flow north to the Potomac. Shallow and placid for most of its length, the Shenandoah River draws mineral nutrients from limestone springs to provide sustenance for minnows, crayfish, and their larger predators. Most of Virginia's other major rivers also have their headwaters in or beyond the Blue Ridge, including the York, James, and Rappahannock. The **New River,** to the southwest, is actually the oldest in North America, and the second most ancient in the world—only the Nile is older. It began flowing before the Appalachians were formed, explaining why it's one of the few major rivers that flow south to north, across the grain of the mountains.

spruce in the mountains, then head east and find alligators in cypress swamps and shells on sandy beaches, all in the same day.

THE MOUNTAINS

Virginia's hills are part of the **Appalachian chain** that separates the watersheds of the Atlantic Ocean and the Gulf of Mexico. Once as tall and jagged as the Rockies, the much older Appalachians have mellowed with age into a soothing western skyline. Though the mountains appear gentle, looks can be deceiving— frozen snowdrifts can still trap your four-wheel-drive vehicle at the right time of year if you're not careful. The entire chain runs from Alabama to Canada, but "Appalachia" (as much a cultural term as a geological one) only reaches as far north as south-central New York. In Virginia, narrow crests and steep slopes ease into smoother mountaintops in the south part of the range. Weathered granite outcroppings top many peaks, while slightly acidic groundwater has eroded an underlying stratum of limestone into a myriad of caves, bridges, sinkholes, and pillars.

The **Blue Ridge Mountains** form the easternmost fringe of Virginia's slice of the Ap-

Flora and Fauna

Temperate forests include 26 tree species from deep green eastern hemlocks to fragrant-budded tulip trees, whose trunks have measured more than 25 feet in diameter. Indians fashioned dugout canoes from these giants, and settlers boiled and ate the acorns of white oaks before cutting down the trees for their fine wood. Flowering dogwoods erupt in the spring along with azaleas and purple flame, or rose rhododendrons (called laurels locally). The pink and white flowers of trilliums blanket the northeast foothills. Green and yellow violets, Dutchman's-breeches, lady's slippers, skunk cabbage, and 85 species of ferns all sprout in the undergrowth at various times.

Common animals in the mountains include rabbits, foxes, chipmunks, skunks, and raccoons. Many of Virginia's million or so white-tailed deer browse roadside grasses in Shenandoah National Park, while bobcats are rarely seen. Black bears are also present, but shy. Classified as omnivores, they subsist mostly on nuts, berries, and the tender parts of trees. Among the birdlife, the turkey vultures (buzzards) are the most impressive to watch, riding updrafts on their six-foot wings. Their red heads are a good field mark. Black vultures are smaller and less common. Another big blackbird, the raven, alternates flapping with gliding, and croaking in one of a dozen particular ways. Wild turkeys, the largest birds in the hills, really look like those Thanksgiving decorations, and if you do enough hiking you'll probably lose a few heartbeats to the sudden launch of ruffed grouse. Red-tailed hawks can spot rodents and small reptiles from hundreds of feet in the air before diving for a meal.

CENTRAL VIRGINIA

Virginia's midsection runs from the base of the Blue Ridge (hence the term Piedmont, which translates roughly as "foot of the mountain") east across low, rolling hills rising no higher than 1,000 feet. It's separated from the coastal plain by the **fall line,** a topographic stripe where the central plain's harder metamorphic rock crumbles into the sandier soils of the coast. Many of the state's rivers, winding slowly across the flat countryside, turn into white water over the edge of the fall line, which roughly parallels I-95 as it runs from Alexandria to Petersburg.

Ranging from 50 miles wide in the north to almost 200 miles wide at the North Carolina border, Virginia's central plain has endured more human impact over the years than other parts of the state. Centuries of tree-clearing, farming, city-building, and suburb-spreading have turned much of the gently forested slopes into pastures, ponds, and pavement. Though transformed, the Piedmont still retains a patrician grace most evident in the horse country near Charlottesville

and Lexington, where miles of whitewashed fences border deep green meadows.

Flora and Fauna

Oaks prevail among the trees that are left, though mostly in second- and third-stage stands of chestnut, red, and white varieties. Maples, cypress, and black gum line the meandering rivers, while south of the James coniferous forests of pine begin to replace deciduous species. Springtime brings the vibrant pink and magenta blooms of redbud and the creamy white petals of flowering dogwoods. Morning glories and bluebells display two of the more gaudy blossoms among the flowers.

Those animals that have learned to coexist with people are abundant, including deer, raccoons, opossums, and squirrels, along with the occasional quail and wild turkey in the underbrush. Edge communities (where two ecosystems meet, such as pastures and forests) are good places to spot wildlife, especially birds. Indigo buntings can be spotted in hedgerows, and red-winged blackbirds prefer marshy land near water. Artificial lakes and riverbanks are prime habitat for muskrats, beavers, and kingfishers. By night your flashlight might catch the reflecting eyes of an opossum or bobcat. Reptiles include snapping and eastern box turtles and a nighttime cacophony of bullfrogs, gray treefrogs, and spring peepers. The northern water snake is most common, bearing a superficial resemblance to the poisonous (but nonswimming) copperhead.

THE COAST
The Tidewater

Once past the fall line, the coastal plain begins its gentle descent to sea level. Virginia's 3,300 tortuous miles of shoreline display a vast network of marshes, creeks, and rivers that widen into estuaries drained and filled by the ocean tides. Dry hardwood groves likewise transform into **flooded forests** of bald cypress and black gum. Unlike their upland relatives, many of these wetter, less accessible forests have escaped the logger's ax, allowing their rich soils to support largely unaltered ecosystems. Sixteen species of warbler flit through the Spanish moss in the Great Dismal Swamp, which continues south across the state line into North Carolina. Unusual species like green anole—a lizard that looks like a salamander—and Creole pearly eye butterflies inhabit the otherworldly recesses of Virginia's coastal swamps. Tannin, a natural acid, stains the waters brown and keeps bacteria from growing (which led early sea captains to prefer these waters for long journeys). Impenetrable, boggy tangles of shrubs and trees called **pocosins** are rare and little-studied.

Mixing mineral salts from the ocean and fertile soil washed downriver from central Virginia, **salt marshes** are some of the richest habitats in the state—indeed in all of North America. Each acre can generate up to twice as much organic material as an acre of farmland, attracting migratory birds by the millions every spring and fall. Swans, geese, and ducks all float in the brackish waters at different times of year. Look for the black-tipped blue bill of the redhead, a diving duck, and listen for the supernatural hoot of barred owls at night.

Chesapeake Bay

The coastal plain flows into one of the largest estuaries in the world, fed by 100,000 streams and rivers in Maryland and Virginia. With an average depth of only 20 feet, the Chesapeake Bay meets the Atlantic at the superb natural harbor of Hampton Roads. Here, fresh and salt water mix into a rich blend that supports a staggering diversity of life. The bay's name comes from the Algonquian word *Chesepioc* (great shellfish bay), and bushels of oysters and crabs are still yanked up to the sunlight by the unique breed of Chesapeake watermen (or waterpeople, nowadays) like they have been for generations. Wading birds such as ibis, egrets, and great blue herons stalk the shoreline in search of smaller creatures. Ospreys and bald eagles—once brought to the edge of extinction by pesticides, hunting, and habitat destruction—soar overhead in renewed numbers.

The Shore

At the ocean's edge stretch long, shallow lagoons and salt flats just a shell's throw from open water. Change is the only constant along the beaches, especially in the case of the **barrier islands** that line

the seaward side of the Eastern Shore. These narrow strips of sand are thought to shelter a greater variety of birds than any other ecosystem in the country. Here the whistle of the endangered piping plover echoes over beaches simultaneously eaten away and built up by the constant pounding waves.

Tall marsh grasses provide protection against erosion—at least long enough for stumpy trees to gain a foothold before being inundated by the ocean to begin the cycle again. Muskrats ply tidal pools for shellfish as the rare least tern lays its eggs in shallow pits in the dunes. Thanks to the warming effect of the Gulf Stream, you'll find many southerly plant and animal species at the northern extreme of their range along the Virginia coast, including live oak, sea oats, sawgrass from the Everglades, and the chicken turtle, with a neck longer than its shell.

CLIMATE

It's hard to decide whether summer's gentle prelude or its fiery swan song is more beautiful, but weather-wise, spring and fall are Virginia's most enjoyable seasons. On average the state manages to escape both the frigid northern winters and the incapacitating summer swelter of the Deep South, though high humidity levels can make temperatures in both seasons feel more extreme.

The warm weather of **spring** brings forth buds and blossoms throughout the mountains and Piedmont, though temperatures can still dip into the 30s at night (or even 20s in the mountains). Rivers swollen with melting snow surge past electric groves of blooming bluebells, marigolds, violets, and daffodils. According to local lore, spring climbs the Blue Ridge 100 feet a day, pushing skyward the green line of new leaves dotted with the flowers of dogwoods, pink azaleas, and purple and white rhododendrons. Migrating birds leave their winter nesting grounds along the coast, while others arrive in breeding plumage ready to build a nest and start a family.

Summer brings high temperatures and humidity. Averages of 80°F seem more like 100°F when there's enough water in the air to drink through a straw. Suddenly the coast is a lot more attractive than the muggy countryside, even with the sudden thunderstorms that condense in the afternoons. The mountains are also cooler than the lowlands in summer; nights can be downright nippy, making jackets and sleeping bags necessary for overnighters. Wildflowers bloom in succession the entire season, as newborn fawns and chicks take their first wobbly steps.

Virginia's famous **fall** colors peak near the middle of October with a vivid palette of yellow, gold, orange, and red, courtesy of maples, oaks, and hickories. Bird migrations peak during this season, sending hawks, shorebirds, and songbirds for the warmer climates of the southern United States, the Caribbean, and Latin America. Harvest time brings roadside produce stands and huge rolls of hay scattered throughout farmland in the Shenandoah and central Virginia. Balmy Indian summer weather gradually gives way to nighttime temperatures in the 40s by October.

In **winter,** the shore is bleak but still beautiful in its emptiness, as boardwalks stand empty and the wind shoves whitecaps across the gray water. Snowfall in the Piedmont quickly turns into slush, but can still block unplowed back roads for

days. Temperatures in both regions average near 30°F, rarely dipping into the teens for long. You can experience clear, cold air and bare-branch views from the mountains, as long as the Skyline Drive and Blue Ridge Parkway aren't closed by snow. Waterfalls and seeps turn into garlands of ice, and the occasional ice storm or freezing fog can coat everything in a glittering film of frost.

CONSERVATION

Virginia's Department of Conservation and Recreation (DCR) began the comprehensive **Virginia Natural Heritage Program,** www.dcr.state.va.us/dnh/index.html, in 1989 with a goal of identifying, protecting, and managing Virginia's wide range of ecosystems. In less than a decade, scientists, resource managers, landscape architects, and computer jockeys have worked together to identify more than 1,000 conservation sites to date containing rare species or communities—making the statewide program the most comprehensive of its kind in the United States. It was recognized by The Nature Conservancy in 1994 as one of the

CONSERVATION ORGANIZATIONS AND STATE AGENCIES

Alliance for the Chesapeake Bay
P.O. Box 1981
Richmond, VA 23218
804/775-0951
800/662-CRIS
website: www.acb-online.org

Chesapeake Bay Foundation
Virginia State Office: Capitol Place
1108 E. Main St., Ste. 1600
Richmond, VA 23219
804/780-1392, 888/SAVE-BAY (888/728-3229)
website: www.cbf.org

The Conservation Fund's Civil War Battlefield Campaign
1800 N. Kent St., Ste. 1120
Arlington, VA 22209-2156

703/525-6300
fax 703/525-4610
website: www.conservationfund.org/conservation/civilwar

Friends of the North Fork of the Shenandoah
P.O. Box 746
122 South Commerce St.
Woodstock, VA 22664
540/459-8550
fax 540/459-8805
website: www.gmu.edu/bios/shenando/north

Friends of the Shenandoah River
P.O. Box 410
Front Royal, VA 22630
540/636-4948
website: www.fosr.org

most outstanding natural heritage programs in the Western hemisphere.

Save the Bay

One of Virginia's main environmental challenges is keeping the Chesapeake Bay healthy. This incredibly complex ecosystem—or rather, collection of ecosystems—is doing better than it was 25 years ago, thanks to strict fishing limits and restrictions on the flow of industrial pollutants and nutrient-laden farmland runoff, but there's still plenty of work to be done. Algae and silt cloud the water to the point of inhibiting the growth of underwater grasses that shelter crabs and fish. Annual algal "blooms" thrive on the nitrogen, phosphorus, and other chemicals introduced into the bay by polluting industries, car exhaust, and agricultural and residential runoff. The tiny plants then decompose through a process that eats up the oxygen in the water, creating "dead zones" incapable of supporting fish.

In 1996 health problems such as skin rashes, respiratory trouble, and memory loss began to appear among bay fishermen. Fish soon started showing up dead by the thousands, covered with strange red skin lesions. By August 1997, these "kills" had spread from the Pocomoke River in Delaware through Maryland to the top of Virginia's Eastern Shore, claiming as many as 10,000 fish at a time. When the culprit—a bacteria called *Pfiesteria piscicida*—was discovered, Maryland closed the Pocomoke and two other tributaries and local seafood sales plummeted. It's thought the bacteria, which is normally harmless, is turned toxic by excessive nutrients running into the bay from local pastures, where chicken manure is used as fertilizer (chickens outnumber people in the area by 500 to 1). Three-quarters of the fish in the Rappahannock River were found to have lesions.

One proposed solution to restore the bay to its former glory is to bring oyster populations back to their ancient levels. A century ago, the bay sheltered so many oysters that their huge shell banks were a navigation hazard to boats, and together they could filter the entire volume of water in the bay in 3–4 days. Only 1 percent of that population is left now, meaning it takes a year to filter the same water. Scientists' computer models predict that even 10 percent of the original

---

Sierra Club—Virginia Chapter
6 N. 6th St.
Richmond, VA 23219
804/225-9113
website: virginia.sierraclub.org

The Nature Conservancy—Virginia Chapter
490 Westfield Road
Charlottesville, VA 22901
804/295-6106
website: nature.org/states/virginia

Virginia Conservation Network
1001 East Broad St., Ste. LL 35-C
Richmond, VA 23219
804/644-0283
website: www.vcnva.org

Virginia Department of Conservation and Recreation
203 Governor St., Ste. 213
Richmond, VA 23219-2094
804/786-1712
website: www.dcr.state.va.us

Virginia Department of Environmental Quality
P.O. Box 10009
Richmond, VA 23240
804/698-4000, 800/592-5482
website: www.deq.state.va.us

oyster populations would go a long way toward restoring the ecosystem. They point to the example of zebra mussels in the Great Lakes: even though they're considered nonnative pests, the mussels have cleaned the water enough to bring back aquatic animals and plants gone for three decades. Bumper crops of stinging jellyfish might be reduced in the Chesapeake Bay as a side benefit of increasing oyster levels.

Virginia and Maryland are developing disease-resistant strains of oysters, and dumping more than three million bushels of oyster shells on old reef spots every year in the hope of reseeding faded breeding grounds. The most vocal resistance is coming from local fishermen, who balk at the idea of setting aside a quarter of the current oyster beds as sanctuaries to prevent overfishing. They argue that natural biological rhythms and disease are the culprits, not human activity. In the end it might take a nonfishing subsidy to equal the success achieved with the rockfish population, which was brought back from the edge of disaster though a cooperative effort among Maryland, Virginia, and Delaware agencies. With the bay area's population expected to grow 12 percent or more by 2010, the pressure is on.

The Blue Ridge Turns Purple

Visibility has never been perfect from the crest of the Blue Ridge; even early accounts of the views begin, "On a clear day . . ." Just like in the Smoky Mountains of North Carolina, water vapor combined with airborne dust and organic compounds given off by trees forms a natural hill-shrouding haze, especially in summer. In recent years, though, industrial smog and auto exhaust have added a new purple tinge that began reaching the peaks around 1976. Increasing amounts of acid rain, originating in the emissions from old coal-fired power plants in the Ohio and Tennessee valleys, hurt trees and fish in Shenandoah National Park. Runoff churned up by livestock and poultry produces the same results in mountain rivers and streams as it does in the Chesapeake Bay. Thanks to levels of ozone, acid rain, and smog that occasionally exceed those of nearby major

cities, Shenandoah National Park is the second most polluted national park in the country. Local conservation groups and state government branches try to keep tabs on water quality and industry, but the job can be overwhelming.

This type of pollution is having a terrible effect on the region's streams. The rivers and creeks of southwestern Virginia are home to 48 rare and endangered mussels and fish, the highest number of imperiled species in any ecosystem in the United States outside Hawaii. Virginia's mountain streams, widely known as some of the finest brook trout habitat left in the United States, are faring no better. The Paine Run River on the western slope of Shenandoah National Park ranked number 11 on the list of the country's 13 most endangered rivers in 2001, according to the conservation group American Rivers (www.americanrivers.org). Acid rain is slowly making the Paine Run and other mountain streams and rivers in the Mid-Atlantic region too acidic to support populations of native brook trout. Already five of eight local trout species have vanished. If this type of pollution is not reduced by 70 percent soon, say conservationists, the Paine Run may suffer the same fate as the St. Mary's River in the George Washington National Forest, which made the American Rivers list in 1993. Since then, it has become a "zombie river": moving but dead, too acidic to host self-sustaining trout populations. (The U.S. Forest Service is injecting massive doses of limestone into the water in the hopes of reducing the stream's acidity enough to support trout once again.) According to a University of Virginia study, 6 percent of the state's 304 trout streams are already too acidic for brook trout.

One promising example of conservation in the high country is a compromise reached over the Laurel Fork Special Management Area in Highland County). In July 1996, Thornwood Gas of Pennsylvania received permission from the U.S. Forest Service to build a 34-mile pipeline along the boundary of the management area. Local residents, worried that the company would start to drill in the pristine woodlands, formed an opposition coalition and began to consider prohibitive lawsuits. The Nature Conservancy then stepped in and brokered an unprecedented agreement. Thornwood Gas was allowed to build the pipeline, but only by burying it alongside existing roads.

Plus the company agreed not to drill, but instead to transfer 1,700 acres of surface rights to the Nature Conservancy and to draw gas in compliance with nondamaging subsurface rights owned by the U.S. Bureau of Land Management.

History

Good Old Dominion, blessed mother of us all.

—Thomas Jefferson

PRECOLONIAL ERA

No one is sure when the first humans crossed the ice bridge over the Bering Strait to enter the Americas—estimates range as high as 50,000 years ago—but anthropologists generally agree that they subsisted on seasonal hunting and gathering once they arrived. Musk ox and caribou fell to stone-tipped spears and wooden clubs, supplying the primitive nomads with food, clothing, and material for tools. Roots, nuts, and berries filled in when game was scarce, and temporary encampments were moved to follow the herds or flee the harsher seasons.

Approximately 11,000 years ago, the glaciers of the most recent ice age retreated to 200 miles north of present-day Virginia. The future state's first inhabitants arrived from the west to find unfamiliar species of bison, deer, turkeys, bears, and elk moving up from the south. These family groups often camped alongside streams, leaving behind only chipped stone tools and discarded flakes to record their passing.

Within a few thousand years, this ice age had ended completely, taking with it larger mammals like mastodons and mammoths, with help from the spears of early natives. Temperatures continued to climb, relegating cold-weather tree species such as hemlocks, birches, and firs (which had flourished at lower elevations) to the Appalachian peaks. Human populations increased slowly but surely, so that by the time of Christ, the **Woodland Period** was in full swing. Amid lowland forests of hickory, oak, and chestnut a

more settled lifestyle emerged. Rudimentary agriculture produced crops of corn, squash, and beans, while fragile pottery made continuous migration less practical. The discovery of the bow and arrow made hunting and warfare more efficient. Relatively small numbers kept native Virginians' impact on their environment to a minimum, though they occasionally burned large swaths of forest to flush out game and drove herds of bison over cliff edges, killing more than they could use at one time.

Welcome to the "New" World

When they arrived in 1607, the first European settlers found the Tidewater area under the control of the **Powhatan Confederacy,** an Algonquian native group whose lands stretched from North Carolina to the Potomac River. Thirty tribes containing some 10,000 people lived in palisaded villages by rivers or on hillsides under the leadership of Wahunsonacock, called Chief Powhatan by the Europeans. The Powhatans fished, hunted, and grew corn, squash, pumpkins, and herbs in summer gardens. Dressed in animal hides and woven plant fibers, they decorated themselves with feathers, tattoos, and jewelry made of shells, clay beads, and pearls. High priests called *Periku'* offered sacrifices to *Okee* or **Mannith,** worshipped as the "Creator of All Things."

Farther west and north lived the **Monacans** and **Manahoacs,** occupying the eastern edge of the Blue Ridge and the upper banks of the James, Potomac, and Rappahannock rivers into the Allegheny Mountains. These traditional enemies of the Powhatans shared a common Siouxan cultural heritage and language. Other native groups included the **Nansemond,** who were such good farmers they became known as the "granary" of

reconstructed Indian village at the Jamestown settlement

the early English colony; the **Rappahannock** near present-day Richmond; and small groups of **Cherokee** up from the south.

THE COLONIAL PERIOD

Jamestown

At the turn of the 17th century, England was painfully aware that it needed to get a foothold in the New World. Spain, after all, had been busily colonizing, converting, and pillaging for the last century. Three decades of attempts finally bore fruit in 1607, when three ships—the *Sarah Constant*, the *Goodspeed*, and the *Discovery*—brought 143 settlers to the mouth of the Chesapeake Bay. In contrast to the conquistadors financed by the Spanish Crown, the English expedition was a private venture organized by the London-based Virginia Company. Captain Christopher Newport led the ships 30 miles up the James River, which he named after the English king. On May 14, 1607, the colonists tied their ships to trees, disembarked, and set about building the first permanent English settlement in the Americas.

Soon James Fort stood guard over Virginia, the name given to all of North America not under the control of the Spanish or French, after the English Virgin Queen (Elizabeth I). The land was rich, game plentiful, and the natives, at least at first, were friendly, but the colony still almost failed within its first few years. Inept leaders, with the exception of adventurer John Smith, were ill-suited to the hard decisions and harder labor. Despite warnings to avoid damp, low-lying areas, they built their settlement in a salt marsh, which led to famine and disease. The winter of 1609–1610 became known as the Starving Time, during which things got so bad one colonist killed and ate his wife ("for which hee was executed, as hee well deserved," wrote a fellow sufferer; "now whether shee was better roasted, boyled or carbonado'd I know not"). The colony was abandoned in May 1610 by its 60 remaining colonists; however, their departing boat was met by two ships bearing Gov. Thomas Gates from England, and the survivors were convinced to stick it out.

Colonist John Rolfe, who had married John Smith's alleged 13-year-old savior Pocahontas in 1609 (not for any "carnall affection; but for the good of this plantation, for the honour of our countrie"), began a legacy a few years later by

VIRGINIA'S TRIBES TODAY

In 1990, the state's native groups—defined by proof of existence for a minimum of 200 years—made up 0.2 percent of the population. The **Pamunkey** (pa-MUN-kee) live along the river of the same name in King William County, which contains the supposed burial site of Chief Powhatan. In the same country live fewer than 100 **Mattaponi** (ma-ta-poe-NYE) on a reservation along the Mattaponi River dating to 1658. A smaller group called the Upper Mattaponi live off the reservation. Charles City County is home to 1,000 **Chickahominy** mingled with the nonnative population. Half that many **Monacans** make up the westernmost surviving group, and 300 **Nansemond** live in Norfolk, Chesapeake, Virginia Beach, and Portsmouth near their ancient hunting grounds around the Great Dismal Swamp. About 750 of the **United Rappahannock** were moved from Richmond County to King and Queen County.

Events

Typical powwows echo with heavy drums, dancing, and chanting by participants in buckskin clothes and eagle and turkey feathers. Native American veterans proudly display their U.S. Army uniforms beneath the flags of their county and tribe. Chiefs lead processions, followed by braves in war paint, women, and children. Native American food and crafts are featured. The **Monacan Pow-Wow,** 804/929-0334, is held in June, along with the **Virginia Indian Heritage Festival** in Jamestown and a **Mattaponi Pow Wow.** The United Rappahannock tribe hosts the **American Indian Heritage Celebration** at the George Washington Birthplace in Westmoreland County, 804/769-1508, in early August, followed closely by the **Nansemond Indian Tribe Association Pow Wow and Festival** at Lone Star Lakes Lodge, off Route 10 and Pembroke Lane near Suffolk, 804/232-0248. A general **Indian Heritage Festival and Pow Wow** happens at the Virginia Museum of Natural History, 1001 Douglas Ave., Martinsville, 540/666-8600, in early September.

planting the first crop of West Indian tobacco (*Nicotiana tabacum*). With some selective breeding, the large-leaf tobacco plant would prove a stable revenue crop in high demand back home in England. Representative government, in a limited sense, began in June 1619, when the first legislative assembly in the New World convened for six days in a "generall Assemblie" in the Jamestown church. The first boatload of 20 African slaves arrived that same year.

Things Get Worse Before They Get Better

Fewer than 1,200 out of 4,000 arrivals survived to 1624, victims to Indian attacks and a major epidemic in 1622–1623 that killed 500 people. Though friendly at first with gifts of food and advice, the Powhatans turned hostile when they realized the Europeans were here to stay. Within two years all the main native towns had been seized, Chief Powhatan had fled, and any colonists venturing beyond the walls of the settlement took their lives in their hands. A temporary truce followed the marriage of Powhatan's daughter Pocahontas to colonist John Rolfe in 1614, but relations quickly deteriorated. A surprise attack in March 1622 under Powhatan's successor Opechancanough killed 400 settlers. In 1624 the Virginia Company's charter was revoked and Jamestown came under British government rule, making it the first royal colony.

Nonetheless, by 1634 the colony counted 5,000 inhabitants, who were concentrated along the James and York rivers, the Eastern Shore, and the Hampton Roads area. Most settlers under Gov. Sir William Berkeley (1642–1652 and 1660–1677) were small-scale farmers, artisans, and tradesmen, many of whom had worked their way out of indentured servitude and found themselves owning land for the first time. Tobacco quickly became the major crop, creating a demand for slave labor. The first boatload of "20 and odd Negroes" had arrived in Hampton Roads in 1619 as indentured servants rather than slaves, but by 1660—the year before slavery was legalized—the colony counted one black for every 20 whites. Five hundred more colonists were killed in a 1644 Indian attack, one that

CAPTAIN JOHN SMITH

The savior of Jamestown saw more action before setting foot in the New World than most of us see in a lifetime. Born in 1580 in Lincolnshire, England, Smith spent his childhood on his family's farm before being apprenticed as a teenager to a local merchant. At age 16 he ran away to fight in France for Dutch independence from Spain, worked on a merchant ship in the Mediterranean Sea, and went to Transylvania to battle the Turks. Knocked out in battle and left for dead, Smith was captured and sold to a Turkish *pasha* who sent him as a present to his heartthrob in Constantinople. The lady, though reportedly smitten with her English prisoner, sent him to her brother, who abused him so badly that Smith killed his latest master and fled. With an iron collar still around his neck, he escaped through Russia, ending up back in England in time to buy stock in the newly formed Virginia Company in 1605; he was 26 years old.

On December 20, 1606, Smith and 142 other hopeful setters sailed west. A stubborn, disputatious nature quickly got him in trouble with the trip leaders, who accused the adventurer of conspiracy and had him arrested. At their arrival in Chesapeake Bay, though, the sealed expedition orders were opened and revealed that Smith had been named a member of the governing council. When other leaders kept him from assuming the position, he set out west to look for a passage to the Pacific. He got far enough to discover the falls on the James River near Richmond, then returned to find the settlement in dire straits. Local natives had become increasingly hostile, and the ill-prepared colonists were reduced to a daily ration of one pint of wormy grain boiled in water. In the words of one settler, "Our drinke was water, our lodgings, castles in the air."

Smith assumed leadership and set out to whip the settlement and its inhabitants into shape. Sturdy houses and defenses were constructed, and relations with the Powhatans were improved to allow colonists to trade for corn, fish, and other food. Around this time, Smith began a series of expeditions up the "Patawomeck" and "Topoahannock" rivers, on which he based his famous 1606 map of Virginia. Accurate enough to serve local navigators for a century, Smith's map was used to survey the Mason-Dixon line between Pennsylvania and Maryland, which separated free states from slave states during the Civil War.

While searching for the source of the "Chickahamania" River in December 1607, Smith was captured by the Powhatans, who took him to a lodge on the banks of the York River. In a later account, he described Chief Powhatan as "a tall well propotioned man, with a sower looke . . . proudly lying uppon a Bedstead a foote high, upon tenne or twelve Mattes, richly hung with manie Chaynes of great Pearles about his necke . . . with such a grave Maiesticall countenance, as drave me into admiration to see such state in a naked Savage."

According to his own account, Smith was then condemned to death and laid out on the clubbing block. As the story goes, Powhatan's 13-year-old daughter Pocahontas rushed forward and pleaded successfully with her father to spare Smith's life. Whatever the case, he was eventually freed and returned to lead the colony, which had been hampered by laziness and inept leadership and was struggling through the winter of 1607. Appointed president of Jamestown in September 1608, Smith enforced a rigid discipline, strengthened fortifications, and started general military training. Idlers were spurred on with the edict, "He who does not work, will not eat." His efforts saw the group through the next hard winter until more settlers arrived with provisions in the summer of 1609. That September he was wounded severely enough in a gunpowder explosion to force him to return to England. He never went back to Virginia.

On later journeys, Smith explored and mapped the Maine and Massachusetts coastlines, dubbing the area New England with the approval of Prince Charles. On another voyage he was captured by pirates, escaped, and returned to England penniless. One final colonizing attempt in 1617 ended in failure. For the rest of his life, Smith praised the wonders of the Western continent in books such as *A Description of New England* (1625), *The Generall Historie of Virginia, New England, and the Summer Isles* (1624), and *The True Travels, Adventures and Observations of Captaine John Smith in Europe, Asia, Africa and America* (1630). He died in London in 1631.

lead to the capture and murder of the blind, elderly Chief Opechancanough. A treaty of submission signaled the beginning of the long, slow displacement of native tribes.

Early Unrest and Bacon's Rebellion

Supporters of Charles I, who was deposed and killed in 1644, fled to the New World and set down the roots of a gentry society with firm historical ties to England (hence Virginia's nickname of the Old Dominion). Tobacco sales were funneled through a handful of London merchants, driving prices down and making it increasingly difficult for small Virginia farms to turn a profit. Charles II, placed in power in 1660 after the English Civil War, tried to grant all of Virginia's northern neck—at the time, the entire colony—to English nobility.

Further impolitic decisions provoked a rebellion in 1676 led by 26-year-old Nathaniel Bacon. After the Colonial government had refused to help frontier settlers fight off repeated Indian attacks, Bacon spearheaded an unauthorized campaign against the Susquehanna tribe, for which he was labeled a rebel and traitor by aging Governor Berkeley. During the fighting that ensued, Bacon occupied the General Assembly, burned Jamestown, and spoke out against the increasingly corrupt and self-serving government. The rebellion collapsed soon after Bacon's untimely death that October, but the point had been made.

Expansion and the Golden Age

Through the late 17th and most of the 18th centuries, the colony spread steadily west. In March 1669, German scholar John Lederer became one of the first white men to reach the crest of the Blue Ridge. Scotch-Irish and Germans moved down from Pennsylvania into the Shenandoah Valley near the middle of the 18th century, sparking friction with French settlers and their native

Our men were destroyed with [such] cruell diseases as Swellings, Flixes, Burning Fevers, and by warres, and some departed suddenly, but for the most part they died of meere famine. There were never Englishmen left in a foreigne countrey in such miserie as wee were in this new discovered Virginia.

—George Percy, early colonist

allies that resulted in the French and Indian War (1754–1763).

This same era also became known as the "Golden Age" of plantations, financed by huge tobacco profits and based largely on the aristocratic society of English estate owners. A core of First Families with names such as Carter, Randolph, and Byrd formed a "bourgeois aristocracy" that defended self-government jealously, as long as it served their own interests. Speculation in land and slave trading brought in even more money, while the basic concepts and advocates of American liberal thought were being born. By 1715, the colony counted one black for every three whites.

The Eve of Revolution

The more than 120,000 persons living in the British colony in 1715 lived modestly in a stable, if narrowly based, plantation economy. Colonists were still prohibited many rights extended to English subjects across the Atlantic, though, and royal edicts kept overriding acts passed by the Virginia House of Burgesses. In 1763 a ridiculous, unenforceable law prohibiting westward expansion angered frontier settlers and coastal land speculators alike. Taxation without representation reached its peak when Britain passed the Stamp Act of 1765, designed to help extract money from the colonies for the recent war in England. A fiery speech in Williamsburg by gifted orator Patrick Henry implied that the colonies might be better off without George III. (His words "Caesar had his Brutus, Charles the First his Cromwell, and George III . . ." were interrupted by cries of "Treason!") The Virginia General Assembly followed by passing the Stamp Act Resolves, which decreed that only Virginia had the right to tax Virginians. Repealed in 1766, the Stamp Act was replaced by heavy import duties the next year.

In 1773 the perpetrators of the Boston Tea

INTRODUCTION

Party received the support of the local government, even as the British Parliament closed the port to all commerce and sent in troops to maintain order. When Virginia's Governor Dunmore dissolved the General Assembly in response, the burgesses met at Raleigh Tavern in Williamsburg to propose a meeting in Philadelphia to seriously discuss separation from England. George Washington, Patrick Henry, and Benjamin Harrison all made it to the first Continental Congress in September 1774, where a militia was organized to defend the colonies. At the March 1775 Virginia Convention at St. John's Church in Richmond, Patrick Henry made his most famous speech. Although nobody present actually wrote it down, witnesses recalled it ending along these lines: "I know not what course others may take; but as for me, give me liberty, or give me death."

THE REVOLUTIONARY WAR

Virginia managed to escape most of the fighting of the first three years of the American Revolution, beyond supplying leaders, troops, supplies, and the occasional landmark document. In May 1776, the same month Gov. John Dunmore fled to England, radicals and conservatives united in the decision for independence at the Virginia Convention in Williamsburg. By the time the ink had dried on the U.S. Constitution (penned mostly by Virginian Thomas Jefferson), two other papers had been completed: George Mason's Virginia Bill of Rights, asserting that "all power is vested in, and consequently derived from, the people" (this later served as the model for the Federal Bill of Rights); and Virginia's first constitution, ending 169 years as an English colony. Patrick Henry was chosen as governor of Virginia, and no one seemed to notice the irony that although Virginians had sounded the loudest demands for liberty, Virginia was still closest in sentiment to England of all the colonies. The Virginia gentry lead the struggle for independence: "These gentlemen from Virginia appear to be the most spirited and consistent of any," wrote John Adams upon the arrival of the Virginia delegates to the first Continental Congress.

George Washington had been elected commander-in-chief of the Continental Army soon after the first shots were fired at Lexington and Concord. Many of his fellow Virginians made a name under him, including cavalry leader Col. Harry "Lighthorse" Lee, father of Civil War legend Robert E. Lee, and George Rogers Clark, who managed to win the Northwest Territory from Britain in 1778–1779 after a hard-fought winter campaign. Help from French forces under the Marquis de Lafayette proved crucial.

When Thomas Jefferson became governor of Virginia in 1779, he found the state treasury practically emptied by the expense of supplying the scrappy Continental Army. Life in Virginia remained more or less unaffected by the war until English ships invaded via Hampton Roads in 1779, forcing the capital to be moved to Richmond for safety. Jefferson resigned his position in June 1780, narrowly avoiding capture by the British, thanks to Capt. Jack Jouett, who rode all night to warn him at his Monticello home. Seven other legislators were captured.

Infamous traitor Benedict Arnold—one of Washington's most trusted commanders before becoming a brigadier general in the British Army—and troops destroyed Richmond in January 1781. Before the year was out, however, Britain's Gen. Lord Charles Cornwallis found himself surrounded on the Yorktown peninsula between 10,000 Continental troops under Washington and 8,000 under Lafayette, with the French fleet preventing escape by sea. On October 19, Cornwallis marched his troops (many of whom were, according to one witness, "much in liquor") across Surrender Field between the ragged Continental Army and the spotless French forces. A band played "The World Turned Upside Down," and a new country was born.

After the Revolution

The U.S. Constitution was adopted at the Philadelphia Constitutional Convention in 1787. Virginia's approval of it spurred a debate that pitted Virginians who had helped draft it, including George Washington and James Madison, against fellow statesmen wary of an omnipotent national government, led by Patrick

Henry and George Mason. The Bill of Rights proved a good compromise, and proratification forces prevailed by a vote of 89–79. In 1788, Virginia became the new nation's 10th state, and a year later George Washington was elected its president, with Thomas Jefferson as secretary of state. The new nation was off and running.

BETWEEN THE WARS

Setting Up a Country

Early American politics were marked by conflict over how much power the national government should have. Thomas Jefferson and James Madison championed states' rights, arguing that the federal apparatus should stick to what was specifically outlined in the Constitution and leave everything else to state and local governments. Federalists, on the other hand, followed the lead of New Yorker Alexander Hamilton in pushing for the widest possible role of the federal government. Regardless, Virginians dominated national politics for the first four decades, supplying four of the first five presidents, including an uninterrupted stretch from 1801–1825. Virginian John Marshall served as chief justice of the U.S. Supreme Court from 1801–1835.

Antebellum Life

The first half of the 19th century is still remembered as one of the more idyllic times in Virginia's history, evoking the plantation nostalgia of hoop skirts, gentlemen on horses, and sun-drenched fields of cotton and tobacco. Of course, it *was* an ideal time for a select few. All others worked themselves to the bone to make a living (or, in the case of slaves, simply to survive). Small-scale agriculture was still the norm—an average farm in 1850 was only 340 acres—and most farmers were too poor to own slaves, instead relying on family members for help in raising peanuts, potatoes, corn, hogs, chickens, and cattle. Rutted roads connected scattered towns where courthouses served as social hubs and mercantiles sold everything from medicines to bolts of cloth. Any necessary tools or buildings were fashioned by the farmers themselves or hired artisans.

Family connections were paramount, and served to emphasize—in a polite way—the gap between the gentry and the rabble. The gap existed even in worship: the upper class attended Presbyterian and Episcopal services while the populace primarily attended Methodist, Lutheran, and Baptist churches. Above all, the concepts of civility, humility, and honest hard work shaped Virginia society. "The Virginian," wrote historian Percival Renier, "liked to think of himself as a plain and homespun-appearing gentleman with a noble pedigree, which naturally put him above airs and snobbery and fine clothes. . . ." State politics were split between the demands for representation from burgeoning western counties, universal taxpayer suffrage, and freedom for slaves on one hand, and on the other the interests of wealthy eastern landowners and merchants who granted certain grudging concessions.

The Slavery Issue

The narrow-minded policies and political conservatism of the aspiring aristocrats of the east eventually began to mire Virginia's antebellum ("prewar") period in economic and political stagnation. Granted, the Founding Fathers were a hard act to follow, but still Virginia politicians faltered again and again, allowing the port of Hampton Roads to fall far behind those in New York, Baltimore, and Boston and resisting the construction of a canal between the Potomac and the Ohio rivers. New England became the nation's textile center instead of Richmond, public education suffered (with the exception of the University of Virginia), and a population exodus caused the state to lose 13 congressmen between 1810 and 1860.

Fostering the decline was the increasingly inefficient but entrenched plantation economy. Tobacco exhausted the soil and brought in less and less money, but even though the slave trade had been abolished in 1778, the practice of slavery continued, and came to be seen as the rotten root of a weakening tree. By the turn of the 19th century, more than one-third of Virginia lived in bondage. Thomas Jefferson, the slave owner who had written about the equality of man, had foreseen the conflict:

Indeed I tremble for my country when I reflect that God is just: that His justice cannot sleep forever: that considering numbers, nature and natural means only, a revolution of the wheel of fortune, an exchange of situation, is among possible events. . . .

Northern states began to clamor for emancipation as slave revolts gained momentum. In 1800 a huge slave named Gabriel was said to have led 1,000 others in a thwarted rebellion in Richmond. Thirty years later, black preacher Nat Turner led 60 slaves to kill 58 whites—mostly women and children—in Southampton County near the North Carolina line. Though the rebels were caught within 48 hours, the event threw gasoline on the fire. Pro-slavery forces blamed abolitionist propaganda and killed innocent blacks in retaliation.

Most arguments against slavery came from the industrialized North, where factories provided plenty of work for men of any color and smaller farms made a large labor force unnecessary. The disregard for slaves' human rights was an issue in the new western territories, while Southern abolitionists resented the political stranglehold held by the pro-slavery planter aristocracy. In the end, economics was probably the most important factor: the poor farmer in Georgia and the owner of a Massachusetts textile factory found it equally impossible to compete against slave labor.

Slave owners dreaded the idea of these regions unifying against them. They found too much of their declining income tied up in human beings—close to half of the taxable wealth of the Tidewater was in slaves—and argued that the system was better, for everyone but the slaves, than the alternative of wage slavery for whites. It was also argued that there were too many slaves to simply set free, or so their owners said. Most southern whites found it impossible to imagine the transition to a stable, prosperous society in which two races worked side by side as equals. And who would pay to ship the freed slaves out west, or back to Africa?

An 1832 plan for gradual emancipation failed in the Virginia General Assembly, putting the issue to rest until the Mexican-American War (1846–1848), which again raised a central issue last heard in the Missouri Controversy of 1819: the status—slave or free—of new territories admitted into the Union. A slight economic recovery in the 1850s, including Virginian Cyrus McCormick's invention of the mechanical reaper in 1831, the construction of more railroads, and the flourishing of Richmond's slave-powered Tredegar Iron Works, did little to distract from the debate.

Prelude to War

In October 1859 the country was rocked by a raid on the federal arsenal at Harper's Ferry (now in West Virginia) led by militant abolitionist John Brown. Seventeen whites and five free blacks tried to steal enough weapons to arm slaves for a rebellion, and in the process killed the mayor and other townspeople. The group was eventually captured by U.S. Marines under the command of a young lieutenant colonel named Robert E. Lee, but their death sentences gained the abolitionist cause a white martyr and forced slave owners to face the reality that opponents of slavery were willing to fight, and die, for their cause. Brown's dying words echoed over the widening chasm: "The sins of this guilty land can only be purged with blood."

The final straw came in 1860 when Abraham Lincoln was elected president on a Republican platform, pledging to keep slavery out of the territories. On December 20, South Carolina seceded from the Union, followed soon after by Mississippi, Alabama, Florida, Georgia, Louisiana, and Texas. When Fort Sumter on the South Carolina coast was attacked by Southern artillery on April 10, Lincoln called for 75,000 volunteers to put down the "insurrection." Originally against secession, Virginia nonetheless withdrew on April 19. Fireworks exploded above Richmond as "ten thousand hurrahing men and boys" carried torches through the streets to celebrate the occasion. Six days later, Virginia became part of the Confederate States of America.

"They say Virginia has no grievance," reported one contemporary writer; "she comes out on a point of honor."

VIRGINIA'S EIGHT PRESIDENTS

The Old Dominion has supplied more U.S. presidents than any other state.

George Washington
1789–1797

William Henry Harrison
1841
(died during term)

Thomas Jefferson
1801–1809

John Tyler
1841–1845

James Madison
1809–1817

Zachary Taylor
1849–1850
(died during term)

James Monroe
1817–1825

Woodrow Wilson
1913–1921

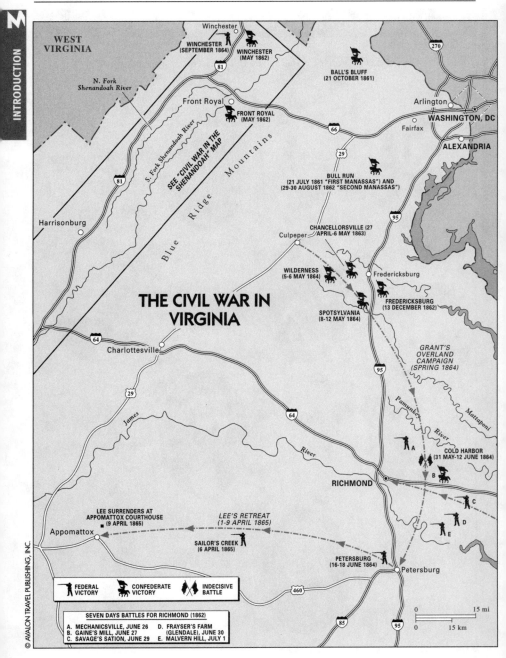

THE CIVIL WAR IN VIRGINIA

WEST VIRGINIA

Winchester

WINCHESTER (SEPTEMBER 1864)

WINCHESTER (MAY 1862)

N. Fork Shenandoah River

S. Fork Shenandoah River

SEE "CIVIL WAR IN THE SHENANDOAH" MAP

Front Royal

FRONT ROYAL (MAY 1862)

BALL'S BLUFF (21 OCTOBER 1861)

Arlington

WASHINGTON, DC

Fairfax

ALEXANDRIA

Blue Ridge Mountains

BULL RUN (21 JULY 1861 "FIRST MANASSAS") AND (29-30 AUGUST 1862 "SECOND MANASSAS")

Harrisonburg

CHANCELLORSVILLE (27 APRIL-6 MAY 1863)

Culpeper

WILDERNESS (5-6 MAY 1864)

Fredericksburg

FREDERICKSBURG (13 DECEMBER 1862)

SPOTSYLVANIA (8-12 MAY 1864)

GRANT'S OVERLAND CAMPAIGN (SPRING 1864)

Charlottesville

Pamunkey River

Mattaponi

James River

COLD HARBOR (31 MAY-12 JUNE 1864)

A

B

C

D

E

RICHMOND

LEE SURRENDERS AT APPOMATTOX COURTHOUSE (9 APRIL 1865)

LEE'S RETREAT (1-9 APRIL 1865)

Appomattox

SAILOR'S CREEK (6 APRIL 1865)

PETERSBURG (16-18 JUNE 1864)

Petersburg

FEDERAL VICTORY

CONFEDERATE VICTORY

INDECISIVE BATTLE

SEVEN DAYS BATTLES FOR RICHMOND (1862)
A. MECHANICSVILLE, JUNE 26
B. GAINE'S MILL, JUNE 27
C. SAVAGE'S STATION, JUNE 29
D. FRAYSER'S FARM (GLENDALE), JUNE 30
E. MALVERN HILL, JULY 1

0   15 mi
0   15 km

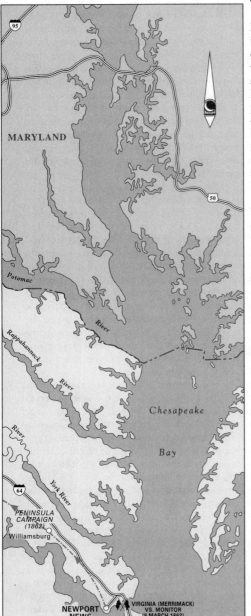

THE CIVIL WAR

In creating a new country, the American Revolution had left two major issues unresolved: the true dominion of the federal government over individual states, and the contradiction between the assertion of the equality of man in the Declaration of Independence and the fact that in America, more people owned other people than in any other country in the world. Before those questions would be answered, four years of fighting would make muddy wastelands of the same acres fought over in the Revolutionary War less than a century before, and close to 700,000 Americans—more than in both World Wars put together—would die.

As a border state located only a rifle shot from Washington, D.C., and home to the Confederate capital, Virginia suffered more major battles and witnessed more casualties than any other state. Both the first major clash of the Civil War and the peace treaty that signaled its end happened in the Old Dominion (on property owned by the same man), while the four intervening years left her graveyards full, her society in ruins, and literally tore the state in half.

Early Fighting

The Civil War began in earnest at the **First Battle of Bull Run** on July 21, 1861. Convinced the Rebels would turn and flee at the first hint of trouble, Washingtonians rode out from the city and spread out picnics on a hillside near Manassas to watch the battle. Fewer than half of the 57,000 troops present actually fought, and confusion reigned. Blue and gray uniforms appeared on both sides, along with highland kilts and baggy trousers straight from North Africa. The early Confederate flag resembled the Stars and Stripes so closely that gunners mistakenly fired on their own troops. On their retreat to Washington, routed Federal soldiers found themselves entangled with the carriages of fleeing spectators, and all hopes of a quick victory were extinguished.

Battle of the Ironclads

Union troops retreating from Portsmouth had burned, among other things, a steam frigate called the **Merrimac.** Desperate for any kind of

SOLDIERS AND POLITICIANS

Seven U.S. presidents served in the Union army during the Civil War. All were generals except McKinley, who was a major.

Chester A. Arthur   Rutherford B. Hayes
James A. Garfield   Andrew Johnson
Ulysses S. Grant   William McKinley
Benjamin Harrison

naval weapon to help break the tightening noose of the Union blockade, Confederate shipbuilders restored the charred hulk, covered it with steeply sloping iron plates, and rechristened her the *Virginia.* In March 1862, the reborn ship steamed into Hampton Roads like a "floating barn belching smoke," according to one witness, rammed a carriage-sized hole through one Union warship, sank another with cannon fire, and drove off three more as shells and bullets bounced off her sides. The next morning the Union unveiled its own metal ship called the *Monitor,* built with a round turret and a flat deck even with the waterline (a "Yankee Cheese Box on a raft"). Four hours of fighting and maneuvering accomplished little besides demonstrating both ships' resistance to gunfire. Hampton Roads remained under Union control, Gen. George B. McClellan was able to move troops by water to occupy Norfolk, and the *Virginia* was blown up to escape capture. The *Monitor* sank in a storm off North Carolina in December.

The Rebels Forge Ahead

Virginia's Confederate Tidewater area was evacuated after the defeat of the *Virginia,* and the first struggles for Richmond began. During what became known as the **Seven Days Battles** in late June 1862, Gen. McClellan propelled his newly trained Army of the Potomac to within sight of Richmond, but was pushed back by Robert E. Lee's inspired tactics. Gen. Thomas "Stonewall" Jackson helped Lee by tying up Union reinforcements in the Shenandoah Valley. Close to 35,000 soldiers died, but the threat to Richmond

was lifted, for the moment. At the **Second Battle of Manassas** in August and September, Union Gen. John Pope made the mistake of ordering pursuit when the Confederates weren't really retreating. Lee, Jackson, and Gen. James Longstreet took advantage, attacking with such ferocity that Pope barely managed a nighttime withdrawal back across the Bull Run River to safety.

With renewed confidence, Lee moved north, but the capture of a copy of Confederate marching orders led to a clash with McClellan at Antietam (an-TEET-um) near Sharpsburg, Maryland, on September 17. This battle remains the single deadliest day in American history, leaving 12,410 Union soldiers and 10,700 Rebels sprawled in the dirt. Lincoln saw an opportunity he had been waiting for, and on January 1, 1863, he issued the Emancipation Proclamation, freeing all slaves in areas not held by Union forces. This edict, which Lincoln called "the central act of my administration, and the greatest single event of the 19th century," thus turned the Civil War into a fight over slavery, pure and simple. England and France couldn't afford diplomatic recognition of the Confederacy without appearing to support the "peculiar institution" they had outlawed long ago, and the Southern cause became forever linked with human bondage.

Lee still seemed invincible, beating back Federal attacks on Virginia time and again. At **Fredericksburg** on December 13, 1862, Gen. Ambrose Burnside, though warned by Lincoln, didn't move quickly enough in crossing the Rappahannock, allowing Lee to entrench his forces on higher ground and win the battle. The battle of **Chancellorsville,** April 27–May 6, resulted in triumph and tragedy for the Rebels. Lee sent Jackson on a daring flanking maneuver toward a weak point in Gen. Joseph Hooker's line of 160,000. The Federals were pushed back across the Rappahannock in defeat. During the evening of May 2, however, Jackson was mistakenly fired on by his own troops, and died eight days later. "I know not how to replace him," mourned Lee, who had no choice but to press on without his star commander. Union forces were carrying the war's western theater,

the C.S.S. Virginia and the Monitor

threatening the South's control of the Mississippi River and occupying Tennessee. Nevertheless, General Lee and Jefferson Davis, president of the Confederacy, plotted an attempt to take the Federal capital. In June the Army of Northern Virginia crossed the Potomac.

The Tide Turns

Three days of fighting at **Gettysburg** in early July 1863 ended Confederate hopes of taking Washington, D.C., despite a final desperate charge by 11,000 Rebel soldiers under Gen. George Pickett into the face of point-blank gunfire. During the retreat, Lee told Pickett, "The men and officers of your command have written the name of Virginia as high today as it has ever been written before." One in three soldiers survived Pickett's Charge. When the smoke cleared, the Battle of Gettysburg—the bloodiest of any American war—had claimed more than 50,000 casualties. Vicksburg, Mississippi fell on July 4, 1863, and though two more years of fighting would follow, the Confederate cause was all but lost.

Virginia's westernmost districts had voted against secession in 1861, and now that Union forces controlled the entire region from the Ohio River to the mountains, they took action. In 1863 all of Virginia's counties beyond the Alleghenies and two at the northern end of the Shenandoah Valley were accepted into the Union as West Virginia.

A Slow End

By 1864, the Confederate economy was in shambles. The Union naval blockade kept the shoreline sealed, causing barrels of flour to sell for $200 and spurring bread riots in Richmond. Morale plummeted and Confederate soldiers began to desert in droves as it became obvious that only a miracle would bring a Southern victory. Though few citizens publicly suggested surrender, many blamed Jefferson Davis and the Confederate government for the deteriorating situation. The last realistic hope was that the Southern armies could prolong the fighting long enough for public disgust in the North to unseat Lincoln in the 1864 elections, bringing about the possibility of a negotiated peace.

Instead, Ulysses S. Grant, newly appointed commander of all Union armies, moved south with Richmond and General Lee's battle-weary Army of Northern Virginia in his sights. "Wherever Lee goes," Grant ordered Gen. George Meade, "there you will go also." Lee repeatedly outguessed Grant's flanking maneuvers as the Confederate army, undersupplied and half as large, dogged the Federals in a string of fierce battles that led slowly southward. During the **Battle of the Wilderness** (May 5–6, 1864), the opposing forces clashed in dense undergrowth. More than 25,000 troops—two-thirds of them Federals—died in the confused fighting, many in wildfires set by cannon bombardment. At lea

© JULIAN SMITH

ruins in Northern Virginia

12,000 more fell struggling for one square mile of ground called the "Bloody Angle" in the **Battle of Spotsylvania Court House** (May 8–21) nearby. Union victories came at a heavy price. In two months during the spring of 1864, the Federals lost 77,452 men in Virginia—more soldiers than there were in Lee's entire army.

Realizing he stood little chance of defeating Lee in straightforward combat, Grant moved south to lay siege to Richmond and Petersburg, the Confederate capital's vital supply center. Through the summer and fall of 1864, the Confederates watched helplessly as Gen. Philip Sheridan razed the fertile Shenandoah Valley and Gen. William Sherman began his famous "March to the Sea" from Atlanta to Savannah, cutting a swath of destruction through the Georgia heartland.

Richmond was evacuated and burned by its inhabitants on April 3, 1865, sending the Confederate government fleeing west to Danville. After fighting a final series of skirmishes in retreat across Virginia, Lee asked Grant for a meeting six days later on April 9. Grant later wrote, "I felt . . . sad and depressed at the downfall of a foe who had fought so long and valiantly, and had suffered so much for a cause, though that cause was, I

believe, one of the worst for which a people ever fought." The terms of surrender were drawn up and signed in the parlor of the Wilmer McLean House at Appomattox Court House, and on April 12 the ragged but unbowed Confederates turned over their arms and flags in a formal ceremony. The opposing armies saluted each other, and the war was over.

The Dust Settles

Virginia was readmitted to the Union in 1870, three years after Congress had placed the South under military rule. It's hard to overestimate the effect of defeat on the consciousness of the South, and Virginia and her inhabitants in particular. Society as they knew it had been utterly transformed from orderly and stratified to chaotic. Richmond and most of Fredericksburg and Petersburg lay in ruins, along with large sections of dozens of other cities and towns. Local currency was worthless, 350,000 slaves no longer had to take orders, and the rest of the work force—two whole generations of men—was left demoralized, wounded, or dead. By 1877, Virginia's total war loss was estimated at $457 million, a staggering amount when divided among only 1.2 million inhabitants.

Paying the debt, including $45 million owed even before the war, became the central political issue of the late 19th century. Decades of dissension followed as "Readjusters" took the reins of government in an effort to reduce the debt and interest. Before a compromise was reached, hundreds of schoolhouses were shut down due to lack of funds. By the turn of the 20th century, the economy had begun to gain momentum again. Once it had been freed from the narrow-minded control of the planter aristocracy, Virginians were able to diversify into smaller-scale agriculture, mining, commerce, and manufacture. Railroads again stretched across the state, and suburbs sprouted as the larger cities were rebuilt.

In contrast, the decades following the Emancipation Proclamation marked one of the lowest points in the history of American blacks. Slavery was over, but freedom was still drowned by the hostile voices of many white Southerners. Even though a new state constitution drawn up in

1867 ratified universal male suffrage for both races, a series of rulings preserved slavery in everything but name for years. Restrictive "Black codes," poll taxes, and the 1896 Supreme Court decision in *Plessy v. Ferguson* kept minorities in a parallel existence that was definitely "separate" but far from "equal." Voting by blacks fell 90 percent (as did the turnout of poor whites, though not as much) when handwritten applications were required for voter registration. While there was much less racial violence in Virginia than in states farther south, the mere appearance of the Ku Klux Klan in certain regions was enough to discourage any protest.

Meanwhile the myth of the Old South began to take root in books, songs, and popular culture. The past, real or imagined, provided comfort during the hard times following the Confederate defeat. The horrors of the war—still evident in missing limbs, ruined buildings, and mass graves—began to take on the sheen of chivalry, with gallant young soldiers fighting and dying in vain defense of their homeland. Nineteenth-century novelist James Branch Campbell noted that Southerners were creating "in the same instant that they lamented the Old South's extinction, an Old South which had died proudly at Appomattox without ever having been besmirched by the wear and tear of existence."

20TH CENTURY

As the digits clicked over from nines to zeros, Virginia found itself increasingly a contender on the national playing field. Chemical fertilizers made farmers less dependent on tobacco and diversification into industry continued. World War I stimulated the economy even more by sparking an enormous expansion of the Newport News shipyard, bringing in money and workers. Tourism began to bring in significant income, and once again a Virginian sat in the White House—Woodrow Wilson served two presidential terms from 1913–1921. The Great Depression slowed mining and the wheat and tobacco markets, but the state suffered less than others thanks to the frugality of a new captain at the helm.

The Byrd Years

The governorship of 1926–1930 marked the beginning of half a century of political impact for Democrat Harry F. Byrd., Sr. Tracing his lineage to 17th-century merchant and land speculator William Byrd, this leading Southern progressive brought Virginia's government into the modern age with a policy of honesty and efficiency. During his tenure as governor, various laws revised the tax system, expanded highways, set aside more money for social-welfare programs including schools and mental hospitals, and promised severe penalties for lynching. A solid core of Virginia conservatism remained, though; in 1928 the state voted for a Republican presidential candidate for the first time since 1872. Roosevelt's New Deal was viewed with skepticism even as it made the government the state's leading source of revenue from 1932 on. World War II brought thousands of soldiers to military camps throughout the state and caused Hampton Roads to mushroom even more to support the shipyards and the Norfolk Naval Base.

By mid-century, Virginia had shifted from a rural state to an urban one as its population, which had doubled since the turn of the century, leapt by 25 percent from 1940–1950. Thanks to the stability of the Byrd administration, employment rose and rural blacks and big labor began to emerge as potent political forces.

Race Relations

Blacks in Virginia continued to struggle against a statewide system of segregation that kept nonwhite schools inferior and prohibited minorities from sitting on juries and holding public office. Even without the incidents of violence that plagued the deeper South, many black citizens emigrated from Virginia to Washington, D.C. and the northeast in search of better lives. When the unanimous 1954 Supreme Court decision in ***Brown v. Board of Education*** declared segregation inherently unequal and therefore illegal, a massive statewide resistance blossomed. This would mark the last attempt to hold onto the old order in an embarrassing departure from the usual Virginian civility.

Spurred on by Sen. Harry Flood Byrd (son of

KEY DATES IN VIRGINIA HISTORY

1607	Jamestown settled
1610	Jamestown almost fails due to winter famine, inept leadership, and poor planning
1612/13	John Rolfe plants first crop of West Indian tobacco
1788	House of Burgesses, the first representative assembly in the New World, convenes at Jamestown
	First blacks brought to Virginia
1624	Virginia becomes a royal colony when Virginia Company's charter is revoked
1676	Bacon's Rebellion against Governor Berkeley's administration fails
1693	College of William and Mary founded in Williamsburg
1699	Colonial capital moved to Middle Plantation (now Williamsburg)
1774	British Gov. John Murray dissolves House of Burgesses
	Newly formed Virginia Convention calls for first Continental Congress
1775	Patrick Henry advocates rebellion in famous speech to House of Burgesses
	Revolutionary War begins at Lexington and Concord, Massachusetts
1776	Declaration of Independence signed in Philadelphia
	Virginia Convention adopts state constitution and bill of rights
1779	Richmond becomes state capital

1781	Lord Cornwallis surrenders to Gen. George Washington at Yorktown, ending American Revolution
1788	Virginia ratifies U.S. Constitution
1789	George Washington becomes first president of United States
1831	Nat Turner's slave rebellion
1859	John Brown's raid on Harper's Ferry
1861	Civil War begins
	Virginia secedes from the Union, joins Confederate States
	Richmond becomes Confederate capital
1863	West Virginia splits from Virginia, admitted to Union
1865	Lee surrenders to Ulysses S. Grant at Appomattox, ending Civil War
1870	Virginia readmitted to Union
1889	Newport News opens Simpson Dry Dock, the largest in the world
1954	U.S. Supreme Court decision to end segregation in public schools meets massive resistance in Virginia
1957	Chesapeake Bay Bridge-Tunnel completed
1969	First Republican elected governor of Virginia since 1886
1971	State constitution rewritten
1990	L. Douglas Wilder, the country's first African American governor, is elected in Virginia

Harry, Sr.), the General Assembly voted to withhold state funds from any school honoring integration. By 1958, intergrated public schools in Charlottesville, Norfolk, and Front Royal had closed. One year later, Gov. Lindsay Almond bowed to popular protest, business pressure, and the federal courts by accepting limited integration (all the while railing against the "livid stench of sadism, sex immorality, and juvenile pregnancy" that he believed resulted from the integration of public schools in Washington, D.C.). Schools in Prince Edward County remained closed until 1964, focusing national attention on the fact that black children were receiving no

education while white children attended private institutions. The 1965 Civil Rights Voting Act and the 24th Amendment to the Constitution ended the struggle, at least in the eyes of the law, and assured minorities in Virginia and elsewhere of their right to representation.

Recent History

Virginia's economic and technological boom is best evidenced in the northern part of the state. Fairfax County, home to 41,000 residents in 1940, counted 533,000 in 1973—a 1,200 percent increase. The result has been, in the eyes of many, a lesson in development gone wrong as pastoral farmlands are transformed into faceless suburbs. On a brighter note, the country's first test-tube baby was delivered at Norfolk General Hospital on December 28, 1981.

Meanwhile, state politics have made the transition to a true multiparty democracy controlled for the most part by Democrats. Harry F. Byrd, Sr., died in 1966, and a series of liberal Democrats then came to power. After three successive gubernatorial elections were won by Republicans, a Democrat again carried the election in 1981. In 1990, L. Douglas Wilder became the first elected black governor in the state and the country. Born in Richmond to children of former slaves, Wilder received a Bronze Star for heroism in the Korean War and a law degree from Howard University. He gained attention as the state's first black senator in 1969 for his efforts to change the state song and to es-

tablish a holiday for the birthday of Martin Luther King, Jr. Wilder won the race for governor by fewer than 7,000 votes.

By the early '90s, Virginia's population was well over 6 million, with two-thirds of Virginians living in cities; the state's per capita income ranked 12th in the country. The extraordinary transformation from half a century ago—when two-thirds of only 2.7 million people lived in rural areas—owes much to the release of the past, primarily in the form of segregation. Crossing the Potomac from Washington, D.C. used to be a step back in time to a proud but impoverished land living out its dreams of yesterday and insulated from the rest of the nation. Today it's a step forward into busy financial and manufacturing centers and a modern agricultural system tied into the global market, where the past still echoes but no longer impedes.

Economy and Government

ECONOMY

With the nation's capital just across the Potomac, it's no surprise the federal government dominates Virginia's financial picture. Four hundred fifty square miles of military facilities, including the Pentagon in Arlington and the Marine Corps base in Quantico, provide a substantial chunk of the state's gross product. In 1990 the Department of Defense employed 108,000 people spread throughout 29 military installations. It's slightly ironic that this traditionally conservative state has been buoyed so much by the mid-century expansion of military and federal agencies within her borders. Virginia is one of the top five recipients of federal funds in the country, with the federal government responsible for almost one-seventh of the state's gross product.

Shipbuilding leads the manufacturing sector, followed by tobacco processing and light industry, producing chemicals, clothing, machinery, wood products, and food. High-tech firms are concentrated in northern Virginia, while mining consortiums supervise the extraction of coal, granite, sand, clay, and other minerals from the

southwestern hillsides. Tourism brought in almost $10 billion in 1995, making it the third-largest retail industry and employer.

Agriculture is the next big earner, centered on dairy products, livestock, fruit, and grains. More than 30 percent of Virginia's 93,000 acres of peanut farms crowd the mouth of the Chesapeake Bay. As the productivity demands of the 20th century forced farms to become more and more mechanized, many smaller family operations closed, sending ex-employees to the cities in search of work. Surviving farms have tended to shrink. In 1990 there were about 46,000 farms throughout the state averaging 193 acres each, and farming—once the backbone of the state's economy—had fallen to about 1 percent of Virginia's annual economy. The coastal fishing industry is the state's smallest revenue producer, despite hundreds of millions of pounds of fish and shellfish pulled from the Chesapeake Bay each year.

GOVERNMENT

The executive branch of Virginia's state government consists of three elected positions: governor, lieutenant governor, and attorney general. Each serves a four-year term, but governors cannot be reelected. Seven judges are appointed to the supreme court, the highest of four judiciary levels, for 12-year terms. The 10-member Virginia Court of Appeals was started in 1985.

Virginia's legislative body is the General Assembly, consisting of 40 senators serving four-year terms and 100 delegates elected every two years. It meets every January in Richmond for sessions of 30 or 60 days. The state constitution, adopted in 1971, is Virginia's seventh since 1776.

A moderately conservative electorate has voted for Republican presidents in nine out of 12 elections since 1948. Democrats, though, dominated state politics from 1883–1970, when Linwood Holden became the first Republican governor in 87 years. However, the General Assembly has remained mostly Democratic, and the party reclaimed the gubernatorial office in 1982 and held it until George Allen's 1994 gubernatorial victory. In 2001, both of Virginia's senators, Allen and John Warner, were Republicans. Allen's narrow defeat (52–48 percent) of incumbent Democratic Sen. Chuck Robb ended a long era of Democratic control over Virginia politics that began in the 1970s.

Current Republican Gov. Jim Gilmore was elected in 1997 on a platform of tax cuts and improvements in education. The Richmond native and U.Va. alumnus, formerly the state Attorney General, has already cut tuition and fees at Virginia's public colleges and universities by 20 percent, provided $26 million in funding for the state's historically black universities, and delivered the biggest tax cut in Virginia's history.

The People

SETTLEMENT

For a group with such a strong historical identity, Virginians are a surprisingly diverse lot. And it's not as if they haven't had time to blend; the first settlers stumbled ashore and kissed the earth in 1619, and people have been arriving ever since. Early colonists almost all came from rural England, mostly the midland and southern counties near London. Arrivals from Wales and France in the 18th century had to make room for the large numbers of Irish, German, and Scotch-Irish farmers who flowed into the Shenandoah Valley from New Jersey, Pennsylvania, and Maryland. Native tribes were decimated by imported diseases they had no immunity against, until a mere fraction of tens of thousands of Native Americans remained.

The first blacks arrived in 1619 as indentured servants, but by the end of the century thousands of African slaves were being hauled ashore and sold as labor on huge Tidewater plantations. Virginia quickly became the most crowded state in the New World, relatively speaking, with a population that doubled every quarter century after 1680. By the eve of the Revolutionary War, the colony counted 550,000 inhabitants, almost half of whom were black.

The state broke the one-million mark near the beginning of the 19th century, but lost many during the carnage of the Civil War and as a result of the secession of several western counties, which became West Virginia in 1863.

CURRENT STATISTICS

In 2000, nearly three-quarters of Virginia's more than seven million inhabitants lived in the metropolitan corridor stretching south from Washington, D.C., to Richmond and east to Hampton Roads. Virginia Beach led in population, followed by Norfolk, Richmond, Newport News, and Chesapeake. Just under 75 percent of Virginians describe themselves as Caucasian. Almost 20 percent are black, concentrated in the Piedmont and coast area (central Richmond and Charles City county on the Historic Peninsula are both more than three-quarters African American).

Other minorities, mostly Hispanic, Asian, and Middle Eastern, make up the remaining population. In the last decade, Hampton Roads had

INTRODUCTION

© JULIAN SMITH

Holy Land USA

one of the country's fastest-growing Jewish communities, as well as growing numbers of immigrants from India.

The state's per capita income is the highest in the southeast and slightly above the national average, with about 11 percent below the poverty line and about 11 percent earning more than $75,000 in annual household income.

ATTITUDES

It's almost impossible to summarize a state this varied, but if any quality holds true across the board, it's affability. A wave is the surest sign, whether it's from the driver of a pickup passing on a back road or a complete stranger helping you parallel park. Locals are more than happy to point you in the right direction or to give you their two cents on the most recent scandal across the Potomac; just be patient because folks tend to choose their words carefully.

A mild but deeply rooted conservative streak, also called "a touch of old Southern values," runs beneath day-to-day affairs in more traditional parts of the state. This pride in the past can alternately—or simultaneously—glorify Virginia's

rich heritage and sustain less welcome parts of it. Race relations, while better than in most Southern states, have been slightly inflamed in recent controversies over the designation of the third Monday in January as Lee-Jackson-King Day (rather than just Martin Luther King, Jr. Day) and former Gov. George Allen's quickly rescinded decree that April be declared Confederate History and Heritage Month.

In the early '90s, former Gov. L. Douglas Wilder, the grandson of former slaves, led the fight to retire the state song "Carry Me Back To Old Virginia," written by black minstrel James Bland in the 1870s. The song, which depicts a slave fondly remembering the days when he "labored so hard for old Massa/Day after day in the fields of yellow corn," infuriated black legislators and mortified many white legislators as well. It hadn't been played at official functions since the 1970s but wasn't officially retired by the General Assembly until 1997. A new state song will be selected in January 2002, when a special committee will select from several entries, including songs by Donna & Jimmy Dean and A.P. Carter. Click on the "State Song" link at www.acir.state.va.us for an update.

Virginia is a pious state, too, with a religious conservatism evidenced by broadcasts of the "700 Club" from Pat Robertson's Christian Broadcasting Network in Norfolk and by Jerry Falwell's Liberty University near Lynchburg. A tradition of religious acceptance dates back to Thomas Jefferson's 1785 Statute for Religious Freedom. Today Protestants—mostly Methodists, Southern Baptists, and Presbyterians—outnumber other religious groups. You will come across pockets of Quakers and Mennonites in the Shenandoah and Hunt Country, and Richmond has one of the largest Jewish populations of any city its size in the country.

On the Road

With so many activities readily available, it's a surprise Virginians ever get anything done. Simply put, if you can do it on the East Coast, you can probably do it here, from shopping to surfing and most everything in between.

Hours and admission prices vary depending on the season. Children's prices generally apply to kids under 12, with tots admitted for free. Senior admission falls somewhere in between the adult and child price. Taking pictures is against the rules in many museums and historical houses; ask first.

Outdoor Recreation

GENERAL RESOURCES

Information on the state's incredible range of open-air activities can be ordered from the **Virginia Department of Conservation and Recreation** (DCR), 203 Governor St., Suite 302, Richmond, VA 23219, 804/786-1712 or 800/933-7275, www.dcr.state.va.us. This is also the place to go for information on Virginia's 65 **state parks and natural areas** (www.dcr.state.va.us/parks), which together cover almost 75,000 acres. See individual park listings for more details.

The Virginia section of the Great Outdoor Resource Page (**GORP**) (www.gorp.com/gorp/location/va/va.htm) lists activities, tour operators, and links for the entire state. Finally, a great source for articles and activity listings in the Mid-Atlantic states is *Blue Ridge Outdoors,* a free monthly tabloid-format magazine distributed

Shenandoah

throughout Virginia. You can also get it directly from Portico Publications, Ltd., 222 South St., Charlottesville, VA 22902, 434/817-2755, www.blueridgeoutdoors.com.

HIKING AND CAMPING

The simplest way to enjoy Virginia often reveals her humblest, but most profound, pleasures. Whether it's an evening amble down a country lane or a predawn slog up some rocky peak, walking only requires two legs, a pair of boots, and a little time and effort. For this small investment you can find yourself in a nearly forgotten corner of the state, resting by an icy waterfall or enjoying a 50-mile view—or maybe just down the road, discussing bait fish with the folks at the local market.

Shenandoah National Park draws D.C. residents by the station-wagon full, and for good reason because it encloses some of the choicest acres in Appalachia. Most visitors never go more than an hour from the asphalt, though, leaving the backcountry to the more determined. Through the park coils part of the famous Appalachian Trail, tramped by hundreds of through-hikers and thousands of day-ramblers every year. Further south lies the Mount Rogers National Recreation Area and Breaks Interstate Park, both rugged and less trafficked.

Other established trails such as the Washington and Old Dominion, Virginia Creeper, and New River started out as railroad beds before being reborn as foot-power freeways. For details on these routes (which are also open to bikes and horses), refer to the relevant chapters in this book or call the **Rails-to-Trails Conservancy** in Washington, D.C., at 202/797-5400, www.railstrails.org.

Underlying it all is more than three million acres of the **George Washington and Jefferson National Forests,** covering most of the mountains and more than one-eighth of the entire state. More information on the national forests can be found at local district offices (listed in the regional sections) or the Supervisor's office at 5162 Valleypointe Pkwy., Roanoke, VA 24019-3050, 800/265-0019 or 540/265-5100, www.southernregion.fs.fed.us/gwj.

The **Potomac Appalachian Trail Club,** 118 Park Street SE, Vienna, VA 22180-4609, 703/242-0693, fax 703/242-0968, email: info@patc.net, www.patc.net, is a great resource for information on hikes, excursions, and work trips on the AT and elsewhere. Call their Activities Information Line at 703/242-0965 for trips scheduled the following week. (For more information on the Appalachian Trail, see the special topic in the Shenandoah chapter.)

Swimming holes statewide (and along the entire East Coast, for that matter) are listed online at www.swimmingholes.org, and you can create and download a custom topographic map from **TopoZone** (www.topozone.com).

BICYCLING
Mountain Biking

Fat-tire fanatics will quickly find that Virginia's high country offers some of the best steep dirt on the East Coast. *Mountain Bike* magazine voted Charlottesville the number 8 "Dream Town" in the country for mountain bikers, while *Dirt Rag* has called Harrisonburg one of 11 great biking destinations around the world. Many excellent foot trails are also open to knobby tires—just heed the creed. Difficulty ranges from countless miles of easy-grade dirt roads to single-track descents that will turn your hair white. These last are taken full advantage of by annual downhill events throughout the state. Interstate 81 provides handy access to trails and approach roads following the length of the Blue Ridge.

Various books can tell you where to go, and a handful of tour companies can take you there. National Forest district offices are good sources of information on trail conditions and maps, as are local bike shops, some of which also rent bikes. If you're looking for a more sedate ride, every former-railroad trail has a host of agencies that offer rentals and shuttle service to cyclists; obtain information from **Rails-to-Trails Conservancy** 1100 17th St. NW, Washington, DC 20036, 202/331-9696, fax 202/331-9680, email: railstrails@transact.org, www.railstrails.org.

The **Eastern Virginia Mountainbike Asso-**

DIRT RULES

The **International Mountain Biking Association (IMBA),** 1121 Broadway, Ste. 203, P.O. Box 7578, Boulder, CO 80306, 303/545-9011 or 888/442-4622, email: info@imba.com, www.imba.com, advocates a set of guidelines designed to ensure that mountain bikers will always be welcome in the backcountry:

Ride on Open Trails Only. Stay out of wilderness areas, don't trespass on private land, and respect road and trail closures.

Leave No Trace. Stick to well-worn, hard-packed trails and forest roads whenever possible, and don't encourage erosion by mud-bogging right after a rainstorm.

Control Your Bicycle. Don't give fellow bikers a bad rap by hitting someone else.

Always Yield Trail. Cyclists should give way to both hikers and horses on the trail. Let them know you're coming, then slow down or even stop to let them pass.

Never Spook Animals. Give horses a wide berth (consider dismounting), and leave the cows alone.

Plan Ahead. Don't strand yourself by overestimating your abilities, and always wear a helmet.

Cycling Events

Bike Virginia, 757/229-0507, fax 757/259-2372, email: info@bikevirginia.org, www.bikevirginia.org, is an annual five-day ride down back roads, past historical monuments and natural wonders covering about 50 miles per day. Some 2,000 cyclists a year sign up to explore a different part of the state. Vehicles carry your luggage, and the trip organizers can help arrange meals and accommodations every evening. The tour costs $185 adults, $125 kids 13–17, $75 kids under 12.

The **Tour de Chesapeake,** P.O. Box 552, Mathews, VA 23109, 804/897-8867, fax 804/768-2259, email: info@tourdechesapeake.org, www.tourdechesapeake.org, sticks close to the water in mid-May. Choose from rides of 15–62 miles for $40 adult, $20 children. In October the **Shenandoah Fall Foliage Bike Festival** P.O. Box 3187, Staunton VA 24402, fax 540/885-2669, email: info@shenandoahbike.org, www.shenandoahbike.org, has road rides of 10–76 miles starting and ending in Staunton ($70 adults, $50 kids 13–17, $30 kids under 12).

For more information on events, look up the **Virginia Cycling Association,** www.vacycling.org, an organization of a dozen or so local cycling clubs. The Virginia State Bicycle Coordinator offers an annual list of biking events on its website (www.vdot.state.us/info/vabikeing/bikevent.html).

ciation, P.O. Box 7553, Hampton, VA 23666, 757/722-4609 ext. 33, fax 757/723-4870, email: membership@emva.org, www.evma.org, specializes in the Tidewater area. Other good sources of biking information are the **International Mountain Biking Association,** P.O. Box 7578, Boulder, CO 80306-9899, 303/545-9011, email: imba@aol.com, www.imba.com, and the **Virginia State Bicycle Coordinator,** Virginia Department of Transportation, 1401 E. Broad St., Richmond, VA 23219, 800/835-1203, email: vabiking@vdot.state.va.us, www.vdot.state.va.us. *Blue Ridge Outdoors* magazine publishes an annual Virginia Bicycling Guide, listing local bike clubs and good rides.

Road Biking

Paved roads running through the rural countryside make road riding just as rewarding as off-road adventures. A weekend in the saddle can be as diverse as a salt-breezed spin along the Eastern Shore to a turn through the rolling hills of the Piedmont, all along back roads far from the roar of the interstates. Both the Tour DuPont and the Tour de Trump follow the Skyline Drive and Blue Ridge Parkway along the crest of the mountains. Colonial Parkway connects Jamestown, Williamsburg, and Yorktown across the neck of the Historic Peninsula. Three major cycling circuits (part of Interstate Bicycle Routes 1 and 76) cross the state, including 500 miles of

ON THE ROAD

VIRGINIA CYCLING CLUBS

Central Virginia Mountain Bike Association
207 Hunters Creek Rd.
Forest, VA 24551
804/522-6581
email: ckrhodes@worldnet.att.net
website: www.go.to/cvma

The Discovery Program
200 Macon Rd.
Orange, VA 22960
540/672-2296
email: amink@ns.gemlink.com

Eastern Virginia Mountain Bike Association
P.O. Box 7553
Hampton, VA 2366
email: patandjudyhurley@worldnet.att.net
website: www.evma.org

Explore Park Trail Association
P.O. Box 8508
Roanoke, VA 24014
540/427-1800
email: jvodnik49@aol.com
website: www.exploresingletrack.com

Iron Mountain Trail Club
P.O. Box 1085
Damascus, VA 24236
540/475-6108
email: thorsch@naxs.com
website: bikeguy.naxs.com

Mid-Atlantic Off-Road Enthusiasts
P.O. Box 2662
Fairfax, VA 22031
703/707-6576
email: brionm@erols.com
website: www.more-mtb.org

the Trans-America Bicycle Trail from Breaks Interstate Park to Yorktown and sections of Maine-to-Virginia and Virginia-to-Florida routes, both of which hit Richmond. For maps and more information, contact the State Bicycle Coordinator, who can also send you brochures on state cycling laws.

Riders from both camps can benefit from the **Adventure Cycling Association** (ACA), 150 East Pine Street, P.O. Box 8308, Missoula, MT 59807, 800/755-2453 or 406/721-1776, fax 406/721-8754, email: info@adventurecycling.org, www.adventurecycling.org, a nonprofit organization that helps support the development and maintenance of more than 25,000 miles of roads and off-road trails nationwide. Among other benefits, members can join organized tours and transport their bicycles free on Northwest Airlines. The ACA stocks long-distance gear, books, and excellent route maps (both the TransAmerica Bicycle Trail and the Atlantic Coast Route cross Virginia). Their annual TransAmerica ride from Williamsburg to Portland, Oregon, spread out more than 93 days, costs $3,200 pp with full support.

Wherever you go, don't overestimate your abilities or underestimate the terrain. Take foul-weather gear, tire patches, a pump, and enough food and water to keep you going in case the next rest stop is farther than you thought. In the countryside, angry dogs can be a nuisance and occasionally a danger. Outrunning them is an option (most will give up the chase once you leave their territory), as is shouting and dismounting to put your bike between Cujo and yourself. Save kicking, Macing, or whacking with a pump for a last resort.

HORSEBACK RIDING

Hundreds of miles of trails are open to riders, including the Virginia Creeper and New River. The Virginia Highlands Horse Trail in the Mount Rogers National Recreation Area is probably the state's most popular, with campsites specifically designed for horse traffic. Various lodges, farms, and outfitters throughout the Shenandoah and southwest Virginia can set you up for a day ride, including guided rides from Skyland Lodge in Shenandoah National Park. The Virginia Horse

Mountain Bike Virginia
14200 Birds Eye Terrace
Chester, VA 23831
email: bikewright@earthlink.net

Potomac Velo Club
15611 Rhame Dr.
Dumfries, VA 22026
website: www.potomacvelo.com

Shenandoah Mountain Bike Club
132 New York Ave.
Harrisonburg, VA 22801
540/568-6777
email: carpenmc@jmu.edu
website: www.shenandoahbicycle.com

Virginia Beach Bicycle Association
2642 Holland Rd., Ste. 103
Virginia Beach, VA 23452
757/498-3873
email: ttntcycles@aol.com
website: www.importservice.com

Williamsburg Area Bicyclists
106 Indian Springs Rd.
Williamsburg, VA 23185
email: rsmcki@mail.wm.edu

Winchester Wheelmen
P.O. Box 1695
Winchester, VA 22604
540/662-7654
email: mollyg@asti-usa.com

Center near Lexington hosts national equine events. Contact the **Virginia Horse Council,** email: vhj@virginiahorse.com, www.virginiahorse.com/council, for a statewide list of stables and public horse trails—or take a look at their publication, *The Virginia Horse Journal,* www.virginiahorse.com.

Riding takes on a more patrician air in the Piedmont area and the Hunt Country of northern Virginia, where horses have been a cornerstone of life for generations. **Fox hunts** in spring and fall evoke Old England (and horrify animal-rights activists) with groups of riders in traditional uniforms galloping after packs of baying hounds. In American hunts, the event itself is more important than the actual fox, which is

© JULIAN SMITH

Steeple-chasing is a rich tradition in Virginia.

rarely caught. You'll have to be invited by a member of a hunt (local club) to ride even on a mock hunt; most observers follow by car and enjoy tailgate picnics along the way—don't forget the corkscrew. During the November–March season, you might be able to catch the blessing of the hounds, a ritual in which a priest or minister invokes divine guidance on the pack.

Long before Virginia-born Secretariat won the Triple Crown in 1973, **horse races** raised the blood pressure of both species involved. Dozens of steeplechases and assorted flat-track events take advantage of the state's prime horse stock, which goes back to thoroughbred stallions like Bulle Rock, imported from England in 1730. Races are held from spring to fall at places such as Foxfield near Charlottesville, where dressy tailgate parties distract college students and race fans alike. The Plains, near Middleburg, hosts the Virginia Gold Cup in May and the International Gold Cup in October.

The Middleburg visitors center or the **Virginia Steeplechase Association,** www.middleburgonline.com/steeplechase/steeplchase.html, can provide a listing of seasonal horse events. For information on some two dozen local hunts, steeplechase, and "point-to-point" races, contact the *Chronicle of the Horse,* P.O. Box 46, Middleburg, VA 20118, 540/687-6341, fax 540/687-3937, www.chronofhorse.com, and then contact the local clubs themselves.

Polo matches usually include the traditional divot-stomping at halftime. Recent referendums have begun to reverse religious-inspired prohibitions on pari-mutuel betting, making new tracks like the Colonial Downs in Richmond the place to lay your money down.

CLIMBING

At least 30 recognized climbing areas scattered along the Blue Ridge provide a respectable alternative to West Virginia's Seneca Rocks, with a fraction of the crowds. Most cliffs are 40–60 feet high and can be top-roped. Access is easy and legal to routes in national forests and state and national parks, and you might even find some winter ice at places such as Crabtree Falls and White Oak Canyon. Great Falls on the Potomac is one of the most popular sites in the D.C. area, with more than 100 routes of all levels.

Don't trespass on private land, and clean up any mess you make to help ensure that future climbers will be welcome. Jeff Watson's *Virginia Climber's Guide* and Eric Hörst's *Rock Climbing Virginia, West Virginia, and Maryland* are both good sources. The Mountaineering Section of the Potomac Appalachian Trail Club (PATC, see "Hiking and Camping" section) organizes rock or ice climbs most weekends. Contact the PATC for details.

RAFTING, KAYAKING, AND CANOEING

Few things embody the Virginia landscape as much as flowing water, etching the Piedmont before widening into the watery highways of the Tidewater and the Chesapeake Bay. Some 380 miles of Virginia's waterways have been declared State Scenic Rivers for their beauty, historic significance, or recreational value. All told, nearly 200 rivers, creeks, and channels are open to boaters of every kind, many with excellent public access. Calmer waters fill tidal estuaries and more than 30 lakes ranging 500–50,000 acres. Dozens of outfitters and tour companies can put you on the water.

The foothills of the Blue Ridge are only the beginning of the journey for Virginia's biggest rivers, whose upper reaches often churn with white water, like the Russell Fork as it roars through the canyons of Breaks Interstate Park. Rafters and kayakers in search of a challenge should also look east to the fall line, where wide, slow rivers suddenly gush over a natural ledge that runs the length of the state. Even though the park itself is closed to boaters, the Potomac River seethes near Great Falls Park into one of the finest white-water stretches in the east. The James River can reach Class V, depending on the season, within sight of Richmond.

Between the chutes and holes lie placid stretches ideal for canoes and inner tubes—the Clinch, Maury, Mattaponi, upper James, and the South Fork of the Shenandoah are just a few of the most popular watercourses. A canoe is also the best way to explore the spooky depths of the

Great Dismal Swamp or the boggy reaches of the Nottaway and Blackwater rivers near Suffolk. Always bring food, drinking water, sunscreen, and a change of clothes in a waterproof container (trash bags work). River shoes and insect repellent can also come in handy.

The **Virginia Professional Paddlesports Association,** 540/635-1553, email: info@vappa.com, www.vappa.com, is a good place to direct water sports questions. Member businesses are listed on their website, which also has paddle-trip tips. **Blue Ridge River Runners,** P.O. Box 10243, Lynchburg, VA 24501, 434/929-1313, www.hovac.com/wa4pgm/brrr.htm, is a group that advocates river safety and the protection of Virginia's waterways and can help arrange paddling instruction. Likewise, **American Whitewater,** 1430 Fenwick Ln., Silver Spring, MD 20910, 866/262-8429, email: Nick@amwhitewater.org, www.amewhitewater.org, lists conservation information and river level readings. Some rafting companies are listed under **Organized Tours,** otherwise look under individual city listings.

BOATING

On the Chesapeake Bay and the Atlantic, it may take more effort and money to hit the water, but it's almost guaranteed to be well worth it. **Excursion** or **cruise** boats, from restored wooden schooners to modest motorboats, take passengers on sightseeing junkets. The trips, which can last anywhere from an hour to all day, usually feature narration on points of interest and drinks, snacks, or even a full sit-down meal (on the luxury dinner yachts up the Potomac). You'll find more locals than tourists aboard **water taxis** and **ferries,** which simply shuttle between one shore and another.

Charter boats, under both sail and mechanized power, can be rented for a day or longer to go after trophy fish or to explore the farthest reaches of the seaward islands. Expect to have your references and credentials thoroughly checked if you plan to rent one "barebones," meaning without a captain. A hired skipper will tack on at least $100 to the price, which tends to be around $250 for two days (often a minimum rental). Charters often leave from **marinas,** shoreside establishments that

are combination truck stop, mini-mart, and RV campground. Mooring slips, electrical hookups, holding-tank pumps, fresh water fill-up, bait, tackle, and crusty advice are standard, with the occasional laundry, grocery, and shower facilities thrown in for good measure.

Various local schools offer classes in the operation and navigation of sailing and power boats. Your next step will probably be a rental, either of a full-sized craft or a smaller day sailer, windsurfer, or rowboat. Most major lakes and countless locations along the bay and coast have public launching ramps for boat trailers. Contact the DCR for a map of public access to the Chesapeake Bay and its tributaries, and look at the *Virginia State Road Atlas* for other river and lake access points.

SURFING

Virginia Beach is without a doubt the most popular surfing area on the coast. Be careful of local regulations: surfing is prohibited in some spots and within 300 feet of piers; wear a leash to avoid a fine. Summer surfing hours typically run from sunrise to 10 A.M. and 5 P.M. to sunset. A good break curls near the jetty off 1st Street near the Lighthouse Restaurant. Conditions are just as promising along the Eastern Shore, but difficult access keeps many surfers away. You'll need a flat-bottomed boat to explore the outer islands of the Virginia Coast Reserve.

Swells are usually small (1–5 feet), but can grow to 9–10 feet during the winter and spring nor'easters or late summer hurricanes. Early fall is most dependable. You'll probably need at least a partial wetsuit in the spring and fall, and an early start is essential to enjoy the summer warmth without the crowds. Bottoms are sandy. Virginia Beach is full of surf shops, some of which rent boards.

For more details, order *The Surf Report,* Vol. 8, #12, from Surfer Publications, P.O. Box 1028, Dana Point, CA 92629, 714/496-5922, fax 714/496-7849. The Virginia District of the **Eastern Surfing Association** can be contacted at P.O. Box 4619, Virginia Beach, VA 23454, email: va@surfesa.org, www.surfesa.org. For online surf conditions, try www.mcnetwork.com/surf.

FISHING

The more than 75,000 registered anglers (annually) have statewide conservation efforts to thank for the quality of fishing in Virginia. Both fly and bait casters can go after native Eastern brook trout in the hillside streams of Shenandoah National Park, part of 2,800 miles of trout waters within the Blue Ridge. Bass are ubiquitous throughout the state—the upper James River can't be beat for smallmouth, with more trophy fish per mile than any other Virginia river. Sunfish and catfish are also plentiful, joined by crappie and white perch downstream near Richmond. Head to the South Fork of the Shenandoah River for redbreast sunfish, then try the New River for yellow perch, muskellunge, and walleye, and the Chickahominy near Walker's Dam in late spring for bluegill, chain pickerel, and herring. Almost all of the state's lakes and reservoirs also offer excellent fishing: Smith Mountain Lake near Roanoke is Virginia's top spot for striped bass, and largemouth bass fishing in the John H. Kerr Reservoir along the North Carolina border can't be beat. Charter boats ply the Chesapeake Bay for trout, bluefish, flounder, drum, and sharks, while deep-sea boats leave Virginia Beach in search of marlin, sailfish, and sea bass. Peak saltwater season is May–September.

The **Virginia Department of Game and Inland Fisheries,** 4010 West Broad St., Richmond, VA 23230-1104, 804/367-1000, www.dgif .state.va.us, can provide details on fishing spots and regulations, along with an annual guide to freshwater angling throughout the state. Freshwater licenses are available to nonresidents over 16 for $30 from sporting goods stores, bait shops, and marinas (stocked-trout permits are another $30, and tack on $3.50 to fish in the National Forest). No permits are required for saltwater fishing from Cape Henry to North Carolina. They're required except for the first weekend in June, when nontrout fishing is free statewide. For information on fishing in the Chesapeake Bay, try www.chesapeakeangler.net.

HUNTING

Hunting ranks near the top of the list of Virginia's most popular activities—though more among lo-

ONE NATION, UNDERGROUND

If you're interested in something more adventurous than a stroll down a well-lit, well-trodden underground path, then spelunking in private caves may be just your speed. Numerous regional grottoes (clubs) can get you started and recommend private guides.

Blue Ridge Grotto
2528 Montgomery Ave. SW
Roanoke, VA 24015-4225

Battlefield Area Troglodyte Society (BATS)
P.O. Box 3472
Fredericksburg, VA 22402-3472
website: www.halifax.com/bats

Charlottesville Grotto
P.O. Box 625
Ivy, VA 22945-0625

Fairfax Underground Network (FUN)
7713 Shreve Rd.
Falls Church, VA 22043-3315
email: gmoss@nova.org

Front Royal Grotto
4001 Tanager Ct.
Front Royal, VA 22630

James River Grotto
215 Coffee Rd.
Lynchburg, VA 24503
website: jamesrivergrotto.home.att.net

Madison University Student Grotto
UREC Bldg.
James Madison University
Harrisonburg, VA 22807

cals. So many permits are sold every year that, when combined with the sale of fishing licenses, it's almost enough to completely support the Virginia Department of Game and Inland Fisheries. More than 350,000 licenses are sold annually for every type of hunting imaginable, starting with guns, arrows, trapping, and falconry. In the western part of the state, most hunting occurs in the national forests, while back east hunters use private land or hunting clubs. With close to a million deer roaming the state, it's no surprise that whitetails are one of the most popular targets during the November–January season (dates vary for black-powder and bow hunters). Other fall seasons encompass duck, small-game (rabbit and squirrel), quail, and bear. Waterfowl season includes Canada geese along the Eastern Shore, and turkey season spans five weeks in the spring.

Licenses and regulations vary locally, and a hunter education certificate is necessary for first-timers and younger hunters. Order the annual *Virginia Hunter Guide* from the **Virginia Department of Game and Inland Fisheries,** P.O. Box 1104, 4010 West Broad St., Richmond, VA 23230-1104, 804/367-1000, www.dgif.state.va.us.

Local hunt clubs will know about public and private shooting ranges for clay, trap, and skeet.

BIRDWATCHING

The uninitiated may dismiss it as a mysterious, pointless waste of time and energy, but once you've caught the birding bug, you'll always wince at how much you were missing before peering through binoculars and poring over checklists taught you to see all of nature in a vivid new way. The spring and fall migration periods are the best times for birding in almost any part of the state, from hawk-spotting along the Blue Ridge to waterbirds following the Atlantic Flyway up and down the coast. Several guidebooks are indispensable for birders, and most Virginia parks and reserves can supply, or at least point you toward, a list of local species.

CAVES AND CAVERNS

Though not technically *out*doors, Virginia's underground acres can provide a glimpse of a fascinating side of the state—the underside. Virginia is

Mid-Virginia Underground
1218 Stover Shop Rd.
Churchville, VA 24421
email: tadams@cfw.com

New River Valley Grotto
P.O. Box 3056
Radford, VA 24143
website: www.runet.edu/~jfox/nrvg

Richmond Area Speleological Society
P.O. Box 6708
Richmond, VA 23230-0708
804/673-2283
email: rass@richmond.infi.net
website: www.caves.org/grotto/rass

Rockingham County Speleological Society
5803 Goldenview Dr.
Linville, VA 22834
email: mmcav6@worldnet.att.net

Tidewater Grotto
P.O. Box 62642
Virginia Beach, VA 23462
email: astubbe@gte.net

VPI Cave Club
P.O. Box 558
Blacksburg, VA 24063-0558
website: www.vt.edu:10021/org/cave

ON THE ROAD

among the top cave states in the country, with more than 3,200 at last count. Most of them were formed when carbonic acid, a weak natural acid carried in groundwater, ate away at underground limestone (calcium carbonate) deposited as sediments on the floors of shallow seas eons before.

Over millions of years, the steady drip of mineral-laden water has worn away rooms and passages and filled them with a moonscape of fantastic formations with names like soda straws, cave drapery, and flowstone. Stalactites hang tight to the ceiling, often bearing a drop of water at the tip ready to slide off and leave another hairsbreadth of ore behind. Stalagmites grow up underneath, occasionally meeting their suspended twin and joining into a column. Everything down here happens excruciatingly slow—it can take more than 100 years for a feature to grow one inch.

Expect cool temperatures year-round (55–65°F), confusing passages, and one of the only opportunities on earth to experience total darkness. Tight squeezes might mean you have to push your backpack though first, or assume the "Groucho walk"—bent over at the waist, with your head up to watch for stalactites. Guides show the way and provide assurance and helmets with carbide lamps. Emergency kits, instruction in their use, and three sources of light per person should be standard. Wear sturdy boots and reasonably warm clothes you won't mind getting muddy, and bring food and water in a small backpack. *Never* go underground without an experienced guide.

No matter how sturdy they seem, don't touch any formations; the oils from your fingertips can stop the accumulation of minerals (notice how slick and dead-looking the places you're allowed to touch are). Keep an eye out for bats hanging asleep along the walls and ceiling; if they're woken up in the middle of their winter hibernation, they'll use up too much stored energy and won't be able to survive until spring. (Just for the record, bats are not dangerous; just imagine them as mice with wings.)

Virginia's most impressive and accessible caves—almost all in the Shenandoah—have been tamed and opened to the public. These commercial caverns feature paved paths, handrails, colored lights, and towering monuments with ridiculous names like "Dairy Queen Cone." Wide reflective lakes (always called "Fairy" something) are often only inches deep and peppered with dozens of tiny growths. Guided tours are mandatory.

For more information on caving in Virginia, contact a local club or the **Virginia Cave Board,** part of the Virginia Department of Conservation and Recreation's Division of Natural Heritage, 217 Governor Street, 3rd Floor, Richmond, VA 23219, 804/786-7951, fax 804/371-2674, www.dcr.state.va.us/dnh/cavehome.html.

SKIING

In 1959, The Homestead, in the Shenandoah area, added the first ski slopes in the South to its long list of activities. Since then three other resorts have opened on Virginia's western mountains. Conditions can be great for this far south: I've carved six inches of fresh powder at Massanutten on a few occasions. During the ski season of mid-December to mid-March, temperatures seldom drop below the teens even at night. All four resorts welcome snowboarders (The Homestead boasts a 250-foot halfpipe), and most offer snowmaking and slopeside lodging.

GOLF

With its mild climate and endless undulating acres, Virginia has sprouted more than 150 public, resort, and semi-private golf courses. A few rival any in the country, including Wintergreen Resort and The Homestead. One course in Williamsburg clings so tightly to its Highland roots that sheep roam the grounds and a Scottish bagpiper plays at dusk each day. The **Virginia State Golf Association,** 830 Southlake Blvd., Suite A, Richmond, VA 23236, 804/378-2300, www.virginiagolf.com, lists courses, shops, tournaments, and instruction available statewide. Call 800/932-2259 for a copy of the annual *Virginia Golf Guide,* or try the **Williamsburg Area Golf Association,** 888/2-GOLF-WB, the **Virginia Beach Golf Association,** 800/446-8038, or the **Roanoke Valley Golf Association,** 877/GOLF-MTN.

FLY THE FRIENDLY SKIES

Should you become interested, for some strange reason, in experiencing the Virginia airspace up close, you have a few options. First (and most straightforward) is by drifting through it attached to a parachute. You can learn enough for a tandem jump in as little as half an hour, then take the plunge strapped to an instructor's chest for $200. Static-line courses, in which your ripcord is pulled automatically (remember those World War II movies where the poor saps line up, clip in, and jump?) cost about the same. An all-day Accelerated Free Fall (AFF) level one course (it's the learning that's accelerated, not the fall) will have you yanking your own ripcord and set you back a little over $300 pp.

Take the plunge on the Middle Neck at the **West Point Skydiving Center,** 804/785-9707 or 804/304-9954, email: lostmymind@skydivewestpoint.com, www.skydivewestpoint.com; or with **Skydive Virginia** in McGaheysville, 540/967-3997, email: info@skydive-virginia.com, www.skydive-virginia.com, in Louisa, between Charlottesville and Richmond. **Skydive Orange,** 540/943-6587, email: skydive@cfw.com, www.skydiveorange.com, operates a small but respectable school out of the Orange County Airport (I jumped with them, and I'm still here), and the **Hartwood ParaCenter,** 540/752-4784 or 800/422-7870, www.skydiving-center.com, is in Hartwood near Fredericksburg.

For a slightly more relaxed approach, you can learn how to hang glide with John Middleton of **Silver Wings** in Arlington, 703/533-1965, email: silverwingshg@netzero.net, www.silverwings-hanggliding.com. Mandatory "ground school" is $10 pp and after that lessons cost $70. Most people attain a novice rating after 10 to 20 lessons, allowing you to launch from a mountainside— with supervision.

For a special gift for that barnstorm-dreamer, **Front Royal Fighter Command,** 800/809-5482 or 540/635-2203, email: info@giftflight.com, www.giftflight.com, offers flights in a World War II North American AT-6 "Texan" fighter trainer. Prices range from $270 for a 15-minute test flight to $490 for an hour-long session, with an optional tail-mounted videotape of the flight. Passengers on rides of a half hour or longer will be given a chance to fly the thing (under supervision, of course), and can opt to hold on as the pilot demonstrates a series of aerobatic maneuvers.

MORE OUTDOOR RECREATION

A host of **water sports,** including sailing, scuba diving, and jet-skiing, is offered by various businesses along the coast, concentrating around Virginia Beach. **Hot-air balloons** and **skydiving** planes lift enthusiasts above the fields of the Piedmont and northern Virginia (bringing them back to earth at slightly different speeds). Seasonal **college sports** like football, basketball, soccer, and baseball demonstrate local spirit like nothing else. See pertinent chapters for details on all of these pastimes and more.

Contact the Virginia Department of Agriculture and Consumer Services, www.vdacs.state.va.us, for a copy of **"Virginia Grown,"** an annual booklet describing spots around the state where you can pick your own berries and farm produce, as well as month-to-month produce availability chart and farmers' market listings.

ON THE ROAD

Civil War–Related Activities

With the most Civil War battlefields and sites of any state—one-third of the country's total—Virginia has the market cornered on Civil War sightseeing. From the first major battle at Bull Run to Robert E. Lee's surrender at Appomattox Court House, the Old Dominion boasts more than two dozen spots where you can appreciate the war's effects on the lives of soldiers and everyday citizens. Most of the National Battlefield Parks, administered by the National Park Service, are concentrated in the northern and eastern parts of the state. All charge entrance fees, but several special passes are available. A Golden Eagle Passport—good at any national park for a year—costs $50. U.S. Citizens over age 62 can buy a Golden Age Passport ($10) for lifetime access to any National Park, while disabled visitors can receive a free Golden Access Passport with similar privileges. Fees in all national parks are suspended on August 25 for Founders Day, celebrating the establishment of the National Park Service.

Presentations, exhibits, brochures, and park rangers are there to teach you about the history of each site before you take the tour, which can be self-guided or led by rangers. Picnic areas and gift shops are part of the package, but you'll have to look elsewhere for food and lodging.

REENACTMENTS

Even if history isn't your thing, you may well become more interested after watching one of these events. Held on various anniversaries at sites throughout the state, reenactments are history brought to vivid life, worlds away from dull textbook prose. The attention to detail is amazing—for serious reenactors *everything* has to be authentic, down to the scratchy wool of their pants and the frames on their eyeglasses. Many carry original weapons and accessories (antique sabers and firearms can run in the thousands of dollars). Although rifle fire is prohibited in national battlefield parks except under carefully controlled circumstances, in other areas you'll

see antique arms put to every intended use save actually perforating another soldier.

In the field, the smoke of campfires and artillery firings mingles with the rattle of drums and the clop of horse's hooves. Back in camp you can watch a surgeon demonstrate his amputation technique, or a local matron hand out hoecakes to hungry soldiers. Tens of thousands of spectators gather for the larger events, each paying a small fee to watch. Individual battlefields and sites can tell you about reenacting schedules or put you in touch with local reenactment organizations. **Page One Publications,** P.O. Box 4232, Richmond, VA 23220-4232, 804/232-2395, www.civilwartraveler.com puts out magazines such as *The Guide to Historic Virginia, Mid-Atlantic Civil War Traveler, and The Guide to Virginia's Civil War,* each published one to three times per year. These magazines are available free or for a small change at most local-regional visitors centers, historic sites, and National Parks in Virginia, and through their ultra-handy website.

The range of publications dealing with Civil War travel alone shows how popular the subject is to many people. Good magazines to check out include *America's Civil War,* email: amcivilwar@palmcoastd.com, www.thehistorynet.com/AmericasCivilWar; *Civil War Times Illustrated,* email: civilwarti@palmcoastd.com, www.thehistorynet.com/CivilWarTimes; and *Blue & Gray Magazine,* www.bluegraymagazine.com, with driving tours, color maps, and plenty of photographs. The *Camp Chase Gazette,* P.O. Box 707, Marietta, OH 45750-0707, 740/373-1865, fax 740/374-5710, email: info@campchase.com, www.campchase.com, is primarily for reenactors, and is put out 10 times per year.

Working to preserve historic battlefields from the encroachments of modern civilization are organizations such as the **Central Virginia Battlefields Trust,** 604A William St., Ste. 1, Fredericksburg VA 22401, email: webmaster@cvbt.org, www.cvbt.org, and the **Civil War Preser-**

vation Trust, 1331 H Street NW, Ste. 1001, Washington, DC 20005, 202/367-1861, email: civilwartrust@civilwar.org, www.civilwar.org. They also have lots of handy links on their websites for Civil War–related travel information.

CIVIL WAR TRAILS

Inaugurated in 1997, these travel itineraries focus on five different phases of the conflict in Virginia. Three special driving routes ("1862 Peninsula Campaign: Civil War in the Tidewater," "Lee vs. Grant: The 1864 Campaign," and "Lee's Retreat") and two regions (the Shenandoah Valley and northern Virginia) link more than 250 sites of historic significance. Some are in National Parks or Battlefields, and for the rest, special arrow signs point you down remote back roads far from the recent world, past private homes still bearing bullet scars, churches that once housed the wounded, and streams where soldiers rested more than a century ago. Maps and information can be ordered free by calling 888/248-4592 or stopping by the website www.civilwartraveler.com/about/trailsFAQ.html.

Organized Tours

In addition to local tour companies, several national operators can lead you through Virginia's tourist attractions, back roads, or outdoor recreation. Reservation and cancellation policies vary; you usually have to reserve your spot with a deposit, which can be refunded as long as you don't cancel too close to the date of departure. All prices quoted are per person (pp) based on double occupancy.

BUS TOURS

Most of these tours are primarily booked through travel agents. **Globus,** www.globusandcosmos.com, offers "The Historic East," covering Washington, D.C., the Shenandoah Valley, northern Virginia, Richmond, Maryland, and Pennsylvania (8–10 days, $1,110–1,340). Their **Cosmos** budget branch covers much of the same area in "America's Glorious Heritage" (9–11 days, $900–1,190). **Colette Tours,** 800/340-5158 or 401/728-3805, fax 401/728-1380, www.collettevacations.com, has "Heritage of America" ranging from New York to Williamsburg (nine days, $1,200–1,330). **Maupintour,** 800/255-4266, email: info@maupintour.com, www.maupintour.com, covers "Philadelphia, Washington, and Williamsburg" (eight days, $1,700), and also offers a "Williamsburg Christmas" tour (eight days, $2,270).

Gadabout Tours, 800/952-5068 or 760/325-5556, email: cally@gadabouttours.com, www.gadabouttours.com, visits Washington, D.C. with stops in Alexandria and Mount Vernon for a week in the spring or fall ($1,700).

Gray Line, 303/433-9800, email: glsightseeing@aol.com, www.graylinedc.com, sends daily bus tours to Colonial Williamsburg ($68), Busch Gardens ($68), Monticello and Charlottesville ($68 pp), and Mount Vernon and Old Town Alexandria ($28); most are from spring to fall and end at Union Station in Washington, D.C. after a morning hotel pickup in the Capitol.

Old Virginia Tours, 12 Wachovian Way, Raphine, VA 24472, 800/685-7265 (PIN 7315), or 540/377-2110, email: info@oldvatours.com, www.oldvatours.com, offers smaller bus tours of Monticello, Charlottesville, the Shenandoah Valley, Williamsburg, and various Civil War sites. They can also arrange custom-designed tours.

OUTDOOR TOURS

Sierra Club Outings, 85 2nd St., 2nd Floor, San Francisco, CA 94105, 415/977-5500, fax 415/977-5795, email: national.outings@sierraclub.org, www.sierraclub.org/outings, organizes hikes through the fall colors of the Shenandoah (six days, $800). They'll also arrange for you to work alongside U.S. Forest Service personnel in the Mount Rogers Wilderness Area during a one-week service trip ($265). **New England Hiking**

ON THE ROAD

VIRGINIA'S OFFBEAT BEST

Dinosaur Land, White Post: Fiberglass Tyrannosaurs and a 60-foot shark are just the beginning.

Bull Run Castle, Aldie: A cement-and-steel stronghold waiting for the next Civil War—and a B&B.

Yogaville, Buckingham, and **Holy Cross Abbey,** Berryville: Two different takes on spiritual room and board.

Holy Land USA, Bedford: Full-size replicas of Bible scenes on a central Virginia farm.

Jolly Roger Haggle Shop, Staunton: More than one million items piled to the ceiling.

Jeff Matthews Museum, Galax: A Kodiak grizzly and more than 1,000 knives.

Garlic Festival, Rebec Vineyards, Amherst (October): The "stinking rose" in just about every form imaginable.

Natural Bridge Wax Museum, Natural Bridge: What does this have to do with a 215-foot limestone span? I give up, too.

Tangier Island: A unique fishing community in the bosom of the Chesapeake Bay.

Pocahontas Exhibition Coal Mine, Pocahontas: Go underground with a former miner, hardhats and all.

Holidays, P.O. Box 1648, North Conway, NH 03860, 800/869-0949 or 603/356-9696, email: nehh@aol.com, www.nehikingholidays.com, rambles through the Blue Ridge, exploring Civil War history and country inns along the way (five days, $1,200–1,300). The Potomac Appalachian Trail Club and Appalachian Trail Conference both organize day and overnight hikes as well; see "Hiking and Camping."

Birders could do much worse than **Field Guides Incorporated,** 9433 Bee Cave Rd., Bldg. 1, Ste. 150, Austin, TX 78733, 800/728-4953 or 512/263-7265, fax 512/263-0117, email: fieldguides@fieldsguides.com, www.fieldguides.com. Their "Virginia and Carolina Capes" tour looks for raptors, seabirds, shorebirds, and passerines along the coasts of both states in September (nine days, $1,750). **Smithsonian Study Tours and Seminars,** 1100 Jefferson Dr. SW, Washington, DC, 20560, 877/338-8687 or 202/357-4700, fax 202/633-9250, email: tours@tsa.si.edu, smithsonianstudytours.si.edu, offers a wide range of educational seminars and study tours in Virginia covering topics as diverse as classic railroads, architecture, and winter birding. They range from $50 for a one-day Civil War tour to $2,000 for a nine-day tour from historical sites from Williamsburg to Washington, D.C.

Holidays and Festivals

Every town has its own list of annual celebrations, from Monterey's Highland Maple Festival to Norfolk's Harborfest. At any given event, chances are you'll find live music, dancing, parades, displays of regional crafts, and tables groaning under platters of local food. Historical figures from a particular city are often remembered—or even brought to life by reenactors—on their birthdays, and local events are commemorated in services or parades. Some events charge admission, anywhere from $5–20 per adult, and the more popular ones start selling tickets months ahead of time.

Most national holidays, including Easter, the Fourth of July, and Labor Day, get their own celebrations, while Christmas and the week after bring religious services, buildings lit with strings of bulbs,

and candlelight tours of historical sites. **First Night** heralds in the New Year in many cities, often an alcohol-free, family-oriented, cultural-performance event. During **Historic Garden Week,** 804/644-7776, email: gardenwk@erols.com, www.vagardenweek.org, at the end of April, the grounds and gardens of more than 250 locations statewide (most otherwise closed to the public) are open to visitors. Tickets for individual events range from $10–30 pp. Order a 220-page guidebook, available February to April, for $5 from Historic Garden Week, 12 E. Franklin St., Richmond, VA 23219.

A good source on festivals in Virginia, besides the Virginia Tourism Corporation (VTC) and local chambers of commerce, is the Old Dominion edition of the bimonthly newspaper

© JULIAN SMITH

ON THE ROAD

Posters at Cockram's General Store in Floyd attest to Virginia's musical heritage.

Southern Festivals, 888/257-0956, email: jlowry@ipass,net, www.southfest.com. On the Internet, search for "Virginia" at the Festivals.com website (www.festivals.com).

Many businesses and all government offices are closed on national holidays. These include New Year's Day (January 1), Dr. Martin Luther King Jr. Day (third Monday in January, sometimes called Lee-Jackson-King Day), President's Day (third Monday in February), Memorial Day (last Monday in May), Independence Day (July 4), Labor Day (first Monday in September), Columbus Day (second Monday in October), Veteran's Day (November 11), Thanksgiving Day (fourth Thursday in November, as well as the following day), and Christmas Day (December 25).

VIRGINIA'S BEST MUSIC EVENTS

American Music Festival, Virginia Beach, September

Carter Family Memorial Festival, Carter Family Fold (Maces Spring), August

Floyd Flatfoot Jamboree, Floyd, every Friday

Hampton Jazz Festival, Hampton, June

Old Time Fiddler's Convention, Galax, August

Shenandoah Valley Music Festival, Orkney Springs, August

Town Point Jazz and Blues Festival, Norfolk, August

Shopping

CRAFTS

Virginia handicrafts come in an amazing range of styles and quality. Pottery is near the top of the list, produced in historic ceramics centers like Strasburg. Along the coast you can watch decoy carvers at work, or take a class yourself. Keep an eye out for bronze wildlife sculptures and signs advertising "woodcarvings for sale" outside private homes. Craftspeople in Jamestown and Colonial Williamsburg keep historical skills alive as they produce silver pitchers, hand-blown glass, shoes, and musical instruments, many of which are for sale.

Heading west you'll come across hooked rugs, table linens, and quilts from the looms of local weavers, along with hand-forged iron and brass from places such as Virginia Metalcrafters in Staunton. Woodcrafters turn out tools, toys, musical instruments, and cane-seat chairs and other furniture. Throughout the state artisans benefit from **art centers** like the Torpedo Factory, housed in an old munitions plant in Alexandria. Some, including Norfolk's d'Art Center and The Arts Depot in Abingdon, offer classes as well as display and sales areas.

ANTIQUES

Serious buyers and casual browsers agree that shopping for antiques can eat up a week as easily as an afternoon. Barns and attics throughout the state have been raided to stock tiny shops and huge antique malls, with old stuff by the truckload for sale restored or "as is." Prices are lower in Virginia than in Washington, D.C., drawing many shoppers down from the Capitol in search of that elusive but always possible Great Find. The list is practically endless but includes old toys, quilts, magazines, food cans, advertising posters, clothing, and lawn ornaments. **Furniture** ranges from country standbys like cupboards, dressers, wardrobes, rope beds, and blanket boxes to distinctive Hepplewhite, Sheraton, and empire desks, chairs, and chests.

Civil War relics such as swords, guns, uniforms, and utensils can get pricey, but smaller items—for instance prints, maps, and minnie balls (bullets)—are often more affordable. Packaging and/or delivery can often be arranged on the spot.

Before you plunk down $400 on that creaking, weather-beaten farm table, it helps to know a little about antique pricing. Shop around to get an idea of price ranges, and look for various reference books that advise how to get the most for your money. A wide range of **publications** cater to antique buyers and sellers, including *Antique Week*, P.O. Box 90, 27 N. Jefferson, Knightstown, IN 46148, 800/876-5133 or 765/345-5133, www.tias.com/mags/antiqueweek; *Southeastern Antiquing and Collecting Magazine*, P.O. Box 510, Acworth, GA 30101, 770/974-6495 or 888/388-7827, email: antiquing@go-star.com, www.go-star.com/antiquing; and *Antiques and the Arts,* published by The Bee Publishing Co., P.O. 5503, Newtown, CT 06470-5503, 203/426-3141, www.antiquesandthearts.com. A good online resource is **AntiqueWeb Collecting News,** www.antiqueweb.com.

LOCAL SPECIALTIES

For a souvenir you can eat, consider taking home a particularly Virginian food: hams, pound cakes, wine, preserves, and peanuts are the most typical. Local cookbooks, especially those found along the coast, will bring back dinner-table memories for years.

Minerals are popular, especially at "rock shops" at the entrance to most commercial caverns. Some sell geodes (hollow stone balls filled with crystals) that you can crack open yourself.

TAXES

The state levies a 3.5 percent retail sales tax, which is augmented by a local tax of 1 percent. As of 2001, taxes on food were going to be reduced by 2 percent over four years.

Accommodations

PRICE RANGES

This book uses the following rate categories, based on double occupancy during high season: **Under $50, $50–100, $100–150, $150–250,** and **Over $250.** A 5 percent **lodging tax** is added to the statewide retail sales tax, for a total increase of 9.5 percent.

HOTELS AND MOTELS

Virginia law dictates that maximum prices must be posted in rooms. Beyond that, though, accommodation rates can vary drastically depending on the timing, your persistence, and the manager's desire to fill an otherwise empty room. **High season** (May–September and the October fall foliage displays) can jack up prices as much as 50 percent, as can holidays and local events such as college athletic games and graduations.

Always ask about discounts—business/corporate, government, senior (AARP), auto club (AAA), and military rates are almost always lower. Weekend rates, except in resort areas like Virginia Beach, can save you a bundle if you stay Friday and/or Saturday night. Longer stays of a week or more are also discounted. Simply checking around in the evening can often score you a good deal because hotels are eager to fill empty rooms. Websites such as Priceline (www.priceline.com) allow you to bid for available rooms and can often net amazing deals—start by bidding much lower than you would think.

Hotel chains' main reservation numbers can tell you the location of their nearest representative, list facilities, and even keep a room waiting; however, calling a hotel directly for a reservation (especially on a Sunday night) is often better than calling the chain's toll-free number or booking over the Internet. Ask to speak to the manager on duty or someone in the sales office, and ask the reservationist to put a note in your record requesting a room upgrade, just on the off chance that one is available and offered.

MORE PERSONAL

Bed-and-breakfasts, though more expensive, can often be a reason for visiting in themselves. Staying at one is like being a guest in someone's house, which is often exactly what you are, except that someone caters to your every whim and the building is often an outstanding antique. Nobody opens a B&B to retire early (though many owners already are), so you know your hosts are in it for the joy of meeting people and sharing their love of the area. Owners have often grown up nearby or even in the same house, making them an ideal source of local guidance and trivia. Multi-course, silver-service breakfasts are the norm instead of the exception—no muffin-and-instant-coffee "Continental" fare here. Smoking is usually permitted outside only, if at all (one brochure reads, "The house is 200 years old and the fire department five miles away."). Private bathrooms are standard, or at least there's a separate bath just down the hall—these always seem to have large clawfoot tubs. Guests can often use a kitchen or kitchenette to prepare food.

Country inns straddle the line between hotels and B&Bs, with the formalized quality of

Shirley's Bay View Inn, Tangier Island

© JULIAN SMITH

ON THE ROAD

VIRGINIA HOTEL CHAINS

Best Western	800/780-7234	www.bestwestern.com
Comfort Inn	800/228-5150	www.comfortinn.com
Days Inn	800/544-8313	www.daysinn.com
Econo Lodge	800/553-2666	www.econolodge.com
Hampton Inn	800/426-7866	www.hamptoninn.com
Hilton Hotels	800/445-8667	www.hilton.com
Holiday Inn	800/465-4329	www.holiday-inn.com
Howard Johnson Lodge	800/406-1411	www.hojo.com
Hyatt Hotels	888/591-1234	www.hyatt.com
Marriott Hotels and Resorts	800/932-2198	www.marriott.com
Microtel Inns & Suites	888/222-2142	www.microtelinn.com
Motel 6	800/466-8356	www.motel6.com
Omni Hotels	800/843-6664	www.omnihotels.com
Quality Inn	800/288-5151	www.qualityinn.com
Radisson	800/333-3333	www.radisson.com
Ramada Inn	800/298-2054	www.ramada.com
Sheraton Hotels	800/625-5144	www.starwood.com/sheraton
Super 8 Motels	800/800-8000	www.super8.com
Travelodge	800/835-2424	www.travelodge.com

service of the former and much of the distinct charm of the latter. Led by the world-class Inn at Little Washington, Virginia's inns offer privacy and luxury in a romantic, indulgent setting.

Advance reservations are desirable for both inns and B&Bs, especially during weekends, high season, and special events. Popular ones fill up months or even years in advance. A deposit in the form of one night's fee is often required, and a minimum length of stay may be imposed during the high season. Cancellation requires prior notice—at least 24 hours, or as much as one week—to avoid paying a service charge. Deals on multi-night stays are possible. Rates given are per room, double occupancy.

The **Bed and Breakfast Association of Virginia,** P.O. Box 1077, Stanardsville, VA 22973, 888/660-BBAV or 540/672-6700, www.bbav .org, lists its members online. Other helpful sources are the **Bed and Breakfast Line** of the Virginia Tourism Corporation, 800/262-1293,

and **Bed & Breakfast Inns Online,** www.bbon-line.com/va. Regional B&B associations are listed in the various chapter introductions.

CAMPING

Whether you want to get completely away from it all or just relocate and bring most of it with you, camping is the most flexible and affordable way to travel for an extended period. Campgrounds vary widely, but most are open from March or April through November or December. Reservations and/or deposits may be necessary at private campgrounds in resort areas or during peak seasons.

Public campgrounds include those at 24 state parks, state fishing lakes, and wildlife management areas. Eight state parks (Hungry Mother, Claytor Lake, Douthat, Fairy Stone, Twin Lakes, Seashore, Staunton River, and Westmoreland) also have cabins for rent from March–December. You can reserve these and state park campgrounds online at www.dcr.state.va.us/parks/reserve.htm or by calling 800/933-7275 or 804/225-3867. Free primitive camping is permitted in the backcountry of the Jefferson and George Washington National Forests except where specifically prohibited. Backcountry and campsite camping are possible in the Shenandoah National Park.

Private campgrounds usually include grills, drinking water, flush toilets, hot showers, coin laundry, and a camp store. More elaborate sites, typified by **KOA Kampgrounds**, 406/248-7444, www.koakampgrounds.com, come complete with pools, game rooms, hot tubs, saunas, and volleyball courts. Occasionally they'll have small cabins with air-conditioning and heat for about the price of a budget motel room. Features such as bicycle rental, miniature golf, and summer children's programs cost extra. You can reserve their campsites online.

VIRGINIA'S BEST ROMANTIC GETAWAYS

Hope and Glory Inn, Irvington (Coast): A former schoolhouse with a (private) shower in the English cottage garden.

Inn at Little Washington (Central): The granddaddy of them all—five stars in food and lodging.

L'Auberge Provençale, White Post (Shenandoah): A French country inn with gourmet cooking.

Liberty Rose B&B, Williamsburg (Coast): Designer fabrics and old-time hospitality in a historic setting.

Sampson Eagon Inn, Staunton (Shenandoah): "Skip-lunch" breakfasts and period antiques in an 1840 home.

Other Ideas:

• Grab a bottle of wine and enjoy Shakespeare and a picnic among the historic ruins at the **Barboursville Winery** near Charlottesville.

• Soar in a **hot-air balloon** over the Hunt Country scenery, and land to a champagne toast.

• Take a thermos of coffee to the top of **Humpback Rocks**, on the northern Blue Ridge Parkway, for a 360-degree sunrise view.

Hookups for water, electricity, and sewer are charged as a whole or occasionally available separately. RV drivers can contact the **Recreation Vehicle Industry Association,** 1896 Preston White Dr., P.O. Box 2999, Reston, VA 20195-0999, www.rvia.org or www.gorving.com, for information on choosing and operating an RV. **Camper Clubs of America,** P.O. Box 25286, Tempe, AZ 85282-5286, 800/369-2267), www.camperclubs.com, offers a $10-per-night guarantee to 250 affiliated campgrounds nationwide for a fee of $100 per year.

YOUTH HOSTELS

Virginia has official Hostelling International (HI) outposts in Bluemont, Urbanna, Virginia Beach, and on the Blue Ridge Parkway near Galax. Even without the member's discount, these modest lodgings are much cheaper than a hotel room at around $15 pp per night (less for members). Hostels are usually closed during the day and lock their doors at 10 P.M.

HI membership is $25 per year and can be acquired at any hostel, from Council Travel or STA Travel, or from the source: **Hostelling International–American Youth Hostels,** 733 15th St. NW, Ste. 840, Washington, DC 20005, 202/783-6161, fax 202/783-6171, www.hiayh.org. HI memberships are compatible with those from other organizations such as the Europe-based **International Youth Hostels Federation,** www .iyhf.org. The online directory **Hostels.com** (www.hostels.com) list hotels worldwide.

HOME STAYS

U.S. Servas, Inc., 11 John St., Ste. 407, New York, NY 10038, 212/267-0252, fax 212/267-0292, email: servas-info@servas.org, www.servas.org, oversees a worldwide network designed to promote peace and foster intercultural understanding through person-to-person contact. After an initial interview, travelers 18 and older pay $55 per year to rent a list of hosts who offer room and board for two nights. Becoming a Servas traveler is an excellent way to meet interesting local people and can easily repay your initial investment.

HOME EXCHANGES

If you're interested in a longer-term stay, consider a home exchange. **HomeExchange.com,** P.O. Box 30085, Santa Barbara, CA 93130, 805/898-9660 or 866/898-9660, fax 805/898-9199, email: admin@homeexchange.com, www.homeexachange.com, currently has the most listings in Virginia. The use of cars is often included, and you can also trade boats or RVs for homes–temporarily. Their list is free to search, but listing costs $30 per year. You can also try **Trade to Travel** 800/899-1096 or 434/246-2099, email: info@tradetotravel.com, www.tradetotravel.com; **SunSwap,** email: info@sunswap.com, www.sunswap.com; or **Home Exchange and Rental Homes,** email: info@erhomes.com, www.erhomes.com.

TRAVELING WITH PETS

Smaller pets are accepted at some hotels and motels (often with a small surcharge), but most B&Bs do not allow your furry friends to accompany you during your stay. Remember that pets must stay in vehicles or on roads in Shenandoah National Park.

Food

CLASSIC COUNTRY CUISINE (A.K.A. HOME COOKIN')

As soon as the Jamestown settlers were able to make it through a few winters in a row, they set about starting a tradition of rich dining that lives on in Virginia homes and restaurants today. All the fruits of the fertile land went into the pot and onto the table, including fish from the rivers, bays, and ocean; corn from the Indians; produce brought from the Old World; and farm animals of every description. Every well-stocked dining room had a "groaning board" bent under the weight of overflowing platters.

Today restaurants like Williamsburg's Shield Tavern, Charlottesville's Michie Tavern, and Leesburg's Green Tree serve the legacy in its truest form. Wherever you go in Virginia, though, you're liable to enjoy local specialties in some form or another. Odds are better farther into the countryside or at a restaurant that advertises home cookin' as a specialty.

One quick disclaimer—this is not health food. Deep-fried, salted for weeks, and loaded with butter, home cooking Virginia-style can pack on the pounds quicker than a chocolate tour of Switzerland. But heck, people have been eating it for generations, and they keep living to a ripe old age, so it's not as if your arteries will clog overnight.

And anyway, it is *good*. The classic meal, served at a restaurant such as The Homeplace near Roanoke, goes something like this: sides of coleslaw, beans (butter or baked), black-eyed peas, mashed potatoes (plenty of gravy), cornbread, grits, and fresh, flaky, steaming biscuits sidle up to a centerpiece of crispy fried chicken, juicy roast beef, or salty country ham. Occasionally soup— vegetable, chili, or hearty Brunswick Stew (with the original rabbits and squirrels replaced with chicken, ham, or beef)—is served on the side. Peanut soup is a local staple, just the right balance of sweet and spicy. Salad can mean anything from tossed greens and dressing to canned fruit served on cottage cheese. Iced tea is the drink of choice, followed closely by local apple cider. Dessert is often homemade peach cobbler or pecan pie.

Main courses almost always include some kind of meat. "Country-fried" or "chicken-fried" steak is covered in batter before cooking, and barbecue usually means pork, with a more delicate flavor than the vinegar-fueled kick of barbecue served farther south. Pot roast, rib-eye steak, chicken and dumplings, and baked pork chops are all popular, but ham is by far the most distinctive Virginia centerpiece. The tradition began in Colonial days, when pork proved easier to preserve by smoking, drying, sugar-curing, or pickling than other meats. Over the years, ham (technically the thigh of a hog) has evolved into a few variations. Virginia ham, also known as Williamsburg or country ham, is dry-cured with salt and then smoked. Smithfield ham,

CRAB LINGO

backfin large fin containing choice meat
buster crab within hours of shedding
dead men gray lungs (and how you'll feel if you eat them)
doubler male and female crab caught in mating embrace
jimmy legal-sized male
peeler crab ready to molt
pot crab trap
sook mature female

named after the small town on the James River west of Norfolk, is slowly smoked over a hickory fire and then aged, skin and all, for up to a year. This, along with a coating of pepper applied during curing, gives it a stronger, smokier taste than other, less mature hams. Local stores often have Smithfield hams hanging in burlap sacks, which customers remove before soaking overnight and cooking. The secret is to slice it paper thin, ideal for the traditional ham biscuit.

Breakfast is often as serious an undertaking. Biscuits and gravy, chicken-fried steak, and ham slices may all make an appearance next to your eggs and coffee.

SEAFOOD

The daily catch, served up in weather-beaten cafés on the Eastern shore and Virginia Beach's great oceanfront restaurants, is the state's other gourmet specialty. Ask your server whether the selection is native or not—fresher is better. Dozens of Virginia's 200 species of fish, including rockfish (striped bass), bluefish, shad, trout, pike, and crappie, are served broiled, fried, smoked, and baked.

The most famous Chesapeake shellfish is *Callinectes sapidus,* the famous **Chesapeake blue crab,** whose scientific name translates as "savory, beautiful swimmer." An average of 50 million pounds of these crabs are plucked from the bay every year, making up half the nation's entire catch. Cracking open and eating crabs is an acquired art form, but well worth the effort; males are easier to pick apart, while the millions of eggs inside females can make

the experience even messier. Crab cakes, made with cornmeal or cracker crumbs and eggs, are a more manageable alternative.

Soft-shell crabs are brought up within an hour after molting, as they sit dazed on the bottom waiting for their new shells to harden. Those caught just before shedding are stored in floating boxes and watched around the clock until they get around to it. They're fried in batter and eaten whole, often on a bun—a true saltwater delicacy. Crab imperial (mixed with bread, egg, mayonnaise, and Worcestershire), deviled crabs with horseradish and chili powder, and cream-based soups like bisque and sherry-laced "she-crab" are all recipes worth trying. If you're interested in catching your own, try renting a small crab pot from a sporting goods store or netting crabs in the shallows with fish or chicken leftovers as bait.

It was a brave soul who ate the first raw **oyster,** but somehow the slimy mouthful caught on. Chincoteague oysters on the halfshell are the best. Oyster season runs September–April, with a peak around the holidays. **Clams** are served raw or steamed and are usually cherrystones (a.k.a. littlenecks, hard-shells) or manoes (steamers, longnecks, or soft-shells). True Virginia-coast chowder isn't the creamy New England style or red Manhattan style; here it's made with a clear base filled with potatoes, celery, onions, and herbs. Everything comes with a handful of small balls of fried cornmeal dough called **hush puppies.**

VIRGINIA WINE

Of all the eastern states, Virginia enjoys the best climate—and mindset—for growing and enjoying quality vintages. Vineyards between 37–39°north latitude, the same as California's north coast, avoid both the harsh northern cold and the prolonged humid southern summers. Production is limited, with most bottles sold at wineries, festivals, wine shops, and supermarkets alongside beer (hard liquor by the bottle is found only in state-run Alcohol Beverage Control stores). Quality of Virginia wine has taken a quantum leap in the 1990s, according to one winemaker. Maybe the state's little-brother complex to the West Coast wine country will some day carry it to first place.

ON THE ROAD

History

Early Jamestown settlers grew grapes with the help of French *vignerons* sent by the Virginia Company, but even with the Assembly's "Acte 12" compelling each farmer to plant 12 grapevines or be punished, imported vines died and hardy local varieties turned sour. Cold weather, insects, disease, and the American Revolution undermined the 1769 Act for the Encouragement of the Making of Wine. Thomas Jefferson, the "Father of American Wine," shipped in an Italian expert to help him plan Monticello's vineyards, but it wasn't until 1835 that Richmond viticulturist Dr. D.N. Norton bred the first "non-foxy" American wine grape, encouraging local vintners to give it another go.

By 1979 Virginia counted six wineries, and in 1988 Ronald Reagan presented former Soviet president Mikhail Gorbachev with a bottle of Virginia Seyval at the Moscow summit. Four years later, *Wine Spectator* magazine dubbed Virginia "the most accomplished of America's emerging wine regions." The awards had started rolling in, including the 1993 and 1995 *Wine Spectator* Critic's Choice awards bestowed on Williamsburg Winery, placing it among the world's 200 best. By 1997, Virginia was sixth in the country in fine wine production, and in 2001 counted 63 wineries spread over thousands of acres.

Varieties

Whites like chardonnay and Riesling grow best in the Old Dominion. They tend to be light- to medium-bodied, closer to wines from Burgundy or the Pacific Northwest than California, thanks to Virginia's comparably cooler climate. More complex whites bear the mark of oak-barrel aging.

Chardonnay is the most widely planted variety, resulting in a balanced, crisp bottle that's easy to match with food. Riesling comes next, producing a semi-dry to dry wine. Reds like cabernet sauvignon are more temperamental—"God couldn't grow a good merlot in Virginia," says one vintner.

Visiting Wineries

Wineries can be found from the coast to the mountains, with the highest concentration in the Piedmont. Visiting one combines a drive through beautiful countryside with the satisfaction of buying a quality vintage directly from the person who made it—and prices are always best at the winery.

Tastings are given free or for a small charge, allowing you to pick your favorite from a wide selection. Tours of the facilities can be guided or self-guided, leading you past crusher-stemmers, presses, fermentation tanks, oak aging barrels, and bottling setups. Many wineries allow you to enjoy your purchase immediately with a picnic on the grounds, and a few offer gourmet restaurants on the premises. October has been dubbed Virginia Wine Month, with dozens of different events held at wineries. During the rest of the year, wineries host everything from jazz concerts to food festivals.

Local wineries are listed in special topics in each chapter. Visiting hours vary, so it's always a good idea to call before showing up. When driving, look for small grape-cluster road signs that point the way to wineries.

Resources

For a free list of wineries and events, contact the **Virginia Wine Marketing Office,** P.O. Box 1163, Richmond, VA 23209, 800/828-4637, www.virginiawines.org.

Transportation

BY CAR

Like most of the United States, Virginia is best explored in your own vehicle. Luckily a convenient network of interstate highways provides easy access to every corner. I-81, running the length of the western border, and I-95, connecting Washington, D.C. with Richmond and North Carolina, are the main north-south arteries. Interstate 66 links the nation's capital with I-81, and I-64 runs from the Norfolk area through Richmond to Staunton, continuing west from Lexington into West Virginia.

The speed limit on rural interstates is 65 mph; otherwise it's 55 mph or as marked. Radar detectors are illegal in Virginia. State-maintained routes may have a name (i.e., Old Mill Road) as well as a number (Rt. 645), so keep this in mind

ON THE ROAD

RESOURCES FOR DRIVERS

Virginia Department of Highways and Transportation,
800/835-1203, www.vdot.state.va.us

Highway Help and Information
Statewide 800/367-7623, TTY 800/432-1843
Blue Ridge Parkway 828/298-0398, www.nps .gov/blri
Hampton Roads Area 800/792-2800 or 757/928-1111 ext. 7623
Chesapeake Bay Bridge-Tunnel 757/331-2960
Jamestown Ferry 757/331-2960
Metro Washington D.C. 202/863-1313 or 211 cellular
New River Valley Area 540/382-0200, ext 7623
Roanoke Valley Area 540/981-0100, ext. 7623
Skyline Drive 540/999-3500

Virginia Travel Websites
Hampton Roads Traffic Cameras: www.gohamp-tonroads.com/partners/traffic
Hampton Roads Traffic Information: www.vdot .state.va.us/roads/tunnel.html
Ferry Information email: ferryinfo@vdot.state.va.us; www.vdot.state.va.us/info/ferry_info.html
Map of Road Conditions in Virginia: www .vdot.state.va.us/roads/eocstate.html
Traffic Conditions: www.vipnet.org/portal/virginia/travel_traffic.htm
Travel Weather: www.vipnet.org/portal/virginia/travel_weather.htm
Metro Washington D.C.: www.smartraveler.com/wdc

Virginia State Police Offices
Administrative Headquarters
Rt. 60, one mile west of Richmond, 804/674-2000, www.vsp.state.va.us

Division 1 (Northern Coast, Petersburg, Richmond)
Rt. 1, three miles north of Richmond, 804/553-3444 or 800/552-9965

Division 2 (Northern Shenandoah)
Rt. 29, three miles northeast of Culpeper, 540/829-7401 or 800/572-2260

Division 3 (Central Virginia, Middle Shenandoah)
Rt. 613, two miles west of Appomattox, 434/352-7128 or 800/552-0962

Division 4 (Southwest Virginia)
I-81, two miles east of Wytheville, 540/228-3131 or 800/542-8716

Division 5 (Southern Coast, Eastern Shore)
Rt. 13 in Chesapeake, 757/424-6820 or 800/582-8350

Division 6 (Southern Shenandoah, West-central Virginia)
Rt. 11, one mile west of Salem, 540/375-9500 or 800/542-5959

Division 7 (Northern Virginia)
Rt. 620 in Fairfax, 703/323-4500 or 800/572-4510

© JULIAN SMITH

driving the Blue Ridge Parkway

as you look for that out-of-the-way B&B. Give the state tourism office a call for a free map of the state's thousands of miles of official and proposed **scenic byways.**

If you plan on doing a lot of driving, then joining the **American Automobile Association (AAA)** can come in handy. Emergency roadside assistance, free maps, tourbooks, and campbooks are all included in the year-long membership. Contact your local AAA office for details.

Driving Hazards

In winter, state-maintained roads are generally plowed quickly, thought a fast, heavy snowfall can take a day or two to clear. Nearly invisible black ice is the biggest winter driving hazard, especially at night and in the early morning before the sun melts it. Fog on the mountains is another concern; it's most often encountered along the Skyline Drive and Blue Ridge Parkway. Visibility can plunge to 50 feet or less, so go slow and turn on your headlights. (Some passes, like I-64 near Waynesboro, have lights in the roadway to make driving in fog safer).

Car Rental

To save money, shop around for the best rates and consider local companies. Fly-drive packages and long-term rentals, especially if booked ahead of time though a travel agent, can be much

MAJOR CAR RENTAL COMPANIES

Alamo	800/462-5266	www.goalamo.com
Avis	800/230-4989	www.avis.com
Budget	800/404-8033	rent.drivebudget.com
Dollar	800/800-3665	www.dollarcar.com
Enterprise	800/325-8007	www.pickenterprise.com
Hertz	800/654-4173	www.hertz.com
National	800/227-7368	www.nationalcar.com
Thrifty	800/847-4389	www.thrifty.com

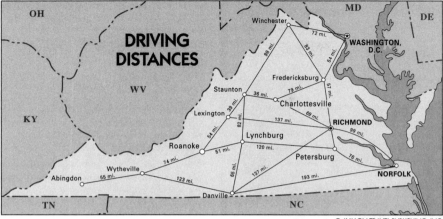

DRIVING DISTANCES

© AVALON TRAVEL PUBLISHING, INC.

less expensive. Ask if the quoted price includes local taxes and unlimited mileage, and ask about dropoff/refueling charges, cancellation penalties, one-way fees, insurance coverage, and deposits so you know what to expect ahead of time.

BY BUS

Greyhound, 800/231-2222, www.greyhound .com, connects most Virginia cities and tourist destinations. Tickets are cheaper if you buy them 7–21 days in advance. Their Ameripass program offers discounted unlimited travel for certain periods (weeks or months). Ask about other discounts for students, seniors, and military personnel. Children 2–11 travel for half-price, and companions assisting a disabled traveler are free with 48 hours' notice. Call the toll-free number for route and fare information; local terminal numbers will handle all other inquiries.

TRAVEL INSURANCE COMPANIES

Access America	P.O. Box 90315, Richmond, VA 23286	800/284-8300 or 804/673-1491
Carefree Travel Insurance	P.O. Box 9366, 100 Garden City Plaza, Garden City, NY 11530	516/294-0220 or 800/323-3149
Tele-Trip	P.O. Box 31716, Mutual of Omaha Plaza, Omaha, NE 68131	800/228-9792
Travel Assistance International	1133 15th St. NW, Ste. 400, Washington, DC, 20077	202/828-5894 or 800/821-2828; fax 202/828-5896
Travel Guard International	1145 Clark St., Stevens Point, WI 54401	715/345-0505 or 800/782-5151; fax 800/826-1300
Wallach and Co., Inc.	107 W. Federal St., P.O. Box 480, Middleburg, VA 20118-0480	540/687-3166 or 800/237-6615; fax 540/687-3172

ON THE ROAD

AMTRAK VIRGINIA LINES

Train	Route	Virginia Area Stops
Cardinal	Washington, D.C. to Chicago, IL	Alexandria, Manassas, Culpeper, Charlottesville, Staunton, Clifton Forge
Carolinian and Piedmont	Washington, D.C. to Charlotte, NC	Alexandria, Quantico, Fredericksburg, Richmond
Crescent	New York City to New Orleans	Washington, D.C., Alexandria, Manassas, Culpeper, Charlottesville, Lynchburg, Danville
Northeast Direct	Boston to News, VA	Washington, D.C., Alexandria, Newport Woodbridge, Quantico, Fredericksburg, Ashland, Richmond, Williamsburg
Silver Service	New York City to Miami	Washington, D.C., Alexandria, Richmond, Petersburg
Twilight Shoreliner	Boston to Newport News, VA	Washington, D.C., Alexandria, Quantico, Fredericksburg, Ashland, Richmond, Williamsburg

BY TRAIN

Traveling on **Amtrak,** 60 Massachusetts Ave. NE, Washington, DC 20002, 800/872-7245, www.amtrak.com, is closer in price to flying to the state but more comfortable and convenient. Amtrak's *Metroliner* connects New York City to Washington, D.C.'s **Union Station,** 50 Massachusetts Ave. NE, 202/371-9441, www.unionstationdc.com. From there, Metrorail lines run to destinations in northern Virginia.

In the rest of the state, service varies between one or more roundtrips daily to 3–6 per week with Amtrak Thruway buses connecting some cities. Student, senior, veterans', and children's discounts are available. Special seating, boarding assistance, and discounts for disabled travelers are available with 24 hours' notice, and service dogs ride free. Once again, use the toll-free number for route and fare questions; otherwise, local terminal numbers for baggage and other questions are given under individual city listings.

MAJOR AIRLINES SERVING VIRGINIA

American Airlines	800/433-7300	www.aa.com
Continental Airlines	800/525-0280	www.continental.com
Delta Airlines	800/221-1212	www.delta-air.com
Midway Airlines	800/446-4392	www.midwayair.com
Northwest Airlines	800/225-2525	www.nwa.com
Trans World Express	800/221-2000	www.twa.com
United Airlines, United Express	800/241-6522	www.ual.com
USAir, USAir Express	800/428-4322	www.usair.com

BY AIR

Most major airlines fly into one of two major airports in northern Virginia: **Washington Dulles International Airport** near Herndon or **Ronald Reagan National Airport** on the Potomac between Arlington and Alexandria. National handles domestic flights from east of the Mississippi. There are also major airports near Richmond, Norfolk, Newport News/Williamsburg, Charlottesville, and Roanoke.

The cheapest flights are almost always round-trip and date-restricted (usually requiring a Saturday-night stay). You'll have to book in advance and purchase within a day or two of making a reservation to secure the fare. Try different airports and smaller or regional carriers, and look in the Sunday travel sections of larger U.S. newspapers for up-to-the-minute deals. (Due to the vagaries of airline computer reservation systems, the best times to make reservations are weekdays between midnight and 1 A.M.—especially Wednesdays—and the worst times are on weekends.)

Information and Services

WHEN TO GO

If you're lucky enough to choose the time of year you visit Virginia, then seasonal weather will be one of your prime concerns. Overall, spring and fall are probably the best times to visit Virginia. In April, May, and September you'll find lulls in the tourist season *and* great weather.

In the spring, equestrian events like races and hunts thunder through northern Virginia, and crowds aren't yet a problem. Be warned that many tourist attractions don't open until April or May. Summer is high tourist season, even though high temperatures and humidity send most visitors to the beaches, historic sites, and theme parks along the coast. Fall's famous colors bring a second high season, though smaller than in the summer. In winter, the least crowded season, you can have entire days to yourself if you can handle the cold. Many sights close, especially in the mountains. Local festivals happen throughout the year.

HEALTH AND SAFETY

For emergencies anywhere in the state, dial 911 from any phone (no charge), or phone the Virginia State Police. Hospitals in larger cities are excellent, though emergency-room treatment is always more expensive than visits scheduled with an appointment.

Outdoors

Whenever you go into the wild, always tell someone where you're going and when you expect to be back, and then contact them when you return. It's a good idea to carry a first-aid kit, available prepackaged at most camp, drug, or large discount stores, and bring extra clothing layers (including a waterproof layer) and a safety kit that includes a Swiss army knife, waterproof matches, compass, topographical map, flashlight, emergency blanket (pocket-sized, mylar), signal whistle, and emergency food.

Even the clearest, highest mountain streams stand a good chance of containing **giardia,** a bacteria transmitted in human and animal waste that causes severe diarrhea. Filter or treat all water with iodine pills or drops. **Mosquitoes** are an annoyance everywhere in the summer and fall, along with **bees, wasps, yellowjackets,** and **hornets.** Female **black widow spiders,** identifiable by a tiny red hourglass on the abdomen, live in dark, woody places like rotting logs and under benches and tables. Their bite causes severe abdominal pain. If you are bitten, consult a physician. **Lyme disease** is transmitted through deer tick bites. It's not as common here as in New England but still appears every so often. Use insect repellent and check yourself after passing through tick territory—high grass or underbrush. If you notice a large red circular rash around a bite, seek medical treatment—it's life-threatening if untreated.

Virginia is home to three species of poisonous snakes. **Rattlesnakes** live in the mountains, **cottonmouth moccasins** inhabit swamps, and **copperheads** are everywhere. Don't stick your feet or hands anywhere you can't see, and if you encounter a snake, back off slowly. They're more afraid of you than you are of them and strike out of fear at sudden movements. Swimming in the ocean could expose you to a brush with a **jellyfish.** The best thing to minimize the sting (besides staying out of the water) is—believe it or not—meat tenderizer.

Plants to avoid include **poison ivy, poison oak,** and **poison sumac.** To help watch out for offending flora, remember the saying, "leaves of three, let it be." The irritating oil transmitted by contact with these plants can be washed off with soap and water, and over-the-counter cortisone creams can relieve the itching. Several local types of **mushrooms** and **berries** are also dangerous if ingested—don't eat any if you don't know what you're doing.

Weather-Related Problems

Being wet and tired in the cold mountains can lead to **hypothermia,** a dangerous plunge in the body's core temperature. Symptoms include shivering, slurred speech, and loss of coordination and mental clarity. Warm the affected person up by skin-to-skin contact, warm them with liquids (no alcohol), and evacuate as a last resort. **Lightning** is a danger on exposed ridges—stay away from lone trees and conductive materials such as power lines and metal fences. The summer sun along the coast can cause a nasty **sunburn,** so cover up with clothes and sunscreen, at least for the first week or so.

Crime

Although things have improved in the last few decades, the downtown areas of larger cities like Richmond and Norfolk still pose a threat of **robbery,** especially at night. Check with hotel staff regarding safe and dangerous areas. To discourage **break-ins** and **car theft,** don't leave valuables in plain view in your vehicle, and always lock the doors. Consider using an antitheft device like The Club in questionable neighborhoods.

MAPS

The **AAA map** of Virginia is the handiest for general navigation. For every last back road and some city maps, pick up a copy of the large-format *Virginia Topographic Atlas and Gazeteer* published by DeLorme ($19.95). Hikers can order U.S. Geological Survey (USGS) **topographical maps,** from Virginia dealers listed online (mapping.usgs.gov/esic/map_dealers/va.html) or from **Omni Resources,** 1004 South Mebane St., P.O. Box 2096, Burlington, NC 27216-2096, 336/227-8300, fax 336/227-3748, email: custserv@omnimap.com, www.omnimap.com, which also carries city and recreational maps and the *Virginia Atlas & Gazetteer.* Call the U.S. Geological Survey, 888/275-8747, www.usgs.gov/pubprod/index.html, for lists of maps and more information.

If you're into maps as art, order a catalog from **Raven Maps & Images,** P.O. Box 850, Medford, OR 97501-0253, 800/237-0798 or 541/773-1436, fax 541/773-6834, email: info@ravenmaps.com, www.ravenmaps.com. At 35 feet by 65 feet, their *Virginia, Maryland, Delaware, & DC* map is too large to carry in the car with you, but with tinted elevation and shaded relief, it's nice enough to frame and hang on the wall ($30 plain, $50 laminated).

INFORMATION

The **Virginia Tourism Corporation** (VTC), 901 E. Byrd St., Richmond, VA 23219, 800/321-3244, email: VAinfo@Virginia.org, www.virginia.org, can send you information on almost anything having to do with tourism in the state. The **state government** is also a good resource: 1111 East Main St., Ste. 901, Richmond, VA 23219, 804/786-4718 or 877/482-3468, www.state.va.us.

MONEY
Credit Cards

These are handy because not only do you not need to have cash on hand, but you can also contest charges for unsatisfactory services after the fact. They're accepted in cities, but in small towns you'll occasionally come across restaurants and museums that won't take them. In an emergency, you may be able to convince a local merchant or gas station attendant to give you cash change on a credit card purchase. The most commonly accepted credit cards are **Visa,** 800/632-3300, **Mastercard,** 800/456-7880, **Discover,** 800/487-2978, and **American Express,** 800/221-7282. The latter has offices in Alexandria, Arlington, Blacksburg, Charlottesville, Colonial Heights, Fairfax, Falls Church, Leesburg, Mclean, Norfolk, Richmond, Roanoke, and Virginia Beach.

Automatic Teller Machines

ATMs are widely available in midsized and larger cities but uncommon in smaller towns. For the locations of ATMs accepting cards bearing the **Mastercard/Cirrus** logo, call 800/424-7787 or log on to www.mastercard.com/cardholderservices/atm; for **Visa/Plus** call 800/843-7587 or stop by www.visa.com/pd/atm/main.html.

STUDENT TRAVEL

The **Council Travel,** 800/226-8624, www.counciltravel.com, issues the International Student Identity Card (ISIC) and under-26 Youth Cards that can secure you cheap flights and the occasional admission deal. **STA Travel,** 800/781-4040, www.sta-travel.com, is another student-oriented travel agency with offices across the country. Canadian students should contact a local branch of **Travel CUTS,** 866/246-9762, www.travelcuts.com, for rail passes and discounted flights. They also have offices in California and London.

GAY AND LESBIAN TRAVELERS

Even though it's not part of the Deep South, Virginia still leans toward the conservative end of the moral spectrum, so discretion is advised. Some larger cities support some sort of gay scene, which you can find out about through several channels. The **Dulles Triangles,** P.O. Box 3411, Reston, Virginia 20195, 703/787-0744, www.dullestri-

angles.com, is a gay social club in the northern Virginia area. **Gaytravel.com,** 800/429-8728, www.gay-travel.com, combines gay-oriented travel information, agents and operators.

Out & About, 995 Market St., 14th Floor, San Francisco, CA 94103, 415/644-8044, fax 415/644-7985, www.outandabout.com, is a monthly newsletter ($50 per year) covering resorts, hotels, cruise lines, and airlines' and **Viajar Travel,** email: info@viajartravel.com, www.viajartravel.com, is an online clearinghouse of gay and lesbian travel information.

TRAVELERS WITH DISABILITIES

Wheelchair access varies, so it's always best to call ahead and check. Upscale hotels are usually accessible, but B&Bs—often in old houses—probably aren't. Some theaters and restaurants have ramps and elevators, and some caverns and Civil War sites feature paved trails. All National Park Service visitors centers are wheelchair accessible. Most restrooms and buildings in Shenandoah National Park are accessible, along with some picnic grounds and campgrounds.

Resources

The VTC provides a special number, 800/742-3935, for fielding questions regarding special-needs travel. Reach its TDD Relay Center at 800/828-1120. The **Opening Door, Inc.,** 8049 Ormesby Lane, Woodford, VA 22580, 804/633-6752, www.travelguides.org, is a local nonprofit organization that publishes the free *Virginia Travel Guide for Persons with Disabilities,* now in its fifth edition, with 300 pages of access information on Virginia hotels, restaurants, shops, and attractions.

For more information on disabled travel, contact **Mobility International USA,** P.O. Box 10767, Eugene, OR 97440, 541/343-1284, fax 541/343-6812, email: info@miusa.org, www.miusa.org, or the **Society for the Advancement of Travel for the Handicapped,** 347 5th Ave., Ste. 610, New York, NY 10016, 212/447-7284, fax 212/725-8253, email: sathtravel@aol.com, www.sath.org.

ON THE ROAD

TRAVELING WITH CHILDREN

Dozens of spots in Virginia are as fun for children as their parents—if not more. Theme parks like Paramount's Kings Dominion, Busch Gardens, and Water Country USA are obvious first choices. You may be surprised how quickly children warm up to history when it's brought to life at places like Colonial Williamsburg, the Museum of American Frontier Culture, and Virginia's Explore Park. (Nothing sparks a kid's interest like a mountain man in full buckskin explaining how to hunt bear or a blacksmith pounding red-hot iron over a forge.)

Even Civil War sites, which could easily bore young minds to tears, offer the occasional battle reenactment or fascinating museum. Other hands-on exhibitions are designed with kids in mind, like the Shenandoah Valley Discovery Museum in Winchester, Richmond's Children's Museum, or Roanoke's outstanding Science Museum of Western Virginia. Theaters often host children's plays, and storytellers, musicians, face-painters, and puppeteers frequent festivals.

Local baby-sitting agencies can be found in the yellow pages or through hotel desks. **The Family Travel Times,** 40 5th Ave., New York, NY 10011, 888/822-4388 or 212/477-5524, email: info@ familytraveltimes, www.familytraveltimes, publishes a bimonthly newsletter, with subject headings like "Country Inns That Really Like Kids" and "Mountains of Fun," for $40 per year. Also, try the "Travel With Kids" section of the **About.com** website (travelwithkids.about.com).

SENIOR TRAVELERS

Many hotels and attractions offer discounts for seniors—ask when making reservations or at the gate. The **American Association of Retired Persons,** 601 E St. NW, Washington, DC, 20049, 800/424-3410 or 978/323-4141, fax 617/426-0701, email: member@aarp.org, www.aarp.org, is the country's largest seniors' organization, with discounts for members ($10 per year) on hotels, car rentals, air travel, and tours worldwide. **Elderhostel,** 11 Avenue de Lafayette, Boston, MA 02111-1746, 877/426-8056, email: registra-

tion@elderhostelorg, www.elderhostel.org, organizes worldwide "extraordinary learning adventures" for people 55 and over (one-half of a couple is sufficient).

TRAVEL INSURANCE

Several agencies offer specialized travelers' insurance in various combinations of health, accident, trip-cancellation and trip-interruption, and lost-luggage protection. Two dependable choices are **Travel Guard International,** 1145 Clark St., Stevens Point, WI 54481, 800/826-4919, www.travel-guard.com, and **Access America,** email: service@accessamerica.com, www.accessamerica.com.

TIME ZONES

Virginia is in the eastern time zone, five hours behind Greenwich mean time. **Daylight savings time** sets clocks one hour ahead on the first Sunday in April ("spring forward") and one hour back on the last Sunday in October ("fall back").

BUSINESS HOURS

Stores are generally open Monday–Friday 10 A.M.–6 P.M., and occasionally on Saturday. Shopping centers can be open daily, late on weeknights, and Sunday noon–5 or 6 P.M. Public and private office hours run Monday–Friday 9 A.M.–5 P.M., and banks are open Monday–Friday 9 A.M.–5 P.M., with occasional extended hours on evenings and Saturday mornings. Post office doors open at 8:30 A.M. on all days but Sunday and stay open until 5 P.M. on weekdays and 12:30 P.M. on Saturday. Museum and gallery hours vary, but many are closed on Monday (the same goes for restaurants). Just about everything closes on Thanksgiving, Christmas, and New Year's Day (even sites listed as open daily), and other national holidays may mean closings as well.

TIPPING

As any former restaurant server will tell you (and there are plenty of us out there), a 15 percent tip on bills is standard because waiters make considerably less than minimum wage before tips. Leave 20 percent or more to reward outstanding service. Taxi drivers typically receive 15 percent and airport porters and bellhops about $1 per bag.

Central Virginia

The Piedmont, Virginia's heartland, is also known as "Mr. Jefferson's Country." Two and a half centuries later, the man who left his indelible stamp on the central part of the state is still spoken about with a curious mixture of awe and familiarity, like a distinguished uncle who's just in the next room. These rolling hills, achingly beautiful in the late-afternoon sunlight, echo almost every aspect of a true renaissance life.

Thomas Jefferson was born on his father's farm at Shadwell in 1743, and plows still turn the rich soil of large parts of Albemarle and Orange counties every spring. Along with the land for Monticello, Jefferson inherited a taste for things patrician, a value system carried on with gusto by the Piedmont's current upper crust. Grand 19th-century homes anchor wealthy neighborhoods in Richmond, while in rural areas shaded country lanes

lead to historic estates, each with its own name and legion of caretakers. Packs of foxhounds in the care of riders on purebred horses are blessed outside Grace Episcopal Church on Route 231 in an annual ritual Jefferson would have undoubtedly appreciated.

Though the author of the Declaration of Independence failed in his first few attempts at coaxing a decent grape from the fertile Virginia soil, central Virginia now cradles the most wineries in the state. Jefferson's fascination with classical architecture lives on in the neoclassical lines of the state capitol in Richmond, the porticoes of Monticello, and the unmistakable rotunda of the University of Virginia in Charlottesville.

Above all, the third American president carried himself with an air of

THE STAR
HIDE ALIX STILL
SEEK HIM!

Holyland, USA

humility—he described how he found the greatest happiness when up to his elbows in his gardens or tinkering on one of the items on an endless list of projects and mechanical schemes. Despite all the new money that has poured into the Piedmont lately—along with celebrities like Rita Mae Brown, Sam Shepherd, and media billionaire John Kluge—central Virginia is still simple at heart. Whether it's the hand-poled Hatton Ferry across the James River at Scottsville, a well-worn tractor resting in a field of alfalfa, or the way everyone knows your name down at the general store after a couple of visits, this part of the state carries on Jefferson's greatest, quiet legacy: that of things of quality, appreciated slowly.

© JULIAN SMITH

the gardens at Monticello

HIGHLIGHTS

Almost all Virginia interstates lead to Richmond, which has been bursting with history ever since Patrick Henry gave his "liberty or death" speech in St. John's Church in 1775. As headquarters of the Confederacy, Richmond guarded the home of Jefferson Davis; the home is now part of the state's foremost Civil War museum. Today Richmond remains Virginia's political and commercial capital, humming with life in restored historic neighborhoods full of museums, restaurants, shops, and nightclubs.

Other Piedmont cities well worth a visit include the traditional tobacco center of Lynchburg, frighteningly cozy Charlottesville, and Fredericksburg, contested in some of the Civil War's hottest fighting. Civil War buffs have made a living out of exploring the Piedmont's wealth of battlefields and sites, from the trenches around Richmond to Appomattox Court House, where Robert E. Lee surrendered in April 1865.

Many founding fathers picked the Piedmont to build their homes, which survive today as museums, including Thomas Jefferson's Monticello and Poplar Forest, James Madison's Montpelier, and James Monroe's Ash Lawn-Highland. Outdoor enthusiasts can cycle down the Piedmont's asphalt ribbons for weeks or shoot the James rapids through the heart of Richmond. Rivers such as the Rapidan, Rappahannock, and James snake from one end of the region to the other, providing ample opportunities for boating, swimming, and fishing. To the southwest, Smith Mountain Lake offers all of the above and more.

ACCESS

All roads lead to Richmond—or interstates, in this case. I-64 connects Virginia's capital with the Blue Ridge, Charlottesville, and the coast, while I-95 skewers Richmond on its way from Washington, D.C. to North Carolina. I-85 is an alternate route south, while I-295 encircles Richmond and reaches down to Petersburg. Beyond the interstates, federal highways such as US 15, US 60, and US 522 offer more direct (and scenic) drives between major Piedmont cities. US 29 is the quickest route between Charlottesville and Washington, D.C. via I-66—just watch those speed traps around Culpeper. Smaller state roads like Rt. 20, Rt. 231, and Rt. 40 are the slowest and prettiest yet, taking their sweet time as they meander across the farmlands and up into the Blue Ridge foothills.

CENTRAL VIRGINIA

Richmond and Vicinity

Since its miraculous rebirth from the ashes of the Civil War, the capital of Virginia has learned to look forward as well as back. Without ignoring its role as one of America's consummate Southern cities—and all the respect for tradition that entails—Richmond has become a busy, affluent, eclectic metropolis that's more than sufficient to anchor its mother state in the past and propel it toward the future.

Visitors, swayed by descriptions a decade or two out of date, might expect a crumbling, dreary place full of unrepentant ghosts and the stale smell of tobacco. Granted, some parts of downtown still aren't all that pleasant. Others, though, have undergone an amazing transformation. Some of the liveliest nightlife in the state has bloomed by the James River, while to the west streets are packed at noon with browsers and the business lunchtime crowd. Other historic neighborhoods go about their business and tend their historic buildings as proud and conservative as ever.

Greater Richmond, which includes the city and Chesterfield, Hanover, and Henrico counties, is home to 850,000 people, of whom 30 percent are African American. The number climbs to 80 percent when focused on the 203,000 inhabitants of the city itself. A high percentage of younger residents are here attending schools such as the University of Richmond, Virginia Commonwealth University and its Medical College of Virginia branch, Virginia Union University, and the Union Theological Seminary.

Richmond has always been one of Virginia's commercial hubs, and even as trade along the James has faded it has found new ventures to take over. More than a dozen Fortune 500 companies have their corporate headquarters here, including Reynolds Metal, which introduced Richmond and the world to aluminum foil in 1947. Richmond's title of "Tobacco Capital of the World" lives on in cigarette billboards, cigar shops, and the sprawling, state-of-the-art headquarters of Philip Morris—the city's second-largest private employer—south of the James. Nonetheless, *Health* magazine recently rated the Richmond metro area as the healthiest city in the country.

Revitalization is a never-ending process, and Richmond's latest direction is the $1-billion Downtown Master Plan, designed to guide development until 2010. In the blueprints are a biotechnology research park, the restoration of the Jefferson Hotel and Main Street Station, and complete facelifts to the Richmond Convention Centre and the Sixth Street Marketplace. The transformation of 32 acres of Tobacco Row along the river from 5th to 17th Streets, complete with walkways, plazas, and apartment buildings, is considered one of the most ambitious redevelopment projects in the country.

HISTORY

Christopher Newport and Captain John Smith scouted the stretch of the James by Richmond in 1607, within weeks of the English settlers' landing. The name came from William Byrd II, who decided the falls at this spot on the James reminded him of Richmond-on-Thames in England. Several forts protected the bustling port, which was plotted out in 1737.

In April 1780 the Colonial capital was moved from Williamsburg to Richmond to protect it from the invading British, but to no avail. Famous traitor Benedict Arnold put the town of 700 to the torch in January 1781. Richmond recovered, largely because of a canal system completed in 1840 that connected to the western Piedmont. The canal bypassed the falls and helped the city become a regional hub for transport, milling, banking, and trade. By the turn of the 19th century, Richmond's population had passed 5,000, and local culture blossomed. Planters brought their families into town in the winter to enjoy the stars of Europe and America performing on city stages. Edgar Allan Poe wrote brilliant, scathing book reviews for *The Southern Literary Messenger* from August 1835 through January 1837, and at one party Charles Dickens acquired his nickname of the "artful

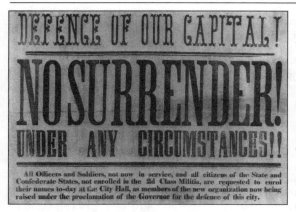

DEFENCE OF OUR CAPITAL!

NO SURRENDER!

UNDER ANY CIRCUMSTANCES!!

All Officers and Soldiers, not now in service, and all citizens of the State and Confederate States, not enrolled in the 2d Class Militia, are requested to enrol their names to-day at the City Hall, as members of the new organization now being raised under the proclamation of the Governor for the defence of this city.

riverside commercial district, set ablaze to keep its supplies out of Yankee hands.

Once again Richmond rebuilt itself. Still an important shipping center, the city enjoyed an economic boom near the turn of the 20th century. During this time, tobacco factories, flour mills, and iron foundries were constructed. Three major railways fed 1,245 manufacturing plants. Prohibition and the Great Depression came and went, shaking but sparing the city that by the late 1930s was the fastest-growing industrial center in the country. The historian Mary Newton Standard wrote how "business buzzes, traffic roars, skyscrapers soar to heaven, and numberless smokestacks proclaim that everything in the world, from matches to locomotives, is made in Richmond."

dodger" as his host boasted how the famous author had dodged Philadelphia and Baltimore in favor of Richmond.

The most industrialized city in the south at the start of the Civil War became the Confederate capital on May 29, 1861. Jefferson Davis presided over this city flush with Southern pride and host to lavish balls where hoop-skirted belles flirted with officers in crisp uniforms. After three years of fighting, however, hope had given way to reality. Richmond's population tripled as wounded and captured soldiers flooded the city. Belle Isle in the James became one of the war's largest prison camps; local factories cranked out thousands of weapons for Confederate troops; and basic necessities such as food and clothing grew scarce as the sound of gunfire approached with enemy armies.

The Union army marched within hearing distance of the city's church bells in 1862 and again in 1864, but it wasn't until April 1865 that Robert E. Lee's Army of Northern Virginia found itself cornered. Davis and the Confederate government fled to Danville as the defensive lines at Petersburg collapsed on April 3. Retreating troops marched out by the light of fires raging in the

The Army of the Confederate Government having abandoned the City of Richmond, I respectfully request that you will take possession of it with organized force, to preserve order and protect women and children and property.

—**Mayor Joseph C. Mayo's message to Ulysses S. Grant at the fall of Richmond, April 2, 1865**

Dozens of antebellum homes in the downtown area fell to the wrecking ball of progress while wealthy citizens built Tudor estates to the west. A growing black population made the integration of city schools an inevitability and has shifted the political power structure away from its traditional Southern paradigm.

ORIENTATION

Downtown Richmond, the heart of the Greater Richmond Metropolitan Area, spreads along the northern side of a bend in the James River. Navigation is simple: the only kink in the simple grid street layout is in Carytown and The Fan, where everything has a 30-degree slant. Aside from this, and the fact that most main avenues are one-way, Richmond is an easy city to navigate. Parking is another matter—tickets appear quicker than flies at a barbecue, and the main nightlife districts in Shockoe are notorious

CENTRAL VIRGINIA

for their lack of spaces (even though they're free on weekends). Broad Street (US 60) is the main east-west thoroughfare, running the entire length of the city. As you'll soon find out, Richmonders love to carve their city up into neighborhoods, though they're not always so eager to delineate them clearly.

SAFETY

In 1996 the violent crime rate for the metro area was 597 crimes per 100,000 people, about the same as in Raleigh-Durham, North Carolina, and Boston, Massachusetts. The city proper experienced a jump in crime in the late 1980s and early 1990s, but lately crime is down again. This is thanks in part to the state's new Project Exile, which sets a minimum five-year sentence, without parole, for crimes committed with a gun. The heavily advertised and enforced program has led to a 21 percent decrease in violent crime from 1997–2001 and is being copied by other cities nationwide.

Still, it's better to drive than walk through the downtown area at night, especially from one neighborhood to the next (say, Jackson Ward to Shockoe Slip). Wandering within popular, well-lit districts like Carytown and The Fan is considered safe. Some hotels offer shuttle service; beyond that, drive or call a cab.

CENTRAL RICHMOND

Richmond's historic heart beats in the neighborhood of **Court End,** between Leigh Street and the state capitol. Centuries-old mansions and churches sit next to the dome of the Richmond Coliseum, modern office buildings, and the halls of the Medical College of Virginia (MCV), a branch of Virginia Commonwealth University.

White House and Museum of the Confederacy

The largest collection of Confederate relics in the world starts with pieces of the C.S.S. *Virginia* out front and continues inside. For its location in the heart of the rebel capital, the

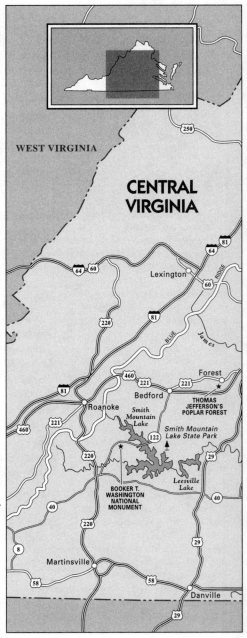

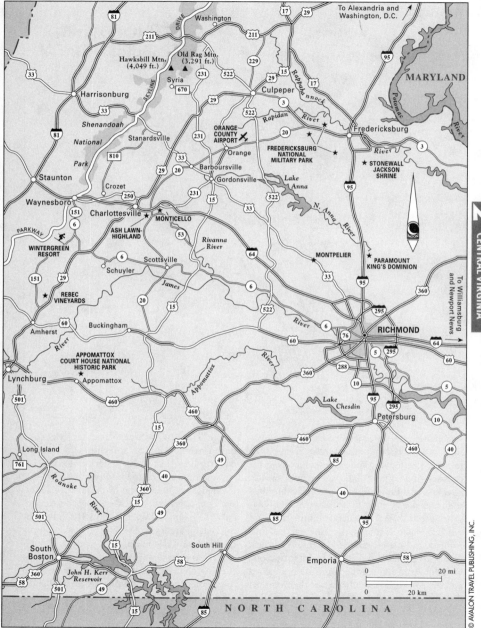

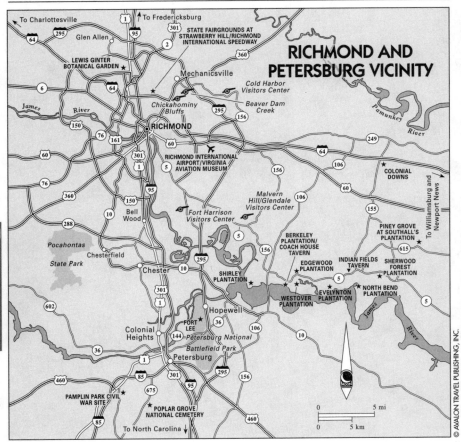

RICHMOND AND PETERSBURG VICINITY

presentation is surprisingly objective, with only a slight Southern slant peeking through from time to time. The moving collection ranges from the prosaic—more than 500 flags, dozens of swords, pistols, and rifles, and soldiers' letters home—to the particular, in its prized assortment of personal effects from Confederate luminaries.

J.E.B. Stuart's plumed hat, Stonewall Jackson's revolver, and a re-creation of Robert E. Lee's field tent with his table inside are highlights, along with the sword and coat Lee wore to Appomattox and the pen with which he signed the surrender documents. Upstairs you'll find changing exhibits addressing the experiences of blacks, women, and other civilians during the war, while downstairs

hangs "The Last Meeting of Lee and Jackson," a monumental 1869 oil painting depicting the commanders' final parley at Chancellorsville.

Next door stands the building leased by the Confederate government as a home for Jefferson Davis, his family, and a dozen or so slaves August 1861–April 1865. Built in 1818, it became the Federal headquarters during Reconstruction. Lavish period decorations include many original Davis pieces, such as his favorite horsehair rocking chair (sat in by Lincoln less than 48 hours after the evacuation of Richmond) and a marble bust of the president of the Confederacy buried by a neighbor to keep it safe from Union troops. Notice the "gasaliers," hanging glass globes

FIGHTING FOR RICHMOND

The Confederate capital saw two major Civil War campaigns reach her doorstep. The first, in 1862, crushed the possibility of a short war, and the second two years later set the stage for the war's end.

The Seven Days' Battles

Gen. George B. McClellan's Peninsular Campaign advanced to within sight of Richmond in June 1862. Robert E. Lee, recently named commander of the Confederate army, recalled Stonewall Jackson and his troops from the Shenandoah Valley and struck first on June 26 with 90,000 men. McClellan's army was flushed out of Mechanicsburg, but struck back at Beaver Dam Creek with a vengeance that left earthworks "waist deep in blood," in the words of one officer.

General Robert E. Lee

The next day 55,000 Rebels attacked at Gaines' Mill, securing a last-ditch victory after being driven back repeatedly from the blue line along Boatswain's Creek. The heaviest fighting of the Seven Days' Battles resulted in 15,000 casualties, twice as many Confederate as Federal. McClellan began a fighting retreat, clashing with Lee at Savage's Station on June 29 and White Oak Swamp and Glendale (Frayser's Farm) on June 30. On July 1 the Union army managed to reach the safety of gunboats on the James River at Harrison's Landing. Under orders to protect the withdrawal, Maj. Gen. Fitz-John Porter lined his troops up in battle formation

General George P. McClellan

along Malvern Hill and mowed down enemy ranks forced to cross open ground. Gunboat artillery helped slaughter 6,000 advancing troops, causing Confederate Gen. E.M. Law to remark, "It was not war—it was murder."

The Seven Days' Battles convinced McClellan to abandon his advance on Richmond for the time being, refusing Lincoln's offer of another 50,000 men by saying it wouldn't be enough. A week of fierce combat had cost 35,000 lives and untold suffering. One Georgian soldier wrote home, "I have seen, heard, and felt many things in the last week that I never want to see, hear, nor feel again."

The Beginning of the End

By 1864 Richmond was heavily defended behind two rings of defensive earthworks and a series of forts on the outskirts of the city. Ulysses S. Grant had taken command of Union forces and put Richmond in the crosshairs once again. After much maneuvering by both sides, Confederate troops dug in at Cold Harbor just in time for Grant's assault on June 3.

A massive frontal attack in sweltering heat threw 60,000 men against the impregnable Confederate lines in what quickly became the bloodiest charge of the war. More than 7,000 Federal soldiers were cut down with appalling speed by Rebel rifles and artillery. Some witnesses said the outcome was decided in 15 minutes; others said eight. Knowing they were doomed, Union soldiers pinned their names to their uniforms to notify their next of kin of their death—the early origin of dog tags. A diary found on one soldier's body ended with: "June 3. Cold Harbor. I was killed."

Ten more days of fighting in 100-degree weather proved the futility of infantry assaults against strongly held trenches, changing the course of the Civil War and all wars thereafter. Grant eventually withdrew and crossed the James toward Petersburg, where a 10-month siege would lead to the fall of Richmond and the end of the Civil War.

CENTRAL VIRGINIA

lit by coal gas, and the toy cannon in the nursery (the Davis kids were apparently hellions).

Both buildings are on the Medical College of Virginia campus at 1201 E. Clay St., 804/649-1861. Open Mon.–Sat. 10 A.M.–5 P.M., Sun. noon–5 P.M.; $7 adults, $4 children 7–18 (separate admissions are available).

Capitol Square

A statue of George Washington on horseback surveys this grassy oasis dominated by the classical lines of the **Virginia State Capitol,** 804/698-1788. The original central section, begun in 1785, was designed by—who else—Thomas Jefferson, based on the Maison Carrée, a 1st-century Roman temple in Nîmes, France. Even though it wasn't yet completed, the Virginia Assembly held its first meeting here in 1788. The Jean-Antoine Houdon statue of George Washington that stands under the cupola was unveiled the same year. It's considered one of the most valuable marble sculptures in the country because it was the only one Washington posed for in person. House and Senate chambers were added to the structure in 1904–1906. Open daily 9 A.M.–5 P.M. Apr.–Nov. (Sun. 1–5 P.M. the rest of the year), with free tours every half hour.

To one side is the **Executive Mansion,** 804/371-2642, the oldest continually inhabited governor's residence in America. Call for a current schedule of free 15-minute tours. **Old City Hall** fills Leigh Street with a block of Victorian Gothic pomp in gray stone. Built in 1886–1895, the structure was restored in the mid-1980s. The first floor is open to visitors—don't miss the ornate splendor of the painted pillars and two-story atrium. Across Leigh Street stands **New City Hall** with a 19th-floor observation deck (open daily until dusk), and a **visitors information center** fills the bottom of the Old Bell Tower (1824) at the southwest corner of the square.

The Valentine Museum

A collection of photos, old clothing, and antique tobacco tools captures the "Life and History of Richmond" from the 17th to 20th centuries. The museum abuts the Wickham House, built in 1812 by John Wickham, Richmond's wealthiest citizen and the lawyer who defended Aaron Burr against charges of treason in 1807. It's hard to decide which is more beautiful—the rare set of neoclassical decorative wall paintings or the Oval Parlor, designated one of the "100 most beautiful rooms in America." Behind the museum is a small garden, café, and the studio of Richmond sculptor Edward Valentine, moved here in 1937 from its original spot at Leigh and 8th streets. The museum, 1015 E. Clay St., 804/649-0711, www.valentinemuseum.com, is open Mon.–Sat. 10 A.M.–5 P.M., Sun. noon–5 P.M.; $5 adults, $3 children 7–12.

John Marshall House

The home of the third U.S. Supreme Court chief justice (1801–1835) reflects the astonishing career of one of the most brilliant men to ever hold the post. Revolutionary War veteran, lawyer, ambassador to France, secretary of state—Marshall did it all. He even had the temerity to oppose his cousin, Thomas Jefferson, in the political arena. The house was built in 1788–1790 in the federal style and contains many original architectural features and relics from Marshall's life and times. The house, 818 E. Marshall at 9th St., 804/648-7998, is open Tues.–Sat. 10 A.M.–5 P.M. (Oct.–Dec. until 4:30 P.M.); $3 adults, $1.25 children 7–12.

JACKSON WARD

This National Historic District is best known as a cradle of African American business and culture in the early- and mid-20th century. Many black business and social leaders found a home along Quality Row, as Leigh Street west of 2nd Street was known. Banks, fraternal organizations, and other businesses benefited from a foundation of prominent figures such as Maggie Walker and Bill "Bojangles" Robinson. The Hippodrome Theater on 2nd Street (called The Deuce) swung through Prohibition to the tunes of Duke Ellington, Cab Calloway, and Billie Holiday, who handed down the crown to Ella Fitzgerald, Nat King Cole, and James Brown in later years.

Today many of Jackson Ward's stately row

houses have been restored as homes and offices, many with shallow covered front porches and fine ornamental ironwork (the neighborhood has more decorative wrought iron than any other outside of New Orleans). Sadly, enough of Jackson Ward has fallen into disrepair that the neighborhood was listed by the National Trust for Historic Preservation as one of the 11 most endangered historic places in America in 2001. The construction of I-95 in the 1950s destroyed 200 homes, and today it's estimated that $200 million is necessary for a full restoration.

Maggie L. Walker National Historic Site

The daughter of a former slave, Maggie Walker overcame physical disability and racial prejudice to become the first female bank president in America, as well as owner of a newspaper, insurance company, and department store. Her St. Luke Penny Savings Bank is now called The Consolidated Bank and Trust Company, the oldest black-operated bank in the United States. Walker lived at this two-story brick rowhouse with her family from 1904–1934, leaving many family pieces behind. The house, 600 N. 2nd St., 804/771-2017, www.nps.gov/malw, is operated by the National Park Service, which has restored it to its 1930s appearance. Open Wed.–Sat. 9 A.M.–5 P.M., with free admission and tours on the hour.

Black History Museum and Cultural Center of Virginia

Exhibits on Richmond's black history with a focus on the immediate area are displayed in this 1832 house, which served as a high school and black public library over the years. The center, 804/780-9093, is at 00 E. Clay St. at St. James Street. Open Tues.–Sat. 11 A.M.–4 P.M., Sun. 1–5 P.M.; $4 adults, $2 children under 18.

Statue of Bill "Bojangles" Robinson

The "King of Tapology" got his break in 1907 as a waiter in the Jefferson Hotel, supposedly dancing his way out of a mixed-up order all the way back to the kitchen. He went on to perform his trademark stair dance on Broadway and in the movies, appearing in the first black "talkie" and starring alongside Shirley Temple in *The Little Colonel*. The 10-foot aluminum sculpture was erected in 1973 at the corner of Adams and Leigh streets, where the dancer had donated a traffic light to help local children cross in safety.

THE FAN

In addition to thrift shops, worn-in apartments, and combination deli-laundromats, students of Virginia Commonwealth University (VCU) enjoy living in one of the largest intact Victorian neighborhoods in the country. The Fan takes it name from the way the streets spoke out from Monroe Park at the corner of Belvedere and Franklin. Million-dollar mansions and renovated early-1900s townhouses along Monument Avenue contrast funky pastel buildings along Main Street west toward Carytown, with rooftop gardens and cobblestone alleys adding an extra touch of character. South of the I-95 downtown expressway, The Fan turns purely residential, with brightly painted houses along tree-lined streets.

Monument Avenue

The northern border of The Fan has been called one of the most beautiful boulevards in the world, and even if statue-happy Richmond has worn you down already, it is impressive. Huge likenesses of Confederate heroes—with one notable exception—pose on raised platforms, each surrounded by a traffic circle and linked to the next by grassy medians. **J.E.B. Stuart** sports his trademark plumed hat at Monument Avenue and Lombardy Street, followed by **Robert E. Lee** at Allen Avenue and **Jefferson Davis** at Davis Street. **Stonewall Jackson** faces boldly north (on purpose) at Boulevard, and **Matthew Fontaine Maury,** the father of modern oceanography, stands at Belmont Avenue. (Ironically, Maury's work helped the Union blockade seal up the Southern coast during the Civil War.)

Monument Avenue's latest addition almost didn't make it. Born in Richmond in 1943, **Arthur Ashe, Jr.** began playing tennis at age seven and went on to win the U.S. Open and Wimbledon, becoming the first black man to receive a number-one international ranking. After

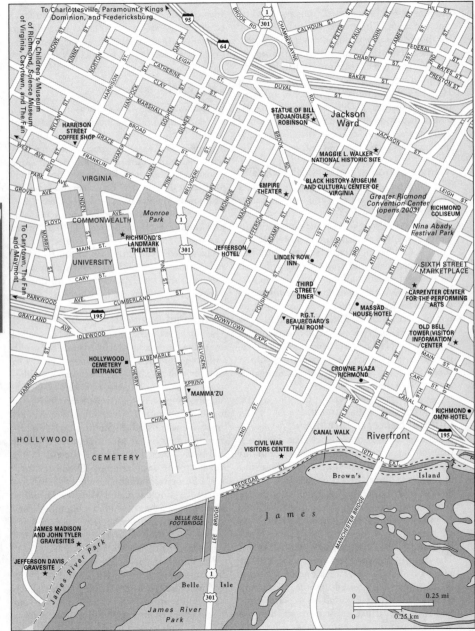

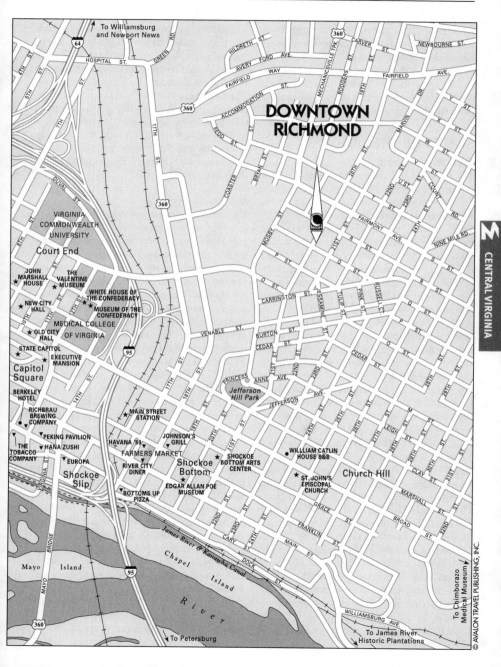

CENTRAL VIRGINIA

retiring, Ashe used his fame to promote black athletics and education, even writing a book about the history of black athletes. Controversy surrounded the decision to erect Ashe's likeness in such traditional company, but it was unveiled in 1996 nonetheless. Fittingly, the statue renders him offering a tennis racket and book to children reaching up at his feet.

SOUTH OF THE FAN

Civil War Visitors Center

The squat brick buildings of the Tredegar Iron-works, once so crucial to the doomed Confederate cause, are now the main visitors center for the **Richmond Battlefield National Park,** 804/226-1981, www.nps.gov/rich. Churning day and night, the ironworks produced 1,100 cannons, ammunition, and the armor plating that protected the *C.S.S. Virginia.* Armed workers prevented its destruction at the hands of a mob during the burning of Richmond, and the factory went on to produce cast iron artillery shells until 1957.

Three floors of exhibits and artifacts tell the story of the desperate fighting that encircled the city for most of the war. Park rangers can answer any questions left after your tour of the museum and a short film, and they rent out tapes for a self-guided **auto tour,** which runs to the east and south of the city. The 130-mile loop takes you past 10 sites from the 1862 campaign (Chickahominy Bluff, Beaver Dam Creek, Gaines Mill/Watt House, Glendale/Frayser's Farm, Malvern Hill, and Drewry's Bluff) and the fighting in 1864 (Garthright House, Parker's Battery, Cold Harbor, and Fort Harrison). There are smaller visitors centers at **Chimborazo Hospital** and **Cold Harbor** (on Rt. 156 five miles southeast of Mechanicsville) as well as at **Fort Harrison** (off Rt. 5) and **Glendale Cemetery,** both open seasonally. Visitors centers are open daily 9 A.M.–6 P.M. (5 P.M. out of season). Living-history demonstrations include Richmond Civil War Day at Tredegar (late April) and the anniversaries of the battle of Cold Harbor (early June), Fort Harrison (late September), and Seven Days Battle at Malvern Hill (late June).

Byrd Park

Three lakes, picnic shelters, sports fields, trails, and tennis courts fill one of Richmond's most popular parks, along Boulevard south of I-195. During the summer you can rent paddle boats on Boat Lake and feed the ducks on the other two. **The Carillon,** a 240-foot tower with 56 bells, recently underwent $1.4 million worth of renovations and is a centerpiece of the city's Fourth of July fireworks. Outdoor concerts, children's performances, and the Festival of the Arts in July and August are held in the **Dogwood Dell** outdoor amphitheater.

Maymont

The former dairy farm of Maj. James Dooley, Confederate veteran and millionaire, and his wife Sallie May has become the city's most family-friendly sanctuary. Their Romanesque Revival mansion, completed in 1893, is full of European and Asian curios acquired over years of traveling, including oriental rugs, stained glass, frescoes, and porcelain. Maymont's grounds, though, are its real treasure: 100 acres of rolling open parkland, a riot of buds, birds, and blossoms in the spring and inviting at any time of year. Three decades of work went into the herb, formal Italian, and Japanese gardens that slope down toward the James River. Children love the aviary, farm barn, and the new Nature & Visitors Center, with exhibits on the James River hydrology, flora, and fauna, from fish to river otters.

Maymont is run by the nonprofit Maymont Foundation, 804/358-7166, www.maymont.org. A donation of $4 is suggested for admission to the house and the nature center, which are open Tues.–Sat. noon–5 P.M. along with the farm and barn. The grounds, gardens, and visitors center are open daily 10 A.M.–5 P.M. A wealth of children's activities include tram tours (daily year-round, $2 adults, $1 children), carriage rides (Sundays Apr.–Oct., $3/2), and hayrides (weekends June–Aug., $2/1). Annual events start with a Flower and Garden Show in February and continue to a Family Easter and Christmas open house. Call about periodic Barn Days, garden tours, and history and nature programs.

To get to Maymont's main entrance at 2201

CENTRAL VIRGINIA

Shields Lake Dr., take Boulevard (VA 161) south two miles from I-64/I-95 exit 78. (You can also reach Boulevard by heading west on Cary St.) Bear right at the Columbus statue, left at the Carillon (on Boulevard the whole way), then turn left onto Shirley Road. Bear left after one block into Byrd Park, and take a right after another block onto Shields Lake Drive.

Hollywood Cemetery

It's hard to imagine a more tranquil resting place than this bluff over the James River. Acres of headstones, winged monuments, and mausoleums alternate between eerie and almost inviting, depending on the whims of weather and the time of day. Jefferson Davis, James Monroe, and John Tyler are the three most famous residents, along with J.E.B. Stuart and 21 other Confederate generals, six Virginia governors, and the first battle casualty of the Civil War. A 90-foot pyramid of rough stone marks the graves of 18,000 Confederate soldiers. The cemetery, 804/648-8501, is open daily 8 A.M.–5 or 6 P.M. Enter off Albemarle Street. **Richmond Discoveries,** 804/222-8595, offers guided walking tours of Hollywood Cemetery the last Sunday of each month Mar.–Oct. for $5 pp.

James River Park

A substantial chunk of southern riverbank and several islands have been set aside as a nature and recreational reserve in the middle of Richmond. Four hundred fifty acres of urban wilderness stretch from the Robert E. Lee (US 1/301) bridge upriver to the **Pony Pasture** and **Huguenot Woods** sections beyond the Powhite Parkway (Rt. 76) bridge. There are entrances to the south side from 22nd Street, 42nd Street, and at Reedy Creek, where you'll find park headquarters. An elevated footbridge leads from the 22nd Street entrance to **Belle Isle,** with a great view of the Richmond skyline, 19th-century industrial ruins, and the remains of a notorious Civil War POW camp that held as many as 8,000 prisoners at one time. Migrating thrushes and warblers flock to Pony Pasture in the spring, accompanied by the blooms of Virginia bellflowers, morning glories, and Dutchman's breeche.

A **visitors center,** 804/646-8491, sits along Riverside Drive on the south bank, one mile east of Huguenot Bridge. Pick up information on fishing and multiuse trails like the Geology Interpretive Trail near Belle Isle, crossing a favorite 19th-century dueling ground. Naturally, floating draws the most visitors: the calm stretch of river from Huguenot Woods to the visitors center is fine for tubing, but beyond that you'll need a raft or kayak and an experienced guide.

CARYTOWN

Cary Street, west of Boulevard, strings together an eclectic mix of antique stores, unusual restaurants, and students on skateboards clattering down brick sidewalks.

Virginia Museum of Fine Arts

Richmond's most outstanding collection is on par with any along the eastern seaboard. Everything from Egyptian sculptures to Andy Warhol's "Triple Elvis" makes an appearance in the multifarious museum, which boasts original works by Monet, Renoir, Picasso, and Degas, along with strong showings from the ancient Mediterranean, medieval Europe, and American art nouveau and art deco.

The museum, 2800 Grove Ave. at N. Boulevard, 804/340-1400, www.vmfa.state.va.us, is open Tues.–Sun. 11 A.M.–5 P.M. (Thurs. until 8 P.M.) for a $5 suggested donation. Free guided tours of highlights are offered. Locals rate the museum shop as outstanding, and the **Arts Cafe** is convenient for a bite on the outside patio in the sculpture garden.

Virginia Historical Society Center for Virginia History

Next door to the art museum, this collection has a state's worth of portraits, weapons, tools, and books on display to catalogue Virginia's cavernous past. Dugout canoes and Richmond streetcars are displayed near the library and murals of Virginia history. The center, 408 N. Boulevard, 804/348-4901, is open Mon.–Sat. 10 A.M.–5 P.M., Sun. 1–5 P.M.; $4 adults, $2 children (free on Mondays).

CENTRAL VIRGINIA

Agecroft Hall

For a truly unique house tour, visit this 15th-century Tudor mansion, 4305 Sulgrave Rd., 804/353-4241, that was dismantled in England in the 1920s and moved to the ritzy Windsor Farms neighborhood of Richmond to save it from destruction. The mansion offers a general 30-minute tour as well as specialty kids' tours or lectures on period dining habits. The house features period furniture and decorations, original woodwork, and magnificent gardens overlooking the James River. Performances of various Shakespearean works are staged on the lawn during summer. Open daily 10 A.M.–5 P.M., closed Mondays; $5 adults, $4.50 seniors and students, $3 children 12 and older.

RIVERFRONT

The former riverside site of Richmond's Tredegar Iron Works, origin of most Confederate cannon balls and artillery pieces during the Civil War, is now home to a **World War II and Korean War Memorial. Brown's Island,** at the bottom of 7th Street, is one end of Richmond's **Canal Walk** along the old James River–Kanawha Canal. Richmond's canal was part of a network first envisioned by George Washington to reach all the way to Mississippi. It was extended through Lynchburg to Buchanan, where bateaux boats carried cargo in the early and mid-19th century, but eventually overtaken by railroads and mostly forgotten. Historic markers tell the history of the riverfront from here to the other end near the "Triple Crossing" in Shockoe Slip; in the early 20th century, Richmond was the only city in the world with a triple main-line railroad crossing, which is still in use today.

SHOCKOE SLIP

The Confederate capital's warehouse and commercial district, reduced to charred rubble in 1865, has been resurrected within the last few decades into a lively local hot-spot. Fashionable shops and art galleries are open by day, and at night old-fashioned street lamps light the cobblestone avenues in front of renovated warehouses now holding restaurants and nightclubs. A portion of Thomas Jefferson's Virginia Statute for Religious Freedom has been emblazoned on the wall of a parking lot at the corner of Cary and 14th streets.

SHOCKOE BOTTOM

Farther east under the I-95 overpass, Shockoe Bottom was once Richmond's oldest commercial district, replete with produce markets and warehouses. Tall sailing ships hailed from Africa with bodies for the district's slave auction houses, while canal barges and rail lines brought in raw materials for towering brick tobacco factories. Until recently, Shockoe Bottom was plagued by periodic flooding—a 1972 surge courtesy of Hurricane Agnes caused $350 million in damage—but a multimillion-dollar flood wall now protects dozens of restaurants, pubs, and shops.

Tobacco Row, between 20th and Pear streets, is the target of Richmond's latest urban redevelopment project, aimed at transforming crumbling warehouses into apartment buildings. There are also plans to restore the unmistakable **Main Street Station,** whose ornate clock tower once welcomed countless rail travelers to the city, to its former glory. The **17th Street Farmers' Market,** which is closed on Sundays but open year-round, has been active since 1779, making it perhaps the oldest in the country.

Shockoe Bottom Arts Center

In 1994 artist Deanna Brizendine and her son Rusty Davis acquired the bottom floor of an abandoned American Tobacco Company factory. With Old Town Alexandria's Torpedo Factory in mind, they opened dozens of studio spaces to artists of all stripes. The Arts Center holds monthly juried exhibitions and an evening reception the second Friday of each month. The first Saturday of each month is said to be the best time to catch artists in their studios. The center, 2001 E. Grace St. at 21st, 804/643-7959, is open Tues.–Sat. 10 A.M.–5 P.M., Sun. 1–5 P.M.

Edgar Allan Poe Museum

The genius of ghoul was raised and married in Richmond, spending more time here than in any other city. Poe gained his first national attention here on the staff of the local *Southern Literary Messenger.* The Old Stone House—actually the oldest residence in Richmond, built in the 1730s—houses his personal effects and daguerreotypes of that famous haunted visage. Sip a lemonade in the Enchanted Garden before embarking on a guided tour of the house, where you'll see his walking stick, childhood bed, and a model of Richmond in Poe's day.

The museum, 1914 E. Main St., 804/648-5523 or 888/213-2763, www.poemuseum.org, is open Tues.–Sun. 10 A.M.–5 P.M.; $6 adults, $5 children. Guided tours begin on the hour.

CHURCH HILL

A mosaic of 19th-century architectural styles adorns the city's oldest residential neighborhood, named for St. John's Church. Lovingly restored homes in Victorian, Greek Revival, and Federal style gaze out over the city and river.

St. John's Episcopal Church

Built in 1740–1741, Richmond's oldest house of worship is also one of the oldest wooden buildings in Virginia. It's best known as the site of Patrick Henry's "Give me liberty or give me death" speech to George Washington, Thomas Jefferson, and the rest of the Second Virginia Convention on March 23, 1775. The parish dates to 1611, and services are still held here. Edgar Allen Poe's mother is buried in the surrounding cemetery, which was the only public burial ground in Richmond until 1826.

Half-hour tours of the church, 2401 E. Broad St., 804/648-5015, are given Mon.–Sat. 10 A.M.–4 P.M., Sun. 1–4 P.M.; $3 adults, $1 children 7–18. Tours are given until 3:30 P.M., and Henry's speech is reenacted in full the Sunday closest to March 23, with a smaller-scale reading every Sunday at 2 P.M. from June–Sept.

Chimborazo Medical Museum

The site of one of the Confederate's largest wartime hospitals is now the headquarters of the Richmond Battlefield National Park, 3215 E. Broad St, 804/226-1981, and a medical museum.

At its peak, Chimborazo Hospital was the largest of its kind in the world, eventually treating 76,000 patients in 150 buildings and 100 tents. Displays trace the practitioners and unenviable recipients of late-19th-century war medicine. Open daily 9 A.M.–5 P.M.

OTHER SIGHTS

Virginia Holocaust Museum

Opened in 1997 by a group of volunteers, some of whom are concentration camp survivors themselves, this small museum offers a poignant look into the horrors of Europe during World War II. Self-guiding tours with CD players and headphones lead you through a re-created box car and family room frozen in mid-capture. Archives and a library are available to researchers.

The museum, 213 Roseneath Rd., 804/257-5400, www.va-holocaust.com, is behind Temple Beth-El at Roseneath and Grove streets. It's open Mon.–Fri. 9 A.M.–5 P.M., Sat. 2–5 P.M., Sun. 1–5 P.M. for free, but donations are appreciated.

Science Museum of Virginia

It's hard to miss the monumental Union Station (topped by a green copper dome), which houses an excellent body of hands-on displays on neat-o subjects like aviation, computers, crystals, astronomy, and static electricity. A 100-foot Foucault pendulum in the rotunda lobby is so big its swing is nudged by the rotation of the earth, and even the infrared toilet flushers have explanatory cards. IMAX films and planetarium shows are shown in the 270-degree Ethyl Universe Theater.

The museum, 2500 W. Broad St., 800/659-1727 or 804/367-6552, www.smv.org, is open Mon.–Thurs. 9:30 A.M.–5 P.M., Fri. and Sat. 9:30 A.M.–7 P.M., Sun. 11:30 A.M.–5 P.M. (limited hours Sept.–May) for $9 adults, $8 children 4–12 including a theater show. Admission to the museum only ($5 adults, $4 children) and theater only ($5 pp) is also available.

Richmond Children's Museum

The M-word can strike fear into the heart of the bravest 10-year-old, but this playhouse will leave youngsters age 2–12 begging for more. After dressing up for the kid-sized doctor's office, TV studio, and grocery store, children can learn about computers or explore a 40-foot replica of a Virginia limestone cave. For the artistically inclined, there's a stage and materials for painting, drawing, and sculpting. Special family programs year-round bring storytellers, puppeteers, chefs, and musicians to explain their crafts or just entertain. The museum, 2626 W. Broad St., 804/474-2667, is open year-round Mon.–Sat. 9 A.M.–5 P.M., Sun. noon–5 P.M., for $5 pp.

Virginia Aviation Museum

Fans of the early days of air travel will love this hangar full of restored vintage planes at the Richmond International Airport. The impressive collection, 804/236-3622, includes the 1927 Fairchild FC-2W2 used by Admiral William Byrd (a Virginian) to make the first flight over Antarctica, a Cold War–era SR-71 spyplane, and a luxury monoplane that carried Clark Gable, Carole Lombard, and William Randolph Hearst. Open daily 9:30 A.M.–5 P.M.; $5 adults, $3 children 4–12.

Lewis Ginter Botanical Garden

Patrick Henry once owned these grounds north of Richmond where Lewis Ginter, founder of the American Tobacco Company, opened the Lakeside Wheel Club in the 1880s for Richmond's cycling gentry. Ginter's niece began converting the property into gardens, which she named Bloemendaal after Ginter's home in the Netherlands and left to the city at her death. The largest perennial gardens on the East Coast include plants native to Africa, Asia, and the Americas, including the Standard Reference Collection of the American Ivy Society. Streams gurgle past wildflower meadows, a formal Victorian garden, and a typical English "cottage" garden.

The gardens, 1800 Lakeside Ave., 804/262-9887, are at the intersection of Hillard Rd. (Rt. 356) and Lakeside Ave. (Rt. 161), 1.5 miles north of I-95 exit 80. They're open daily 9 A.M.–5 P.M. $5 adults, $3 children 2–12. The Bloemendaal House has a horticultural gift shop, and the Lora and Claiborne Robins Tea House serves light meals.

ACCOMMODATIONS

A construction boom in the 1980s resulted in a new hotel opening up just about every other month in Richmond, leaving the city with 11,000 rooms in 150 hotels and motels. The most distinctive—and expensive—lodgings congregate downtown, led by the truly unique Jefferson Hotel. More generic options scatter into the Greater Richmond area, with a concentration near the Richmond International Airport.

Downtown

Lowest rates near the James go to the passable **Massad House Hotel,** 11 N. 4th St., 804/648-2893, fax 804/780-0647 ($60). The 363 rooms at the **Omni Richmond Hotel,** 100 S. 12th St., 804/344-7000, fax 804/648-6704, start in the $100 range and rise to around $200. The 16-story hotel overlooks the canal and river and has a restaurant and deli. A row of 1840 Greek Revival townhouses has been converted into the lovely **Linden Row Inn,** 100 E. Franklin St., 804/783-7000 or 800/348-7424, fax 804/648-7504. Period Victorian furnishings decorate 71 rooms and parlor suites, and guests have access to the first-class sport facilities of a YMCA a few blocks away. Rates are $100–190.

Because it's in The Fan historic district, the **Emmanuel Hunzler House,** 2036 Monument Ave., 804/355-4885, can't hang a sign out front, but the fully restored 1914 Italian Renaissance townhouse is well worth searching out. Dark mahogany paneling starts in the entry and leads into the living room, with a large marble fireplace. An elevator and shallow stairs—legacies of a former disabled owner—lead upstairs to four guest rooms, one of which has a jacuzzi and its own fireplace. Rates include a full breakfast and a big gray cat (to pet, not to keep). Rates are $110–160.

Bensonhouse of Richmond, email: be.our.guest @bensonhouse.com, www.bensonhouse.com, operating out of the Emmanuel Hunzler House, can arrange stays in the Greek-Revival **William Miller House,** 1129 Floyd Ave. ($115–135), as well as in Williamsburg and Fredericksburg.

The **William Catlin House Bed & Breakfast**

Inn, 2304 E. Broad St., 804/780-3746, was built for its namesake in 1945 by one of the country's finest masons. Robert and Josephine Marin have since outfitted it with oriental rugs, crystal chandeliers, and canopied four-poster beds with goose-down pillows. A full breakfast is included with rooms and suites ($100).

The best high-rise hotels in central Richmond are the **Crowne Plaza Richmond,** 555 E. Canal St., 804/788-0900, fax 804/788-7087, overlooking the River and within easy walking distance of the Shockoe neighborhoods, and the **Richmond Marriott,** 500 E. Broad St. at 5th, 804/643-3400, fax 804/788-1230. On the other end of the scale, in size if not in luxury, is the **Berkeley Hotel,** 1200 E. Cary St., 804/780-1300, fax 804/648-4728, www.berkeleyhotel.com. This small, European-style place in the heart of Shockoe Slip earned four AAA stars for its excellent service and terraces over the street. Its Berkeley Restaurant, open daily, is whispered to be as good as, and perhaps a better value than, The Jefferson's hallowed Lemaire. These three hotels are in the $150–200 price range.

Jefferson Hotel

Maj. Lewis Ginter, of botanical-garden fame, spared no expense when he created the country's finest hotel in Richmond's most fashionable neighborhood near the turn of the 20th century. Millions from Ginter's cigarette fortune went into its design and construction, and in 1895 the Jefferson opened in time for the wedding of the year—the union of Charles Dana Gibson and Irene Langhorne, the original "Gibson Girl." An eye-popping smorgasbord of styles from rococo to Edwardian has wowed a who's-who of famous guests over the years, including Charlie Chaplin, Sarah Bernhardt, and nine presidents. After a steady decline through the 20th century, this National Historic Landmark received a multimillion-dollar facelift in the late 1980s and early 1990s that brought back much of its original splendor.

A tourist destination almost as much as it is a hotel, the Jefferson starts with the opulent Rotunda Lobby, with a 70-foot ceiling and huge faux-marble pillars dripping with carved nuts and fruits. A central staircase (often credited, though wrongly, with inspiring the set designers of *Gone With the Wind*) flows upward to the Palm Court, where sunlight pours through a Tiffany stained-glass dome onto a life-sized statue of Thomas Jefferson by Edward Valentine. The court once featured a grass lawn around a pool filled with live alligators; today classical music wafts over guests enjoying a traditional afternoon tea.

Along with a salon, gift shop, and health club, the Jefferson, at Franklin and Adams Sts., 800/424-8014 or 804/788-8000, fax 804/225-0334, www.Jefferson-hotel.com, offers the formal **Lemaire Restaurant,** 800/649-4644, whose seven dining rooms have earned it not only awards for best brunch and best overall restaurant in Richmond, but also five AAA stars. Open for all meals Monday through Friday, Saturday for breakfast and dinner, and Sunday brunch. **T.J.'s Grill and Bar** serves more casual and less expensive fare like black-eyed pea hummus and grilled focaccia pizzas. Rates for the 274 units start at $250.

Outside of Downtown

Several hotel choices in the $50–100 range can be found a short drive outside downtown Richmond. Near the intersection of Broad Street and I-64 are a **Fairfield Inn by Marriott,** 7300 W. Broad St., 804/672-8621, and a **Comfort Inn Executive Center,** 7201 W. Broad St., 804/672-1108, decorated with a Colonial touch. Near the airport are the **Airport Inn Motel,** 515 S. Laburnum Ave., 804/222-4200, fax 804/222-2828, and the **Wingate Inn Richmond Airport,** 491 International Centre Dr., 804/222-1499, fax 804/222-1498.

Camping

The closest campgrounds to Richmond are still some distance out of the city center. In Ashland, off I-95 exit 89 nine miles north of downtown, the **Americamps Richmond-North/Best Holiday Trav-L-Park,** 11322 Air Park Rd., 800/628-2802 or 804/798-5298, email: Americamps@aol.com, www.Americamps.com, has hookup sites for $20–25. **Pocahontas State Park,** 804/796-4255, www.dcr.state.va.us/parks/pocahont.htm, about eight miles south of Richmond, has sites with water and electric hookups for $18 (along with a 17,000-square-foot pool, one of the largest on the East coast), and the Paramount's Kings Dominion theme park welcomes campers for $20–28.

FOOD

For a conservative city, Richmond has an astonishing variety of restaurants. From cheap retro diners to upmarket haute cuisine, almost every style and ethnicity you can imagine is represented among hundreds of eateries. You might even detect a postmodern jab at the city's slowly eroding traditionalism in places that mix the traditional with the irreverent.

Central Richmond

East meets South at **P.G.T. Beauregard's Thai Room,** 103 E. Cary St. at 1st St., 804/644-2328. Richmond's first and still by far best Thai restaurant is set in a 19th-century townhouse. Waitresses in traditional costume take your orders for satay (skewered) beef, spring rolls, and specials like salmon steamed in a bamboo basket. Cool down after a spicy plate of green curry beef with a dish of homemade ice cream. The open brick café in back is perfect for warm summer evenings. Open for lunch and dinner Mon.–Sat.

The '50s-style **Third Street Diner,** 218 E. Main St., 804/788-4750, is a good place for a late-night bite, open 24 hours, seven days a week. Dozens of small eateries in the north section of the **Sixth Street Marketplace** on Broad Street cater to tourists and downtown lunch-breakers.

The Fan

A cheery air pervades **Stella's,** 2132 W. Main St., 804/257-9885, offering an arty take on traditional Greek fare such as spanakopita and moussaka. There's lots of fish on the menu, where entrees like the polenta crusted sea bass are $8–12 for lunch and around $20 for dinner (open Mon.–Sat.) Lunch sandwiches including a tasty portabella are $6–8, and there are Greek beers and a long wine list to choose from as well.

Occupying a deep red building at 2232 W.

Main St. is **Sticky Rice,** 804/358 7870, a stylish Japanese restaurant with a sushi bar. Appetizers like edamame (crunchy fried beans) are $2–7 and sushi rolls are $3–6. Entrees, served for lunch Mon.–Fri. and daily for dinner, run $10–14, or slightly less for vegetarian specials, rice plates, and the Tokyo burger.

Opposite sits **Southern Culture,** 2229 W. Main St., 804/355-6939, with an interesting, well-seasoned amalgam of Louisiana, Caribbean, southwestern, and Mexican flavors. If the entrées like pasta jambalaya and seafood okra gumbo ($7–17) look too big, then one of the huge salads—or even desserts—might well be enough. They have music and dinner specials at night (served daily), or stop by on Sunday for the gospel brunch.

The only all-vegetarian menu in the city is found at the **Harrison Street Coffee Shop,** 402 N. Harrison St., 804/359-8060, along with a $2.50 bottomless cup of coffee and space for local artists, musicians, and poets to display their talents. Open for breakfast and lunch Mon.–Fri., and lunch on Saturday and Sunday. At **World Cup,** 204 N. Robinson St., 804/359-5282, you can enjoy coffees and teas from around the world on map-topped tables. They also offer sodas and light fare like bagels and sandwiches, along with live music on Monday evenings in the summer. Open daily for all meals. The **Strawberry Street Cafe,** 421 N. Strawberry St., 804/353-6860, is always packed for lunch with fans of its healthy, filling food and bathtub salad bar. Homemade soups, amazing gourmet sandwiches (try the open-faced crab), and entrées like spinach lasagna and Mediterranean wraps are served daily for lunch and dinner.

Mamma'Zu, 501 S. Pine St., 804/788-4205, inhabits an unpretentious old diner, but it's a hidden gem with some of the best Italian food in Richmond. Made-to-order pizzas and calamari Napoletana run $8–10 for lunch (served Mon.–Fri.), and dinner entrées from the chalkboard list are $10–15 (Mon.–Sat.). Get there early or expect to wait a long time because word of this hot spot is spreading quickly.

North of the Fan

Named for a 19th-century Virginia governor who always gave just a little bit more, **Extra**

Billy's, 5205 W. Broad St., 804/282-3949, offers button-popping servings of baby-back ribs, pork barbecue, and beef brisket. Grab an onion-string appetizer and bucket of beer, and dig in. Open Mon.–Sat. for lunch, dinner daily.

Carytown

Look for the big sun over the outdoor patio to find **Nacho Mama's,** 3449 W. Cary St., 804/358-6262, serving Richmond's best burrito along with combo dinners and a mouthwatering Mexican crab cake platter. Lunch specials are around $6, along with a few vegetarian options and the requisite range of margaritas. **Ristorante Amici,** 3343 W. Cary St., 804/353-4700, serves fresh Northern Italian cuisine and great *tiramisu.* Entrées are around $10 for lunch (Mon.–Sat.) and closer to $20 for dinner (daily), with pastas in the $12 range.

For a quick Carytown bite, stop by the vegetarian deli inside **Ellwood Thompson's Natural Market,** 4 N. Thompson St., 804/359-7525, or **Mary Angela's Pizza, Pasta & Subs,** 3345 W. Cary St., 804/353-2333, where they whip up New York–style pizza and subs for $4–5 (open for lunch Mon.–Sat., dinner daily). **Farouk's House of India,** 3033 W. Cary St., 804/355-0378, has an inexpensive lunch buffet and a wide vegetarian selection. Subcontinental specialties like tandoori chicken and naan bread are available for lunch Tues.–Sun. and dinner Mon.–Sun.

Carytown Burger and Fries, 3500-1/2 N. Cary St., 804/358-5223, is said to serve Richmond's best burger in Ukrop's Shopping Center, open Mon.–Sat. 11 A.M.–9 P.M. The **Cary Street Cafe,** 2631, W. Cary St., 804/353-7445, sits a few steps outside the bustle of Carytown. Another range of veggie options include the ELT (eggplant instead of bacon), spinach lasagna, and sautéed summer squash cakes. A weekday happy hour takes advantage of the room-length bar inside. Open Mon.–Fri. 3 P.M.–2 A.M., Sat. and Sun. 11 A.M.–2 P.M.

Shockoe Slip

If there's one restaurant you shouldn't miss in Richmond, even if only to peek inside, it's **The Tobacco Company,** 1201 E. Cary St., 804/782-9555. Dim light, wicker chairs, iron scrollwork, and plenty of plants evoke Richmond's early-1900s heyday when this restaurant began as a tobacco warehouse. An antique elevator rises slowly through the three-story glass-roofed atrium toward a brass chandelier from the lobby of a Federal Reserve Bank in Chicago. A wooden cigar-shop Indian and roaming cigarette girl complete the picture.

The Victorian lounge on the first floor is great for a mint julep in the afternoon and is only one of The Tobacco Company's options for live music in the evenings. Amid all this spectacle is some of the city's better food. A "Contemporary American" menu is heavy on the seafood, beef, and veal, with an excellent four-seafood pasta ($16–22). The second-floor dessert buffet has to be one of the best refined-sugar-for-your-dollar deals in the state. Open daily for lunch and dinner.

The **Richbrau Brewing Company,** 1214 E. Cary St., 804/644-3018, owns the distinction of being the first brewpub to open in Richmond. It's classier than you might think, with everything from beer-battered fish and chips to maple pecan chicken ($10–18) to go along with the homemade beers. Try a Big Nasty Porter (it's not so bad) or the Old Nick Pale Ale. They also make root beer and cream soda. Open daily for dinner 4–11 P.M.; the bar and pool room upstairs are open later.

Two of the best Asian restaurants in the city face each other across Cary Street in the center of Shockoe Slip. Stone lions flank the entrance of **Peking Pavilion,** 1302 E. Cary St., 804/649-8888, an elegant Chinese dining room that's packed at lunch (specials are $7–8) and often dinner as well. Dinner specials like Szechwan Three Delicacies and Peking Imperial ($11–23) are worth the splurge. Open Mon.–Fri. for lunch and dinner. **Hana Zushi,** 1309 E. Cary St., 804/225-8801, is Richmond's only true sushi bar, serving the Japanese delicacy à la carte at the bar ($3–4 each) or on combination plates for $10–12. Eight different styles of *bento* lunch boxes are around $7. They also have a full selection of teriyaki, tempura, and sake and Sapporo beer to top it off. Open Mon.–Fri. for lunch and Mon.–Sat. for dinner.

CENTRAL VIRGINIA WINERIES

Afton Mountain Vineyards
540/456-8667
Near Afton; 234 Vineyard Lane

Autumn Hill Vineyards/Blue Ridge Winery
434/985-6100, email: autumnhill@mind-spring.com
Near Stanardsville; 301 River Dr.

Barboursville Vineyards and Historic Ruins
540/832-3824; email: bvvy@comet.net,
www.barboursvillewine.com
Near Barboursville; south on Rt. 687 and Rt. 777

Burnley Vineyards & Daniel Cellars
540/832-2828, email: burnleywines@rlc.net,
www.burnleywines.com
Near Barboursville; west on Rt. 641 off Rt. 20

Cooper Vinyards
540/894-5253
Near Louisa; I-64 exit 148 (Shannon Hill Rd.),
eight miles north

Dominion Wine Cellars
540/825-8772
Near Culpeper; Rt. 3 exit off US 29

Grayhaven Winery
434/556-3917, www.grayhavenwinery.com
Near Orchid; I-64 east exit 159 to Rt. 522 north

Hill Top Berry Farm & Winery
434/361-1266, email: hilltop1@intelos.net
Near Nellysford; I-64 exit 107 to Rt. 151 south,
10 miles to Rt. 612

Horton Cellars Winery/Montdomaine Cellars
540/832-7440, email: vawinee@aol.com,
www.hvwine.com
Near Gordonsville; Rt. 33 west for four miles

Jefferson Vineyards
434/977-3042, email:
info@jeffersonvineyards.com, www.jefferson-vineyards.com
Near Charlottesville; three miles past Monticello

on right, 1399 Thomas Jefferson Parkway (Rt. 53)
Site of Thomas Jefferson's first *vinifera* vines.

The Kluge Estate Winery and Vineyard
434/977-3894 ext. 55
Near Charlottesville; Rt. 20 south to Rt. 627 to
right on Blenheim Rd.

Lake Anna Winery
540/895-5085, www.lawinery.com
Near Glenora; I-95 Thornburg exit to
Rt. 208 west

Misty Mountain Vineyards & Winery
540/923-4738
Near Madison; Rt. 231 north from US 29 to Rt.
651 west

Mountain Cove Vineyards and Winegarden
434/263-5392
Near Lovingston; Rt. 718 to Rt. 651

Oakencroft Vineyard & Winery
434/296-4188, email: fwr@oakencroft.com,
www.oakencroft.com
Near Charlottesville; 3.5 miles west of US 29 on
Barracks Road

Prince Michel & Rapidan River Vineyards
540/547-3707 or 800/869-8242,
www.princemichel.com
Near Leon; US 29 south of Culpeper
Wine museum, AAA four-diamond restaurant,
800/800-9463

Rebec Vineyards
434/946-5168
Near Amherst; Rt. 29 five miles north of town
Garlic festival in October.

Rockbridge Vineyard
540/377-6204 or 888/511-9463, email:
rocwine@cfw.com, www.rockbridge.com
Near Staunton; I-81 exit 205 to Rt. 606 west

Rose Bower Vineyard & Winery
434/223-8209
Near Farmville; south on US 15 to Rt. 665 to Rt. 604 to Rt. 686

Rose River Vineyards & Trout Farm
540/923-4050
Near Syria; west on Rt. 670, left on Rt. 648

Sharp Rock Vineyards
540/987-9700, email: darmor@sharprock.com, www.sharprock.com
Near Sperryville; Rt 522 to Rt. 231 to Rt. 601 to Rt. 707 intersection
Cottage and carriage house bed-and-breakfast

Smokehouse Winery
540/987-3194, email: smokehouse@tidalwave.net, www.smokehouse-winerybnb.com
Near Sperryville; Rt. 29 to Rt. 522 to Rt. 231 to Rt. 608
19th-century log cabin bed-and-breakfast

Stone Mountain Vineyards
434/990-9463
Near Stanardsville; Rt. 810 to Rt. 627 in Dyke, VA to Rt. 632

Stonewall Vineyards & Winery
434/993-2185, email: stonewall@juno.com
Near Concord; north five miles on Rt. 608, left on Rt. 721

Tomahawk Mill Winery
434/432-1063, email: tomahawk@gamewood.net
Near Chatham; Rt. 57 west 4.5 miles, right on Rt. 799, 3.4 miles, left on Rt. 649, three miles

White Hall Wineyards
434/823-8615, www.whitehallvineyards.com
Near White Hall; Rt. 810 north, left on Rt. 674 (Breakheart) to Sugar Ridge Rd.

Wintergreen Winery
434/361-2519, www.wintergreenwinery.com
Near Nellysford; Rt. 151 south to Rt. 684 west

CENTRAL VIRGINIA

A short walk farther down Cary Street brings you to **Europa**, 1409 E. Cary St., 804/643-0911, a classy Mediterranean café and tapas bar with food that lives up to its atmosphere. Sangria, paella, and excellent tapas attract a younger hip crowd, especially on weekends when the cave-like Bodega lounge is open downstairs, velvet sofas and all. They offer tapas and paella deals Monday nights and serve lunch ($5–10) Mon.–Fri. and dinner ($10–25) Mon.–Sat.

Shockoe Bottom

For a healthy dose of soul food (meaning cooked by any means necessary, but with plenty of love), stop by **Johnson's Grill**, 1802 E. Franklin St., 804/648-9788. If the meatloaf, pork chops, and spare ribs ($4–6.50) don't bring tears to your eyes, the homemade peach and apple cobbler will. Open Mon.–Fri. for breakfast and lunch from 6 A.M.

Lazy ceiling fans, palm trees, and a haze of

cigar smoke evoke the heyday of pre-Revolutionary Cuba in **Havana '59,** 16 N. 17th St., 804/649-2822. Step up to the wide bar under strings of tiny lights and order a *mojito,* the Cuban mint julep, or take a table and enjoy a bowl of Cuban black bean soup or a plate of *ropa vieja,* a quintessential mix of barbecued shredded beef with peppers, tomatoes, onions, and garlic. Open daily for dinner and Sunday for brunch.

Despite an unfortunate location right under the I-95 overpass, **Bottoms Up Pizza,** 1700 Dock St., 804/644-4400, thrives thanks to outstanding pizza with thick sourdough crusts served inside or on two open decks. Try one of their specialty pies like the Remocaldo Renegade, with crabmeat, spinach, and artichoke hearts, to learn why this place keeps getting voted the best pizzeria in the city. Upstairs, with its pink-lit bar, is a popular place to meet for a late-night bite before hitting the Shockoe scene. Open for lunch and dinner daily.

All the things that make a classic diner—table jukeboxes, breakfast all day, and the "Rochester Garbage Plate"—come together in the **River City Diner,** 1712 E. Main St., 804/644-9418. This endearing '50s throwback is open for all meals except dinner Sunday, and 24 hours on Friday and Saturday. **Millie's Diner,** 2603 E. Main St. at 26th St., 804/643-5512, puts a gourmet spin on countertop meals with entrées like Thai spicy shrimp and grilled quail on polenta. Once a lunch spot for tobacco-plant workers, Millie's is still definitely a diner—there's a jukebox on the counter and the grill sizzles right next to the door—but the food guarantees you'll have to wait for a table if you don't show up early. Open daily for lunch and dinner (from 9 A.M. on Sunday for the "Devils' Mess" brunch).

NIGHTLIFE

With so many college-age residents, Richmond certainly has no deficit of bars, pubs, and music halls, but the city's traditional attitude ensures plenty of more refined alternatives (some of which may require dressing up). Most of the action centers on Shockoe neighborhood restaurants, thanks to Virginia licensing laws, which require establishments that serve alcohol to serve food as well.

Look for up-to-the-minute information on evening entertainment in the *Richmond Times-Dispatch,* various entertainment papers like *Punchline,* or the handbills plastering any utility pole.

Shockoe Bottom and Shockoe Slip

Richmond's main nightlife districts throb with music on weekend evenings. If your tastes don't run to beer-fueled frat-rock, there are still plenty of higher-brow choices. Across the street from Bottom's Up Pizza is the **Canal Club,** 1544 E. Cary St., 804/643-2582, whose entrance is on S. 17th Street and Dock Street facing the canal. A relatively new entry into the Shockoe Bottom music scene, it's already becoming known as a dependable spot for good live tunes.

Once one of Richmond's premiere live-music venues, The Flood Zone has become the **Have a Nice Day Cafe,** 11 S. 18th St., 804/771-1700.

Anyone who can pass the "neat and clean" dress code can enjoy a huge bar and tunes from the '70s and '80s. **Poe's Pantry and Pub,** 2706 E. Main St., 804/648-2120, tends toward bluegrass, acoustic, and jazz. Poe's also has open-mike nights and blues jams.

The **Tobacco Company** lounge brings quality blues, rock, acoustic, and jazz acts Tues.–Sat. evenings. The **Tobacco Club** downstairs draws the professional crowd for pop and top-40 music, with a moderate dress code befitting the classy setting. Just as stylish is the rooftop of **Havana '59,** where patrons sip rum-and-Cokes while a DJ spins below. A Victorian billiards lounge/sport bar above the **Richbrau Brewing Co.** dining room is popular with twenty- and thirty-somethings, offering foosball, darts, and live music.

Carytown and The Fan

Coffeeshops and alternative tunes, mostly along Main Street from VCU to Boulevard, cater to a hip college crowd. **Trademarks,** 1707 E. Franklin, 804/649-1079, and **Twisters,** 929 W. Grace St., 804/353-4263, both feature up-and-coming local bands. The latter also has DJs and disco nights. **The Sidewalk Cafe,** 2101 W. Main St., 804/358-0645, may look like a sports bar from the outside—notice the TV eight feet above the street—but inside it's a well-worn, friendly place that's been around since 1991. It's a restaurant, too, with a simple menu, but stick around for the disco ball to be called into play and find out why it's near the top of many locals' lists.

On weekends, jazz floats from the intimate confines of **Bogart's Backroom,** 203 N. Lombardy St., 804/353-9280, one of the oldest clubs in the area, in the back of Bogart's restaurant. The **Cary Street Cafe** welcomes an eclectic mix of acoustic and bluegrass, and you can enjoy more local talent in between loads at **The Lost Sock,** 1319 W. Main St., 804/358-0646, a laundromat with food, darts, and open-mike nights on Thursdays.

Elsewhere

The **Hole in the Wall,** 309 N. Laurel St., 804/225-7103, is a centrally located spot for an evening's entertainment, and the nearby **Fire-**

ballz, 623 E. Main St., 804/783-0202, offers live bands and the "Big Ass Pizza" (two feet across). Tuesday night is movie night at the **Legend Brewing Co.,** 321 W. 7th St., 804/232-3446, with campy 16-mm classics shown for free. They're on the south side of the river near the end of Manchester Bridge.

Alley Katz, 10 Walnut Alley Ave., 804/643-2816, is a distinctive venue for local and national bands that tend toward the mainstream more than the dissonant. It's off Laburnum Avenue near the state fairgrounds. Finally, **Potter's Pub,** 7007 Three Chopt Rd., 804/282-9999, is the place for folk music. This one is in the Village Shopping Center—take Kensington Avenue west until it turns into Patterson, and keep going until it intersects with Three Chopt Road at the city limits.

THE ARTS

Music

The **Virginia Opera,** 804/643-6004, has gained national attention since its inception as the Official State Opera in 1975. Eleven productions per season are held at the Carpenter Center. Even older, the **Richmond Symphony,** 804/788-1212, began in 1957 and went on to receive the American Society of Composers, Author and Publishers' Award for the fifth time in 1996. Two hundred annual performances range from classical masterworks to all-star pops with guest artists like Itzhak Perlman and Bruce Hornsby. Most of the shows happen at the Carpenter Center and the Landmark Theater.

Dance

A beloved holiday performance of *The Nutcracker* is only one great production of the **Richmond Ballet,** 804/344-0906, the state's only professional troupe and one of the finest on the East Coast. The **Concert Ballet of Richmond,** 804/798-0945, performs more modern works at the Women's Club Auditorium at 211 E. Franklin Street and various outdoor festivals.

Theaters and Performance Spaces

Everyone who visits Richmond should see a movie at the **Byrd Theater,** 2908 W. Cary St.,

804/353-9911, in a setting as palatial as anything on Broadway. Tickets are only $2, and if you're lucky you'll come on a night when the organ player rises out of the stage before the show. Another Roaring '20s movie house has been transformed into the **Carpenter Center for the Performing Arts,** 600 E. Grace St. at 6th St. Marketplace, 804/225-9000. A ceiling painted to look like the open sky caps a lavish array of Moorish adornments, plush rugs, and a sweeping grand staircase. With 2,000 seats, the Carpenter Center is large enough to host the Richmond Ballet and opera performances as well as concerts and traveling Broadway productions.

Richmond's Landmark Theater, 6 N. Laurel at Main, 804/780-4213, began in 1927 as a Shriner meeting hall with 4,600 seats, six lobbies, 42 hotel rooms, and a bowling alley. With an Arabic tile design in the lobby, it was known as The Mosque until 1995, when a $6-million renovation brought back 3,500 seats. It has hosted the same range of performances as the Carpenter Center, including Garrison Keillor's "American Radio Hour." The **Empire Theater,** 114 W. Broad St., 804/344-8040, is Richmond's oldest (1910) and home to Theater IV, offering family, off-Broadway, and adventurous performances for older audiences.

Outdoor concerts, children's performances, and the Festival of the Arts in July and August come to **Dogwood Dell** in Byrd Park. The **State Fairgrounds at Strawberry Hill** accommodates Virginia's largest monthly flea market, 804/431-9500, along with many annual festivals. Major rock acts such as Sting and Tina Turner swing by the **Classic Amphitheater,** 804/228-3213.

Groups and Organizations

TheatreVirginia, 804/353-6161, based in the Virginia Museum of Fine Arts, puts on a nationally acclaimed variety of drama, comedies, and musicals during its Sept.–April season. The **Arts Council of Richmond,** 1401 W. Main St., 804/355-7200, is a nonprofit organization aimed at the promotion of arts in the metro area, while **Downtown Presents,** 804/643-2826, sponsors events and festivals in central Richmond.

SHOPPING

Funky gift, thrift, and clothing shops share space in Carytown with pricey boutiques and stores selling housewares and furniture. Drop in on places like **World of Mirth,** 3005 W. Cary St., 804/353-8991, for a taste of the kitschy and the unusual. **La Lune Design,** 3407 W. Cary St., 804/358-6505, sells clothing, jewelry, and art, as does **Bygones Vintage Clothing,** 2916 W. Cary St., 804/353-1919, next to the Byrd Theater.

Carytown is also the first stop for antiques, where places such as **Martha's Mixture Antique Sales & Restoration,** 3445 W. Cary St., 804/358-5827, have good selections. Elsewhere, try the **Antique Boutique and Delectable Collectibles,** 1310 E. Cary St., 804/775-2525, in Shockoe, and **Adams' Antiques,** 1423 W. Main St., 804/355-0254, in The Fan.

Millie Jones sewed her first flag ("It's a Boy") 25 years ago, and since then her colorful banners have become a Richmond tradition that's spreading to the rest of the state. Other flag shops have followed, but Millie's **Festival Flags,** 322 West Broad St., 804/643-5247, is the real thing. The **Richmond Arsenal,** 7605 Midlothian Tpk., 804/272-4570, doesn't sell firearms, but it is full to the rafters with Civil War relics. For new, used, and rare books on all things American, Southern, and Virginian, stop by **Owens & Ramsey Booksellers,** 2728 Tinsley Dr., 804/272-8888. They also have a selection of maps and fine art prints.

North of The Fan, **Ghana House by Rawquartz,** 517 N. Harrison St., 804/355-2962, stocks a kaleidoscopic array of wooden masks, sculptures, crafts, and clothing from West Africa. **Tinkers,** 2409 Westwood Ave., 804/359-3301, is Richmond's choice for folk art. The section of the marketplace south of Broad Street has a host of smaller gift shops. **My Romance,** 1206 E. Cary St., 804/643-4438, is typical of Shockoe's upscale offerings. Chandeliers and classical music provide a luxurious setting for their lingerie, soaps, candles, and fragrances.

RECREATION

Tours

The paddle wheeler **Annabel Lee,** 804/644-5700, leaves from 3011 Dock St. in Shockoe Bottom for leisurely dining cruises on the James River from March to December. On Tuesdays a three-hour Plantation tour leaves at 8 A.M. for the Westover, Evelynton, and Berkeley plantations downriver. Two-hour lunch tours leave at 11 A.M. Wed.–Sat. Prices are $23–59 pp. **Kanawah Cruises,** 1701 Dock St., 804/649-2800, run half-hour narrated tours of the James River and Kanawah Canal. The tours leave from the Turning Basin at Canal and Virginia streets for $3 adults, $3 children 5–12. Also available are six-person electric boats for $35 per hour.

Daily guided bus tours of Richmond are the specialty of **Richmond Tours,** 915 N. Allen Ave., 804/213-0151 or 877/913-0151, www.richmondtours.com. Their city tours range from $18–20 adults ($16–18 children under 12), and they offer more expensive weekend excursions to Civil War sites and the James River plantations as well.

Spectator Sports

The **Richmond Braves,** 804/359-4444, continue a strong local baseball tradition that has left Richmond without a baseball team only one year since 1884. The Atlanta Braves' top AAA farm team plays Apr.–Sept. at the 12,000-seat Diamond ballpark, 3001 N. Boulevard, one of the finest minor-league stadiums in the country. The **Richmond Kickers,** 804/643-7825, compete in the United States Interregional Soccer League (USISL) and won the U.S. Open Cup in 1995. Their Apr.–Sept. season takes place at the University of Richmond Stadium at Douglas Avenue and McCloy Street.

Puck-heads will want to catch the **Richmond Renegades,** 804/643-7825, who won the East Coast Hockey League's Riley Cup championship in 1994–1995, only four years after forming. The Renegades play at the **Richmond Coliseum,** 601 E. Leigh St., 804/780-4956, which at 14,000 seats is the largest indoor entertainment facility in Virginia. The Coliseum hosts a wide range of professional and college sports and other events, from pro wrestling and monster-truck extravaganzas to ice shows and the circus.

All of the universities and colleges in town have their own sports teams, from the U of R's Spiders on down, that compete on campus and in city venues such as the Coliseum. Call the athletic departments of the University of Richmond, 804/289-8388, and Virginia Commonwealth University, 804/828-7267, for schedules and locations.

Horse-racing fans breathed a sigh of relief in 1997 with the opening of **Colonial Downs,** 804/966-7223 or 888/482-8722, the first parimutuel betting racecourse in the state since the 1800s. With a five-level grandstand, restaurants, lounges, and monitors, the track is one of the largest and most luxurious of its kind in the country. The fall thoroughbred season culminates with the Breeder's Cup. Colonial Downs is near exit 214 off I-64 heading east to Williamsburg and Newport News, and there's a 200-screen Off-Track Wagering Facility at 4700 Broad St., 804/342-2211.

On weekends in May and September, crowds of close to 100,000 descend on the **Richmond International Raceway,** 804/345-7223, in the state fairgrounds at Strawberry Hill, to watch one of America's fastest-growing spectator sports, that thunderous mix of gas fumes and adrenaline known as NASCAR. The track, Virginia's largest sports facility, hosts various Winston Cup events, from the Pontiac Excitement 400 in March to the Miller Genuine Draft 400 in September, among others. Tickets can get scarce, so call ahead.

Rafting and Kayaking
As one of the few cities in the world with serious white water churning through its center, Richmond knows its rapids. The James River can hit Class IV and V near Hollywood Cemetery and Belle Isle, making Richmond enough of a whitewater destination that many people live here just to paddle—some local executives even commute by kayak. Milder sections of the James welcome paddlers and tubers during the Mar.–Nov. season. A licensed outfitter is definitely the way to go if you're up for tackling the urban froth: the **Rich-**

mond Raft Company, 4400 E. Main St. at Water St., 804/222-7238 or 800/540-7238, email: raft@richmondraft.com, www.richmondraft.com, is your best bet. They lead trips for $46–62 pp, both Class III and IV quickies to serious spills over the fall line. The guides are first rate and the paddling as tough as you want it.

Adventure Challenge, 8225 Oxer Rd., 804/276-7600, email: info@adventurechallenge.com, www.adventurechallenge.com, organizes white-water kayaking, sea kayaking, river tubing, and skiing shuttles in the winter.

Other Outdoor Recreation
Call the **Richmond Area Bicycling Association,** 804/266-2453, for information on group rides for families, mountain bikes, and racers, along with local cycling maps and tips. The **Richmond Department of Recreation and Parks,** 804/646-5733, in City Hall at 900 E. Broad St., is the best source of information on Richmond's 60 parks. They organize various outdoor adventure classes, trips, and seminars throughout the year.

Disc Golf is a popular pursuit in the Richmond area (and nationwide, see www.pdga.org) that is growing quickly because it requires little athletic ability, is free except for the cost of discs, and allows you to spend time outdoors with friends or alone. A nice, wooded, free 18-hole course can be found at the bottom of Church Hill, which has been restored so that the neighborhood is now safer than it was in the past. Tournaments are held on Wednesday nights, and Professional Disc Golf Association (PDGA)–approved discs can be purchased at the recreation store Beck & Little in Carytown.

EVENTS
Many of Richmond's annual events happen at the Strawberry Hill Fairgrounds, 804/228-3200, north of downtown at the intersection of Laburnum Avenue (Rt. 197) and Meadowbrook Rd. (Rt. 627). To get there from downtown, take 5th Street north from Leigh Street 1.5 miles to Brookland Park Boulevard, take a left, bear right onto Meadowbrook Road after two blocks, and keep going another mile.

CENTRAL VIRGINIA

April's **Easter on Parade,** 804/643-2826, fills Monument Avenue with an old-fashioned parade, carnival rides, and jazz, blues, and Dixieland music. That same month brings Richmond's rite of spring: the **Strawberry Hill Races,** a steeplechase event and so much more. Citywide carriage parades and balls get everyone in the mood for the extravagant tailgate parties on the day of the races, some of which are so elaborate there's a competition for the best theme and costumes. All proceeds go to charity.

May's perfect softball weather ushers in the **Round Robin Softball Tournament,** said to be the largest in the world. More than 400 teams from 20 states compete on Memorial Day weekend in parks around the city. That same month the **Tour DuPont,** one of America's premier cycling events, rolls through downtown Richmond on a different course every year. Tens of thousands of onlookers line the streets to watch riders sprint to the finish line at 10th and Cary streets.

Up to 50 free concerts comprise **The Big Gig,** 804/643-2826, in July. Jazz, rock, country, and classical performances are held for two weeks in the Nina Abady Festival Park, the Carpenter Center, and elsewhere. More summer concerts are held at the **Riverfront** on Wednesdays, **Nina Abady Festival Park** ("Friday Cheers"), and at the **Canal Turning Basin** near the south end of 14th Street. Call 804/643-2826 for a schedule. Maymont has classical **Musical Mondays** outside on the lawn as well; call 804/261-6200 for information. The second weekend in August the **Carytown Watermelon Festival,** 804/353-1525, fills nine blocks of Carytown with melons and music. The next weekend is the **Down Home Family Reunion,** 804/644-3900, with African dancing and music and "down-home" food in Abner Clay Park.

Everything that makes fairs great—rides, livestock exhibits, fattening food, the circus—happens for 10 days in late September at the **State Fair of Virginia** at the Richmond Raceway Complex.

In early October the **Second Street Festival** celebrates Jackson Ward's African American heritage with theater, soul food, vendors, and ragtime and gospel music. Also in early October, the **Richmond Children's Festival** in Byrd Park is modeled on a different culture every year, with music, entertainers, crafts, and food.

The December holidays bring open houses at historic homes like Maymont and the Lewis Ginter Botanical Gardens, along with **Holiday House Tours** in the Fan. Call 804/254-2550 for information. Area boats are festooned with lights during the **James River Parade of Lights,** 804/706-1340, the first weekend in December. A local favorite is the **Grand Illumination** of the tree and holiday displays at the James Center, 804/344-3232, accompanied by choral concerts and wagon rides. Richmonders are also fond of the **Tackiest Christmas Decorations Tour,** which links places so gaudy they stop traffic. Look in the *Richmond Times-Dispatch* in early December or late November for a map.

TRANSPORTATION

Getting Around

Richmond is served by the **Greater Richmond Transit Company,** 804/358-4782, www.ridegrtc.com. Call them for bus schedules and routes.

Local taxi companies, including **Yellow Cab,** 804/222-7300; **Veterans Cab Association,** 804/276-8990; and **Metro Taxicab Service,** 804/353-5000, can take you to the airport from downtown for $15–20.

Getting There and Away

Plans are afoot to restore Main Street Station in Shockoe Slip to serve as a train depot once again, but until then there's **Amtrak,** 7519 Staples Mill Rd., 804/553-2903, north of I-64 exit 185 in western Richmond. Taxi fare to downtown runs around $15. The **Greyhound-Trailways** terminal, 2910 N. Blvd., 804/254-5910, is near I-95 exit 78.

Once known as Byrd Field, the **Richmond International Airport,** 804/226-3052, www.flyrichmond.com, sits off I-64 exit 197 east of downtown. There's no bus service into the city, but **Groome Transportation,** 800/552-7911 or 804/222-7226, offers 24-hour service ($20 per couple). Most downtown luxury hotels also run shuttles. Car rental agencies include Thrifty, 804/222-3200; Budget, 804/222-5310; National, 804/222-7477; Avis, 804/222-7416; and Hertz, 804/222-7228.

INFORMATION

The **Richmond Metro Convention & Visitors Bureau,** 550 E. Marshall St., 888/742-4666 or 804/782-2777, email: mrcvb@richmondva.org, www.RichmondVA.org, operates three **visitors centers:** the main one at 1710 Robin Hood Rd., at exit 78 off I-95/I-64, 804/358-5511; one at the Richmond International Airport, 804/236-3260; and one in the Bell Tower on the State Capitol grounds, 804/648-3146. The main one is open daily 9 A.M.–5 P.M. (June–Aug. until 7 P.M.), while the others are open 9:30 A.M.–4:30 P.M. Each sells the **Richmond City Pass,** which gives admission to any five of the city's 19 major attractions for $15. The pass is valid for one month and includes free access to the **Richmond Cultural Conection,** an air-conditioned shuttle that runs between most of these sites from June–Nov. ($1 pp otherwise).

For Richmond information online, try the websites of *Richmond* magazine (www1.richmond.com/richmondmagazine), *Style Weekly* (www1.richmond.com/StyleWeekly), and the *Richmond Times-Dispatch* (www.gatewayva.com).

NEAR RICHMOND
Paramount Kings Dominion

Ten roller coasters—the most on the East Coast—are the main draw to the Piedmont's favorite amusement park. Start with a few of the classic wooden rattlers, like the 1975-vintage Rebel Yell and The Grizzly, consistently voted one of the best in America by enthusiast groups,

before risking gastrointestinal distress on something more modern. The Hypersonic XLC, new in 2001, dispenses with all the formalities and simply rockets passengers straight up and straight down, using compressed air. Volcano: The Blast Coaster shoots passengers from the top of a "live" volcano at 70 mph, and The Outer Limits: Flight of Fear uses an electromagnetic launching system to shoot cars horizontally onto a darkened indoor track.

Other rides include the Xtreme Skyflyer in Wayne's World, sort of a swinging bungee jump, and guaranteed soakers such as Whitewater Canyon, the Log Flume, and WaterWorks, a 19-acre water park with slides, rafts, and a 650,000-gallon wave pool. For children, there's KidZville and Nickelodeon Splat City, and a one-third model of the Eiffel Tower with a view of the whole park.

Kings Dominion, 804/876-5000 or 876-5561, www.kingsdominion.com, is on Rt. 30 off I-95 exit 98. Tickets are $32 for adults and children over seven, and $27 for children 3–6. It's open late Mar.–Oct. (weekends only outside of June–Aug).

Metro Richmond Zoo

In Moseley, just south of Richmond, the Metro Richmond Zoo, 8300 Beaver Bridge Rd., 804/739-5666, is a little-known gem that kids and parents alike will enjoy. Even many longtime Richmonders don't know they have a zoo in the area, so you're likely to have some breathing room as you gaze at the penguins, giraffes, kangarros, and a rare white Siberian tiger. Open Mon.–Sat. 9:30 A.M.–5 P.M.; $6.75 adults, $5.75 seniors, $4.75 children 3–11, free children two and under.

Petersburg and Vicinity

Best known as the site of the last major battle of the Civil War, Petersburg (pop. 36,000) sits sleepily alongside the Appomattox river within day-trip distance of Richmond. The friendly residents of historic Olde Towne still recall with a shiver the tornado that passed through in August 1993, causing more damage in a few minutes than the Union army did during a 10-month siege. Luckily, most of the city's major sights escaped unharmed. Petersburg is only a short drive from the many historic plantations along the upper James.

HISTORY

Established in 1784, Petersburg weathered a destructive visit by Benedict Arnold and 2,500 British soldiers on their way to Yorktown during the Revolutionary War. For the next hundred years, the town served as a popular stopover for travelers drawn to its theater, race track, and taverns.

By June 1864, Ulysses S Grant realized the key to taking Richmond was this vital road and rail junction just a day's ride to the south. He managed to sneak 75,000 troops almost within striking distance before Robert E. Lee caught on and scrambled to reinforce Gen. P.G.T. Beauregard's force of 15,000 before the Federals arrived.

Poor coordination kept Union forces from taking advantage of an early victory on June 15 over the northern Confederate bulwarks, and five days later the two armies settled down to 10 months of trench warfare and waiting. Opposing lines were so close that soldiers on both sides could tell time by the tolling of the courthouse clock. Supplies quickly ran low inside the city, but the unflappable Confederates held thrifty Starvation Balls rather than submit.

In time Grant was able to lengthen Union lines until they stretched from here to Richmond. Scattered skirmishes peaked on March 25, 1865, when Lee tried to break out with a failed attack at Fort Stedman to the east. The Confederate commander realized his hopeless position, and on the night of April 2, Lee evacuated Petersburg and Richmond and led his army on its final march west.

SIGHTS

Olde Towne

Petersburg's historic hub centers on the Appomattox River where the **Appomattox Iron Works** hunkers on aptly named Old Street. Call the visitors center for details on the following sights.

The beautiful Exchange Building, built in the 1840s as a commodities market, is the home of Petersburg's **Siege Museum,** 15 W. Bank St. Farmers once gathered to trade and auction produce under the Greek Revival dome in the two-story central hall, but now the focus is on civilian life during the terrible 10 months before the city fell. Hoop skirts, tourniquets, and cannon balls show what civilians faced from day to day as Grant waited on their doorstep. Unusual pieces, like an experimental revolving-barrel cannon and the shell-dented brass steeple of the Tabb Street Presbyterian Church, round out the collection. Open daily 10 A.M.–5 P.M.; $3 adults, $2 children under 12.

The prominent Bolling family built **Centre Hill Mansion,** 1 Centre Hill Circle between Adams and Tabb Sts., in 1823. Originally in the Federal style, Centre Hill was remolded as a Greek Revival building in the 1840s. Victorian antiques, ornate woodwork, and plaster designs adorn the main floors, while downstairs is the mouth of a tunnel that once went all the way to the river. Don't miss the nine-foot 1886 grand piano. Open daily 10 A.M.–5 P.M.; $3 adults, $2 children.

Outside of Olde Towne

Proving it's not just for backyard barbecues and company picnics, the **Softball Hall of Fame,** 3935 S. Crater Rd., 804/732-4099, honors the men and women who have left their mark in the ranks of the professional U.S. Slo-Pitch Softball Association (USSSA). World Champion jerseys, trophies, and videos fill the museum, which is open Mon.–Fri. 8:30 A.M.–4 P.M.; free.

The story of the U.S. Army Quartermaster Corps, the oldest corps in the army, is told in the **Quartermaster Museum,** 804/734-4203, at Fort Lee three miles east of downtown along

Washington Street (Rt. 36). Everything from Ulysses S Grant's saddle to General Patton's Jeep (with custom Mercedes seats) is on display, including the collection of the U.S. Army Women's Museum. Open Tues.–Fri. 10 A.M.–5 P.M., Sat. and Sun. 11 A.M.–5 P.M.; free.

Petersburg National Battlefield Park

Comprising six major units, this park protects Petersburg's substantial Civil War legacy. Nine months—almost a quarter of the entire war—was fought near Petersburg, mostly during what is still the longest siege in American history. Start at the main unit, 2.5 miles east of downtown on Washington Street (Rt. 36), where the **Eastern Front visitors center,** 804/732-3531, www .nps.gov/pete, has an hourly map presentation that relates an overview of the battles. Take the trail past the grassy knolls of Confederate defensive earthworks to the massive Dictator mortar that once hurled 250-pound shells into the heart of Petersburg (at night citizens could watch the lit fuses arc overhead before impact). From here a 26-mile auto tour leads past other spots along the battle line, including the gaping hole left by the surreal Battle of the Crater.

Other units include the **Poplar Grove National Cemetery** southwest of downtown, filled with 6,000 Union casualties, and Grant's siege headquarters at **City Point,** 804/458-9504, where the Appomattox empties into the James. There's a ranger station at the **Five Forks Battlefield,** 804/265-8244, farther west along Rt. 460, where Gen. Sheridan took 2,000 Confederate prisoners on April 1, 1865.

Most of the siege's 30,000 Confederate casualties are buried in **Blandford Cemetery,** off Crater Rd. (US 301/480) south of Washington St. A set of Tiffany stained glass windows was donated to the **Blandford Church,** 319 S. Crater Rd., by Southern states in memory of their Civil War dead. (Open daily 10 A.M.–5 P.M.; $3 adults, $2 children.) The sight of girls putting flowers on Confederate graves at Blandford Cemetery later prompted Union General John A. Logan to push for Memorial Day to be established.

The visitors center is open daily 9 A.M.–5

AFRICAN AMERICAN HISTORY IN PETERSBURG

Petersburg's rich vein of African American history starts with the First Baptist Church at 236 Harrison St., which opened in 1774 as the earliest organized black church in America (guided tours by appointment). By the mid-19th century, the city had the largest free black population in Virginia, though two-thirds remained slaves. Former slaves who had been manumitted (given their freedom) or bought it themselves organized small, self-contained communities in places like Pocahontas Island on the Appomattox River near Petersburg. Joseph Jenkins Roberts, the first president of Liberia 1848–1855 (and again 1871–1876), left his hometown in 1829, and 1888 saw the election of Virginia's first black congressman, Petersburg resident John Mercer Langston. The visitors center has more information.

P.M., $10 per car, $5 per bicycle or pair of shoes ($5/3 Sept.–May). During the summer, costumed interpreters add a living touch to the experience.

Pamplin Park

This private Civil War site south of Petersburg features a high-tech interpretive center with a fiber-optic battle map, interactive video programs, and war relics in a $10.5-million Battlefield Center. Trails lead along some of the best-preserved Civil War fortifications in existence. Get an idea of what life was like during the winter of the Petersburg siege (1864–1865) in a reconstructed soldier's hut, and across the road stop by Tudor Hall, an 1812 plantation home that was used as headquarters by a Confederate general. Guided tours and reenactments happen periodically; call for a schedule. You can grab a bite at the Hardtack & Coffee Cafe.

Pamplin Park, 6125 Boyton Plank Rd., 877/615-6435 or 804/861-2408, www.pamplinpark.org, is on Rt. 670, a little more than one mile south of I-85 exit 63 via US 1. It's open daily 9 A.M.–5 P.M. (6 P.M. Memorial Day–Labor Day); $12 adults, $6 children 6–11.

CENTRAL VIRGINIA

CENTRAL VIRGINIA

© VIRGINIA TOURISM CORPORATION

Living history programs at Petersburg National Battlefield Park re-create life during the Civil War.

ACCOMMODATIONS

$50–100

A treasury of French antiques fills **La Villa Romaine,** 29 S. Market St. at Market St., 804/861-2285 or 800/243-0860 ext. 1234, lavilla.tierranet.com, from a carved armoire to matching twin Louis XVI beds. A full European breakfast is included, and guests after a lit-

tle something special can opt for a chauffeured Rolls Royce tour of the area.

A **Comfort Inn,** 11974 S. Crater Rd., 804/732-2900, and a **Hampton Inn,** 11909 S. Crater Rd., 804/732-1400, are both on US 301 near I-95 exit 45.

$100–150

A turret tops the gorgeous Queen Anne Victorian mansion now known as the **High Street Victorian Inn,** 405 High St., 804/733-0505 or 866/477-8466, email: highst@ctg.net, www.highstreetinn.com. Rooms have antique four-poster beds and brass washbasins, and a full breakfast is included. On August 6, 1864, the Federal Court of Inquiry of the Battle of the Crater was held at the **Walker House,** 3280 S. Crater Rd., 804/861-5822, email: walkerhouse@mindspring.com, www.walkerhouse.com. Four rooms are each named after a season, and the spacious spread includes a walnut-paneled library and koi goldfish in the lily pond. The 1815 farmhouse is one mile off I-95 exit 48B.

Three miles west of downtown on Washington Street is the **Mayfield Inn,** 3348 W. Washington St., 804/733-0866 or 800/538-2381, one of the few buildings in town that survived both the Revolutionary War and the

GEORGE'S LIE

G eorge Washington visited Petersburg near the turn of the 19th century and recorded being forced to tell a lie in order to leave in peace:

Having suffered very much by the dust yesterday, and finding that . . .
a number of other Gentlemen were intending to attend me part of the way today, I caused their enquiries respecting the time of my setting out, to be answered that, I should endeavor to do it before eight o'clock; but did it a little after five.

Civil War. Robert E. Lee stayed here with his staff in 1750 before abandoning Petersburg. Four acres of grounds around the 1750s mansion include a pool and enchanting gardens. A full country breakfast comes with a night in one of the four rooms.

Built in 1763, the **Folly Castle Bed & Breakfast**, 323 W. Washington St., 804/861-3558 or 800/863-0089, www.follycastle.com, takes its name from the fact that such a large Georgian home for its childless owner seemed, well, a bit ill-advised. In 1885 its owners moved it 100 feet so they could enjoy a fashionable West Washington Street address. Suites include access to a peaceful garden with waterfall and lily pond.

Camping

The **South Forty KOA**, 2809 Courtland Rd., 804/732-8345, is south of Petersburg, half a mile beyond I-95 exit 41 on Rt. 35. Sites are $23–28.

FOOD

Next to the visitors center on Old Street, the **Farmer's Market**, 804/732-3378, occupies an octagonal brick building built in 1888 on the site of Petersburg's first tobacco warehouse. Local farmers still sell seasonal produce from stalls outside, a stipulation of the building's 1806 deed of sale for $1. Economical lunch salads and sandwiches are in the $5 range, and dinner entrées from BBQ to surf and turf run $10–15. Line dancing, comedy shows, karaoke, and live bands fill the center stage throughout the week. Open Tues.–Sun.

Next to the farmer's market, **Leonardo's Deli & Cafe**, 7 Bollingbrook St., 804/863-4830, serves light fare, including homemade bread and sandwiches, along with coffees and Italian sodas. It's open for lunch Mon.–Fri. and dinner Tues.–Sat. A block beyond down Sycamore is the **Dixie Restaurant**, 250 N. Sycamore, 804/732-5761, a local institution with rock-bottom prices and famous hot dogs (ask about the Dixie Dog song). Open Mon.–Sat. for all meals.

Longstreet's Cafe, 302 N. Sycamore, 804/722-4372, is an inviting coffee shop that sells

THE CRATER FIASCO

The idea was simple and daring: covertly dig a 500-foot tunnel under the Confederate trenches at Petersburg, fill it with explosives, and with one lit match avoid a torturous siege and perhaps even end the Civil War early. Union officials dismissed the idea as "claptrap and nonsense," but Lt. Col. Henry Pleasants managed to convince Maj. Gen. Ambrose E. Burnside that his corps of Pennsylvania coal miners could pull it off.

Burnside in turn persuaded a reluctant Ulysses S Grant to give the go-ahead, and on June 25, 1864, digging began. How Union sappers managed to dig a tenth of a mile directly under hundreds of listless Confederate troops without being heard is anyone's guess, especially with two Confederate counter-tunnels in the vicinity, but on July 23 the cramped passage was completed. It took four days to pack the end with 8,000 pounds of gunpowder and seal the shaft for 38 feet, and at 3:30 a.m. on July 30 the fuse was lit.

Nothing happened. A nervous volunteer was sent below with another match, and at 4:45 a.m. the earth beneath the sleeping Confederates erupted. Nine entire companies were suddenly airborne above a hole 170 feet wide and 30 feet deep. Nearly 300 men were killed outright or mortally wounded.

Members of Brig. Gen. James Ledlie's division spearheaded the assault into the smoking hole, but were so shocked by the carnage they found that they milled about in confusion. The enraged Rebels regrouped and struck back, firing on the clump of blue uniforms without mercy. A black Union division (originally picked to lead the attack, but switched at the last minute to avoid charges of racism) was ordered in to help, but found itself trapped as well. Many were shot by Confederates after surrendering. By 1 p.m. the Union troops had been pushed back to their original line after suffering 3,798 casualties, more than twice as many as their opponents.

Grant later called the event "the saddest affair I have witnessed in the war."

CENTRAL VIRGINIA

FOOD AND FUN IN EMPORIA

Emporia, a small city in south-central Virginia, hosts two annual events celebrating regional food. The second weekend in June the **Virginia Pork Festival,** 800/482-7675 or 434/634-6611, www.VAporkfestival.com, one of the East Coast's largest food festivals, features 43,000 pounds of the Other White Meat, from ribs to chitterlings. All you can eat, along with five stages of country, bluegrass, and rock, is yours for $22 pp.

The **Virginia Peanut Festival** arrives in late September with music, carnival rides, and a classic car show. Some 12,000 visitors show up to appreciate the peanut butter–sculpting contest and the Peanut Parade, culminating in the Miss Emporia–Greensville Peanut Festival Pageant. (This is distinct from the **Suffolk Peanut Fest,** www.suffolkfest.org, held in mid-October).

Leading in to Emporia's peanut celebrations is the **Great Peanut Bicycle Tour,** 800/449-2453, www.greatpeanuttour.com, which winds through the peanut country of southern Virginia and northeast North Carolina in early September. The four-day tour typically draws around 1,500 cyclists.

For more information, contact the Emporia–Greensville Chamber of Commerce, 400 Halifax St., 434/634-9441, www.emporia-greensvillechamber.com/contact.htm.

Boar's Head sandwiches ($6–7), box lunches ($6–8), and lots of wine and beer. Open Mon.–Sat. 10 A.M.–7 P.M. Next to the visitors center, **The Brickhouse Run,** 407 Cockade Alley, 804/862-1815, is a classic British pub á la Petersburg, with friendly proprietors and great pub fare such as fish and chips and shepherd's pie ($10–15). Open for dinner Tues.–Sat.

Look for the wrought iron tables and vine-covered fountain outside **Betsy's Courtyard,** 21 W. Old St., 804/733-6600, to track down New Orleans food served daily for lunch and Wed.–Sat. for dinner. Entrees like seafood etouffé and pecan-crusted salmon are $15–17 for dinner. Daily lunch specials include salads and quiches ($6–8).

ENTERTAINMENT AND RECREATION

Shopping

The sign says Complete Home Furnishings at the **Trading Post,** 314 N. Sycamore, 804/733-4772, but you'll find much more in this salvage shop supreme. Everything from railroad collectibles to coffee and spices trades hands at the **South Side Station Flea Market,** 804/733-5050, a flea market housed in two buildings along the river. It's open Tues.–Sun. Antique addicts can get their fix within a few blocks of the visitors center at **Woody's Antiques,** 3 W. Old St., 804/861-9642, and **American Hurrah Antiques,** 406 N. Market St., 804/861-9659.

Nightlife

The **Cockade City Grill,** 305 N. Sycamore, 804/862-2537, has a big bar and live entertainment until 11 P.M. on weekdays and 2 A.M. on weekends. On Thursday evenings in the summer, live music shows are held under the I-95 overpass behind the visitors center. The shows are $5 pp and move indoors after dark.

EVENTS

A Civil War–themed **Starvation Ball** on New Year's Day brings period costumes, music, and Jeff Davis punch to Centre Hill Mansion. In mid-April the Petersburg Art League sponsors a citywide **Artfest** at Poplar Lawn Park at Sycamore and Fillmore. You can take **Hallows Eve tours** of Blandford Cemetery in late October. Call the visitor's center for more information.

TRANSPORTATION

Amtrak, 804/526-4077, has a station at 3516 South St. in Ettrick, across the river on US 36 past Virginia State University. **Greyhound/Trailways,** 804/732-2905, is at 108 E. Washington St. at Adams. Local bus service is provided by **Petersburg Area Transit,** 804/733-2413.

INFORMATION

The 1815 home of mayor George Jones has become the Petersburg **visitors center,** 425 Cockade Alley at Old St., 800/368-3595 or 804/ 733-2400, www.petersburg-va.org. Just south of the US 1/301 bridge, the McIlwaine House is open daily 9 A.M.–5 P.M. From Apr.–Oct. you can buy block tickets to certain Petersburg sights.

Fredericksburg and Vicinity

The largest city between Washington, D.C. and Richmond, Fredericksburg eases up against a bend in the Rappahannock River just below its tumble over the fall line. The home of Mary Washington College and dozens of antique and relic shops, Fredericksburg (pop. 22,000) counts estates, battlefields, and a historic riverfront area among its attractions. Herb and flower gardens bursting with tulip magnolias, crepe myrtles, and Bradford pear blossoms separate trim, neatly spaced houses in the downtown National Historic District. It's a popular escape from the Capitol and a good base for exploring the Northern and Middle Necks.

HISTORY

Fredericksburg was established in 1727, named for the Prince of Wales and father of King George III. Wagons loaded with tobacco, flax, wheat, hemp, and flour rolled into the port city from surrounding farms for shipment downriver and on to Europe. George Washington spent part of his childhood at Ferry Farm across the Rappahannock. He attended school briefly in town and returned decades later to buy his mother Mary a house on Charles Street. Trade was brisk at the Rappahannock falls, and Fredericksburg thrived for a time. Three-masted schooners docked in her port, and wealthy plantation owners enjoyed horse races and lavish balls.

Revolutionary fervor reached a peak in Fredericksburg in the 1770s as the courthouse green rang with the shouts of officers drilling their troops. In 1777, Thomas Jefferson, George Mason, and other founding

THE VIRGINIA STATUTE OF RELIGIOUS FREEDOM

Passed by the Virginia Senate on January 16, 1786, Thomas Jefferson's landmark Virginia Statute of Religious Freedom separated church and state so effectively that it became the basis for the First Amendment to the U.S. Constitution. Along with the University of Virginia and the Declaration of Independence, it was one of three things he ordered to be included in his epitaph: ". . . and not a word more . . . because by these, as testimonials that I have lived, I wish most to be remembered." (About one-third of the statute appears here.)

I. WHEREAS Almighty God has created the mind free, so that all attempts to influence it by temporal punishments or burdens, or by civil incapacitations, tend only to beget habits of hypocrisy and meanness. . . .

II. BE IT . . . ENACTED BY THE GENERAL ASSEMBLY that no man shall be compelled to frequent or support any religious worship, place, or ministry whatsoever, nor shall be enforced, restrained, molested, or burdened in his body or goods, nor shall otherwise suffer on account of his religious opinions or belief; but that all men shall be free to profess, and by argument to maintain, their opinion in matters of religion, and that the same shall in no wise diminish, enlarge, or affect their civil capacities.

III. . . . AS WE ARE FREE to declare, and do declare, that the rights hereby asserted are of the natural rights of mankind, and that if any act shall hereafter be passed to repeal the present, or to narrow its operation, such act will be an infringement of natural right.

M

CENTRAL VIRGINIA

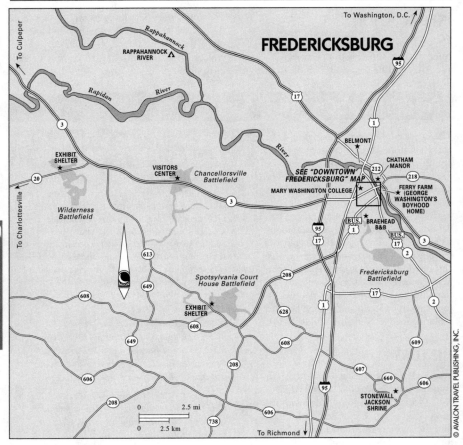

fathers met in the Rising Sun Tavern to draw up the Virginia Statute of Religious Freedom, which would eventually become the First Amendment to the U.S. Constitution.

Its strategic position on the river, midway between the Federal and Confederate capitals, put Fredericksburg and its 4,000 inhabitants in the middle of some of the Civil War's hottest fighting. From 1861–1865 it changed hands seven times, but it was in 1862–1863 that the city saw its worst moments. A Union bombardment two days before the Battle of Fredericksburg reduced most of the city to rubble. Thirty thousand occupying soldiers found little left to loot before their officers imposed order. Lincoln visited on

May 23 to meet with his generals, and Clara Barton tended wounded Federal soldiers inside the Presbyterian church. In 1863 and 1864, Lee repeatedly trounced Grant in the fields to the west, resulting in 17,000 bodies to fill the Fredericksburg National Cemetery, part of the Fredericksburg and Spotsylvania National Military Park.

SIGHTS

Most of Fredericksburg's historic sites are preserved in a 40-acre National Historic District along the river. Opening hours are shorter from Dec.–Feb.

George Washington's younger brother Charles built the **Rising Sun Tavern,** 1306 Caroline St.,

DOWNTOWN FREDERICKSBURG

CENTRAL VIRGINIA

540/371-1494, around 1760. It served as a stagecoach stop and post office during its heyday, when a beer cost three times as much as a bed (which you might have had to share with four other people) and the bathwater was changed after every third person. Self-described "wenches" in colonial costume guide you through the separate rooms for women (resting and primping) and men (drinking and gambling), explaining along the way why tankards have glass bottoms and the genesis of expressions such as "mind your Ps and Qs" and "cold shoulder." Open Mon.–Sat. 9 A.M.–5 P.M., Sun. 11 A.M.–5 P.M.; $4 adults, $1.50 children.

Some of the remedies at the **Hugh Mercer Apothecary Shop,** Caroline and Amelia Sts., 540/373-3362, are guaranteed to make you glad you weren't born 200 years ago. Mercer practiced here for 15 years, treating George Washington, among many other patients. He was killed in the Revolutionary War. Nowadays tour guides demonstrate tooth extractors, amputation tools, and the 18th-century inoculation technique for smallpox. Don't miss the tools for inducing bleeding, including a jarful of live leeches and a hand-held razor device (back then it was thought that human bodies held 12 quarts of blood, a

© JULIAN SMITH

the Virginia countryside

mistake that may have helped kill Washington). Others medicines aren't so bad: cobwebs for open wounds, coltsfoot for asthma, and saffron to "quicken the brain." A pair of handblown glass bottles, exquisitely painted from the inside, stands on the shelves. Open Mon.–Sat. 9 A.M.–5 P.M., Sun. 11 A.M.–5 P.M.; $4 adults, $1.50 children.

Mary Ball Washington spent the last 17 years of her life in the **Mary Washington House,** 1200 Charles St., 540/373-1569, bought for her by her son George. The simple home still contains some original pieces like china bearing the Washington family wheat pattern. Behind the building is a separate kitchen and a small garden that's been restored to Mary's standards. Open Mon.–Sat. 9 A.M.–5 P.M., Sun. 11 A.M.–5 P.M.; $4 adults, $1.50 children.

Furnishings, arts, weapons, and personal objects make up the collection of the **James Monroe Museum and Memorial Library,** 908 Charles St., 540/654-1043, www.JamesMonroeMuseum.mwc.edu. The fifth President was the only one besides Washington to fight in the Revolutionary War, and the only one to have a foreign capital named after him (Monrovia,

Liberia). Mary Washington College administers the museum, which holds many pieces from the Monroe White House. Open daily 10 A.M.–5 P.M.; $5 adults, $1 children.

The **Fredericksburg Area Museum and Cultural Center,** 907 Princess Anne St., 540/371-3073, holds three floors of excellent exhibits from the prehistoric to the present. The first floor is geared toward kids, with changing exhibits like "The Age of Reptiles." They'll also like the Indian wigwam. On the second floor, Revolutionary-era pieces include a beautiful inlaid Hepplewhite sideboard and early-18th-century survey documents. Firearms and a shell-splintered door represent the Civil War, followed by Ku Klux Klan relics and whites-only signs that touch on 20th-century racial issues. A re-created council chamber and Civil War photos fill the third floor. Open Mon.–Sat. 10 A.M.–5 P.M., Sun. 1–5 P.M.; $4 adults, $1 children.

Incredible plasterwork by the same itinerant artist who decorated Mount Vernon is a highlight of the **Kenmore Plantation and Gardens,** 1201 Washington Ave., 540/373-3381, www.kenmore.org. One of the rooms in the elegant 18th-century mansion, built for George Washington's brother-in-law and his wife, is considered one of the 100 most beautiful in the country. A wide lawn balances the elaborate boxwood gardens behind. Stop by the kitchen for a nip of tea and a cookie. Open Mar.–Dec. Mon.–Sat. 10 A.M.–5 P.M., Sun. noon–5 P.M.; $6 adults, $3 children.

In 1752, Washington entered the **Masonic Lodge No. 4,** 803 Princess Anne St. at Hanover St., 540/373-5885, as an apprentice. Now a museum, the lodge includes the Bible on which Washington swore his Masonic oath. Open by appointment (check at the visitors center) for $2 pp. A few other buildings in downtown Fredericksburg are worth a visit, starting with the Greek Revival **Presbyterian Church,** at George and Princess Anne streets. Built in 1833, it still has a cannon ball from the Union barrage imbedded in one wall. **St. George's Episcopal Church,** on Princess Anne Street between George and William streets, has several Tiffany windows. Union troops set up temporary barracks in the basement of the Victorian Gothic **courthouse** across George Street and watched the nearby battles from its cupola.

Colonial ladies once mounted horses from the small **slave auction block** at the corner of Charles and William streets, and the **horse-chesnut tree** on Faquier Street between Charles and Edward is the only one left of 13 planted by George Washington to symbolize the original states.

ACCOMMODATIONS

$50–100

There's a **Quality Inn,** 543 Warrenton Rd., 540/373-0000, fax 540/373-5676, near the intersection of US 17 and I-95; and the **Best Western Central Plaza,** 3000 Plank Rd., 540/786-7404, fax 540/785-7415, sits next to the Spotsylvania Mall. Try the **Days Inn Fredericksburg South,** 5316 Jefferson Davis Hwy., 540/898-6800, fax 540/891-6256. Fountains, flags, and kites decorate the atrium of the **Ramada Inn,** 5324 Jefferson Davis Hwy., 540/898-1102, fax 540/898-2017.

$100–150

The **Kenmore Inn,** 1200 Princess Anne St., 540/371-7622 or 800/327-7622, fax 540/371-5480, www.kenmoreinn.com, has an award-winning restaurant with outdoor dining and an English pub with jazz and blues on weekends. Guests can relax on the veranda facing Princess Anne Street or in front of the fireplace in the sitting room. Rates are $105–145, or $200 for a two-bedroom suite. Facing the visitors center is the **Richard Johnston Inn,** 711 Caroline St., 540/899-7606, occupying a pair of joined townhouses built in the late 1700s by the mayor of Fredericksburg. Six sumptuous bedrooms and two suites are dressed out with antiques such as a huge mahogany queen bed from the 1830s. Rooms at the **Holiday Inn Select,** 2801 Plank Rd., 540/786-8321, fax 540/786-0397, are around $110.

FOOD

Breakfast and Lighter Fare

Start things off with a $4 breakfast under the purple awning of the **Caroline Street Cafe,** 1002 Caroline St., 540/374-1136, which also sells burgers and sandwiches such as their famous crabcake ($6.50) from 8 A.M. (10:30 on Sunday). **Goolrick's Pharmacy,** 901 Caroline St., 540/373-9878, is a step back in time with its 1940s soda fountain and lunch counter. (By some estimates it's the oldest continually operating soda fountain in the country.) They serve an inexpensive breakfast, homemade soups, and sandwiches along with the obligatory egg creams and floats. Pick up a box lunch for the battlefields at the **Olde Towne Wine and Cheese Deli,** 707 Caroline St., 540/373-7877, with Boar's Head sandwiches, fresh soups, and a Friday evening New Orleans dinner. Open Mon.–Sat. 11 A.M.–8 P.M.

Hyperion Espresso, 301 William St., 540/373-4882, serves the black diesel in an eye-catching setting daily from 7 A.M., and the **Java and Cone Connection,** 615 Caroline St., 540/371-4435, also has snacks, sweets, and a gift shop. **Barefoot Green's,** 1017 Sophia St., 540/373-2012, is a restaurant, market, and carryout with seafood platters for $7–9. Open for lunch Thurs.–Sun.

CENTRAL VIRGINIA

More Substantial

An alternate take on French is **Le Petit Auberge,** 311 William St., 540/371-2727, home to yet another D.C. chef who fled to the quieter reaches downstate. Local paintings hang on bare brick walls in the dining room adjoining a small pub. Excellent entreés like wild bay rockfish and baked brie are $6–10 for lunch and $10–20 for dinner, and there's an early-bird dinner deal Mon.–Thurs. for $16. Next door is **Bistro 309,** 309 William St., 540/371-9999, which serves modern cuisine with Southern flair for dinner Tues.–Sat. Appetizers like smoked chicken quesadillas and zatar (Lebanese flatbread) are $5.50–7.50, and entreés like wood-oven–roasted salmon are $17–25.

Chef Salvador Del Rosario of **Six-twenty-three,** 623 Caroline St., 540/361-2640, serves contemporary bistro cuisine in a 1771 Georgian home known as The Chimneys. Dinner entrees cost $18–24, and tapas (small dishes originated in Spain) are $4–10 each. They're open for lunch and dinner Wed.–Sun., with full bar service and live jazz on the first Wednesday night of every month.

Smythe's Cottage and Tavern, 303 Faquier St., 540/373-1645, squeezes into a tiny, blue 19th-century cottage. Notice the upside-down picture of Ulysses S Grant in the tap room, and enjoy local staples like ham and biscuits, peanut soup, and Brunswick stew for $5–8 for lunch and $12–19 for dinner. Dining is available inside or on outside tables. Open for lunch and dinner Mon.–Sun.

Generous portions of authentic northern Italian dishes are standard at the **Ristorante Renato,** 422 Williams St., 540/371-8228. Lunch and dinner specials includes side dishes, dessert, and even a glass of wine (for dinner). Most dinner entreés are around $20, except for the pastas ($15), and all breads, pastas, and pastries are cooked on the premises. Open for lunch Mon.–Fri., dinner daily. It may seem like an oxymoron, but **Sammy T's,** 801 Caroline St. at Hanover St., 540/371-2008, serves healthy pub fare, like bean and grain burgers and an apple-cheddar melt. Sandwiches are around $6 and entrées, including many vegan and vegetarian options, cost $6–10. Open daily for lunch and dinner.

ENTERTAINMENT AND RECREATION

Shopping

You could outfit a mansion (or a brigade) with all the antiques and Civil War artifacts for sale along Caroline Street. Try the **Picket Post,** 602 Caroline St., 540/371-7703; **Way Back When,** 918 Caroline St., 540/371-7841; and the **Antique Corner of Fredericksburg,** 900 Caroline St., 540/373-0826, for starters. Every weekend starting at 7 A.M. you can peruse seasonal produce, crafts, and antiques at the **Manor Mart Flea Market,** along US 1 just south of town.

At the **Art First Gallery & Studios,** 108 Hanover St., 540/371-7107, you can peruse the works of local artists and buy whatever catches your fancy. Across the street is the workshop and studio gallery of local potter **Dan Finnegan,** 540/371-7255, 106 Hanover St., with gas and wood-fired stoneware. **The Copper Shop,** 1707B Princess Anne St., 540/371-4455, specializes in the handcrafted Fredericksburg lamp, a glass and candle creation made by local coppersmiths Allen H. Green II and III.

Outdoors

The folks at **Outdoor Adventures,** 4721 Plank Rd., 540/786-3334, 800/357-9710, www.outdooradventures.net, run canoe and kayak trips on Potomac Creek and the Rapidan and Rappahannock rivers. They also rent camping gear and have classes in kayaking, rock climbing, and backpacking. **Friends of the Rappahannock Ecotourism,** 3219 Fall Hill Ave., 540/373-3448, is a volunteer group aimed at preserving the river's beauty and health. They offer interpretive canoe tours, guided hikes, and overnight trips. For more paddle sports, check with **Rappahannock Outdoors,** 3219 Fall Hill Ave., 540/371-5085, or **Clore Brothers Outfitters,** 5927 River Rd., 540/786-7749, 800/704-7749, http://members.aol.com/clorebros/.

Tours

The Living History Company, 904 Princess Anne St., 540/899-1776, 888/214-6384, www.history-experiences.com, leads a wide range of guided tours, from daylight history walks to lantern-lit "Phantoms of Fredericksburg" battlefield rambles. Town tours are $15 adults and $8 children, and battlefield rambles cost $60–120 for 2–4 hours. Buy tickets at the visitors center for **Trolley Tours of Fredericksburg,** 540/898-0737, which cover the major sights in town and on the battlefield in an hour and 15 minutes. These tours leave from the visitors center daily from Apr.–Nov. and on weekends in Dec. and cost $12.50 adults, $5 children. Horse-drawn **carriage tours** of the historic center, 540/654-5511, leave daily 9 A.M.–5 P.M. from George and Sophia streets for $15 adults, $7.50 children.

Nightlife

Mary Washington students name **The Underground,** under the George St. Grill at 106 George St., 540/371-9500, as the place in town for acoustic and rock acts. Live music also happens at **J. Brian's Tap Room,** 200 Hanover St., 540/373-0738, and the **Santa Fe Grill and Saloon,** 216 William. St., 540/371-0500.

EVENTS

In June, the **Great Rappahannock Whitewater Canoe Race** paddles past. Some people take it seriously, and some slap together the most ridiculous craft that will float. Fredericksburg's **Heritage Festival** around the 4th of July brings live music, crafts, food, and a raft race on the river. The story of October's **Dog Mart** begins in pre-Revolutionary days when Indians were said to have traded furs for the settler's exotic animals. Revived in 1927, it's evolved into a small festival with music, food, and a dog parade.

TRANSPORTATION

There's an **Amtrak** station at Princess Anne Street and Lafayette Boulevard, with commuter service via Alexandria to D.C.'s Union Station, and a **Greyhound/Trailways** depot, 1400 Jefferson Davis Hwy., 540/373-2103.

INFORMATION

Stop by the **Fredericksburg Visitor Center,** 706 Caroline St., 800/678-4748 or 540/373-1776,

www.fredericksburgva.com, for walking-tour maps and a short movie on the area. They also have free parking passes and a block ticket to eight area sights, including Belmont, Ferry Farm, and Kenmore for $19.75 adults, $8 children. Open daily 9 A.M.–5 P.M. (7 P.M. in summer).

ACROSS THE RIVER

Belmont

The home of American painter Gari Melchers (1860–1932) has been turned into a museum and park overlooking the river and city. The house dates to the turn of the 18th century and was left untouched during the Federal occupation because its owner was a Union sympathizer. Many of Melchers's original furnishings, including a linen press and a series of plates designed to teach children the story of the Prodigal Son, reflect his fascination with Holland and the simple lives of the Dutch peasants that he painted repeatedly. A granite studio holds these works and famous portraits of Teddy Roosevelt and Mark Twain.

The house and studio, 540/654-1015, are open for tours Mon.–Sat. 10 A.M.–5 P.M., Sun. 1–5 P.M. (Dec.–Feb. Mon.–Sat. 10 A.M.–4 P.M.) $4 adults, $1 children. By dictate of his widow's will, the gates to the peaceful parklike grounds—perfect for a picnic—are never locked.

Ferry Farm

In 1738 the Washington family moved to a small farm on the east bank of the Rappahannock, near a dock from which ferries ran to the newly founded city of Fredericksburg. Here, the future president, still only a child, would begin his education and grow up alongside three brothers and a sister. Ferry Farm is also the source of two of the more enduring Washington myths—the cherry tree and the silver dollar thrown across the river. At his death in 1743, Augustine Washington left Ferry Farm to George, who turned to surveying for income. Nine years later he inherited Mount Vernon from his half-brother Lawrence, leaving his mother in possession of Ferry Farm until he sold it in 1774 and moved her into town.

Excavations are still in progress, so there's not much to see beyond an archaeology lab, surveying office, and icehouse pit. Self-guided tour brochures point out what used to be where. The farm is under the auspices of Kenmore Plantation, 540/373-3381, and open Mar.–Dec. Mon.–Sat. 10 A.M.–5 P.M., Sun. noon–5 P.M.; $2 adults, $1 children.

FREDERICKSBURG AND SPOTSYLVANIA NATIONAL MILITARY PARK

From 1862–1864 some of the most brutal engagements ever fought on North American soil shook the landscape around Fredericksburg. It's estimated that 100,000 soldiers were killed on four major battlefields within 15 miles of the city.

Park headquarters are across the Rappahannock from Fredericksburg in **Chatham Manor,** 120 Chatham Ln., 540/371-0802, www.nps.gov/frsp. This Georgian mansion was built in 1771 with a commanding view from the riverside heights. A series of Union officers established command posts here, and Walt Whitman, Clara Barton, and Abraham Lincoln all passed through during the fighting (making it the only building both Lincoln and George Washington visited). Open daily 9 A.M.–5 P.M. Entrance to the park is $4 pp, good for a week.

Battle of Fredericksburg

During the cold winter of 1862, Union Gen. Ambrose Burnside, who had replaced McClellan after his defeat at Antietam, Maryland, pursued Robert E. Lee south toward Richmond. Despite Lincoln's urgings for speed, Burnside had hesitated long enough to allow the Army of Northern Virginia to dig in on the high ground west of Fredericksburg by early December. Pontoon bridges across the icy Rappahannock were finally erected, in the face of Confederate sniper fire, and on December 13, 120,000 Federal troops poured across the river to attack Lee's force of 70,000.

Stonewall Jackson initially drove Gen. George Meade's forces back from Prospect Hill. Burnside then sent 30,000 troops to take Marye's Heights from 5,000 Confederate soldiers, who were crouched behind a stone wall along the Sunken Road, and the real slaughter began. Wave after wave of Federal soldiers were mowed down by rifle fire from ahead and artillery shells from above. None came closer than 100 feet to the wall, but Burnside's orders held and the futile attacks continued until 8,000 men lay broken and dying.

A 19-year-old South Carolina infantryman named Richard Kirkland was so tormented by the cries of the wounded that he left the safety of the stone wall to offer men water from his canteen. Union gunners ceased fire at this act of mercy, and the Angel of Marye's Heights entered Civil War legend. Kirkland's deed is commemorated on the Sunken Road in a monument done by the same sculptor who created the Marine Corps Iwo Jima Memorial in Arlington.

Never had anyone present seen such a massacre. Viewing the battle, Lee said to Gen. James Longstreet: "It is well that war is so terrible, or we should grow too fond of it." "It can hardly be in human nature," wrote a Northern war correspondent, "for men to show more valor, or generals to manifest less judgment." Pacing in his tent the next day, Burnside was overheard muttering "Those men. Those men."

The **Fredericksburg National Cemetery** now occupies Marye's Heights in the center of the city. More than 15,000 soldiers are buried here, of whom only 15 percent have ever been identified. As you stand on the crest of the hill, imagine thousands of Federal troops swarming from the fields to the east "like some huge blue serpent," in the words of one Confederate witness, "about to encompass and crush us in its folds." At the foot of the slope a **visitors center,** 540/373-6122, sells admission tickets, and you can also rent a tape to guide you along the 75-mile auto tour. It's open daily 9 A.M.–5 P.M.

Battle of Chancellorsville

Union spirits ran low after the debacle at Marye's Heights. In late April 1863, Gen. Joseph "Fighting Joe" Hooker replaced Burnside and set about reorganizing the Union forces and restoring morale. So as not to repeat Burnside's mistake, Hooker divided his 134,000 troops into two groups and moved them across the Rapidan and Rappahannock Rivers to attack Lee from the west in a pincher movement.

True to form, Lee took the initiative and rushed west to attack first at Chancellorsville, after making the risky decision to leave 10,000 men under Maj. Gen. Jubal Early to defend the Fredericksburg position. Though outnumbered more than two to one, Lee threw his forces against the Union defensive lines. Jackson was sent with 25,000 troops on a 12-mile march to attack the Federal army from the west, which the savvy commander managed to pull off undetected—had he failed and Hooker attacked Lee's remaining 15,000, the Confederates would have been crushed.

As it happened, Jackson's brigade charged from the woods behind a terrified horde of deer and rabbits, destroying the Union right flank. Fierce gunfire left nearby trees useless as lumber afterward. The victory was short-lived, though, because Jackson was mistakenly shot by his Confederate guards while out scouting the battlefield at dusk on May 2. He died eight days later.

Meanwhile, Gen. John Sedgewick had finally wrested Marye's Heights from Jubal Early. J.E.B. Stuart took over Jackson's position and drove Hooker back to the Rappahannock. The Union general withdrew his forces across the river and was relieved of command by Lincoln shortly thereafter. The Confederates had won a huge victory but lost one of their finest commanders.

The **Chancellorsville Visitor Center** on Rt. 3, 540/786-2880, is open daily 9 A.M.–5 P.M. A four-mile loop trail covers major sites and can be shortened to a 20-minute walk. Historians lead guided walking tours daily in summer and on weekends in the spring and fall.

Battle of the Wilderness

In March 1864 Ulysses S Grant became commander-in-chief of all Union forces. He also gained a determination to track down and annihilate Lee at all costs. By May 5 Grant had marched almost within sight of the Confederate position around Fredericksburg. Once again Lee struck first in the tortured undergrowth west of Chancellorsville known as The Wilderness.

Federal coordination and their advantage of numbers dissolved in the confusion. Heavy gunfire ignited the dense brush, burning wounded soldiers to death in a hellish confusion of smoke and bullets. One Union survivor remembered it as "a blind and bloody hunt to the death, in bewildering thickets, rather than a battle." After two days of fighting, both armies had lost close to 15 percent of their ranks: the Federals 17,500 and the Confederates 8,000.

The **Wilderness Exhibit Shelter** is on Rt. 20, 1.3 miles west of Rt. 3.

Battle of Spotsylvania Court House

Refusing to accept defeat at The Wilderness, Grant resolved to lead his army south, a decision greeted with cheers by his soldiers. Lee, however, won the race to Spotsylvania Court House, which controlled the shortest route to Richmond. Federal troops found themselves facing an entrenched Confederate army of 50,000, dug in behind hastily constructed earthworks.

"I propose to fight it out on this line if it takes all summer," Grant wrote Lincoln, but the battle was decided in just two weeks of the war's most savage combat. On May 20 the Battle of Bloody Angle raged around a bulge in the Rebel line called the Mule Shoe. Twenty hours of desperate hand-to-hand combat in the pouring rain saw men trampled into knee-deep mud and others shot and bayoneted through gaps in the wooden breastworks. Point-blank cannon fire cut two-foot oaks in half, prompting one solider to remark later, "We had not only shot down an army, but also a forest." Days later the square-mile patch of ground that had cost 13,000 lives was abandoned by both sides.

Both armies, each a third smaller, eventually moved southeast together for 11 more months of fighting. While the Union could replace its fallen soldiers, the Confederacy could not, and Lee's goal changed to delay instead of victory.

The **Spotsylvania Exhibit Shelter** is on Rt. 613. Loop hiking trails up to seven miles long pass the Bloody Angle and Lee's final line.

Stonewall Jackson Shrine

After his accidental wounding, Jackson was moved to a plantation office in Guinea Station, where he died on May 10. Historians on duty lead tours through the building, 804/633-6076, which is open daily 9 A.M.–5 P.M. (Fri.–Tues. in spring and fall; Sat.–Mon. in winter).

Camping

Campers can choose from **Aquia Pines Camp Resort,** 540/659-3447, on US 1 just north of I-95 exit 143 ($22-30), or the **Fredericksburg KOA Kampground,** 7400 Brookside LAne (I-95 exit 126), 540/898-7252. The latter has 115 sites ($26–31) and 9 cabins ($42), along with a free train shuttle, hayrides, and a heated pool.

Charlottesville

Home to an eclectic mix of old values and liberal intellectualism, "C-Ville" combines fraternity parties and yoga groups, Colonial architecture and Wal-Marts, all in a setting that's close to perfect—the Blue Ridge Mountains half an hour west, the ocean two hours east, and in every direction the acres roll and rivers wind. It's no wonder, then, that *Money* and *Outside* magazines have listed Charlottesville (pop. 40,000) as one of the most livable cities in the country.

It's a wealthy town (just head out into the countryside in any direction to find estates galore) but surprisingly down-to-earth, with a strong community feeling. Coffee shops and bookstores abound near the University of Virginia, and the vibrant Downtown Mall scene teems with locals and tourists alike on summer evenings. In contrast, traffic chokes the glass-and-plastic corridor of US 29 north toward D.C., lined with shopping malls, office buildings, and supermarkets. A diverse local music scene boasts some impressive talent, and new plays and gallery shows open like dogwoods in the springtime.

HISTORY

Named in 1762 for Queen Charlotte, wife of George III, Charlottesville depended on Rivanna River trade until well into the 1800s. English soldiers and officers and Hessian mercenaries were incarcerated in barracks from 1799–1780 (the origin of the name of Barracks Rd.), and a year later Col. Banastre Tarleton raided the town intent on capturing Thomas Jefferson and other revolutionary leaders. British troops destroyed stores of tobacco and seized the county courthouse, but a heroic 40-mile ride by Capt. Jack Jouett through pitch-dark forests—on a par with Paul Revere's historic gallop—enabled Jefferson to escape.

Along with Jefferson, Charlottesville has hosted over the years James Monroe, James Madison, and the exploring duo of William Clark (born in Buena Vista) and Meriwether Lewis (born near Ivy). Though it was positioned along one of the main roads from the coast to the mountains, it remained a small town until the early 19th century. In 1822 Jefferson wrote:

In our village . . . there is a good degree of religion, with a small spice of fanaticism . . . Episcopalian and Presbyterian, Methodist and Baptist meet together . . . listen with attention and devotion to each others' preachers, and all mix in society in perfect harmony.

When Jefferson opened the University of Virginia in 1825, the town consisted of 600 people, a courthouse, a church-in-progress, and a handful of taverns. River traffic faded after the Virginia Central Railroad reached Charlottesville in 1848, and many University buildings became hospitals during the Civil War. Sheridan's troops did little damage when they occupied the town in 1865. When chartered as a city in 1888, Charlottesville's population was 4,200.

ORIENTATION

Charlottesville really has two downtown areas: the elbow of University Avenue/Main Street known as "The Corner," and the historic district around the Downtown Mall. West Main Street connects the two. The first few miles of

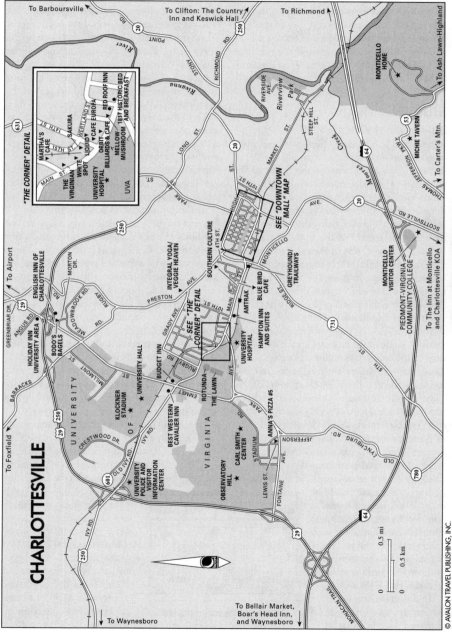

CENTRAL VIRGINIA

US 29 north toward Culpeper is crammed with shopping centers, fast-food restaurants, and service stations. Often the easiest way to get from one end of town to the other is to hop on the US 250 bypass, which loops around the northern side, or on I-64 as it cruises between Staunton and Richmond to the south.

SIGHTS

University of Virginia

In his epitaph, Thomas Jefferson wished to be remembered—right next to penning the Declaration of Independence—as the father of the University of Virginia. At the time, his idea of an "academical village" was pushing the envelope; in the guise of the first secular college in the country, Jefferson planned to bring the values and intellectual excitement of the Enlightenment to America. Ground was broken in 1819 within sight of Monticello, where in his later years Jefferson could gaze down on his pet project. The school opened in 1825 with 68 students and 10 teachers, consisting of the present-day central Lawn and surrounding buildings.

Today, UVA ("U-V-A," or simply "The University") is one of the highest-rated state universities in the country, excelling in English and its numerous graduate schools: business, law, and medicine. Most of the approximately 20,000 Cavaliers (the nickname comes from the school's nationally ranked football team) hail from northern Virginia suburbs, and competition for admission among out-of-staters is fierce. It's an interesting place that combines history and high-powered academics with a healthy dose of school spirit, leading to jokes such as: How many UVA students does it take to change a lightbulb? Three: one to change the bulb, one to hold the keg he's standing on, and another to expound on how Mr. Jefferson discovered electricity.

Tradition lives on in the fraternities and sororities clustered along Rugby

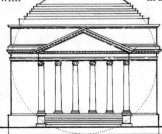

UVA's Rotunda was modeled after the Pantheon in Rome.

BOB RACE

Road, where parties reach epic proportions (one house fills its entire ground floor with sand for a beach blowout in February). In school lingo, a "freshman" is called a "first-year" and so on up the ladder—and don't let anyone hear you call the *grounds* a "campus."

But gradual change seeps in among the most entrenched traditions. Once an old-boy's club of the highest order, UVA went coed in the early '70s.

The Lawn has been declared a World Heritage Site as well as an "outstanding achievement of American architecture" by the American Institute of Architects. At the head of the grassy, sloping expanse stands the striking white dome of the Rotunda, modeled after the Pantheon in Rome. Jefferson envisioned the grounds as a living architectural museum where students couldn't help but be inspired to learn, so each of the 10 **pavilions** reflects a different classical style. Notice how they're set farther apart heading downslope, to account for perspective when seen from the Rotunda. The pavilions are still divided between professors' residences and classrooms, though now only a select few seniors—sorry, *fourth-years*—get to live in the Lawn's tiny brick rooms, which is still considered an honor even if the bathrooms are outside and around the corner. Many rooms have their own story—one occupied by Edgar Allan Poe has been sealed off with glass. Behind each is a unique garden lined by distinctive serpentine brick walls (for stability as well as beauty).

Free, lively tours are offered five times a day year-round by the University Guides, 434/924-7969, whose competitive ranks are filled in an annual competition. For more information on the University and events, call 434/924-0311 or stop by their website at www.virginia.edu.

The outstanding **Bayly Art Museum,** 434/924-3592, www.virginia.edu/~bayly/bayly.html, is a block down Rugby Road from the Rotunda. Opened in 1935, it boasts a permanent collection of art from the 15th to 19th centuries with an emphasis on American works, especially those from Jefferson's era (1775–1825). A dozen or so temporary exhibits, from Rodin to Australian aboriginal bark paintings, get floor space every year. Open Tues.–Sun. 1–5 P.M., free.

Downtown Mall

Charlottesville's pedestrian mall on W. Main Street between 2nd Street East and 6th Street East has become an example for similar structures around the country. Trees, fountains, benches, and whimsical statues mingle with outdoor cafés, unique shops, and vendors selling everything from Mennonite bread to Rastafarian incense. The controversial addition, in the mid-1990s, of a six-screen movie theater and ice rink to the west end has turned out to be a crowd-drawing blessing in disguise, even though it opened one cross-street to traffic.

At the eastern end is the **Virginia Discovery Museum,** 434/977-1025, www.vadm.org, with hands-on science and history exhibits, including an authentic Colonial log house and a working beehive. It's open Tues.–Sat. 10 A.M.–5 P.M., Sun. 1–5 P.M.; $4 adults, $3 children under 13.

Other Downtown Sights

A few blocks off the mall sits the **Albemarle County Courthouse,** 501 E. Jefferson St. at 5th St. E, the historical hub of downtown activity since its completion in 1860. Jefferson's will and some of his correspondence are stored inside. The **McGuffey Art Center,** 201 2nd St. E. between Jefferson and Market, 434/295-7973, occupies an old school named for Dr. William McGuffey, author of the *McGuffey Eclectic Reader* series for children at the turn of the 20th century. Close to 50 artists have workshops and studios here, sharing gallery space with rotating exhibits and dance performances. Open Tues.–Sat. 10 A.M.–5 P.M., Sun. 1–5 P.M.; free.

Monuments

Robert E. Lee astride his faithful steed Traveler graces a small park at the corner of Jefferson and 1st Street East, and a dynamic **Stonewall Jackson** urges Little Sorrel forward from Jefferson and

4th Street East. The statue of **Lewis and Clark** at Main Street and Ridge Street is the subject of occasional protests for its depiction of Sacajawea (who basically kept them alive through the Louisiana Territory) in a kneeling, subservient position. **William Clark,** explorer of the Northwest territory, stands at West Main Street and Jefferson Park Avenue.

ACCOMMODATIONS
Services

Guesthouses Bed and Breakfast, 434/979-7264, fax 434/293-7791, email: info@va-guesthouses.com, www.va-guesthouses.com, arranges stays in B&Bs and private cottages throughout Albemarle County.

$50–100

The **Red Roof Inn,** 1309 W. Main St., 434/295-4333, fax 434/295-2021, is right on the corner. At the intersection of Emmet Street (US 29) and Ivy Road/University Avenue are a **Budget Inn,** 140 Emmet St., 434/293-5141, fax 434/979-4529, and the **Best Western Cavalier Inn,** 105 N. Emmet St., 434/296-8111, fax 434/296-3523.

The Tudor **English Inn of Charlottesville,** 2000 Morton Dr., 434/971-9900, fax 434/977-8008, sits in the elbow of US 29 and the Rt. 250 bypass, opposite the **Holiday Inn University Area,** 1600 Emmet St., 434/977-7700, fax 434/296-2425. Farther up 29 N, a **Super 8,** 390 Greenbrier Dr., fax 434/973-0888, also falls in this category.

$100–150

Take Monticello Avenue (Rt. 20) south past I-64 and the visitors center to reach **The Inn at Monticello,** 1188 Scottsville Rd. (Rt. 20), 434/979-3593, fax 434/296-1344, email: stay@innatmonticllo.com, www.innatmonticello.com. Built around 1850 at the foot of Monticello Mountain, this country inn roared in the 1920s with a horse racing track and swimming pool in the front yard. Twin fireplaces face each other across the main entrance room where famous gourmet breakfasts are served. Upstairs are five bedrooms, some of which

CENTRAL VIRGINIA

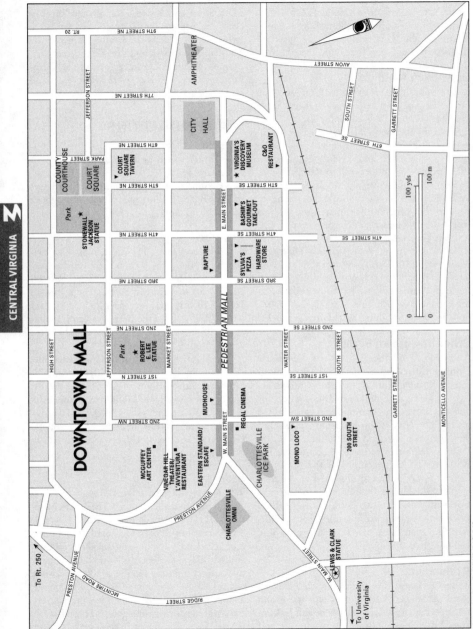

DOWNTOWN MALL

- HIGH STREET
- JEFFERSON STREET
- PARK STREET
- 9TH STREET NE
- RT. 20
- 7TH STREET NE
- 6TH STREET NE
- 5TH STREET NE
- 4TH STREET NE
- 3RD STREET NE
- 2ND STREET NE
- 1ST STREET N
- 2ND STREET NW
- W. MAIN STREET
- MARKET STREET
- PRESTON AVENUE
- MCINTIRE ROAD
- RIDGE STREET
- E. MAIN STREET
- 5TH STREET SE
- 4TH STREET SE
- 3RD STREET SE
- 2ND STREET SE
- 1ST STREET SE
- SOUTH STREET
- WATER STREET
- GARRETT STREET
- MONTICELLO AVENUE
- AVON STREET
- 6TH STREET SE
- GARRETT STREET

AMPHITHEATER

CITY HALL

COUNTY COURTHOUSE

COURT SQUARE

Park

★ STONEWALL JACKSON STATUE

★ COURT SQUARE TAVERN

★ VIRGINIA'S DISCOVERY MUSEUM

▼ C&O RESTAURANT

▼ BASHIR'S GOURMET TAKE-OUT

RAPTURE

▼ SYLVIA'S PIZZA

▼ HARDWARE STORE

Park

★ ROBERT E. LEE STATUE

PEDESTRIAN MALL

MUDHOUSE

■ REGAL CINEMA

■ MCGUFFEY ART CENTER

■ VINEGAR HILL THEATER/ L'AVVENTURA RESTAURANT

■ EASTERN STANDARD/ ESCAFE

CHARLOTTESVILLE ICE PARK

▼ MONO LOCO

● 200 SOUTH STREET

CHARLOTTESVILLE OMNI

★ LEWIS & CLARK STATUE

To Rt. 250

To University of Virginia

100 yds

100 m

0

0

© AVALON TRAVEL PUBLISHING, INC.

CENTRAL VIRGINIA

have fireplaces, private porches, and period antiques. To fill the afternoons there's croquet, a hammock, and checkers on the front porch.

$150–250

The centrally located **1817 Historic Bed & Breakfast,** 1211 W. Main St., 434/979-7353 or 800/730-7443, fax 434/979-7209, email: The1817Inn@aol.com, www.bbonline.com/va/1817, fills two townhouses built by Thomas Jefferson's master craftsman James Dinsmore, who left his mark on Monticello, Montpelier, and Poplar Forest. If anything in the convertible clutter strikes your fancy, you might be able to take it home: Candice Deloach runs the place as an antiques store too, with the help of Mississippi and Virginia, a pair of black labs. Rates include a "continental plus" breakfast, and The Tea Room Cafe serves lunch daily, featuring entrées such as tarragon chicken salad and avocado melts.

The **Omni Charlottesville,** 235 W. Main St., 434/971-5500, fax 434/979-4456, anchors the east end of the Downtown Mall. It has two pools, a fitness center, and the Virginia Wine Country Restaurant featuring local vintages. Since it was built in 1856, **200 South Street,** 800/964-7008 or 434/979-0200, fax 434/979-4403, email: southst@cstone.net, www.southstreetinn.com, has passed through various phases as a boarding house, brothel, and girls' finishing school. A columned neoclassical veranda wraps all the way around the cream-colored building, perfect for an evening cup of tea. English and Belgian antiques and a private collection of local historical photos decorate the interior. Rooms include whirlpool baths, canopy beds, and a continental breakfast.

The **Boar's Head Inn & Country Resort,** 200 Ednam Dr., 800/476-1988 or 434/296-2181, fax 434/972-6019, www.boarsheadinn.com, is on Rt. 250 two miles west of town. The 53-acre country estate has 175 rooms and suites furnished with Colonial art and reproductions overlooking green hills and a lake. Dining choices include the four-star Old Mill Room and the more casual Racquets Restaurant. A daily wine tasting is held off the main lobby. Guests have access to their famous Sport Club with its Birdwood championship golf course, a top-rated tennis facility, pool, and

gym. If this isn't enough, try an afternoon at the Just Rewards spa or a flight in a hot-air balloon. In-season rates range from $185 for a room to up to $500 for a suite. They also have bed-and-breakfast packages for $100 pp.

It's a little farther to **Keswick Hall,** 701 Club Dr., Keswick, 434/979-3440 or 800/274-5391, fax 434/977-4171, email: keswick@keswick.com, keswickhall.orient-express.com, but guests who can afford it won't be disappointed. Sir Bernard Ashley (husband of designer Laura) turned this 1912 Italianate villa into an exclusive country club/resort intended to feel like someone's home rather than a hotel. Hence there's no concierge desk, but there is a lounge with a fireplace opening onto a patio overlooking the hills rolling into the distance. Laura Ashley fabrics decorate each room in a different theme, all reflecting the couple's hobbies, such as sailing and lepidopterology (butterfly watching). Guests are spoiled with head chef Rick Small's French and Italian cuisine. Accommodations include temporary membership to the Keswick Club, boasting one of Arnold Palmer's favorite golf courses on the East Coast, tennis courts, spa, and pools. To get there, take Rt. 250 east to Shadwell, take Rt. 22 east for 1.5 miles, and follow the signs.

In the same direction off Rt. 729 is **Clifton: The Country Inn,** 1296 Clifton Inn Dr., 434/971-1800 or 888/971-1800, fax 434/971-7098, email: reservations@cliftoninn.com, www.cliftoninn.com, named by *Country Inns* magazine as one of the 12 top inns in America. The manor house was built around 1800 as an office for Thomas Mann Randolph, Thomas Jefferson's son-in-law, who liked it so much he moved in. Each of the 14 rooms is unique, and private guest cottages like the Livery, Carriage House, and Randolph's Law Office are all within a stone's throw of the Rivanna River. A lap pool flows into a waterfall near the hot tub and clay tennis court. The *Washington Post* calls Chef/Innkeeper Craig Hartman's nightly five-course gourmet dinners "stunning."

Camping

The **Charlottesville KOA,** 3825 Red Hill Rd., 434/296-9881, is on Rt. 708 south of the city.

You can get there via I-64 east exit 118A and US 29 south, or I-64 west exit 121 and Rt. 20 south. It's open Mar.–Oct., with full hookup sites for $20–27 and cabins for $34.

FOOD

On the Corner

Two UVA alumni opened the smoothie bar and sandwich shop **Liquid,** 104 14th St. W., 434/295-3775, a vegetarian café with a brain-freezing array of fruit smoothies. Sandwiches like roasted red pepper hummus on wheat fall in the $5 range, accompanied by homemade soups (try the ginger and apple with squash), wheatgrass shots, and soya milk chai. If you need a boost, ask for an extra shot of ginseng, kava-kava, or St. John's Wort in your Energizer or Mood Enhancer. Open Mon.–Fri. 8 A.M.–10 P.M., Sat. 10 A.M.–10 P.M., Sun. 11 A.M.–8 P.M. Across 14th Street is **Sakura,** 105 14th St., 434/923-3339, a Japanese restaurant and sushi bar with daily lunch specials ($6–8) and dinner entrées for $10–16. Udon and soba noodles dishes run $7–10, with yakitori and other appetizers for $4–6.

Just around the corner, **Cafe Europa,** 1331 W. Main St., 434/295-4040, offers a Greek version of light, healthy fare, with soups, salads, sandwiches, and baklava served daily for all meals. The vibe is relaxed at the **Mellow Mushroom,** 1509 W. Main St., 434/972-9366, where calzones, subs, salads, and "monumental" hoagies are turned out for $6–8. The popular spot specializes in pizzas ($7–20) with such creative titles as Kosmic Karma and Gourmet White, and there's sidewalk seating in the summer.

Martha's Cafe, 11 Elliewood Ave., 434/971-7530, has healthy, vegetable-heavy entrées inside and on the patio of a charming old house. Don't miss the goldfish in the bathtub or the spinach-crab soup that's just one choice for lunch (served daily) for $5–7. Dinner entrées ($10) such as herbed chicken linguine are served Wed.–Sat. At the end of the same street, the **Buddhist Biker Bar & Grill,** 434/971-9181, has a contemporary menu with a wry twist. Lamb lentil chili, duck tacos, and the "Big ol' hunk of beef" (ribeye) are $10–14, served on the brick

patio and on two outdoor decks in nice weather. Open daily for dinner.

The Virginian, 1521 W. Main St., 434/984-4667, is Charlottesville's oldest restaurant. It's been a keystone of The Corner since 1921 and still offers the same dependable eats and beer as always. Entrées start at $9 for pasta and include an $11 catfish platter and $13 filet mignon. Sandwiches, soups, and quiches run $5–6, as do steamed mussels and eggplant brochette appetizers. Open daily for lunch and dinner. By now we've left the realm of the heart-friendly, but that's the attraction of the **White Spot,** 1407 University Ave., 434/295-9899. This quintessential greasy spoon is famous for its Gusburger, topped by a fried egg and usually devoured at 2 A.M. during the stumble home. Open daily for all meals.

West Main Street

Down West Main is **Southern Culture,** 633 W. Main St., 434/979-1990, true to its roots with baked Virginia ham, Georgia peach cobbler, and sweet potato pie. Cajun and Caribbean influences put jambalaya and jerk pork on the menu—served leisurely but worth the wait. A popular bar almost fills the first floor. Open daily for breakfast and dinner.

Another few steps brings you to the **Blue Bird Cafe,** 625 W. Main St., 434/295-1166, a good place for a sunny California-style lunch on the front patio. Jumbo salads, veggie burgers, and tuna steaks barely leave room for homemade desserts like chocolate bourbon pecan pie. Open Mon.–Fri. for lunch, dinner daily, and Sunday brunch.

Downtown Mall

Asian-leaning fusion fare is the idea at **Eastern Standard,** 434/295-8668, where pomegranate lamb chops and other entrées are $15–22 for dinner Wed.–Sat. It's on the second floor above **Escafe,** which is more economical but just as stylish. (The bar is a choice spot for people-watching.) Appetizers like spicy sesame noodles are $2–8, followed by pasta and chicken entrées for $7–14. Open for dinner Tues.–Sun. A lot of research went into creating the ultimate coffeehouse, resulting in the **Mudhouse,** 213 W. Main

St., 434/984-6833, with comfy sofas, Internet computer, and live music some weekend nights.

Relative newcomer **Rapture,** 303 E. Main St., 434/293-9526, leads the pack of pricey nouvelle cuisine eateries that have started to take over the Downtown Mall (including **Bizou, Metropolitan,** and **Oxo**), offering eclectic Asian dishes such as Thai, peanut, and dragon noodle bowls ($7–8). Steaks and fish and chips round out the menu. In back the atmosphere borders on bordello, with pool tables and red velvet around a modish bar. Open daily 11 A.M.–2 A.M.

Sylvia's Pizza, 310 E. Main St., 434/977-0162, has the best pizza on the mall; order it by the slice or a whole pie. Just next door is the **Hardware Store,** 316 E. Main St., 434/977-1518, a real (former) hardware store more than a century old. Shelves perch over the old-time soda fountain and condiments are served in a tool box. An encyclopedia of inexpensive sandwiches ($4–6) fills the menu, along with meter beers, sundaes galore, crepes, and knishes. **Bashir's Gourmet Take Out,** 414 E. Main St., 434/923-0927, was twice voted Best Ham in New York City for its apricot-glazed ham sandwich, served on a roll with a slice of brie. Other dishes show Greek, Hungarian, Algerian, and Brazilian influences. Open Mon.–Sat. 7 A.M.–7 P.M.

The Pepsi sign out front doesn't seem to promise much, but the **C&O Restaurant,** 515 E. Water St., 434/971-7044, across from the old train station, is often called the best in town. Brick walls and worn wood floors give this former railroad flophouse the feel of an old country home, the perfect setting for innovative (but not overly expensive) French cooking. Try an appetizer like wild mushrooms in puff pastry ($4–9) before digging into a Cuban steak or rockfish baked in parchment ($12–18). Open Mon.–Fri. for lunch, daily for dinner. Down Water Street is **Mono Loco,** 200 W. Water St., 434/979-0688, a colorful slice of Cuba. Lobster conch fritters and other appetizers run $6–7, with roasted pork and corn tamales for $9–16 for dinner. Don't miss the Crazy Monkey cookies for dessert. Open Mon.–Fri. for lunch and dinner and Sunday brunch.

On the other side of the Mall, the **Court Square Tavern,** 500 Court Square at 5th and Jef-ferson Sts., 434/296-6111, offers tavern favorites like shepherd's pie and a brewer's bible of beers in an atmosphere fitting its historic location.

Elsewhere

The **Bellair Market,** 2401 Ivy Rd., 434/971-6608, is another case where looks are deceiving. From the deli inside this Exxon gas station comes specialty sandwiches good enough to earn write-ups in *Southern Living* and *Outside* magazines. Mouthfuls like the Keswick, Montpelier, and Ednam are $4–6, with some vegetarian options. Open daily. Who knows what happened to the first four, but **Anna's Pizza #5,** 115 Maury Ave., 434/977-6228, serves some of the best in town. The family-owned place has been going for 25 years. Open daily for lunch and dinner.

Foods of All Nations, 2121 Ivy Rd., 434/296-6131, is an international gourmet grocery *par excellence,* with everything from sandwiches to sushi available to go. The **Integral Yoga Health Food Market,** 923 Preston Ave., 434/293-4111, stocks more wholesome goods, and their **Veggie Heaven** natural food café serves organic, vegetarian, and vegan dishes ($6–9) for lunch and dinner daily.

And last is a Charlottesville tradition: **Bodo's Bagel Bakery,** serving thousands of authentic New York–style "water" (i.e., boiled) bagels every day. A long line at mealtimes is a given at both locations—1418 N. Emmet St. (Rt. 20), 434/977-9598, and 505 Preston Ave., 434/293-5224—but whether you're on a budget or not, you just can't beat the bagel sandwiches for $1.50–3, famous Caesar salads, and homemade soups. Open breakfast and lunch daily.

ENTERTAINMENT

The local *C-Ville Weekly,* www.c-ville.com, is a good source for entertainment news and schedules. The Piedmont Council of the Arts operates an **Artsline,** 434/980-3366, with details on local happenings, and offers more information on their website at www.monticello.avenue.org/Arts/Piedmont.

Performing Arts

Charlottesville's premiere performance company is **Live Arts,** 609 E. Market St., 434/977-4177, www.livearts.org, with a Sept.–June schedule of theater, poetry, dance, performance art, and music. Call the **Charlottesville and University Symphony Orchestra,** 434/925-6505, for their most recent performance schedule.

At the University, the **McIntire Department of Music,** 434/924-3052, is the place to ask about shows by the Jazz Ensemble, Collegium Musicum, or various singing groups such as the University Singers and Hullabahoos. Tuesday Evening Concerts, among others, are held in the Cabell Hall auditorium, 434/924-3984. Call the **Drama Department,** 434/924-3376, for information on seasonal plays held in the Heritage Repertory Theater.

Theater

Independent cinema is the hallmark of the **Vinegar Hill Theater,** 220 W. Market St., 434/977-4911, www.vinegarhilltheater.com, which has opened a contemporary Italian restaurant called L'Avventura, 434/977-1912, open for dinner Tues.–Sat. Opened in 1912, the **Jefferson Theater,** on the Downtown Mall, 434/980-1331, has hosted the Three Stooges and Harry Houdini over the years. Now it's one of those second-run movie houses that mysteriously—but thankfully—stays in business despite only charging a few dollars per seat. The **Espresso Royale Cafe,** 1415 University Ave., 434/923-3226, holds movie screenings in its back room, where you can bake your own pizza for $5. For film times and locations in town, call 434/917-3456, or stop by their website at www.917-FILM.com.

Nightlife

For its size, Charlottesville has an astonishing amount of local musical talent. It's best known as the home of The Dave Matthews Band (and as the "next Seattle" in an often-scoffed *Newsweek* quote). Dave himself used to tend bar at Miller's, and local jazz guru John D'Earth has toured with Bonnie Raitt and Bruce Hornsby. Other star-quality resident performers include guitarist Tim Reynolds and drummer Robert Jospe.

If you only have one night to go out, catch D'Earth's jazz group on a Thursday night at **Miller's,** 434/971-8511, on the Downtown Mall—you don't often hear bop this hopping

for so little money. Red neon lights the smoky bar, which used to be a hardware store.

On the Corner is **Orbit Billiards,** 102 14th St. NW, 434/984-5707, which hosts the occasional folk or blues jam. Open daily 5 P.M.–2 P.M. **Trax,** 120 11th St. SW, 434/295-8729, has been Charlottesville's top live-music club for years, hosting everyone from Wynton Marsalis to Pavement. Tickets are available at the door, Plan 9 record stores, or Mincer's on the Corner. **Max** next door has country music and line dancing.

Sushi bar by day, musical hot-spot by night, **Tokyo Rose,** 434/295-7673, books cacophonous local groups and established indie-rockers. If you're going to catch the Next Big Thing, chances are it'll be here. The **Outback Lodge,** 917 Preston Ave., 434/979-7211, brings regional and national blues and rock to the Down Under Dance Club in Preston Plaza at Rose Hill Drive. Hidden among the fraternity mansions of Rugby Road is the **Prism Coffeehouse,** 214 Rugby Rd., 434/977-7476, www.theprism.org, a local gem that hosts national bluegrass, folk, and acoustic acts.

RECREATION

Spectator Sports

Cavalier football games at UVA's Carl Smith Center are as much a display of tradition as school spirit. Semi-formal attire is the norm, especially among the fraternities and sororities. Wait for the song after each home-team touchdown, sung (or at least hummed) to the tune of "Auld Lang Syne." A strong soccer program has turned out powerhouse teams and sent members to the Olympics. Games are held in **Klockner Stadium** next to University Hall, where you'll catch basketball games. Call 800/542-8821 or 434/924-8821 or browse the website www.virginiasports.fansonly.com for schedules.

Two major steeplechase events are held every year at **Foxfield,** 434/295-9501, about five miles out Barracks Road into the countryside after it turns into Garth Road. One event occurs the last Saturday in April, and the other on the final Sunday in September; both are full-day occasions complete with tailgate picnics, socializing, and hip-flask nipping (among Cavaliers, at least).

Outdoors

At the **Ivy Creek Natural Area,** 13 trails explore 215 acres of maples, walnut, poplars, and hemlocks. To get there, head 2.3 miles west on Hydraulic Road from US 29 north, then turn left at the fourth light; there will be a sign after another half a mile. Call the Ivy Creek Foundation, 434/973-7772, for information. **Riverview Park** borders a bend of the Rivanna River east of downtown. The paved Rivanna Greenbelt trail is part of the Rivanna Trail, a pedestrian path that circles the city. For more information on local parks and outdoor pursuits, contact the city Parks and Ground Division, 434/970-3589, or the county Department of Parks and Recreations, 434/296-5844.

For the best view of Charlottesville—as good as Monticello's, if not better—take a right turn on the way up to the historic home (see Monticello entry for directions). A steep, winding dirt road tops the next mountaintop over, where you'll find the Carter Mountain Orchard, 434/977-1833, and 360-degree views from the observation deck.

Hot-air balloon flights can be booked through the **Bear Balloon Corporation,** 434/971-1757 or 800/932-0152, email: flybehr@aol.com, www.2comefly.com, which operates in conjunction with the Boars Head Inn, or **Bonaire Charters,** 434/589-5717 or 434/293-3561. Prices are typically $135–185 pp.

Other Activities

You can carve the rink at the **Charlottesville Ice Park,** 434/817-1423, even in the middle of the Piedmont's summer swelter. Anchoring one end of the Downtown Mall, it has a skating school, hockey leagues, and public skating time along with a pro shop, rentals, and lessons. Public skating is $3 adults, $2 children under five, with skates to rent for 50 cents. A **walking tour** with the Charlottesville Historical Society, 434/296-1492, is a pleasant way to see the historic downtown area. One-hour walks leave from the McIntire Building, at 200 2nd St. NE, from Apr.–Oct. at 10 A.M. on Saturdays; suggested donation is $3 pp. **Extreme Sports,** 434/975-1900, in the Berkmar Crossing Shopping Center up Rt. 29 North, rents kayaks and mountain bikes for $35 per day.

SHOPPING

The Downtown Mall has Charlottesville's best browsing-per-block quotient. Here you'll find **Copernicus,** 100 E. Main St., 434/296-6800, with a wide range of brain-rousing children's toys, and **Vivian's Art to Wear,** 301 E. Main St., 434/977-8908, which sells clothes, sculpture, and other crafts from regional artists. The front section of the **Hardware Store** restaurant, 434/977-1518, is a mini-mall complete with confectioner, bookstore, and small shops selling Mexican art and jewelry.

Stop by the **Signet Gallery,** 212 5th St. NE, 434/296-6463, for ceramics, wood, leather, and glass goods, and if you have room in your luggage for an oriental rug, try the **Sun Bow Trading Co.,** 401 E. Main St., 434/293-2159. For a great selection of Virginia wine and good advice on choosing, visit the **Market Street Wineshop and Gourmet Grocery,** 311 E. Market St., 434/979-9463.

The **Charlottesville City Market** is open in the spring and summer from 7 A.M.–noon in the H&R Block parking lot on Water Street It's also held at Central Place on the Downtown Mall on Wednesdays from 7:30 A.M.–1:30 P.M.

EVENTS

Mid-April's **Dogwood Festival** is Charlottesville's largest. For two weeks the delicate blooms are the occasion for fireworks, a carnival, barbecue, and citywide parade. Students and townspeople alike pack the grassy amphitheater at the western end of the Downtown Mall for the beer truck and live music during Charlottesville's **Fridays After Five** concerts, www.fridaysafter5.com, sponsored by the Charlottesville Downtown Foundation, 434/296-8548, www.cvilledowntown.org. Bring a blanket and a snack and get down to everything from funk and rock to blues and country. Concerts are held Apr.–Oct.

The **Monticello Wine and Food Festival** in early October starts with a seven-course Bacchanalian Feast at the Boar's Head Inn. That same month the U.Va. Drama Department holds the **Virginia Film Festival,** email:

CENTRAL VIRGINIA

filmfest@virginia.edu, www.vafilm.com, focusing on American films with a different focal theme every year (e.g., film noir or animals). Showings range from classics and Hollywood premieres to documentaries and experimental films, drawing big-name stars and critics such as Roger Ebert and Anthony Hopkins.

TRANSPORTATION

Getting Around

Charlottesville is best appreciated by foot, especially since convenient parking is at a premium. Things are a bit spread out, though, so it's a good thing the **Charlottesville Transit Service** (CTS), 434/296-7433, sends buses around the city Mon.–Sat. A fee of $2 will get you unlimited rides for a day on all CTS buses. Tickets are available at the CTS offices, 314 4th St. NW, or at the visitors center.

Free trolleys run from the Downtown Mall to The Corner and U.Va. every 15 minutes Mon.–Fri. from 6:30 A.M.–midnight. Hop aboard the **University Transit Service** to get around the U.Va. grounds. For taxi service, try **Yellow Cab**, 434/295-4131.

Getting There and Away

There's a **Greyhound/Trailways** bus terminal at 310 W. Main St., 800/231-2222. Trains leave the **Amtrak** station, 810 W. Main St., 434/296-4559, for Washington, D.C. and New York. The **Charlottesville-Albemarle Airport**, 434/973-8341, www.gocho.com, is eight miles north of town on the west side of US 29. It's served by USAir Express, Comair, Continental Express, United Express, and Colgan Air. It also has three car rental agencies: Avis, 434/973-6000; Budget, 800/527-7000; and National, 434/974-4664.

INFORMATION

The **Monticello Visitor Center**, 434/293-6789, 434/977-1786, or 877/386-1102, email: visitorcenter@ci.charlottesville.va.us, www.charlottesvilletourism.org, is just south of the intersection of Monticello Avenue (Rt. 20 south) and I-64. Among the best equipped in the state, it has a gift and book shop and a small museum on Thomas Jefferson. If you have time before you head uphill to Monticello, catch the free 30-minute film on Jefferson's life and home shown hourly. On sale is a President's Pass block ticket that covers Monticello, the Michie Tavern, and Ash-Lawn Highland for $27 adults, $13 children 6–11 (also available at each location). Open daily 9 A.M.–5:30 P.M., Sun. 11 A.M.–3 P.M.

There's also a satellite **visitors center** on the Downtown Mall at 108 Second St. SE, 434/977-6100, open daily 8 A.M.–6 P.M.

Charlottesville Vicinity

NORTH OF CHARLOTTESVILLE

Barboursville Vineyards and Historic Ruins

Virginia governor James Barbour lived here from 1810–1815, in a mansion designed by Thomas Jefferson (which accounts for the octagonal central room). It burned on Christmas Day 1884, leaving a roofless brick hulk with columns pointing skyward. The ruins are a great place for a picnic accompanied by a bottle of wine from the winery. If you can, come by in late July or early August when the Four County Players, 540/832-5355, monticello.avenue.org/fourcp,

perform their annual **Shakespeare in the Ruins** under the stars.

The winery, 540/832-3824, email: bvvy@barboursville.com, www.barboursvillewine.com, is near the intersection of Rt. 20 and Rt. 23. Open Mon.–Sat. 10 A.M.–5 P.M., Sun. 11 A.M.–5 P.M., with winery tours offered on weekends 10 A.M.–4 P.M.

Montpelier

James Madison, known as the chief proponent of the Federal Bill of Rights, was actually the third generation to make his home here on 2,700 acres of Piedmont farmland. His father built the orig-

THE INN AT LITTLE WASHINGTON

Virginia's flagship country inn sits at the main (and only) crossroads of a small village at the eastern foothills of the Blue Ridge. Washington itself, long ago prefixed by "Little" to distinguish it from the capital, was surveyed by its 17-year-old namesake in 1749 and is the only place that was named for him before he became the first president. Almost abandoned by the 20th century, Washington now brims with B&Bs and antique stores. Much of this is thanks to the Inn, which was bought in 1977 by Patrick O'Connell and Reinhardt Lynch.

After 100 years as a general store, gas station, and dance hall, the building needed some serious renovations. But the work was worth it: the Inn was the first place ever to get five stars from both the Mobil Travel Guide and AAA for its accommodations and food. One reviewer gave it five stars out of a possible four.

Flags and flowers drape the white clapboard facade of the modest two-story building. Inside, rich fabrics and wall-coverings set off the owners' collection of art and antiques. Eight rooms and two suites were decorated by a London stage designer whose drawings hang on the walls. Personal touches like framed tarot cards, crystal balls, and bouquets of flowers create a small world of exotic luxury. The rooms don't have TVs or radios, but they do have king-sized canopied beds and chilled champagne waiting at check-in. Suites have Jacuzzis and loft bedrooms; two more rooms fill detached guest houses.

It's hard to believe, then, that what the Inn is really known for is its cuisine. Chef Patrick O'Connell derives inspiration from the 18th-century portrait of French gastronome Anthelme Brillat-Savarin ("Tell me what you eat and I'll tell you what you are") in turning out meals that one critic described as "so good it makes you cry." None less than Craig Claiborne of the *New York Times* called his dinner "the most fantastic meal of my life." Something perfect from the 14,000-bottle wine cellar is only one highlight of the five-course masterpieces, whose entrees add a French zest to regional Virginia favorites like Chesapeake Bay crabmeat and wild duck. Breakfast can be served in your room or in the Terrace Room overlooking the garden, and picnic lunches are available.

The Inn is in the center of town at Middle and Main Sts., 540/675-3800, fax 540/675-3100, email: washington@relaischateaux.com. Rooms are $340–800 and suites are $550–850 (prices rise on weekends, in the month of October, and on certain other dates). Prix-fixe dinners are $90–130, served daily except Tuesday. Rooms and tables fill up months ahead (on some Saturday nights they've received 3,000 requests for only 65 seats), so book your stay as far in advance as possible. The Inn is popular for getaways, both romantic and illicit: 10 engagements happened on one Valentine's Day, and the maitre d' has likened his job to directing a French movie.

CENTRAL VIRGINIA

inal red-brick Georgian house, which Madison himself enlarged twice under the advisement of Thomas Jefferson. In 1817 he retired to Montpelier with his wife Dolly after serving four congressional terms and the fourth presidency. He died in 1836 and was buried on the property; his wife died in 1849.

In 1900 the property was purchased by William and Anna Rogers DuPont, who enlarged the house further, creating a total of 55 rooms plus added outbuildings. Their daughter Marion, one of Virginia's foremost horsewomen, took over the property in 1928 and began the well-known Montpelier Hunt Races.

Today the restored house and grounds, formally opened in 1987 by the National Trust for Historic Preservation, are a memorial to Madison's life and work. The view of the Blue Ridge Mountains is impressive, as are 2,700 acres of replanted formal gardens, pasturelands, and forests.

Montpelier, 540/672-2728, www.Montpelier.org, is just south of the town of Orange on Rt. 20 and is open daily 9:30 A.M.–5 P.M. (4:30 Dec.–Mar.); $9 adults, $4.50 children 6–11. Admission includes a short movie on Madison's life and a prerecorded audio tour of the house and grounds. The birthdays of James and Dolly Madison are celebrated on March 16 and May 20, respectively, with graveside ceremonies and receptions at the home. The **Montpelier Hunt Races** 540/627-0027, the first weekend in November features Jack Russell Terrier Races, the Dolley Madison Tailgate Competition, and the Virginia Hunt Cup.

Graves Mountain Lodge

The Graves family has offered food and lodging in Syria for almost 150 years, starting with stagecoaches crossing the Blue Ridge and now five generations later with this rustic retreat within sight of Hawksbill and Old Rag mountains. Thirty-eight motel rooms are $70–85 pp, eleven cottages and cabins cost $53–107 pp, and six rooms in an old farmhouse are $70–78 pp. Rates include three meals a day of honest farm fare served family-style at long wooden tables. Locally caught catfish and baked ham, sugar-cured on the premises, are augmented by fruits and vegetables grown on the 5,000-acre farm. For nonguests, meals are still available (breakfast $8, lunch $10, and dinners around $20), but reservations are suggested.

Here at the foot of the Blue Ridge, the opportunities for hiking and fishing are almost endless. The lodge stables, 540/923-5071, organizes horseback rides by the hour or day, and there's even a pool. Yearly events pack the place to the gills, starting with the **Spring Fling Festival** the last weekend in April. May brings the **Graves' Mountain Music Festival**— bluegrass, that is—the weekend after Memorial Day. The second and third weekends in October are claimed by the **Apple Harvest Festival,** with hayrides, apple-picking, cider-making, and country music.

Graves Mountain Lodge, 540/923-4231, fax 540/923-4132, email: info@gravesmountain.com, www.gravesmountain.com, is near Syria, reached from Rt. 231 via Rt. 670. It's open mid-Mar.–Nov.

WEST OF CHARLOTTESVILLE
Crozet

The only reason most people have heard about this tiny burg is because it's the home of **Crozet**

Pizza, Rt. 240 at Rt. 810, 434/823-2132. Owner/chef Bob Crum has been topping the best pizza in the state for 25 years, ranging from the usual (pepperoni) to the unusual (asparagus, eggplant, jalapeños). Photos of fans from around the world wearing Crozet Pizza shirts decorate the walls. Open Tues.–Sat. 3–10 P.M.; reservations are definitely recommended for dinner.

SOUTH OF CHARLOTTESVILLE
Michie Tavern

On Rt. 53 to Monticello, you'll pass this restored tavern, which was originally in Earlysville, 17 miles northwest of Charlottesville. Built by William Michie (MICK-ee) in 1784, it served stagecoach travelers for decades before falling into disrepair. In 1927, a wealthy businessman paid to have it moved here and restored.

Behind the tavern proper are reproductions of "dependencies," including a smokehouse, ice house, and root cellar. The Meadow Run grist mill is said to have seen no rest since 1797. After perusing the general store and crafts shops, try an Old Dominion vintage. Admission is $8 adults, $2 children 6–11.

If you didn't pack a lunch for your visit to Monticello, a stop at the "Ordinary" will leave you bursting at the seams. This log cabin sports original wood-beam walls and ceilings, creating the perfect atmosphere for a Colonial-style southern buffet served on pewter plates. The Tavern, 434/977-1234, www.michietavern.com, serves lunch year-round for $12 adults, $6 children 6–11.

Monticello

Even if you're not a history fanatic, you know this landmark—it's on the back of a U.S. nickel, a portrait of its creator on the flipside. If you're

© MICHIE TAVERN

into history, or architecture, or at the very least can appreciate a stunning spread, don't miss Monticello, one of the country's outstanding architectural achievements.

Monticello (mon-ti-CHELL-o) was Thomas Jefferson's pet project, which he designed, expanded, and refined over four decades. The first version of the house itself was radically redesigned after a five-year trip to France, where the future president acquired a loathing for the British-style Georgian brickwork so common to contemporary Colonial architecture. (Williamsburg's design, he wrote, was "the most wretched I ever saw.")

What took its place was a blend of the Italian style of architect Andrea Palladio and the French design of the court of Louis XVI. Eight rooms became 21, and Monticello Mark II was finished in 1809. Jefferson died here on July 4, 1826, on the 50th anniversary of the signing of the Declaration of Independence. He's buried in a family plot on the grounds.

The manor house tops a columned, classical portico with a large dome, the first of its kind in the state. Notice how the outside windows are continuous between floors, making the facade look smaller while giving it a more unified appearance. Touches of Jeffersonian whimsy fill the interior, where the first floor is open to the public. A private museum in the entrance hall holds mastodon bones, a model of the Great Pyramid of Egypt, and relics from Lewis and Clark's expedition to the Pacific Ocean. In the corner a seven-day clock has weights that slowly fall from the ceiling to the basement through a special hole in the floor.

Almost every room is a different size and shape. In the study an ingenious handwriting copier allowed Jefferson to pen two letters at once, and don't miss the view from the parlor. The president's private suite features a bed alcove open to both the dressing room and the study, allowing him to rise in either room depending on his mood and the time of day.

The estate's true kingly feel, though, comes from the grounds. More than 1,000 acres of lush gardens have been restored to their original glory, doing proud Jefferson's sentiment that "no occupation is as delightful to me as the culture of the earth, and no culture comparable to that of the garden." Service quarters in Mulberry Row were placed so as not to obscure the stunning view (Monticello means "little mountain" in Italian). Even though he called slavery an "abominable crime," Jefferson did own about 200 slaves, whose homes and lives are currently being excavated and examined.

The estate commands a hilltop three miles southeast of Charlottesville on Rt. 53 (Thomas Jefferson Pkwy.). From I-64, take exit 121 (westbound) or 121A (eastbound) to Rt. 20 South (if traveling westbound, turn south, or left, on Rt. 20); make a left on Rt. 53, just after the first stoplight. The entrance to Monticello is located on the left, approximately 1.5 miles from Rt. 20. You'll have to park at the bottom, and from there you can walk or take a shuttle bus half a mile up to house. Weekends can be crowded, but there are always picnic spots among the trees. The **Little Mountain Luncheonette** near the ticket window serves snacks from 10:30 A.M.–4 P.M., Apr.–Oct. Admission ($11 adults, $6 children 6–11) includes a 25-minute guided tour. Open daily 8 A.M.–5 P.M. (Nov.–Feb. 9 A.M.–4:30 P.M.), 434/984-9800 or 984-9822, www.monticello.org.

Ash Lawn-Highland

It seems that Jefferson's sense of style was contagious. In 1793 James Monroe, whom some historians call Jefferson's protégé, bought 1,000 acres just south of Monticello. When George Washington sent Monroe to France for three years, Jefferson hired gardeners to give his friend's orchards a jump start. From 1799–1823 Monroe lived at Highland with his family. He felt comfort in the view of Monticello to the north and borrowed from his mentor's style in designing his own house (which remained a much more modest affair).

Sadly, one year after his second term as president ended in 1825, Monroe was forced to sell Highland, where he had hoped to retire, to pay off a $75,000 debt. Subsequent owners added the name Ash Lawn in 1838 and in 1884 built a Victorian-style house next to the original building.

The College of William & Mary, Monroe's alma mater, maintains Ash Lawn-Highland as a working farm. It's 2.5 miles southeast of Monticello

CENTRAL VIRGINIA

THOMAS JEFFERSON

I have sworn upon the altar of God eternal hostility against every form of tyranny over the mind of man.

President, author of the Declaration of Independence, and potent political philosopher, Thomas Jefferson began his life on April 13, 1743, in what is now Albemarle County. When his father, surveyor and cartographer Peter Jefferson, died in 1757, Jefferson followed his father's wishes and pursued a classical education, at the College of William & Mary. In school he made friends among the faculty and local government, who introduced him to the pleasures of urbane society, as well as the law, the natural sciences, and the pursuit of knowledge for its own sake.

After a five-year study of law and admittance to the bar, Jefferson entered politics in 1769 as a member of the Virginia House of Burgesses. Relations with Britain were already sliding downhill, and Jefferson soon found himself leading Patrick Henry and others who favored strong resistance to the mother country. In 1776, as a member of the Second Continental Congress, Jefferson found an outlet for his growing intellectual radicalism and profound, passionate writing skills by drafting the Declaration of Independence.

As his country struggled to fight itself free, Jefferson tried to put the ideas of the declaration into action as governor of Virginia 1779–1781. This proved easier said than done; his Statute of Religious Freedom encountered vigorous opposition that delayed its enactment until 1786, and his lackluster performance during the British invasion of 1780–1781 inspired the editor of a local paper to label him "a coward, a calumniator, a plagiarist, [and] a tame, spiritless animal." On September 6, 1782, the worst blow fell. Martha Wayles Skelton Jefferson, with whom Jefferson had enjoyed "ten years of unchequered happiness," died soon after the birth of their sixth child. "A single event," he wrote, "wiped away all my plans and left me a blank which I had not the spirits to fill up." He never remarried.

Jefferson was able to escape somewhat on a five-year diplomatic trip to France from 1784–1789 in the company of Benjamin Franklin and John Adams, who had helped him draft the declaration. Here he wrote his only full-length book, *Notes on the State of Virginia* (1787). This volume, which answers a series of questions posed by a French diplomat on North America and its rapidly changing society, is considered by many to be one of the most insightful works of the 18th century.

After stints as secretary of state and vice president, Jefferson became the third U.S. president in 1801, narrowly defeating Aaron Burr in a close race that characterized the early polarization of American politics. In contrast to Burr's Federalists, Jefferson's Republicans supported policies claimed both by today's Democrats, in their championship of human rights and opposition to plutocracy and oligarchy, and modern Republicans, in the idea that the best federal government is small, noninterfering, and decentralized.

During his first term (1801–1805), Jefferson nearly doubled the size of the United States through the Louisiana Purchase. He originally intended to buy only a small part of the Mississippi River valley, but when a cash-poor Napoleon offered to sell everything from the Great Lakes to the Rockies and beyond for only $15 million, Jefferson jumped at the chance (even though, as he freely admitted, he had no constitutional authority to do so). Under his orders the Lewis and Clark expedition left to explore the territory, resulting in one of the greatest adventures the country has ever seen.

Jefferson's second term didn't go as well, thanks in part to growing controversy over the role of the federal government. His efforts to avoid involvement in the Napoleonic Wars led to more charges of timidity and vacillation. In 1809, deeply in debt, he handed over the reins of office to James Madison.

Jefferson's later life at Monticello gave him ample time to pursue the endless interests pushed aside by a career in politics. Over his lifetime Jefferson wrote volumes of letters that give a remarkably detailed picture of the man himself. He considered himself part of an educated gentry that owed its existence to the same public that held it responsible to govern justly. At six feet two inches tall, Jefferson was lanky, angular, and carried himself with a relaxed dignity.

Jefferson observed the construction of the University of Virginia by telescope until its opening in 1819, when he was finally able to indulge what he called his "canine appetite" for learning. He was one of the most educated men of his time—able to understand Latin, Greek, French, Spanish, Italian, and Anglo-Saxon—to the point where, at age 71, he read Plato's *Republic* in the original Greek and pronounced it overrated.

His interest in architecture left its neoclassical stamp on dozens of buildings in Virginia and Washington, D.C., and as an amateur naturalist Jefferson collected and tried to classify fossils from all over the country. Mathematics and meteorology both fascinated him, and he always had some experiment in planting going in the fields of Monticello in the hopes of improving the prosperity of American farmers.

Yet, even as almost every event of his daily life went down on paper, certain aspects of the private man have remained a mystery. In 19,000 surviving letters, for example, not one exists between him and his wife. Then there's the question of how the country's foremost champion of natural rights and the equality of man could own hundreds of slaves. His *Notes on the State of Virginia* addresses the issue most directly, calling it a "great political and moral evil." But from there Jefferson falls back on limp arguments reflecting the prevailing prejudices of his era. Arguing that blacks were inferior to whites in physical beauty, foresight, and imagination, Jefferson couldn't bring himself to imagine both races living peacefully side by side. Slavery, in his view, was a necessary evil, crucial to the economy of the state and preferable to the "dynamite of class struggle" between rich and poor white planters.

Jefferson died on July 4, 1826, the 50th anniversary of the signing of the Declaration of Independence and only hours before his friend John Adams. He lies at Monticello under the inscription:

Here was buried Thomas Jefferson, author of the Declaration of American Independence, of the Virginia Statute of Religious Freedom, and father of the University of Virginia.

© JULIAN SMITH

the famous Monticello

on Rt. 795 (James Monroe Pkwy.). A collection of period furnishings fills the main house, including some from the Monroe White House and others that were presented as gifts from South American republics in thanks for the Monroe Doctrine of noninterference in political matters. The small screens protected ladies' caked-on makeup, lard- and wax-based as was the style, from melting in the heat from the fireplace.

Keep an eye out for the chair that's been seen to rock on its own on repeated occasions. Legend says it was Monroe's favorite, so some think the spirit is his. Another story says that a nanny died in the chair when a stray spark from the fireplace caught her long hair on fire.

A gift shop and picnic tables await after a 40-minute house tour, which is included in the admission ($8 adults, $5 children 6–11). Open daily 9 A.M.–6 P.M. (Nov.–Feb. 10 A.M.–5 P.M.), 434/293-9539, email: AshLawnJM@aol.com, www.monticello.avenue.org/ashlawn. In April, period music drifts through the gardens, lit with 1,000 candles, during the **Champagne and Candlelight Tour** that coincides with Garden Week. **James Monroe's birthday** on April 28 is obviously a special day as well. The annual **Summer Festival,** 540/293-4500, starts with the Mid-Summer Eve Music Gala in late June and features outdoor opera performances and a bonfire finale in August. **Plantation Days** in July include crafts, historical reenactments, and dressage (horse dancing), and the house is lit with candles during the holidays.

Walton's Mountain Museum

Earl Hamner, Jr., based his famous TV series on vivid memories of growing up in the rural village of Schuyler during the Depression. The show won six Emmys and two Golden Globes its first year and went on to run for 211 episodes over eight more years. Fans will recognize locations like the Waltons' kitchen and living room and John-Boy's bedroom, all re-created in the Schuyler Community Center—once Hamner's own elementary school. Ike Godsey's country store now houses a gift shop. The museum, 888/266-1981 or 434/831-2000, www.the-waltons.com, is open Mar.–Nov. daily 10 A.M.–

4 P.M.; $5 adults, $4 children 6–12. To get there, take US 29 south to Rt. 6 east, go five miles, take a right and follow Rt. 800 to its end, and then a right onto Rt. 617.

Scottsville

The first seat of Albemarle County occupies a horseshoe bend in the James River, a choice location that made it the chief port above Richmond for freights and passengers during a golden era in the mid-1800s. The barges are long gone, but you can still drift downstream on a canoe or inner tube from **James River Reeling and Rafting,** 434/286-4386, email: canoetown@aol.com, www.reelingsandrafting.com. Rentals with shuttle service are $14–30 pp, and they also offer overnight camping and fishing trips for $36–70 pp. **James River Runners,** 10082 Hatton Ferry Rd., 434/286-2338, email: info@jamesriver.com, www.jamesriver.com, also run the James on canoes, kayaks, and rafts.

Wintergreen Resort

Nineteen ski slopes ranging from novice to expert has earned Wintergreen *Skiing Magazine's* title of "best ski resort in the South." Five lifts serve the 1,000-foot vertical drop of the Highlands, and there's a snowboard park and a learn-to-ski area

THE VIRGINIA GARLIC FESTIVAL

The humble, pungent bulb of *Allium sativum* is the subject of a weekend's worth of fun in mid-October at the **Rebec Vineyards,** 434/946-5168, five miles north of the town of Amherst. Virginia's most fragrant fair has 100 vendors selling garlic in just about every form imaginable, along with pony rides for children and music on four stages. Some 12,000 people turn out to see the selection of the Garlic King and Queen and the Best Garlic Costume, taste the entries in the Garlic Cook-off, and watch and wince at the garlic-eating contests. (Think you can eat three ounces of raw garlic in 30 seconds? Only three out of 40 contestants accomplished the feat one year.)

nearby. Sip a cappuccino in front of the fireplaces in the cozy stone lodge, recently improved along with other facilities to the tune of $10.5 million. Adult lift tickets are $35–47 or $20–25 at night. Ski rentals are $26–30 adults, $20–25 children (snowboards are $25–35), and private lessons are $80 for two adults for one hour.

Two outstanding golf courses (one designed by Rees Jones) draw guests during the summer, along with 25 tennis courts, six pools, and 20-acre Lake Monocan. You can rent bikes, horses, and ponies, or simply hike from the nature center along 30 miles of trail operated by the Wintergreen Nature Foundation. The Wintergarden Spa has hot tubs, a Jacuzzi, saunas, and workout rooms. Dining options include the **Copper Mine Restaurant and Lounge** and the **Devils Grill.** The Out of Bounds Adventure Center boasts facilities for paintball, rock climbing, basketball, in-line skating, volleyball, and skateboarding. Rental choices include hundreds of mountaintop villas and dozens of slopeside homes, most of which have kitchens and fireplaces.

Wintergreen, 800/266-2444, www.wintergreenresort.com, is on Rt. 644, off Rt. 151 south of Nellysford. You can also get there from the Blue Ridge Parkway via the Reeds Gap exit at milepost 13.

Lynchburg and Vicinity

Virginia's classic tobacco town goes by a few different monikers. As the "City of Seven Hills," Lynchburg (pop. 66,000) bulges with lofty historic districts and stately inns. As the center of Virginia's conservative religious heartland, it's also called the "City of Churches," with more than 130 houses of worship as well as Jerry Falwell's Liberty University, Dial-the-Bible listings in the White Pages, and radio preachers who end every sentence in "-uh." Even its tourist slogan "The Real Virginia" rings true thanks to Lynchburg's combination of the new—ideas debated in several medium-sized colleges—and the old—Thomas Jefferson's Poplar Forest and Appomattox Court House, both nearby.

HISTORY

After earning his freedom from a wealthy Quaker planter, indentured Irish servant Charles Lynch went on to marry the boss's daughter and build the town's first warehouses and commercial buildings on land he had acquired along the upper James River. In 1757, his son John set up a ferry terminal at the bottom of today's 9th Street, and Lynchburg was off and running as a regional commercial center.

Trade poured in along the river itself, the James River and Kanawha Canal from Richmond, and railroads from Petersburg and Alexandria. A dark, coarse-leafed local variety of tobacco soon became the area's main cash crop. Farmers humming popular songs like "Goin' Down to Lynchburg Town To Carry My Tobacco Down" brought huge hogsheads in from surrounding fields to dozens of warehouses along the riverbanks. Small boats called *bateaux*, usually manned by a trio of skilled, brawny slaves, waited on the water to take the containers to Richmond.

By the mid-19th century, Lynchburg was second only to New Bedford, Massachusetts, in per capita income nationwide (whale oil still brought in more money than tobacco). Soon more than 30 million pounds of tobacco were passing through the city's warehouses every year. Lynchburg served as a major Confederate storage depot during the Civil War and as one of four quartermaster (horse) depots in the Confederacy. On June 18, 1864, Gen. Jubal Early narrowly managed to save the city from destruction by running empty trains back and forth with much noise and commotion, convincing Union generals that imaginary rebel reinforcements had arrived.

The tobacco trade carried Lynchburg into the early 20th century, but as demand slackened, the city turned to its wealth of antiquity to lure visitors. Many antebellum houses marred by mid-century neglect have been restored as homes and offices.

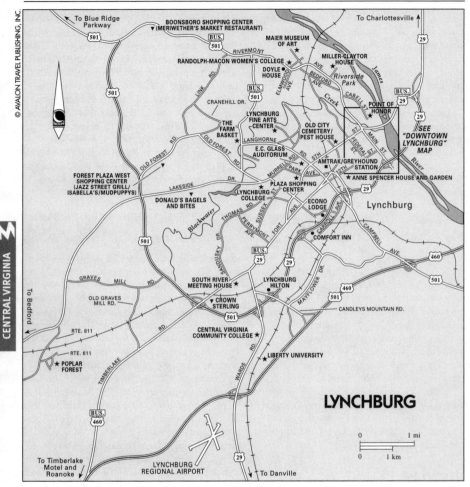

Lynchburg

LYNCHBURG

0   1 mi

0   1 km

SIGHTS

Five of Lynchburg's seven hills are now historic districts near the river. Two Baptist church spires bookend **Court House Hill,** where the 139 steps of **Monument Terrace** lead past a row of war memorials to the steps of the **Old City Court House Museum,** 901 Court St., 434/847-1459. The dome-capped Greek Revival temple was used from 1855–1955 and displays a working clock made in Boston in 1925 with weights that drop through hollow

columns in front. It was opened in 1976 as a local history museum entered through the restored Hustings Courthouse. Exhibits range from native Monacan tribes to life in Lynchburg during the tobacco boom. Open daily 10 A.M.–4 P.M.; $1 pp over 12.

Many of the grand houses on **Diamond Hill** were built during Lynchburg's golden age near the turn of the 20th century. Once one of the city's most exclusive neighborhoods, Diamond Hill embraces a wealth of architectural styles, including Queen Anne and Greek, Gothic, and Geor-

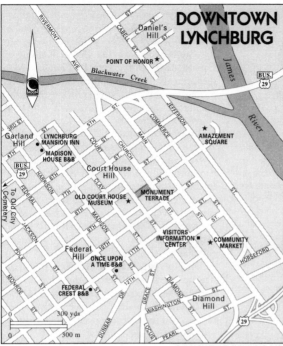

DOWNTOWN LYNCHBURG

© AVALON TRAVEL PUBLISHING, INC.

M

CENTRAL VIRGINIA

campus of Randolph-Macon Women's College. An impressive collection of 19th- and 20th-century American works includes paintings by Edward Hopper, Winslow Homer, and Georgia O'Keefe. Open Wed.–Sun. 1–4 P.M. (off-season Tues.–Sun. 1–5 P.M.); free.

The **Old City Cemetery,** open daily dawn to dusk, came into use in 1806. A loop trail starting at Taylor and 4th streets passes ancient family plots, Revolutionary War graves, and the final resting place of Blind Billy, a local street musician and former slave whose freedom was paid for by Lynchburg residents. Beyond the Confederate section, containing 2,200 soldiers from 14 states, you'll find butterfly and medicinal herb gardens, a lotus-studded goldfish pond, and a row of 60 varieties of antique roses from the 16th to 19th centuries. The Cemetery Center includes the **Museum of 19th Century Mourning Customs,** open daily 11 A.M.–3 P.M.

Along the path is the **Pest House Medical Museum,** once the medical office of local physician John J. Terrell. During the Civil War, Dr. Terrell turned it into a "House of Pestilence" for his experiments isolating victims of smallpox and measles. The 1840s building, viewed through glass doors, contains medical tools from the era, including an amputation kit, "asthma chair," and "poison chest" (presumably for medicines). You can take a self-guided audio tour outside, but the inside is open only by prior appointment. Call the Lynchburg visitors center for information.

At the **Anne Spencer House and Garden,** 1313 Pierce St., 434/845-1313, www.lynchburgbiz.com/anne_spencer, the Lynchburg poetess who wrote of love and reverence of beauty in mankind and nature is memorialized in her home and the gardens that inspired many of her stanzas. Spencer (1882–1975) is considered part of the

gian revival. **Federal Hill** to the west was Lynchburg's first residential suburb, filled with Federal-style homes along steep, dead-end streets. Once known as Quality Row as it passed through the **Garland Hill** district, Madison Avenue is still partially paved in century-old brick.

On the far side of Blackwater Creek rises **Daniel's Hill,** dominated by the octagonal bay facade of **Point of Honor,** 112 Cabell St., 434/847-1459, www.pointofhonor.org. Built in 1815 by Dr. George Cabell, Sr. (doctor to Patrick Henry, among other revolutionary figures), the Federal mansion is named for duels once fought over matters of principle on this bluff over the James. Among other activities, cooking demonstrations are given in a reconstructed kitchen. Open daily 10 A.M.–4 P.M., with admission ($4 pp over 12) including a guided tour.

A few blocks farther up the James you'll find the **Maier Museum of Art,** 1 Quinlan St., 434/947-8136, www.rmwc.edu/maier, on the

THE BEALE TREASURE

Virginia's best-known lost fortune is said to consist of close to 3,000 pounds of gold, 5,000 pounds of silver, and thousands of dollars in jewels. Some say it's a hoax, but hundreds of hopeful treasure hunters would like to believe otherwise.

In 1817, a party of 30 Virginians led by Thomas Jefferson Beale left to try their luck mining in Colorado. They struck a rich vein of gold and silver in the south-central part of the state, which they worked for a year and a half before the accumulating wealth started to make some uncomfortable. Beale and eight others were sent back to Virginia to bury two truckloads of nuggets while the others stayed and mined.

The party arrived at Goose Creek in Bedford County in November 1818, following a faint trail through a gap in the Blue Ridge foothills near the Peaks of Otter. Snow covered their tracks as they dug a square pit six feet deep, lined it with flat stones, and placed inside iron cooking pots filled with treasure. The last concealing spadeful fell in December, and within two months they had rejoined their comrades.

After two more years of mining, Beale led another trip back to the same spot and a second load joined the first. This time he decided to leave a message for his partners in Colorado in case something happened to his group on the return. Three numerical ciphers detailing the location of the hoard, the contents of the vault, and the name of the party were put in a strongbox and given to Lynchburg innkeeper Robert Morris, with instructions to open it if no one returned in 10 years.

Beale and his crew left once more for Colorado, and Morris never saw any of them again. Two months later he received a letter saying the keys to the code were in the mail, and then nothing. As the years passed, Morris gradually forgot about the strongbox, until he happened upon it decades later while searching for a harness in a shed. After trying for years to decipher the codes, Morris showed them to a friend, who managed to break the one describing the vault using a key based on the Declaration of Independence. The other two were made public but remain a mystery despite the efforts of decoding experts and computer codebreakers.

Harlem Renaissance and is the only Virginian included in the *Norton Anthology of Modern American and British Poetry*. While living here she entertained visitors like George Washington Carver, Martin Luther King, Jr., Thurgood Marshall, and W.E.B. DuBois, when she wasn't composing in the small garden cottage she called Edenkraal. Open Mon.–Sat. 10 A.M.–4 P.M.; $5 adults, $2 children under 12.

Amazement Square, 27 9th St., 434/845-1888, is a new hands-on learning center oriented toward kids, but exhibits with names like "Your Amazing Body" and "Once Upon a Building" might end up intriguing grownups as well. At the center of the building is a four-story agglomeration of tunnels, stairs, and paths called the Amazement Town. Open Tues.–Sat. 10 A.M.–5 P.M., Sun. and Mon. 1–5 P.M., $3.50 adults, $4 children under 13.

The city's first house of worship (1757) still stands as the **South River Meeting House,** 5810 Fort Ave., 434/239-2548, also called the Quaker Meeting House. It's open daily 9 A.M.–3 P.M. for free, and tours can be given with a few days' prior notice.

Parks and Natural Areas

Daniel's Hill continues upriver into **Riverside Park**—look for a sign along Rivermont at the Virginia School of the Arts building. Trails along the hillside lead to the keel of the packet boat the *John Marshall,* typical of the 19th-century craft that were pulled by mules as far as Richmond. This particular one carried Stonewall Jackson's body to Lexington for burial.

Three hundred acres along **Blackwater Creek Natural Area** as it snakes through downtown Lynchburg from Cabell Street to Old Forest Road have been set aside, enclosing the 155-acre Ruskin Freer Nature Preserve and interlaced by bicycle and foot trails along old railroad beds. To find the northern end of the seven-mile Creekside Trail, take Rivermont Road to Bedford Road and then Hollins Mill Road, following this 0.7 mile to a parking lot at Hollins Mill Dam. Another entrance off Rivermont follows signs along Elmwood Avenue, Woodland Avenue, and E. Randolph Place.

For more information on parks in the area, contact the Lynchburg Park and Recreation Department at 301 Grove St., 434/847-1640.

ACCOMMODATIONS

$50–100

Two of Lynchburg's most economical hotels are the **Econo Lodge,** 2400 Stadium Dr., 434/847-1045 or 800/553-2666, and the **Timberlake Motel,** 11222 Timberlake Rd., 434/525-2160 or 800/289-4201.

Children are welcome at **Once Upon a Time,** 1102 Harrison St., 434/845-3561, since the owners have four daughters themselves. A different fairy tale theme decorates each bedroom, from the Frog Prince Room to the Three Bears Suites, and guests can write their own tales in the blank journals while relaxing in a clawfoot tub. The French Second Empire mansion was built in 1874 atop Federal Hill by the brother-in-law of the city's first millionaire, so he could overlook his factories.

Also in this price range are a **Hampton Inn,** 5604 Seminole Ave., 434/237-2704, fax 434/239-9183, and a **Comfort Inn,** 3125 Albert Lankford Dr., 434/847-9041, fax 434/847-8513.

$100–150

In the Garland Hill district stands the **Madison House Bed and Breakfast,** 413 Madison St., 877/901-1503 or 434/528-1503, email: info@madisonhousebb.net, www.madisonhousebb.com, an Italianate Victorian mansion built for a tobacco baron in the 1880s. Beautiful wrought-iron porch decorations and leaded glass in the front door window are only the beginning. Inside you'll find a library with volumes dating to the 18th century, crystal chandeliers, and original china bathroom fixtures from the early 1900s. Meals come on Limoges and Wedgwood china, and tea is served every day at 4 P.M.

Just next door stands the **Lynchburg Mansion Inn,** 405 Madison St., 800/352-1199 or 434/528-5400, mansioninn@aol.com, www .lynchburgmansioninn.com, built in 1914 for James Gilliam, president of six banks, five coal firms, and the Lynchburg Shoe Company. The manor is one of Virginia's finest Spanish Georgian buildings, featuring 22 columns under a 105-foot veranda, rich cherry woodwork in the cavernous Grand Hall, and a three-story oak and cherry staircase with more than 200 balustrades. Four rooms and two suites include use of the five-person spa out back.

The **Federal Crest Inn,** 1101 Federal St., 800/818-6155 or 434/845-6155, fax 434/845-1445, email: inn@federalcrest.com, www.federalcrest.com, commands a stately view from the top of Federal Hill, especially from the Eagle's Nest Theater on the third floor, built as a stage for the original owner's children (and now home to a large-screen TV). Seven fireplaces, each with a unique mantel, are spread throughout the house, which has five guest rooms with down comforters and gas-log fireplaces.

FOOD

Snacks and Starters

The **Lynchburg Community Market,** 434/847-1499, is the place for picnic fixings, baked goods, and exotic takeout. It's been open since 1783 (current hours daily 7 A.M.–2 P.M.). Just inside the entrance, **Moore's at the Market** serves a no-frills breakfast from $2–3. **The Farm Basket,** 2008 Langhorne Rd., 434/528-1107, offers box lunches and healthy fare along the lines of cucumber sandwiches on fresh-baked bread. The small eatery is open for lunch Mon.–Sat. At **Donald's Bagels and Bites,** 2225 Lakeside Dr., 434/385-9277, you can find breakfast bagels, pastries, salads, and sandwiches along with scrumptious pies, cakes, and cheesecakes. Open Mon.–Sat. for breakfast and lunch from 6:30 or 7 A.M.

More Substantial

New Orleans cooking lives in Lynchburg at the **Jazz Street Grill,** 434/385-0100, in the Forest Plaza West Shopping Center. Louisiana favorites like catfish and Cajun popcorn shrimp ($8–14) share the menu with $6–7 po' boys and andouille sausage sandwiches. Try a Deep South microbrew while enjoying the live weekend entertainment. Open daily for lunch and dinner. Next door is **Isabella's,** 434/385-1660, a trattoria serving the cuisine of northern Italy in a casually upscale atmosphere. Lunch plates—soups, pizzas, and panini sandwiches—are $7–8, and dinner entreés are $14–18, slightly less for pasta. They specialize in brick-oven cooking; try the stuffed Portobello appetizer or the oven-roasted oysters. Open Mon.–Fri. for lunch and Mon.–Sat. for dinner.

Crown Sterling, 6120 Fort Ave. at US 501, 434/239-7744, bills itself as "Central Virginia's Oldest Fine Dining Restaurant," serving aged beef charcoal-grilled to perfection for dinner Mon.–Sat. Steaks, chicken, and seafood entreés run $12–24, including teriyakis, grilled swordfish, and filets galore. A contemporary contrast comes in the form of **Meriwether's Market Restaurant,** 434/384-3311, in the Boonsboro Shopping Center. This cheery, moderately upscale bistro is run by the same folks as Isabella's, offering various soup/salad/sandwiches combinations for $6–7 (try the orzo salad and oyster spinach bisque) and healthy, Mediterranean-style entreés for $14–21 during dinner. Lynchburg's best wine list and dozens of beers compliment a hand-crafted bar near a small market selling various cooking concoctions. Open for lunch Mon.–Sat. and dinner daily, with live jazz on Wednesday.

ENTERTAINMENT

Nightlife

Cattle Annie's, 4009 Murray Pl., 434/846-3206, features both kinds of music—country *and* western—and a 4,500-square-foot dance floor. Wednesday is family night, and Friday is ladies' night. Patrons of **Mudpuppy's Pub and Sports Emporium,** 434/385-4304, in the Forest Plaza West Shopping Center, can choose from 10 TVs usually showing sports, a beer at the bar, and live blues on Friday and Saturday nights until 2 A.M. The **Jazz Street Grill,** 434/835-0100, in the Forest Plaza West Shopping Center, sounds like Dixieland on weekends.

Fine Arts

One of the oldest continuous community theater groups in America, the **Lynchburg Fine Arts Center,** 1815 Thompson Dr., 434/846-8451, presents pop chorus concerts, resident ballet company shows, and assorted children's performances

year round. Two free galleries show changing exhibits. The **Lynchburg Symphony Orchestra,** 621 Court St., 434/845-6604, puts on seven concerts per year at the Lynchburg City Stadium or the E.C. Glass Auditorium. Call **Lynchburg College,** 1501 Lakeside Dr., 434/544-8100, for details on events at the Dillard Fine Arts Building, and the Daura and Dillard galleries.

SHOPPING

Two dozen antique shops sell bits and pieces of Lynchburg's rich history, from Victorian hatpins to antique linens. Many are along Main Street, like **Haleys,** 1024 Main St., 434/528-1329; **Scarlet's Main Street Antique Mall,** 1026 Main St., 434/528-0488; and **Sweeney's Curious Goods,** 1220 Main St., 434/846-7839. In the Boonsboro Shopping Center, **Pheasant's Eye,** 434/384-3568, displays and retails works by local and regional artists, including photographs, pottery, handblown glass, clothing, and lamps.

The Farm Basket shopping complex, 2008 Langhorne Rd., 434/528-1107, is a fun collection of shops offering art, flowers, jewelry, and crafts. Wander around inside to unearth the gems offered at places such as **Farm Basket Papers,** featuring unique stationery, and **Virginia Handicrafts Inc.,** with kaleidoscopes, games, and paintings. Then take a break on the deck overlooking Blackwater Creek with a box lunch from the food shop (and don't miss the homemade foods like apple butter and hot pepper jelly).

EVENTS

At the end of April, the **Celtic Festival,** 434/297-5080, features music, crafts, vendors, and Scottish games. The Community Market rings with music and smells like supper during **Friday Cheers,** with live music and drinks in the early evening from May–Aug., and the **Thomas Jefferson Tomatoe Faire** in early August, commemorating the founding father's first taste of the feared fruit (which was once thought to be poisonous).

In June the **James River Bateaux Festival** brings a week of one of the East Coast's most unusual waterborne celebrations, centered on reproductions of 18th-century shallow-draft merchant boats. Each 60-foot craft could carry up to 20 tons of goods to Richmond and back much faster than horses and wagons. A few were discovered near Richmond in the early 1980s, allowing carpenters to rebuild the time-tested design. The festival follows the river, stopping at towns along the way for various activities.

The **James River Blues Festival** arrives at the Riverfront in mid-August, and September's **Kaleidoscope** starts with the Italian Festival of the Seven Hills and keeps going the entire month. Kaleidoscope is Lynchburg's main fall celebration and involves everything from a barbecue jamboree and bike race to a teddy bear parade and bocce ball tournament, plus the usual concerts, crafts, and cooking.

TRANSPORTATION

Getting Around

The **Greater Lynchburg Transit Company,** 434/847-7771, serves the city and surrounding area from its main terminal at the Plaza Shopping Center.

Getting There and Away

The **Lynchburg Regional Airport,** 434/582-1150, is eight miles south of downtown on US 29. It's served by USAir Express, United Express, and Atlantic Southeast Airlines/Delta. Airport Limo, 434/239-1777, will take you into town, or you can rent a car from Avis, Budget, or Hertz. The Crescent line between New York and New Orleans stops at the local **Amtrak** station, 434/847-8247, at Kemper Street at Park Avenue, daily. **Greyhound/Trailways,** 434/846-6614, has moved to the same building.

INFORMATION

For walking-tour brochures and advice on anything in the region, stop by the **Lynchburg Visitors Information Center,** 216 12th St., 800/532-7821 or 434/847-1811, email: RealVA@aol.com. Open daily 9 A.M.–5 P.M. the **Lynchburg Regional Chamber of Commerce,** 2015 Memorial Ave., 434/845-5966, email: info@lynchburgchamber.org, www.lynchburg chamber.org, is another good resource, as is Lynchburg Online, www.lynchburgonline.com.

THOMAS JEFFERSON'S POPLAR FOREST

In 1773 Thomas Jefferson inherited a 4,812-acre working tobacco farm from his father-in-law, providing the future president with a welcome source of cash income. In 1806 he laid the foundation there for a house he would come to cherish even more than Monticello: a year-round retreat from that "curiosity of the neighborhood," which had already become a magnet for visitors. Eventually Jefferson was making the three-day ride from his official residence three or four times a year and staying here anywhere from two weeks to two months at a time.

Poplar Forest was sold at Jefferson's death and became a private home. In 1984 it was bought by a nonprofit organization that began restoration in the early 1990s. Restoration is an ongoing process; as of 2001 the interior was finished but mostly unfurnished, emphasizing the simple, classical lines of the structure itself. Guided tours are included with admission.

A winding gravel drive leads to the north portico of the house, which forms a perfect octagon reflected in the shape of two brick privies on the opposite side. Similarities to Monticello appear in the skylight over the 20-foot central room, alcove beds, and the three-piece windows that fill the parlor with light from floor to ceiling. Twin earth mounds on either side of the house were formed during the leveling of the lawn and once planted with aspens and weeping willows—two of 14 species that graced the property.

To reach Poplar Forest, 804/525-1806, www.poplarforest.org, head south on VA 811 from US 221, then take a left on VA 661 (Bateman Bridge Rd.) and follow the signs. It's open Apr.–Nov. daily 10 A.M.–4 P.M.; $7 adults, $1 children 6–16 (grounds only $3 pp). The Hands-on History tent, open daily 11 A.M.–2 P.M. in summer, allows kids to learn Colonial-era skills such as writing with a copy of Jefferson's polygraph and using a drop spindle.

BEDFORD

The self-proclaimed "World's Best Little Town" lost a larger percentage of its population to the horrors of World War II than any other community in the country; 21 of 35 local boys sent to Europe were killed in the landing at Normandy. This explains why the otherwise unremarkable town was chosen as the location for the **National D-Day Memorial,** 800/351-3329, 540/586-3329, www.dday.org, dedicated in 2001. Set on a hilltop, the memorial re-creates the beach landing down to sculptures of fallen soldiers and jet fountains that simulate bullets pinging off metal and cratering the reflecting pool. A large arch is striped like Allied planes, and walls record the names of the dead. A D-Day Memorial Educational Center is planned for 2004. The memorial is near the intersection of the US 460 bypass and VA 122, open Tues.–Sun. 10 A.M.–5 P.M., $10 per vehicle.

Bedford is also home to the inimitable **Holy Land USA,** 1060 Jericho Rd., 540/586-2823, www.holyland.pleasevisit.com, a curious mix of faith and farming on the property of retired supermarket owner Bob Johnson. Sheep graze and geese waddle among life-sized dioramas depicting the life of Jesus and scenes from the Bible using unmistakable imagery: the wise man's house stands firm on a rock, while the foolish man's house built on sand is a pile of scrap. A three-mile trail into placid fields passes old farm machinery and enough Bible quotations for a month of Sundays.

Holy Land USA is three miles west on Dickerson Mill Rd. (Rt. 746) from Rt. 122 just south of town, open daily 9 A.M.–5 P.M.; free.

APPOMATTOX COURT HOUSE NATIONAL HISTORIC PARK

Following the falls of Petersburg and Richmond in early April 1865, Robert E. Lee led his exhausted Army of Northern Virginia on a fighting retreat west. The goal was to link up with Gen. Joseph Johnston and his Army of Tennessee in Danville, but Ulysses S Grant's forces harried the Rebels at every step. On April 6, the Battle of Saylor's Creek cost 7,000 Confederate casualties and one-third of the remaining ranks captured, including Lee's son Custis and seven other generals. Two days later, Lee answered Grant's re-

Holy Land USA

quest for a discussion of surrender, though saying he would rather "die a thousand deaths."

On Sunday morning, April 9, the two generals met in the parlor of Wilmer McLean's humble home in Appomattox Court House. The terms of surrender were quickly written up—the Confederates would be allowed to return home unmolested, all could keep their horses and officers their sidearms—and Lee signed the paper, ending four years of bloodshed and chaos. At a ceremony on April 12, the ragtag Rebel army laid down its flags and weapons and each man was handed a hastily printed parole. "The war is over," said Grant, prohibiting any celebration among his troops out of respect. "The rebels are our countrymen again." Instead he ordered his men to present arms to their former enemies, who returned the salute in kind.

The McLean House was dismantled in 1893 amid plans to ship it to the capital and rebuild it as part of a war museum, but this never happened and the pieces lay rotting for decades. Luckily the decaying village was designated a National Historical Park in 1954 and eventually restored to its 1865 appearance.

Visiting Appomattox Court House

Appomattox Court House National Historical Park is on Rt. 24, three miles north of US 460 and the town of Appomattox. Start at the **visitors center,** 804/352-8987 ext. 26, www.nps.gov/apco, which is open daily 8:30 A.M.–5 P.M.; $4 pp over 16 in summer ($2 pp otherwise). Get your bearings with two 15-minute slide presentations and a map display of Lee's retreat, and take a look at the museum, which holds relics such as little Lula McLean's doll, the "silent witness" to the signing.

In the village, a reconstructed version of the McLean House is decorated as accurately as possible from paintings and first-hand accounts. None of the furnishings are original, thanks in part to many of those at the signing who quickly snapped up mementos of the event (i.e., anything that wasn't nailed down). Nearby Clover Hill Tavern, on the other hand, dates to 1819. The park includes a section of the Richmond-Lynchburg Stage Road where the Confederates stacked their arms during the surrender ceremony.

LUCKLESS WILMER McLEAN

In the summer of 1861, a Union shell that tore through his kitchen convinced an aging farmer named Wilmer McLean it was time to move. Two huge armies were clashing on his farm near Manassas, and it seemed like the fighting might go on for a time. Declaring he hoped "never to see another soldier," McLean took his family south and west to where he thought the war could never reach—to the dusty burg of Appomattox Court House, where on April 9, 1865, Gen. Robert E. Lee surrendered to Gen. Ulysses S. Grant in McLean's living room, ending the Civil War. As Wilmer later said, "The war began in my front yard and ended in my front parlor."

Park interpreters can answer questions and point you down the trails to both Lee's and Grant's final headquarters. Living-history programs are held daily in summer, and reenactments are held yearly the weekend closest to April 9 on Rt. 667, three miles north of US 460 toward Lynchburg. Call 804/352-0493 for information.

Appomattox Court House Town

Stop by **The Caboose Sandwich Shop,** 804/352-2638, at the intersection of Rt. 24 and US 460 in the town of Appomattox, for inexpensive subs and ice cream. Camping is available at the same crossroads at the **Parkview Mobile Home & RV Park,** 804/352-2366 ($20) and at **Yogi Bear's Jellystone Camp Resort,** 757/993-3332, six miles west on US 460 next to Paradise Lake; $20–25. You can also find sites near the 150-acre lake in **Holiday Lake State Park,** 804/248-6308, www.dcr.state.va.us/parks/holliday.htm, in the Appomattox Buckingham State Forest east on Rt. 24, for $15–18.

For more information on the area, including details on the **Railroad Festival** in mid-October, contact the **Appomattox Chamber of Commerce visitors center,** 434/352-2621, www.appomattox.com, in the restored railroad depot at 5 Main St. (open daily 9 A.M.–5 P.M.).

Local historian Patrick Schroeder assumes the persona of George T. Peers, former sheriff and

Appomattox Court House county clerk in 1867, for **walking tours** of the town on Friday and Saturday evenings from May–September. The tours focus on the fateful days of April 1865, but also include gossip on local celebrities and other juicy tidbits. They start at the Confederate Cemetery at 6:30 P.M. for $10 adults, $6 children under 12. Tickets are available at the visitors center.

YOGAVILLE

Born in India in 1914, Integral Yoga guru Sri Swami Satchidananda established the **Satchidananda Ashram—Yogaville,** 800/858-9642, email: iyi@yogaville.org, www.yogaville.org, to further his goals of peace, universal understanding, and enlightenment. The 750-acre rural retreat centers around the Light of Truth Universal Shrine (L.O.T.U.S.), shaped like a 100-foot blooming lotus. Inside is a neon-lit meditation chamber and 12 altars symbolizing the 10 major religions, "Other Known," and "Those Still Unknown." Shrine open Mon.–Fri. 10 A.M.–noon, 2–5 P.M., Fri. 7–9 P.M., Sat. 10 A.M.–7 P.M., Sun. 10 A.M.–5 P.M., (longer hours in the summer); free.

The ashram hosts workshops and retreats year-round, and guests are welcome to stop by for an afternoon, day, week, or longer. Lodging options include camping ($35 weekdays, $45 weekends), dorms ($55/60 or $65/70 for private room with shared bath), and the Lotus Inn ($75/80), all of which include buffet vegetarian meals, yoga classes, and meditation sessions every day.

SMITH MOUNTAIN LAKE

Central Virginia's favorite aquatic escape was formed in 1966 by the damming of the Roanoke River in Smith Mountain Gap. The resulting 40-mile lake has more than 500 miles of gorgeous shoreline (featured in the movie *What About Bob?* with Richard Dreyfus and Bill Murray). Oak and pine forests shelter wild turkeys, deer, and woodchucks, and year-round bird species like pine warblers, tanagers, ospreys, and the rare bald eagle are joined by migratory ducks, geese, loons, and occasionally great tundra swans.

Information and Activities

At Bridgewater Plaza, on the south side of Hales Ford Bridge (Rt. 122 south from Bedford), you'll find a **visitors center** operated by the Smith Mountain Lake Chamber of Commerce, 800/676-8203 or 540/721-1203, email: smlc-cp@aol.com, www.sml-chamber.com, along with one of two dozen marinas scattered along the shoreline. At just about any of these you can rent Jet-Skis, canoes, sailboats, paddleboats, and fishing boats by the hour or day as well as buy bait and equipment; try **Webster's Marine Center,** 800/325-9110 or 540/297-5228; **Captain's Quarters Boat Rental,** 540/721-7777; and the **Saunders' Parkway Marina,** 540/297-4412, at the end of Rt. 626 on the north side.

Fishing in Smith Mountain Lake is outstanding, especially for black bass, muskie, and walleye. Striped bass are in season year-round—the state record (45 pounds, 10 ounces) was taken here in 1995. Guides like **Reel Time Charters,** 888/202-3474 or 540/970-3524, and **My Time Guide Service,** 800/817-5007 or 540/721-5007, provide equipment and advice. Trips of two to four people can be either four or eight hours long.

The *Virginia Dare* paddlewheel tour boat, 800/721-3273 or 540/297-7100, www.vadare-cruises.com, takes passengers on sightseeing lunch and dinner cruises from Apr.–Dec. Tours are $40 pp for lunch and $33–40 for dinner, and run daily. Contact **Bridgewater Parasail,** 540/721-1639, for a short flight behind a drag-boat over the water. **Virginia Air Services,** 540/297-4500, runs sightseeing flights in a high-wing Wilga out of the small local airport.

Of course there are plenty of shopping possibilities in the gourmet markets and antique stores along Rt. 122 on both sides of the bridge. Three lakefront golf courses—**Mariner's Landing,** 540/297-7888, www.marinerslanding.com; Sycamore Ridge, 540/297-6490; and **The Westlake,** 800/296-7277 or 540/721-4214—are open to the public. You can tour the **Smith Mountain Dam,** 540/985-2587, in the Recreation Area of the same name, at the east end of the lake daily 10 A.M.–6 P.M.

Smith Mountain Lake State Park

Sixteen miles of shoreline and the only public swimming beach in the lake fall within this small park, 540/297-6066, www.dcr.state.va.us/parks/smithmtn.htm, on the north shore of the lake off Rt. 626. Not all the fun is in the water: four short hiking trails wind through pine and hardwood forests to secluded coves. Facilities include paddleboats for rent, hiking trails, and campsites for tents and vehicles ($8–18) open March–December. Two- and three-bedroom cabins with docks and wood-burning stoves can fit 4–6 people each for $80–100 per night and $500–560 per week in season. Park admission is $3 per vehicle ($2 weekdays; $1 off-season).

Accommodations and Food

Don and Mary Davis's **Stone Manor Bed & Breakfast,** 1135 Stone Manor Place, 540/297-1414, fax 540/297-5154, www.stone-manor.com, is at the west end of the lake. The beautiful stone house has three rooms ($85–115), private docks, a pool, and a lighted boardwalk along 690 feet of waterfront. To get there, take Rt. 757 from Rt. 24, pass Goodview, take a right onto Rt. 653, another right at the Sycamore Ridge Gold Club sign, and continue one mile.

A plethora of real-estate agencies can help with lakeside lodging rentals. Try **Lake Retreat Properties,** 800/421-6980 or 540/297-6002, fax 540/297-8902, email: info@lakeretreat.com, www.lakeretreat.com; or **Lakeshore Rentals,** 800/572-6098 or 540/297-5610, fax 540/297-6848, email: tturner@btitelecom.net, www.lakeshorerentals.com.

Campers can hole up at the state park, or the **Crazy Horse Campground & Marina,** 540/721-2792, on Rt. 122 one mile north of Hale's Ford Bridge ($20–25). The **Camper's Paradise Marina,** 540/297-6109, www.campersparadise.com, is along Rt. 616 on the south side, with sites for $17–22 and motel rooms for $80–90. Their homestyle restaurant is famous for its breakfasts.

Bridgewater Plaza offers a few dining options of the burgers-wings-and-beer school: **R.T.'s Dock-N-Dine** has live music on weekends; **Moosie's,** 540/721-5255, cooks up BBQ and Mexican dishes; and the **Pizza Pub** explains itself.

The Landing restaurant, 540/721-3028, is nearby at 773 Ashmeade in Moneta. It's a more upscale place, with appetizers such as blood orange and fuji apple salad for $7–10 and entreés like Roasted Vegetable Napoleon for $15–25 served for dinner Thurs.–Sun. Lunch plates (Wed.–Sun.) are $8–12.

Events

Saunders Marina hosts an **Antique and Classic Boat Show and Rally** in August, with mahogany and cedar cruisers, runabouts, and sailboats on display for free. Fifteen wineries come for the **Smith Mountain Lake Wine Festival** at Barnard's Landing in late September. Call the Smith Mountain Lake Chamber of Commerce for more information.

BOOKER T. WASHINGTON NATIONAL MONUMENT

Early-1900s America's most influential and powerful black activist was born a slave on a small Virginia tobacco farm in 1856. Freed by the Emancipation Proclamation, the Washington family moved to West Virginia, where young Booker struggled to take advantage of a startling new opportunity: education. First he rose every day before dawn to work in a salt mine so his afternoons would be free for school. Then, at age 16, Booker walked most of the 500 miles back to Virginia to attend the Hampton Institute, one of the country's leading schools for blacks, where he would eventually become a teacher.

In 1881 Washington opened his own school, the Tuskegee Institute in Alabama. A low point in race relations, personified by the rising Ku Klux Klan, intensified the fine balance between educating fellow blacks in useful skills and antagonizing whites. His nonconfrontational stance, calling for interracial cooperation without abolishing social segregation too abruptly, drew protests from within his own race.

Nonetheless, Washington endured critical attacks and racial slurs to become the leading black figure of his day. His famous Atlanta

Compromise Address of 1895 crystallized his conservative viewpoint, which gradually became more liberal in his later years. In 1901 he published an autobiography, *Up From Slavery*, and he died at Tuskegee in 1915.

The farm where Washington was born into servitude is on Rt. 122 west of Smith Mountain Lake. The visitors center, managed by the National Park Service, 540/721-2094, www.nps.gov/

bowa, has a short video and museum displays on Washington's life. From there, a short walking trail leads past reconstructed buildings and stone outlines of the original structures, including the owners' home and the building where Washington was born. Costumed interpreters lead guided tours during the summer, and the 1.5-mile Jack-o-Lantern Trail heads off into the woods. Open daily 9 A.M.–5 P.M.; free.

Danville

The manufacturing center of southern Virginia, just a hair over the North Carolina line, Danville (pop. 55,000) is also one of the most important tobacco auction centers in the country. Along with one million square feet of auction space, the legacy of its Victorian era economic heyday lives on in the stunning architecture along Millionaires' Row.

HISTORY

William Byrd, trying to determine the true boundary between North Carolina and Virginia in 1728, was so captivated by the surrounding scenery that he said he felt as if he had wandered "from Dan to Beersheba." The Biblical praise stuck in the name of the Dan River and, in 1793, the town itself, which was named the same year its first tobacco warehouse was established. "Twelve fit and able men" elected the first mayor in 1833, and during the Civil War, Danville's population of 5,000 expanded when Federal soldiers were imprisoned there.

After the destruction of Richmond in April 1865, Jefferson Davis and the rest of the Confederate cabinet moved into the home of prominent Danville citizen Maj. William T. Sutherlin. Less than two weeks later, the rebels would lay down their arms—long enough, however, to earn Danville the title of Last Capital of the Confederacy.

In the meantime, Danville's manufacturing industry kept growing. Riverside Cotton Mills, founded in 1882, today is called Dan River Inc., the largest single-unit textile facility in the world.

In January 1886, electric lamps flickered to life across Danville, signaling the activation of the first municipal power plant in the United States.

ORIENTATION

Danville is spread on both sides of the Dan River, which runs roughly east to west. Downtown is mostly on the southern side of the river, sandwiched above the North Carolina line.

SIGHTS

The section of Main Street near the 1000 block, listed in the "National Register of Historic Places," is the architectural equivalent of a wedding cake catalog. Dripping scrollwork and sweeping porches decorate mansion after mansion, each one gaudier than the one before. Cupolas and minarets thrust skyward as stately columns keep everything grounded. Every architectural style of the Victorian era, plus a few more to boot, is represented: Queen Anne (#926), High Victorian Gothic (#878), Early Federal (#770), Georgian Revival (#776), even Italianate (#753). The gorgeous monster at #1020 is simply known as the "Wedding Cake House."

Danville Museum of Fine Arts and History

This 1857 Italianate mansion on Millionaires' Row was home to Maj. William T. Sutherlin, tobacco merchant and wartime quartermaster for Danville, before Jefferson Davis and company arrived on April 3, 1865. Davis issued his

THE WRECK OF THE OLD 97

September 27, 1903, began as just another quiet Sunday morning in Danville. At the helm of locomotive No. 1002, Engineer Joseph A. Broady, a 20-year veteran of the Southern Railroad, was running late from Lynchburg. Luckily the "Old 97" was the fastest engine on the Southern Line, and Broady opened the throttle wide. At the top of White Oak Mountain, however, he realized he was going too fast for the three-mile downhill grade that loomed ahead. A 500-foot curved trestle above the Dan River sealed the train's fate.

In vain Broady reversed the engine, locking the wheels in a scream of metal. As the five-car train hit the trestle, it leapt from the rails and vaulted 75 feet into the rocky creek bed below. Nine passengers were killed and seven were injured in the disaster. Images of the twisted wreckage leapt from front pages nationwide.

The famous ballad inspired by the crash inspired controversy of its own. Initially recorded by Virginia musicians Henry Whitter and G.B. Grayson, it was released by singer Vernon Dalhart and went on to become the country's first platinum record, before the term was even invented. It eventually sold five million copies. The song's true author, however, was still in dispute. In 1933, the first major copyright lawsuit was resolved when the courts ruled against the RCA Victor Company, stating that David George, a telegraph operator at the scene of the accident, was the original author. Notwithstanding the fact that George himself probably added new lyrics to an older folk tune, he was awarded $65,000. RCA Victor, in turn, tied up the case through appeals for so long that George never collected a penny for "The Wreck of the Old 97."

A plaque marks the crash site on US 58 between Locust Lane and North Main Street.

final proclamation as Confederate President a day later, and left for North Carolina on April 10 after the arrival of the news that Lee had surrendered at Appomattox Court House. Today the museum, 975 Main St., 434/793-5644, houses exhibits of local history and art, with a small auditorium where local groups perform. Open Tues.–Fri. 10 A.M.–5 P.M., Sat. and Sun. 2–5 P.M., for a $2.50 suggested donation.

The Crossing at the Dan

The former Southern Railroad Yard at 667 Craighead Street in the tobacco warehouse district has been renovated and filled with shops, restaurants, and entertainment facilities. The 1899 passenger station is now the **Danville Science Center,** 434/791-5190, www.smv.org/wdanvil.html. A satellite of Richmond's Science Museum of Virginia, the center is full of hands-on family-oriented displays of science and natural history. Open Tues.–Sat 9:30 A.M.–5 P.M., Sun. 1–5 P.M.; $4 adults, $3 children 4–12.

Danville's **Community Market,** 434/797-8961, occupies the 1904 Southern Railroad Freight Warehouse. Farm-fresh produce, baked goods, and crafts are among the offerings Apr.–Dec., Fri. and Sat. from 8 A.M.–5 P.M. and Sun. noon–5 P.M. Nearby **Auctioneers Park,** 434/799-5215, has an amphitheater with room for thousands. This is where you'll find one end of a 3.5-mile bike and foot trail along the riverfront to Dan Daniel Park, passing over an early-1900s railroad bridge along the way.

Birthplace of Lady Astor

Born here on May 19, 1879, Nancy Witcher Langhorne would grow up to become the Viscountess Astor, the first woman to sit in the British Parliament. Her sister Irene would make a name for herself in turn by marrying artist Charles Dana Gibson and providing the inspiration for the famous "Gibson Girls." The house itself, 117 Broad St. at Main St., is undergoing renovations and open by appointment only; call the visitors center for information.

American Armoured Foundation

The largest private collection of American armored combat vehicles was recently moved to Danville from New York—no small feat, considering it consists of almost 100 pieces spanning 200 years of history, including a 62-ton tank and a missile transport.

The museum, 3401 US 29 N, 434/836-5323, www.aaftankmuseum.com, is impressive in its breadth as well, from 500 pieces of military headgear to 140 weapons, such as bazookas, flame throwers, and machine guns. As soon as everything gets settled, nine vehicles, including Panzer and Patton tanks, will be on display next to eight artillery pieces and more than 100,000 pieces of military memorabilia. Call for hours and prices.

Virginia International Raceway

Originally built in 1957, this racetrack situated 12 miles east of Danville got a facelift in the 1990s. A year-round schedule of motor events includes motorcycle races and historic sports car rallies. An 1830s plantation home serves as a clubhouse, complete with restaurant and lounge. Most events are held from Apr.–Oct., led by the Ferrari Challenge in late April and the Virginia Festival of Speed in late June and early July. Lodging plans are in the works, but in the meantime you can camp for $10 (tents) to $25 (RVs).

The raceway, 888/611-2099 or 434/822-7700, www.virclub.com, is in Alton, Virginia. To get there, take US 58 east to Rt. 62 south. In Milton, North Carolina, take Rt. 57 onto Racetrack Road back over the state line. Tickets are $10–55 pp; contact the raceway for events listings and information.

ACCOMMODATIONS

$50–100

The **Innkeeper Danville West,** 3020 Riverside Dr., 434/836-1700, fax 434/799-9672, is on US 58 west of the US 29 junction, and its sister the **Innkeeper Danville North,** 1030 Piney Forest Rd., 434/836-1700, fax 434/836-1700, is on US 29 2.5 miles north of US 58.

Cabins made of logs from century-old tobacco barns make up the **Fall Creek Farm B&B,** 2556 Green Farm Rd., 434/791-3297. Inside are stone fireplaces and whirlpool tubs, and outside are porch rockers. To get there, take US 29 north (Main St.) to Rt. 726 East (Malmaison

Rd.) and go 3.5 miles to Rt. 360 South (Old Richmond Rd.). From there it's another mile to Rt. 719 (Green Farm Rd.). **Breezy Oaks,** 800/783-6344 or 434/822-5866, is a country farmhouse run by a certified massage therapist. Handmade furniture fills the 19th-century structure, 13 miles east of Danville; from US 58 east, take Rt. 119 south 1.5 miles.

$150–250

Near the intersection of US 29 and US 58 is the **Stratford Inn,** 2500 Riverside Dr., 434/793-2500, with 150 units and suites, some with whirlpools, along with a heated pool and exercise rooms. The dining room, probably the classiest eatery in town, serves all meals beneath Early American décor. (The icebox lemon pie is justifiably famous.) Cozy booths and piano music in the Library Lounge round things out.

FOOD

Danville isn't a gourmet town; most restaurants are simple and straightforward. **Macy's Diner,** 1203 Piney Forest Rd. (Alt 29N), 434/836-5034 or 434/836-0132, has been family owned and operated since 1951. It's open daily 11 A.M.–9 P.M. Don't miss the banana pudding at the **Danview Restaurant,** 116 Danview Dr., 434/793-3552, another homestyle place that serves all meals Mon.–Fri. from 6 A.M.

In the Riverside Shopping Center, **Joe & Mimma's Italian Restaurant and Pizza,** 3336 Riverside Dr., 434/799-5763, has pastas for $6–8 and entreés for $10–16, along with healthier and vegetarian entreés, gourmet pizzas, and seafood. Open for lunch and dinner Tues.–Sat. **The Brown Bean,** 1799 Memorial Dr. at Park Ave., 434/791-2700, is attached to the Gingerbread House Gift Shop. Open 8:30 A.M.–5:30 P.M., Mon.–Fri. (4:30 P.M. Saturdays), they offer plenty of muffins and other breakfast fare as well as soup, salad, sandwich lunch combinations for $4–5.

EVENTS

From August through mid-November, Danville's six warehouses are filled with earthy brown leaves and the barks of auctioneers during **tobacco auction** season. Contact the visitors center for schedules. Mid-May's **Festival in the Park** brings arts and crafts, entertainment, and food to Ballou Park, which is also the site of the Virginia State Barbecue Championships during **Pigs in the Park** the same month.

Concerts are held at the Crossing of the Dan the first Friday evening of every month in summer during **Fridays at the Crossing,** while the **Virginia Cantaloupe Festival** in mid-July brings all the vine-ripened cantaloupes you can eat.

Danville's next big event is the **Fall Festival & Halloween at the Crossing,** with a petting zoo, costume contests, and carnival rides. Call 434/799-5200 for information on local events.

INFORMATION

The Danville Chamber of Commerce runs a **visitors center** out of their offices at 635 Main St., 434/793-5422, email: danchamb@gamewood.net, www.danvillechamber.com. Open Mon.–Fri. 9 A.M.–5 P.M., Sat. 9 A.M.–2 P.M.

CENTRAL VIRGINIA

The Coast

A simple concept—Virginia meets the ocean—becomes much more complex in reality. Comprising both the state's largest city and towns so small that everyone in the phone book could ride a school bus, the coast embraces some of Virginia's greatest diversity in both its landscape and its people. Aside from the sea, its major defining feature is the Chesapeake Bay, whose mouth opens onto one of the finest, largest, and busiest natural ports in the world. Around this harbor spreads Hampton Roads, officially the Norfolk–Virginia Beach–Newport News Metropolitan Statistical Area, home to 1.4 million people—one-quarter of Virginia's population and more than the total population of 13 other entire states.

Second only to northern Virginia in growth, the Hampton Roads area boasts the world's largest coal-shipping port, privately owned shipyard, and naval facility. One-third of its workers are employed by the Department of Defense or private defense contractors. Yet around this megalopolis—close enough, in parts, to see its glow at night—stretch some of the state's most pristine natural acres, covering miles of undisturbed shoreline, barrier islands, marshes, and estuaries.

HIGHLIGHTS

Most of the 2.5 million people who visit Virginia's coast every year have their sights set on the Historic Peninsula, where the United States began—twice. Only a short drive apart are Jamestown, the first European settlement in the New World in 1607, and Yorktown, site of the final battle of the American Revolution. Between them is Colonial Williamsburg, one of America's most popular family destinations, where life in the 18th century is re-created down to belt buckles and bootstraps. Venerable historic plantations, including Shirley, America's oldest,

Hampton

and Berkeley, site of the first Thanksgiving, preside over the James River.

Along with plentiful nightlife, restaurants, and hotels, Hampton Roads offers some of Virginia's most outstanding museums, including the Mariner's Museum in Newport News and the Virginia Marine Sciences Museum in Virginia Beach. The city of Hampton is rich in African American history, and Portsmouth—birthplace of almost 200 World War II warships—sits just across the Elizabeth River from Norfolk, home to the U.S. Navy Atlantic fleet. To the east, Virginia Beach boasts 38 miles of beaches and a scrubbed-up version of a classic boardwalk.

Hikers, boaters, and bikers need only insect repellent, sunscreen, and a water bottle to explore the depths of the Great Dismal Swamp and amazingly unsullied coastal preserves such as First Landing State Park, almost within walking distance of downtown Virginia Beach, and False Cape State Park to the south. Reaching toward the interior of the bay, "the Necks" (local parlance for the area's skinny peninsulas split by rivers) offer a quiet rural escape dotted with historic mansions and Indian reservations. In a category of its own is the Eastern Shore, home to archaic harbor towns, gourmet crab shacks, and Chincoteague's wild ponies.

ACCESS

The only Virginia interstate that heads seaward is I-64 from Richmond, threading the Historic Peninsula as it runs east to Williamsburg and the Hampton Roads area. US 17 leaves Fredericksburg for the Middle Neck, where it crosses US 360 before crossing the York River at Yorktown. The Northern and Middle Necks each have their own backbone: Rt. 3 runs the length of the former, and US 17 skewers the latter. US 360 runs from Richmond across both to Reedville.

Farther south, US 460 connects Petersburg with Suffolk near Hampton Roads, and US 58 rolls east from Emporia more or less along the North Carolina state line toward Portsmouth. Two of the most scenic ways to reach the coast are Rt. 5, which passes half a dozen James River plantations southeast of Richmond, and US 13 down the length of the Eastern Shore from Maryland.

Northern Neck

Reaching bayward between broad, patient rivers, the Necks evoke the Piedmont, but with a shoreside twist. A hazy light filters across the flat farmland, where the odor of freshly mown fields mixes with the slightly salty breeze off the Chesapeake Bay. Talk at the local store is as likely to be about fixing outboards as about maintaining Chevies. Replete with local color—John Boy's Market, Ernie's Gas Station, an annual "Ugly Pick-Up" contest in the town of Village—it's even more rural than much of central Virginia. Most visitors come for quiet walks, fishing, boating, and shopping from spring to fall. (In the off-season, many towns shut down their tourist facilities completely.)

For more information on the Northern Neck, contact the **Northern Neck Tourism Council** in Warsaw, 800/393-6180, www.northern-neck.org.

GEORGE WASHINGTON BIRTHPLACE NATIONAL MONUMENT

The father of his country squalled into the light on February 22, 1732, on Pope's Creek Plantation, on the southern bank of the Potomac. It doesn't seem like a bad place to spend the first three and a half years of one's life, in among the trees here where the meandering creek empties into the river. Although the building in which Washington was born is gone, an outline in crushed oyster shells shows where it stood, next to a reconstructed farm complete with outbuildings and animal pens.

Pleasant paths lead from the visitors center, 804/224-1732, www.nps.gov/gewa, to the Memorial House, which contains an original tea table. George's father, grandfather, and great-grandfather lie in the family cemetery nearby.

THE COAST

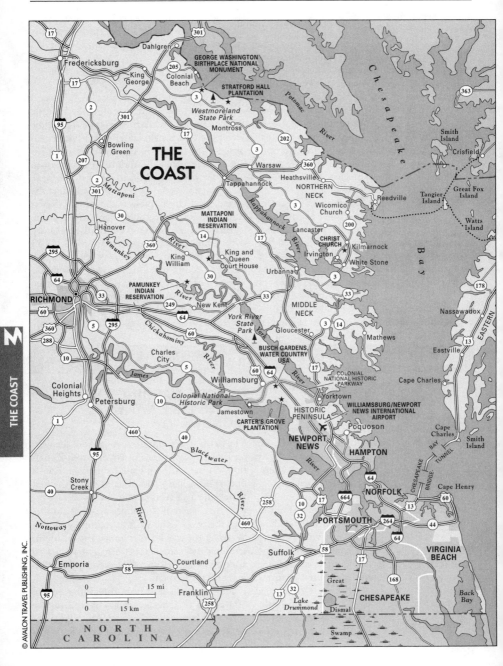

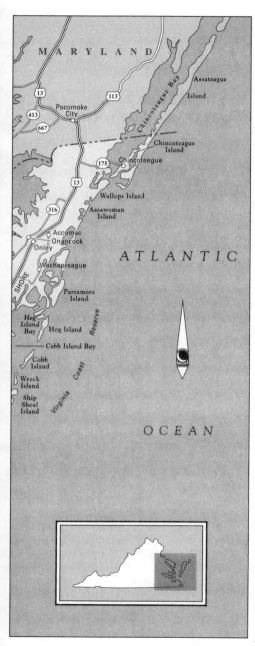

Costumed interpreters manage the working farm, which provides a window into 18th-century life in the Tidewater. A nature trail continues to a picnic area, and at the end of the road is a family burial ground and a beach on the Potomac. The monument is on Rt. 204 off Rt. 3, open daily 9 A.M.–5 P.M.; $2 pp.

WESTMORELAND STATE PARK

Ancient marine fossils trapped in Horsehead Cliffs attest to the age (more than 127 million years) of the sediments that make up this peninsula between the Rappahannock and Potomac rivers. It was set aside in 1936 as one of Virginia's first six state parks. Behind the beach and steep riverside bluffs stretch 1,295 acres of meadows and forest populated by beavers, hawks, and turkeys.

The park, on Rt. 347 off Rt. 3, has horse and hiking trails, a swimming pool, picnic areas, and a playground. You can spend the night in a one, two-, or three-bedroom cabin ($60–90) or at one of the park's 133 campsites ($11–22) open Mar.–Dec. The Potomac River Retreat can hold 16 people in two fully contained living areas and has deck areas facing the Potomac River ($233). A camp store sells supplies, and the visitors center, 804/493-8821, rents rowboats and paddleboats in season. Ask about kayak trips along the Horsehead Cliffs on Wed. and Sun. ($10). Open daily dawn–dusk; $2 adults, $1 children from Memorial Day to Labor Day, $1–3 per car the rest of the year. Check out their website at www.dcr.state.va.us/parks/westmore.htm.

STRATFORD HALL PLANTATION

Robert E. Lee, the Northern Neck's other famous son, was born on an estate his family had occupied for almost a century. In the late 1730s on a bluff near the Potomac, Thomas Lee built a huge mansion—shaped like an H in honor of his wife, Hanna. His nephew, Henry, moved in in 1782 and married Annie Hill Carter of Shirley Plantation. Henry went on to make a name for himself in the Revolutionary War as Harry "Light-Horse" Lee. But on January 19, 1807, just four years before Henry lost his fortune in

WESTMORELAND BERRY FARM AND ORCHARD

You can pick your own raspberries, blackberries, blueberries, and strawberries at this 80-acre farm along the Rappahannock. Or you can stop by just to sample more than a dozen seasonal fruits, including apricots, peaches, cherries, apples, plums, and pumpkins. A snack bar serves fruit sundaes, frozen yogurt, and other toothsome mouthfuls. Families from Fredericksburg and beyond come to enjoy wagon rides, farm animals, and crafts at the Tri-Berry Festival in June.

The Farm, 800/997-2377, is southwest of Oak Grove on Rt. 638, reached from Rt. 3 via Rt. 634. It's open during growing season (May–Oct.) Mon.–Sat. 8 A.M.–6 P.M. and Sun. 10 A.M.–6 P.M. Check out their website, www.westmorelandberryfarm.com, for a harvest schedule and a list of annual events.

land speculation and moved the family to Alexandria, Annie gave birth to a son who was destined for even greater fame: Robert E. Lee.

The Great House, one of the most majestic edifices in the state, looks like a brick castle set back a short distance from the river. Sixteen fireplaces and numerous 17th- and 18th-century furnishings fill the cavernous interior. These include many Lee heirlooms, such as a 1660 clock and the crib where Robert slept as a baby. Notice the 17-foot "inverted tray" ceiling in the Great Hall, and ask about the fireplace angels to which Robert bid good-bye as the family was packing to move. Downstairs are servants' quarters, the original kitchen, bedrooms, and a schoolroom where the teacher slept.

Stratford Hall, 804/493-8038, www.stratfordhall.org, is on Rt. 214 off Rt. 3. A reception center houses a museum where you can learn about estimating the age of clay pipes by the diameter of their stems, and a gift shop selling fresh-ground corn and oats from the estate's fully functional mill. There's also a snack bar and a log-cabin dining room serving a hearty plantation lunch daily. Three miles of nature trails explore the working plantation's 1,700 rural acres. Annual events include a free open house on Robert's birthday (Jan-

uary 19), another on African-American Heritage Day (usually the last weekend in February), and chamber-music concerts in the summer and fall with plantation dinners by candlelight. Open daily 9 A.M.–4:30 P.M.; $8 adults, $4 children.

REEDVILLE

Founded in 1867 ("by Northerners," grumbles one pamphlet), this small city was reportedly the richest per capita in the country around World War I, thanks to the abundant menhaden fishing in Chesapeake Bay. Today, boats sit in the driveways of tidy houses along Main Street (Rt. 360), which dead-ends at the water along Millionaires' Row, named for a succession of gorgeous Victorian mansions.

Sights
A **Fisherman's Museum,** 804/453-6529, www.rfmuseum.com, has been set up in an 1875 waterman's house along Main Street just before Millionaires' Row. Displays of ship models, photos, and tools lead visitors to a crabbing skiff and traditional workboat moored to the rear dock. Open Wed.–Mon. 10:30 A.M.–4:30 P.M. (weekends only Nov.–May); $2 adults.

Accommodations
The Gables Inn, 804/453-5209, occupies the unmistakable brick mansion at the end of Main Street, built in the late 1800s by a local captain who brought the bricks by schooner from New England. (The boat's three masts were also used in the construction.) Rooms are $105–118. In the nearby village of Fleeton is the **Fleeton Fields B&B,** 800/497-8215, 804/453-5014, with two rooms and two suites for $70–130, along with a rose-filled garden, antiques, and fireplaces.

The **Chesapeake Bay/Smith Island KOA,** located 2.5 miles northeast of the intersection of Rt. 652 and US 360, 804/453-3430, has campsites for $22–27. Boats to Smith Island, Maryland, leave from here from May–October.

Food
Elijah's Restaurant, 804/453-5359, offers waterfront dining overlooking Cockrell's Creek. Seafood,

of course, is the specialty, along with homemade bread, desserts, and soups served outside on the wide porch. Elijah's is open seasonally for breakfast and dinner Wed.–Sun. Reservations are suggested.

Down at the end of Main street by the marina is **The Crazy Crab,** 804/453-6789, with an outdoor deck, plenty of wine, and daily chef specials of seafood, steak, and chicken. Open for lunch and dinner Tues.–Sun.

The deli counter at **Cockrell's Creek Seafood,** 804/453-6326, south on Seaboard Rd. off Fleeton Rd., sells scallops, shrimp, crabs, and other marine delicacies to take out or eat there. Open in season Mon.–Thurs. 10–4, Fri.–Sat. 10 A.M.–5 P.M.

Recreation
Pittman's Charters, 804/453-3643, www.chesapeakeangler.net/mysticladyII, sends fishing groups after stripers, croaker, trout, and bluefish aboard the 42-foot *Mystic Lady* May–Dec. Charters, including gear, run $60 pp for up to 23 people. **Captain Billy's Charters,** 804/580-7292, www.captainbillyscharters.com, runs similar trips from the Ingram Bay Marina, near Wicomico Church, for $390 per day (maximum six people). Sunset cruises are $15 pp (four-person minimum), and they also offer evening and overnight trips.

Anna Campbell's **Northern Neck Eco Tours,** 804/580-6639, email: info@northernneckecotours.com, www.northernneckecotours.com, runs guided kayak tours out of nearby Wicomico Church that can be customized and combined with bird-watching, fishing, and berry picking. They also offer equipment rental and kayak courses.

Tours and Transportation
Day trips to Tangier Island and lunch cruises up the Rappahannock to the Ingleside Plantation Winery are only two of the trips offered by **Tangier and Chesapeake Cruises,** 804/453-2628, www.eaglesnest.net/tangier. The *Chesapeake Breeze* leaves daily at 10 A.M. for Tangier Island, returning about 3:45 P.M., for $20 adults, $10 children with an optional $12.25 lunch. Reservations are recommended during the summer. They also offer narrated lunch and dinner tours aboard a paddlewheeler to Fredericksburg, with

onboard dancing on Friday and Saturday. Boats leave May–Oct. from the Buzzard's Point Marina, reached by taking a right before Reedville onto Fairport Road (Rt. 626), followed by a left onto Buzzard Point Road.

Events
The **Waterman's Festival and Blessing of the Fleet,** held during the first full weekend in May, packs tiny Reedville with crowds hankering for tons of seafood, boat rides and tours, and demonstrations of crab picking and crab-pot building. The second weekend in June brings the **Bluefish Derby,** at Buzzard's Point Marina. Anyone whose catch beats the standing state record of 25 pounds 4 ounces can claim a $50,000 cash prize plus a new pickup, boat, and trailer.

The **Traditional Small Boat Show,** around the Fourth of July, showcases handcrafted boats under 20 feet, and the traditional **Oyster Roast and Bluegrass on the Lawn** takes place the second Saturday in November.

IRVINGTON AND VICINITY
Christ Church
The centerpiece of this small fishing town is a monolithic house of worship completed in 1735 by Robert "King" Carter. This is one of the few unaltered Colonial churches in the country. It features a high arching ceiling, shoulder-high walls between family-sized pew "boxes," and a three-level pulpit, although it has no bell tower. Services are still held here from June to Labor Day, and a museum/visitors center, 804/438-6855, www.christchurch1735.org, is open Apr.–Nov. Mon.–Sat. 10 A.M.–4 P.M., Sun. 2–5 P.M. The church is on Christ Church Road (Rt. 646) off Rt. 200 just north of Irvington.

Accommodations and Food
Along Carter's Creek you'll find both sections of the first-class **Tides Inn** on King Carter Drive (Rt. 634), 800/843-3746 or 804/438-5000, fax 804/438-5222, www.the-tides.com. This all-inclusive getaway is rated among the top 20 in the country by Condé Nast *Traveler*. Open Apr.–Dec., it features the top-rated Golden Eagle golf course,

THE COAST

a sandy beach, a saltwater pool, and yacht cruises aboard the *Miss Anne*. Rooms are $150–300, and suites are $300–450.

In 1890, a schoolhouse opened in an old Methodist church near the center of Irvington. Today the building houses **The Hope and Glory Inn,** 634 King Carter Dr., 800/497-8228 or 804/438-6053, www.hopeandglory.com. This award-winning place is decked out with folk art and a large central lobby where classrooms once echoed with children's voices. If the four upstairs bedrooms ($130–185) are full, there are also four guest cottages ($155–210) out back near an enclosed outdoor bath with

clawfoot tub, shower, and sink. The English cottage garden features a moon patch that blooms in the evening. Their "Big Chill" weekends are becoming popular, when groups of friends rent the entire place. (The website alone is worth a look.)

The **White Stone Wine and Cheese Co.,** 804/435-2000, on Rappahanock Drive (Rt. 3) in the town of White Stone, offers the largest local wine selection and sandwiches in a small café. In Irvington, the chic little **Trick Dog Cafe,** 4557 Irvington Rd., 804/438-1055, serves tasty bites like grilled salmon roulade and roasted leg of lamb ($16–22) for dinner Tues.–Sat.

Middle Neck

URBANNA

One of 20 port towns established by a 1680 Act of Assembly, Urbanna was named for England's Queen Anne, as was Annapolis, Maryland. The town has weathered pirate attacks and three wars during its centuries as a tobacco export center and fishing village. Watermen still unload their day's catch on wharves shared by recreational boaters and anglers, only a short walk from Victorian homes on the National Register of Historic Places.

Sights

Opened in 1876, the **R.S. Bristow Store,** Virginia St. at Cross St., 804/758-2210, once sold patent medicines, live chickens, and wood by the cord. More than 125 years later, it's still going strong, selling clothes, gifts, and household goods. There's a shoe section where the post office used to be and an old-fashioned rolling ladder to reach the higher shelves. The nearby **courthouse building** dates to 1748, making it the oldest structure in Urbanna. It has served various functions over the years, shifting from a church to Confederate Civil War barracks to its present role as a women's club headquarters.

Accommodations

In addition to 13 modest rooms ($65), the **Urbanna Inn,** 250 Virginia St., 888/758-4852 or

804/758-4852, fax 804/758-0516, has one of the nicest restaurants on the Middle Neck. Entrées include seafood, poultry, meat, and pasta selections, and sorbet comes between courses. There's a fun raw bar toward the rear. Open for lunch and dinner Mon.–Fri., all meals Saturday and Sunday. The **Atherson Hall B&B,** 250 Prince George St., 804/758-2809, was originally the home of a 19th-century schooner captain and has rooms in the same price range.

Half a mile outside of town on Rt. 602, **Hewick Plantation,** 804/758-4214, fax 804/758-3115, email: hewick@oonl.com, occupies a brick manor home built around 1670. Set on 66 wooded acres, it's on both the National Register of Historic Plantations and the Virginia Historic Landmark List and is run by the 11th-generation descendent of its original owner, Christopher Robinson, Esq. of Yorkshire, Member of the House of Burgesses and original trustee of the College of William and Mary. Two rooms are $85–150.

The cozy **Sangraal By-The-Sea,** 804/776-6500, has hostel rooms for $17 pp. The owners give occasional environmental education programs, and you can walk the surrounding nature trails to your heart's content. It's a little tricky to find, especially at night; take Rt. 628 off Rt. 33/3 about three miles east of the turnoff for the Rt. 3 bridge across the Rappahannock. Turn north at the Wake Post Office onto Carlton Road

(Rt. 626), and it's about one-half mile farther, on the left. Waterfront campsites at the **Bethpage Camp Resort,** 804/758-4349, email: bethpage@oonl.com, www.bethpagecamp.com, about 15 miles west near the intersection of Rt. 17 and Rt. 684, are $25–30 with full hookups. This huge place has two pools, a tennis court, a grocery store, and a marina. Open April–November.

Food

Other than the Urbanna Inn, the town's dining options are more modest. **Jimmie's Grill,** 230 Virginia St., 804/758-5213, has Boar's Head deli sandwiches and microbrews, while **Marshall's Drug Store,** 50 Cross St., 804/758-5344, offers an authentic lunch counter with real milkshakes.

INDIAN RESERVATIONS

A museum on the 1,200-acre **Pamunkey Indian Reservation,** 804/843-4792, www.baylink.org/Pamunkey, traces the history of the largest Powhatan chiefdom, established in 1607. Exhaustive displays include beautiful ceremonial garments and a collection of mean-looking weapons, including the world's largest collection of modern handmade flint points. Several local potters have formed a guild to begin reviving traditional methods, and their wares are for sale in the museum shop. Open Tues.–Sat. 10 A.M.–4 P.M.; Sun. 1–4 P.M.; $2.50 adults, $1.25 children. Take Rt. 633 or Rt. 626 south from Rt. 30, then follow the signs.

Officially designated in 1658, the **Mattaponi Reservation,** www.baylink.org/Mattaponi, has been whittled down to only 150 acres. It's located off Rt. 30 opposite the Pamunkey reservation via Rt. 626 or Rt. 640, and hosts an annual powwow in mid-June, with dancing, drumming, food, and crafts. Every year the tribal chief presents the governor of Virginia with a gift of peace in accordance with original treaties.

Colonial Williamsburg

America's largest and most popular living-history museum presents the Colonial capital as it existed on November 11, 1775, the tense eve of the Revolutionary War. One of the most ambitious historical projects ever, this isn't just a re-created farm or household—this is an entire town brought back to life and inhabited by people portraying a cadre of craftspeople, slaves, merchants, and aristocrats.

It may not be everyone's cup of tea (or ale), but Colonial Williamsburg is a remarkable feat, the product of decades of research, experiment, and refinement. The realism—aside from the hordes of tourists—is amazing. Horse-drawn carriages clop past a merchant arguing with his neighbor over the best course of political action, while nonplussed ducks wander down a dusty lane where a smith stands sweating over his forge. Best of all, you can even take part in it yourself. Join a tipsy Colonial gentleman singing bawdy tavern songs, learn the finer points of baking apple fritters from his decorous wife, immerse yourself in the latest findings at an archeological dig, or sit on a courthouse jury to decide whether a pig thief deserves a flogging or just a day in the stocks.

Children especially love the "living" aspect of Williamsburg, rolling hoops across the Palace Green in three-cornered hats or taking lessons from the Dancing Master in the Governor's Palace. Colonial Williamsburg has done an enviable job of marketing itself as the ultimate family destination covering both the educational and entertainment angles—and a million visitors a year seem to agree.

HISTORY

Rural acreage known as Middle Plantation got a rude awakening when it was picked as the site for the new Colonial capital in 1699. The planter aristocracy of the day had decided it needed a more sophisticated spot for the business of governing and socializing than damp Jamestown, and this site, near the newly established "Free Schoole & College" of William and Mary, seemed suitable.

THE COAST

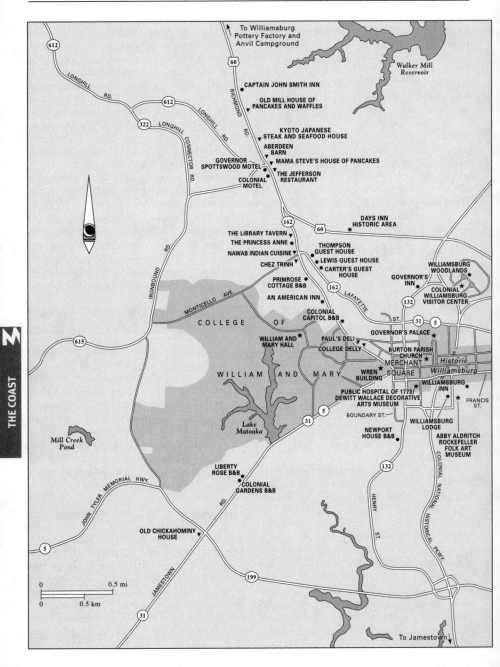

THE COAST

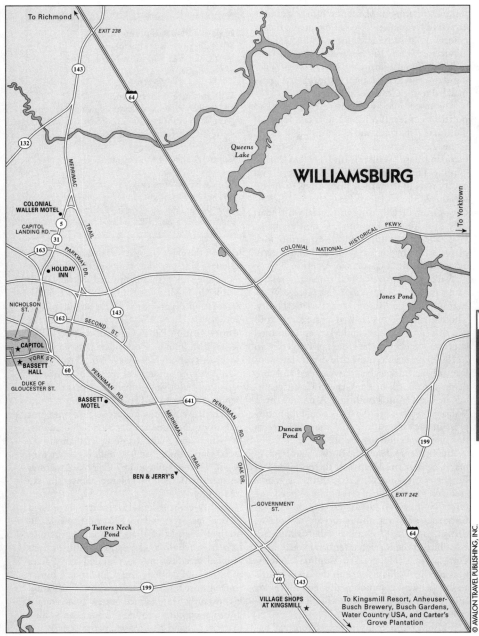

To Richmond

EXIT 238

143

64

132

MERRIMAC TRAIL

Queens Lake

WILLIAMSBURG

To Yorktown

COLONIAL WALLER MOTEL

CAPITOL LANDING RD.

5

31

163

PARKWAY DR.

HOLIDAY INN

COLONIAL NATIONAL HISTORICAL PKWY

Jones Pond

NICHOLSON ST.

162

143

SECOND ST.

CAPITOL

YORK ST.

BASSETT HALL

60

DUKE OF GLOUCESTER ST.

PENNIMAN RD.

BASSETT MOTEL

641

PENNIMAN RD.

Duncan Pond

199

MERRIMAC TRAIL

OAK DR.

BEN & JERRY'S

EXIT 242

GOVERNMENT ST.

Tutters Neck Pond

64

199

60

143

VILLAGE SHOPS AT KINGSMILL

To Kingsmill Resort, Anheuser-Busch Brewery, Busch Gardens, Water Country USA, and Carter's Grove Plantation

THE COAST

© AVALON TRAVEL PUBLISHING, INC.

Plans were immediately set in motion to transform a scattering of plantation buildings into a capital fit for the New World's oldest and richest colony. First to be laid out was the Duke of Gloucester Street, 100 feet wide and almost one mile long, from William and Mary's Wren Building at one end to the capitol at the other. A grassy mall led to the Governor's Palace.

The town quickly became the cultural and political center of Virginia and the focus of Colonial America's most fashionable social scene. As a ceremonial city with little manufacturing base, Williamsburg swelled during "Public Times" in April and October. Rural gentry rode in from their plantations to attend sessions of the House of Burgesses and Governor's Council, delighting in a social whirl that, they said, rivaled London's. Countless balls, fairs, and races competed for attention with performances by English actors and musicians in one of the earliest theaters in America.

Williamsburg welcomed some impressive names during its heyday, including George Washington, George Mason, and Patrick Henry. Thomas Jefferson first arrived in the early 1760s as a student at William and Mary and returned later as a member of the House of Burgesses. In 1719, 13 pirates from the ship of the notorious Edward Teach (Blackbeard) were tried and condemned to death in the General Court chamber in the Capitol building. A decade later, Williamsburg boasted the first successful printing press in the colony, followed soon after by its first newspaper and paper mill.

Patrick Henry defied the British Stamp Act in his "Caesar-Brutus" speech to the House of Burgesses on May 30, 1765, throwing sparks ever closer to the fuse of revolution. When Governor Spotswood dissolved the House of Burgesses as it was about to vote to boycott British goods in 1769, its members simply reassembled at the Raleigh tavern and voted there. On May 6, 1776, the first Virginia Convention met in Williamsburg to declare Virginia an independent commonwealth, and four years later the capital was moved to Richmond to escape the invading British.

British, Continental, and French forces all bil-

COAST AREA WINERIES

Ingleside Plantation Vineyards
804/224-8687; www.ipwine.com
Near Oak Grove (Northern Neck); Rt. 638 south of Oak Grove

Williamsburg Winery, Ltd.
757/229-0999; www.williamsburgwineryltd.com
Near Williamsburg; I-64 exit 242A to Rt. 199 west, left onto Brookwood Dr., left onto Lake Powell Rd. for 0.75 miles
Gabriel Archer Tavern next door.

Windy River Winery
804/499-6996; www.windyriverwinery.com
Near Beaverdam; I-95 N exit 98, Rt. 684 west 10 miles, Rt. 738 north 1.5 miles

leted on the city's grassy lawns during the Revolutionary War, providing temporary relief from an economic slump that continued into the 19th century by buying goods from local merchants. Restoration began in the 1920s at the instigation of Rev. Dr. W.A.R. Goodwin, rector of the historic Bruton Parish Church. Bankrolled by no less than John D. Rockefeller, Jr. (who signed documents anonymously as "Mr. David"), the plan met with some local resistance until residents realized it was probably the best thing to happen to the city in 150 years.

Exhaustive research in libraries and museums in Europe and America uncovered documents, drawings, and maps detailing Williamsburg's faded glory. More than 450 buildings were torn down, 91 were built, and 67 Colonial structures restored (with their inhabitants allowed to stay on for life).

Eighty-eight original buildings have been meticulously restored on 173 of the town's 220 original acres. More than 500 other structures have been rebuilt as closely as possible to their original specifications, surrounded by 90 acres of lawns and gardens and a 3,000-acre buffer zone against further development. Restoration is constantly being refined as new archeological information comes to light, from hearth-stone material to hand-painted wallpaper designs.

© JULIAN SMITH

truly colonial transportation

VISITING COLONIAL WILLIAMSBURG

If you don't plan ahead, visiting Colonial Williamsburg can be an exercise in patience. Reservations for hotels and special events are essential during peak months (April, May, July, August, October, late November, and December), and early morning is always the best time to visit the more popular stops, such as the Governor's Palace and Capitol building. You can do the highlights in one day, even a single tiring morning, but a much better plan is to leave yourself a few days—even a week—to wander the back lanes, chat with the interpreters, and linger over a pint at one of the taverns.

Williamsburg is open 365 days a year, with its main attractions open Apr.–Oct. 9:30 A.M.–5 P.M. and Nov.–Mar. 10 A.M.–4 P.M. Restaurants and taverns bustle until after dark, and the streets are always free to wander, but you'll need to buy passes to enter the historic buildings.

First stop is the visitors center run by the **Colonial Williamsburg Foundation,** 800/447-8679 or 757/220-7286, fax 757/565-8938, www.colonialwilliamsburg.org. The center, off US 60 By-

pass and the Colonial Parkway just east of Rt. 132, is an event in itself, with Burger King and Texaco branches, color-coded parking lots, and a gigantic bookstore. Ticket lines can take awhile, so you might want to designate a volunteer to wait while everyone else in your party catches the 35-minute orientation film, *Williamsburg—The Story of a Patriot.*

Admission passes come in a few different versions. You can always upgrade to the next level by paying the price difference, and all tickets can be purchased online though the Foundation's website. A basic **Day Pass** ($32 adults, $16 children 6–17) gives admission to all the museums and exhibits, including Carter's Grove Plantation, until 5 P.M. The **Freedom Pass** ($38/19) adds admission to Williamsburg by Night activities and is good for one year. The **Liberty Pass** ($55/23), also good for one year, includes access to exclusive events and special visitor services, and discounts on shopping, dining, and other activities in the Williamsburg area. Some evening programs, including music, dancing, and theater performances, require advance reservations and separate admission. With any ticket, you'll receive a copy of the tabloid

THE COAST

Visitor's Companion, which contains a map and details on the week's events.

The Colonial Williamsburg Foundation has concocted several discount vacation packages involving accommodations, meals, golf, and seasonal events. Packages like the Patriot Plan and Colonial Escape run anywhere from $200 to 450 per night, combining food, lodging, and admission to attractions such as Colonial Williamsburg, the Jamestown Settlement, and the Yorktown Victory Center. Call the Foundation, or check their website, for more details. Free parking near the visitors center is included with every ticket, and shuttle buses run to the historic area.

HISTORICAL SIGHTS

Governor's Palace

This mammoth building was constructed from 1708–1722 to symbolize the power of the Crown in the colonies. Thomas Jefferson and Patrick Henry stepped through the door as the capital's first two governors, shortly before it burned to its foundation in 1781. It's been restored to the era of Governor Norborne Berkeley, Baron de Botetourt (1768–1770), one of the last royal governors who was actually respected by his Colonial subjects—maybe the lavish dinner parties had something to do with it.

An astounding rosette of muskets on the ceiling of the entrance hall, along with dozens of criss-crossed swords on the walls, show the true basis of British power in the colonies. Don't miss the birdcages in the butler's pantry and the 10 acres of restored gardens with topiary works, a holly maze, and a fish pond. The Governor's Palace is the single most popular building in Colonial Williamsburg, receiving 650,000 visitors annually, so try to get there early in the day.

The Capitol

Shaped like a bulbous H, this brick building is a reconstruction of the original structure finished in 1705 and burned in 1747. Large round windows admit light to twin chambers for the House of Burgesses and Governor's Council, as well as the General Courtroom, with its dark wood paneling, snakelike glass chandelier, and semicircular bench with chairs for the governor and council. George Washington, Thomas Jefferson, and Patrick Henry all polished their oratory in the House of Burgesses, the lower elected body that sent proposed laws to the Council for consideration. Interpreters explain how jury duty today is a garden party compared to what it was in the 18th century, when juries were denied heat, food, and water in order to encourage a speedy verdict. A military encampment in the Capitol Square explains why the House of Burgesses is currently dissolved (or was, in November 1775).

Courthouse of 1770

Many a criminal quaked at the sight of the cupola and weathervane atop Williamsburg's Courthouse, where severe punishment followed quick judgment. Criminal cases from wife-beating to murder were tried in this original building, along with more mundane matters such as debtor disputes and the issuing of licenses. Guilty parties were then fined, thrown in jail, or simply flogged at the whipping post outside. Visitors can take part in the dispensation of Colonial justice on either side of the docket—as a member of the jury or a defendant. Punishments are optional.

Magazine and Guardhouse

Weapons and 60,000 pounds of gunpowder were once stored in this octagonal structure, built in 1715 on Duke of Gloucester Street opposite the Courthouse. It later served as a meetinghouse, dance school, livery stable, and market before being fully restored and filled with flintlock muskets, cannons, bayonets, and powder barrels once again.

Raleigh Tavern

The unofficial capitol of Colonial Williamsburg was known for the quality of its entertainment as well as its discussion and gossip. Named for Sir Walter Raleigh, who founded the famous lost colony of Roanoke Island, North Carolina, two decades before Jamestown's founding, the tavern witnessed the birth of the Phi Beta Kappa society and innumerable late-night soireés in its first few decades. Patriots including Thomas Jefferson and Harry "Light-Horse" Lee all endured hangovers after evenings in the Apollo ballroom (time spent plotting the future of their infant country, no doubt). A table in the billiard room dates to 1738, and a bake shop in back sells gingerbread and cider.

Brush-Everard House

Public Armorer John Brush built this house in 1717, making it one of Williamsburg's oldest buildings. Two-time mayor Thomas Everard moved in in the late 18th century, and it was continually occupied until 1946. It's furnished as a typical Colonial craftsman might have been able to afford, with outstanding carved woodwork and a library containing books recommended by Jefferson as "the core of any educated gentleman's collection."

Bruton Parish Church

One of the country's oldest Episcopal churches stands at the foot of Palace Green, built in 1715 in the shape of a cross by Governor Spotswood, who included an enclosed covered pew for his own use. The walls and windows are original. It's not officially part of Colonial Williamsburg, and since services are still held here it's only open 9 A.M.–5 P.M. Mon.–Sat., noon–5 P.M. Sunday. Legend has it that a vault buried in the churchyard by Nathaniel Bacon holds gold chalices, original editions of the U.S. Constitution, the King James Bible, and the Book of Saint Peter, as well as proof that his father, Sir Francis Bacon, authored the plays attributed to Shakespeare. Despite fervent hope of finding that last one, more than one researcher has dug among the graves with no luck.

Peyton Randolph House

One of Colonial Williamsburg's most elegant homes reflects the tastes of its owner, Peyton Randolph, who was speaker of the House of Burgesses, president of the First Continental Congress, and the only native Virginian to be knighted. French military leaders Lafayette and Rochambeau lived here during the Yorktown campaign, enjoying its seven paneled rooms at

the corner of Nicholson and England streets. At Randolph's death, his cousin Thomas Jefferson purchased his books and used them to start the Library of Congress. A recent 2,000-square-foot addition expanded the kitchen, dairy, and smokehouse.

George Wythe House

A more conservative residence belonged to George Wythe, the first Virginian to sign the Declaration of Independence. (He didn't sign the Constitution, however, because it didn't contain antislavery provisions or a Bill of Rights.) As the first professor of law in America, Wythe taught Jefferson, Monroe, and future Chief Justice John Marshall at William and Mary. George Washington stayed in this house before the battle of Yorktown, and Rochambeau passed through after Cornwallis's surrender. A tree box topiary and hornbeam arbor fill the rear gardens, near an outbuilding where you can watch Colonial cooking demonstrations.

Public Gaol

Offenders and the merely offensive, from pirates and runaway slaves to Tory sympathizers and the insane, all enjoyed the hospitality of Williamsburg's public jail. Built in 1704, it was used until 1910 and has been restored to its 1720s appearance. Miserable barred cells still hold the little extras—manacles, leg irons, and the like—that made every stay special.

Public Hospital of 1773

Speaking of madmen, Williamsburg's Public Hospital for Persons of Insane and Disordered Minds opened as the first facility in the country to care for the mentally ill. In the 18th century, insanity was considered a conscious choice, so along with the progressive therapies like sports and music, patients were also kept in cages, dunked in water, and held in manacles to "convince" them to mend their mindset. Conditions grew more humane in the 19th century under the administration of John Galt II, who introduced crafts shops and social gatherings for inmates. Successful treatments, though, remained elusive. Open Wed.–Mon., 11 A.M.–6 P.M.

Trade Sites

Master craftspeople, many of whom have served multiyear apprenticeships, practice Colonial-era crafts at dozens of shops and exhibits throughout the historic area. At the **gunsmith** house, an armorer explains the intricacies of a flintlock musket. You can watch handbills and newspapers being printed on an 18th-century press in the **Printing Office.** One of the best areas to watch demonstrations is near **Robertson's Windmill,** between the Governor's Palace and Randolph House, where coopers build casks and carpenters plane boards for the latest restoration. A shoemaker, silversmith, saddlemaker, and wigmaker operate along **Duke of Gloucester Street,** and elsewhere you can catch a milliner, wheelwright, and blacksmith at work. Stop by the **Pasteur and Galt Apothecary Shop** for a disquieting display of medical knowledge (or ignorance) at the time.

© JULIAN SMITH

Robertson's Windmill

College of William and Mary

America's second-oldest college was chartered on February 8, 1693, by King William III and Queen Mary II, consisting of three buildings in the angle formed by Richmond and Jamestown roads. The **Wren Building** was named for Sir Christopher Wren, though he probably didn't design it, and is the oldest academic building in the country still in use (1695). It's been restored to its 1776 appearance. Two wings containing a chapel and Great Hall embrace a courtyard whose fourth side was never enclosed as planned. Call 757/221-1540 for information on opening hours. To either side stand the **President's House,** still in use, and the **Brafferton,** originally built as an Indian School.

The college severed ties with Great Britain in 1776 and soon became the first school in the United States to have branches of law and modern languages and operate under an honor system. Thomas Jefferson, James Monroe, and John Tyler are among its more prestigious alumni. The school became state-supported in 1906 and went coeducational in 1918. Today it counts close to 8,000 students, most of whom take advantage of one of the top undergraduate programs in the country, taught by more than 667 faculty.

Some 3,000 works of art dating to 1732 are displayed in the **Muscarelle Museum of Art,** 757/221-2700, open Mon.–Fri. 10 A.M.–4:45 P.M., Sat. and Sun. noon–6 P.M.; free.

Bassett Hall

The 19th-century home of John D. and Abby Aldrich Rockefeller has been restored to its 1930s splendor of Chippendale furniture, original paneling, and needlepoint rugs made by Abby. It sits amid 585 acres of woodlands across Francis Street from the Capitol. It's usually open daily 10 A.M.–5 P.M., but as of 2001 was closed for renovations; call 757/246-2099 for information.

OTHER SIGHTS

DeWitt Wallace Decorative Arts Museum

A gift of $14 million (the largest in Williamsburg's history) from DeWitt Wallace, the owner of *The Reader's Digest,* funded construction of this modern exhibition hall. Entered through the Public Hospital at Francis and N. Henry streets, the DeWitt Gallery, 757/220-7724, houses an astonishing collection of 10,000 objects from England and America. Furniture, paintings, ceramics, textiles, silver, and glass on display date to the 17th and 18th centuries. Highlights in the Masterworks Gallery upstairs include a Charles Wilson Peale portrait of George Washington and a case clock made for King William III in 1699. The **Gallery Cafe** serves light sandwiches, salads, soups, and wine for lunch Wed.–Mon. Open daily 10 A.M.–5 P.M.

Abby Aldrich Rockefeller Folk Art Museum

This world-class collection of folk art, ranging in age from the 1730s to the present, was the passion of John D. Rockefeller's wife, one of the first collectors to search out untutored rural artists in the 1920s and '30s. Everything from toys and weathervanes to painted furniture and tinware show that true inspiration can have the most humble beginnings. Notice the ship carvings and embroidered mourning pictures. The museum, S. England St. across from the Williamsburg Lodge, 757/220-7690, is open daily 10 A.M.–5 P.M.

Carter's Grove Plantation

Carter Burwell, grandson of Robert "King" Carter, built this grand mansion from 1750 to 1754 along the shore of the James. The 200-foot-long manor house is described as the epitome of the Georgian style, even though later owners added Victorian and Colonial revival touches. A wide arch in the paneled entrance hall leads to a sweeping flight of stairs, with sword gashes on the railing said to be the work of British brigadier Banastre Tarleton (on whom the bad guy in Mel's Gibson's movie *The Patriot* was based) as he spurred his horse up the stairs. Both George Washington and Thomas Jefferson were reportedly turned down for marriage in the "Refusal Room" upstairs.

Around the 750-acre estate are reconstructed slave quarters, whose pine-log cabins each held as many as 24 people, and the ongoing excavation of **Wolstenholme Towne**—all that's left of a Colonial settlement wiped out by Indians on March 22, 1622. Only 60 of the original 220 colonists known as the "Society of Martin's Hundred" escaped. Recent finds are displayed in the **Winthrop Rockefeller Archeology Museum.**

Carter's Grove, 757/229-1000 ext. 2973, is eight miles east of Williamsburg on Rt. 60. It's

open daily 9 A.M.–5 P.M. Mar.–Dec. Admission is included in Williamsburg tickets; separate admission is $18 adults, $11 children 6–12.

ACCOMMODATIONS

With close to 10,000 hotel rooms, Williamsburg has no shortage of places to stay. Still, this is such a popular destination that reservations are always helpful—and essential during peak months of April, May, July, August, October, late November, and December. The **Williamsburg Hotel and Motel Association,** 800/999-4485, email: innkeepers@williamsburghotel.com, www.williamsburghotelassoc.com, operates a reservation service that can help set up lodgings and meals in the area.

Colonial Williamsburg Foundation Hotels

For information and reservations for these accommodations in the historic area, call 800/447-8679.

What could be more authentic after a long day in the 18th century than curling up in an actual Colonial home? The foundation operates 27 Colonial houses, each with its own unique history and from 1–16 rooms. The **Market Square** Tavern is where Thomas Jefferson lodged as a student at William and Mary; the **Quarter** was a favorite of Cary Grant in the 1940s. Some of the buildings, including the **Bracken Tenement** and **Ewing House,** are original, whereas others are reconstructed. Many have canopied beds, fireplaces, and views of Duke of Gloucester Street.

The **Williamsburg Inn,** 137 Francis St., 757/229-1000, fax 757/220-7096, is probably the finest hotel in the city, if not on the entire Historic Peninsula. Rennovations completed in 2001 enlarged the hotel to 62 rooms and upped its AAA category to four diamonds. No two rooms in this posh place are alike, but all are lavishly decorated with antiques. The Inn's formal Regency Dining Room is justly famous for its elegant setting and extensive wine list; the Regency Lounge provides a more casual option. English tea is served on Saturday and Sunday, and a convincing facsimile of Martha Washington

THE COAST

attends occasionally. Guests have access to full sports facilities and three golf courses, including the nationally known Golden Horseshoe. Rates are in the $450 range.

Across England Street from the Abby Aldrich Rockefeller Folk Art Center stands the **Williamsburg Lodge,** 310 S. England St., 757/220-7600, fax 757/220-7799, a resort hotel popular with conference groups. Two hundred sixty-seven rooms alternate between Colonial and modern decor, and the sunken garden is perfect for an after-dinner ramble. Dining choices include the Bay Room Restaurant and the relaxed Lodge Cafe—their Chesapeake Bay Feast on Friday and Saturday evenings, and the Sunday brunch buffet, are justly famous. Prices are around $250. The **Woodlands Hotel,** 102 Visitors Center Dr., 757/229-1000, fax 757/221-8942, offers 202 contemporary rooms ($125) and 98 suites in comfortably wooded surroundings next door to the Colonial Williamsburg visitors center. The **Governor's Inn,** 506 N. Henry St., 757/229-1000, fax 757/220-7019, began its career as a Sheraton a short walk from the visitors center and the historic area. It has 200 rooms ($100) and a pool.

Bed-and-Breakfasts

Century-old beech, oak, and poplar trees welcome you to the **Liberty Rose B&B,** 1022 Jamestown Rd., 800/545-1825 or 757/253-1260, www.libertyrose.com, called the most romantic bed-and-breakfast in Williamsburg. Set on a hilltop, the two-story home features rooms with names like "Magnolia Peach" and "Savannah Lace" ($155–205), decorated with designer wallcoverings and vintage fabrics. Soak in an antique clawfoot tub or savor a gourmet breakfast on the sunny porch.

Colonial Gardens, 1109 Jamestown Rd., 800/886-9715 or 757/220-8087, fax 757/253-1495, email: colgdns@widomaker.com, www.ontheline.com/cgbb, is just next door, with rocking chairs on the front porch and plush robes in the bedrooms ($125–155). Breakfast is served on fine china in the formal dining room, and over the holidays a Christmas tree brightens each room. German-born Inge Curtis opened **A Prim-**rose **Cottage,** 706 Richmond Rd., 800/522-1901, email: ingecurtis@aol.com, www.primrose-cottage.com, as an outlet for her interests in cooking, gardening, and carpentry, and it shows in the beds of pansies and primroses in the front yard and her famous "Dutch Babies" for breakfast. Four bedrooms are $95–155.

The **Colonial Capital Bed & Breakfast,** 501 Richmond Rd., 800/776-0570 or 757/229-0233, fax 757/253-7667, email: ccbb@widomaker.com, www.ccbb.com. occupies a 1926 Colonial Revival home across the street from William and Mary. Oriental rugs and family heirlooms fill the three-story house, whose large plantation parlor is warmed by a roaring fire in the winter. (Rates $130–145.)

For historical accuracy, it's hard to beat the **Newport House,** 710 S. Henry St., 757/229-1775, fax 757/229-6408, www.bbonline.com/va/newport/index.html, a reconstruction of a 1756 home designed by Colonial architect Peter Harrison. Wood siding is carved to look like cut stone (Harrison's solution for a client who couldn't afford a stone house), and the two rooms ($130–155) are furnished with museum-quality English and American antiques, accurate down to the bedspread patterns. Hosts John and Cathy Miller teach English country dancing in the ballroom some evenings and often include a historic recipe or two for breakfast.

Other noteworthy B&Bs in the Williamsburg area include Laura Reeves' **Williamsburg Manor Bed & Breakfast,** 600 Richmond Rd., 800/422-8011 or 757/220-8011, fax 757/220-0245, www.bbonline.com/va/williamsburgmanor/index.html, with optional but delectable dinners; and the **Williamsburg Sampler Bed and Breakfast,** 922 Jamestown Rd., 800/722-1169 or 757/253-0398, fax 757/253-2669, email: wbg.sampler@aol.com, www.bbonline.com/va/sampler/index.html, proclaimed "Inn of the Year" by Gov. George Allen in 1995. Both offer accomodations for $150–160.

Hotels, Motels, and Guest Houses

Several private homes in Williamsburg have been opened to guests. Try **Carter's Guest House,** 903 Lafayette St., 757/229-1117; the **Lewis Guest House,** 809 Lafayette St., 757/229-6116;

or the **Thompson Guest House,** 1007 Lafayette St., 757/229-3455. The **Bassett Motel,** 800 York St., 757/229-5175, has rooms for around $50.

Slightly more expensive options include the **Governor Spottswood Motel,** 1508 Richmond Rd., 757/229-6444, fax 757/253-2410; the **Colonial Waller Motel,** 917 Capitol Landing Rd., 757/253-0999, fax 757/253-0276; and the **Captain John Smith Inn,** 2225 Richmond Rd., 757/220-0710, fax 757/220-1166.

The **Days Inn Historic Area,** 331 Bypass Rd., 757/253-1166, fax 757/221-0637, goes for a country-inn atmosphere in its 120 rooms, including some suites. There's a **Holiday Inn** at 814 Capitol Landing Rd., 757/229-0200, fax 757/220-1642, with a dining room, gym, and cocktail lounge. Finally, **The Princess Anne,** 1350 Richmond Rd., 757/229-2455, fax 757/229-0122, has 71 attractive rooms decorated with Colonial fabrics set on wooded grounds.

Resorts

Five miles east of Colonial Williamsburg on US 60 is **Kingsmill Resort,** 800/832-5665 or 757/253-1703, www.kingsmill.com, the state's largest golf and spa resort. Three golf courses on the banks of the James River include the difficult River Course, site of the Michelob Championship at Kingsmill and the Anheuser-Busch Golf Classic. Fifteen tennis courts, a racquetball court, nature trails, and a full fitness center/spa round out the amenities. Guestrooms and suites, with one to three bedrooms and kitchens, range from $220–1,000. Call for information on various packages including admission to Colonial Williamsburg and nearby attractions.

Camping

The **Anvil Campground,** 5243 Mooretown Rd., 800/633-4442, email: stay@anvilcampground.com, www.anvilcampground.com, is the closest to central Williamsburg, but the nearby train tracks may take some getting used to. Full-hookup sites are $29 and tent sites are $21, and the fourth and seventh nights are free.

Take Rt. 646 north from I-64 exit 234 (Lightfoot) to reach the **Colonial KOA Resort,** 4000 Newman Rd., and the **Williamsburg KOA Re-sort,** 5210 Newman Rd. The same phone number, 800/KOA-1733, lets you reserve campsites ($27–46) or one- and two-room cabins ($28–70) at either place.

FOOD

Historic Area Dining

Four reconstructed taverns carry on the tradition of "savory victuals expeditiously served after the best manner." Low beamed ceilings, roaring fireplaces, and pewter plates evoke the days when wealthy planters gathered to dine on classic dishes such as peanut soup, Sally Lund bread, and Brunswick stew. All the taverns have garden seating in cooperative weather, and entrées range $6–8 for lunch and $13–22 for dinner. Call 757/229-2141 for reservations, which are recommended.

Christina Campbell's Tavern, on Waller St. behind the Capitol, specializes in seafood. Mrs. Campbell's gumbo and Carolina fish muddle were favorites of George Washington, who probably would have also enjoyed the strolling balladeers. Open daily for dinner and Tues.–Sat. for brunch. Grilled poultry, seafood, and Colonial game pie are served in candlelit elegance at the **King's Arms Tavern** on Duke of Gloucester Street. Top it off with a slice of pecan pie and goblet of Colonial punch. Open Wed.–Sat. for lunch and daily for dinner.

The **Shields Tavern** next door is the oldest and largest in Williamsburg, re-creating a rustic eatery of the late 1740s. Eleven dining rooms fill with the smell of pork chops baking and beef roasting on a specially designed spit. Other tempting choices, including the catch of the day and filet mignon, go well with a mug of sparkling cider. Open Thurs.–Tues. for lunch and daily for dinner. Adjacent to the Courthouse is **Josiah Chowning's Tavern,** opened in 1766. Mr. Chowning's black walnut ice cream is a standout after a heaping plateful of baked stuffed pork chops. After 9 P.M., you can knock back a tankard or two in a setting rich with 18th-century music and games in Gambol's pub. Open daily for lunch and dinner.

Award-winning chef Marcel Desaulniers, author of the popular dessert manuals *Death by*

Chocolate and *Dessert to Die For,* is reason enough to visit **The Trellis Restaurant,** 757/229-8610, a California-style restaurant hung with whimsical paintings. Lunch offerings such as herbed couscous sandwiches and grilled eggplant and scallion salad run $8–10. Dinner entrées include vegetarian and vegan selections alongside thin-cut calf's liver and sauteed rabbit. Full dinners run $25. Desserts, of course, are lethal. Open daily for lunch and dinner.

Berrett's Restaurant and Raw Bar, 199 S. Boundary St., 757/253-1849. This casual seafood place runs with a nautical theme because it offers every kind of fresh local seafood imaginable. Try the Crabmeat Imperial, served on puff pastry with Virginia ham.

Starters

Two places with good breakfast selections are the **Old Mill House of Pancakes & Waffles,** 2005 Richmond Rd., 757/229-3613, with more than a dozen varieties, and **Mama Steve's House of Pancakes,** 1509 Richmond Rd., 757/229-7613, run by the same folks who own The Jefferson. Both are open daily for breakfast and lunch. The Hunt Breakfast buffet at the Cascades Restaurant, by the Colonial Williamsburg Visitors Center, also earns wide praise.

Student Favorites

Inexpensive pizzas, subs, sandwiches, and steamed seafood are the standard favorites at **The Library Tavern,** 1330 Richmond Rd., 757/229-1012, "where silence isn't golden" and which also has a full bar and pool tables in the back. The **College Delly & Pizza Restaurant,** 336 Richmond Rd., 757/229-6627, is similar, with spaghetti and hot sandwiches, and **Paul's Deli Restaurant & Pizza,** 761 Scotland St., 757/229-8976, has Greek and Italian plates. All three are open daily for lunch and dinner until 2 A.M.

Plenty of fast-food joints line Richmond Road heading north, with many seafood and breakfast buffet options. No matter how big the meal, there's always room for a scoop of ice cream at **Ben & Jerry's,** 3044 Richmond Rd., 757/565-3800, which is open daily 11 A.M.–10 or 11 P.M.

More Substantial

In 1950, Harriet Petrell opened **The Jefferson Restaurant,** 1453 Richmond Rd., 757/229-2296, making it one of the first eateries on the Richmond strip. She can still be found knitting behind the counter while the kitchen turns out tried-and-true Virginia specialties from grain-fed catfish to Southern-fried chicken. Entrées are $13–22 including soup and salad. This unpretentious but dependable place is open daily from 4 P.M. Half restaurant, half antique shop, the **Old Chickahominy House,** 1211 Jamestown Rd. (Rt. 31), 757/229-4689, resembles an old farmhouse and serves food to match. Plantation meals in the 18th-century dining room include chicken and dumplings and homemade pie; hearty country breakfasts of ham, bacon, sausage, eggs, and biscuits are around $8 (the pancakes are to die for). Open daily for breakfast and lunch.

The **Aberdeen Barn,** 1601 Richmond Rd., 757/229-6661, claims the best beef in town, and a bite of the slow-roasted prime rib might convince you. Their signature dessert involves a croissant, ice cream, and peach sauce—let your imagination go from there. Reservations are suggested for the rustic, candlelit restaurant, open daily for dinner.

Le Yaca, 757/220-3616, in the Village Shops at Kingsmill, serves the best French food for miles around in a rustic setting around a large open hearth. For lunch, the salad table is filled with a dozen kinds of French salads, and no dinner is complete without the outstanding onion soup and something off the lengthy wine list. Open Mon.–Sat. for lunch and dinner.

For a taste of Asia, try the chargrilled Vietnamese entrées at **Chez Trinh,** 757/253-1888, 157 Monticello Ave., in the Williamsburg Shopping Center. More tastes of Asia can be found at **Kyoto Japanese Steak & Seafood House,** 1621 Richmond Rd., 757/226-8888, with a teppanyaki grill show out front or sushi in the quieter back room (open daily for dinner, around $20); and at **Nawab Indian Cuisine,** 204 Monticello Ave., 757/565-3200, with sampler platters and a lunch buffet (open daily for lunch and dinner).

RECREATION

Historical Diversions

Colonial Williamsburg offers a full roster of activities by day and night, from guided walking tours of the historic area to an evening of Vivaldi at the Palace of the Governors. Some events, such as a candlelight walk around the city's haunted spots, are scheduled. Others just happen—as when wandering reenactors allow you to debate the rights of man with Thomas Jefferson or gossip with Martha Washington about her husband's snoring.

You can ride a carriage down Duke of Gloucester Street, attend a witch trial, and march to the beat of the Colonial Williamsburg Fife and Drum Corps—all in the same day, if you want. The African-American Interpretation and Presentations staff reflects the fact that half of Williamsburg's population in the 18th century were slaves. Check your *Visitor's Companion* for a daily schedule of events. Most are free, but evening Colonial performances require a $12 ticket ($9 for Liberty Pass holders).

Music and Other Nightlife

J.M. Randall's Restaurant and Lounge, 4854 Longhill Rd. in the Olde Towne Square, 757/259-0406, features acoustic rock and blues. Live bands also play at **The Library Tavern,** 1330 Richmond Rd., 757/229-1012, which is popular with William and Mary students.

The Music Theatre of Williamsburg, 7575 Richmond Rd., 757/546-0200 or 888/687-4220, is similar but with a wider range of music. Opened in 1998, it hosts variety shows covering the spectrum from big band and jazz to show tunes and gospel, with a dash of comedy. At William and Mary, 757/221-1540, concerts come to **Phi Beta Kappa Hall** and the larger **William and Mary Hall,** which can hold up to 10,000 people.

The Corner Pocket, 757/221-0808, in the Williamsburg Crossing Shopping Center at Rt. 5 and Rt. 199, is an upscale, 18-and-over pool hall with a moderate dress code and high-quality tables.

Outdoors

You can rent bicycles from **Bikes Unlimited,** 759 Scotland St. at Richmond St., 757/229-4620, or **Bikesmith of Williamsburg,** 515 York St., 757/229-9858, to explore Colonial Williamsburg and the Colonial National Historical Parkway.

Shopping

Williamsburg is one of Virginia's shopping meccas, so the trick becomes figuring out what you want to buy, not where to buy it. Outlets galore fill malls and shopping centers in every direction from the historic center, but the most distinctive souvenirs come from specialty shops in and around Colonial Williamsburg.

Most of the items you can see being made by Williamsburg craftspeople are also for sale, either at the shops themselves or in two **Craft Houses** run by the Colonial Williamsburg Foundation. One is in the Colonial shopping district of Merchant's Square, which fills the last block of Duke of Gloucester Street before William and Mary; the other is near the Folk Art Center. At both you can buy authorized reproductions of furniture, wallpaper, china, glassware, and many other items made in Williamsburg workshops.

Alternately, head to the shops themselves to meet the artisans and discuss their work. Choose from handmade jewelry at the **Golden Ball Shop,** cakes from the **Raleigh Tavern Bakery,** and antique prints at the **Colonial Post Office** (which can cancel your postcards with an original 18th-century postmark). General stores including **Greenhow** and **Tarpley's** carry tricornered hats, candles, soaps, and baskets, while **Prentice Store** sells fine linens.

Merchant's Square is home to upscale shops such as the **J. Fenton Gallery,** with unique handicrafts by Virginia artists; **Quilts Unlimited, Shirley Pewter Shop,** and **The Toymaker of Williamsburg.**

Five miles north on Richmond Rd. sprawls the **Williamsburg Pottery Factory,** 757/564-3326, more of a settlement than a store, with 32 buildings spread over 200 acres. Begun as a roadside stand in 1938, Williamsburg Pottery stocks tens of thousands of discounted items—not just pottery but also prints, glassware, ceramics, and much more—and draws five million visitors a year.

EVENTS

In late September, the **Williamsburg Scottish Festival and Celtic Celebration,** email: info@wfsonline.org, www.wsfonline.org, brings bagpipes, brogues, and a Balmoral reception to the Williamsburg Winery at 639 Lake Powell Rd., off Rt. 31 south of the city. Celtic dancing, clan tents, and a *Ceilidh* (Scottish musical party) round out the festivities.

The Christmas holiday season is one of Williamsburg's busiest times, beginning with the **Grand Illumination,** on December 6, when the entire historic area flickers with candlelight. Homes are decorated with 18th-century ornaments made from natural materials such as pine cones and evergreen boughs, and the streets echo with concerts and carols. Special holiday programs, feasts, fireworks, and military salutes continue through the New Year.

TRANSPORTATION

Getting Around
Public buses along US 60, passing Williamsburg Pottery and Busch Gardens, is managed by James City County Transit (JCCT), 757/220-1621. Buses ($1 pp) run daily from 9 A.M.–9 P.M. Colonial Williamsburg's **shuttle buses** are the easiest way to get around the historic area, stopping at the visitors center, Merchants Square, the Magazine, Governor's Palace, and Capitol building.

Getting There and Away
The **Williamsburg Transportation Center,** 468 N. Boundary St. at Lafayette, houses the terminals of Greyhound/Trailways, 757/229-1460, and Amtrak, 757/229-8750. Fourteen miles east of Williamsburg, at I-64 exit 255 in Newport News, is the **Newport News-Williamsburg International Airport,** 757/877-0221, www.nnwairport.com, served by United Express, US Airways Express, and AirTran. Shuttle services include Yellow Cab of Williamsburg, 757/722-1111, and Towne & Country Limousine, 757/564-4450.

Both the transportation center and the airport have a handful of car rental agencies.

INFORMATION

In addition to the Colonial Williamsburg Visitors Center, you can contact the **Williamsburg Area Convention & Visitor Bureau,** 421 N. Boundary St., 800/368-6511 or 757/253-0192, www.visitwilliamsburg.com, for general information, or stop by **Williamsburg Online** at www.williamsburg.com.

NEAR WILLIAMSBURG

York River State Park
A rugged landscape of gorge, forest, marsh, and bluff fills 2,500 acres where Taskinas Creek meets the York River. The site of public tobacco warehouses in the 17th and 18th centuries, when it was known as Taskinas Plantation, this park has a much longer history than that: fossilized whale vertebrae, sharks' teeth, and coral up to five million years old have all been found nearby.

More than 25 miles of trails connect the river, creek, and freshwater ponds plied by anglers during fishing season (boat rental are available). You can also rent mountain bikes for a six-mile single-track and five easier trails. Guided canoe trips up the brackish tidal waters of Taskinas Creek leave from the **Taskinas Point Visitors Center,** 757/566-3036, www.dcr.state.va.us/parks/york rive.htm, and interpretive programs explore the park's fossils and natural offerings. The visitors center is off I-64 exit 231 to Rt. 507 north; continue to Rt. 606; within one mile, take a right, continue 1.5 miles, and take a left onto Rt. 696. Admission is $2 adults, $1 children.

Busch Gardens Williamsburg
Historic recreation takes on a slightly different meaning in Virginia's largest amusement park, repeatedly voted America's Most Beautiful for its Old World theme. Roller coasters are the stars, beginning with Apollo's Chariot, whose first drop (out of nine) is 210 feet high. On the Alpengeist, passengers hang from the track as if on a ski lift, although the similarity ends when the ride hits 67

mph and 3.7 Gs during the "cobra roll." In 2001, *Amusement Today* magazine awarded Busch Gardens Williamsburg three of the top steel roller coasters in the world: the Alpengeist (#2), the Big Bad Wolf (#9), and the Loch Ness Monster (#15).

Get an up-close look at the gray wolves at Jack Hanna's Wild Reserve, and you won't believe how big and beautiful the Anheuser-Busch Clydesdales near the petting zoo are. If you get hungry (tip: wait until *after* you ride the Alpengeist) you'll find wurst, beer, and an oompah band in the 2,000-seat Festhaus. Ireland recently became the sixth country to be added to the park's European palette, and a monorail runs to the Anheuser-Busch brewery.

Busch Gardens, 800/253-3350 or 757/253-3350, www.buschgardens.com, is off US 60 three miles southeast of Williamsburg. It's open 10 A.M.–7 to 11 P.M., daily Apr.–Aug. and assorted weekends and other days in March, September, and October. Tickets are $41 adults, $34 children 3–6. You can buy a two-day pass for Busch Gardens and Water Country USA for $50 pp ($65 for three days).

Water Country USA

Anheuser-Busch also administers the mid-Atlantic's largest waterpark, which offers more than 30 ways to escape the summer swelter. Splash through the darkened tunnels of the Aquazoid, team up for the Meltdown, a four-person water toboggan, or hit escape velocity on the superspeed, 320-foot Nitro Racer waterslide. The H2O UFO and Cow-A-Bunga areas are geared toward kids, and whole families can enjoy the wave pools and dive shows.

Water Country USA, 800/343-7946 or 757/253-3550, www.watercountryusa.com, is on Water Country Parkway (Rt. 199) near Busch Gardens. It's open daily 10 A.M.–6 to 8 P.M., late May–Aug., plus weekends through May and September; $30 adults, $23 children 3–6.

Anheuser-Busch Brewery

Fans of suds can visit the source at one of the world's largest breweries, 757/253-3036, only a few miles east of Williamsburg along US 60. A free self-guiding tour teaches you about the history of beer from George Washington's own recipe to the modern mega-brewing process. At the end, there's a hospitality center with free samples (two per person), a snack bar, and a gift shop. Open daily 11 A.M.–5 P.M.

JAMESTOWN

The first permanent European colony in America began as James Fort, hastily erected in 1607 by a handful of nervous English settlers who had traded three cramped sailboats for an endless, untamed wilderness. A combination of sickness, inexperience, hostile natives, and bad management almost spelled the colony's doom in the first few years, but the leadership of Capt. John Smith and a series of fragile truces with the local tribes allowed 5,000 inhabitants to survive to 1634.

Settled in 1607, Jamestown, site of the first permanent European colony in America, fell to ruins after the Colonial capital was moved to Williamsburg in 1699. A Confederate fort took the place of the original wooden stockade in 1861, a year before Jamestown Island was occupied by Union troops. In 1933, the island became part of the Colonial National Historical Park. In the late 1980s, an archaeological reassessment led to the discovery of the original

reconstructed ship at Jamestown settlement

© JULIAN SMITH

THE COAST

settlement (part of which had been hidden by the shifting currents of the James River). Further excavations uncovered the triangular footprint of the Jamestown fort in 1996.

Two separate locations provide contrasting interpretations of the site. First comes Jamestown Settlement, a re-creation of life on the pitiless frontier. Across the bridge is the real thing, on Jamestown Island, a much more low-key but equally affecting spot maintained by the National Park Service.

Jamestown Settlement

Hardy colonists and their native counterparts come to life in this living-history museum of life in 17th-century Virginia—albeit a slightly sanitized and user-friendly version—down to the smell of cooking fires and the roar of gunpowder muskets. Start at the museum, packed with artifacts and information on the English pioneers and their alternating allies and enemies, the Powhatan Indians. Catch the short movie on the settlement before you step outside for the real attractions.

First comes the **Powhatan Indian village,** a cluster of domed houses made of woven reeds over sapling frames. Here, interpreters costumed in animal skins show you how to make bone fishhooks, scrape hides, and build a canoe. Kids will enjoy grinding corn (at least for awhile) and will probably ask about the ceremonial circle of wooden poles carved with faces.

A short walk down the path brings you to the river pier, where three full-size **ship reproductions** of the vessels that brought the European settlers are tied up. Cormorants fish in the water next to the *Discovery,* the *Godspeed,* and the *Susan Comfort.* Climb aboard and imagine crossing 6,000 miles of open ocean in quarters this cramped—the smallest craft is only 50 feet long, with roughly as much space as a small school bus. The *Susan Comfort,* the largest, is 116 feet long with a brightly painted hull. Re-enactors will point out the brick hearth (surprising on a wooden ship) and demonstrate various shipboard activities including furling sails and dropping anchor. These are fully functioning ships, and they occasionally sail away to participate in nautical events.

The colonists must have breathed a sigh of relief to step out of the fo'c'sle (forecastle, or upper deck) and into the safety and relative spaciousness of **James Fort.** Tall wooden palisades connect three raised circular platforms at each corner. Farm fields stretch beyond the walls, while inside stand wattle-and-daub homes, a church, a guardhouse, and storehouses. Try your hand at ninepins (an early version of bowling) and cover your ears for the periodic firing of militia rifles.

Yearly events start in mid-March with **Military Through the Ages,** with reenactors demonstrating weapons, tactics, and camp life. May 12 is **Jamestown Landing Day,** with more living-history demonstrations, and the Virginia Council on Indians co-sponsors the music and dance of the **Virginia Indian Heritage Festival** in mid-June, which brings crafts, storytelling, and food. Two holiday events happen simultaneously at the Yorktown Victory Center: **Foods & Feasts of Colonial Virginia,** a three-day Thanksgiving event focusing on Colonial and native food; and **A Colonial Christmas,** showcasing 17th- and 18th-century holiday decorations and traditional activities.

The whole place is gearing up for the 400th anniversary of the original settlement in 2007; new facilities will include a new Powhatan Indian village and an educational center that will double the existing exhibit space.

Jamestown Settlement is open daily 9 A.M.–5 P.M. and has a gift shop and small café. Tickets are $10.75 adults, $5.25 children 6–12, with a combination ticket including the Yorktown Victory Center available for $15.75 adults, $7.50 children. For more information, contact the **Jamestown-Yorktown Foundation,** P.O. Box 1607, Williamsburg, VA 23187, 888/593-4682 or 757/253-4838, www.historyisfun.org.

Jamestown Yacht Basin

At the end of Rt. 31, the **Jamestown Ferry,** 800/VA-FERRY (823-3779), heads to Scotland Wharf on the south side of the river once or twice an hour. Narrated nature cruises on the *Jamestown Island Explorer,* 757/259-0400, also head from here into the marshes and streams of the lower James. Accounts of local history and folklore are interrupted with glimpses of native birds, fish, and animals during the 90-minute tours ($15 adults, $10 children). **Jamestown Beach Campsites,** 757/229-7609, has sites for $20–28 along with a beach, pool, playground, and boat ramp.

Jamestown Island (Colonial National Historical Park)

The earlier end of this elongated park begins with the **Jamestown Glasshouse of 1608,** next to the ruins of the original brick and river-stone furnaces. The first factory industry in the colonies folded after one shipment to England, but artisans in the reconstructed workshop still sell lovely handblown glassware made from the same mixture of ash and sand. Open daily 8:30 A.M.–5 P.M.

Keep driving across a narrow spit of land into the island to reach the National Park Service **visitors center,** 757/229-1733, with a museum housing one of the largest collections of 17th-century artifacts in the country. Everyday utensils including hairpins, buckles, and candlesticks invoke the real people who suffered, survived, and died on this swampy island an ocean away from anything safe and familiar.

Pick up a map of the **James Cittie townsite,** then explore on your own or join one of the four or so ranger-led walks per day. Part of the original townsite has been inundated as the James shoreline shifted, but brick outlines mark where certain buildings once stood. The oldest standing structure is the 1639 tower of the Memorial Church, near statues of Pocahontas and Captain John Smith. A memorial cross marks 300 shallow graves dug during the Starving Time of 1609–1610. The Association for the Preservation of Virginia Antiquities (APVA), which co-manages the site, operates an archeology lab in the Dale House that displays recent finds in the ongoing excavations (open daily 10 A.M.–4 P.M.).

Along the five-mile loop drive (which can be shortened to three), you'll stand a good chance of spotting descendants of the same deer, muskrat, and waterbirds hunted by the Jamestown settlers. To augment historical markers along the way, you can rent an audio tour tape at the visi-

tors center ($2). Living-history programs and children's activities are held at the visitors center from spring to fall. Annual events include **Jamestown Day,** celebrating the founding of the colony, in early May; the **First Assembly Day Commemoration,** in late July; and an evening walking tour and symbolic torching of the town in late September near the anniversary of **Bacon's Rebellion** in 1676. Open daily 9 A.M.–5 P.M.; $6 adults over 16 ($9 with the Yorktown Battlefield).

For more information on Jamestown island, contact the **National Park Service,** P.O. Box 210, Yorktown, VA 23690, 757/898-3400, www.nps.gov/colo. **Clark Transportation,** 757/565-0042, offers car service from Williamsburg to Jamestown ($11 one-way) and Yorktown ($20).

YORKTOWN

One of Virginia's major ports in the 18th century, Yorktown rivaled Williamsburg with its thriving waterfront at the base of a bluff beneath Main Street's regal homes. Almost 2,000 people lived here when Lord Cornwallis arrived in 1781, pursued by the American army and the French navy just offshore. Days of bombardment convinced the British general to request a meeting on October 17 and to surrender officially two days later.

Yorktown Visitors Center (Colonial National Historical Park)

The earth ramparts erected by George Washington's troops now defend this museum, filled with various relics saved from the final confrontation of the Revolutionary War. George Washington's field tents are displayed next to surrendered flags and a rifle stock broken by a British soldier in disgust. Walk through a partial reconstruction of a British warship (watch your head), and get your bearings through a narrated map presentation.

Walking tours, led by interpreters in costume and character, leave from here for the British Inner Defensive Line and the town of Yorktown. You can rent an auto tour tape ($2) for two battlefield loops, passing Surrender Field, George Washington's headquarters, and earthworks

THE COAST

reconstructed through archaeological excavations and detailed studies of 18th-century military maps.

The visitors center, 757/898-3400, is open daily 9 A.M.–5 P.M. for $5 pp over 16 ($9 with Jamestown Island). It's administered by the National Park Service, P.O. Box 210, Yorktown, VA 23690, 757/898-3400, www.nps.gov/colo. A free trolley runs down into town and back every half hour or so during summer.

Historic Yorktown

Still a sparse but working village, Yorktown counts dozens of homes more than two centuries old, many of which occupy their own "lots" (blocks) on the fringes. A path from the visitors center takes you past the 84-foot **Victory Monument,** topped by a winged statue of Liberty, to **Cornwallis' Cave** on the riverbank, a dank hole where the British general is said to have made his headquarters during the shelling. The **Nelson House** was once home to Thomas Nelson, Jr., a signer of the Declaration of Independence. It still bears scars from cannonballs directed by Nelson himself, who suspected Cornwallis was inside. The terms of surrender were drafted in the **Moore House.**

History of a different sort is remembered in the **Watermen's Museum,** 309 Water St., 757/887-2641. Boat models, marine life, and a boat-building area out back honor the "iron men and wooden boats" who have fished the local waters since the first Indians ventured out in dugout canoes. A gift shop sells work by local artists. It's near the US 17 bridge by the water. Open Tues.–Sat. 10 A.M.–4 P.M., Sun. 1–4 P.M.; $3 pp.

Accommodations: The **Duke of York Motel,** 508 Water St., 757/898-3232, fax 757/898-5922, sits right on the riverside, with a restaurant that serves breakfast and lunch. The **Yorktown Motor Lodge,** 8829 George Washington Hwy., 757/898-5451, fax 757/898-1766, has 42 comfortable rooms ($55–90) and an outdoor pool, three miles south of the bridge along US 17. Set on a high bluff above the Waterman's Museum, the **York River Inn,** 209 Ambler St., 800/884-7003 or 757/887-8800, fax 757/887-5939, email: info@yorkriverinn.com, www.yorkriverinn.com, is an elegant little place with two rooms and a suite ($110–130).

Food: You can grab a bite along the water at the **Yorktown Pub,** 757/886-9964, with live music on Friday and Saturday nights. Open daily for lunch and dinner, cash and travelers' checks only. **Waterstreet Landing,** 757/886-5890, serves gourmet pizzas, soups, and sandwiches at the foot of Church Street. **Nick's Seafood Pavilion,** 757/887-5269, is a classier affair at the foot of the US 17 bridge. Friendly service complements a Mediterranean melange of mirrors, statues, greenery, and even a fountain pool. Seafood dishes are $10–15, with combination plates around $15. Open daily for lunch and dinner.

Shopping: Colonial goods, including ceramics, brass, and wrought iron, can be found at **Period Designs,** 757/886-9482, and local artists give demonstrations and sell their work at the **On The Hill Cultural Arts Center,** 121 Alexander Hamilton Blvd., 757/898-3076.

Annual Events: In late April, a **Revolutionary War weekend** features encampments and demonstrations, followed by a **Civil War Weekend** in late May. Yorktown's biggest celebration is **Yorktown Day** near October 19, with the victory commemorated by costumed skirmishes, parades, patriotic music, and military drills here and at the Yorktown Victory Center. Holiday celebrations include **Foods & Feasts of Colonial Virginia** in late November and the **Colonial Christmas** in December.

Activities: From May–Oct. **Erin Kay Charters,** 757/879-8276 or 804/642-5096, runs fishing trips and pleasure cruises on the York River and Chesapeake Bay from the Watermen's Museum aboard the *Miss Yorktown.*

Yorktown Victory Center

This well-done museum and living-history center sits across US 17 from Yorktown itself. Brush up on your background knowledge along the outdoor timeline that leads inside the main building, where exhibits on people affected by the war—from slaves to common women to soldiers—are told through narrated recordings,

© JULIAN SMITH

Yorktown Victory Center

relics, and documents. A military section displays pistols owned by the Marquis de Lafayette near the waterlogged remains of British ships raised from the York River.

Outside, at the Continental Army encampment, you can learn about medicine, food, and music in Colonial armies, and become one of the 17 people needed to fire a cannon (unloaded, of course). A short distance away is a reconstructed farmsite typical of a lower- to middle-class family of the late 18th century. A tobacco barn, forge, and modest home stand next to vegetable and herb gardens and animal pens, managed by costumed interpreters who demonstrate Colonial cooking, farming, and games.

The Yorktown Victory Center, 757/887-1776, is open daily 9 A.M.–5 P.M.; $7.75 adults, $3.75 children 6–12. A combination ticket including the Jamestown Settlement is available for $15.75 adults, $7.50 children. There's also a snack bar and large gift shop.

The Victory Center operates under the auspices of the **Jamestown-Yorktown Foundation,** P.O. Box 1607, Williamsburg, VA 23187-1607, 888/593-4682 or 757/253-4838, www.historyisfun.org.

JAMES RIVER PLANTATIONS

The fertile banks of the lower James have been prime real estate ever since the days of the Powhatan capital at Sandy Point. During the 18th and 19th centuries, lavish mansions served as business and social centers for huge tobacco plantations. Carriages no longer clatter down long, tree-shaded gravel lanes where servants wait to escort visitors into the parlor for tea and talk of planting, but the area is still mostly forest and farmland with no major town center.

Rt. 5, also called the John Tyler Highway, leads straight from Richmond to six major plantations along the river's north bank. Annual events like garden tours, special teas, birthday celebrations, and progressive luncheons happen almost every month of the year. Block tickets granting admission to Shirley, Berkeley, Evelynton, and Sherwood Forest cost $33 pp and are sold at each. For more information on the plantations, call Sherwood Forest at 800/704-5423, or stop by **Virginia's James River Plantations** on the Internet (www.james-riverplantations.org).

THE COAST

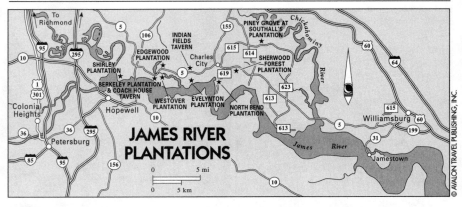

JAMES RIVER PLANTATIONS

© AVALON TRAVEL PUBLISHING, INC.

Shirley Plantation

Virginia's oldest plantation sits on land settled in 1613 by Sir Thomas West. The Queen Anne mansion was begun in 1723 by Edward Hill III for his daughter Elizabeth and her new husband, John Carter, eldest son of agricultural tycoon Robert "King" Carter. Finished in 1738, the house survived both the Revolutionary and Civil wars and is the birthplace of Anne Hill Carter Lee, mother of Robert E., who married Light-Horse Harry in the parlor. Today it's home to the 11th and 12th generations of the Hill-Carter family, plenty of heirlooms, and centuries of stories.

Highlights of the mansion include hand-carved woodwork and a unique square flying stairway that ascends for three stories without any visible means of support. A laundry house where Robert E. Lee was tutored for a time stands among the original brick outbuildings in the unique Queen Anne forecourt, next to an inviting bench under a huge willow oak overlooking the river. Corn, soybeans, and wheat have taken the place of tobacco on the remaining 800 acres of farmland.

Shirley Plantation, 800/232-1613, email: information@shirleyplantation.com, www.shirleyplantation.com, is open daily 9 A.M.–5 P.M.; $9 adults, $5 children 6–12. Half-hour tours are given until 4:30 P.M.

Berkeley Plantation

On December 4, 1619, 38 English settlers had kissed the earth and thanked the heavens upon landing partway up the James River after three months at sea. A monument marks the spot of the original Thanksgiving (followed only two years later by the first batch of bourbon whiskey distilled in the New World).

The Harrison family bought this property in 1691. Benjamin Harrison IV built the manor house in 1726, leaving his and his wife's initials in a datestone over a side door. His son Benjamin V signed the Declaration of Independence and served three terms as governor of Virginia. *His* son William Henry became the ninth president of the United States after making his name on the western frontier. George Washington stopped by from time to time, the first in a string of 10 presidents to enjoy the Harrisons' hospitality. Although he didn't live at Berkeley, William Henry's grandson Benjamin Harrison did the family proud by becoming the 23rd president of the United States.

During Union occupation in 1862, Gen. Dan Butterfield composed the haunting melody of "Taps" shortly before Lincoln visited to review McClellan's army. In this century, the property has been lovingly restored through the efforts of Malcolm Jamieson—whose father, ironically, was a Federal drummer boy. Worth a stop in themselves are Berkeley's terraced boxwood gardens, spread between the house and wide lawns leading down to the river, where geese and sheep wander. The view of the James here is unparalleled and peaceful.

Berkeley, 804/829-6018 or 888/466-6018,

www.berkeleyplantation.com, is open daily 8 A.M.–5 P.M. for $9.50 adults and $6.50 children 6–12. The **First Thanksgiving Festival,** on the first Sunday in November, commemorates the original ceremony of gratitude with Colonial and native reenactors. At Berkeley's **Coach House Tavern,** 804/829-6003, costumed waiters serve Colonial favorites in a restored outbuilding (open daily for lunch, dinner by reservation only).

Westover Plantation
William Byrd III, founder of Richmond and Petersburg, built this Georgian manor house in the 1730s. It's famous for its elegant proportions, view of the James, and ancient tulip poplars around the lawn. Westover is also known as one home of the ghost of Byrd's daughter Evelyn, who pined to death at age 18 after her Catholic parents forbade her to marry a Protestant. She told friends she would be back from the beyond, and her glowing ghost has since been reported here and at Evelynton (witnesses describe it as nonthreatening).

Westover, 804/829-2882, www.jamesriver-plantations.org/Westover.html, shares an access road off Rt. 5 with Berkeley Plantation. The house is only open during Historic Garden Week in April, but the grounds and garden are open to visitors daily 9 A.M.–6 P.M. for $2 pp.

Evelynton Plantation
Originally part of the Westover property, Evelynton (EVE-lin-ton) was named after Byrd's daughter, who is said to haunt both mansions. Since 1847, it has been home to the Ruffin family, whose patriarch, Edmund, fired the first shot of the Civil War at Fort Sumter, South Carolina, and pioneered agricultural techniques that rescued Virginia's declining tobacco economy in the 19th century. The original house and outbuildings were burned during the Civil War Battle of Evelynton Heights, between Gen. George McClellan, J.E.B. Stuart, and Stonewall Jackson.

Architect Duncan Lee designed the current manor house, built in 1937. The Ruffins still farm 2,500 surrounding acres but allow guests to peruse the house's period antiques and formal gardens outside. Evelynton, 800/473-5075 or

804/829-5075, www.evelyntonplantation.org, is open daily 9 A.M.–5 P.M. for $9.50 adults, $6.50 children 6–12.

Sherwood Forest
The only home owned by two U.S. presidents was begun in 1730 under the name Smith's Hundred. William Henry Harrison inherited it in the 1790s but never lived here, in part because he died one month after his inaugural speech. Harrison's vice president, John Tyler, took over both the presidency and the ownership of this white clapboard house, where he retired in 1845. Tyler's grandson still lives upstairs.

Additions to the original building have made Sherwood Forest the longest wooden-frame house in the country—more than 300 feet. A 68-foot ballroom was designed to accommodate guests dancing the Virginia reel. Scars in the woodwork bear witness to Civil War action, and many of the furnishings and decorations belonged to President Tyler. Original outbuildings, terraced gardens, and more than 80 varieties of trees brighten the grounds. Sherwood Forest is also home to a ghost—the Gray Lady, whose rocking has been heard in the Gray Room for more than two centuries.

Sherwood Forest, 804/829-5377, www.sherwoodforest.org, is open daily 9 A.M.–5 P.M. for $9.50 adults, $6 children.

Accommodations and Food
Edgewood Plantation, 4800 John Tyler Hwy., 800/296-3343 or 804/829-2962, email: edgewoodplnatation@williamsburg-virginia.com, www.edgewood-plantation.com, hosts guests in a Gothic Revival home built in 1849 that has since served as post office, church, and Confederate signal post. Fireplaces and a two-story free-standing spiral staircase wait inside, while a 1725 gristmill, formal gardens, and pool surround the house. (Look for the "Lizzie" etched in an upstairs window by a woman who supposedly died of a broken heart waiting for her lover to return from the Civil War.) Eight guest rooms—six in the house and two in the former slave's quarters–are $200.

Between Evelynton and Sherwood Forest sits the **Indian Fields Tavern,** 9220 John Tyler Hwy.,

804/829-5004, an early-1900s farmhouse praised by *Bon Appetit* magazine for its "New Southern" specialties and fresh Chesapeake seafood. It's open daily for lunch and dinner, but make reservations ahead of time or be ready to wait in a rocking chair on the veranda until a table opens up.

Across Rt. 5 is the **North Bend Plantation,** 12200 Weyanoke Rd., 800/841-1479 or 804/829-5176, fax 804/829-6828, www.ontheline.com/nbbb, built in 1819 for William Henry Harrison's sister Sarah. Union Gen. Philip Sheridan made his headquarters here in 1864 and dug trenches that still exist at the eastern edge of the property. The owners, the fifth generation of the Copland family to own North Bend, are happy to point out Sheridan's plantation desk, the 1914 billiard table, and a library full of rare and old books. Rates ($115–135) include a full country breakfast and use of the swimming pool.

Northern Hampton Roads

NEWPORT NEWS

Virginia's fifth-largest city (pop. 180,150), Newport News was named for Capt. Christopher Newport, pilot of the *Susan Constant* in 1607, whose "news" was word sent back to England that the settlers had arrived safely. With no real downtown area, Newport News stretches along I-64 and US 60 toward the largest privately owned shipyard in the country, the massive Newport News Shipbuilding and Dry Dock Company facility.

Recently overtaken by Food Lion as the state's largest private employer, the shipyard still employs about one-tenth of the city's population. Despite recent military cutbacks, it still churns out nuclear attack submarines and aircraft carriers for the U.S. Navy, still according to its founder's 19th-century credo: "We shall build good ships here at a profit—if we can—at a loss—if we must—but always good ships."

Dust-blackened trains rattle south, bound for the largest coal-shipping port in the country, passing one of the country's largest municipal parks and the outstanding Mariners' Museum (well worth a day's detour in itself).

Mariners' Museum

A 3,200-pound, 18-foot golden eagle figurehead ushers you into one of the best nautical collections in the world. Thirteen galleries display the distress lantern that signaled the end of the Union's steel-hulled *Monitor,* gleaming Chris Crafts from the 1920s and 1930s, and intricate scrimshaw carved by bored but talented whalers.

Especially remarkable are the 16 miniature model ships made over two decades by August Crabtree. Magnifying glasses built into the display cases let you appreciate the stunning detail, down to inch-tall figureheads carved with modified dental tools. It's a wonder Crabtree didn't go blind during the 20 years it took to finish the collection, which comprises everything from Indian dugouts to Columbus's ships.

On interactive video displays in the Chesapeake Bay gallery, you can learn how to navigate. Other displays include knot-tying lessons, the evolution of the U.S. Navy, well-worn boatbuilding tools, and changing exhibits covering topics such as pirates, the slave trade, and (of course) the *Titanic.* The museum, 800/581-7245 or 757/596-2222, www.mariner.org, is open daily 10 A.M.–5 P.M., $6 adults, $4 students, free children 5 and under, $14 family of four.

The same turn off US 60 leads to the **Peninsula Fine Arts Center,** 757/596-8175, www.pfac-va.org, with changing exhibitions of local and national artists such as Norman Rockwell (open Mon.–Sat. 10 A.M.–5 P.M., Sun. 1–5 P.M.; $4 adults, $3 students, senior citizens, and active duty military, $2 children 4–15), and the 550-acre **Mariners' Museum Park.** A five-mile trail circles Lake Maury, where you can rent canoes, johnboats, and fishing tackle from the boathouse, 757/591-7799.

Newport News Park

Covering more than 8,000 acres, the largest city park east of the Mississippi is a patchwork

YOU CAN'T DRIVE THE HAMPTON ROADS

Spend a little time near the mouth of the Chesapeake Bay and you'll probably start to get confused by a fair amount of the local terminology. Most important, and least distinct, is the term "Hampton Roads" itself.

In maritime parlance, "roads" means a safe anchorage, usually in a sheltered natural harbor, which the lower Chesapeake Bay has in abundance. "Hampton" comes from English nobleman Henry Wriothesley (RIZ-lee), the third Earl of Southampton, who financed early colonizing expeditions. What was originally the "Earl of Southampton's Roadstead," then, has been shortened over the years to "Hampton Roads."

You'll also hear Hampton Roads used to refer not only to where the James, Nansemond, and Elizabeth rivers flow into the Chesapeake Bay, but to the entire metropolitan area surrounding it, from Newport News to Virginia Beach. Hampton Roads itself is usually divided further into the "South Side" (of the James)—including Norfolk, Virginia Beach, Chesapeake, Portsmouth, and Suffolk—and "the Peninsula" (as in Historic) to the north, the setting of Newport News and Hampton itself.

Even though "Tidewater" technically refers to the entire region affected by the ebb and flow of the ocean (basically all of Virginia east of the fall line), it's often used the same way "South Side" is—to refer to everything south of the James River.

Historic Plantations

Wealthy planter Richard Decauter Lee built **Lee Hall Mansion,** 163 Yorktown Rd., 757/888-3371, www.leehall.org, in 1848–1859. The Italianate Renaissance house served as headquarters for Union Maj. Gen. John Macgruder and Gen. Joseph E. Johnson during the early stages of the 1862 Peninsular Campaign. Most of the Virginia War Museum's Civil War collection has been moved into the basement, and the grounds are being landscaped with 19th-century bulbs and plantings. It's open Mon.–Sat. 10 A.M.–4 P.M., Sun. 1–5 P.M.; $5 adults, $4 children. Tours are given every half hour.

Endview Plantation, 362 Yorktown Rd., 757/887-1862, www.endview.org, was erected around 1760 by William Harwood, Jr. One of the few surviving wooden buildings from the 18th century, Endview was visited by George Washington and 3,000 Virginia militia and served as a training ground for troops during the War of 1812. George B. McClellan paid a visit during the Civil War, as did a Confederate captain who made it his home. Both sides of the conflict eventually used the building as a hospital. Thus it's one of the few places in the United States with archeological evidence from three separate wars. Open Mon.–Sat. 10 A.M.–4 P.M., Sun. 1–5 P.M.; $5 adults, $3 children. Civil War reenactments in late March commemorate the Battle of Williamsburg, and an artillery weekend arrives in mid-June.

Virginia Living Museum

It doesn't have statues that walk or paintings that talk, but this semi-zoo does boast a bevy of wild animals in outdoor pens modeled after their natural habitats. Start in the main building, where different sections of the James River—complete with plants, catfish, and bass—have been reproduced in a series of aquariums. At the touch tank, find out why horseshoe crab blood sells for $30,000 an ounce, and try not to wake the screech owl in the World of Darkness.

Then step outside onto the nature trail to reach open-air enclosures where raccoons scurry, bobcats pace, and otters zoom away from an underwater window in streams of bubbles. Past the

of meadows, swamps, lakes, and hardwood forest threaded by mountain-bike, horse, and nature trails. There's an 18-hole disc golf course, a five-star archery range, and the kaleidoscopic azaleas of the Peace Garden. Visitors can rent bikes to explore 10 miles of Civil War fortifications or take out a canoe or paddleboat to fish on Lee Hall Reservoir. The **Newport News Golf Club at Deer Run,** 757/886-7925, has two full courses, and an interpretive center offers naturalist walks and nature programs. You can even spend the night at one of 188 campsites, 800/203-8322 or 757/888-3333, with full hookups for $18.

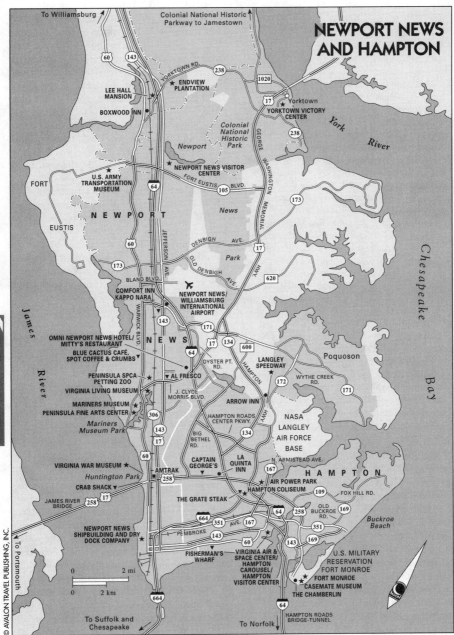

NEWPORT NEWS AND HAMPTON

To Williamsburg

Colonial National Historic Parkway to Jamestown

60 143

YORKTOWN RD.

238

1020

LEE HALL MANSION

★ ENDVIEW PLANTATION

17 Yorktown ★ YORKTOWN VICTORY CENTER

BOXWOOD INN

York River

Colonial National Historic Park

238

Newport

GEORGE WASHINGTON MEMORIAL

★ NEWPORT NEWS VISITOR CENTER

FORT

★ U.S. ARMY TRANSPORTATION MUSEUM

64 FORT EUSTIS BLVD.

105

173

N E W P O R T

News

EUSTIS

60 DENBIGH AVE.

173 OLD DENBIGH AVE.

Park

17

620

BLAND BLVD.

COMFORT INN KAPPO NARA

JEFFERSON AVE.

★ NEWPORT NEWS/ WILLIAMSBURG INTERNATIONAL AIRPORT

Chesapeake

143

WARWICK BLVD.

N E W S

171

OMNI NEWPORT NEWS HOTEL/ MITTY'S RESTAURANT

17 134

600

BLUE CACTUS CAFÉ, SPOT COFFEE & CRUMBS ▼

64

OYSTER PT. RD.

LANGLEY SPEEDWAY

Poquoson

▼ AL FRESCO

172 WYTHE CREEK RD.

171

PENINSULA SPCA PETTING ZOO ★

VIRGINIA LIVING MUSEUM ★

J. CLYDE MORRIS BLVD.

ARROW INN

MARINERS MUSEUM ★

PENINSULA FINE ARTS CENTER ★

306

NASA LANGLEY AIR FORCE BASE

Mariners Museum Park

HAMPTON ROADS CENTER PKWY.

143

17

BIG BETHEL RD.

134

VIRGINIA WAR MUSEUM ★

Huntington Park

60

CAPTAIN GEORGE'S

LA QUINTA INN

N. ARMISTEAD AVE.

H A M P T O N

AMTRAK

258

167

CRAB SHACK ▼

★ AIR POWER PARK

109 FOX HILL RD.

HAMPTON COLISEUM

JAMES RIVER BRIDGE

258 17

THE GRATE STEAK ▼

64 258

OLD BUCKROE RD.

169

Buckroe Beach

664 351 167

AVE.

351

NEWPORT NEWS SHIPBUILDING AND DRY DOCK COMPANY

PEMBROKE

143

60

143 169

FISHERMAN'S WHARF

VIRGINIA AIR & SPACE CENTER/ HAMPTON CAROUSEL/ HAMPTON VISITOR CENTER

U.S. MILITARY RESERVATION FORT MONROE

FORT MONROE

★ CASEMATE MUSEUM THE CHAMBERLIN

0 ——— 2 mi

0 ——— 2 km

664

64

To Suffolk and Chesapeake

To Norfolk

HAMPTON ROADS BRIDGE-TUNNEL

James River

To Portsmouth

© AVALON TRAVEL PUBLISHING, INC.

THE COAST

NATURALLY YOURS TOUR

An excellent introduction to the natural wonders of the mouth of the Chesapeake Bay is this three-day circuit of five state parks in the Hampton Roads region. York River, First Landing, False Cape, Chippokes Plantation, and Kiptopeke are all on the itinerary, along with canoeing in Taskinas Creek, optional night hikes, and a tour of the Virginia Marine Science Museum's Chesapeake Bay Center in First Landing. The tour runs six times a year from Apr.–Oct. and costs $230 pp including meals and accommodations. Reserve a spot by calling the state's Department of Conservation and Recreation at 800/933-PARK (933-7275).

raucous wetlands aviary, home to great blue herons and snake-necked cattle egrets, are more pens containing white-tailed deer, wild turkeys, and bald eagles. A $21-million-dollar expansion began in 2001 with the addition of a raised outdoor aviary, housing birds from Virginia's coastal plains such as ibis, herons, and egrets. In the works are an ocean aquarium and more outdoor habitats for red wolves and peregrine falcons.

The main building has a planetarium and a gift shop full of neat stuff along the lines of ant farms and glowing floating plastic jellyfish. Various educational programs and outings include Chesapeake Bay eco-safaris and winter whale-watching trips. The museum, 524 J. Clyde Morris Blvd., 757/595-1900, www.valivingmuseum.org, is open Mon.–Sat. 9 A.M.–5 P.M., Sun. noon–5 P.M.; $7 adults, $5 children, $3 planetarium.

Huntington Park

At the east end of the James River bridge (Rt. 258), you'll find the **Virginia War Museum,** 9285 Warwick Blvd., 757/247-8523, www.warmuseum.org, with hundreds of artifacts from centuries of combat. From flintlock pistols to M-16s, sabers to World War II Japanese officers' samurai swords, anything and everything having to do with conflict in all its forms is displayed next to actual pieces of the Dachau concentration camp and the Berlin Wall. Open

Mon.–Sat. 9 A.M.–5 P.M., Sun. 1–5 P.M.; $2 adults, $1 children 6–15.

Younger kids will love the big wooden **Fun Fort** overlooking the water by a children's fishing pier and picnic area. Farther on, the **James River Fishing Pier,** 757/247-0364, sells bait and supplies and rents poles. At nine-tenths of a mile, this is one of the longest on the East Coast, open daily Mar.–Nov. 9 A.M.–11 P.M.; $6 adults, $4 children (including a fishing license).

Other Sights

Even more animals live across J. Clyde Morris Boulevard at the **Peninsula SPCA Petting Zoo,** 757/595-1399. A surprising collection of exotic animals, including lions, tigers, jaguars, snow leopards, mountain lions, and mandrills (a type of ape) shares a rear lot with a petting barnyard, home to goats, ducks, sheep, peacocks, and a few nervous llamas. You can't take any of these home with you, but you might be inspired to adopt a dog or cat inside. Open Mon.–Fri. 10 A.M.–5 P.M., Sat. 10 A.M.–4:30 P.M., Sun. 11 A.M.–5 P.M.; $2 adults, $1 children.

The history of the transport wing of the U.S. Army (motto: "Nothing happens until something moves") is the subject of the **U.S. Army Transportation Museum,** 757/878-1115, www.eustis.army.mil/dptmsec/museumn.htm, on the grounds of Fort Eustis off 164 exit 250A. If it ever carried men or equipment, it's here, from a Conestoga wagon to Desert Storm HUMVs. Experimental designs are the most interesting—check out the one-man "aerocycle" helicopter and the 20-foot silver disk of the Avro Car Mark II, a real-life flying saucer now claimed by nesting birds in the yard outside. Open Tues.–Sun., 9 A.M.–4:30 P.M.; free.

Accommodations and Food

The **Omni Newport News Hotel,** 1000 Omni Blvd. 800/843-6664 or 757/873-6664, fax 757/591-3502, has rooms for $140–170, an indoor heated pool, a nightclub, and Mitty's Ristorante and Piano Lounge, the best Italian eatery this side of Hampton Roads. Rooms at the **Relax Inn,** 12340 Warwick Blvd., 800/951-7829 or 757/881-9670, fax 757/596-0482, are in the

THE COAST

ROCKIN' ROADS

The Hampton Roads area is awash in early rock 'n' roll history. In his classic "From Four Til' Late," bluesman Robert Johnson sang of the "16-hour drive" from Memphis to Norfolk. Early rockers Link Wray and Gene Vincent grew up in the area, and Gary "U.S." Bonds recorded many of his early classics, such as "Quarter to Three," at Frank Guida's Norfolk studio in 1959. Ace Records (www.acerecords.co.uk) offers the excellent compilation "Frank Guida Presents The Norfolk Virginia Rock 'n' Roll Sound."

$60–75 range. The **Mulberry Inn,** 16890 Warwick Blvd., 800/223-0404 or 757/887-3000, fax 757/887-3665, has a total of 100 rooms and efficiencies for $70–90. A **Holiday Inn Express** is open on the same site, 757/887-3300, fax number 757/887-0300 offering 57 rooms.

The **Boxwood Inn,** 10 Elmhurst St., 757/888-8854, fax 757/887-3986, www.boxwood-inn.com, began as the early-1900s home of Simon Curtis, railroad baron and unofficial "boss-man" of Warwick County. Set along the train tracks that made Curtis his fortune, the building was gradually expanded and altered into a general store, boardinghouse, post office, and county hall of records. It fell into disrepair, but through the tireless efforts of Bob and Barbara Lucas, it's been reborn as a B&B and restaurant. Barbara studied at French culinary school, so the food is excellent, and the couple plans seasonal "dinnertainments" with various themes—a medieval banquet, Civil War costume ball, Dickens Christmas dinner, and so on. Four rooms are $75–125, with packages including accommodations, dinner, breakfast, and wine for $100 per couple. The restaurant is open Tues.–Fri. for lunch and afternoon tea, and for dinner on Fridays by appointment.

On the James River Fishing Pier sits the **Crab Shack,** 7601 River Rd., 757/245-2722, with a window-lined dining room and outdoor deck overlooking the James River. Fresh softshell crabs and the catch of the day come in sandwiches ($5–9) and on platters ($15–20). Open daily for lunch and dinner. If you think it can't

get any fresher, try the sushi and sashimi ($2–4) at **Kappo Nara,** 550 Oyster Point Rd., 757/249-5396, open for lunch Mon.–Fri. and dinner daily.

Al Fresco, 11710 Jefferson Ave., 757/873-0644, comes recommended for authentic Italian fare (especially the lobster ravioli), with dinner entrées in the $10–15 range. Open for lunch and dinner Mon.–Fri. and dinner on Saturday. Another welcome recent addition is the **aria fifty one café,** 605 Pilot House Dr., 757/873-2200. Chef Michael Toepper pulls off the Italian–alien combination with flair (Roswell risotto, anyone?), serving imaginative and tasty dishes for lunch and dinner Mon.–Fri. and dinner on Saturday.

Transportation

Newport News is connected to Hampton, Norfolk, Virginia Beach, Portsmouth, and Chesapeake by **Hampton Roads Transit,** 757/222-6100, www.hrtransit.org. Call or check their website for routes, hours, and fares. **Amtrak,** 9304 Warwick Blvd. in Huntington Park, 757/245-3589, is the closest station to Hampton Roads, with shuttle bus service to Norfolk and Virginia Beach. To reach the terminal of the **Newport News-Williamsburg International Airport,** 757/877-0221, www.nnwairport.com, turn onto Bland Blvd. off Jefferson Ave. (Rt. 143) near I-64 exit 255.

Information

The **Newport News Visitors Center,** 13560 Jefferson Ave., 888/493-7386 or 757/886-7777, www.newport-news.org, is at the entrance to Newport News Park at I-64 exit 250B. It's open daily 9 A.M.–5 P.M.

HAMPTON

The oldest English community in America leapt into the modern age with the seven Mercury astronauts, who trained at the NASA Langley Air Force Base. Hampton (pop. 141,000) overflows with history—especially about African Americans—and boasts an attractive, modern waterfront jammed with masts and fishing boats.

History

A settlement of Kecoughtan (KICK-o-tan) Indians was overrun in 1610 by a band of settlers sent by Capt. John Smith to build a fort at the mouth of the James River. Fort Henry and Fort Charles both came in handy when relations with the native tribe went downhill. Formally established and named in 1680, Hampton was plagued by pirates during its early years. In 1718, Lt. Robert Maynard is said to have captured and killed Edward Teach, alias Blackbeard, and displayed his head at the entrance to the bay as a warning to other pirates.

Hampton was spared during the Revolutionary War but attacked and occupied by the British in 1813. The *Monitor* and the *Virginia* battled within sight of Fort Story in March 1862, eight months after Hampton's inhabitants had burned most of the city to the ground to prevent its falling into Federal hands.

A rich vein of black history in the area began in August 1619 with the arrival of British America's first shipment of "20 and odd" Africans to Old Point Comfort, and continued with the establishment of the Hampton Normal and Agricultural Institute in 1868.

Hamptons Carousel

This ornate merry-go-round, 757/727-6374, graced an amusement park on Buckroe Beach from 1921–1985. It's been fully restored and enclosed from the elements, with all the original paintings, mirrors, and organ music intact. Open Apr.–Sept. Mon.–Sat. 10 A.M.–8 P.M., Sun. noon–6 P.M. (Oct.–Nov. daily noon–6 P.M.); 50 cents pp.

Virginia Air and Space Center

Imagine an airplane hangar opening like a beetle's wings and you'll have a good picture of Hampton Roads' temple of aeronautics, full to its curving roof with jets, spacecraft, and all the high-tech gizmos that keep them in the air. The Apollo 12 command module and a three-billion-year-old moon rock commemorate the moon race, and dozens of hands-on displays explain the principles of flight and space travel. You can hop on the Internet, have your height scanned electronically, and try to keep lunch down in the tri-axis astronaut trainer.

The **Hampton Roads History Center,** upstairs, traces the area's past and includes what archaeologists believe is a pirate's skeleton. There's also a five-story IMAX theater.

© JULIAN SMITH

ships steaming through Hampton Roads

The Air and Space Center, 600 Settlers Landing Rd., 800/296-0800 or 757/727-0900, www.vasc.org, is open daily 10 A.M.–5 P.M. (to 7 P.M. Thurs.–Sun. from Memorial Day–Labor Day); $6 adults, $4 children ($9.50/$7.50 with an IMAX movie). In the summer, tour buses leave for the NASA Langley Base, now devoted mostly to basic aerospace research.

Air Power Park

If the kids are still clamoring for more planes, this should do the trick: one of the largest privately owned collections of aircraft in the country. Plenty of airborne lethality is on display, from a Nike surface-to-air missile to supersonic jets. It's at 413 W. Mercury Blvd., 757/727-1163, open daily 9 A.M.–4:30 P.M.; free.

St. John's Church

Elizabeth City Parish, the oldest continuous English-speaking parish in the country, was established the same year Europeans arrived at Hampton. This small cruciform church at 100 W. Queens Way, 757/722-2567, open Mon.–Fri. 9 A.M.–3 P.M., Sat. 9 A.M.–noon, is the fourth on this site, erected in 1728. Eight-foot-thick walls are graced by stained-glass windows dating to 1883, one of which portrays the baptism of Pocahontas. Take a minute to wander the surrounding graveyard, with its ornate monuments and Confederate tombstones.

Little England Chapel

The only remaining African American missionary chapel in the state (c. 1879), 4100 Kecoughtan Rd., 757/723-1710, contains exhibits on the religious lives of blacks in Virginia after the Civil War. Call for hours.

Hampton University

The story of America's foremost black university goes back to the Civil War, when escaped slaves sought refuge at Union-held Fort Monroe. Federal officers declared the runaways "contraband of war" to ensure their safety, and in 1868 Gen. Samuel Chapman Armstrong answered their pleas for education by opening the Hampton Normal and Agricultural Institute in the center of the city. Initially consisting of only three teachers and 15 students, Hampton University has grown into a model for African American schools in the United States, counting Booker T. Washington among its many distinguished alumni. Still standing near the entrance is Emancipation Oak, under whose branches slaves once labored over the alphabet and the Emancipation Proclamation was first read to Hampton's populace.

Nine thousand pieces of African American, Native American, Asian, and Pacific art occupy the galleries of the **Hampton University Museum,** 757/727-5308, including works by John T. Biggers, Elizabeth Catlett, and Henry O. Tanner's *The Banjo Lesson*. The pen Lincoln used to sign the Emancipation Proclamation is also on display, and the museum store sells handcrafted ethnic art. In 1997 the collection was moved to the Huntington Building on Frissell Avenue, a former Beaux-Arts library renovated to the tune of $5 million. Open Mon.–Fri. 8 A.M.–5 P.M., Sat. and Sun. noon–4 P.M.; free.

Fort Monroe

Fort Monroe, the largest stone fortification ever built in the United States was preceded by Fort George, which was washed away in a hurricane in 1749. This version was constructed from 1819–1834 at Old Point Comfort to protect the strategic entrance to the Chesapeake Bay. Edgar Allan Poe was stationed here from 1828–1829, and Robert E. Lee was here from 1831–34 as a second lieutenant and engineer. Manned by 6,000 soldiers, Monroe was the only Union-controlled fort in the upper South during the Civil War. In May 1862, Abraham Lincoln visited "Fort Freedom," two months after Federal troops watched the *Monitor* and the *Virginia* shell it out from the ramparts.

Today the fort, still surrounded by a moat with a bridge wide enough for only a single car, is headquarters for the U.S. Army Training and Doctrine Command. Visitors can walk around the walls for the view of Norfolk across the water and visit the **Casemate Museum,** 757/788-3391, in whose cool, dank chambers Jefferson Davis was imprisoned for six months after the end of the war. Displays on the history of the fort and coastal artillery include relics of Davis's stay, including his intricate meerschaum pipe. Open daily 10:30 A.M.–4:30 P.M.; free.

Accommodations

The **Arrow Inn,** Semple Farm Rd., 800/833-2520 or 757/865-0300, www.arrowinn.com, is a motel near the Speedway with rooms for less than $50. Only a few blocks away from the Hampton Coliseum, the **La Quinta Inn,** 2138 W. Mercury Blvd., 757/827-8680, fax 757/827-5906, has rooms for $60–83. Nearby you'll find a **Comfort Inn,** 1916 Coliseum Dr., 757/838-3300, fax 757/838-6387, with rooms for $110–140.

On the grounds of Fort Henry stands **The Chamberlin,** 888/729-7705 or 757/727-9700, fax 757/722-4557, built in 1928 to replace two previous buildings that both burned. The first, called the Hygeia, was a prime seaside escape in the 19th century, with a veranda where Edgar Allan Poe read poetry a month before his death. A full-scale renovation near the turn of the 21st century brought it up to par with its choice location and amenities, including tennis, golf, a private beach, and a pool on the edge of the bay. Rooms are $85–105.

You can camp at **Gosnold's Hope Park,** 757/850-5116, for $7 per night with (no hookups, but a dump station and flush toilets). It's north of downtown Hampton off Little Back River Road, open year-round.

Food

Goodfellas Restaurant and Bar, 13 E. Queen St., 757/723-4979, offers a burgers-and-pizza menu with an outdoor patio. Open daily for lunch (entrées less than $6) and dinner ($6–12).

Look for the Dionysian painting on the wall of **The Pottery Wine and Cheese Shop,** 22 Wine St., 757/722-8466, to find this gourmet deli and espresso bar. Homemade bread and signature sandwiches are among the edible offerings. Open Mon.–Sat. 9 A.M.–6 P.M., Sun. 11 A.M.–4 P.M. (Both of these places are within a few blocks of the visitors center.)

The **Blue Cactus Café,** 10367 Warwick Blvd., 757/596-7372, offers better-than-average Mexican dishes like quesadillas in the $6–8 range. This one is in Historic Hilton Village near Main Street, an interesting little strip of real estate built for ship workers in the 1920s. Here you'll also find **Spot Coffee & Crumbs,** 10369 Warwick Blvd., 757/596-7768, a comfy coffee nook open daily.

For seafood head to **Captain George's Seafood Restaurant ,** 2710 W. Mercury Blvd., 757/826-1435, with a huge buffet ($15–22). They're open daily for dinner and Sunday at noon, as is **The Grate Steak,** 1934 Coliseum Dr., 757/827-1886, where you can cook your own on their open grill.

Recreation and Entertainment

Buckroe Beach, 757/727-6347, is a wide, clean stretch of sand on the Chesapeake Bay. Concerts and outdoor movies are held at a pavilion during the summer; big-band tunes are on the bill every Sunday. NASCAR races roar through **Langley Speedway,** 3165 N. Armistead Ave., 757/865-1100, during the Winston Series, March–October.

Head down to the public piers near the visitors center to find the *Miss Hampton II,* a double-decker motor boat that explores the Chesapeake Bay on sightseeing cruises Apr.–Oct.; $18 adults, $9 children. On sunny days, it passes the Norfolk Naval Base and stops at Fort Wool, a pre–Civil War citadel built on a 15-acre manmade island. Call the visitors center for tickets and reservations. The 62-foot *Venture Inn II,* 800/853-5002 or 757/850-8960, www.ventureinncharters.com, leaves from the same place for deep-sea fishing excursions Oct.–Dec. ($26 adults, $18 children half-day), and whale-watching trips Dec.–March ($35/$27). Their Holiday Lights cruises ($15/7) are also popular.

For an evening out, it's hard to beat the **Hampton Coliseum,** 757/838-4203, www.hamptoncoliseum.org, which has welcomed everyone from the Rolling Stones to Metallica. (The Coliseum even has an Elvis Door, cut into the side of the arena in the 1970s so the King could escape straight to his limo after the show.) Blues bands play at Goodfellas Tues.–Sat.

Events

Hampton's big yearly event is the **Hampton Jazz Festival,** 757/838-0836, boasting three decades of some of the world's best musicians. It's shifting toward more soul, blues, and pop, with performers like Aretha Franklin, Ray Charles, and B.B. King. Hotel rooms fill up months ahead of time for the two-day festival in late June, so plan accordingly.

Block Parties bring local music, eats, and kid's events to Queen's Way near the visitors center on Saturday and Sunday evenings throughout the summer. More entertainment comes to Mill Point Park during the **June, July & Jazz** series on Fridays in those months. Crustaceans galore accompany the **X-Crab-A-Ganza!** in mid-May. Mid-June's **Seafood Fling,** 757/788-3151, fills Fort Monroe with children's games, a volleyball tournament, and a five-kilometer race.

The **Hampton Cup Regatta,** 757/722-5343, in mid-August is the oldest of its kind in the country. Nine classes of hydroplane boats hit 140 mph on their way from the Mercury Blvd. Bridge to Fort Monroe. In early September, the Chesapeake Bay itself is cause for celebration during **Hampton Bay Days,** 757/727-6122. The city's biggest event, held the weekend after Labor Day, includes carnivals, seafood, sports, music, water events, and fireworks. The end of that month is when you'll find the **Antique & Classic Boat Show** docked on the downtown waterfront. For more information on local events stop by www.hamptoneventmakers.org on the Internet.

Information

Hampton's **visitors center,** 800/800-2202 or 757/727-1102, occupies an octagonal building on the waterfront reminiscent of a screw-pile lighthouse. It's open daily 9 A.M.–5 P.M. The Newport News **visitor center** can be reached at 888/493-7386, www.newport-news.org.

Transportation

During the summer, the antique-styled **Hampton Trolley** runs from the downtown waterfront to the coliseum every half hour daily until late afternoon for 25 cents pp, May–Nov. Hampton is connected to Norfolk, Newport News, Virginia Beach, Portsmouth, and Chesapeake by **Hampton Roads Transit,** 757/222-6100, www.hrtransit.org. Call or check their website for routes, hours, and fares.

There's a **Greyhound/Trailways** terminal at 2 W. Pembroke Ave. and Jefferson Ave. (Rt. 143), 757/722-9861 or 800/231-2222. The **Harbor Link Ferry** to Norfolk, 757/722-9400, leaves every hour in the summer, 7:15 A.M.–7:30 P.M. Mon.–Thurs., 7:15 A.M.–11:30 P.M. Fri., 9:15 A.M.–11:30 P.M. Sat., and 9:15 A.M.–9:30 P.M. Sun.; $5 adults, $4 children one-way. The **Newport News-Williamsburg International Airport** can be reached at 757/877-0221, www.nnwairport.com.

Norfolk and Vicinity

Norfolk (pop. 232,000), Virginia's second-largest city and the unofficial hub of Hampton Roads, is more than home to the world's largest naval base. The city also gives the region a "real" downtown and city-style skyline and is home to a galaxy of great restaurants, outstanding museums, three schools (Old Dominion University, Norfolk State, and the Eastern Virginia Medical School), and enough nightlife and shopping to keep even visiting sailors happy—now that most of the off-color waterfront joints have closed. Norfolk is a surprisingly pleasant city, with a spanking new Waterfront marketplace, plenty of green parks, and blue water in every direction. (By the way, it's pronounced NOR-fik—or NAW-fik, if you want to sound like a true old-time local.)

HISTORY

The original townsite of about 500 acres was bought near the turn of the 18th century for 10,000 pounds of tobacco. It quickly became one of Colonial Virginia's largest trade centers, sending out tobacco, flour, meat, and lumber to be exchanged for sugar and molasses in the West Indies. With a spring at Main and Church the only source of drinking water, visiting sailors

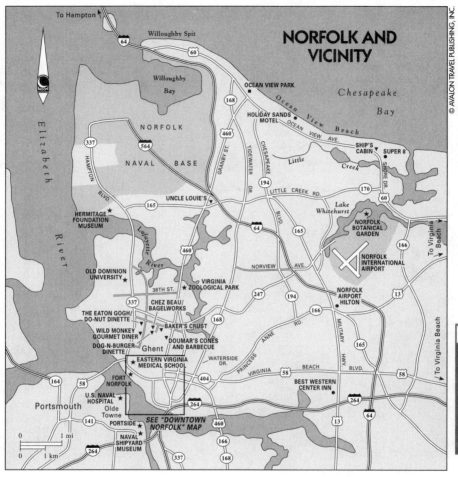

naturally steered for the taverns (and have been doing so, more or less, ever since).

With a little more than 1,000 residents by the latter 18th century, Norfolk almost ceased to exist on New Year's Day 1776, when an 11-hour British bombardment leveled two-thirds of the city. Within two months, colonists had destroyed the rest to prevent it from sheltering Lord Dunmore's soldiers. Only a few brick structures were left standing in "chimney town," including the cannon-scarred walls of St. Paul's Church.

Such a great location couldn't go to waste,

though, and Norfolk soon rebuilt itself into the largest town in Virginia. Many of its 7,000 inhabitants worked on the docks and in the warehouses that exchanged produce from the Piedmont for goods from abroad. Some historians blame the economic jealousy of upriver cities for Norfolk's failure to become a great ocean port akin to Boston or New York.

Tens of thousands of Confederate troops stationed nearby couldn't keep Norfolk, along with Portsmouth and Suffolk, from falling into the hands of the Federals in March 1862. The first

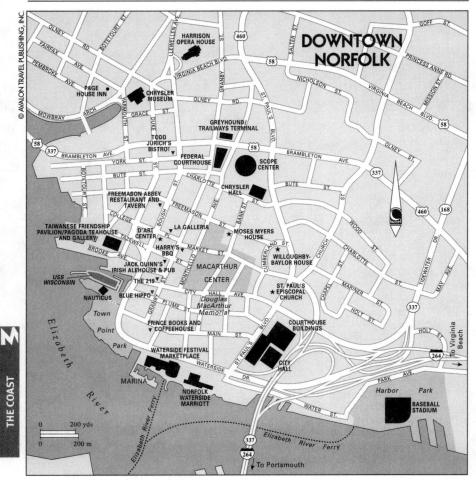

DOWNTOWN NORFOLK

steps to becoming the world's largest coal port came with the first load, which arrived in 1882 on the Norfolk & Western Railroad. In 1907, the Jamestown Exhibition drew national attention to Norfolk and planted the seeds of the naval base in a few abandoned buildings used for offices and barracks. Three years later, Eugene Ely made the first airplane flight from a ship (an honor turned down by the Wright brothers).

A friendly force of soldiers, sailors, and officers invaded Norfolk during World War I, prompting construction of a working base in 1917. Huge ships steamed in and out of Hampton Roads, dropping off men for training and R&R and picking up munitions turned out by the thousands. By the end of the war, Norfolk counted 34,000 enlisted residents and was well on its way to becoming synonymous with the U.S. Navy.

Even with the base closings of the 1990s, Norfolk is still the world's largest naval center. A recent downtown renaissance cleaned up seedy sections of the waterfront and saw the creation of the Waterside Festival Market, a 12,000-seat baseball stadium for the AAA Norfolk Tides, and the futuristic NAUTICUS aquarium and maritime center. A 260-foot whale mural gracing a parking garage on Waterside Drive illustrates the revival.

SIGHTS

NAUTICUS

The $52-million National Maritime Center was opened in 1994 to much fanfare (and some controversy over the price tag). Designed to resemble an aircraft carrier down to a Blue Angel fighter landing on top, this high-tech gallery offers children and adults a plethora of interactive computer displays on all things nautical, from ship design to cleaning up after an oil spill.

Experience warfare at sea in the AEGIS theater, which simulates the bridge of a destroyer. Beautiful tropical fish and moray eels flit through aquariums near a touch tank and working aquatic laboratories maintained by Old Dominion University and the Norfolk State University. On the second floor, the **Hampton Roads Naval Museum** covers two centuries of local naval history through archaeology, models, and photographs.

The latest addition to NAUTICUS is parked next door and easily as big as the center itself. The 887-foot *USS Wisconsin* is one of four Iowa-class battleships in the U.S. Navy, and it's almost unbelievably big. Nine 16-inch guns saw action in World War II, Korea, and the Persian Gulf. Some 2,700 men served on board during World War II—1,000 more than there were room for, leading to such crowding that one sailor searched for a friend for three days, then ended up sending him a postcard in frustration. Because the Navy has to have two battleships on call at all times (currently this one and the *USS Iowa*), the *Wisconsin* could technically be called into service at any time, thus the lower decks remain sealed off to visitors. For more information, contact the USS Wisconsin Foundation, 757/664-4795, www.battleshipwisconsin.org.

NAUTICUS, One Waterside Dr., 800/664-1080 or 757/664-1000, www.nauticus.org, is open Tues.–Sat. 10 A.M.–5 P.M., Sun. noon–5 P.M. (daily 10 A.M.–5 P.M. Memorial Day–Labor Day); $7.50 adults, $5 children 6–17. The first

floor, open to anyone who crosses the "gangplank" entrance ramp, has storage lockers, a gift shop, and a cafeteria.

Hermitage Foundation Museum

The 12-acre summer retreat of William and Florence Sloane, built 1908–1932 on the shore of the Lafayette River, now houses the largest private collection of Asian art in the country. The Mock Tudor house itself is a wonder, filled with hidden doors and stairways and incredible woodcarvings by Charles Woodsend. Then there's the collection: 1,400-year-old Chinese marble Buddhas, unique Persian prayer rugs, and a collection of minutely detailed Chinese and Japanese snuffboxes. Other ancient cultures are represented by glass vials to catch the tears of Roman mourners, intricately carved Spanish *varqueños* (traveling desks), Bronze Age burial containers for food more than 6,000 years old, and other items.

The museum, 7637 North Shore Rd., 757/423-2052, is open Mon.–Sat. 10 A.M.–5 P.M., Sun. 1–5 P.M.; $4 adults, $1 children 6–18. Mandatory tours last one hour, and the lush wooded grounds are free.

Douglas MacArthur Memorial

Norfolk's 19th-century City Hall, a neoclassic monolith designed by the same architect as the U.S. Capitol, was chosen as the final resting place for Douglas MacArthur (1880–1964), one of this century's most intriguing military figures, who is buried in the building's rotunda. Displays include many personal curios, including his ever-present corncob pipe and a 1950 Chrysler Imperial limousine. A theater shows a short film on his life, and thousands of books and mementos fill the library and archives. It's open Mon.–Sat. 10 A.M.–5 P.M., Sun. 11 A.M.–5 P.M.; free.

St. Paul's Episcopal Church

The only building to survive the leveling of Norfolk in 1776 stands in an island of trees and ancient gravestones amid the clutter and clamor of downtown. The first church on this site was built in 1639; this one dates to 1739 and still has a British cannonball embedded in its south wall. At St. Paul's Blvd. and City Hall Ave., the church, 757/627-4353, still supports an active Episcopal parish. It's open for tours Tues.–Fri. 10 A.M.–4 P.M.

Huntington Tugboat Museum

The 1933 *Tug Huntington,* built in Norfolk, pushed and pulled hundreds of submarines, aircraft carriers, and passenger vessels during its half-century career. It's been restored from crew's quarters to mighty engine room and now displays photos and videos on the history of tugboats through the years. The tug, 757/627-4884, is docked at the Waterside Marina, between Town Point Park and the Waterside. Open daily 11 A.M.–5 P.M.; $2 adults, $1 children.

Norfolk Naval Base

The home of NATO's Atlantic operations and the U.S. Atlantic Fleet—all 150 ships and 100,000 workers—the Norfolk Naval Base stretches for 15 miles along the Elizabeth River and Willoughby Bay. Visitors can ogle monstrous aircraft carriers, amphibious assault vessels, submarines, cruisers, and destroyers on narrated tours leaving 2–4 times daily Mar.–Dec. from the Waterside or the Naval Base Tour Office, 9079 Hampton Blvd., 757/444-7955; $5 adults, $2.50 children. Free ship tours are given on weekends—check at the base tour office.

Norfolk Botanical Gardens

This is the perfect antidote to Hampton Roads' urban sprawl—155 acres of trees, shrubs, and flowering plants sandwiched between the Norfolk International Airport and Lake Whitehurst. It's easy to spend a whole day wandering among beds brimming with so many varieties of plants that something's almost always in bloom. Every known variety of azalea—250 in all—bloom March–May, followed by the 4,000 plants in the Bicentennial Rose Garden. Add 600 camellias and one of the largest collections of rhododendrons east of the Mississippi, and you have a flower-lover's nirvana. More than 30 special gardens include a tropical plant pavilion, Colonial herb garden, and a unique garden in a bog, where unfortunate Confederate POWs were held during the Civil War.

The gardens, 6700 Azalea Garden Rd., 757/441-5830, are open daily 9 A.M.–7 P.M. (5 P.M. Oct–Apr.) for $6 adults and $4 children 6–18. Twelve miles of trails wind through the greenery, including the Fragrance Garden Trail for visitors with impaired vision. You can walk or drive the paths (no bikes) or take a tram tour. A boat tour on the lake costs the same. In the main building, you'll find a horticultural gift shop and the **Garden House Café,** with a patio over the Japanese garden. It's no surprise that the gardens are popular with wedding parties and, especially the third week in April, with picnickers, who flock for the **International Azalea Festival.** The four-day event celebrates Norfolk's role in NATO, honoring a different country every year and ending with the coronation of an Azalea Queen in a special garden pavilion. (The only thing to disturb the peace of the place are the airlines taking off overhead from the airport next door, but at least there's an overlook to get a good view.)

Virginia Zoological Park

A century old, this is the state's largest zoo, with 350 animals in its collection. Most popular are three white rhinos, the African elephants, and the Siberian tigers. Peacocks and guinea hens wander near the monkey house. In 1998, ground was broken for a special 10-acre African Okavango Delta exhibit, which will expand the zoo by one-third with lions, zebras, giraffes, and warthogs displayed in natural surroundings near a replica of an African village. Special children's events include summer safaris, crafts, and games, and changing exhibits pass through regularly. The zoo, 3500 Granby St., 757/441-5227, www.virginiazoo.org, is open daily 10 A.M.–5 P.M.; $3.50 adults, $1.75 children 2–11. It's free 4–5 P.M. on Sunday and Monday.

Chrysler Museum of Art

Named one of the 20 best art museums in the country by *The Wall Street Journal,* the Chrysler boasts a collection ranging from pre-Columbian to modern and touching on Greco-Roman, Asian, Islamic, Egyptian, and Indian along the way. Works by Mary Cassatt, Paul Gauguin, and Edward Hopper hang alongside an outstanding collection of decorative glass, including dozens of gorgeous Tiffany lamps, windows, and the famous flower-form vase. On the second floor resides the 6.5-pound sterling silver mace presented to the city in 1754 by Governor Robert Dinwiddie in recognition of wealthy local merchants' support of the Tory party.

The museum, 245 W. Olney Rd., 757/664-6200, www.chrysler.org, is open Tues.–Sat. 10 A.M.–5 P.M., Sun. 1–5 P.M.; $4 adults, $2 children. It's free on Wednesday, and you can buy combination tickets including admission to the three historic houses administered by the museum—the Moses Myers and Willoughby-Baylor houses and the Adam Thoroughgood House in Virginia Beach. **Phantoms Restaurant,** 757/333-6291, serves lunch, coffee, and dessert.

Historic Houses

The **Moses Myers House,** 323 E. Freemason St., 757/664-6283, was built 1789–1791 by one of Norfolk's first Jewish residents, a consul and merchant originally from New York. His family lived here until 1931, when the house was opened as a museum concentrating on the lifestyle and traditions of Virginia's early Jewish immigrants. Most of the furniture, including a beautiful tall case clock, is original. Open Tues.–Sat. 10 A.M.–5 P.M., Sun. 1–5 P.M. A blend of Georgian and Federal styles characterizes the **Willoughby-Baylor House,** 601 E. Freemason St. at Cumberland, 757/664-6283, restored to reflect the middle-class 18th-century life of Capt. William Willoughby's family. Cooking and medicinal herbs have been replanted in the kitchen garden. It's open the same hours as the Moses Myers House, with tours given at 2 P.M. with advance reservations. Admission to either house is $5 adults, $3 children. Tours start at the Freemason Reception Center, 401 E. Freemason St., 757/441-1526.

ACCOMMODATIONS

With so many hotels right next door in Virginia Beach, Norfolk has slid a little in the lodging department. Thanks to unusual local regulations, there's only one B&B in the whole city.

$50–100

Only a short walk from the Chesapeake Bay and Ocean View Beach is a **Super 8,** 7940 Shore Dr., 757/588-7888, fax 757/588-6783.

$100–150

Closest to the airport is the **Norfolk Airport Hilton,** 1500 N. Military Hwy., 757/466-8000, fax 757/466-8802, with two lighted tennis courts and a spa. The **Best Western Center Inn,** 235 N. Military Hwy., 757/461-6600, fax 757/466-9093, has a pool, sauna, and gym near I-264; and some of the rooms at the 23-story **Norfolk Waterside Marriott,** 235 E. Main St., 757/627-4200, fax 757/628-6452, have views of the Elizabeth River just outside. Two restaurants serve all meals.

$150–200

Stephanie and Ezio DiBelardino bought a condemned 1899 Georgian Revival mansion near the Chrysler Museum in 1990 and transformed it into the **Page House Inn,** 323 Fairfax Ave., 800/599-7659 or 757/625-5033, fax 757/623-9451, email: innkeeper@pagehouseinn.com, www.pagehouseinn.com. Business is booming at Norfolk's only B&B (and AAA four-diamond-rated property), furnished with four-poster beds, clawfoot tubs, and 19th-century artwork. Four rooms ($135–150) and three suites ($165–200), including the Bath Suite with its gas-log fireplace and sunken hot tub, are available in the house. They also offer a singular Boat and Breakfast option aboard their 43-foot motorsailer the *Bianca,* with optional private crewed excursions ($200–300).

The **Holiday Sands Motel,** 1330 E. Ocean View Ave., 757/583-2621, fax 757/587-7540, ranges in price from $70–175, depending on season.

FOOD

What it lacks in hotels, Norfolk more than makes up for in food. From $1 cones on the world's first ice-cream-cone machine to dinner in a restored abbey, the city has it covered—and with the headquarters of People for the Ethical Treatment of Animals (PETA) in town, you can be sure there are plenty of vegetarian options. All are open daily for lunch and dinner unless otherwise noted.

Downtown

Head to the international food court at the **Waterside complex** for Cajun, pizza, tacos, sushi, burgers, and Ben & Jerry's. One standout, the **Mongolian Express,** lets you choose as much meat, veggies, noodles, and sauces as you can fit in a bowl before a cook stir-fries it in front of you for $5. Upstairs, **Reggie's British Pub,** 757/627-3575, offers fish and chips and shepherd's pie in a dark-green, oiled-wood ambiance. Entrées are around $7 for lunch and $10–15 for dinner, and, of course, there's plenty of beer, ale, and hard ciders. Live entertainment on weekends builds up to one of the biggest St. Patrick's Day parties in town.

Joe's Crab Shack, 757/625-0655, is a somewhat self-consciously "fun" place overlooking the river. It's boisterous at night, with entrées in the $10 range. The coffeeshop at **Prince Books and Coffeehouse,** 109 E. Main St., 757/622-9223, serves pastries, panini sandwiches, salads, and desserts Mon.–Fri. 8 A.M.–8 P.M., Sat. 10 A.M.–8 P.M., Sun. 11 A.M.–5 P.M.

Produce from small, ecologically sound farms goes into the food at **Todd Jurich's Bistro,** 210 W. York St., 757/622-3210. Jurich, one of the best chefs in the area, mixes the innovative with the down-home in dishes like a vegetarian Reuben and country-style meatloaf. Open Mon.–Fri. for lunch, Mon.–Sat. for dinner, with entrées around $20. A high arched ceiling and stained-glass windows show that the **Freemason Abbey Restaurant & Tavern,** 209 W. Freemason St., 757/622-3966, occupies a real late-19th-century abbey. Daily specials such as lobster, prime rib, and tempura fried shrimp are around $10 for lunch and $13–19 for dinner. Lighter choices like seafood quiche and house sandwiches are also available.

Thanks in part to the opening of the MacArthur Center nearby, Granby Street has undergone a culinary renaissance of sorts. Places like **The 219,** 219 Granby St., 757/627-2896, are typical: a friendly, offbeat little spot serving pot-

stickers and other appetizers ($5–7), pizzas ($9–10), and entrées such as Southeast Asian catfish for $13–17. Open Mon.–Fri. for lunch, daily for dinner. **Jack Quinn's Irish Alehouse & Pub,** 241 Granby St., 757/274-0024, sums itself up neatly. Beers and single-malt Scotch whiskey are on the menu, of course, as are entrées such as corned beef and cabbage, shepherd's pie, and Boxty, a traditional Irish potato pancake with various mix-ins ($9–12). Sandwiches are around $6, and there's often traditional music at night.

Named after 12th Dynasty Egyptian sculpture, the **Blue Hippo,** 147 Granby St., 757/533-9664, lives up to the motto, "Life is too short to eat boring food." It's an upscale, candlelight-and-jazz kind of place with an extensive wine selection at the bar and iced Russian caviar service for those so inclined. Appetizers are $8–12 and entrées such as sushi-grade ahi tuna $20–30. Exactly the opposite sits across the way: look for the neon sign for **Harry's Famous BBQ & More,** 250 Granby St., 757/625-1355, a no-frills eatery with every conceivable version of barbecue for $5–15.

Next to NAUTICUS and the *USS Wisconsin* in the ornate Taiwanese Pavilion is the **Pagoda Teahouse and Gallery,** 265 Tazewell St., 757/646-8856, selling tea, coffees, snacks, soup, salad, and sushi for $5–6. They have an Asian art gallery and shop and an upstairs balcony overlooking the surrounding fountains and flowers.

Ghent and Vicinity

This neighborhood, once one of Norfolk's classiest zip codes, has been rescued from a mid-century decline and turned into a hotspot of boutiques, fine restaurants, and historic homes within walking distance of Old Dominion University. Here the **Wild Monkey Gourmet Diner,** 1603 Colley Ave., 757/627-6462, offers a chic spin on the traditional diner. A large wine selection is displayed, bottles and all, on the chalkboard menus advertising heaping portions of jambalaya, pork chops with port wine, and their "famous" $10 meatloaf.

More than fresh, crusty breads are on the menu at the **Baker's Crust,** 330 W. 21st St., 757/625-3600, a popular local café with a crepe bar and bakery attached. Big salads, herb rotisserie chicken, and Cajun pasta have gone over so well that there's already one in Virginia Beach and another opening in Richmond. **Chez Beau,** 742 W. 21st St., 757/624-2455, serves Thai and French fare, including curries, leg of lamb, and duck breast Tues.–Sun. for lunch (entrées around $8) and dinner ($11–13). Another good spot for a quick bite in Ghent is **Bagelworks,** 757/622-2955, in the same shopping center.

You can munch a bit of history at **Doumar's Cones and Barbecue,** Monticello Ave. and 20th St., 757/627-4163. "Uncle" Abe Doumar invented the ice cream cone at the 1904 World's Fair, and his original hand-rolling machine is still in use at this true-as-they-come drive-in with curb service and famous limeades. Even the prices haven't changed in decades: cones are only $1, and burgers, hot dogs, and barbecue sandwiches are $2.

If you're in a hurry, **The Eaton Gogh,** 806 Harrington St., 757/640-0233, offers takeout service for she-crab soup, roll-up sandwiches, and box lunches, or you can have a seat inside or on the outdoor patio. Open for breakfast and lunch daily. Two classic delis in the vicinity are the **Dog-N-Burger Grill,** 2001 Manteo St., 757/623-1667, an old-time place with great ribs, and **Donut Dinette,** 1917 Colley Ave., 757/625-0061, under the second generation of ownership of the same family.

Elsewhere

Joe Hoggard's **Ship's Cabin,** 4110 E. Ocean View Ave., 757/362-4659, serves elegant seafood overlooking the Chesapeake Bay and on tables in the sand during the summer. Open daily for dinner. In the Ward's Corner shopping center near the Navy Base is **Uncle Louie's,** 132 E. Little Creek Rd., 757/480-1225, a local institution with two faces. On one side a cozy restaurant hides behind a gourmet deli, serving everything from deli sandwiches to whole lobsters topped off by great desserts shipped in from out of town. The other side is a bar and grill with diner-style meals by a pink neon-lit bar and pool tables. Open daily for all meals, with karaoke on Wednesday and live entertainment on Saturday nights.

ENTERTAINMENT AND RECREATION

To find out what's going on around Norfolk, pick up a free copy of the *Port Folio* entertainment weekly or the Friday *Preview* section of the *Virginian Pilot.*

Nightlife

The **Tap House Grill,** 931 W. 21st St., 757/627-9172, has a young crowd and a long list of microbrews to go with live music most evenings. Side by side near Old Dominion University are the **4400 Campus Club,** 4402 Hampton Blvd., 757/451-4400, a college dance club that once made a *Playboy* magazine best-party-spot list. The **Riverview Theater,** 3910 Granby St., 757/625-3100, has been converted from movie house to live-music stage, hosting hard-edged and lighter alternative sounds.

The **Fifth National Banque,** 1849 E. Little Creek Rd., 757/480-3600, has been voted "Club of the Year" by the Virginia Country Music Association several times for its huge dance floor and quality booking. **The White House Cafe,** 249 W. York St., 757/533-9290, hosts comedy acts; and **Q-Master Billiards,** 6214 Sewells Point Rd., 757/853-8900, is the largest pool hall on the East Coast, with 50 tables, a full bar, and exhibitions throughout the year.

Other dependable night spots are the **Bienville Grill,** 731 W. 21st St., 757/625-5427; the **Taj Mahal Restaurant and Lounge,** 1215 W. Little Creek Rd., 757/489-8406; and the **NorVa Boathouse,** 317 Monticello Ave., a revamped Jazz Age movie palace dating to 1922, which has hosted acts like Ringo Starr and Prince. Tickets are available through Ticketmaster, 757/518-5550. The beautiful people are reported to gather at **Havanna,** 255 Granby St., 757/627-5800.

In Ghent, the **Naro Expanded Cinema,** 1507 Colley Ave., 757/625-6276, shows independent flicks and the *Rocky Horror Picture Show.*

Performing Arts

Norfolk's eye-catching **SCOPE Center,** 757/664-6464, can seat 12,000 for concerts, ice shows, and circuses. The more intimate **Chrysler Hall,**

757/664-6464, hosts the **Virginia Symphony,** 757/892-6366, going strong since the 1920s, as well as Broadway shows and an annual pops series. The symphony has been performing since the 1920s and gives more than 140 concerts per year. Tickets start at $10.

The **Virginia Opera,** 757/623-1223, is the official company of the Commonwealth, performing at the 1,600-seat Harrison Opera House at 160 Virginia Beach Blvd. Six productions a year are on the schedule for the **Virginia Stage Company,** 757/627-1234, from Sept.–Apr. at the cozy Wells Theater on Monticello Avenue. Call the **Virginia Ballet Theater,** 134 W. Olney Rd., 757/622-4822/7400, for its current schedule.

Spectator Sports

The AAA **Norfolk Tides,** 757/622-2222, aren't the only ones enjoying the new Harbor Park stadium. A four-star restaurant helped earn it a reputation as one of the best minor-league ballparks in the country—perfect for this farm team for the New York Mets (the Tides have already produced stars like Dwight Gooden and Darryl Strawberry). Partners with the Washington Capitols, the **Hampton Roads Admirals** hockey team, 757/430-8873, competes in the East Coast Hockey League in the SCOPE Center Oct.–March.

On the Water

Vacation homes and inexpensive apartment-hotels line the seven miles of **Ocean View Beach,** 757/441-1745, on the Chesapeake Bay, with public bathrooms, picnic facilities, and a 1,600-foot pier where you can rent fishing and crabbing gear. It's a quieter alternative to Virginia Beach's crowds, and lifeguards keep an eye out during the summer, even though there's no undertow. Ocean View Beach Park hosts free movies, concerts, and food festivals May–Aug.; call Norfolk Festevents, 757/441-2345, for a schedule. **Ocean View Watersports,** 1000 E. Ocean View Ave., 757/583-8888, rents jet skis, waverunners, kayaks, windsurfers, paddle boats, and small sailboats.

Certified instructor Randy Gore runs **Tidewater Adventure Kayak Ecotours,** 110 W. Randall Ave., 888/669-8368 or 757/480-1999, email: rgore@infi.net, www.tidewateradventures.com, which offers beginning and intermediate kayak classes, rolling clinics, and private instruction. They also lead tours on beginner-friendly sit-on-top kayaks to the Back Bay, Eastern Shore, and Great Dismal Swamp. Prices range from $35 pp for 2.5-hour trips to $70 for all-day ventures.

Cruises and Tours

Sightseeing and dinner-dance cruises aboard the sleek *Spirit of Norfolk,* 333 Waterside Dr., 757/627-7771, www.spiritofnorfolk.com, leave from the Waterfront year-round. Prices range from $21 for a weekend moonlight party cruise to $23–29 lunches and $36–56 dinners. The *Carrie B,* 757/393-4735, leaves from the Waterside and Portsmouth's Portside for daily tours of the shipyard and naval base ($12–14 adults, $6–7 children under 12) and sunset cruises from Apr.–Oct. Standing 135 feet tall, the red-sailed *American Rover,* 757/627-7245, www.americanrover.com, is the largest topsail passenger schooner flying the stars and stripes. Daily tours of Hampton Roads nautical landmarks past and present run Apr.–Oct. from the Waterside dock; $14–20 adults, $7–10 children.

© VIRGINIA TOURISM CORPORATION

Norfolk's *American Rover* cruises Hampton Roads' nautical landmarks.

Shopping

Designed by the same team responsible for Baltimore's Harborplace and Richmond's Sixth Street Marketplace, Norfolk's **Waterside Festival Marketplace,** 757/627-3300, has dozens of shops selling African art, Southwestern jewelry, clothes, herbs, and Virginiana. Art exhibits and music performances pass through various public spaces, and there are plenty of places to stop for a bite. The complex, open Mon.–Sat. 10 A.M.–9 or 10 P.M., Sun. noon–6 or 8 P.M., also has a TRT bus kiosk and visitors center.

Also downtown is the **d'Art Center,** 125 College Place, 757/625-4211, home to 40 studios where resident artists labor over everything from ceramics and calligraphy to sculpture and masks. You can stop by to chat or browse Tues.–Sat. 10 A.M.–6 P.M., Sun. 1–5 P.M. Every weekend, a different artist gives a discussion and demonstration of his or her work. Call the center for information on art classes and changing exhibits.

Norfolk's trendiest shopping neighborhood is historic Ghent, centered on Colley Avenue and 21st Street. Here you'll find places like **Artifax,** 1511 Colley Ave., 757/623-8840, selling contemporary American crafts, alongside antique stores such as **Nero's Antiques and Appraisals,** 1101 Colonial Ave., 757/627-1111, and **Hollingsworth Antiques,** 819 Granby St., 757/625-6525, in an old livery stable. The **Ghent Market & Antique Center,** 1400 Granby St., 757/625-2897, takes a whole block to accommodate more than 100 dealers, an auction gallery, farmers' market, restaurant, and old-time arcade.

Smack in the center of downtown is the gargantuan **MacArthur Center,** 757/627-6000, a shopping mall with 150 stores and eateries and an 18-screen multiplex.

EVENTS

With as many annual celebrations as any city in the state, Norfolk takes its festivals seriously. It even has an office devoted just to scheduling and information, called **Festevents,** 120 W. Main St., 757/441-2345, www.festeventsva.org. Unless indicated otherwise, all events are held among the trees in the pleasant Town Point Park on the

Waterfront. Along with those listed as follows, the park hosts free **Friday Concerts at The Point** May–August. Sailing fans will want to keep an eye out for regular **tall-ship visitations,** when ships from as far away as South America dock at the park. When you climb aboard you'll find the crews are happy to show you around.

The third weekend in April, the **International Azalea Festival Parade,** 757/022-2312, ends with an air show featuring the Blue Angels, barnstormers, and free-fall teams celebrating Norfolk's importance to NATO. The festival culminates in the coronation of an Azalea Queen. From late April to late May, the **Virginia Waterfront International Arts Festival,** 757/664-6492, attracts world-class performers such as Itzhak Perlman and the Russian National Ballet for a series of concerts in Norfolk, Hampton, Portsmouth, and Virginia Beach.

Cinco de Mayo, on the weekend closest to May 5, brings mariachi bands, spicy food, and Tejano music, followed by the **Town Point Jazz and Blues Festival** in early August. One of the largest free concerts of its kind in the East, this event has featured bands like Spiro Gyra and the Fabulous Thunderbirds in the past. Early June's **Harborfest** is Norfolk's biggest celebration, attracting 100,000 people for water and air shows, live entertainment, fireworks, and seafood the first weekend of the month. A highlight is the Parade of Sails, a procession of fully rigged sailboats through the harbor.

Zydeco and crawdads arrive in late June during the **Bayou Boogaloo and Cajun Food Festival,** followed by the **Summer Breeze Jazz Concert** the weekend nearest the Fourth of July. **Reggae on the River** in late July brings national acts such as reggae/ska band Eek-a-Mouse and the largest drum jam in Hampton Roads. Giant puppets, costumed characters, and theater shows mark the **Virginia Children's Festival and Halloween Spooktacular** in late October. Hone your SPAM-carving skills for the citywide contest during the **River Rib Fest,** simultaneous with a **Clogging Classic,** both also in September.

Twenty-five Virginia wineries are featured during the **Town Point Virginia Wine Festival** in mid-October, which sets the stage for **Fleet Week** in mid-October, celebrating the birthday of the Navy, and the Halloween **Masquerade in Ghent.** **First Night Norfolk,** on New Year's Eve, is a family-style alcohol-free event ending in fireworks over the Elizabeth River.

TRANSPORTATION

Getting Around

Norfolk Electric Transit (NET) runs eight buses from Harbor Park to the Harrison Opera House, stopping at Waterside and NAUTICUS along the way. Buses run Mon.–Fri. from 6:30 A.M.–11 P.M. Norfolk is connected to Newport News, Hampton, Virginia Beach, Portsmouth, and Chesapeake by **Hampton Roads Transit,** 757/222-6100, www.hrtransit.org. Call or check their website for routes, hours, and fares. They offer a bus tour that passes most of the major sights in town for $3.50 adults, $1.75 children, leaving 3–4 times daily.

The ***Elizabeth River Ferry*** is an old paddle wheeler kept around for its charm now that a bridge connects Norfolk to Portsmouth. It churns across the river year-round for less than $1 pp, leaving every hour 7 A.M.–10 P.M. on weekdays and 10 A.M.–11:30 P.M. on weekends. The **Harbor Link Ferry** to Hampton, 757/722-9400, leaves every hour in the summer, 7:15 A.M.–7:30 P.M. Mon.–Thurs., 7:15 A.M.–11:30 P.M. Fri., 9:15 A.M.–11:30 P.M. Sat., and 9:15 A.M.–9:30 P.M. Sun. for $5 adults, $4 children one-way.

Getting There and Away

You can catch a Thruway bus to the Amtrak station at Newport News at Norfolk's **Greyhound/Trailways** terminal, 701 Monticello Ave., 757/625-7500. Reach the **Norfolk International Airport,** 757/857-3351, www.norfolkairport.com, from I-64 exit 279 to Norview Avenue. **Norfolk Airport Shuttle,** 757/857-1231, will take you there and to Virginia Beach.

INFORMATION

The **Norfolk Convention & Visitors Bureau,** 232 E. Main St., 757/664-6620 or 800/368-3097, www.norfolkcvb.com, operates visitors

centers on 4th View St. off I-64 exit 273, in the Waterside complex, and at 9401 4th View St. at Ocean View, all open daily 9 A.M.–5 P.M. Other good sources of information are the city's website, www.Norfolk.va.us, and that of *The Pilot* newspaper (www.HamptonRoads.com).

PORTSMOUTH

A little more than 100,000 people live in this centuries-old seaport across the Elizabeth River from Norfolk. The nation's oldest naval shipyard bristles with cranes and girders south of the narrow, tree-lined brick sidewalks of the Olde Towne district, with more historic buildings than any other city between Alexandria, Virginia, and Charleston, South Carolina.

History

Portsmouth was established in 1752 on the land of a colonist executed for participating in Bacon's Rebellion. The Gosport Navy Yard arrived 15 years later, quickly becoming the busiest in the Colonies during the Revolutionary War. British soldiers ransacked Portsmouth in 1779 and burned ships in the harbor, but by 1798 Portsmouth was again so busy that, according to a witness, "one might walk . . . to Norfolk on the decks of vessels at anchor." In 1799, the shipyard turned out the *Chesapeake,* the first ship built for the new U.S. government. The British paid another visit during the War of 1812, when 2,600 men landed here only to be beaten back by American troops at forts Norfolk and Nelson (today home to the U.S. Naval Hospital).

Federal forces evacuated the city and burned the naval yard soon after Virginia's entry into the Civil War, allowing Confederate shipbuilders to raise the sunken frigate *Merrimac* and turn her into the CSS *Virginia* in time to battle the Union ironclad *Monitor.* In May 1862, it was the Confederates' turn to torch the city as Union troops moved back in. The country's first battleship, the USS *Texas,* rolled off the docks in 1892, followed by the first American aircraft carrier, the USS *Langley,* in 1922. Portsmouth's docks, well on their way to becoming the largest in the country, were renamed the Norfolk Naval Shipyard in 1945.

Sights

Portsmouth's central **Olde Towne** area includes the **Portside** complex, a smaller version of Norfolk's Waterside, with various small eateries open Apr.–Oct.

A $6 Key Pass includes admission to the following four attractions, all within walking distance. At the water end of London Blvd., the retired Coast Guard vessel *Portsmouth* houses the **Lightship Museum,** 757/393-8741. Commissioned in 1915, the ship guided vessels into Hampton Roads's tricky harbor for decades before being restored as a floating museum and National Historic Landmark. Tour the captain's quarters, boiler room, and crew's mess Tues.–Sat. 10 A.M.–5 P.M., Sun. 1–5 P.M. for $1 pp. A kid-sized city, rock-climbing wall, and a $1 million antique toy train collection are only a few of the 90 diversions at the **Children's Museum of Virginia,** 221 High St., 757/393-8393. Open Mon.–Sat. 9 A.M.–5 P.M., Sun. 11 A.M.–5 P.M.; $5 pp.

Ship models, artifacts, and uniforms fill the **Naval Shipyard Museum,** 757/393-8591, at the end of High Street. The collection, dating to the 1700s, includes an 1880 Gatling gun and antique diving helmets. Open Tues.–Sat. 10 A.M.–5 P.M., Sun. 1–5 P.M. for $1 pp. Portmouth's **Courthouse Galleries,** 420 High St., 757/393-8543, fill a restored 1846 courthouse with works by international and regional artists. Open Tues.–Sat. 10 A.M.–5 P.M., Sun. 1–5 P.M.; $1 pp.

A century of local sports heroes, including Arthur Ashe, Bobby Ross, and Sam Snead, are honored in photos and personal equipment at the **Virginia Sports Hall of Fame & Museum,** 420 High St., 757/393-8031, open Tues.–Sat. 10 A.M.–5 P.M., Sun. 1–5 P.M.; free.

Entertainment and Recreation

One of the best sound systems in Hampton Roads makes a movie at the **Commodore Theater,** 421 High St., 757/393-6962, an experience not to be missed. Built in 1945, the Art Deco theater underwent a two-year, $800,000 restoration that brought back 40-foot canvas murals and Italian lead crystal chandeliers. You can enjoy appetizers and light meals during the show in the 200-person dining area downstairs, but up in the balcony you'll have to be content with the usual movie snacks.

Narrated **trolley tours** of Olde Towne are offered by Hampton Roads Transit from May–Sept. They leave from the visitors center four times daily for $3.50 adults, $1.75 children under 12. **Olde Towne Lantern Tours** are led by guides in period costumes on Tuesday evenings June–Aug. ($3 pp). Check at the visitors center for information on these and other tickets, including the "Olde Town Portsmouth Pass" ($18.50 adults, $11.25 children), granting entrance to all museums plus a trolley tour and harbor tour. Paddleboat tours of the inner harbor, shipyard, and Norfolk Naval Base leave from Portside Apr.–Oct. on the *Carrie B,* 757/393-4735, ($12–14 adults, $6–7 children under 12). Portsmouth's **Memorial Day Parade** is the oldest in country.

Information

Portsmouth's visitors center is operated by the **Portsmouth Convention & Visitors Bureau,** 505 Crawford St., Ste. 2, 800/767-8782 or 757/393-5327, email: info@portsva.com, www.portsva.com. Open daily 9 A.M.–5 P.M.

Transportation

Portsmouth is connected to Newport News, Hampton, Norfolk, Virginia Beach, and Chesapeake by **Hampton Roads Transit,** 757/222-6100, www.hrtransit.org. Call or check their website for routes, hours, and fares. The **Elizabeth River Ferry** leaves daily from the Portsmouth visitors center for Norfolk, every hour 7 A.M.–10 P.M. on weekdays and 10 A.M.–11:30 P.M. on weekends.

GREAT DISMAL SWAMP NATIONAL WILDLIFE REFUGE

Steeped in mystery, legend, and dread, this sodden corner of the state is actually more beautiful than it is dreary and still bursts with life despite multiple attempts to tame its wildness. Deep peat bogs echo with the strange cries of concealed animals down long, straight canals that contrast the seething disorder of the bog itself.

History

Estimates put the age of the swamp at close to 10,000 years, when the rivers flowing through it began to slow and accumulate peat. An Indian legend of a great fireball falling from the sky has led some to believe that 3,100-acre Lake Drummond—one of only two natural lakes in the state—was formed by a meteorite. Early colonists saw the swamp as an ugly hindrance rather than a wildlife haven and tried their best to "improve" it. In 1728, after nearly losing his life surveying the state line, Col. William Byrd gave the area its name and called it a "vast body of dirt and nastiness" that "not even a Turkey Buzzard will venture to fly over."

George Washington organized a logging company in 1763, building roads and digging drainage ditches through what he considered a "glorious paradise." One 22-mile canal bearing his name is the oldest artificial waterway in the country. Eventually most of the timber was cut, leaving the swamp a shadow of its former self. In 1973, The Nature Conservancy transferred 49,100 acres to the Department of the Interior to make into a National Wildlife Refuge. Today, the Great Dismal Swamp covers 131,770 acres in Virginia and North Carolina, of which 82,150 are in Virginia.

Habitats and Residents

Ironically, human interference has left a greater variety of habitats than if the swamp had been left alone. Mixed forest, brier thickets, pine barrens, and shrub bogs now surround the original cypress swamps, whose peaty depths can reach 18 feet. Vines, including the tree-strangling supplejack, hydrangea, and Virginia creeper, festoon the branches of maples, black gums, and, of course, bald cypress, with their knobby mud-level "knees" and swollen lower trunks. Poison ivy vines as thick as your arm and a sharp-spined shrub called the devil's walking stick will make you want to hew to the trails. Venture out at night and you'll probably see the ghostly glow of foxfire (a type of fungus) in the distance.

In among the greenery live otters, raccoons, foxes, mink, and white-tailed deer, along with the rare bobcat and black bear. Snakes, including copperheads, rattlers, and cottonmouth moccasins, all are found here, albeit infrequently, as well as 22 species of amphibians and dozens of kinds of birds. The tannic acid is too much for most fish to live in Lake Drummond, whose position in an unusual "perched bog" makes it the highest point in the swamp.

Visiting the Swamp

One hundred forty miles of hiking and biking trails follow old drainage ditches from one end of the swamp to the other. Fishing and boating on Lake Drummond, access via a feeder ditch from the Dismal Swamp Canal, are also popular (there's a public boat ramp north of the feeder ditch). Bring water, good shoes, and *insect repellent*—the mosquitoes are merciless. Spring is the best time to catch migrating birds and the tiny blooms of dwarf trillium. The main **Washington Ditch entrance,** off Rt. 32 south of Suffolk via US 13, is open daily one-half hour before sunrise to one-half hour after sunset and offers access to a one-mile **Boardwalk Trail** over the swamp. For more information, contact the refuge office in Suffolk at 757/986-3705, email: R5RW_GDSNWR@fws.gov, northeast.fws.gov/va/dis.htm.

Virginia Beach and Vicinity

Miles of beaches, inexpensive hotels, surf, sand, and sun—Virginia's premiere seaside resort has it all. It also has tacky gift shops, hotels so tall they block your tan, and more than 425,000 people in residence. Whatever your vacation preference, be it miniature golf or a world-class museum, you can probably find it in Virginia Beach, although you might have to share it with a few thousand new friends.

Tourism, obviously, is the number-one industry, ever since the first beachfront hotel went up, in 1883. Virginia's most populous city didn't really become a national resort, though, until recently. The population doubled between 1980 and 1990, and it currently welcomes 2.6 million visitors annually.

The municipality has invested hundreds of millions of dollars to make its beachside resort area more family oriented. New benches and lighting, wider sidewalks, buried power lines, and a boardwalk bicycle trail have all transformed Pacific and Atlantic avenues. A stepped-up police presence and anti-cruising laws help maintain the crime rate lower than in any other city this size in the country. For a tourist mecca, it's a surprisingly quaint and quiet town.

Repeat visitors will find Virginia Beach wears two faces: one during the summertime tourist season, and a completely different one the rest of the year. Off-season, the city returns to its residents and quiets considerably, becoming just perfect, in some people's opinions, for enjoying nearby state parks, the outstanding Marine Science Museum, and Edgar Cayce's Association for Research and Enlightenment—or simply staring out to sea from your own private stretch of sand.

SIGHTS

Boardwalk and Beach

Virginia Beach's pride and joy, a wide expanse of pure white sand facing the Atlantic, stretches along "the Strip" from 1st to 42nd streets. The city's sandy heart has been significantly spruced up near the turn of the 21st century. The beach itself has been widened by 300 feet by 3.2 million cubic yards of imported sand, and there are now information kiosks and public restrooms at 17th, 24th, and 30th streets. You can rent beach umbrellas and chairs from vendors on the beach for $20 per day until 4:30 P.M.

From Memorial Day through Labor Day, lifeguards are stationed every block or so from 9:30 A.M.–6 P.M., keeping an eye out for wayward vacationers and anybody drinking or tossing a ball or frisbee, all of which are prohibited in the summer. Surfing is also forbidden on the main beach from 10 A.M.–4 P.M. (6 P.M. on weekends), but wave-riders still congregate near Rudee inlet and the 14th Street pier.

The **Norwegian Lady,** at 25th Street, faces the sea, where the bark *Dictator* sank in 1891. A twin of the nine-foot bronze figurehead stands in Moss, Norway.

The sand becomes less crowded (and unpatrolled) as you head north into Fort Story or south to Croatan. Chick's Beach, just west of Lynnhaven Inlet, is the most popular of the calmer beaches along the Chesapeake Bay.

Virginia Marine Science Museum

You'll find yourself eye-to-eye with a harbor seal before you're even inside this place, the most popular museum in the state and one of the best in the country. From the seal tank at the entrance to a drift through a kelp forest in the three-dimensional IMAX theater, this museum draws 650,000 visitors per year (from the sound of it sometimes, mostly schoolchildren) with a collection that's the next best thing to—and in some cases *better* than—strapping on a scuba tank and going diving yourself.

A recent $35-million expansion tripled the size of the museum, giving it 800,000 gallons of fresh and saltwater in aquariums galore. Starting with the new 300,000-gallon Atlantic Ocean Pavilion, these tanks are the highlight of any visit. See if you can count five varieties of sharks in the Norfolk Canyon Aquarium, and don't miss the sea-turtle hatchling laboratory next to

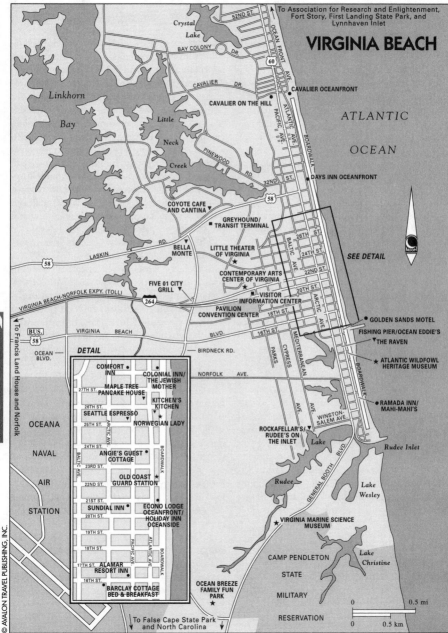

To Association for Research and Enlightenment, Fort Story, First Landing State Park, and Lynnhaven Inlet

VIRGINIA BEACH

Crystal Lake

BAY COLONY DR.

Linkhorn

Bay

Little

Neck

PINEWOOD RD.

Creek

CAVALIER DR.

CAVALIER OCEANFRONT

CAVALIER ON THE HILL

ATLANTIC AVE.

PACIFIC AVE.

BOARDWALK

ATLANTIC

OCEAN

DAYS INN OCEANFRONT

32ND ST.

COYOTE CAFE AND CANTINA

GREYHOUND/ TRANSIT TERMINAL

BELLA MONTE

LITTLE THEATER OF VIRGINIA

CONTEMPORARY ARTS CENTER OF VIRGINIA

FIVE 01 CITY GRILL

LASKIN RD.

VIRGINIA BEACH-NORFOLK EXPY. (TOLL)

264

VISITOR INFORMATION CENTER

PAVILION CONVENTION CENTER

18TH ST.

16TH ST.

BALTIC AVE.

ARCTIC AVE.

26TH ST.

24TH ST.

22ND ST.

20TH ST.

SEE DETAIL

MOON

GOLDEN SANDS MOTEL

FISHING PIER/OCEAN EDDIE'S

THE RAVEN

ATLANTIC WILDFOWL HERITAGE MUSEUM

BUS. 58

VIRGINIA BEACH BLVD.

OCEAN BLVD.

BIRDNECK RD.

DETAIL

NORFOLK AVE.

MEDITERRANEAN

CYPRESS

PARKS

AVE.

RAMADA INN/ MAHI-MAHI'S

BOARDWALK

WINSTON-SALEM AVE.

ROCKAFELLAR'S/ RUDEE'S ON THE INLET

Lake Rudee

Rudee Inlet

Lake Wesley

GENERAL BOOTH BLVD.

VIRGINIA MARINE SCIENCE MUSEUM

Lake Christine

CAMP PENDLETON

STATE

MILITARY

RESERVATION

To Francis Land House and Norfolk

OCEANA

NAVAL

AIR

STATION

COMFORT INN

COLONIAL INN/ THE JEWISH MOTHER

MAPLE TREE PANCAKE HOUSE

27TH ST.

26TH ST.

KITCHEN'S KITCHEN

SEATTLE ESPRESSO

25TH ST.

NORWEGIAN LADY

24TH ST.

ANGIE'S GUEST COTTAGE

23RD ST.

OLD COAST GUARD STATION

22ND ST.

21ST ST.

SUNDIAL INN

20TH ST.

ECONO LODGE OCEANFRONT/ HOLIDAY INN OCEANSIDE

19TH ST.

18TH ST.

17TH ST. ALAMAR RESORT INN

16TH ST.

BARCLAY COTTAGE BED & BREAKFAST

ARCTIC AVE.

BALTIC AVE.

PACIFIC AVE.

ATLANTIC AVE.

BOARDWALK

OCEAN BREEZE FAMILY FUN PARK

To False Cape State Park and North Carolina

0   0.5 mi
0   0.5 km

the aquarium holding the youngsters' cat-eyed parents. A touch tank full of stingrays are so eager to be petted that they pop halfway out of the water. Just down the hall are exhibits on deep-sea diving, beach ecology, and a decoy shack with a resident carver. Try your hand at oyster tonging before taking a walk down the nature trail to the Owls Creek Salt Marsh Pavilion, where you can watch river otters cavort and ospreys nesting on specially built platforms near their brethren enclosed in the outdoor aviary.

The museum, 717 General Booth Blvd., 757/425-FISH (425-3474), www.vmsm.com, is open daily 9 A.M.–5 P.M. with extended summer hours. Admission is $10 adults, $6 children 4–11, with various IMAX combination tickets available. The museum also organizes various **day trips**.

Association for Research and Enlightenment (ARE)

The work of Edgar Cayce, the famous 20th-century American psychic, is the basis for this institution and museum. After entering a self-induced trance, Cayce would deliver predictions on the future and surprisingly accurate diagnoses of patients from just their names and addresses. The ARE has some 14,000 transcripts of the sessions, called "readings," including the one that convinced Cayce to move to Virginia Beach and open the center.

The Association, 67th St. and Atlantic Ave., 757/428-3588, www.edgarcayce.org, is open to the public Mon.–Sat. 9 A.M.–8 P.M., Sun. 11 A.M.–8 P.M. A daily list of free activities includes group meditations, ESP classes, and lectures on Cayce's work. You'll have to pay extra for yoga, meditation instruction, and evening lectures. The **ARE Health Services Center** next door offers massage, hydrotherapy, reiki, and various other spa treatments for $50 pp ($25 students).

Old Coast Guard Station

From 1875 to 1915, more than 600 ships foundered and sank off the Virginia coast, prompting the creation of 11 life-saving stations from the North Carolina border to the Eastern Shore. This 1903 building is the only one left of five along the southern Virginia shore. Formerly called the Life-Saving Museum, the Old Coast Guard Station, 24th St. and Atlantic Ave., 757/422-1587, www.oldcoastguardstation.org, still traces the history of early rescue efforts—which is really the history of Virginia Beach itself, since the town grew up around the five nearby stations.

Videos, models, and full-sized artifacts inside tell the story of the hardy Surfmen, forerunners of today's Coast Guard, who risked their lives to rescue shipwreck survivors. Lyle guns were used to shoot lines to ships in distress, along which a lifecar could ferry as many as four people at a time to safety. Knowledgeable volunteers tell you how the attic is said to be haunted, ever since the bodies of wreck victims were stored there. A roof-mounted "shipcam" allows guests to identify far-off ships. Open Mon.–Sat. 10 A.M.–5 P.M., Sun. noon–5 P.M.; $3 pp.

Atlantic Wildfowl Heritage Museum

The long history of bird hunting is told in the centuries-old DeWitt Cottage, 1113 Atlantic Ave., 757/437-8432, www.awhm.org, in prints, decoys, and marvelously detailed sculptures. Try your hand at painting a decoy on a computer screen before buying one in the gift shop, and don't miss the homemade "O-gauge" Big Gun upstairs, whose homemade barrel started out eight feet long. Open Tues.–Sat. 10 A.M.–5 P.M., Sun. noon–5 P.M.; free.

Historic Houses

Norfolk's Chrysler Museum oversees the **Adam Thoroughgood House,** at 1636 Parish Rd., a 1680s plantation house, built of brick and oyster-shell mortar in the style of an English cottage. Formal gardens and four rooms of antiques reflect the English ancestry of its builder, the grandson of Thoroughgood, who had come to Virginia as an indentured servant around 1620. The house is on the Lynnhaven River directly east of the intersection of Northampton Blvd. (US 13) and Independence Blvd. (Rt. 225). It's open Tues.–Sat. 10 A.M.–5 P.M., Sun. noon–5 P.M. (Jan.–March Tues.–Sat. noon–5 P.M.); $3 adults, $1.50 children 6–18. You can also

THE COAST

BONNY BARBARA ALLEN

O ne of Virginia's most famous folk ballads conforms to the classic, albeit loose, definition: a romantic song with no known author and no definitive text (this is only one of dozens of versions), told by an objective, uninvolved narrator.

'Twas early in the month of May,
The rosebuds they were swelling,
Sweet Jimmy on his death-bed lay
For the love of Barbara Allen.

He called his servant to his side:
"Go to the town she's dwelling,
Say, 'My master's sick and sent for you
For you, Miss Barbara Allen."

So slowly, slowly did she ride,
And slowly she went to him
And all she said when she arrived
Was, "Young man, you are dying."

"Oh yes, Oh yes, I'm very sick
The pain of death's upon me,
I know I'll never see another day
Unless I get you, Barbara Allen."

He turned his pale face to the wall,
She turned her back upon him.
"Farewell, farewell, to all my friends,
Be kind to Barbara Allen."

As she was riding through the town
She heard the bells a-tolling,
And every sound seemed to say,
"Hard-hearted Barbara Allen."

She looked to the east and
looked to the west
She saw the corpse a-coming,
"Driver, drive here to my side
That I may gaze upon him."

The more she looked the more she sighed
And finally burst out crying;
"Mother, father, take me home,
For, mother, I am dying."

Sweet Jimmy died on Saturday night
Barbara Allen died on Sunday,
The mother died the love of them both
And was buried on Easter Monday.

They both were carried to the graveyard
And they were buried together,
And on one grave sprung a red red rose,
And on the other a briar.

They grew and grew to the
church steeple top,
They could not grow any higher,
They linked and twined in a
true lover's knot
For all true lovers to admire.

purchase a combination ticket ($6 adults, $4.50 children) including the Moses Myers and Willoughby-Baylor Houses in Norfolk.

A modest but elegant example of early Virginia architecture, **Lynnhaven House,** 4405 Wishart Rd., 757/460-1688, dates to 1725. Costumed interpreters demonstrate 18th-century skills and crafts between special annual events. Open June–Sept. Tues.–Sun. noon–4 P.M., weekends in May and Oct., for $3.50 adults, $2 children 6–18. It's east of Independence Blvd. and south of the Adam Thoroughgood House. Costumed interpreters lead tours of the **Francis Land House,** 3131 Virginia Beach Blvd, 757/431-4000, built in the mid- to late 18th century by a wealthy local planter. Open Tues.–Sat. 9 A.M.–5 P.M., Sun. 11 A.M.–5 P.M.; $3 adults, $2 children.

Contemporary Art Center of Virginia

The only museum of its kind in the state, the Contemporary Art Center, 2200 Parks Ave., 757/425-0000, www.cacv.org, begins with an airy main atrium filled with trees and windows. The building's angular modern lines complement the paintings and sculpture inside. Studio art classes and outdoor shows are part of the schedule of regularly changing exhibits. It's open Tues.–Fri. 10 A.M.–5 P.M., Sat. 10 A.M.–4 P.M., Sun. noon–4 P.M.; $3 pp.

Parks

The aptly named **Mt. Trashmore,** on your right as you drive on I-264 from Norfolk to Virginia Beach, is the first aboveground solid-waste landfill to become a municipal park. But you'd never guess that underneath two lakes and a skateboard park lie 650,000 tons of garbage. The park includes Kids' Cove, a huge nautical-themed playground designed by children.

Fort Story

In the middle of this U.S. Army base, north of the boardwalk on Atlantic Avenue, stands the **Cape Henry Memorial,** replacing one erected by Jamestown colonists under Capt. Christopher Newport on April 29, 1607, in gratitude for a safe arrival on solid ground. Part of Colonial National Historical Park, the memorial also describes the naval battle that raged offshore on September 5, 1781, between 24 French ships commanded by Adm. Comte de Grasse and 19 British vessels under Rear Adm. Charles Graves. After surprising the French at anchor, the British hesitated long enough for the colonists' allies to line up in battle formation and win after a brief fight. Cornwallis was thus denied reinforcements, and the American Revolution was brought one step closer to success.

The official symbol of Virginia Beach, the **Old Cape Henry Lighthouse,** 757/422-9421, was built in 1791, the first building authorized by the first Congress. Stones from the same quarry that supplied the U.S. Capitol, the White House, and Mt. Vernon went into the 90-foot octagonal tower set on the tallest sand hill in the area. In use until 1881, the lighthouse is now open to the public daily 10 A.M.–5 P.M.; $2 adults, $1 children 6–15. The ascent—up a steep spiral staircase, two ladders, and through a small hole in

© DOVER PUBLICATIONS, INC.

French and British fleets clash off Cape Henry in 1781.

THE COAST

the floor of the upper room—is not for the weak of heart or wide of midsection, but the view from the top is outstanding.

First Landing State Park

The inner half of Cape Henry manages to hide 2,880 acres of dunes, marshes, and cypress forest within sight of the highrises along Virginia Beach's seaside strip. It's the most popular state park in Virginia, drawing more than one million visitors annually, yet remains an amazingly unspoiled nugget of nature for lying so close to the state's largest city.

Habitats ranging from tidal cordgrass salt marshes to live-oak and loblolly pine scrub atop 50-foot dunes shelter prothonotary warblers, also called swamp canaries, and wading birds such as green herons. Spring peepers, bullfrogs, and kingfishers ply the tannin-browned waters of gothic flooded forests in the center, one of the northernmost stands of Spanish moss and bald cypress in North America.

Stop at the **visitors center,** off Seashore Dr. (US 60) at the west end of the park, 757/412-2300, www.dcr.state.va.us/parks/1stland.htm, for a map of 20 miles of hiking trails, including the six-mile Cape Henry trail (which runs the length of the park and is popular with mountain bikers) and the Bald Cypress Nature Trail into the heart of the swamp. The park's **Chesapeake Bay Center,** developed in cooperation with the Virginia Marine Science Museum, houses displays on the aquatic life of the region and its human history. This park can get crowded, especially with trail joggers, so come early and on weekdays to avoid the herds—and bring insect repellent. Primitive campsites near this entrance are $18 (Mar.–Dec.) and require advance reservations in the summer and on weekends year-round. Two-bedroom cabins ($95–101) are also available. Gates are open 10 A.M.–dusk, and parking costs $2 per car ($3 on weekends).

ACCOMMODATIONS

At last count, some 150 places offered more than 11,000 rooms of some sort in Virginia Beach, mostly along Atlantic and Pacific avenues. Keep in mind that rates can vary wildly from one season to the next. High season is loosely defined as May to mid-September, with a week in March for spring break. From November to February or March is the lowest season, leaving Mar.–May and Sept.–Nov. in between. The same room can cost three times as much in June as it does in January. (In the listings below, off-season rates are included in parentheses.)

Bargaining may work at hotels and motels in the off-season, and ask about discounts for extended stays. Many accommodations, like B&Bs and condominiums, are open only during the summer. The city offers a helpful **central reservation telephone number** for securing rooms: 800/VA-BEACH (822-3224).

Under $50

Angie's Guest Cottage, 302 24th St., 757/428-4690, email: info@angiescottage.com, www.angiescottage.com, is a comfy house in the center of the strip with 34 beds in five dorm rooms for $16 ($12) for American Youth Hostel (AYH) and Hostelling International (HI) members and $19 ($16) for nonmembers. Air-conditioned private rooms for one or two people are available to HI members for $27 pp ($21.50). There's a porch, library, and full kitchen, and six B&B rooms available in-season that range from $82–112 for two people. They also run Lacy's Duplex, a separate house with two units that rent in-season for $475–675 per week for up to four people.

$50–100

On Atlantic Avenue you'll find rooms at the **Golden Sands Motel,** 1312 Atlantic Ave., 757/428-1770 for $90 ($60).

$100–150

An 1895 summer cottage, one of Virginia Beach's oldest houses, has become the **Barclay Cottage Bed & Breakfast,** 400 16th St., 757/422-1956, www.barclaycottage.com. It once served as a boarding school where Ms. Lillian Barclay taught until age 80. Double-covered balconies run all the way around the building, decorated with antiques such as an 1810 sleigh bed and items donated by former students. It's open April–October, with five rooms (two with shared bathrooms) for $88–118.

$150–250

Opened in 1927, the original **Cavalier Hotel,** 42nd St. (Cavalier St.) at Oceanfront, 800/446-8199 or 757/425-8555, fax 757/428-7957, www.cavalierhotel.com, was *the* place to stay in Virginia Beach between the wars. Chauffeured limos and Pullman coaches brought seven presidents and celebrities including Jean Harlow, Fatty Arbuckle, and Johnny Weismuller (Olympic swimmer and the original Tarzan) to enjoy the indoor seawater pool and the Cavalier Beach Club, hopping to the sounds of the orchestras of Glenn Miller and Benny Goodman, among others. The hotel on the hill became a radar training school in the 1940s and today is open seasonally. The newer **Cavalier Oceanfront,** open year-round, sits across Pacific Avenue on the beach.

Guests can dine at tables favored by presidents in the Hunt Room Grille, or in the Orion Grill, 11 stories above the beach. Two Olympic-size pools are now filled with fresh water, near hard and clay tennis courts, shuffleboard, and a golf course. The Cavalier Oceanfront has a health club and Camp Cavalier for kids. Room rates are between $200–250 in-season and as low as $80 off-season, depending on whether you're on the hill or the ocean.

The **Alamar Resort Inn,** 311 16th St., 800/346-5681 or 757/428-7582, fax 757/428-7587, www.va-beach.com/alamarresort, has 22 units that sleep up to eight people, set around a courtyard and heated pool for $185 ($110). Thirty-one efficiencies at the **Sundial Inn,** 308 21st St., 757/428-2922, fax 757/491-8218, www.vabeach.sundial.com, have refrigerators and stoves for $170 ($70). At the two-part **Colonial Inn,** 2809 Atlantic Ave., 800/344-3342 or 757/428-5370, www.col-inn.com, rates range from $75–150 for oceanfront accommodations to $45–105 on the opposite side of Atlantic Avenue from the beach.

For more oceanfront highrise rooms in the same price range, try the **Holiday Inn Oceanside,** 2101 N. Atlantic Ave., 757/491-1500, fax 757/491-1945; **Days Inn Oceanfront,** Atlantic Ave. at 32nd St., 757/428-7233, fax 757/491-1936; the **Econo Lodge Oceanfront,** 2109 Atlantic Ave. at 21st St., 757/428-2403, fax 757/422-2530; or the **Comfort Inn,** 2800 Pacific Ave. at 28th St., 757/428-2203, fax 757/422-6043.

Condominiums and Vacation Houses

Usually rented by the week, fully furnished houses and condominiums offer a comfortable alternative for extended stays. Prices range $700–1,200 per week in season for a two-bedroom apartment with full bath, kitchen, and dining room near the beach to $400–600 off-season. Both **The Colony,** 1301 Atlantic Ave., 757/425-8689, ext. 311, fax 757/428-7110, and **Beach Breeze Condos,** 205/207 57th St., 757/646-0530, www.beachbreeze.homestead.com/Home.html, have two-bedroom units within a few blocks of the sand. **Oceanfront Rentals,** 311 24th St., 757/428-7473, www.oceanfrontrentals.homestead.com, has cottages and two-, three-, and four-bedroom houses; and **Mai Kai Resort Condos,** 57th and Atlantic Aves., 800/247-2187, www.maikairesort.com, has a two-bedroom, two-bath beach cottage one block from the sand.

For vacation-house rentals, contact **Siebert Realty,** 601 Sandbridge Rd., 877/422-2200 or 757/426-6200, fax 757/426-6212, email: mail@siebert-realty.com, www.siebert-realty.com; or **Atkinson Realty,** 5307 Atlantic Ave., 757/428-4441, email: info@atkinsonrealty.com, www.atkinsonrealty.com.

Camping

The **Holiday Trav-L-Park,** 1075 General Booth Blvd., 800/548-0223 or 757/425-0249, www.htpvabeach.com, is the size of a small city, with 1,000 sites, four pools, sports courts, restaurant, and a miniature golf course. Campsites with hookups are $30–42 ($16–20), and 24 cabins are $60–80 ($30–40). Just down the road, the **Virginia Beach KOA,** 1240 General Booth Blvd., 757/428-1444, has 500 sites for $30–40 ($16–20) and cabins for $60 ($30).

The **Outdoor Resorts Virginia Beach RV Resort,** 3665 Sandpiper Rd., 757/721-2020, spreads across the beach south of Rudee Inlet.

Two pools, lighted tennis courts, a boat ramp, and a playground are sandwiched between the Atlantic and Back Bay. Waterfront sites are $38–44. Also in this neighborhood is the secluded **North Bay Shore Campground,** 3257 Colechester Rd., 757/426-7911, with 140 sites for $20–27 and four cabins that sleep up to four people for $45–55. To get to both, take General Booth Boulevard south to Princess Anne Road east, and continue east of Sandbridge Road. Colechester Road will be on your right, and Sandpiper Road is the final intersection before the water. Campsites are also available in First Landing State Park.

FOOD

As you might expect, Virginia Beach has plenty of places to eat, with seafood spots leading the pack (about 300 at last count). Many restaurants add gratuities automatically—ask or check your bill.

Snacks and Starters

Both the **Maple Tree Pancake House,** 2608 Atlantic Ave., 757/425-6796, and **Kitchen's Kitchen,** Atlantic Ave. at 26th, 757/491-0813, serve good breakfasts from early morning on. **Seattle Espresso,** 25th and Pacific Ave., 757/425-7650, offers coffee and snacks in a comfortable couch lounge on weekdays 7 A.M.–6 P.M. and weekends 8 A.M.–4 P.M. The **Chesapeake Bagel Bakery,** 296 Constitution Dr., 757/473-9331, also has branches at 1544 Laskin Rd., 757/437-0551, and 2808 Sabre St., 757/631-8230.

Seafood

Near the southern end of the Chesapeake Bay Bridge-Tunnel is **Alexander's On The Bay,** 4536 Ocean View Ave., 757/464-4999, with fine dining in a weathered-wood setting. Escargot and baked brie appetizers ($6–9) lead to lobster, duck, and steak entrées for $15–20. Pasta and sandwiches on the open-air beach deck are $7–15, led by the brimming "Bubba Gump boat" of seafood.

If the Mediterranean-style fresh fish of the day is any indication, the **Lynnhaven Fish House,** 2350 Starfish Rd., 757/481-0003, serves seafood as good as any in Virginia Beach in front

of picture windows overlooking the oceanfront. Dinner entrées run from $15 for Chesapeake Bay crabs to $22 for the King Neptune's Banquet, and lunch plates such as seafood omelets, casseroles, and quiches start at $6. Open daily for lunch and dinner, a little east of Alexander's.

Rudee's on the Inlet, 227 Mediterranean Ave., 757/425-1777, is another popular choice, with an outdoor deck and the requisite nautical decor. Open daily for lunch and dinner; entrées are $11–15. On the fishing pier, **Ocean Eddie's,** 757/425-7742, serves up crab legs, pastas, and sandwiches starting at $5–9, with dinner entrées for $14–18 and live music at the bar.

Locals like the casual **Chick's Oyster Bar,** 2143 Vista Circle, 757/481-5757, open daily for lunch and dinner near the Lynnhaven Fish House at Lynnhaven Inlet, while **Mahi-Mahi's Seafood Restaurant and Sushi Saloon,** 615 Atlantic Ave., 757/425-7800, in the Ramada Inn, is a more lively place, with music and a raw bar (open daily for all meals).

Other Choices

Leaning columns and bloom-spilling baskets give **Bella Monte,** 1201 Laskin Rd., Ste. 100, 757/425-6290, the feel of an explosion in a Tuscan flower shop. Inside the cheery Mediterranean chaos, you'll find a gourmet international market, deli, and café that has won numerous local awards. Choose from 10-inch hand-tossed pizzas, rotisserie chicken, and watercress salads for $6–9, or chicken, pork, and pasta main dishes for $11–18. It's in the Birdneck Point Commons, open Mon.–Sat. for lunch and dinner.

The classy **Coastal Grill,** 1427 N. Great Neck Rd. in the Mill Dam Crossing Shopping Center, 757/496-3348, specializes in ocean-influenced American fare, from oysters mignonette appetizer ($7) to pan-seared fish, pork, veal, and beef entrées ($15–20). It has some sidewalk dining in front. Open daily for dinner. The **Coyote Cafe & Cantina,** 972-A Laskin Rd. in Linkhorne Shops, 757/425-8705, is a little like Santa Fe: based in the Southwest, but evolved into something beyond. A sense of chic fun pervades the restaurant, with its stuffed coyote and cartoon stills from a previous business incarnation, and its menu, from the "kick-ass" chorizo chili to Madre's Meat Loaf. Quesadillas compete with crab cakes on the lunch menu; dinner visits the realm of roast duck and sashimi. Open Mon.– Sat. for lunch, and dinner daily.

An urban artsy theme sustains the **Five 01 City Grill,** 501 N. Birdneck in Birdneck Shoppes, 757/425-7195. Bikes and art hang on the tiled wall under ceiling fans that keep the open kitchen cool. Try the southwest tuna tacos or trademark Michelob Shrimp appetizers for around $6, followed by a "truck-stop" filet mignon, pizza from the wood oven, or grilled Delmonico, with a cappuccino or something from the long wine list to top it off. Open daily for dinner from 4 P.M. **The Raven,** 1200 Atlantic Ave. at 12th St., 757/425-1200, pulls off the usual beach-strip steaks, seafood, and poultry with a little more friendly flair than most. Open daily for lunch and dinner.

In a big old three-story house near Rudee Inlet, **Rockafeller's,** 308 Mediterranean Ave., 757/442-5654, is one of Virginia Beach's most popular standbys. Sit inside among the plants or out on two levels of covered balcony seating, it doesn't matter—the Caesar salads, crab cakes, steaks, and pasta can't be beat. Entrées range $9–17, but they also offer less expensive early-bird specials and kids' plates. Open daily for lunch and dinner, with a moderately priced Sunday brunch.

Inexpensive but tasty Asian fare can be found at **Pho 79,** 4816 Virginia Beach Blvd., 757/687-7844, and **Vietnam Garden,** 2404 Virginia Beach Blvd., 757/631-8048. Both are open daily for lunch and dinner. Vegetarians who don't eat fish should steer to **Azar's Natural Food,** 108 Prescott Ave., 757/486-7778, with healthy Middle Eastern and Mediterranean food, including many no-meat options. They're open daily for all meals.

Virginia Beach's finest restaurant is probably **Le Chambourd,** 3200 N. Great Neck Rd., 757/498-1234, a romantic place serving fine French meals with a touch of Brussels. Entrées such as Salmon en Croute and Crab Montrachet are served daily for lunch and dinner, accompanied by jazz piano on Fridays and Saturdays.

WATER SPORTS

Fishing

An armful of places offer half-day, full-day, and overnight charters in pursuit of the marlin, dolphin, tuna, sailfish, and wahoo that teem offshore at the right time of year. At Rudee Inlet, at the south end of Pacific Avenue at the bridge, the **Virginia Beach Fishing Center,** 200 Winston-Salem Ave., 800/752-0509 or 757/491-8000, runs half-day trips for $22 adults, $12 children, with all equipment provided. They also set up night fishing trips from July–Aug. (Wed.–Sat.) and do offshore sport fishing for marlin, tuna, and wahoo as well. Nearby you can try **Rudee Inlet Fishing Charters,** 200 Winston-Salem Ave., 757/422-5700; and **Action Charters,** 524 Winston-Salem Ave., 757/491-0794. At Lynnhaven Inlet are the **Lynnhaven Seafood Market & Marina,** 3311 Shore Dr., 757/481-4545, and **Bubba's Marina,** 3323 Shore Dr., 757/481-3513.

If all you want is to get a hook in the water, you can rent rods, reels, and crab cages from Apr.–Oct. at the **Lynnhaven Inlet Fishing Pier,** 2350 Starfish Rd. off Shore Dr., 757/481-7071, and the **Virginia Beach Fishing Pier,** 15th St. at Oceanfront, 757/428-2333, near the small amusement park. At the latter it'll cost you $5.50 for a 24-hour fishing/crabbing permit (no separate license required), or $1.25 to watch.

THE COAST

A marlin breaks the surface off the Virginia coast.

© VIRGINIA TOURISM CORPORATION

Scuba Diving

Explore centuries of shipwrecks for $40–50 per dive at places such as the **Lynnhaven Dive Center,** 1413 Great Neck Rd., 757/481-7949, which offers certification courses in its heated indoor pool. Visibility is usually 40–50 feet, and many wrecks have some coral growth. Other places to try for trips, charters, and PADI and NAUI instruction courses include **Undersea Adventures,** at Rudee Inlet, Pier 3, 757/481-3688, www.undersea-adventures.com, offering dives for $55–77 from the 65-foot *Flying Fish.*

Surfing

When James Jordan stood up on a 110-pound redwood board off Virginia Beach around 1912, he became the first person to surf the East Coast. It looks so easy, but be warned—it isn't. A good place to start, for board sales, rentals, and advice, is the **17th Street Surf Shop,** 307 Virginia Beach Blvd., 757/422-6105. Find out if and where the waves are breaking by calling the **17th Street Surf Report** at 757/425-7873, or call **Wave Riding Vehicles,** 1900 Cypress Ave. at 19th St., 757/422-8823.

Rentals

Enticer Water Sports, 308 Mediterranean Ave. at Rudee Inlet, 757/422-2277, rents Jet Skis daily, as does **Rudee Inlet Jet Ski Rentals,** 757/428-4614, at the Virginia Beach Fishing Center. The latter also rents kayaks and Wave Runners. **SeaVenture Rentals,** 800 Laskin Rd. at Browning's Landing, 757/422-0079, has pontoon boats and waterskiing equipment.

Natural History Excursions

Guided kayak tours on Virginia Beach's 120 miles of waterways are only one way to get up close and personal with the amazing variety of life in the surrounding ecosystems. Dolphin kayak trips start at $35 pp for half-day trips and $75 for full-day trips with outfits like **Wild River Outfitters,** 877/431-8566 or 757/431-8566, www.wildriveroutfitters.com, and **Tidewater Adventures,** 888/669-8368 or 757/480-1999, www.tidewateradventures.com. They both also offer sunset and overnight trips, paddling instruction, and gear rental and sales.

The **Virginia Marine Sciences Museum** offers two-hour trips year-round that explore different facets of Virginia Beach's rich waters. Whale-watching excursions (Dec.–March) go after humpbacks and fin whales with cameras instead of harpoons, and dolphin-watching trips in June–Sept. often spot pods of bottlenose dolphins. (The mid-Atlantic's largest population of bottlenose dolphins can often be seen offshore; the museum has begun a photo identification project that currently lists more than 650 individuals.)

Kids love the ocean collection trips June–Aug., on which real marine treasures including seahorses, jellyfish, sand dollars, and crabs are caught and explained, then released back into the water. Each excursion is $10–14 pp. The museum also organizes half-hour excursions aboard the pontoon boat *Coastal Explorer,* www.coastalexplorer.com, through Owls Creek mash, the last undeveloped salt marsh in the city. They leave daily June–Aug. and on weekends in April, May, September, and October. Call 757/437-BOAT for information and reservations on excursions organized by the museum.

OTHER ACTIVITIES

The new paved bike trail along the beach will make you glad you brought your wheels or soon have you looking for some to rent. **Cherie's Bicycle and Blade Rentals,** 2417 Atlantic Ave., 757/437-8888, rents bikes, in-line skates, and safety gear and offers skating classes. Innumerable beach-supply places also rent bikes and in-line skates along with boogie boards, beach chairs, strollers, and umbrellas. Try your hand (and heart) at parasailing in the two-person Skyrider operated by the **Virginia Beach Fishing Center,** 200 Winston Salem Ave. W., 757/422-8359.

The **Ocean Breeze Waterpark,** 849 General Booth Blvd., 800/678-9453 or 757/422-4444, www.oceanbreezewaterpark.com, has a million-gallon wave pool, water flume, and 13 slides in the Wild Water Rapids water park. Tickets are $18 adults, $14 children under 12. You'll have to buy individual passes for miniature golf, batting cages, and rides such as the Grand Prix cars in

Motorworld Thrill Park. Open May–Aug. Another popular (and free) diversion in Virginia Beach is to watch **Navy jets** take off from the Oceana Naval Air Station along Oceana Boulevard and London Bridge Road. Call 757/433-3131 for a schedule.

ENTERTAINMENT

Nightlife

Beach towns always have some of the best after-hours activities going, and Virginia Beach is no exception. Summer crowds tend toward the young, tanned, and beautiful, but whatever your stripe, you'll probably be able to find *some* place that's your speed. Sunburned bodies pack venues such as **The Abyss,** 1065 19th St., 757/422-0748, to sweat a little more after dark. If you'd like a bite with your music, try a restaurant/nightclub such as the sushi bar **Hot Tuna Bar & Grill,** 2817 Shore Dr., 757/481-2888.

The Jewish Mother, 3108 Pacific Ave., 757/422-5430, is one of Virginia Beach's hottest music spots, featuring jazz, folk, and blues most nights. You can catch acoustic performances at the **Abbey Road Restaurant,** 203 22nd St., 757/425-6330, and **Smackwater Jack's,** 3333 Virginia Beach Blvd., 757/340-6638, while **Desperado's Restaurant & Bar,** 315 17th St., 757/425-5566, offers country music, Tex-Mex food, and one of Virginia's few mechanical bulls. Other popular spots for live music are the **Half Shell,** 2917 Shore Dr., 757/481-3642, and the **White Horse Pub,** 757/499-7360, with Celtic and folk music in the Pembroke Mall.

For a game of pool, stop by **Q-Master II Billiards,** 5612 Princess Anne Rd., 757/499-8900, or **Bay Billiards,** 2941 Shore Dr., 757/481-9393. For a chuckle, try **The Thoroughgood Inn Comedy Club,** 757/460-8398, in the Pembroke Meadows Shopping Center, Pembroke Ave. and Independence Boulevard. Laughs happen Wed.–Sat., with national acts appearing Fridays and Saturdays (reservations recommended). The **Comedy Zone** at Liquid 17, 230 Virginia Beach Boulevard, 757/247-2955, is another option.

Completed in 1996 for $1.75 million, the **Virginia Beach Amphitheater,** 3550 Cellar Door Way, 757/368-3000, presents 40 or so concerts per season. Performers include the likes of Jimmy Buffett, Phish, Sting, and No Doubt. There's space for 12,500 people on the lawn in addition to 7,500 covered seats. It's off Princess Anne Road near Princess Anne Park.

Performing Arts

Not all of Virginia Beach's entertainment involves alcohol, flashing lights, and sweating bodies (well, maybe some sweat). Both the **Virginia Beach Symphony Orchestra,** 372 S. Independence Blvd., 757/671-8611, and the **Virginia Beach Ballet,** 4718 Larkspur Square Shopping Center, 757/495-0989, perform at the Pavilion Theater in the Pavilion Virginia Beach Convention Center, 1000 19th St., 757/437-4774. The **Little Theater of Virginia Beach,** 550 Barberton Dr. at 24th St., 757/428-9233, showcases local thespian talent.

SHOPPING

If your tastes don't run to seashell fishermen and sunset ashtrays, a few places in town sell souvenirs of a more memorable kind. **Colonial Cottage Antiques,** 3900 Bonney Rd., 757/498-0600, brings together several dealers in one of the largest antique centers in the Tidewater. **Echoes of Time,** 700 Norfolk Ave., 757/428-2332, offers vintage clothing and books along with well-used furniture. **Caravans International Marketplace,** 302 Laskin Rd., 757/425-7766, offers an eclectic collection of sarongs, batiks, carvings, and toys from Indonesia and Africa, while **Casa Luna Imports,** 323 Laskin Rd., 757/425-4109, tends toward the Latin American in its pottery, jewelry, and wall hangings. **Tidewater Fold Art,** 5312 Kemps River Dr., #102, 757/523-8811, sells local artisan work, pottery, tinware, and quilts.

EVENTS

Most Virginia Beach festivals involve music or sports in close proximity to the ocean. For more information, contact **Beachevents,** 757/463-2300, www.beacheventsfun.com.

Early summer brings two options: **Beach Music Weekend** in mid-May, with performances on beachfront stages at 17th, 24th, and 30th streets, and the **Viva Elvis Festival** in early June. Also in early June, the **North American Sand Soccer Championships** are sponsored by the Hampton Roads Soccer Council, 757/456-0578. It's followed by the **Boardwalk Art Show and Festival,** 757/425-0000, held since 1955, between 14th and 28th streets along the beach.

During **Beach Street USA,** street performers, bands, and magicians wander the sidewalks of Atlantic Avenue between 17th and 25th streets. The family-oriented evening activities take place from Memorial Day–Labor Day. The **Virginia Waterfront International Arts Festival,** www.virginiaartsfest.com, arrives in late April.

Since 1962, the **East Coast Surfing Championship** has determined the best North Atlantic rider in professional and amateur categories. This August event also includes live music, a five-kilometer race, and a catamaran competition offshore. The **American Music Festival** in early September welcomes more than 100 national acts from pop to country in the East Coast's largest music event. Performances are held in oceanfront parks at 5th, 17th, and 24th streets (free at all but 5th St.).

September also brings Virginia Beach's biggest blowout, the **Neptune Festival,** 757/498-0215. Parades, surfing, sailing, and a Sand Castle Classic alternate with the Sandman Triathlon, a U.S. Navy Air Show, and the formal King Neptune's Ball to choose the year's king. Early October's **Blues and Brews,** held in the 17th and 24th street parks, is self-explanatory. From late November to early January, though, two miles of boardwalk are illuminated with glowing sea creatures and sinking ships during **Holiday Lights at the Beach,** with 250 displays sparkling with more than 450,000 lights.

Various fishing tournaments are also held through the year: **the World Striped Bass Championship,** 800/822-3224, www.fishvirginiabeach.com, from Oct.–Dec.; **the Virginia Saltwater Fishing Tournament,** 757/491-5160, year-round (you need a $7.50 license for this one); and **the Red, White, and Blue Billfish Tournament,** 757/422-9319, www.fishvb.com, around the 4th of July.

TRANSPORTATION

Getting Around

Virginia Beach is connected to Newport News, Hampton, Norfolk, Portsmouth, and Chesapeake by **Hampton Roads Transit,** 757/222-6100, www.hrtransit.org. Call or check their website for routes, hours, and fares to these cities. Trolleys run up and down Atlantic Avenue daily from May–Sept., every 10–15 minutes from noon–midnight. The "North Seashore" bus route leaves from Pacific Avenue and 19th Street for Seashore State Park, on weekdays year-round every half hour from 6:30 A.M.–6:30 P.M. The "Museum Express" route (May–Sept.) stops at the Virginia Marine Science Museum and the Ocean Breeze Festival Park. It runs daily every 15–30 minutes from 8 A.M. Fares are 50 cents pp, or you can buy a three-day pass for $3.50. The Discover Tidewater Passport ($9) gives you three days of unlimited access to the Beach Trolley, Elizabeth River Ferry, and Trolley tours.

Street Hogs, 368 Newtown Rd., Ste. 102, 757/493-0070, www.streethogs.com, rents Harley Davidsons for $170 per day to would-be Hell's Angels with motorcycle licenses.

Getting There and Away

Greyhound/Trailways has a terminal at 1017 Laskin Rd., 757/422-2998. The nearest **Amtrak** station is in Newport News, but you can buy tickets at **Great Atlantic Travel,** 1065 Laskin Rd., Ste. 101, 757/422-9001. A Thruway bus connects the terminal to the Amtrak shelter and 24th Street and Pacific Avenue.

If you're driving yourself and continuing on to North Carolina, try this neat route: take Pacific Avenue south to Princess Anne Road (Rt. 615), which ends at Knott's Island at the southern end of Back Bay. From here you can take a free 40-minute car ferry to Currituck, North Carolina, which leaves six times a day. Call the North Carolina Department of Transportation Ferry Information Line at 800/293-3779 for up-to-the-minute ferry information.

INFORMATION

The main **Virginia Beach Information Center,** 2100 Parks Ave., 800/822-3224 or 757/437-4888, is near 21st Street, open daily Memorial Day–Labor Day 9 A.M.–8 P.M. (otherwise 9 A.M.–5 P.M.). There are information kiosks along Atlantic Avenue at 17th, 24th, and 27th streets. Visitor-oriented Internet sites include www.va-beach.com and www.vbfun.com.

BACK BAY NATIONAL WILDLIFE REFUGE

A thin strip of shoreline and a set of islands in Back Bay make up this sanctuary, which preserves 7,700 acres of Virginia's southern Atlantic coast as it was before the highrises and Jet Skis arrived. Once the haunt of wealthy duck hunters from New England, Back Bay National Wildlife Refuge was established in 1938 as an important stop along the Atlantic Flyway for migrating waterbirds, especially greater snow geese.

A wide range of habitats starts among the sea oats on the mile-wide Atlantic strip, a constantly shifting stretch of sand that is predicted to eventually break free from the northern headland near Sandbridge. Maritime forests of scrub oak and loblolly pine cover the higher elevations, interspersed with wax myrtle shrubs and bayberry and blueberry bushes. Three-quarters of the refuge is marsh, covering the bay side of the strip and Long and Ragged islands at the north end of Back Bay.

Three hundred species of birds includes 30 kinds of waterfowl, among them the bald eagle and peregrine falcon. Spring is the peak migration time of songbirds and shorebirds, while hawks arrive in the fall. Tens of thousands of greater snow geese swing through from November–March on their way south from Greenland and Canada's Northwest Territories. Snow goose migration peaks in December, accompanied by Canada geese and tundra swans. The mammal list includes grey foxes, river otters, mink, muskrats, and nutria (a large rodent), which compete with feral horses and pigs introduced by settlers. Back Bay is also one of the northernmost nesting spots for endangered loggerhead sea turtles, who drag themselves ashore in the summer to lay clutches of leathery eggs under the watchful eyes of refuge staff.

Visiting Back Bay

Take Sandbridge Road south to reach the entrance gate, open daily dawn–dusk ($5 per car or $2 per hiker). A **visitors center** (open Mon.–Fri. 8 A.M.–4 P.M., Sat. and Sun. 9 A.M.–4 P.M.) has displays and films on the ecology of the refuge. Boardwalk trails cross the beach, while others along interior dikes are open to mountain bikes. Surf and freshwater fishing is permitted from land or small boats, which many visitors use to explore the bay and islands.

Camping is permitted only in False Cape State Park to the south, reached by a five-mile hike after parking outside the refuge gate. Three-hour guided tram rides through Back Bay and False Cape in open-sided electric trams run twice a day from Apr.–Oct.; $6 adults, $4 children under 12. Call 757/498-2473 for details. For more information on Back Bay, contact the refuge office at 4005 Sandpiper Rd. in Virginia Beach, 757/721-2412, backbay.fws.gov.

FALSE CAPE STATE PARK

This state park encloses six miles of pristine beaches, shore forest, and marsh at the primitive southern end of Virginia's barrier spit. It earned its name—and the reputation as a ship graveyard—because 19th-century sea captains commonly confused it with Cape Henry at the entrance to the Chesapeake Bay. Halfway down the spit lie the brick foundations and old cemetery of the town of Wash Woods, moved because of shifting dunes that threatened to inundate it.

Only environmental education classes are permitted to drive in, so False Cape State Park is accessible to the general public only by a six-mile hike or bike ride though Back Bay National Wildlife Refuge, or by boat through Back Bay. During the winter, the entrance may be closed; check with the **park office,** 4001 Sandpiper Rd. in Virginia Beach, 757/426-7128, www.dcr.state.va.us/parks/falscape.htm, for details and information on various guided hikes and programs. The fat-tire **Terra Gator,** designed for minimal beach impact, runs to False Cape State Park through the Back Bay National Wildlife Refuge for $8 pp on weekends from Nov.–Mar.; reserve space by calling 800/933-PARK. Camping permits for four primitive campsites can be obtained through the First Landing State Park.

The Eastern Shore

"Junk & Good Stuff" reads a sign outside a store on US 13, inadvertently but rather neatly summing up the Eastern Shore in more ways than one. The long, flat neck of the Delmarva Peninsula, dividing the Chesapeake Bay from the Atlantic from Maryland to Cape Charles, is something of an anomaly, a throwback, an often-forgotten corner of crusty watermen, rusty pickups, and salt breezes. It's also one of the most subtly enticing parts of Virginia.

They say that when you cross the Chesapeake Bay Bridge-Tunnel from Virginia Beach you step back in time, and it's not all hyperbole. A rural 1950s feeling pervades all 70 miles of the Eastern Shore, so after a while the modern cars on US 13 start to look out of place, not the vine-covered buildings slowly being reclaimed by the earth on either side. Fewer than 50,000 residents—more than in Charlottesville, fewer than in Lynchburg—are divided into "born-heres" (occasionally "stuck-heres") and recently arrived "come-heres," many of whom have opened B&Bs in small historic towns.

Agriculture is the biggest money-maker on this peninsula, and most of the low-lying fields are covered with acres of potatoes, soy beans, and other crops. Seafood comes next, from net-fuls of finfish to oyster beds and crab pots seeded the length of the bay. Pockets of poverty evidence the recent slipping of both industries.

Visiting the Eastern Shore
A slower pace of life means that it might take a little longer to get your crab cakes on the table and your water refilled here, but use the time to savor your surroundings. There aren't as many things to see and do, per se, as in other parts of the state, but then again that all depends on your point of view. Roadside stands selling produce, shrimp, fireworks, and flowers line US 13, running the length of the Eastern Shore along a historic rail-road route. Countless "creeks"—wide, shallow estuaries—perforate the "bayside" and "seaside," just waiting to be explored by boat. A few public beaches on the bay and ocean are open for swimming and fishing, and trails through miles of marshland are goldmines for birders.

Back in town, fans of historic architecture will have a field day with hundreds of buildings in continual use since before the Civil War. Many fit the classic country-house design of the 19th century, consisting of four connected structures— "big house," "little house," "colonnade," and "kitchen"—with a roofline like a descending bar graph. Towns like Eastville, Accomac, and Cape Charles brim with centuries-old churches, courthouses, schools, and homes.

Local transportation is provided by **Star Transit,** 59 Market St., Onancock, 757/665-1994 or 757/665-4937, whose five bus routes run from Cape Charles to Chincoteague every 5–10s minute from early morning to mid-afternoon, Mon.–Fri. Fares are $1 pp, and the buses have bike racks.

For more information on the Eastern Shore, contact the **Eastern Shore of Virginia Tourism Commission,** P.O. Box 460, Dept. 98, Melfa, VA 23410, 757/787-2460, fax 757/787-8687, email: esvatourism@esva.net, www.esvatourism .org, which runs a visitors center on US 13 just south of Melfa at 19056 Industrial Parkway, 757/787-2460, open Mon.–Fri. 8:30 A.M.–5 P.M. (seasonally 9 A.M.–4 P.M.) You can find local B&Bs online at the website of **Virginia's Eastern Shore Bed & Breakfast Association** (www.bbon-line.com/va/easternshore/index.html).

EASTERN SHORE OF VIRGINIA NATIONAL WILDLIFE REFUGE
The southernmost tip of the Eastern Shore was set aside in 1984 as a sanctuary for migratory

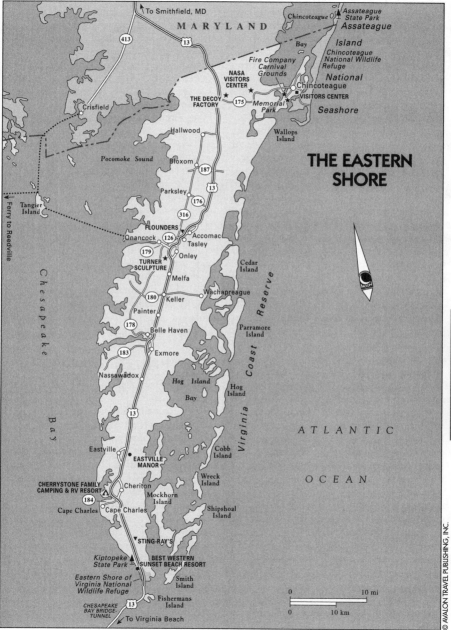

THE EASTERN SHORE

To Smithfield, MD

MARYLAND

413

13

Chincoteague

Assateague
State Park

Assateague

Island

Bay

Fire Company
Carnival
Grounds

NASA
VISITORS
CENTER

THE DECOY
FACTORY

175

Memorial
Park

Chincoteague
National Wildlife
Refuge

National

Chincoteague

VISITORS CENTER

Seashore

Crisfield

Hallwood

Wallops
Island

Pocomoke Sound

Bloxom

187

13

Parksley

176

316

FLOUNDERS

Onancock

126

Accomac

Tasley

Tangier
Island

179

TURNER
SCULPTURE

Onley

Melfa

Cedar
Island

180

Keller

Wachapreague

Painter

178

Belle Haven

Parramore
Island

183

Exmore

Nassawadox

Hog Island

Bay

Hog
Island

13

Eastville

Cobb
Island

EASTVILLE
MANOR

Wreck
Island

CHERRYSTONE FAMILY
CAMPING & RV RESORT

Cheriton

Mockhorn
Island

184

Cape Charles

Cape Charles

Shipshoal
Island

STING-RAY'S

Kiptopeke
State Park

BEST WESTERN
SUNSET BEACH RESORT

Eastern Shore of
Virginia National
Wildlife Refuge

Smith
Island

CHESAPEAKE
BAY BRIDGE-
TUNNEL

13

Fishermans
Island

To Virginia Beach

Chesapeake

Bay

Ferry to Reedville

Virginia Coast Reserve

ATLANTIC

OCEAN

0   10 mi

0   10 km

MOON

THE COAST

birds. Most of the 775 protected acres are salt-water marsh, with some maritime forest, grass-lands, and thickets of myrtle and bayberry. The refuge includes most of Fishermans Island, the northernmost island crossed by the Chesapeake Bay Bridge-Tunnel, as well as Skidmore Island to the east.

The "funneling effect" that occurs when birds gather at the refuge to wait until wind and weather conditions are good enough to cross the bay mean excellent birding opportunities from late August to early November. Bird species resident year-round include great blue herons, great horned owls, woodpeckers, and black ducks. Shorebirds including cattle egrets, glossy ibis, and willets pass through in the spring, but the major migration takes place from late August to early November, when large groups of songbirds and raptors wait at the south side of the bay until weather conditions permit a crossing. Ospreys nest on special platforms in the spring and fall, and in the winter you have a good chance of spotting American kestrels, northern harriers, and snow geese.

The refuge **visitors center** is on the left just past the northern end of the bridge-tunnel. It has hands-on displays on the refuge's natural history and a viewing room over a marsh complete with binoculars and spotting scopes (open daily 9 A.M.–4 P.M. Apr.–Nov., reduced hours off-season). A half-mile interpretive loop trail passes a 60-foot observation tower and old concrete gun emplacements that protected Norfolk's Naval Base during World War II. You can canoe or hike on your own from dawn to dusk, and guided tours of Fisherman Island—part of the same refuge—from 9 A.M.–12:30 P.M. include 4- to 5-mile hikes and wildlife identification pointers. Ask about guided tours of Fishermans Island (Saturday mornings Oct.–March), and contact the U.S. Fish and Wildlife Service at 5003 Hallett Circle in Cape Charles, 757/331-2760, www.east-ernshore.fws.gov, for more information.

KIPTOPEKE STATE PARK

One of the few public beaches on the Eastern Shore started out as the northern terminus of the ferry to Virginia Beach, which moved to Cape Charles in 1949. Kiptopeke, which means "Big Water" in the Accawmack Indian language, now protects half a mile of sand (lifeguarded Memorial Day–Labor Day), as well as trails, a fishing pier, a boat launching ramp, and a full-service campground ($18, $22 with hookups). Entrance is $3 per car ($4 on-season), and naturalist programs are offered during the summer.

The Virginia Society of Ornithology maintains a bird-banding station and raised observation platform to take advantage of the park's location on the Atlantic Flyway. Some 80,000 raptors pass through in early September and October, including sharp-shinned and Cooper's hawks, ospreys, bald eagles, and peregrine falcons. Kiptopeke's hawk observatory is considered one of the top in the country. The tours, presentations, and workshops of the **Eastern Shore Birding Festival,** www.intercom.net/npo/esvabirding, co-incide with the peak fall migration in October. Call the park office at 757/331-2267 or 757/787-2460, 3540 Kiptopeke Dr. in Cape Charles, www.dcr.state.va.us/parks/kiptopek.htm, for information on guided canoe tours through the park's marshes during the hawk migration.

CAPE CHARLES

This quiet town sprang up in 1884 as the southern terminus for the New York, Philadelphia, and Norfolk Railroad. Ferries carried automobiles and freight trains across the Chesapeake Bay to Norfolk and Hampton until the 1950s, when the freight business faded and the newly opened Chesapeake Bay Bridge-Tunnel killed the auto ferry. Today Cape Charles offers only hints that it was once the busiest town on the Eastern Shore, but its appeal hasn't faded completely.

Most of Cape Charles is a historic district. With more than 500 buildings erected between 1885 and 1940, this is one of the largest collections on the East Coast. Colonial revival, neo-classic, and Victorian homes decorated with gingerbread woodwork line residential streets named after famous Virginians, fruits, and trees. Keep an eye out for several Sears Roebuck mail-order-house designs from the 1920s.

THE CHESAPEAKE BAY BRIDGE-TUNNEL

Stretching across the mouth of the Chesapeake Bay like a gap-toothed smile, this engineering wonder lets thousands of drivers a day save a hundred-mile detour between Hampton Roads and the Eastern Shore. Officially named the Lucious J. Kellam, Jr. Bridge-Tunnel, after the Eastern Shore businessman who conceived it, the longest bridge-tunnel system in the world comprises 17.65 miles of US 13 from Virginia Beach to Cape Charles.

Construction began in 1958 to replace ferry service that had operated since the 1930s. Over the following six years, some 825,000 tons of concrete and 55,000 tons of steel were cast into pilings and sections of roadway on shore, hauled out on barges, and fit together like the world's biggest Lego project. The most impressive feat was the raising of four manmade islands in water averaging 40 feet deep. Each one, large enough to hold Yankee Stadium, serves as one end to two mile-long tunnels sunk beneath the main shipping channels.

Two hundred million dollars later, the bridge opened, allowing the first ceremonial vehicle to cross 12 miles of trestled roadway, dip under the bay twice, and pass over two high-clearance bridges near Fisherman Island off Cape Charles. (The idea of one long bridge was scrapped by Navy strategists, who said it would be too easy for enemies to destroy and block the navigable lanes with debris during wartime.) In 1965 it was declared one of the "Seven Engineering Wonders of the Modern World." Total cost: $400 million.

Improvements begun in 1995 are intended to relieve traffic congestion caused by as many as 15,000 vehicles per day in summer months. Another $200 million will add new one-way bridge sections parallel to the original ones, reducing the number of head-on collisions. Traffic lanes will share the same tunnels.

Sea Gull Island, the southernmost of the manmade islands, is home to a restaurant, gift shop, and 625-foot fishing pier, 757/464-4641, with bait and tackle for sale and rent. Even though you might not believe that all this thundering traffic is conducive to wildlife viewing, the artificial islands are among the best places in Virginia to watch migratory seabirds in the winter. Scooters, ruddy turnstones, scaup, eiders, and other duck species, including buffleheads, gadwalls, and common goldeneyes, all make appearances in the winter, especially after a hard freeze.

The bridge-tunnel, by the way, is an exercise in private enterprise, as permitted by Virginia law. A $10 toll is charged each way. Contact the bridge authority at 757/331-2960, www.cbbt.com, for more information.

Sights

The **Cape Charles Museum and Welcome Center,** 757/331-1008, sits across Rt. 184 from the vividly named Meatland supermarket on the way into town. The building the museum occupies used to be a generator house for Delmarva Power and still has one gigantic generator (which still turns over) embedded in the floor. Old photos, decoys, and boat models trace the history of Cape Charles. Open Apr.–Nov. Fri. 2–5 P.M., Sat. 10 A.M.–5 P.M., Sun. 1–5 P.M.; free.

Accommodations

The **Sea Gate Bed & Breakfast,** 9 Tazewell Ave., 757/331-2206, email: seagate@polit.infi.net, www.bbhost.com/Seagate, is in a lovingly restored 1861 house. A curving porch wraps around the entire front of the building, which was once split into a duplex ($80–90). Corinthian columns flank the foyer of the **Cape Charles House,** 645 Tazewell Ave., 757/331-4920, fax 757/331-4959, email: stay@capecharleshouse .com, www.capecharleshouse.com, set in a 1912 Colonial revival frame house with high ceilings and maple plank floors. Five rooms range in price from $85–120.

Rooms in the **Wilson-Lee House,** 403 Tazewell Ave., 757/331-1954, email: stay@wilson-leehouse.com, www.wilsonleehouse.com, embody styles ranging from Victorian to art deco, but each one has terrycloth robes and queen-sized beds. All are $85–95 except the James W. Lee room ($120), decorated with original blueprints of the house.

Only three doors down from the town beach pavilion is the **Sterling House Inn,** 9 Randolph

St., 757/331-2483, fax 757/331-2581, email: SterlingInn@aol.com, www.sterling-inn.com. Four rooms ($95–120) all have air-conditioning, and there's a hot tub on the deck out back and a large library upstairs. The proprietors offer personal guided tours in local natural history and birding, and sunset cruises on the sloop *Adhara*.

The **Best Western Sunset Beach Resort,** 800/899-4786 or 757/331-4786, has 73 rooms ($60–100), campsites ($20–25 for full hookups), and an outdoor pool along with a beachfront café by a small stretch of private beach. It's located a few miles north of the Bridge-Tunnel entrance on US 13. Approximately 1.5 miles west of US 13 on Rt. 680, you'll find the **Cherrystone Family Camping & RV Resort,** 757/331-3063, www.cherrystoneva.com, with three pools, a beach, sports courts, and a playground spread over more than 300 acres. They rent sea kayaks, paddleboats, and bikes, and have 700 campsites for $15–35.

Food

There aren't many service stations where you can get a hand-pulled pork BBQ plate and a glass of merlot, but Cape Charles has one. Head back out to US 13 and a little more than four miles south, where Ray Haynie's **Sting-Ray's,** 757/331-2505, is a local gathering place serving gourmet seafood platters in the back of a big red Exxon station. It may not look like much, but wait until you try the softshells and crab imperial, maybe alongside a bottle from one of the best wine selections on the Eastern Shore. They also serve inexpensive sandwiches, breakfasts, and the usual ribs and chili ($2–5). Open daily from 6 A.M.

In town, **Peppers,** 151 Market St., 757/787-3457, has fresh salads and excellent sandwiches for $3–6 and a noteworthy key lime pie. Open Mon.–Sat. for lunch, Thurs.–Sat. for dinner, with seating inside and out.

Shopping

Charmar's Antiques, 211 Mason Ave., 757/331-1488, inhabits an early-1900s mercantile building that echoes with the tick of clocks. The **Cape Charles Trading Company,** 113 Mason Ave., 757/331-1442, has a little bit of everything—clothes, books, candles, and even a few antiques.

Activities

Operating out of an old service station next to the Sunset Beach Resort, **Southeast Expeditions,** 757/331-2660, www.sekayak.com, run kayak trips ($65–95), as well as sunset excursions and clamming junkets. They also rent kayaks for $15 per hour or $50 per day. The tall schooner *Serenity,* 757/710-1233, leaves from Cape Charles harbor for tours of the bay for $30 pp. Guests can help sail and look for dolphins.

Events

In May, June, and September, Cape Charles holds an **Applaud the Sun Harbor Party,** to celebrate its location on the largest harbor between Norfolk and Maryland. The **Eastern Shore of Virginia Blue Crab Music Festival,** email: musicfest.esva.net, brings country, rock, blues, and R&B in early August, followed by a hometown parade during **Cape Charles Day** in September.

Information

For details on anything else about the town, contact the **Cape Charles–Northhampton County Chamber of Commerce,** P.O. Box 87, Cape Charles, VA, 23310, 757/331-2304, www.ccncchamber.com.

EASTVILLE

In 1766, 10 years before the Declaration of Independence, the county court of this tiny village—then called Peachburg—declared the Stamp Act of Parliament unconstitutional. By the early 19th century, it boasted 217 inhabitants who, in the words of one visitor, were "not to be surpassed for their morality and hospitality to strangers."

The **Old Courthouse** on Courthouse Square guards the oldest continuous court records in America, which have escaped rats, rot, and fire since they were begun in 1632. The building dates to the turn of the 20th century. Next door, the **Clerk's Office** has a small museum inside, including leg irons and a device for measuring slaves' heights. Barred windows mark the **Debtor's Prison,** built around 1814, with an old whipping post in front that may make you

OFFSHORE EDEN

The Nature Conservancy oversees the outermost fringe of Virginia's Eastern Shore, the largest stretch of unspoiled coastal wilderness in the country. With 50,000 acres spread over 14 barrier islands, the Virginia Coast Reserve has been designated one of 10 Last Great Places in America by its custodians and an International Biosphere Reserve by the United Nations.

Beaches, lagoons, pine forests, marshes, and scrub woodlands shelter as many as 80,000 pairs of nesting birds at a time, including every species found along Virginia's coast. Visiting is limited to day use, but the boating, swimming, beachcombing, and picnicking are unsurpassed. Getting there is the only catch because it requires a boat or canoe. Parramore, Shipshoal, and Revel islands are closed to the public, and much of Cedar Island remains in private hands. Check with The Nature Conservancy, P.O. Box 158, Nassawadox, VA 23413, 757/442-3049, www.nature.org/states/Virginia/preserves/art124 4.html, for regulations and information on naturalist-led trips they run every year.

grateful for the comparatively civilized techniques of modern collection agencies. Courthouse green is on Courthouse Rd. (US 13 Business). Step into the modern Circuit Court building, 757/678-0465, for keys to the three buildings above during business hours.

WACHAPREAGUE

Two hundred folks live in the "Flounder Capital of the World," whose name means "Little City by the Sea" in an Indian tongue. Wachapreague (WAH-cha-preeg) is a good base for charter fishing or exploring the islands and marshes of the Eastern Shore's Atlantic edge.

Three brothers named Powell established a wharf and shipping firm here in 1872. Weekly freight and passenger steamers left for points north around the turn of the 20th century, when wealthy visiting sportsmen enjoyed a dance hall, pool room, movie houses, and an elegant hotel (which burned in 1978).

Accommodations and Food

On the waterfront, the **Wachapreague Motel,** 17 Atlantic Ave., 757/787-2105, email: island@ wachapreague.com, www.wachapreague.com, has 30 rooms, efficiencies, and two-bedroom apartments starting at $75 in season and $50 off-season. They also book trips with several local charter boats and run the **Island House Restaurant,** 757/787-4242, overlooking the marsh across the street and enclosing the self-declared finest raw bar on the Eastern Shore. Platters are $8–17, including great crab cakes and Black Angus steaks.

Fifth-generation Wachapreague natives Pat, Tom, and Mike Hart run **The Burton House,** 9 Brooklyn Ave., 757/787-4560, and **Hart's Harbor House,** 11 Brooklyn Ave., 757/787-4848. The two century-old homes have a total of 10 guest rooms and four cabins ($75–95). Rates include full breakfasts and afternoon tea, and guests of both houses can borrow bikes to explore the town.

Recreation

Ask at the Island House, the Wachapreague Motel, or **Captain Zed's Tackle Shop & Marina,** 757/789-3222, about fishing charters starting at $425 for flounder and climbing to $900 for marlin. Four-person, 16-foot skiffs are available for rent for $70 per day.

Events and Information

The Wachapreague **Volunteer Fireman's Carnival** comes to town late June–early August. Several fishing tournaments swing through town as well during the summer: the **M.S.S.A Maryland Saltwater Sportfishermen's Association** in late June; the **E.S. Marlin Club's Billfish Release Tournament** in late July; the **Chick Charter Club Annual Tuna Tournament** in late August; and the **E.S. Marlin Club Fall One Day Marlin Tournament** in early September. Call the Wachapreague Motel or send an email to tourneys@wachapreague.com for more information.

ONANCOCK

One of the Eastern Shore's prettiest towns sits on Onancock Creek near one of the two deepwater harbors on the peninsula. Chock full of

THE COAST

19th-century houses with gingerbread trim and wraparound porches, Onancock (o-NAN-cock) has enough cultural offerings and quiet allure to justify a stay of a weekend or more.

The name, meaning "foggy place" in an Indian language, comes from a native tribe whose king Ekeeks introduced Englishman John Pory to oysters and "batata" (potatoes) in 1621. (After burning his mouth on a steaming tuber, Pory groaned "I would not give a farthing for a truckload.") The settlement, founded in 1680 as Port Scarburgh, weathered frequent raids by British privateers during the Revolutionary War. Growth arrived with steamships plying the Chesapeake Bay, leaving Onancock one of the largest communities on the Eastern Shore.

For more information, try Onancock Online, www.onancock.com.

Sights

On Market St. (Rt. 179) before the center of town stands **Kerr Place,** 757/787-8012, one of the Eastern Shore's finest antique manor homes. Built in 1799 by a Scottish merchant, the elegant Federal mansion once presided over an estate of 1,500 acres. It's been restored by the Eastern Shore of Virginia Historical Society, who have set up offices and a museum of Eastern Shore history inside. Intricate woodwork and plaster carvings decorate the walls and ceiling around period artwork and furniture. Notice the false window in the brick facade, included for symmetry. Open Mar.–Dec. Tues.–Sat. 10 A.M.–4 P.M.; $4 pp.

The venerable **Hopkins & Bro. Store,** www.onancock.net/home.htm, began in 1842 as a feed and farm store and the village post office. One of the oldest general stores on the East Coast, it has been completely renovated and is now owned by the Association for the Preservation of Virginia Antiquities. The attached **Eastern Shore Steamboat Co. Restaurant,** 757/787-3100, serves seafood and prime rib for dinner nightly and lunch on weekends, with a tavern open late.

Accommodations

Marge and Mike Carpenter's **76 Market Street Bed & Breakfast,** 76 Market St., 888/751-7600 or 757/787-7600, email: stay@76MarketSt.com,

www.76MarketSt.com, is only a short walk from downtown and the wharf area. Three rooms in the 19th-century Victorian home ($70–95) all have air-conditiong, and guests can enjoy a TV room and great full breakfasts. Built in 1890, **The Spinning Wheel,** 31 North St., 888/787-0337 or 757/787-7311, fax 757/787-8555, email: b&b@downtownonancock.com, www.1890spinningwheel.com, bills itself as a "folk Victorian" B&B, with rooms for $75–95.

The **Colonial Manor Inn,** 84 Market St., 757/787-3521, fax 757/787-4701, email: hosts@ColonialManorInn.com, www.ColonialManorInn.com, got its start as a boarding house in the 1930s, making it the oldest operating inn on the Eastern Shore. Two acres of grounds and full breakfasts served at the huge dining table are included in the price ($75–115). Back out Rt. 179 toward US 13 sits **Montrose House,** 20494 Market St., 757/787-8887 or 757/787-7088, email: montrose@visi.net, www.bbonline.com/va/montrose, a beautiful country home in the classic four-part design of the early 19th century. A rear screened porch overlooks herb and perennial gardens graced by statues and trellises. Twelve rooms ($90–120) include eight with private baths. Owner Richard Caden also runs **Confetti's Cafe,** 757/787-8887, in Rose's Shopping Center toward US 13.

Food

Chef/owner Armando Suarez from Argentina has decorated **Armando's,** 10 North St., 757/787-8044, with treasures accumulated over a lifetime of music-loving, including antiques, congas, and jazz posters. The menu, replete with Pablo Neruda quotes and a dish named after the chef's daughter, lists pastas and other dishes combining Spanish, Argentine, and Italian influences; the sauces alone are worth a visit. Outside seating is available on an ivy-draped brick patio. Open daily for dinner in-season. In the off-season, they're only open on weekends, but you still might catch them around the corner at **Danielle,** 13 North St., 757/787-1081, serving scrumptious handmade pizza daily for dinner and Mon.–Sat. for lunch.

Bizotto's Gallery-Café, 41 Market St., 757/787-3103, is an antique/gift shop as well as a popular restaurant that's packed at lunchtime. Good food artfully prepared is served daily for lunch and Mon.–Sat. for dinner. Dishes like grilled scallops and Portobello mushroom sandwiches start at $7. The **Market Street Inn,** 47 Market St., 757/787-7626, serves standards including tuna steak and seafood quiche for all meals Mon.–Sat.

Shopping

Crockett's Gallery, 757/787-2288, offers nautical-themed works by a Tangier-born artist. Look to **Walter and Walton's Emporium,** 23 Market St., 757/787-1995, for antiques, furniture, decoys, and Asian art.

Off US 13 south of Onancock, **Turner Sculpture,** 757/787-2818, www.esva.net/~turner, is the largest personal foundry and gallery in the country. Renowned sculptors William and David Turner count the National Audubon Society, the American Museum of Natural History, and the White House among dozens of public commissions for their realistic wildlife bronzes. Here in the gallery, more than 300 different animals are frozen in vivid poses that work especially well in the aquatic creatures—otters, dolphins, humpback whales, and the like. Prices range from $50 for palm-size works to the thousands for larger pieces. Open Mon.–Fri. 8 A.M.–5 P.M., Sat. and Sun. 9 A.M.–5 P.M.

ONANCOCK TO CHINCOTEAGUE

Accomack

A wealth of Colonial architecture fills the tree-shaded streets in this historic burg, founded as Drummondtown in the 18th century. On Courthouse Green stands the early-1900s **Courthouse** next to the Victorian brick **Clerk's Office,** where the Accomack County Orders of 1714–1717 bear the vitriolic inscription "God Damn the King" over the more traditional "God Save the King."

Elaborate paintings inside the Greek revival **St. James Episcopal Church,** built in 1838, simulate columns, doors, and arches. Call 757/787-2462 to arrange a visit to the 1784 **Debtor's Prison,** rendered obsolete in 1849 by a state law that abolished imprisonment for debt.

Parksley

The **Eastern Shore Railway Museum,** 18468 Dunne Ave., 757/665-RAIL (665-7245), starts with a gift shop and collection of antique cars in the 1906 New York, Philadelphia, and Norfolk Railroad passenger station. An original freight station across the yard holds uniforms, maps, and lanterns from back when railroads were the lifeline of the Eastern Shore, while the yard itself is full of dining cars and cabooses from the Richmond, Fredericksburg & Potomac, Norfolk & Western, and Wabash lines, including a 1927 Pullman Diplomat coach and a baggage car with an HO-scale model train layout inside. The museum is two miles west of US 13 on VA 176 (Parksley Rd.), open Mon.–Sat. 10 A.M.–4 P.M., Sun. 1–4 P.M.; $2 adults.

CHINCOTEAGUE

From killdeer nesting in the parking lot at the visitors center to gales that redefine the sandy shoreline, life on Chincoteague Island is shaped by the natural world. Known for its annual pony swim and auction, the largest community on the Eastern Shore combines a seasonal beach resort with a timeless offshore sanctuary, home to plenty of coastal life besides the famous fillies.

History

The story goes that on October 25, 1662, this island, sandwiched between the mainland and Assateague, was granted to Capt. William Whitington by Wachawampe, emperor of the Gingo Teagues. Over time the tribe's name would evolve into Chincoteague (SHINK-a-teeg), meaning "Beautiful Land Across the Water." A tiny settlement was destroyed by a tidal wave that swept over both islands in 1821, but the area gradually resettled over the next decades.

In 1861, a 132–2 vote to remain part of the Union set Chincoteague against the rest of its parent state. Several attempts by mainlanders to storm the island were repulsed. The railroad arrived in 1876, ending an era of lawlessness, illiteracy, and bare feet with the introduction of schools, churches, a newspaper, and new homes.

Incorporated as a town in 1908, Chincoteague

was connected to the mainland by an automobile causeway in 1922. Marguerite Henry's 1947 book, *Misty of Chincoteague,* propelled the town into the collective imagination of children worldwide as only a book about horses can. Many local residents appeared in the movie made from the children's story in the 1960s, and the town's name has been synonymous with ponies on the beach ever since.

Orientation

The town of Chincoteague occupies most of the island of the same name, connected to the mainland and US 13 by Rt. 175. A long, straight causeway crosses marshland and a drawbridge to Main Street, running the length of the island's western shore. Head north (left) on Main Street for a few blocks and turn east (right) onto Maddox Boulevard, where signs lead to the visitors center and the Chincoteague National Wildlife Refuge.

Sights

Decoys of every shape and species fill the cedar-smelling **Refuge Waterfowl Museum,** 7059 Maddox Blvd., 757/336-5800, alongside traps, boats, and hunting weapons. Learn how to reload a shotgun shell like an early-1900s market hunter, and stop by on a weekend when there's a resident carver at work. Don't miss the antique hunting carriage in a side room. Open Thurs.–Mon. 10 A.M.–5 P.M.; $3 adults, $1.50 children. A few blocks farther down the road, the **Oyster and Maritime Museum,** 7125 Maddox Blvd., 757/336-6117, holds the huge fresnel lens from the Assateague Island Lighthouse and exhibits on the history of the local oyster industry. Open daily 10 A.M.–5 P.M. in-season; $3 adults, $1 children.

The new **Island Aquarium,** 757/336-2212, in Landmark Plaza on N. Main St., features touch tanks and other exhibits on life in the marshes and waters of the Chesapeake Bay. Water piped in from the bay fills 1,800 gallons of tanks inhabited by creatures who are periodically re-released into the wild. Open weekdays 10 A.M.–5 P.M., weekends 10 A.M.–9 P.M. in-season; $4 adults, $3 children.

Accommodations

As befits a seasonal resort town, many hotels in Chincoteague close or drop their prices by as much as one-third in the off-season.

The T-shaped **1848 Island Manor House,** 4160 Main St., 800/852-1505 or 757/336-5436, fax 757/336-1333, email: imh@intercom.net, www.islandmanor.com, was built by a local Union surgeon and a postmaster who married a pair of sisters. Apparently the wives didn't get along under the same roof, prompting their husbands to split the house in two. It's since been rejoined and decorated in Federal style. Rates are $80–130.

Miss Molly's Inn, 4141 Main St., 800/221-5620 or 757/336-6686, fax 757/336-0600, email: msmolly@intercom.net, www.miss-mollys-inn.com, occupies a Victorian home built in 1886 by J.T. Rowley for his daughter Molly, who lived there until age 84. Marguerite Henry stayed here while writing *Misty of Chincoteague.* Prices ($85–155) include full breakfasts in the gazebo and scones at teatime. A wraparound veranda and scallop shingles adorn **The Watson House,** 4240 Main St., 800/336-6787 or 757/336-1564, fax 757/336-5776, email: watsonhouse@esva.net, www.watsonhouse.com, built in the late 1800s by David Robert Watson. In addition to the main house, guests can stay in a three-bedroom cottage and two-bedroom townhouse, and have access to complimentary bicycles and beach chairs. Rates are $110–120.

A stone's throw from Chincoteague Sound, the **Year of the Horse Inn,** 3583 Main St., 800/680-0090 or 757/336-3221, email: Richard@yearofthehorseinn.com, www.yearofthehorseinn.com, was the first B&B in town in 1978. It has a private pier and three rooms ($100–125) with private entrances, refrigerators, and balconies with a view of Chincoteague Bay. The "Haven" is a separate two-bedroom cottage that was the original guest house ($150), popular with itinerant fishermen before the town showed up on the tourist radar.

Four large guest rooms ($110–140) and a third-floor sitting room fill **The Inn at Poplar Corner,** 4248 Main St., 800/336-6787 or 757/336-6115, fax 757/336-5776, www.poplarcorner.com, under the same owners as the Watson House. Barbara and David Wiedenheft, the owners of Miss Molly's Inn, also operate the **Channel Bass Inn,** 6228 Church St., 800/249-0818 or 757/336-6148, fax 757/336-6959, email: cbi@intercom.net, www.channelbass-inn.com, dating to 1892. Some of the six rooms and one suite ($100–175) have a view of the Chesapeake Bay, and the public is welcome to stop by for Barbara's famous scones at afternoon tea in the Tea Room—just call ahead for reservations.

A hot tub, crabbing dock, and solarium are only some of the amenities at the **Waterside Motor Inn,** 3761 S. Main St., 757/336-3434, fax 757/336-1878, www.watersidemotorinn.com. Forty-five rooms are $100–145 in-season. Rooms at the **Refuge Inn,** 7058 Maddox Blvd., 888/257-0039 or 757/336-5511, fax 757/336-6134, www.refugeinn.com, top out at $120 in-season, with suites up to $220. They also rent a three-bedroom Cape Cod–style cottage on the north end of the island for $900 per week. The **Driftwood Motor Lodge,** 7105 Maddox Blvd., 800/553-6117 or 757/336-6557, fax 757/336-6558, email: drifwood@intercom.net, www .driftwoodmotorlodge.com, will set you back $90–135.

Furnished Cottages

Another option for extended stays on Chincoteague range in price: $400–800 per week and $200–400 per weekend in-season are typical. Most have cable TV, air-conditioning, full kitchens, picnic tables, and grills. Try the **Chincoteague Cottage Company,** 866/812-1577 or 757/336-5088, email: info@chincoteaguecottages.com, www.chincoteaguecottages.com; **Duck Haven Cottages,** 6582 Church St., 757/336-6290, email: leenoel@shore.intercom.net; or **Holiday Cottages,** 6113 Taylor St., 757/336-6256, fax 757336-6028.

Camping

The **Maddox Family Campground,** 6742 Maddox Blvd., 757/336-3111, www.chincoteague .com/maddox, has 550 sites open Mar.–Nov. for $27–35 depending on whether you want hookups

or not. They also offer a pool, showers, and crabbing equipment. **Tom's Cove Campground,** 8128 Beebe Rd., 757/336-6498, has waterfront sites within sight of the pony swim for $24–30, open Mar.–Nov., along with three fishing piers and an Olympic-sized pool.

Food

Dining in Chincoteague is a lesson in convergent evolution: most of the 23 restaurants are named after someone and offer family-style food, usually seafood, for all meals daily. Many are only open Memorial Day–Labor Day, and most of the rest limit their hours in the off-season. Steak, seafood, and chicken entrées tend to run $10–15.

Popular spots include **Etta's Channel Side Restaurant,** 7452 East Side Dr., 757/336-5644, and the **Island Family Restaurant,** 3441 Ridge Rd., 757/336-1198. **AJ's on the Creek,** 6585 Maddox Blvd., 757/336-1539, is an intimate, romantic place with some of the best seafood in town. Open daily for lunch and dinner (closed Sunday off-season).

The **Landmark Crab House,** Landmark Plaza, 6172 Main St., 757/336-5552, serves Chincoteague's famous oysters for dinner daily, and encloses the Waterfront Lounge, with a Brunswick bar from Chicago dating to 1897. **Don's Seafood Market & Restaurant,** 4113 Main St., 757/336-5715, also has a lounge with a raw bar and dancing past midnight.

Steamers, 6251 Maddox Blvd., 757/336-5478, is an informal seafood joint popular with tourists and locals alike and almost always packed in season. All-you-can-eat feasts start in the low $20s and include soup, salads, biscuits, hush puppies, corn on the cob, sweet potatoes—*and*—the seafood of your choice. Butcher paper and a garbage can for every table keep the mess to a minimum.

Fishing

Dozens of places in Chincoteague rent boats and fishing tackle for visitors interested in exploring the fringes of Chincoteague Bay. Expect to pay $40–50 per day for a midsized fishing boat for 3–4 people, and around $100 for a 12-person pontoon boat for four hours. Rods and reels, crab pots, and clam rakes are $5–10 per day. Try **Barnacle Bill's Bait & Tackle,** 3691 S. Main St., 757/336-5188, www.barnaclebillsbaittackl.com, and **Captain Bob's Fishing Camp,** 2477 S. Main St., 757/336-6654. Both **East Side Rental,** 7462 East Side Dr., 800/889-1525 or 757/336-3409, and **Snug Harbor Marina and Cottages,** 7536 E. Shore Dr., 757/336-6176, rent Jet Skis as well.

Charters let you venture offshore for the big ones: tuna, marlin, swordfish, and shark. Barnacle Bills' has four-hour bay fishing trips for $35 pp, including all bait and tackle, with offshore trips varying in price depending on the size of the party and what you're after. **Captain Wayne Lewis,** 757/336-6835, email: fish@dmv.com, runs trips aboard the 32-foot *Wonderfull I* for $30 pp for a half day, while Captain Fred Gilman of *Reel Time Charters,* 800/982-2818, email: reeltime@bellatlantic.net, offers offshore, big game, and wreck fishing from the 33-foot sport fishing boat of the same name.

Tours and Excursions

Captain Barry's Back Bay Cruises, 4256 Anderson Ave., 757/336-6508, www.captainbarry.bigstep.com, leave from Landmark Plaza on N. Main Street for early-morning bird-watching ($20 pp) and half-day Back Bay Expeditions for $40 pp, with historical tidbits and natural history stops galore. The *Linda J,* 757/336-6214, email: captmilo@shore.intercom.net, is a 24-foot pontoon boat that can be booked for short sightseeing trips for 2–6 people for $15–20 pp.

No less than five tours a day are on the roster for the *Assateague Explorer,* 757/990-1795, www.assateagueisland.com, including pony spotting, bird-watching, fishing, and sunset cruises for $20–30 pp. These leave from Tom's Cove Campground. **Wildlife Expeditions,** 7721 East Side Dr., 757/336-6811, email: cptkyak@intercom.net, jcherrix.tripod.com, is run by Jay Cherrix, whose family tree goes back three centuries on Chicoteague. His sunrise and sunset kayak ecotours come recommended.

The **Intracoastal Kayak Company,** 2257 Spinnaker St. in Greenbackville, 757/336-0070, email: mailto:info@oysterbayoutfitters.com, www.intracoastalkayak.com, runs relaxed, educational, low-impact kayak tours for $60 pp for a half day and $80 for a full day (lunch included), along with early-bird and sunset tours for $40. They also rent touring and surf kayaks ($35–45) as well as car racks.

Other Recreation

If you can't visit during the Pony Roundup, you can still get a close-up view at the **Chincoteague Pony Centre,** 6417 Carriage Dr., 757/336-2776, offering afternoon pony rides daily and a pony show Mon.–Sat. at 8 P.M. Open Mon.–Sat. 9 A.M.–9 P.M., Sun. 1–9 P.M.

Both **Jus' Bikes,** 6527 Maddox Blvd., 757/336-6700, and **The Bike Depot & Beach Outfitters,** at the Refuge Motor Inn, rent beach-cruiser bikes for $3–5 per hour or $10–30 per day. Jus' Bikes also rents mopeds ($60 per day) and Wave Runners ($125).

Shopping

Another unmistakable sign of beach resorts is dozens of stores selling everything from crafts, dolls, and candles to framed seascapes and Christmas goodies, and Chincoteague is no exception. Places such as **Church Street Peddlers,** 6292 Church St., 757/336-6507, stock a little bit of everything. Ronald Justis's **Decoys Decoys Decoys,** 4039 Main St., 757/336-1402 or 800/877-6911, offers one of the largest selections on the East Coast, while copper and folk art are the main offerings at **White's Copperworks,** 6373 Maddox. Blvd., 757/336-1588.

The **Main Street Shop Coffeehouse,** 4288 Main St., 757/336-6782, has an eclectic selection of artwork and great coffee, while **Bay Treasures,** 3845 S. Main St., 757/336-1747, stocks nautical memorabilia and artifacts.

Wildlife prints, sculpture, and paintings are among the offerings of the **Ark II Gallery,** 3777 Willow St., 757/336-6219, and **Skip Jack's Nautical Gifts and Crafts,** 4103 Main St., 757/336-1768, specializes in nautical crafts and gifts. The stone and earthenware at Carol Myers' **Main St. Pottery,** 3891 Main St., 757/336-1546, ranges from whimsical to practical. Local artist Nancy West has woven clothing, oil paintings, and unique jewelry at **Island Arts,** 6196 Maddox Blvd., 757/336-5856, while Wales' native Hal Lott sells silkscreens through **Lott's Arts & Things,** 4281 Main St., 757/336-5773.

Events

Many of Chincoteague's annual events require advance tickets: call the Chincoteague Chamber of Commerce for information.

In April, 150 local and national artists congregate for the **Easter Decoy and Art Festival.** It includes plenty of home-cooked food, but not nearly as much as the **Seafood Festival,** at Tom's Cove Campground the first Wednesday in May. All you can eat of bushels of raw oysters, shoals of fish, and tens of thousands of clams are yours for the price of a ticket—but the event is popular, so you have to buy that ticket in advance from the Eastern Shore Chamber of Commerce in Melfa. If you can, stick around for the **Blessing of the Fleet** at the dock later in the month.

The **Pony Roundup and Swim** is Chincoteague's biggest happening and one of the largest on the Virginia coast. Held since 1925, this event is preceded by the Fireman's Carnival on weekends from late June through July. In late July, members of the Chincoteague Volunteer Fire Company dress up as cowboys and round up the herd of wild ponies that lives in the Chincoteague National Wildlife Refuge. After swimming across the channel, the horses step ashore at Memorial Park at the southern end of the island. Here they're penned until the famous auction, attended by 50,000 or more people. This event fills the town to capacity, so book accommodations well in advance.

Information

The Chincoteague Chamber of Commerce operates a **visitors center,** 6733 Maddox Blvd., 757/336-6161, www.chincoteaguechamber.com, in a traffic circle about one mile west of the bridge to Assateague Island, open Mon.–Sat. 9 A.M.–4:30 P.M., Sun. 12:30–4:30 P.M.

Near Chincoteague

The National Advisory Committee on Aeronautics (NACA) opened an aeronautical research center at Wallops Island in 1945. NACA became a full federal agency, the National Aeronautics and Space Administration (NASA), in 1958, and over the years, the facility has tested and launched thousands of orbital and suborbital rockets and balloons. A recent agreement will allow launches of commercial satellites from the facility. The agency runs a **visitors center,** 757/824-2298 or 757/824-1344, tracing the history of flight, rockets, and space travel through video displays, photos, and real relics of the space program. Space-suit demonstrations and model rocket launchings take place during the summer. Open daily 10 A.M.–4 P.M. (Thurs.–Mon. off-season); free.

On US 13 just north of the turnoff onto Rt. 175 for Chincoteague is **The Decoy Factory,** 757/824-5621, the largest of its kind in the world. You can watch workers put decoys together or buy just about anything you need to make your own, from $10 miniature kits to monthly species specials.

ASSATEAGUE ISLAND AND CHINCOTEAGUE NATIONAL WILDLIFE REFUGE

Assateague Island, a thin ribbon of sand 37 miles long, extends from Ocean City, Maryland to just past Chincoteague Island. The entire spit has been designated a National Seashore, and Virginia's southern one-third of the island was set aside in 1943 as the Chincoteague National Wildlife Refuge to protect dwindling habitat for migrating snow geese.

There's much more to the fishhook tip of sand than the graceful white birds with black wingtips, though. Virginia's portion of the wild pony herd draws plenty of visitors, while enough birds pass through during migrating season to guarantee additions to most birders' life lists. Even though they're not open to camping, 10 miles of wild oceanside beaches offer wave-soothed solitude for hikers who venture off the more popular pathways.

Habitats

Tidal salt marshes and mudflats line the ragged landward side of the island, facing Chincoteague

Island and Chincoteague Bay. Pine and hardwood forests fill the interior, dotted with pools and the large bight of Toms Cove at the southernmost end. The smooth Atlantic edge is almost pure sand, slowly being pushed southward by the endless caress of the ocean.

Species

More than 300 species of **birds** depend on the rich harvest of mollusks, insects, and crustaceans, provided by Assateague Island's freshwater impoundments, marshes, mudflats, and tidal pools. Herons, egrets, gulls, terns, and sandpipers arrive in the summer, followed in the fall by migrating shorebirds and peregrine falcons, which are easier to spot on Assateague than almost anywhere else on the East Coast. Migrating waterfowl, including mallards, pintails, black ducks, Canada geese, and greater snow geese, take advantage of the island's mild winter climate during their thousand-mile journeys. Keep an ear out for the distinctive call of the willet, and be aware of area closures (usually most of Toms Cove Hook) to protect the nesting sites of the endangered piping plover.

Most famous of Assateague's 44 mammal species are undoubtedly the **wild ponies,** separated into two herds by a fence at the Maryland state line. The Virginia herd is technically owned by the Chincoteague Volunteer Fire Company and allowed to graze on federal land by special permit. It's fun to hear that they swam ashore from a shipwrecked Spanish galleon, but it's more probable (and prosaic) that they're the descendants of herds hidden on the island in the 17th century by mainland colonists trying to avoid livestock taxes. (This means they're actually stunted horses, not true ponies.)

With their shaggy manes and stubby legs, they look cute enough to pet, which many people do—bad idea. These are *wild* horses, and visitors get bitten and kicked every year (and promptly blame the refuge staff) for their own foolishness. The horses' short stature, and their bloated bellies (which can't handle human handouts), most likely result from generations of salty marsh grass and brackish water.

Your best chance of spotting them is from the

Woodland Trail in Black Duck Marsh, but you might bump into a few just about anywhere. They tend to stick to the beach in the summer, where the constant breeze keeps the legendary Assateague mosquitoes at bay—at least somewhat.

A small herd of Japanese **sika deer** was released by a Boy Scout troop in 1923 at the northern end of the island, and the deer now outnumber the native **white-tailed deer.** If you come across a large, relatively unfazed rodent with a big bushy tail, it's probably an endangered **Delmarva fox squirrel.**

Visiting the Refuge

The refuge entrance, at the end of Maddox Blvd., is open daily 5 A.M.–10 P.M. in season for $5 per car. A $15 Federal Duck Stamp is good for all federal national wildlife refuges for a year. The U.S. Fish and Wildlife Service operates the **Refuge Visitor Center,** 757/336-6122, www.chinco.fws.gov, open daily 9 A.M.–5 P.M., with wildlife information, trail brochures, and schedules of interpretive activities.

Parts of the beach are open to surfing, fishing, swimming, clamming, and crabbing. Fifteen miles of trails include the 1.6-mile Woodland Trail to an overlook over pony-favored Black Duck Marsh; the 3.2-mile Wildlife Loop, open to vehicles 3 P.M.–dusk; and the Toms Cove Nature Trail, out along the southern tail. Miles of untracked beach stretch north from the National Park Service's **Toms Cove Visitor Center,** 757/336-6577, open daily 9 A.M.–5 P.M., at the entrance to Toms Cove Hook. Cyclists are welcome on paved trails. Boaters should check ahead of time for permitted landing sites.

Camping isn't allowed in the refuge, but it is across the state line in the **Assateague State Park,** 7206 National Seashore Lane, Berlin, Maryland 21811-9742, 888/432-2267 or 410/641-2120. Narrated **tram tours** of the refuge are given from Apr.–Sept., leaving from the Chincoteague Inn at 6262 Marlin Street. These tours last 90 minutes and visit the north end of the refuge where cars aren't permitted. Tickets for tram tours ($8 adults, $4 children) and **boat tours** around the island ($12.50/8) can be bought at the refuge visitors center, or call 757/336-6154 for more details. Information on the **Assateague Island National Seashore** can be obtained by calling 757/336-6577 or 410/641-1441, www.nps.gov/asis.

Both the Park Service and the U.S. Fish and Wildlife Service offer naturalist programs in the refuge daily during the summer and on spring and fall weekends. Annual events start with the **International Migratory Bird Celebration** in May, with guided walks, speakers, and workshops, and continue through **National Wildlife Refuge Week** in October. **Assateague Island Waterfowl Week,** in late November during the southward migration of Canada and snow geese, is the only time visitors can drive to the northern end of the refuge.

The **Assateague Coastal Trust,** 10031 Old Ocean City Blvd., Suite 101A, P.O. Box 731, Berlin, MD 21811, 410/629-1538, fax 410/629-1059, email: act@beachin.net, www.actforbays.org, is a grassroots nonprofit organization dedicated to preserving Assateague Island and its surrounding ecosystem through outreach programs and advocacy efforts. They organize occasional conferences, lectures, and workshops.

TANGIER ISLAND

Only 10 or so miles of Chesapeake chop from the mainland, Tangier is decades away from even the atavistic air of the Eastern Shore. The insularity of this tight little fishing community is something you don't come across every day. The pace of life is a little different and the accent hard to place, making a visit as much a cultural experience as a sightseeing jaunt. Even in a state that has as many curious nooks as Virginia does, Tangier still stands out.

History

Indians fished and hunted on the island for centuries, but Tangier wasn't "discovered" by Europeans—Captain John Smith, to be precise—and named until 1608. The first settlement came in 1686, after native tribes, according to a (probably bogus) legend, sold the island for two overcoats. Cornishman John Crockett, along with his eight sons and their families, was the first to arrive. By the 19th century, the island was home to 100 residents, half of them Crocketts, who made a living fishing and grazing livestock.

Boats are the principal form of transportation on Tangier island.

THE TOWN THAT TURNED PAUL NEWMAN DOWN

The Great Movie Controversy of 1998 showed clearly that increasing tourism hasn't changed the stubbornly independent local attitude of Tangier all that much.

Actor Paul Newman had selected Tangier as the perfect place to film *Message in a Bottle,* a movie starring himself and Kevin Costner. Everything looked great until a core of religious fundamentalists on the town council forced a last-minute change of plans. Despite a petition bearing 200 names, the possibility of $23,000 worth of repairs to the town dock, and work for hundreds of hard-up island residents, a 6-0 vote said that the PG-13 script, with its profanity, sex, and alcohol, was inconsistent with community values and therefore unwelcome.

Many indignant islanders pointed out that swearing, procreating, and even illicit drinking were far from rare on Tangier—and that legions of locals had taken the boat to Salisbury, Maryland, to see the disaster epic *Titanic.* But the arguments fell on deaf ears, and Newman, who had scoped out the island incognito, had to look elsewhere for a film site.

The outside world intruded during the Revolutionary War, when British troops used the island as a base for raiding American ships. During the War of 1812, 12,000 more redcoats stood under the pines in preparation for an attack on Fort McHenry. Local reverend Joshua Thomas harangued the invaders, claiming that the word from above was that they could not take Baltimore. (He was right.) In 1814, Francis Scott Key boarded a British boat on Tangier to negotiate the release of an American prisoner. During his voyage, Key witnessed the American flag "gallantly streaming" through the Battle of Baltimore, inspiring him to write what would become the "Star-Spangled Banner."

A cholera outbreak in 1866 forced an almost total evacuation of the island, and "The August Storm" of 1933 inundated everything on the low-lying island but the top floors of houses. Three years later, the Army Air Corps had to drop supplies onto the school playground when "The Big Freeze" clogged the entire northern bay with a foot of ice. Electricity arrived in 1946, and satellite dishes have begun sprouting in the last decade.

Tangier Today

A little more than five square miles in area, the island consists of three inhabited "ridges," none more than five feet above the Chesapeake waterline, which are split by canals and connected by bridges. Most is marsh and wetlands, hunting grounds for Virginia rails, muskrats, herons, and egrets. About 700 people currently live on Tangier—fewer than half as many as did at the turn of the 20th century—and most are related. A third are Crocketts, with the names of other settlers including Pruitt, Dise, Parks, and Wheatley covering most of the remainder. Crabbing and clamming sustain the community, still considered the "Softshell Capital of the World." Men leave before dawn to check the farms alongshore where the famous local crabs are raised.

Tangier has always been a tightly knit community, in the early 1900s when a book by resident Thomas Crockett rattled so many local skeletons that his descendants later gathered up and destroyed as many copies as they could find. During a World War I visit, President Woodrow Wilson found Tangier's doors locked when islanders suspected his aides of being a German raiding party off a submarine. When Accomack County officials sent over a metal jail in the 1930s, island residents threw it into the water, saying they had no need for one.

A peculiar accent, the product of generations of isolation, evokes England's West Country, turning "time" and "mind" into "toime" and "moind." Front yards (the highest ground on the island) are often crowded with graves and headstones, some centuries old, and highly religious roots continue to sprout—a 1995 revival left one-third of the population born-again Christians. All children attend one school, rebuilt in the mid-1990s, which consistently has the highest percentage of graduates (sometimes six out of six) going on to college in the state. Health care comes in the form of mainland physicians who come twice a week, and dentists and optometrists visit monthly.

Everyone knows each other, of course, and welcomes visitors with a wave from golf carts, bright cruiser bicycles, and a handful of cars and trucks. Stacked crab pots fill backyards lined with chainlink fences, and motorboats zoom around the wharf area, a maze of pilings, crab shanties, and trays called "peeler boxes" where crabs are held until they shed their shells.

Accommodations and Food

Because lodging options are limited, reservations are essential on Tangier. Shirley and Wallace Pruitt run **Shirley's Bay View Inn** on Ridge Rd., 757/891-2396, www.tangierisland.net. Wallace was born in the 1806 house, with a wraparound porch and plantings in abundance. Two rooms in the house and eight cottages behind are open year-round, with air-conditioning, cable TV, and breakfast included for $80. Grace and Jim Brown's **Sunset Inn,** 757/891-2535, is also on Ridge Road, at the south end near the beach, with house and cottage rooms for $75 including breakfast.

Hilda Crockett's Chesapeake House, 757/891-2331, is in town a few blocks south of the church. This local legend, open since 1940, offers rooms in season for $80 including breakfast and dinner. The restaurant is also open to the public, serving all-you-can-eat meals for $13.50 from 11 A.M.– 5 P.M. daily.

Near the docks are the **Fisherman's Corner Restaurant,** 757/891-2900, and the **Islander Restaurant,** 757/891-2249, both serving fresh seafood in season for lunch and dinner. Sandwiches are $6–8 and seafood plates are $10–15—nothing fancy, but as fresh as it comes. On Main Street, **Spanky's Place,** 757/891-2514, serves ice cream to the strains of '50s rock-n-roll, along with lunch and snacks. Almost everything in town closes early (typically 7 P.M.), but you can order pizzas and sandwiches from **Jolly Jim's,** 757/891-2281, a carryout next to the Sunset Inn offering free delivery until 10 or 11 P.M. Alcohol is technically forbidden on Tangier.

Shopping and Recreation

A handful of gift shops are the only places in

THE COAST

Don't speed on Tangier Island.

© JULIAN SMITH

town that take credit cards. Sandy's Gifts, on King Street, has a small museum, and some enterprising islander has set up an honor-fee recipe rack on a fence near the Islander Restaurant. Head to the south end of the island for a nice beach. Several places, including Wanda's Gift Shop, rent bicycles, which can be left sitting around anywhere (where's a thief going to go?). **RB's Rentals,** 757/891-2240, rents golf carts, canoes, kayaks, motor boats, and bicycles from the town dock. They also offer nature cruises around the island on the 46-foot *Elizabeth Thomas,* leaving in the evenings from the dock.

Transportation

The *Courtney Thomas* **mailboat,** 757/891-2240, email: tocruise98@aol.com, leaves Crisfield, Maryland year-round Mon.–Sat. at 12:30 P.M., Sun. at 4 P.M. ($20 pp roundtrip). Also in Crisfield, **Tangier Island Cruises,** 410/968-2338, sends the 300-passenger *Steven Thomas* to the island from May–Oct. at 12:30 P.M., returning the same day at 4 P.M. ($20 pp roundtrip).

Tangier & Chesapeake Cruises, 804/453-2628, sends the *Chesapeake Breeze* from the Buzzard's Point Marina near Reedville, Virginia, daily May–Oct. at 10 A.M., returning at 3:45 P.M. ($20 pp roundtrip), with a narrated tour on the island. **Tangier-Onancock Cruises,** 757/891-2240, email: tocruise98@aol.com, leave from Onancock daily May–Oct. at 10 A.M., returning at 3P.M. ($20 pp roundtrip). The 90-minute cruise aboard the 65-foot *Captain Eulice* is narrated, with an option for a guided tour around the island.

Southwest Virginia

Virginia's rugged western tail—by far the least-tamed, and most-forgotten, part of the state—dangles in the hilly country bordered by North Carolina, Tennessee, Kentucky, and West Virginia. The area has no sweeping Civil War battlefields or well-dressed Founding Fathers to anchor it in memory. History here has a rougher edge to it, beginning with the frontier families who pushed their way into the rippling hills, set up shop, and began a legacy that still exists in force. Pockets of Brethren and Friends (Quakers) keep alive the faith handed down from 18th-century German farmers. The hillsides were gouged into to make way for coal mining and railroads, creating new towns and giving rise to others, while covering everything with a layer of fine grit. Today, countless back roads wind past hillsides laid bare by strip mines, and cities struggle to find a way to fill the economic vacuum left by the departure of the industries.

HIGHLIGHTS

Most visits to southwest Virginia start and end at the "Star City" of Roanoke, a former railroad town reborn as a lively, forward-thinking metropolis. I-81 shoots straight southwest past Blacksburg (wired in more ways than one on the brainpower of Virginia Tech University)

Southwest Virginia

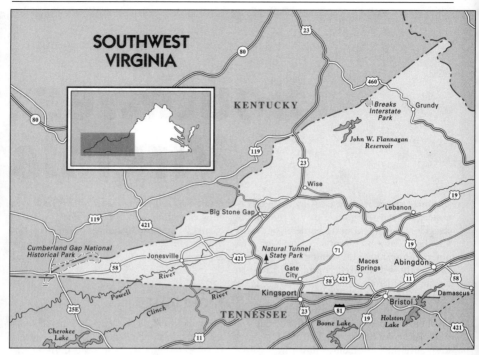

and Abingdon, which is blessed with the outstanding tourist trinity of the Barter Theater, Martha Washington Inn, and the Virginia Highlands Festival.

Beyond that, you have back roads, tobacco barns, and mountain music. The hills here are alive with the sounds of fiddles, banjos, and stomping feet at famous hoe-downs such as the Galax Fiddler's Convention, the Carter Family Memorial Music Center, and the Floyd Flatfoot Jamboree.

Southwest Virginia's true heart, though, is outdoors—the natural wonders of this slice of the Appalachian Plateau rival any in the east. Countless rivers and streams carve the hills with deep, parallel valleys, capped by the quarter-mile-deep gorge of Breaks Interstate Park. The Cumberland Gap National Historical Park preserves the gateway to the American west in much the same condition it was in when Daniel Boone blazed the trail.

Thousands of acres of beech, maple, hickory,

and ash stand within the Jefferson National Forest, including the 117,000 acres of the Mt. Rogers National Recreation Area, which contains the highest peak in the state. Outdoor pursuits are almost endless, from hiking the Appalachian Trail and mountain biking or horseback riding along the Virginia Creeper and New River trails to rafting the Russell Fork River. Even the view from the driver's seat of a car can be worth the trip, especially along I-77 north to West Virginia or the southern section of the Blue Ridge Parkway.

ACCESS

I-81 runs most of the length of southwestern Virginia, paralleled by the slower, more scenic US 11. I-77 slices across briefly from North Carolina to West Virginia. West and north of Abingdon, most rural roads are two-lane, meandering, and gorgeous. The only major airport is in Roanoke, the nearest Amtrak service 45 miles north, in Clifton Forge.

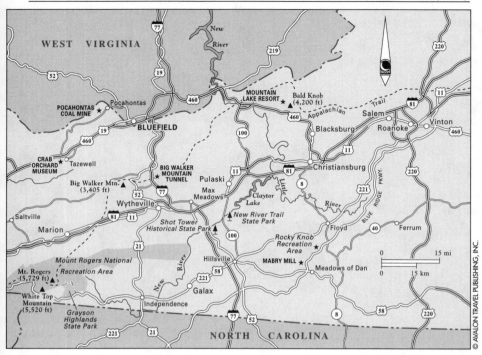

WEST VIRGINIA

New River

POCAHONTAS COAL MINE ★ Pocahontas

BLUEFIELD

CRAB ORCHARD MUSEUM ★ Tazewell

Big Walker Mtn. ▲ (3,405 ft)

Wytheville

Saltville

Marion

MOUNTAIN LAKE RESORT ★ Bald Knob ▲ (4,200 ft) Appalachian Trail Salem

Blacksburg Roanoke Vinton

BIG WALKER MOUNTAIN TUNNEL ★ Pulaski Christiansburg

Max Meadows Claytor Lake Little River BLUE RIDGE PKWY.

Shot Tower Historical State Park ▲ New River Trail State Park Floyd Ferrum

Mount Rogers National Recreation Area

Mt. Rogers ▲ (5,729 ft)

White Top Mountain (5,520 ft) ▲

Grayson Highlands State Park

Hillsville MABRY MILL ★ Meadows of Dan

Rocky Knob Recreation Area ★

Galax

Independence

NORTH CAROLINA

0   15 mi
0   15 km

© AVALON TRAVEL PUBLISHING, INC.

RESOURCES

Both the **Highlands Gateway Visitor Center,** in Max Meadows, 800/446-9670 or 540/637-6766, www.virginiablueridge.org, and the **New River Valley Visitors Alliance,** 7502 Lee Hwy., Radford, 888/398-8988, 540/633-

6788, www.visitnrv.org, are great sources of travel information on the region. If you plan to be among the thousands who flock here during autumn, call the Shenandoah Valley Travel Association's Fall Foliage Hotline at 540/740-3132 to find out when and where colors are peaking.

Roanoke and Vicinity

Settled in a bowl in the mountains and split by the Roanoke River, Roanoke, the largest city in southwest Virginia (pop. 231,000), offers metropolitan convenience with a surprising amount of flair. The "Capital of the Blue Ridge" serves as the transportation and medical center for the entire region and was the first community in North America to offer citywide recycling. Various polls have put it in the top 10 or 20 cities nationwide for quality of life, lack of stress, and tourism potential. Much of this potential is be-

cause of Roanoke's vibrant downtown area, anchored by Market Square and the justifiably famous Center in the Square arts complex.

HISTORY

The city's unenviable original name, Big Lick, refers to the area's salt deposits, sought out by animals, which were in turn hunted by Native Americans. The first European settlers arrived near the end of the 1700s, stopping along the

SOUTHWEST VIRGINIA

© AVALON TRAVEL PUBLISHING, INC.

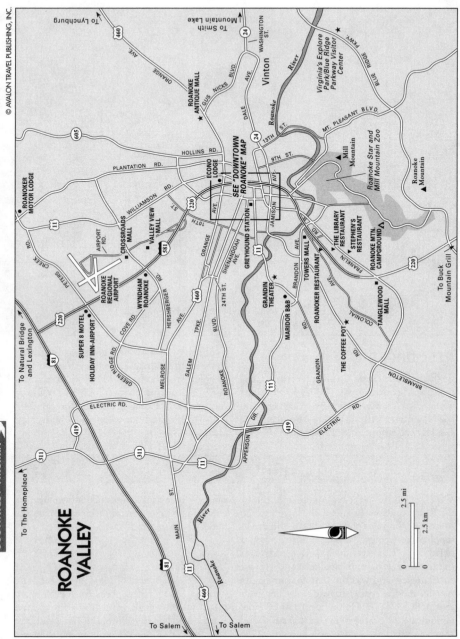

ROANOKE VALLEY

Great Road down the Shenandoah Valley. By the early 1800s, the town's central streets had been laid out and, with the completion of a road over the Blue Ridge from Lynchburg, Big Lick was on its way to becoming a crossroads for western Virginia.

Explosive growth arrived with the steam and clatter of the railroads shortly after the Civil War. In 1881, the Shenandoah Valley and Norfolk & Western railroads chose the town of 700 as a junction point, changing its name in the process to the more presentable Roanoke, from the native word *rawrenock* (shell money). By 1892, some 25,000 people called the valley home. The Virginia Railway arrived in 1906, bringing coal traffic and passengers including Mark Twain, who rode on the first coach into the city. The largest rayon plant in the world opened here in the early 1900s, but even so, toward the middle of the century, Roanoke's economy began to slip.

During the award-winning downtown revitalization in 1979, wise city planners drew heavily on public opinion through questionnaires, interviews, and live television "design-a-thons."

ORIENTATION

Roanoke's rapid blooming has left it a rather scrambled city. The easiest way to navigate is by landmarks and highway exits. Heading south on I-581 from I-81, exit 4 sits between the Roanoke Civic Center on the east and the tan spire of St. Andrew's Catholic Church, one of the highest points in the city. Next, look for the unmistakable Tudor bulk of the Hotel Roanoke and Conference Center, followed by the spaceship tower of the First Union Bank.

Exit 5, onto Williamson Road, carries you past the H&C coffeepot billboard and the Dr. Pepper bottlecap clock on Salem Avenue. Head toward Market Square along Campbell or Salem avenues. (You can park in a garage next to the Center in the Square all day for less than $5.) To reach Mill Mountain and the Blue Ridge Parkway, hop on Walnut Avenue from Jefferson Street south.

Tobacco drying in a barn is a common sight in rural southwestern Virginia.

SIGHTS

Market Square

Begun in the 1880s with only a handful of vendors, this is one of Virginia's oldest markets. After following the city's boom-and-bust cycles through most of the 20th century, the market became the center of Roanoke's recent downtown renaissance. Today, permanent awnings shade sidewalk stands brimming with country market staples: fresh produce in season, baskets of flowers, eggs, dairy products, and meats. Old Victorian shops, now nouveaux country stores, have shelves that groan under gourmet wines, cheeses, and preserves, while for blocks around, restaurants, gift shops, and art galleries take up any extra space.

The historic **City Market Building,** erected in 1922, is home to a neon-lit international food court featuring everything from sushi to Cuban sandwiches. Local legend has it that anyone who drinks from the small **Dog Mouth Fountain,** at Salem Avenue and Market Street, will someday return to Roanoke.

Center in the Square

This converted warehouse at the southwest corner of Market Square houses five floors of

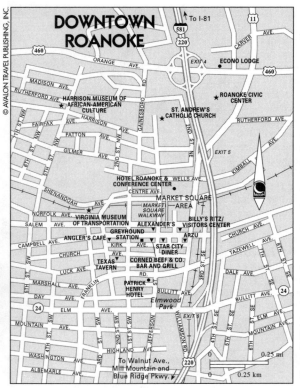

lights that proves that museums can be anything but boring. Hands-on exhibits geared toward kids—but fun for anyone—include holograms, fiber optics, a giant xylophone, and a "body tech" exhibit for budding anatomists. The Hopkins Planetarium and a tank full of live marine animals from the Chesapeake Bay help the museum maintain its consistent status as one of the best in the region. Open Tues.–Sat. 10 A.M.–5 P.M.; $6 adults ($8 with a planetarium show), $4 children ($6 with show). The planetarium alone is $3 pp, and the Mega-Dome Theater shows large-format (70-mm) films for $5 adults, $4 children. The museum is free the second Friday of each month from 3:30–7 P.M.

Each museum also has a gift emporium on the first floor—try dragging your child (or parent) away from the **Science Museum Shop,** next to the **History Museum Store** and the **Art Museum Store.**

An outstanding example of the southwest Virginia's finest cultural attractions. The **Art Museum of Western Virginia,** 540/342-5760, www.artmuseumroanoke.org, features 19th- and 20th-century American art, decorative crafts and works by regional artists, as well as special exhibitions and the Art-Venture, a family-oriented interactive art center. Open Tues.–Sat. 10 A.M.–5 P.M., Sun. 1–5 P.M.; free.

Ten thousand years of local goings-on, from Native Americans to the present day, are covered in the **History Museum of Western Virginia,** 540/342-5770. Open Tues.–Fri. 10 A.M.–4 P.M., Sat. 10 A.M.–5 P.M., Sun. 1–5 P.M.; $2 adults, $1 children (free the second Friday of each month 1–4 P.M.).

Hop the elevator to the **Science Museum of Western Virginia,** 540/342-5710, www.smwv .org, a place full of noises, voices, and flashing

possibilities of regional theater, the **Mill Mountain Theater,** 540/342-5733, www.millmountain.org, shows original works, classics, and children's plays. Tickets are $15–30 for performances on the Main Stage and $10–15 on the Waldron Stage. Call 800/317-6455 or 540/342-5740 for a current schedule.

For more information on Center in the Square, call 540/342-5700 Mon.–Sat. 10 A.M.–5 P.M., Sun. 1–5 P.M. (www.centerinthesquare .org). In the same building, **The Arts Council of the Blue Ridge,** 540/342-5790, can supply information on regional events.

Other Museums

The **Virginia Museum of Transportation,** 303 Norfolk Ave. and 3rd St., 540/342-5670, www.vmt.org, serves as a monument to the glorious methods of simply getting from one place to another. Inside the restored freight station straddling the train tracks three blocks west of Market Square are an O-scale model railroad, a gift shop, and a gorgeous collection of antique autos, including a 1934 Ford V-8 Model A Sedan and a 1950 Studebaker Landcruiser, more spaceship than car. Dozens of train engines and cars—a few of which are open to visitors—fill the lot out back. Steam engines, diesel locomotives, post office cars, and a classic caboose cover virtually the entire history of rail travel. Open Mon.–Sat. 10 A.M.–5 P.M., Sun. noon–5 P.M.; $6 adults, $4 children 3–11.

The Harrison School, opened in 1916 as the city's first public high school for African American students, has reserved a few downstairs rooms for the **Harrison Museum of African-American Culture,** 523 Harrison Ave. NW, 540/345-4818. Changing exhibits relating to African American culture focus on the Roanoke area, and African crafts fill the gift shop. Open Tues.–Fri. 10 A.M.–5 P.M., Sat. and Sun. 1–5 P.M.; free.

Roanoke was home to the country's first volunteer emergency rescue squad, organized in 1928 by a railroad worker who as a child had watched helplessly as two men drowned in the Roanoke River before help could arrive. That small group evolved into today's national Emergency Medical Technician (EMT) system, pioneering the use of cardiopulmonary resuscitation and modern life-saving techniques along the way. More than 50 exhibits (many interactive) at the **To The Rescue Museum,** Tanglewood Mall, 4428 Electric Rd., 540/776-0364, include a memorial to EMTs killed in the line of duty. Open Tues.–Sat. noon–9 P.M., Sun. 1–6 P.M.; $2 adults, $1 children.

Mill Mountain

Sandwiched between the city and the Blue Ridge Parkway sits this lone peak, disconnected from the rest of the Appalachian chain. A trolley to the summit was built in 1910 but was soon abandoned because people preferred to drive up winding Walnut Avenue instead. At the peak stands the **Roanoke Star,** the city's most famous landmark. At 100 feet tall, it's the World's Largest Manmade Illuminated Star,

with 2,000 feet of neon tubing visible for 60 miles. Airplane pilots navigate by it occasionally, and even Elvis Presley once snuck up here after a concert to take a closer look. The view of the city and valley from the base of the star, and the picnic area nearby, are excellent on a clear day.

A short walk away, the **Mill Mountain Zoo,** 540/343-3241, www.mmzoo.org, is a small but professional zoo with more than 50 species of mammals, birds and reptiles, including many exotic, endangered examples such as Japanese macaques, a Nepalese red panda, and Ruby, a huge Siberian tiger with whom the zoo eventually hopes to start a tiger breeding center. Children will love the prairie dog village, petting zoo, and the miniature Zoo-Choo train that circles the park ($1.50 pp). Open daily 10 A.M.–5 P.M.; $6 adults, $4 children under 12.

Virginia's Explore Park

This living-history park, depicting life in Virginia at various points in its history, sits off the Blue Ridge Parkway at milepost 115. Interpreters portraying Native Americans and frontier families tend the working farm and its crops and animals but are happy to demonstrate Colonial skills, including loading and firing flintlock muskets, flint-and-steel fire-making, crafts, and cooking. Eight miles of trails loop past the re-created buildings into the surrounding countryside. You can stop for lunch or dinner at the **Brugh Tavern,** 540/427-2400 (open Tues.–Sun.), a restored inn that once served travelers on the Great Wagon Road in the early 19th century.

The National Park Service recently opened a **Blue Ridge Parkway Visitor Center** here as well, open daily 9 A.M.–5 P.M., May through mid-November. Special events include the Blue Ridge Garden Festival and the Appalachian Folk Festival. Open May.–Oct. Wed.–Sat. 10 A.M.–5 P.M., Sun. noon–5 P.M. (weekends only in April); $8 adults, $4.50 children 3–11. For more information, call 800/842-9163, 540/427-8508, or 540/427-1800, or look at their website: www.explorepark.org.

ACCOMMODATIONS

$50–100

Take I-81 exit 2W to reach the **Super 8** motel, 6616 Thirlane Rd. NW, 540/563-8888. The **Econo Lodge Civic Center,** 308 Orange Ave. and Williamson Rd., tel./fax 540/343-2413, is off exit 4E. On a hilltop just south of the airport, you'll find the **Holiday Inn-Airport,** 6626 Thirlane Rd. NW, 540/366-8861, fax 540/366-1637. Also in this category is the **Colony House Motor Lodge,** 3560 Franklin Rd. SW, 540/345-0411, off I-581/US 220 near the Franklin Rd./Salem exit.

$100–150

With a history almost as long as the city itself, the **The Hotel Roanoke and Conference Center,** 110 Shenandoah Ave., 800/222-8733 or 540/985-5900, fax 540/853-8920, www.doubletreehotels.com, has anchored Roanoke's downtown for more than a century. It was built in a wheat field in 1882, and, thanks to its popularity with vacationers, it's outlasted the railroads that financed it. In the 1930s, major alterations changed the exterior style from Queen Anne to the current classic Tudor. Anyone who's anyone passing through the area has stayed here, from presidents to celebrities, Amelia Earhart to Elvis. The hotel was donated to Virginia Tech University in 1989 and underwent a complete facelift.

Even if you're staying elsewhere, a peek inside the lobby is worth the walk across the glassed-in Market Square Walkway over the train tracks. Florentine marble floors set off vaulted ceilings, while Southern idyll paintings on the walls and ceilings make the Palm Court off the lobby perfect for afternoon tea. Guests enjoy a fitness center, pool, the Regency Room's famous peanut soup, and the hotel's trademark fresh-baked cookies on arrival. Room rates are $90–120.

Dating to between the world wars, the **Patrick Henry Hotel,** 617 S. Jefferson St., 800/537-8483 or 540/345-8811, fax 540/345-8169, is listed on the National Register of Historic Places. Renovations in 1991 preserved the wrought iron, brass, wood, and crystal accents in the lobby area. Most of the rooms include kitchenettes, and suites are also available. Rooms are $100, with suites and one- or two-bedroom units with kitchens going for $110–150.

The **Maridor B&B,** 1857 Grandin Road at Shirley, 540/982-1940, www.bbonline.com/va/maridor, was built in 1916 and is located only a few blocks from the Grandin Theater. Rates for their five rooms range from $95–145 (higher price is for a two-room suite with king-sized bed). The **Best Western Inn at Valley View,** tel./fax 540/263-2400, is in the Valley View Mall complex at 5050 Valley View Dr. ($75–100).

$150–250

Two pools, a spa, tennis courts, and a gym fill the Mediterranean-style **Wyndham Roanoke,** 2801 Herschberger Rd. NW, 540/563-9300, fax 540/366-5846, set on 12 landscaped acres off I-581 exit 3W. Suites are $170–240.

Camping

The National Park Service maintains a 104-site campground at milepost 120.4 on the Blue Ridge Parkway.

FOOD

City Center

A virtual United Nations of eateries fills the Market Square food court, packed at lunch with the downtown crowd. Inside, **Chico & Billy's Prestigious Pizza and Pasta Palace** serves gourmet pizza; **Paradiso** offers authentic Cuban cuisine; and the **Three Li'l Pigs Barbecue** maintains that they "will sell no swine before its time." Most are open daily and have entreés around $5–6.

Blink and you just might miss **Eden's Way,** 104 Church Ave. SE at Williamson, 540/344-3336, a tiny nook serving vegetarian carry-out with spiritual reverence. Everything here is animal-free and excellent, especially the bread. Open for lunch Mon.–Fri. The **Angler's Café,** 310 Second St. SW, 540/342-2436, is another good choice for lunch, with lots of soup and sandwich selections for $5–6. They have lots of fish and vegetarian entreés for $10–16, including a few as fancy as mango cilantro orange roughy. Open for lunch Mon.–Fri., dinner Thurs.–Sat.

SOUTHWESTERN VIRGINIA WINERIES

Abingdon Vineyard & Winery
540/623-1255
Near Abingdon; I-81 exit 19, US 58 east toward Damascus to Rt. 722, go 2.5 miles (road changes to Rt. 710/Alvarado Rd.)

Amrhein's Wine Cellar
540/387-3816
Blue Ridge Parkway milepost 136, south on Rt. 221 for 0.7 miles, right onto Rt. 644 for 1.2 miles, right onto Patterson Rd. for 0.5 miles

Bounday Rock Farm & Vineyard
540/789-7098
Near Floyd; I-81 exit 114 to Floyd, south on Rt. 221 for nine miles, right onto Rt. 750 (Alum Ridge Rd.) for one mile, right onto Rt. 769 (Ferney Creek Rd.) for one mile, left onto Riggins Rd. for 0.5 mile

Chateau Morrisette
540/593-2865
Near Meadows of Dan; From Blue Ridge Parkway milepost 171.5, west on Rt. 726 (Black Ridge Rd.), immediate left onto Rt. 777 (Winery Rd.), 0.25 miles
Gourmet market and deli; Fruity white Our Dog Blue, in blue bottle, is one of the state's best sellers.

Dye's Vineyard
540/873-4659
Near Honaker; US 19, west on Rt. 80, left onto Rt. 620, 0.5 mile

Tomahawk Mill Winery
804/432-1063
Near Chatham; From Rt. 29, west on Rt. 57 for 4.5 miles, right onto Rt. 799 (Climax Rd.) for 3.4 miles, left onto Rt. 649 (Anderson Mill Rd.) for 3 miles
Wines served in 113-year-old water-powered grist mill.

Valhalla Vineyard
540/725-WINE (725-9463)
Near Roanoke; I-81 exit to I-581, take Electric Rd. exit for two miles, left on Rt. 221 (Brambleton Ave.) for one mile, right onto Roselawn Rd. for two miles, left onto Mt. Chestnut Rd. for one mile
Winner of 2000 Governor's Cup and 31 international medals, wines aged in barrel cave beneath vineyards.

Villa Appalaccia
540/593-3100
Near Floyd; on Blue Ridge Parkway between milepost 170 and 171.

The **Texas Tavern,** 114 Church Ave. W., 540/342-4825, is a no-frills, after-midnight kind of place with great chili and actual bottled sodas (open 24 hours a day, seven days a week), while **Billy's Ritz,** 102 Salem Ave. SE, 540/342-3927, is more upscale, serving steaks and pastas near the oak bar and in an open courtyard (open daily for dinner).

Ask around for Roanokers' favorite place for dinner, and chances are good that **Carlos Brazilian & International Cuisine,** 312 Market St. at Church, 540/345-7661, will come up more than once. Casually classy styling, good prices, and outstanding food make this one so popular you'll need reservations on weekends. Try the authentic Brazilian *feijoada*—a full meal that's the national dish—on

Saturday. Entrées run $6–8 at lunch and $8–20 for dinner, open Mon.–Sat.

Arzu, 213 Williamson Rd. SE, 540/982-7160, is another upmarket option specializing in French and Turkish cuisine at the hand of chef Ihsan Demirci. Paintings of Turkey fill niches around the quiet dining room, and upstairs there's a smoking room with fireplace. Lunch plates like Chicken saltimboca and hot sandwiches run $5–7 (served Mon.–Fri.). For dinner (Mon.–Sat.), appetizers like escargot and oysters Rockefeller start at $5, and pasta, beef, chicken, and seafood dishes range $10–17.

One of the city's best nightspots has nothing to do with dancing or alcohol, though intoxicating drinks are still a cornerstone. **Mill Mountain Coffee & Tea,** 112 Campbell Ave. SE,

SOUTHWEST VIRGINIA

540/342-9404, is one of two in Roanoke and four in southwest. Beans roasted here are served in a good, strong brew, alongside dozens of flavors of teas, Italian sodas, and desserts to die for. Open to midnight (1 A.M. Fri.–Sat.). For a quick bite, try one of Roanoke's favorite bagels at **Five-Boro Bagels,** 206A Market Square, 540/342-1494, or 2016 Electric Rd., 540/989-5569.

Elsewhere in Town
The **New Yorker,** 2802 Williamson Rd., 540/366-0935, is a true Manhattan-style deli with great submarine sandwiches and cheese-cake. It's open for lunch and dinner Tues.–Sun. and is often packed around midday. **Montano's International Gourmet,** 3733 Franklin Rd. SW, 540/344-8960, is another popular lunch spot. It's in the Townside Festival Mall, open 10 A.M.–midnight, and has received numerous local awards: best bar, best beer selection, best wine selection, and best healthy business lunch.

    Stephen's, 2926 Franklin Rd. SW, 540/344-7203, serves Roanoke's best—and only—authentic Creole cuisine under high ceilings and wrought iron. Fresh seafood is flown in for the gumbo and étouffée, and softshell crabs and crawfish are available in season. Dinner ($13–22) is served Mon.–Sat.

    With an entryway lined with awards, **The Library,** 3117 Franklin Rd. SW in the Picadilly Square Shopping Center, 540/985-0811, is easily one of the state's better restaurants. Top-notch service, an extensive wine list, and the candlelit atmosphere of book-lined walls set off exceptional French cuisine. Dinner ($15–30) is served Tues.–Sat., and reservations are recommended.

    Don't forget **The Roanoker,** 2522 Colonial Ave. at Wonju, 540/344-7746, a local favorite since 1941. City residents pack several dining rooms for down-home staples like the biscuits-and-gravy breakfast, homemade breads, and fresh vegetables. Open daily for all meals from 7 A.M. (8 A.M. on Sunday).

Out of Town
Eating at **The Homeplace,** Rt. 311 near Salem, 540/384-7252, is like nothing more than dinner at Grandma's. This old country home features a set menu of classic country items—fried chicken, roast beef, or country ham, mashed potatoes, beans, fresh flaky biscuits, cole slaw, gravy, and cobbler for dessert—and they'll keep bringing it out until you beg them to stop. Meals (around $12) are served Thurs.–Sat. 4–8 P.M., Sun. 11 A.M.–6 P.M. To get there, take I-81 exit 140 or 141 to Rt. 311 north, and it's seven miles farther on your left.

SHOPPING

Aside from the farmer's market in Market Square, a wide range of shops provides enough spending opportunities for days. Local artists have studios and shops in the **Studios on the Square Gallery,** 206 Market Square, 540/345-4076. Gourmet country foods are the specialty of **Sumdat Farm Market,** 209A Market St. SE, 540/982-2164, and **Wertz's Country Store & Wine Cellar Inc.,** 215 Market St. SE, 540/342-5133. (The latter also has a restaurant.) **Lee & Edwards Wine Merchants,** 309 S. Jefferson St., 540/343-3900, carries the largest collection of local and international wines in this part of the state, along with beer and homebrewing supplies.

    For antiques, swing by **12 E. Campbell Antiques & Collectibles,** 12 E. Campbell Ave., 540/343-7946; the **Gilded Lily,** 3212 S. Brambleton Ave. SW, 540/725-8665; or **Sweet Repeats Antiques,** 5301 Williamson Rd. NW, 540/342-8123. For the largest selection, try the **Roanoke Antique Mall,** 2302 Orange Ave. NE (Rt. 460) at Gus Nicks Blvd., 540/344-0264, with more than 100 dealers open daily until 6 P.M. And if *that's* not enough, the **Roanoke Antique and Collectable Expo,** 804/431-9500, rolls into the Salem Civic Center one weekend a month, bringing close to 1,000 dealers, food, and outlet stores.

ENTERTAINMENT

Three of Roanoke's major cultural institutions have offices in the Jefferson Center at 541 Luck Street: the **Roanoke Symphony Orchestra,** 540/343-9127; the **Roanoke Ballet Theatre,** 540/345-6099; and **Opera Roanoke,** 540/982-2742. Call each for the latest performance listings. On a more visceral level, the **Roanoke Civic Center** hosts rock concerts and home games with the Roanoke Express pro hockey team (www.Roanokeexpress.com). Phone 540/981-1201 for the box office or 540/343-4500 for hockey tickets.

The **Renaissance Theatre Festival and Virginia Western Theatre,** 540/857-7327, www.vw.cc.va.us/theatre, presents classics and contemporary works during the Summer Renaissance Festival and Spring New Play Festival on the campus of the Virginia Western Community College. **Showtimers,** 540/774-2660 or 540/774-6954, is the oldest continuously performing community theater in Virginia. They put on drama, comedy, music, and dance performances for $12 pp ($10 on Wed.) at a theater on Rt. 419; call for directions.

Two of the city's shopping malls—Valley View and Tanglewood—have multiplex theaters nearby. For a more personal experience, though, head out to the **Grandin Movie Theater,** 1310 Grandin Rd., 540/345-6177. The Grandin is an ornate theater in a style that's all but disappeared (it took a benefit by Bill Murray to keep this one alive). They run current and older films and still occasionally offer ticket specials.

A "Cigar & Billiards" sign outside the **Corned** **Beef & Co. Bar and Grill,** 107 S. Jefferson St., 540/342-3354, advertises the restaurant's major draw after hours, when live and DJ music drifts through the haze in the scotch and cigar lounge toward the pool tables. Established in 1936, **The Coffee Pot,** 2902 Brambleton Ave., 540/774-8256, is a Virginia historic landmark and the oldest roadhouse in the state, hosting acoustic, R&B, and rock on occasion. Look for the big coffee pot on top of the building.

Lowell's, 2328 Melrose NW, 540/344-4884, keeps things cooler with R&B and light jazz, while **The Park,** 615 Salem Ave. SW, 540/342-0946, is a gay and straight dance club open until the wee hours of the morning Fri.–Sun. The **Blueberry Hill Restaurant and Lounge,** 5301 Williamson Rd. NW, 540/362-3622, and **Saltori's,** 202 Market Square SE at Campbell Ave., 540/343-6644, are also popular nightspots.

EVENTS

Roanoke isn't called the Festival City of Virginia for nothing. Call the city's visitors center for details of the following events. For two weeks beginning Memorial Day, the **Festival in the Park**

the beautiful Blue Ridge Parkway

ushers in summer with a concert, a parade, and a black-tie gala. Also in May, the **Virginia State Championship Chili Cook-Off** has participants begging for water at the farmer's market the first Saturday of the month. This often coincides with the **Strawberry Festival.**

Preserves and cobbler are only two of the ways to enjoy the **Virginia Mountain Peach Festival,** held downtown the first weekend in August. The small town of Vinton, just east of Roanoke via US 24 or US 460, is the home of the **Vinton Old-Time Bluegrass Festival and Competition,** held mid-month in the Vinton Farmer's Market and accompanied by crafts and a carnival.

The first Saturday of September, the **Roanoke Symphony Polo Cup** raises funds for the Roanoke Youth Symphony. The national-level tournament is held in Green Hill Park in West Salem and costs $10 pp. Mid-month, Elmwood Park, at the corner of Jefferson St. and Elm Ave., hosts the **Taste of the Blue Ridge Blues & Jazz Festival,** and on the last weekend of the month hosts the **Henry Street African-American Heritage Festival.**

TRANSPORTATION
Getting Around
The **Valley Metro** bus network, 1108 Campbell Ave. SE, 540/982-2222, serves the entire city from its main transfer point at Campbell Court, 17 W. Campbell Ave. Buses run Mon.–Sat., and route maps are available at the visitors center. For cab service, try the **Yellow Cab Co. of Roanoke,** 540/345-7711, or **Liberty Cab,** 540/344-1776.

Getting There and Away
The **Roanoke Regional Airport,** 5202 Aviation Dr. NW, 540/362-1999, www.roanokeairport.com, is the only large airport in southwest Virginia. It's served by Delta Connection, United Express, USAirways, USAirways Express, and Northwest Airlink. Several car rental agencies have offices there: Avis, 540/366-2436; Dollar, 540/563-8055; Hertz, 540/366-3421; and National, 540/563-5050. **Roanoke Airport Limo,**

540/345-7710, and **Prestige,** 540/342-8049, both offer limousine service between the airport and the rest of the city.

There's a **Greyhound** station at 26 W. Salem Ave. SW, 800/231-2222, 540/343-5436. **Amtrak's** nearest station is in Clifton Forge, 45 miles northwest. For information on a Thruway bus there, call 800/872-7245.

INFORMATION
The Roanoke Valley **Visitor Information Center,** 114 Market St., 800/635-5535, 540/345-8622, www.VisitRoanokeVA.com, is on the east side of Market Square. It's open daily 9 A.M.–5 P.M. For more information on the city, try the commercial website, www.roanoke.com.

NEAR ROANOKE
Dixie Caverns
This hole in the earth was discovered by a pair of Civil War soldiers whose dog disappeared while chasing an animal across the hillside. They found the hole the dog had disappeared into (still visible today) and managed, with lanterns and rope, to rescue their canine companion. The caverns the dog—named Dixie—unwittingly discovered creep upward into the mountain instead of down, so for most of the tour you're actually *above* the parking lot where you started.

Fifty-minute tours leave whenever a large enough group materializes. Hundreds of couples have been married beneath the 57-ton Wedding Bell formation (a statement on the beauty of the union or the weight of the commitment—you be the judge). Notice where early tours broke off small stalactites for souvenirs—a practice that would get you thrown in jail today.

The caverns are off I-81 exit 132 just west of Salem, 540/380-2085. Open daily 9:30 A.M.–6 P.M. (to 5 P.M. Oct.–May); $7.50 adults, $4.50 children 5–12. Tent and RV campsites are available.

Dragon's Tooth
A jagged prow of rock juts from the peaks of the Jefferson National Forest, offering great views

© JULIAN SMITH

warming up for the Flatfoot Jamboree at Cockram's General Store

from a moderately strenuous 2.6-mile climb just off the Appalachian Trail. Take Rt. 311 north eight miles from I-81, exit 141, and look for the parking area on the left just past the Catawba Grocery. For more information on this and other hikes in the area, contact the Blacksburg/Wythe Ranger District of the National Forest, 540/228-5551, www.southernregion.fs.fed.us/gwj.

Ferrum

This tiny town erupts every fall with the **Blue Ridge Folklife Festival,** the largest showcase of rural tradition in the state. Animals are the stars, from the State Championship Mule Jumping Contest to coon dog competitions and border collie herding demonstrations. Visitors enjoy all the deep-fried, golden-brown, down-home cooking they can stuff down—barbecue, apple pie, pork rinds, spare ribs, and fried chitterling sandwiches, for starters—while listening to gospel, country, and blues music. Storytellers and a petting zoo will keep the kids busy as parents peruse the quilts and crafts displays.

The festival is held the fourth Saturday in Oc-

tober 10 A.M.–5 P.M.; $6 adults, $4 children. For more information and directions, call the Blue Ridge Institute and Museum of Ferrum College, 540/365-4416, www.blueridgeinstitute.org.

Floyd

One of the more interesting counties in the state, Floyd, south of Roanoke, shelters a small pocket of the 1960s that's apparent in subtle but distinct signs. Earthships (houses made of recycled materials and earth), gasohol, and tie-dyed T-shirts in crafts stores all reflect a countercultural legacy that combines and contrasts intriguingly with the surrounding rural lifestyle. There's only one stoplight in the town of Floyd itself, which makes it easy to find **Cockram's General Store,** 540/745-4563, www.floydcountrystore.com, famous for its weekly Flatfoot Jamboree. Every Friday at 7 P.M., the display cases are pushed aside and the floor given over to *real* country music and shuffling feet. The store is the fourth building on the right to the west of the stoplight, and the show is free.

Before a show, you can grab a pizza across Locust Street at **Mama Lazadro's,** 540/745-4242,

SOUTHWEST VIRGINIA

serving up pizza ($3.50–8) and subs ($5) daily 11 A.M.–8 or 10 P.M. One block away, **The Harvest Moon, Inc.,** 540/745-4366, may be the best-smelling store in the state, full of spices, candles, herbs, produce, and greeting cards. Upstairs wait a coffee and wine shop and a quiet sitting room (open Mon.–Sat. 9:30 A.M.–6 P.M., Sun. noon–6 P.M.). Next door is the **New Mountain Mercantile,** 540/745-4278, with local crafts, an art gallery, and New Age body-and-mind products. The **Jacksonville Center,** 540/745-2784, is an old farm complex that has been transformed into a center for "art, mountain music, theater, dance, crafts, and rural heritage." It's one-half mile south of town on Rt. 8.

The **Floyd County Chamber of Commerce,** 107 E. Main St., 540/745-4407, email: chamber@swva.net, www.community.floyd.va.us, is happy to supply more information on their area, or log on to www.floydvirginia.com.

Southern Blue Ridge Parkway

The **Roanoke Mountain Campground,** 540/982-9242, is off Mill Mountain Road between Roanoke's Mill Mountain Star and the Blue Ridge Parkway. At mile 169, the **Rocky Knob Recreation Area** has a ranger station 540/745-9661, open May–Oct. daily 9 A.M.–5 P.M., and a campground, 540/745-9664, with 109 sites for $12. Housekeeping cabins with fully furnished kitchens and linens are also available; call 540/593-3903 for information, and phone the ranger station for details on backcountry camping nearby.

A National Recreational Trail winds 11 strenuous miles down into Rock Castle Gorge, 1,500 feet deep and studded with outcroppings of quartz. The Black Ridge Trail offers a more moderate hike of 3.1 miles from the visitors center to Black Ridge and Grassy Knoll. A one-mile loop trail also leaves from the parking lot.

Seven miles farther south is **Mabry Mill,** centered on a gristmill operated commercially from 1910–1935. Fresh-ground cornmeal is sold near a restored sawmill and blacksmith shop. There's also a campground, coffee shop, and gift shop (open late Apr.–Oct.)

Cool nights and loamy soil give the **Meadows of Dan** the distinction of raising the sweetest cabbage in the world. The fourth Saturday of every August, more than 3,000 people arrive for the **Cabbage Festival,** at Poor Farmers Farm, 540/952-2560, with country music, games for the kids, and, of course, plenty of cabbage.

Keep going almost to the North Carolina state line to reach the **Blue Ridge Hostel,** mile post 214.5, 540/236-4962. It's a little more than one mile north of the intersection with Rt. 89 and has rooms for $13–14. (For more information on the Parkway, including the northern section, see "Blue Ridge Parkway" in the Shenandoah chapter).

Blacksburg and Vicinity

A quiet residential town on the surface, Blacksburg harbors the secret heart of one of the fastest-growing, most progressive communities in Virginia. Its scenic setting, on a plateau right at the edge of farm country, seduces all ages—Blacksburg is rated one of the best places in the country to retire, while the 25,500 students of Virginia Tech University make up more than 60 percent of the town's population.

This influx of brainpower makes Blacksburg a bit difficult to classify. The town celebrated its bicentennial in 1998—one year after several tattoo parlors downtown hosted the two-day Piercefest VIII. The municipal bus system has won national awards, even as the town lends itself so well to strolling. Over everything spreads the wings of Virginia Tech, southwest Virginia's major learning center. The entire town was one of the first to be wired to the Internet, and Hokie basketball and football are NCAA Division One mainstays.

HISTORY

This gorgeous slice of Appalachia was originally the farming settlement of Draper's Meadow, a mixed community of European settlers and

THE ELECTRONIC VILLAGE

One of the most remarkable things about Blacksburg isn't visible to the naked eye. Some might say it doesn't even exist. But plenty of others, including most of the town's residents, point out that the Blacksburg Electronic Village (www.bev.net), an Internet counterpart to the living, breathing town, is fun *and* useful, making it one of the most famous and successful small-town networks in the world.

The idea began, of course, at Virginia Tech in 1991. With a stated goal to "foster a virtual community to complement and enhance the physical community," the cooperative venture between the city, the university, and Bell Atlantic got off the ground only a few years later. Everybody in town was given free access to the Internet, email, and a host of other Web tools to play with. Two-thirds of the town hopped aboard immediately, either through public-access library terminals or private computers in dorms, offices, or homes (special high-speed phone lines were offered by Bell Atlantic as part of the deal).

Soon the snowball began to roll: restaurants put their menus and coupons online, bands proffered sound clips, and local galleries uploaded images in their collections. The entire range of daily life began to reflect itself in the ether, from businesses advertising sales to people posting obituaries and birth announcements. Blacksburg's "town within a town" has attracted worldwide attention as a model of a successful Internet community and has drawn personal visits from government officials coming from as far away as Japan.

Not all the attention has been positive, though. Critics have voiced worries that the town's shadow twin will actually erode person-to-person connections in the real village. They point out that you don't bump into your neighbors shopping for groceries online and you can't make eye contact in a virtual chat room. Also, critics fear that the silicon doppelgänger may end up driving a wedge between residents who have computers and those who don't.

But an overwhelming percentage of users (185 of 219 in one *USA Today* poll) say that the network enhances connections that already exist outside the net. Public polling for town projects is now a snap. Especially in education, the benefits are hard to deny: schoolkids can correspond with other students overseas, and parents can keep in touch with teachers and track classroom activities.

The key point seems to be Blacksburg's small size. It was already a tightly knit community, so the electronic village brings it closer. Paul Saffo, director of the Institute for the Future in Menlo Park, California, said of the community, "They are very lucky nerds to live there."

---

the first permanent English-speaking colony west of the Alleghenies. Much of the land was granted in 1748 to Col. James Patton's Woods River Company.

A Shawnee attack in July 1775 left all but four settlers dead, wounded, or captured; Patton himself was shot after cutting down two attackers with his sword. One captive managed to escape and make an incredible trek back to the settlements. Another, Mrs. John Draper, was adopted by the chief's family and remained a prisoner until she was ransomed in 1781.

Colonel William Preston arrived in 1772 and built Smithfield Plantation, which still stands on the edge of the Virginia Tech campus. Blacksburg was founded in 1798 on 38 acres donated by William Black and set up as a 16-block grid bounded by today's Draper Road and Wharton, Jackston, and Clay streets.

Dr. Henry Black petitioned the Virginia General Assembly in 1872 to establish a land-grant university in the area. It opened with a single building and 43 students; 125 years later, it thrives as southwest Virginia's largest university and employer.

VIRGINIA TECH

The original Virginia Agriculture and Mechanical College has become Virginia Polytechnic Institute and State University, known simply as Virginia Tech, or more often just "Tech." It's one of the state's powerhouse universities, ranking among the nation's best in research and

SOUTHWEST VIRGINIA

scholarship. A yearly research budget of $100 million makes it easy to understand why there are more computers on campus than phones. Almost 24,000 undergraduate and graduate students study within eight colleges, including Agriculture, Veterinary Medicine, and Forestry.

Stately limestone neo-Gothic architecture dots the 3,000-acre campus in the heart of Blacksburg. Burruss Hall presides over the huge grassy drill field, and the tree-lined duck pond, west of the central campus, provides a peaceful spot to escape the pressures of academics.

Tech's **Museum of Geological Sciences,** 2062 Derring Hall, contains the largest collection of Virginia minerals in the state, alongside full-scale dinosaurs, gemstones, and other fossils. Open Mon.–Fri. 9 A.M.–4 P.M.; free. The university also maintains a **Museum of Natural History,** 428 N. Main St., with a permanent collection of North American mammals and a hands-on Discovery Corner for kids. Open Wed.–Sat. 11 A.M.–5 P.M.; free. For information on either museum, call 540/231-3001.

Smithfield Plantation

Follow signs down Duck Pond Drive to reach this classic plantation home built by Scottish-Irish immigrants William and Susanna Smith Preston in the 1770s. Over the years, two Virginia governors, James Patton Preston (1816–1819) and John Bucanan Floyd (1849–1852), have been born here. Today, the Tidewater-style mansion is a living museum, with costumed interpreters leading tours of the house and the garden, which is planted with culinary and medicinal herbs.

One-hour tours run Apr.–Dec., Thurs.–Sun. 1–5 P.M.; $5 adults, $2 children and students. **Holidays at Smithfield,** the first weekend in December, include musical entertainment and children's activities. Call 540/231-3947 for more information, or stop by their Website at www.mfrl.org/compages/smithfield.

ACCOMMODATIONS

Under $50

The **Red Carpet Inn,** 1615 S. Main St., 540/552-4011, is the least expensive in town at $46.

$50–100

Next to the Tech campus, the **Four Points Sheraton,** 900 Prices Fork Rd., 540/552-7001, fax 540/552-0827, has a tennis court, two pools, and a playground. Rooms are $100. The **Best Western Red Lion Inn,** 900 Plantation Rd., 540/552-7770, fax 540/552-6346, offers a pool and tennis courts and rooms for $85.

$100–150

Blacksburg proper has surprisingly few guesthouses, considering how many students and parents come and go over the course of the year. Several buildings make up the **Clay Corner Inn,** 401 Clay St. SW, 540/953-2604, fax 540/951-0541, www.claycorner.com, from the main home (c. 1929) to the Huckleberry House at 404 Clay Street, with a fireplace in every room and an outdoor Jacuzzi. Twelve rooms provide enough space for the entire Hokie football team, which has stayed here in the past. There's a heated swimming pool out back and a patio perfect for warm-season breakfasts. Rates ($130) include breakfast.

You can also find a heated pool at the **Comfort Inn,** 3705 South Main St., 540/951-1500, with rooms for $140.

FOOD

Coffee Shops and Snacks

Settle into **The Easy Chair Coffee Shop,** 801 University City Blvd., 540/951-1628, for healthy sandwiches, gourmet java, herbal tea, and delicious desserts daily until midnight. **Mill Mountain Coffee and Tea,** 700 N. Main St., 540/552-7442, is a sibling to the downtown Roanoke standby. Local landmark status is claimed by **Carol Lee Doughnuts,** 1414 N. Main St., 540/552-6706. Founded more than 25 years ago, Carol Lee still serves glazed and iced doughnuts and an economical breakfast. Cakes, pies, and bagels are the manna of **Our Daily Bread,** 1317 S. Main St., 540/953-2815. They've expanded to offer daily sandwiches and salads, and even full entrées on Thursdays.

Student Favorites

Sidle up to the counter of **Souvlaki,** 201 College Ave., 540/951-0555, for one of their surprisingly inexpensive foot-and-a-half sandwiches or gyros (don't unwrap until the last bite). Remember, as the sign says, you can't complain about the service: there isn't any.

Techies say **The Cellar,** 302 North Main St., 540/953-0651, has one of the best price-to-volume ratios in town, but they are quick to add that the food is good as well as plentiful. Italian and Greek entrées are $5–7, with normal and specialty pizzas for $6–13. The Cellar is also one of the most popular nightspots in Blacksburg. Speaking of cellars and the goodies therein, the **Vintage Cellar,** 1313 S. Main St., 540/953-CORK (953-2675), stocks more than 750 labels of wine and a few hundred kinds of beer, along with specialty foods and homebrewing supplies.

A Little Fancier

Vincent's Ristorante, 1200 S. Main St., 540/552-9000, offers fine Italian fare for dinner Tues.–Sun. (entrées $10–15) and lunch ($5) on Friday. Other midpriced options include **Zeppoli's Italian Restaurant,** 810 University City Boulevard, 540/953-2000, serving excellent fresh pastas in the University Mall, and **Boudreaux's Restaurant,** 205 M. Main St., 540/961-2330, with Cajun food, lots of seafood, and a Sunday brunch.

ENTERTAINMENT AND RECREATION

Nightlife

For live music, **Top of the Stairs,** 217 W. College St., 540/953-2837, books mostly alternative bands, and **Baylee's** 117 S. Main St., 540/961-7611, hosts live music on weekends. **The Cellar** Restaurant (see above) offers a little cooler atmosphere, with jazz and a great bar open until 2 A.M. The **Lyric Theater,** 135 College Ave., 540/951-0604, is an old-style movie house showing films with a university-town inclination toward the unusual and innovative.

At the College

Virginia Tech football is almost a way of life for diehard fans, who nearly keeled over with joy in 1995 when the hometown Hokies capped their

THE GREAT FRONTIER ESCAPE

Mary Draper Ingles, wife of frontiersman William Ingles, was captured in the Shawnee raid of July 1775 and taken to a spot near Big Bone Kick, Kentucky. There, she managed to escape her captors and struck out for home.

Bearing news of a planned second Shawnee attack, this determined woman followed rivers east and managed to cross 850 miles of some of the wildest country east of the Mississippi before showing up in Adam Harman's cornfield in Giles Country, Virginia, in late November.

Her story was dramatized in a play by Earl Hobson Smith, called the official Historical Outdoor Drama of the Commonwealth (Big Stone Gap already had claim to the Official *State* Outdoor Drama). It's been performed since 1971 at the Ingles Homestead Amphitheater in Radford, off US 11 about 20 miles southwest of Blacksburg, 540/639-0679, www.bev.net/community/NRAC/perform/longwayhome. The play runs from mid-June to the end of August, Thurs.–Sun. at 8:30 P.M. Ticket prices ($10 adults, $5 children 12 and under) include a tour of Mary's cabin and a short walk down a section of the Wilderness Road to Ingles Ferry Landing.

best season ever with a victory over Texas in the Sugar Bowl. (The closest they'd come as of 2001 was a 46–29 loss to Florida State in the 2000 Sugar Bowl.) Games against the archrival Cavaliers of the University of Virginia fill parking lots at either school with tailgate parties and boisterous alumni. For tickets, call 800/VATECH4 (828-3244) or 540/231-6731.

Art happenings on campus range from nationally known musicians and speakers to Virginia Tech's Theater Arts Programs and Audubon Quartet. Call the main campus number, 540/231-6000, for a current schedule.

Outdoors

The surrounding acres of the Jefferson National Forest provide Blacksburg residents»and visitors—with plenty of opportunities to hike, bike, ride horses, and camp. Head west from town on Rt. 460 to reach a few of the more popular trails. Turn left across from the turnoff to Rt. 621 for the entrance to **Pandapas Pond,** an eight-acre pond surrounded by pines and hardwoods with a loop trail around it. (Fishing and canoeing are allowed, but bikes and horses are prohibited within 300 feet.) Keep going up Rt. 460 to Pembroke, then turn right onto Rt. 623 and go four more miles to the parking lot for the **Cascades Recreations Area,** where a National Recreation Trail climbs two miles up a gorge to a 66-foot waterfall.

Both **Blue Ridge Outdoors,** 125 N. Main St., 540/552-9012, and **Back County Ski & Sports,** 3710 South Main St., 540/552-6400, sell outdoor gear and can provide you with information on outfitters in the area.

TRANSPORTATION

Home Ride of Virginia, 620 N. Main St., 800/553-6644, www.bogens.com/homeride, offers weekend bus services for students and anyone else between Blacksburg and Vienna ($36 one-way), stopping at Harrisonburg ($25) and Charlottesville ($25), and between Blacksburg and Hampton ($39), stopping at Richmond ($35). Buses usually leave Blacksburg on Friday and returning on Sunday Septenber–April.

INFORMATION

The Blacksburg Chamber of Commerce operates a **visitors center,** 1995 S. Main St., 800/288-4061 or 540/552-4061, www.blacksburg-chamber.com, open daily 9 A.M.–5 P.M. It's located about one-half mile south of downtown.

MOUNTAIN LAKE AND VICINITY

In the shadow of 4,200-foot Bald Knob, Mountain Lake is Virginia's highest—and one of only two natural lakes in the state (the other lies in the Great Dismal Swamp). No one is quite sure how it formed here, at 4,000 feet, high enough to record the lowest temperatures in the state (it hit –30°F in 1985). One theory holds that a small rockslide blocked a natural outlet sometime during the late 19th century, back when the spot was called Salt Pond by farmers looking for salt for their cattle.

Mountain Lake Resort

It was also around the late 19th century that the first hotel was built on the shore of the chilly lake, providing lodging for people making the east-west trip through the mountains. In the hands of the Porterfield family near the turn of the 20th century, the hotel became known as a luxury stop. Guests were allowed to build their own cottages until the main stone lodge was built in 1936. The movie *Dirty Dancing* was filmed here in 1986, two years after major renovations, and brought the hotel's classic mountain character to the world's attention.

Guests have no excuse to cry boredom. The daily roster overflows with things to do, starting with hikes on a network of trails of different difficulty levels around the lake and into the surrounding hills. You can wander to the Mountain Lake Biological Station, run by the University of Virginia, or as far as Minnie Ball Hill, named for small-caliber Civil War cannonballs still found here more than 150 years after a Union general abandoned his supply wagons because his horses couldn't pull them up the steep grade. Some trails are open to mountain bikes, which are available for rent—as is equipment for volleyball, horseshoes, and croquet.

During warmer months, the small sandy beach is packed with swimmers, while the farther reaches of the lake are open to boats and canoes. Relaxation comes in the form of massages at the health spa, a day camp for children, or simply enjoying the view from a deck chair while families compete at lawn chess nearby.

While you're browsing the row of shops and galleries, notice Bob Evans' whittled wooden Nobbits ("cousins to Hobbits"). He bases them on the German legend of Wurtzelgrabbers (root diggers), said to run around carving their own likenesses out of roots and leaving them on the doorsteps of friends to bring good luck. At the height of fall comes Oktoberfest, with Teutonic food, beer, and live polka music.

Rooms start at $150, with suites available for $140–230. Cottages come with one bedroom ($175–235), two ($210–300), three ($320–370), or four ($540–690). For reservations and information, contact the Mountain Lake Hotel at 800/346-3334 or 540/626-7121, fax 540/626-7172, email: mtnlake@swva.net, www.mountainlakehotel.com.

To get there, take US 460 west (actually north) from Blacksburg, turning right onto Rt. 700, a precipitous backroad that winds through seven gorgeous miles of rural Virginia. As you chug uphill, keep in mind that this stretch was included in a recent Tour DuPont bicycle race as a Category One climb—as hard as it gets.

Near Mountain Lake

This corner of the state conceals one of the wilder chunks of the Jefferson National Forest, marked by high, windswept ridges blanketed with hemlock and spruce. Steep ravines within the 10,000-acre **Mountain Lake Wilderness** conceal stands of centuries-old white oak, with mushrooms, bogs, and berry bushes in more moderate valleys. The **Peters Mountain Wilderness** spreads farther north to intersect with the Appalachian Trail, skirting the West Virginia border near the **White Rocks Recreation Area** off Rt. 613. All three wild areas are open only to primitive camping. For more information, contact the Blacksburg/Wythe Ranger District of the Jefferson National Forest in Wytheville, 540/228-5551, www.southernregion.fs.fed.us/gwj.

A few miles west of the Mountain Lake turnoff is the **Cascades Recreation Area,** known for a four-mile loop trail up Little Stony Creek Gorge. Wooden bridges span the creek as the trail climbs through hemlocks and birch trees to a 60-foot waterfall. Trout fishing is good in the creek. To get here, take a right turn (north) off US 460 onto Rt. 623 in Pembroke, following signs four miles to the Recreation Area.

New River Valley

WYTHEVILLE

First of all, it's pronounced "WITH-vul," and has been ever since the town was incorporated in 1839 along the Wilderness Road (part of which serves as modern Main Street). During the Civil War, Wytheville saw plenty of action because troops from both sides passed through on a regular basis. A Union attack in 1863 was beaten back by a local militia, but by the end of the war, most of the town lay in ruins.

Sights

Wytheville's two museums sit next to each other near the intersection of Monroe and Tazewell streets. The **Haller-Gibboney Rock House Museum,** 540/223-3330, was built of limestone in 1823 and served as a hospital during the Civil War—bloodstains are still visible on the floor of one of the second-story bedrooms, along with a bullet hole in a front parlor window frame. Inside are heirlooms from the Haller-Gibboney family, who owned the house for 150 years. Out back, an herb garden showcases plants used for medicine in the 1800s. Open Tues.–Fri. 10 A.M.–4 P.M., Sat. noon–4 p.m from Apr.–Dec.; $3 adults, $1.50 children 6–12. Tours are given Apr.–Oct.

The historical collection in the **Thomas J. Boyd Museum,** 295 Tazewell St., includes the town's first fire truck (1855), Civil War uniforms, and hands-on displays of local history for children. The hours, admission, and telephone number are the same as for the Rock House. Combination tickets for both museums are $5 adults, $2.50 children 6–12.

In Wytheville's historic downtown district, the **Millward Theatre** is the oldest continuously operating theater in Virginia, built in 1928. Having survived both the advent of television and the Cold War (during which it was designated as a bomb shelter and stocked with emergency rations), the Millward remains an example of an increasingly rare breed of venue. Also on Main Street, the 30-foot **Big Pencil** was built in the late '50s to advertise an office supply store.

THE BIRTHPLACE OF MOUNTAIN DEW AND DR. PEPPER

Southwest Virginia claims parenthood of not one, but two famous soft drinks within miles of each other. Mountain Dew was created about midway between Wytheville and Abingdon, in Marion (I-81 exit 45), where its original spokesperson was a hillbilly shouting, "Ya-hoo, Mountain Dew!" Every Fourth of July, a Chili Cookoff and Mountain Dew Day celebrates the soda.

Just up the highway, at exit 60, pharmacist Dr. Charles Pepper was experimenting with caramel-flavored soda water in the Rural Retreat Drug Store (now a flower shop). As the story goes, his young assistant fled for Texas with the formula after falling in love with one of the pharmacist's daughters. He did, however, eventually name the final product in honor of his former employer.

Accommodations

Look for the pink doors near 7th Street to find the **Travel Lite Motel,** 655 E. Main St., 540/228-5574, the most central and least expensive place in town with rooms for $35–45. The **Wytheville Inn,** 355 Nye Rd., 540/228-7300, fax 540/228-4223, and the **Holiday Inn,** 1800 E. Main St., 540/228-5483, fax 540/228-5417, both have rooms from $70–90.

Just east of town is the **Wytheville KOA Kampground,** 540/228-2601. To get there, take exit 77 off I-81/I-77, then head south one-half mile on Rt. 758. Year-round sites are $32–36, and Kamping Kabins are $56–61. The U.S. Forest Service maintains the **Stony Fork Campground,** 540/228-5551, eight miles north on US 52 and 0.3 mile east on Rt. 717. Forty-nine sites cost $12–16.

Food

The **1776 Log House Restaurant,** 520 E. Main St., 540/228-4139, preserves a touch of creaky country charm; open lunch and dinner Mon.–Sat. After your meal ($9–12), wander to the gardens out back, where you'll find crafts shops and Fran's Deli. At exit 73 off I-81 is

Mom's Restaurant & Country Store, 430 Lithia Rd., 540/228-5068. Sugar-baked ham, country-fried steak, and eggs—you get the picture.

The **Peking Restaurant,** 105 Malin Dr., 540/228-5515, sits on top of a hill near the same exit. This ornate place has tasty Chinese plates for $8–10 and combos for about $8, plus the Flaming Volcano Drink consisting of "rums fired with sacred nectars, served aflame for two people" ($2.50).

Shopping

Both **Snooper's Antique & Craft Mall,** 2114 E. Lee Hwy., 540/637-6441, and the **Old Fort Emporium** 2028 E. Lee Hwy., 540/228-4438, are located on the service road between exits 77 and 80 off I-81. They're both open daily year-round and stock industrial quantities of antiques, collectibles, and snacks.

Information

The **Wytheville Area Chamber of Commerce,** 877/347-8307 or 540/223-3355, email: info@wytheville.com, www.visit.wytheville.com, runs an information center in the city municipal offices, 150 E. Monroe St. at 1st St., open Mon.–Fri. 8 A.M.–5 P.M. For details on the many hikes in the Jefferson National Forest north of town, contact the Blacksburg/Wythe Ranger Districts of the Jefferson National Forest.

Near Wytheville

North of town, the Appalachians crest with surprising speed, forcing I-77 to dive into a tunnel through Big Walker Mountain within a few miles. A small loop beginning at exit 47 has been deemed a Scenic Byway: take Rt. 717 west to the junction with US 52, which you'll climb to the **Big Walker Lookout,** 540/228-4401, email: scenicbeauty@naxs.com. The 100-foot tower sits at 3,405 feet, commanding an Olympian view of the surrounding hills. Admission tickets ($3.50 adults, $2.50 children) are sold in the combination gift shop and deli at the base. Open Apr.–Oct., Tues.–Sun. 10 A.M.–6 P.M., (until 5 P.M. Labor Day–Memorial Day). Afterward, dispel your vertigo by following US 52 north and east back to I-77, crossing Walker Creek.

Walker Mountain Baptist Church

© JULIAN SMITH

GALAX

Early Scottish-Irish settlers would have been proud to know that their fiddles and bagpipes still echo in Galax (GAY-laks), the current World Capital of Old Time Mountain Music. The quiet village is brought to raucous life during the annual **Old Time Fiddler's Convention and Fiddlefest,** the oldest and largest mountain music convention in the country. It was begun in 1935 with the stated purpose of "Keeping alive the memories and sentiments of days gone by and mak[ing] it possible for people of today to hear and enjoy the tunes of yesterday," and that still holds true. The clack of clogs and the slap of flatfoot combine with the usual arts, crafts, and food booths the second week of August. Tickets are $5–10 pp ($30 for all six nights), and campsites are available for $60.

For more information, contact the Old Fiddler's Convention, 540/236-8541, www.oldfiddlersconvention.com, or the **Galax-Carroll-Grayson Chamber of Commerce,** 405 N. Main St., 540/236-2184. If you can't wait for the festival, every Friday evening from 8–10 P.M., WBRF (98.1 FM) and the Galax Downtown

Association sponsor **Blue Ridge Backroads,** one of the few remaining live bluegrass radio shows in the country.

Sights

Turn off the US 58/221 strip (E. Stuart Dr.) onto Main Street to the center of town to reach the massive brick **Grayson County Courthouse,** built near the turn of the 20th century when the town first sprang to life as Bonaparte. From Main Street, head west on Oldtown Street, then south on Old Stuart Drive to reach the **Jeff Matthews Museum,** 606 W. Stuart Dr., 540/236-7874. Barely across the threshold, you're accosted by the biggest stuffed bear you've ever seen, an 8.5-foot Kodiak grizzly from Alaska, presiding over enough animal carcasses to stock a taxidermy shop. Set aside a few hours to browse through everything an early-1900s family (or three) would need to survive, including a fully stocked country store, a 1902 Sears & Roebuck catalog, an 1899 map of Virginia, more than 1,000 knives, and an 800-pound whetstone. Don't miss the antique hair curler, straight out of a Frankenstein movie. Two reconstructed cabins out back, furnished with period artifacts, date to the mid-19th century. Open Wed.–Fri, 1–5 P.M., Sat. 11 A.M.–4 P.M., Sun. 1–4 P.M.; free, but donations are welcome.

This end of the **New River Trail State Park** can be entered from the intersection of US 58/221 and Thomas George Vaughan Jr. Road. The **Galax Farmer's Market** fills N. Main Street with produce, baked goods, crafts, and flowers every Friday and Saturday morning from June–October.

Accommodations and Food

Pickings are slim. Both the **Knights Inn,** 312 W. Stuart Dr., 540/236-5117, fax 540/236-0652, and the **Super 8,** 303 N. Main St. at Washington St., 540/236-5127, have rooms in the $50–60 range. Cheap camping is possible in the **Crooked Creek Wildlife Management Area,** three miles east of town.

The **County Line Cafe,** 956 E. Stuart Dr., 540/236-3201, is also a deli, open daily at 6 A.M. for breakfast. A reasonably authentic Mexican meal runs $8–12 at **Tloquepaque,** 500 E. Stuart Dr. at Caldwell Ave., 540/236-5060.

NEW RIVER TRAIL STATE PARK

This flagship example of a new kind of park, called a greenway, protects a 40-mile stretch of the misnamed waterway and her banks. For 57 miles from Galax to Pulaski, you'll find people hiking, biking, riding horseback, and skiing down the old railroad bed, with occasional stops to fish or admire the cliffs and forest along the river.

Park headquarters, 540/699-6778, www.dcr .state.va.us/parks/newriver.htm, are at 176 Orphanage Drive in Foster Falls, near **Shot Tower Historical State Park,** 17 miles south of Wytheville by either I-77 (exit 24) or US 52. Here, a 70-foot tower was used in the 19th century for making lead rifle shot. From the top, molten metal was poured down through the tower and a 75-foot shaft beneath into a kettle of water at the bottom. The perfectly round balls were then recovered through a horizontal tunnel from the river's edge. Parking ($2) and restrooms are available at the base of the tower,

and a loop trail accesses the New River Trail. Open daily Apr.–Nov., 8 A.M.–dusk. Tours are given weekends and holidays from Memorial Day–Labor Day.

Campsites ($8) are available at the park's Millrace and Cliffview campgrounds, 20 miles apart. Bicycles, canoes, inner tubes, and horses are available for rent at Millrace. Call 800/933-PARK (933-7275) for campsite reservations. Seven other access points stretch along the river from Galax to Draper on I-81 near Pulaski.

Outfitters

In Wytheville, **New River Adventures,** 1007 N. 4th St., 540/228-8311, www.newriveradventures.com, has a full-service bike shop and backpacking and fishing equipment for sale. Daily rental of bikes ($18), canoes ($30), kayaks ($30), and inner tubes ($10) should about cover it (call for details on renting horses). For shuttle service to or from Galax, Fries, or Ivanhoe, add another $12–17, and overnight canoe and fishing trips can be arranged. They have an outlet near Shot Tower State Park.

Guided fishing trips for smallmouth bass are $165–175 pp (two-person minimum) with **Tangent Outfitters,** 4747 State Park Rd., Dublin, 540/674-5202, www.newrivertrail.com. Canoe rentals start at $30 per day, and guided overnight trips are $45–60 pp. Bike rentals with shuttle service on the New River Trail run $35–70 pp ($75 pp for a guided single-track adventure). **New River Canoe and Campground, Inc.,** on US 21 four miles south of Independence, 540/773-3412, www.canoeingthenew.com, rents canoes ($38 including shuttle service) and offers tent sites ($15) and cabins ($25) along the river.

Near the entrance to Shot Tower, the **Cherry Creek Cyclery & More,** tel./fax 540/699-2385, email: shop@cccyclery.com, www.cccyclery.com, has a bike and book shop, with snacks and fishing supplies for sale. They also offer a detailed guide to the trail online at www.cccyclery.com/genin-bg.htm. In Galax, the **New River Riders Bike Shoppe,** 540/236-5900, offers bicycle rental, sales, and service on Rt. 58 at the entrance to the park.

MT. ROGERS NATIONAL RECREATION AREA

To some people, especially residents of the western United States, the idea of a "wilderness" back east tends to elicit mild scoffs. Places like Mt. Rogers, though, prove that there are still spots this side of the Mississippi as wild and gorgeous as any in the country. Throughout the 120,000 acres of the area, massive stone protrusions called "balds" jut skyward from high, wild alpine meadows ringed by fir and spruce forests.

Within the Recreation Area tower Virginia's two tallest mountains. Mt. Rogers (5,729 feet), near the center of the Lewis Fork Wilderness, is covered with enough trees to block any sweeping vistas from the top. Whitetop Mountain (5,344 feet) is more representative of the gently rounded "southern balds" found in Georgia and North Carolina. Some of the best views in the region come from the top of Wilburn Ridge, one mile from Mt. Rogers. Named for an 18th-century hermit and bear hunter, the ridge offers views stretching up to 100 miles.

Hiking

Bring your boots: more than 70 hiking trails creep through the area, offering 400 miles of easy-to-difficult wandering. Most famous of these paths is the **Virginia Creeper National Recreation Trail,** www.cccyclery.com/vacrep.htm, which winds 34 miles along Whitetop Laurel Creek from Abingdon through Damascus to Whitetop Station at the North Carolina line. What began centuries ago as an Indian footpath had been claimed as a railroad bed by the turn of the 20th century. Timber and passengers were ferried from Abingdon to West Jefferson, North Carolina, up grades so steep the engines would slow to a crawl—hence the name.

The last train whistle split the forest silence in 1977, and since then the Virginia Creeper has become a shining example of the nationwide rails-to-trails initiative. It's relatively flat from Abingdon to Damascus, and therefore packed with hikers and horseback riders on weekends. Mountain bikers love to drive to the top of White's Mountain and glide back toward Abingdon. For more information on the trail, contact the Abingdon visitor center or the Virginia Creeper Trail Club online at www.ehc.edu/vacreeper.

Along with the Creeper, the Appalachian Trail snakes through the entire Recreation Area, 64 miles from end to end. The nine-mile Mt. Rogers trail is difficult and doesn't reward you with a view at the end.

Other Options and Events

Although some of the best riding around is found in Grayson Highlands State Park, Mt. Rogers offers the **Virginia Highlands Horse Trail,** running the entire length of the Recreation Area. Horses are also permitted on the Virginia Creeper and Iron Mountain trails within the boundaries of the Recreation Area (the Virginia Highlands Horse Trail lies just outside). Mountain bikes are welcome on many of the same trails.

Even if you don't get out of your car, you can still enjoy the prettiest drive in this part of the state. The **Mt. Rogers Scenic Byway,** consisting of 34 miles of US 58 from Damascus to Volney, earns the title of highest road in Virginia as it climbs the flank of Whitetop. A 23-mile side branch of Rt. 603 to Volney passes closer to Mt. Rogers. Anglers can find trout in Hale Lake and 14-acre Beartree Lake, which also has a small sandy beach for swimming. Whitetop Laurel Creek is popular with fly-casters.

In late March, the **Whitetop Mountain Maple Festival** brings two weekends of country music, maple-tapping demonstrations, art-and-crafts, and food to the community of Whitetop. The **Ramp Festival,** 540/773-3711, salutes the ramp—a wild relative of the onion—the third weekend in May in the Mt. Rogers Fire Hall on US 58. The **Molasses Festival** in mid-October features food, dancing, and molasses making.

Outfitters

In Damascus, the **Blue Blaze Bike and Shuttle Service,** 226 W. Laurel Ave., 540/475-5095, www.blueblaze.naxs.com, rents mountain bikes ($25 for a full day) and runs a bike shuttle service for $20–33 pp. **Adventure Damascus,** 128 W. Laurel Ave., 888/595-2453 or 540/475-6262, email: AdvDam@naxs.com, www.Adventure Damascus.com, rents ($10–19), sells, and repairs bikes, and offers trail maps, private showers, and lockers. Bike tours of 1–3 days are also an option, and their trail shuttle costs $8–17 pp depending on where you want to go ($6 with bike rental).

The **Virginia Creeper Fly Shop,** 540/628-3826, www.vcflyshop.naxs.com, is on US 58 just south of the intersection of I-81 and US 11 near Abingdon. They're a full-service fly shop and offer fly-fishing instruction ($150–190 for one person, $200–240 for two) and catch-and-release drift trips ($250–270 for one person, $300–320 for two). If you didn't happen to bring your own horse, consider a trip aboard a South American camelid with **Treasure Mountain Farm Llama Trekking,** 10436 Echo Lane in Glade Spring, 540/944-4674, email: jcox@naxs.com. Trips to Mt. Rogers and the Virginia Creeper Trail run $60 per day including lunch.

Camping

The Recreation Area has seven camping areas, some of which charge a fee. Most have water, but only three have hot showers. For reservations at any of the sites, call 800/933-7275.

Information

The **W. Pat Jennings Visitor Center,** 800/628-7202 or 540/783-5196, sits off Rt. 16 six miles south of Marion (I-81 exit 45). It's open Mon.–Fri. 8 A.M.–4:30 P.M., Sat. 9 A.M.–5 P.M., and Sun. 1–5 P.M.

Grayson Highlands State Park

On the southern side of the Mt. Rogers National Recreation Area is this hidden gem, off US 58 just west of Volney. Virginia's only state park with horse camping facilities has 25 campsites and stalls for more than 50 animals. Special orange-blaze equestrian trails climb Haw Orchard Mountain—named for the prickly hawthorne trees found there in abundance—for 360-degree views from Big Pinnacle and Little Pinnacle. Not only equestrians love this place—hikers and backpackers can also access the Appalachian Trail and Mt. Rogers from the park, and mountain bikers find that the eight-mile Virginia Highlands Horse Trail makes a great moderate loop ride.

The wingbeats of wild turkeys thunder in the underbrush, while wild ponies—part of a herd of 150 released years ago—may sidle up looking for handouts. They're rounded up twice a year and checked for disease, and some are auctioned off during the **Grayson Highlands Fall Harvest Festival** at the end of September, which also includes Appalachian crafts and music. The **Wayne C. Henderson Music Festival & Guitar Competition,** www.ls.net/~wayne, the third Saturday in June, features music, instrument-making demonstrations, and, of course, food.

A parking fee of $1 ($2 on weekends) allows access to Grayson Highlands. A total of 165 campsites are available, with rates varying by season (around $10–15). Information is available from park headquarters in Mouth of Wilson, 540/579-7092, www.dcr.state.va.us/parks/graysonh.htm.

Abingdon

As the oldest English-speaking settlement west of the Blue Ridge Mountains, Abingdon is the genteel nexus of southwest Virginia, a town that is aware and proud of its history. Abingdon centers on the historic streets of Main—split into East and West at Court Street—and Valley, more residential but just as charming. In places it seems as though every building along the rolling brick sidewalks is an antique, either original or restored to its former grandeur through the careful ministrations of its latest owners. Along with two of southwest Virginia's biggest draws—the Barter Theater and the Martha Washington Inn—Abingdon is the nearest town of substance to the Mt. Rogers National Recreation Area, making this quiet burg of about 7,000 one of the area's most popular destinations.

HISTORY

Abingdon's first name, Wolf Hills, came during a visit by Daniel Boone in 1760, when a group of wolves attacked the dogs in his hunting party near where the town is today. The name stuck until 1774, when Joseph Black erected Black's Fort on this site to protect hundreds of local set- tlers from Cherokee raids. Abingdon proper, named for Martha Washington's home parish, in Oxfordshire, England, was established two years later as the seat of Washington County.

The early 19th century saw Abingdon bloom into a focal point of southwest Virginia, han- dling most of the mail and traffic to the west- ern frontier along the Wilderness Road. It escaped the damage of the Civil War until December 1864, when 10,000 Federal troops under Gen. George Stoneman burned several buildings, in- cluding the depot and the town jail, that were being used to store Confederate supplies. Over the years, other fires have claimed other historic structures, but many more remain standing.

SIGHTS

A good place to start your stroll down Main Street is **The Arts Depot,** in Depot Square at W. Main St. and Russell Rd., 540/628-9091, www.eva.org/artsdepot. Built in the late 19th century as a loading point for the Virginia & Tennessee Railroad, the old freight station was abandoned for years before being rescued and claimed by Abingdon's visual, performing, and literary artists. You can watch artists at work in

THE SALTVILLE MASSACRE

Not as visible as men or munitions but almost as important, salt played a major role in the Civil War. It was used in medicine and gunpowder, and to preserve meat for army rations. Only two spots in the entire South produced significant amounts— one mine near Atlanta and one here, the "Salt Cap- ital of the Confederacy."

Saltville also saw one of the war's worst mas- sacres, on October 3, 1864. The day before, about 3,600 Union troops, including 400 members of the U.S. Colored Cavalry, had been beaten back re- peatedly as they tried to take the town from 2,800 ragtag Confederates under Capt. Champ Ferguson and Brig. Gen. Felix Robertson. By nightfall, hun- dreds of Federal wounded covered the ground after the rest had retreated.

The next morning, Confederate soldiers ad- vanced across the field, shooting black soldiers as they lay helpless. It's uncertain exactly how many were killed this way, but accounts from both sides put the total at well over 100.

Union troops managed to occupy and level much of the town within a few months, but justice took time. Ferguson was eventually captured, tried, and hanged for murder in October 1865. Robert- son, amazingly, not only escaped punishment but lived well into the 20th century. He died, the last surviving Confederate general, in 1928.

SOUTHWEST VIRGINIA

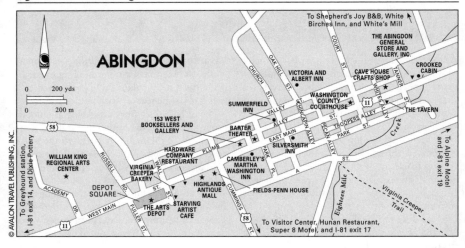

their studios, browse the sales galleries, or attend various workshops and lectures held throughout the year. Both the Sow's Ear Press and the Appalachian Center for Poets and Writers operate out of the building, too. Open Thurs.–Sat. 11 A.M.–3 P.M.

More exhibits and classes are held in the **William King Regional Art Center,** 415 Academy Dr., 540/628-5005, www.wkrac.org. An affiliate of the Virginia Museum of Fine Arts, the center concentrates on the artistic heritage of Appalachia and hosts the works of national artists along the lines of Ansel Adams, Andrew Wyeth, and Winslow Homer. Open Tuesday 10 A.M.–9 P.M., Wed. 10 A.M.–5 P.M., Sat. and Sun. 1–5 P.M.; free.

Head east to the **Fields-Penn House,** 208 W. Main St., 800/435-3440 or 540/676-0216. James Fields built many of the homes in the area in the mid-19th century, including the Washington County Courthouse farther down Main Street. This building dates to 1860 and was home to Fields and his wife, their eight children, and a maiden Aunt Jane. It's now a period museum open Apr.–Dec., Wed. 1–4 P.M., Thurs.–Sat. 1–4 P.M., and guided tours are available.

One block away stands **Camberley's Martha Washington Inn,** one of the town's outstanding landmarks (and a functioning inn). Across

the street is Abingdon's other landmark, the **Barter Theater.**

East Main Street starts to dip and rise as it reaches the old commercial and administrative center of town. Soon you'll pass the **Washington County Courthouse,** the fifth such building to stand at Main and Court streets. This one was built in 1869 and boasts a World War I memorial stained-glass window designed by the Tiffany studio. In the "jockey lot" behind the courthouse, horse merchants used to gather on the first Saturday of each month while court was in session for a boisterous day of trading and gambling (women and children were encouraged to keep their distance).

A short walk farther brings you past **The Tavern,** Abingdon's oldest building and finest restaurant. It'll take a bit longer to get to **White's Mill,** 12291 White's Mill Rd., 540/676-0285. Southwest Virginia's only remaining water-powered grist mill sits a short drive or moderate bicycle ride into the countryside north of town. Built around 1840, it's painfully photogenic and literally redolent of history, with a great musty smell, creaking floorboards, and antique machinery filling four floors. It's open more or less regularly (free, though donations are welcome) and still grinds flour and cornmeal offered for sale across the street in White's Mill Mercantile.

© JULIAN SMITH

the Washington County Courthouse in Abingdon

bircheinn.com, www.whitebirchesinn.com, features three rooms named after playwrights who traded words for food at the Barter Theater: Tennessee Williams, Thornton Wilder, and Noel Coward. Just off the back porch, a small pond is stocked with koi and goldfish.

The **Victoria and Albert Inn,** 224 Oak Hill St., 800/475-5494 or 540/676-2797, email: v&ainn@naxs.com, www.abingdon-virginia.com/v&ainn.html, sits across from the town library. It was built in 1892 and features rooms named for the deep colors of their walls: blue, raspberry, gold, and burgundy. A large front deck graces the **Summerfield Inn B&B,** 101 West Valley St., Abingdon, 800/668-5905 or 540/628-5905, email: stay@www.summerfieldinn.com, www.summerfieldinn.com. The entire house is sunny and spacious, with four large rooms in the main Parsonage and three more modern ones in the newer Cottage, featuring whirlpools.

ACCOMMODATIONS

$50–100

The classic 1960s-era **Alpine Motel,** 822 E. Main St., 540/628-3178, fax 540/628-4217, offers well-kept rooms with mountain views and cable TV for $60.

$100–150

Most of Abingdon's B&Bs fall in the same price category. Built in 1971 on the site of Abingdon's only silversmith shop, the **Silversmith Inn,** 102 E. Main St., 800/533-0195 or 540/676-3924, www.bbhost.com/silversmithinn, was recently restored with a wide balcony and outdoor hot tub in back.

Joyce Ferratt was born in the same house in which she and her husband, Jack, now operate the **Shepherd's Joy Bed & Breakfast,** 254 White's Mill Rd., 540/628-3273. The friendly couple runs a small sheep farm out back, complete with well-trained sheep dogs. The house is decorated with family heirlooms and a sheep motif. Just next door, the **White Birches Inn,** 268 White's Mill Rd., 800/247-2437 or 540/676-2140, fax 540/676-2146, email: stay@white-

$150–200

Known locally as "the Martha," **Camberley's Martha Washington Inn,**, 800/555-8000 or 540/628-3161, fax 540/628-8885, www.camberlyhotels.com, is a gargantuan structure that fills an entire block of W. Main Street with true colonial class. It began in 1832 as the home of Gen. Francis Preston, who built the original central brick structure for his family. Preston made his fortune on the nearby salt mines, allowing him to shell out $15,000—a huge sum at the time—for the construction. In 1858, the building became the Martha Washington College, a high-class school for young women.

During the Civil War, students served as nurses for soldiers wounded in skirmishes near Abingdon, and the Martha became a makeshift hospital while the Washington Mounted Rifles trained on the grounds outside. By 1934, the place had become a true hotel, housing actors in town for productions at the Barter Theater and such presidential luminaries as Harry Truman, Eleanor Roosevelt, Lady Bird Johnson, and Jimmy Carter. An $8-million renovation in 1984 transformed the Martha into a fully modern luxury inn while preserving much of the original architecture and antebellum appeal.

SOUTHWEST VIRGINIA

The building's changing roles over the years reverberate through the various rooms. The west parlor, formerly the master bedroom, became a study hall for the college. The lobby was the original family dining room before serving as the school library. On Washington's birthday, student belles would descend the central staircase in full Colonial costume to dance the Virginia reel in the parlors.

Antique treasures wait around almost every corner. Notice the marble fireplaces, crystal chandeliers, and the beautiful paintings in the Grand Ballroom, formerly the school chapel. Other paintings on the walls of the entranceway are copies of ones in the White House, depicting Niagara Falls, Natural Bridge, Boston Harbor, West Point, and New York City as they looked in the 1830s. Oscar Bachtecit, designer of Rockefeller Center in Manhattan, fashioned the 16-foot brass and silver table in the dining room. The oval glass weighs 300 pounds, and the entire table has been appraised at $100,000. For more history, including a few hotel ghost stories, track down Pete Sheffey, a walking encyclopedia of Martha lore who has served as a bellhop for the past three decades. Fifty-one rooms and 10 suites are filled with rich fabrics and antiques. Room rates ($160–175) include daily Continental breakfast and afternoon tea on weekends. Some suites have fireplaces and Jacuzzis.

Rooms at the **Comfort Inn Abingdon,** 170 Jonesboro Rd., 540/676-2222, fax 540/576-2222, run around $200.

$200–250

The original **Crooked Cabin,** 303 E. Main St., 540/628-8382, fax 540/643-1414, email: jferreira@naxs.com, www.crookedcabin.com, was built in 1780, making it one of Abingdon's oldest buildings. Today it's a cozy, self-contained cottage appointed with antiques and quilts, featuring three bedrooms, a dining room, and a patio and garden out back. The same owners also rent the Meadow Cottage, which can sleep four people in two bedrooms (call for rates and details), and other meals can be arranged from the Abingdon General Store next door.

Camping

The **Riverside Campground,** 18496 North Fork River Rd., 540/628-5333, lies seven miles north of town on Rt. 19, then two miles east on Rt. 611. More than 200 tent and RV sites ($18–21) are open Apr.–Nov., with facilities that include a convenience store, game room, swimming pool, and a sports field.

FOOD

The **Virginia Creeper Bakery,** 284 W. Main St., 540/623-2253, offers a wide range of baked goods and coffees. The specialty is breads—the gingerbread with lemon sauce is excellent. A gift shop and gourmet deli fill **The Abingdon General Store and Gallery, Inc.,** 301 E. Main St., 540/628-8382. Fresh ingredients fill the sandwiches in the deli, while farther back are two restaurants open in different seasons: the Plum Alley Eatery, downstairs, opens for the summer, and the Dumbwaiter, upstairs, serves during winter. Prices range $6–10.

Typical American fare fills the bill at the **Hardware Company Restaurant,** 260 W. Main St., 540/628-1111. Sandwiches run $5–8, and dinner entrées are $8–20. The great old wooden bar, decorated with brass and antique signs, is open until midnight for aprés-theater drinks. The **Hunan Restaurant,** 558 Cummings St., 540/676-2875, is in a shopping center near I-81 exit 17. Here the service is gracious, the prices reasonable, and the food tasty.

Serious Dining

Abingdon's oldest building (and that's saying something) houses **The Tavern** (540/628-1118), serving excellent continental food with a German flair. It was built in 1779 as a tavern and overnight stop for stagecoach traffic on the Wilderness Road. President Andrew Jackson and Louis Phillippe, king of France, were both among the many guests. The first post office west of the Blue Ridge operated out of the east wing, where the mail slot is still visible in the door.

Over the years the building passed through various incarnations as a private residence, general store, bank, barber shop, bakery, and, oh yes, tavern. During the Civil War, wounded soldiers from both armies were tended to on the third floor—the charcoal numbers for each bed are still visible on the plaster walls. In 1984, it was restored using original materials and techniques, including hand-forged hinges, hand-planed lumber, and handmade bricks in the two-foot walls. It was reopened in 1994 by German native Max Harmann with his wife, Kathy, from nearby Damascus. Tilted tables, rustic fixtures, low ceilings, and dark worn wood evoke the informal air of an old tavern, but the food is excellent. German standbys like wiener schnitzel and kasseler rippchen occupy the menu along with salmon, jambalaya, and ostrich. Prices are around $8 for lunch sandwiches to about $15 for dinner entrées.

On one corner of Depot Square, the **Starving Artist Cafe,** 134 Wall St., 540/628-8445, displays works by local artists as a background to a high-powered menu featuring seafood and some sandwiches. Dinner entrées range $10–20.

ENTERTAINMENT AND RECREATION

Barter Theatre

In 1933, aspiring but frustrated Virginia actor Robert Porterfield opened a theater in this structure, built in 1832 as a church on W. Main and College streets, with the novel idea of bringing theater to the masses. Not only would hungry, out-of-work actors and playwrights be given a place to perform their works, but theatergoers short of the cash for a ticket could exchange produce for seats. Playwrights would be given a Virginia ham for the use of their works. The barter system caught on, and farmers and townspeople began exchanging "hams for Hamlet" along with, perhaps, cabbages for Coward and spinach for Shaw (who was a vegetarian). The first season's profits amounted to $4.35 in cash, two barrels of jelly, and a collective weight gain among the actors of more than 300 pounds.

Declared the State Theater of Virginia, the Barter stage has hosted stars including Ernest Borgnine, Gregory Peck, and Kevin Spacey over the decades, making it the longest-running professional repertory theater in the country. Productions, including many world premieres, range from musicals to farce and Shakespeare. Between productions, storytellers take the stage to entertain children. Visitors hail from around the world; the guests coming the longest distance receive a door prize every evening. Tickets run $16–30 for adults, $3 less for children 5–18, and any unsold seats go for $12 to students 15 minutes before the curtain goes up. Major renovations (to the tune of $1.7 million) in the mid-1990s resulted in a vastly improved—yet still intimate—theater. Call the box office at 540/628-3991 for information and ticket sales, or see their website at www.bartertheatre.com.

Outdoor Recreation

The western end of the **Virginia Creeper Trail** starts off Pecan Alley just across the train tracks, near the huge Norfolk and Virginia locomotive—the last one to run these rails. **Highlands Ski & Outdoor Center,** E. Main St., 540/628-1329 or 540/628-9672, rents mountain bikes for $15 per half day or $20 per day. They also stock camping, hiking, and climbing gear for anyone eager to tackle Mt. Rogers. (More bike and outdoor shops can be found in Damascus.)

Black's Fort Stables, 410 Green Springs Rd., 540/628-6263, www.blacksfortstable, organizes guided horseback rides along the trail. Rates range from $10 pp for a half-hour ride to $210 pp for an eight-hour ride. They also offer a Fri.–Sun. "Romantic Getaway" for two with lodging, horseback rides, some meals, and a bonfire at night for $450. Lodging at their eponymous inn, which has a full kitchen and dining room and space for four people, is $125 per night.

EVENTS

As if it didn't already have enough going for it, Abingdon also hosts one of the top 100 tourist events in North America, known as the **Virginia Highlands Festival,** 800/435-3440, www.va-highlands-festival.org. Officially a showcase for Appalachian musicians, artists, craftspeople, and writers, the festival—held for two weeks near the beginning of August—features one of the largest antique markets in the southeast, wine tasting, garden workshops, and a hot-air balloon rally. For kids, there's storytelling, writing workshops, puppetry, and interactive theater.

Get down to music from rock to swing, funk to Celtic, in between sampling food from around the world and choosing your favorites from the exhibits of local and national artists. About 200,000 people pack the town during the festival, so make reservations as early as possible.

During the second week in September, the **Washington County Fair and Burley Tobacco Festival** brings country music and the sounds of livestock to the fairground on US 11 west of town. Carnival rides, tractor pulls, and the Miss Washington County pageant round out the fun. Call the Abingdon Convention and Visitors Bureau.

SHOPPING

Close to a dozen antique shops line Main Street in the center of town. The largest is probably the **Highlands Antique Mall,** 246 W. Main St., 540/676-4438. Craftaholics shouldn't miss the **Cave House Crafts Shop,** 279 E. Main St., 540/628-7721, named for the cave beneath the store, from which, according to legend, the wolves

that attacked Daniel Boone's dogs emerged. The historic home, built in 1858, was used in the 1950s and 1960s to house Barter Theater actors and is graced with a three-story walnut stair railing and a solid burled walnut mantel. In 1971, the Holston Mountain Arts and Crafts Cooperative moved in and began selling crafts of every description: quilts, musical instruments, clothing, baskets, pottery, and toys, to name a few.

Across from the Martha, **153 West Booksellers & Gallery,** 153 W. Main St., 540/628-1232 or 540/628-4506, exhibits fine handicrafts, especially pottery, alongside a peaceful bookstore. **Dixie Pottery** is a warehouse full of crafts and pottery—enough to justify the slogan, "Shop the World." It's five miles south of the center of Abingdon on US 11, near I-81 exit 13. It's open Mon.–Sat 9:30 A.M.–6 P.M., Sun. 1–6 P.M., but there's no phone number, so just stop by.

INFORMATION AND TRANSPORTATION

The Abingdon Convention and Visitors Bureau runs a **visitors center** at 335. W. Cummings St., 800/435-3440 or 540/676-2282, fax 540/676-3076, email: acvb@abingdon.com, www. abingdon.com/tourism, open daily 9 A.M.–5 P.M. **Greyhound** has a station at 465 W. Main St., 540/628-4409.

Far Southwest

TAZEWELL AND VICINITY

From Marion, drive north on Rt. 16—a gorgeous corkscrew of a road—to the hub of Tazewell (TAZ-wul) County, incorporated in 1866 after a fistfight settled a dispute over where to establish the local government seat. Before, between, or after visiting the two sights in the area, stop by the **Piggy Bank Cafe,** 540/988-2560, at 106 E. Main St. in the Old Clinch Balley Bank building—which explains the Prime Rate Burger, Default Dog, and BLT (Bank Loan Transaction). If you stop by in late June, you might catch the **Main Street Mo-**

ments Festival, with carriage rides, street dancing, and an antique show. Check out their website (www.mainstreet.netscope.net) for more information.

Crab Orchard Museum and Pioneer Park of Southwestern Virginia

Nearly every phase of the state's history finds a voice on this 110-acre archaeological site, three miles west of Tazewell on US 19/460, 540/988-6755, www.histcrab.netscope.net. Mastodon fossils and frontier furniture and weapons fill the central gallery building, while the nearby Pioneer Park consists of log homes dating to the

1800s. Park staff discuss crops typical of the pioneer era and explain the uses of various buildings, including a blacksmith shop, lardhouse, and dairy. Near a recently discovered Cherokee burial ground, descendants of local Cherokee groups have built indigenous houses typical of the 16th century. Farther on, a barn contains horse-drawn farm equipment and antique cars.

The park is open Mon.–Sat. 9 A.M.–5 P.M. (Sun. 1–5 P.M. from Memorial Day–Labor Day); $7 adults, $3 children 6–11, $20 family.

Pocahontas Exhibition Coal Mine

Some time during the 19th century, a blacksmith discovered a small outcropping of coal poking out of a nearby hillside. Finding himself with more than enough to power his forge, he amiably allowed neighbors to take home wagonloads for their own homes—despite his wife's warning that there soon wouldn't be enough even for them. In 1882, the Pocahontas Coalfield opened with the arrival of the Norfolk & Western Railroad, giving birth to the town. Over the next 73 years, it would produce more than 44 million tons of coal, including the "famous" Pocahontas Number Three, chosen by the U.S. Navy for its ships for its clean burning.

Today, a short section of the mine is open to the public, providing a fascinating glimpse into the industry that underpinned the economy of this section of Appalachia for most of the past century. In the Coal Heritage Museum, 540/945-2134, wvweb.com/www/pocohontas_mine/web.html, formerly the power house for the mine, visitors learn just how dangerous the industry was. Peruse accounts of the coal-dust explosion in March 1884 that killed everyone in the mine, filling the cemetery on the other side of town. Look for the mine-accident diagrams in the old shower room.

Tours into the mine begin with a video on modern mining. Then you enter the shaft itself, lined with rusted equipment and the famous 13-foot coal seam. The shaft remains a cool 52°F year-round, so wear a coat.

To get here, take Rt. 102 nine miles northwest from Bluefield on the West Virginia border. The mine is on the other side of the town of Pocahontas, over the bridge and railroad track. Open Apr.–Oct. Mon.–Sat. 10 A.M.–5 P.M., Sun. noon–5 P.M.; $6 adults, $3.50 children.

BREAKS INTERSTATE PARK

What could break a mountain? In this case, it took the Russell Fork River and a few hundred eons to carve through Pine Mountain on the border between Virginia and Kentucky. The result is said to be the deepest canyon in the country east of the Mississippi. Numerous overlooks line this five-mile gorge along a broad curve in the river, so deep that you can't even hear the Class V whitewater 1,600 feet below the famous pyramidal Towers.

The Cherokee once hunted here, though by 1769 (only a few decades after English silversmith John Swift supposedly buried a fortune in silver near the Towers) they had relinquished rights to the area. Daniel Boone passed through twice on a reconnaissance mission through the canyon, carving his name in trees in both 1767 (coming) and 1771 (going). Shawnee raids during the late 18th and early 19th centuries only slowed the inevitable influx of settlers.

Park headquarters, 800/982-5122 or 540/865-4413, email: bip@mounet.com, www.breakspark.com, are in the village of Breaks, eight miles north of Haysi on Rt. 80.

Accommodations and Food

Overnight guests can choose from among 140 **campsites** ($7–10) or more permanent accommodations. The **Rhododendron Lodge & Conference Center** has 34 rooms overlooking the canyon ($65–70). Two-bedroom **cottages** are available for $400 per week and can hold up to four people. The **Rhododendron Restaurant** boasts an impressive view from its deck and serves all meals.

Recreation

It may be hard to spot from the top, but the Russell Fork River rages within the confines of the park. Class III-V+ rapids make the run one of the most challenging on the Eastern Seaboard—names like "Triple Drop" and "El

KING COAL

The legendary coal deposits of Appalachia began taking shape hundreds of millions of years before Loretta Lynn's daddy ever made a living out of the side of a mountain. Over the centuries, organic matter was compressed, dried, and hardened into the black substance known as bituminous or "soft" coal, the most common type still found in the Norton formation, which underlies Kentucky, West Virginia, Tennessee, and Virginia.

Coal mining took off with the country's economic expansion after the Civil War, especially at the turn of the 20th century, when fresh-cut passages through the hills allowed railroads to transport the fuel to ships and factories for the first time. Demand for coal peaked in the 1920s, both to power vehicles and to make coke, a precursor to the steel used in gleaming new structures that sprouted from the heart of expanding metropolitan cities. The industry declined after World War II as oil and natural gas began to take over the market, but in the 1970s—about the time women began to work in the mines—the worldwide oil crisis drove demand and coal prices back up. The most recent trend has been back down because worldwide competition, the decline of the steel industry, and a decreasing demand for electric power have all cut demand for coal.

The Industry in its Infancy

Conditions during the early heyday of mining in southwest Virginia (roughly 1910–1930) were brutal and dangerous. Labor was cheap, and mining was often the only work around. Miners had to supply their own tools, which included a soft hat, carbide lamp, and low-vein shovel, so-called because its shallow bend allowed a miner to work under a ceiling only a few feet high. A strong worker could swing a short, double-pointed miner's pick at 40 strokes per minute.

Mines were laid out in grids, with long "main streets," or "headings," crisscrossed by "cross streets," or "rooms," up to 20 feet wide and 60 feet high. The 50-foot square pillars of coal in between were mined (or "robbed") last, to hold the ceiling up as long as possible. In the meantime, hand-cut timbers supported the ceiling, at least most of the time.

To blast out the coal, a miner would drill holes by hand using a six-foot breast auger braced against his sternum. A tamping bar was used to place the explosive charge, filled with the miner's own black powder, and ignited with a small firecracker-type charge called a "squid." The final steps were to light the fuse and run for cover.

The resulting broken pieces of coal were then loaded into carts pulled to the surface by ponies or mules, a method that persisted into the 1950s. Miners noted bitterly that the animals seemed more valuable than they did, and the beasts of burden were certainly harder to replace. The horses and mules were brought out of the mines on weekends to keep them from going blind in the darkness, though many still did.

Flammable methane, which seeps naturally from

Horendo" emphasize that this river is for experienced rafters and kayakers only. **Wahoo's Adventures,** 800/444-7238 or 828/262-5744, www.wahoosadventures.com, send rafts and kayaks downstream.

Twelve miles of short hiking trails lead down to the river or out to overlooks. (Clinchfield Overlook has the best view of the gorge here but is outshone by the Towers Overlook.) Twelve-acre Laurel Lake is stocked with bluegill and bass, and boats can be rented Memorial Day through Labor Day. Likewise, horse rentals and a pool are limited to the summer season.

Information

A **visitors center** is open daily Apr.–Dec. 7 A.M.–11 P.M.; 7:30 A.M.–6 P.M. the rest of the year. A parking/entrance fee of $1 per car is charged Memorial Day–Labor Day. Inside is a small museum on the history of the area, with a focus on coal mining.

BIG STONE GAP

Southwest Virginia's "other" gap has played second fiddle to Cumberland since the early days of the republic, when passages through the mountains were few and precious. The various names of

exposed coal, was the most immediate danger in the mines. The slightest spark could ignite the invisible gas and set fire to coal dust or the coal itself, causing explosions of awesome power. One blast in the Pocahontas mine in March 1884 killed at least 114 people beneath the surface and hurled coal cars out the mouth of the tunnel with enough force to dash them to pieces against the distant bank of a ravine. Such explosions were frighteningly common and were economic as well as human disasters, as noted in the official report of the Pocahontas explosion: ". . . it being the wish of those in authority to have the fullest and widest publicity given to the facts of the circumstances attending this sweeping calamity . . . instantly deprived so many human beings of life and blighted . . . the fair prospects of a mining company just as it was entering upon a career of prosperity." It was the unenviable job of the fire boss to track down methane pockets with the help of caged canaries (who succumbed to the odorless fumes more quickly than humans). The gas was ignited before it became too big a risk.

Other dangers included falling rocks and "widowmakers"—petrified tree stumps that slid from the ceiling with surprising frequency. The most insidious threat by far, though, was black or miner's lung (pneumoconiosis), a chronic pulmonary condition caused by breathing coal dust.

For all this, miners received an average of $2.15 per hour in 1952, which works out to less than $1 for a hand-blasted load of 2.5 tons of coal. Sometimes they were paid in company scrip good only in the overpriced company store, with the excuse that real U.S. currency was hard to come by in such rural areas.

Modern Mining

Plastic hard hats and electric lamps have replaced leather and carbide, and self-rescue kits with 30-minute breathing filters are now carried by every miner. Six-foot roof bolts are epoxied into holes drilled in the ceiling, and blasting has become a less hazardous activity thanks to safety fuses, detonating cords, and electric blasting caps.

The days of digging by hand are also long gone. Massive machines called shearers, armed with twin cutting drums, can gouge out 50 tons of coal—enough to supply the electricity needed by one household for 15 years—every minute. Hydraulic roof supports called shields, each of which can support 500 to 1,000 tons, are electronically controlled to follow the shearer and set themselves in place. A typical shearer can work strips up to 1,000 feet wide and two miles long, eating through 30–40 inches at a time over a period of 9–12 months.

Dust controls imposed by the government in 1969 have cut cases of miner's lung dramatically, and digital methane and oxygen monitors make sure the underground environment is safe. Pay has improved significantly as well, but a few things haven't changed: miners still rid themselves of coal dust in the bathhouse with common kitchen detergent, which has always worked better than regular soap.

its central town over the years reflect its strategic location. Initially called Three Forks, for tributaries of the Powell River that meet in or near the town center, the settlement became Mineral City from 1882 to 1888, thanks to major coalfields nearby. By the end of the late 19th century, three separate railroads served the gateway settlement, hauling out the black gold and leaving a rather drab mining town behind.

Sights and Entertainment

Big Stone Gap's favorite son, John Fox, Jr., made this corner of Appalachia famous in the 19th century with his short stories and novels, most notably in *The Trail of the Lonesome Pine*. The bare-knuckled romance between the Virginia mountain girl and the Eastern mining engineer has metamorphosed into the Official State Outdoor Drama of Virginia, presented at the **June Tollivar Playhouse,** Clinton Ave. near E. 4th St., 800/362-0149 or 540/523-1235, named for its real-life heroine. A rollicking mix of humor and heartbreak, folk music and fantasy, the melodrama unfolds Thurs.–Sat. at 8 P.M. July–Aug.; $12 adults, $10 children.

The mountain girl is also memorialized at the

BURKE'S GARDEN

Discovered in 1748 by surveyor James Burke, this small bowl-shaped valley east of Tazewell is almost entirely circled by Garden Mountain. Even though it's only 10 miles long (hence its nickname of "God's thumbprint"), it's considered one of the prettiest corners of the state. At 3,100 feet, it gets chilly up here, but that doesn't stop local farmers from taking advantage of some of Virginia's richest limestone soils.

To get there, take VA 61 east from Tazewell, then turn right onto Rt. 623 after about eight miles, which takes you up and over the edge of the mountain "bowl." From here you can explore the valley at will. The town of Burke's Garden is little more than a store, a post office, and a church, where some headstones in the graveyard date to the 16th century. Leave the same way you came in, or else Rt. 623 continues up over Garden Mountain to the south—a twisting dirt road that can get sketchy quickly—and passes through the Jefferson National Forest before connecting with VA 42.

June Tollivar House & Craft Shop, Jerome St. at Clinton St. The historic home is open Tues.–Sat. 10 A.M.–5 P.M., Sun. 2–6 P.M., with free tours throughout the day. Like most other sights in town, the Tollivar house is run by volunteers, so hours may vary.

The author is immortalized in the **John Fox, Jr. Museum,** Shawnee Ave. between E. 2nd St. and E. 3rd St., 540/523-2747, built in 1888. Ask the employees about Fox's wife, the opera star Fritzi Scheff (a.k.a. Mademoiselle Modiste), who, according to one account, "dazzled the world with jewels, gowns, pompadour, wasp waist, and sprightly charm." She married Fox less than 24 hours after divorcing her previous husband, a baron, but didn't last long in this decidedly uncosmopolitan neck of the woods. Open Wed.–Sun. 2–5 P.M.; $3 adults, $1 children.

One of southwest Virginia's best regional museums is called, fittingly, the **Southwest Virginia Museum,** W. 1st St. and Wood Ave., 540/523-1322. This former mansion of a state attorney general houses well-presented exhibits tracing the boom-and-bust cycles of the area's coal and iron industries, along with the household utensils, clothes, and furniture of everyday citizens. Open Memorial Day–Labor Day, Mon.–Thurs. 10 A.M.–4 P.M., Fri. 9 A.M.–4 P.M., Sat. 10 A.M.–5 P.M., Sun. 1–5 P.M.; $3 adults, $1.50 children.

Finally, the **H.W. Meador Coal Museum,** Shawnee Ave. and E. 3rd St., 540/523-9209, concentrates on Big Stone Gap's bituminous legacy. You'll know the place by the hulking mine equipment rusting out front, courtesy of the Westmoreland Coal Co., which also runs the museum. Open Wed.–Sat. 10 A.M.–5 P.M., Sun. 1–5 P.M.; free.

Accommodations and Food
Both in-town lodging options sit along US 23 on the way into the center of town. The **Country Inn & RV Park,** 540/523-0374, offers 12 rooms for around $50, and the **Comfort Inn,** 1928-B Wildcat Rd., 800/228-5150 or 540/523-5911, has rooms for just under $100 as well as the **Huddle House** Restaurant, open 24 hours daily.

Fast food has taken over Big Stone Gap, with the usual plastic-roofed representatives scattered about. Across the Powell River from the center of town, **Stringer's Restaurant,** 412 E. 5th St., 540/523-5388, is family run and moderately priced. **Ms. Fritzi's Tea Room** at the early-1900s Victorian House, 606 E. Wood Ave., 540/523-6245, serves lunch Tues.–Sat. and dinner during the Lonesome Pine season, Thurs.–Sat.

Information
Interstate Private Railroad Car number 101 was built in 1870, but today it houses Big Stone Gap's **Regional Tourist and Information Center,** 540/523-2060, email: gaptourism@va-village.com, www.coalfield.com/touristinfo, on US 23 next to the Country Inn Motel. The wooden car is open Mon.–Sat. 9 A.M.–5 P.M., Sun. 1–5 P.M. Memorial Day–Labor Day (Tues.–Fri. 10 A.M.–5 P.M. otherwise), offering walking-tour maps and assistance.

NATURAL TUNNEL STATE PARK

Another monument to geological persistence has been carved by modest little Stock Creek, whose carbonic acid gradually dissolved an 850-foot tunnel through limestone bedrock. The southern entrance opens off the amphitheater, a semicircular gallery with sheer walls that drop 150 feet to creek level. The gaping hole is large enough for the creek and a pair of train tracks, installed in the 19th century to take advantage of the natural passageway to and from the coalfields.

Several short trails, open until dusk, lead to the bottom and around the rim. Careful near the edge at Lover's Leap, where an ancient myth holds that a Native American man and his love, prohibited from marrying by their warring tribes, leapt to their deaths. A chairlift runs into the gorge for $2 pp. About 10 coal trains per day still chug through the tunnel, so a guided tour is the only way to explore beyond the entrance. Tours are given on Sundays in season, and canoe trips on the Clinch River are offered on Saturday (call for information and reservations).

At the top, the **Cove Ridge Center,** 540/940-2674, email: nattunl@mounet.com, www.dcr .state.va.us/parks/naturalt.htm, houses a pool, bathhouse, snack bar, gift shop, and a small museum on the geology and history of the immediate area. It's open 10 A.M.–5 P.M. (until 6 P.M. on weekends) Memorial Day–Labor Day; 10 A.M.–4 P.M. weekends Mar.–May and Sept.–Oct. Car entrance fees are $1 during the week and $2 on weekends. Campgrounds on the hilltop by the entrance cost $11 for tents and $15 with water and electric hookups, and include use of the pool (both open Mar.–Nov.).

Natural Tunnel State Park is off Rt. 871 off US 23 between Clinchport and Duffield.

CUMBERLAND GAP NATIONAL HISTORICAL PARK

One of frontier America's most famous landmarks is more accurately an absence of land: a break in the long Appalachian chain that allowed migrating deer and buffalo, Native Americans, and pioneers alike to pass through into the Ohio River Basin. It was discovered by European settlers in the mid-18th century to be the easiest way to the Kentucky Territory, easing crowding east of the mountains. Named after the Duke of Cumberland, son of King George II, the pass had already been called the Warrior's Path by the Cherokee raiding parties that came from as far as North Carolina to attack western tribes.

Daniel Boone made the pass famous, and vice versa. In 1796, the budding frontiersman set his legend on track when he and 30 "axemen" hacked out the Wilderness Road through the gap. Also known as Boone's Trace, the historic highway was barely a rutted track in spots as it wound from Kingsport, Tennessee, to Boonesborough, Kentucky. Still, between 1775–1810, more than 200,000 settlers crossed through "the first doorway to the West" as the new nation spread its wings.

Today this rugged corner of the Cumberland Mountains is preserved in the nation's second largest historical park (20,271 acres). It's also one of the least visited parks, so any trip to the corner of Kentucky, Tennessee, and Virginia is automatically a step away from crowds as well as into the past.

Visiting the Gap

The visitors center is actually over the border in Middlesboro, Kentucky, 606/248-2817, email: CUGA_Superintendent@nps.gov, www.nps.gov/cuga, open daily 8 A.M.–5 P.M. (until 6 P.M. Memorial Day–Labor Day), and contains exhibits and films on the history and geology of the park. Almost 55 miles of trails wind through hemlock, pine, and oak forests (lusher here than farther north because scouring glaciers didn't make it this far south). Views from the 21-mile Ridge Trail and the Pinnacle Overlook (reached by road) can be spectacular, weather permitting. On a clear day, it's possible to see all three states spread out below and even as far as the Great Smoky Mountains in North Carolina. A curvy four-mile road leads to Pinnacle Overlook (2,440 feet), from which it's possible to see into Virginia, Kentucky, and Tennessee.

Other spots on the itinerary include Hensley Settlement, a self-sufficient homestead dating to the turn of the 20th century and now under restoration by the Park Service. Countless caves creep underground, including Cudjo Caverns, possibly Virginia's largest and containing what

SOUTHWEST VIRGINIA

COUNTRY MUSIC'S LEGENDARY CARTER FAMILY

One of the taproots of American country music reaches all the way back to Maces Spring in southwest Virginia. It's well worth a side trip to visit the music center, especially if you're already in the vicinity of Natural Tunnel State Park.

It all began with carpenter Alvin Pleasant "A.P." Carter, who grew up here and operated a grocery store on Rt. 614. His true passion, though, was collecting and playing the pure, haunting mountain music that recorded the loves, losses, and everyday events of life in Appalachia.

In 1927, Ralph Peer, a talent scout from RCA Victor Records, discovered A.P. playing in a trio with his wife Sara and sister-in-law Maybelle. They soon had a contract to record, turning out the "Bristol Sessions," which are today considered a watershed in commercial country music. Between 1927 and 1942, the Carter Family recorded more than 300 songs, including classics such as "Bury Me Under the Weeping Willow," "I'm Thinking Tonight of Blue Eyes," and "Keep on the Sunny Side," which is inscribed on A.P.'s tombstone in a cemetery just down the road from his store.

In addition to the songs the family wrote, A.P.

also collected songs on countless forays into the hills, where he'd obsessively scribble down lyrics and memorize tunes with the help of Sara and their daughter, Janette. This priceless form of musical anthropology introduced dozens of timeless tunes, including "Will the Circle Be Unbroken?", to the country and the world.

The trio's career ended in 1940 with the breakup of A.P. and Sara's marriage, but its effect on country music still echoes. In 1993, their faces appeared on U.S. postal stamps along with Patsy Cline, Hank Williams, and others. That same year, Rounder Records began to re-release the complete Carter Family Victor recordings, a nine-CD set that includes almost 150 songs recorded from 1927–1934.

A.P.'s grocery store fell into disrepair, serving briefly as a tobacco warehouse, before Janette cleaned it up and began to hold regular concerts in an effort to preserve the family legacy. Soon the crowds drawn to the Saturday-night shows were packing the place to the roof. So with the help of friends and relatives (including Johnny Cash, who married Maybelle's daughter, June), the Carter

Janette and Joe Carter

© JULIAN SMITH

SOUTHWEST VIRGINIA

Family Fold was erected in 1976 and has been going strong ever since.

Shows begin every Saturday at 7:30 p.m. ($4 adults, $1 children 6–12), presenting a wide range of traditional acoustic mountain music, including gospel and bluegrass. Janette still MCs, introducing local and regional artists and occasionally stepping aside while her brother Joe warms the crowd up with a humorous "coon tale." Up to 900 people can squeeze into the dirt-floored arena, although 200–400 is more typical. On summer evenings, the sides and back are opened to the night air, cooling down the cloggers and buck dancers who gyrate on the small concrete dance floor. A concession stand sells CDs, T-shirts, drinks, and snacks, but no alcohol—it's strictly prohibited, as are swearing and misbehaving.

A.P.'s old store is now the **Carter Family Museum,** open every Saturday 6 A.M. to showtime for 50 cents pp. Alongside A.P.'s work clothes and tools you'll find Janette's first autoharp, bought at age 13 with her earnings from performing with the family (25 cents per show); original 78 rpm records; photographs; and show clothes including those worn by Johnny Cash and June when they performed for President Nixon in 1970.

Every August, even more music lovers congregate in Maces Spring for the **Carter Family Memorial Festival,** held to commemorate the family's first recording session. Banjos, fiddles, guitars, and bass fill the Fold all weekend from 2–11 P.M., while local artisans set up booths outside. National acts bring slightly higher prices ($10 pp per day).

Call the Center at 540/386-6054 or 540/386-0035 for show lineups and other questions, or log on to www.scarlet.org/carter/index.html or www.fmp.com/orthey/carter.html. To find the Fold, head toward the town of Hiltons on Rt. 58/421 from Weber City (east) or Bristol (west). In Hiltons, turn onto Rt. 709 and then immediately left onto Rt. 615, also known as the A.P. Carter Highway. Maces Spring is three miles farther, and you can't miss the Fold.

may be the world's largest stalagmite (closed for renovations as of 1997). On the Virginia side, 160 campsites with restrooms and hot showers are available for $10 (28 have hookups for $15). There's no cost for backcountry camping permits, available from the visitors center. Otherwise, admission to the park is free.

A $265-million pair of tunnels completed in 1996 rerouted US 25 to the south of the original mountain pass, which is being restored to its unpaved, "Boone-era" condition. Once the roadbed is removed, the trail will be narrowed and replanted with native shrubs and trees, allowing visitors to cross the gap much as their frontier predecessors did. Work is scheduled to be completed around 2010.

The Shenandoah

Virginia naturalist Henry Heatwole's description of Virginia's rolling, off-center spine as a place full of "small and subtle pleasures" is right on the mark, but it also raises the question: What *is* the Shenandoah, exactly? In name, it's the lazy-winding river—two, actually—that join near Front Royal before flowing north into the Potomac. In legend, it's the wide, fertile valley dividing the Blue Ridge Mountains from the Alleghenies, elevated to near-mythic status by some of the most dramatic fighting of the Civil War. In essence, it's a state of mind, embodied in the odors of rich farmland in morning mist, snow on rugged granite peaks, and the simple pleasures of small-town hospitality evident even in the larger cities.

inhabitants called it. Scattered villages of Shawnee here were prey to frequent raids by Catawbas from the south and Delawares from the north. Later, first- or second-generation German farmers moved down from Pennsylvania to the promising valley—where, it was said, the summer grass grew high enough to tie across a horse's saddle. During the Civil War, the valley's productivity and strategic importance almost proved its undoing. Over three years, the area endured more battles than any other region in the country. Traditionally isolated from the political centers of the Piedmont and the coast, the Shenandoah was long considered the domain of backwoods "clay-

Dinosaur Land

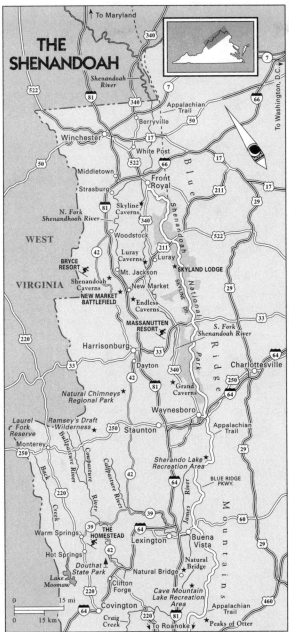

eaters," causing many an argument over how much trade and money for development should be sent from the East.

HIGHLIGHTS

Aside from its intangible enticements of atmosphere, the Shenandoah is replete with things to do and see. Cultural attractions tend toward the historic, led by places affected or begotten by the Civil War. The apple city of Winchester saw the most action, while Stonewall Jackson lived briefly in the antique college town of Lexington before being buried there. Battlefields like New Market and Cedar Creek keep the valley's past alive in year-round displays and annual reenactments.

Stretch your legs with a hike or ride through the seemingly endless George Washington National Forest, then relax with a soak at The Homestead in Hot Springs, the most venerable and lavish resort hotel in the state. In the winter, skiing at Bryce and Massanutten resorts is respectable for being this far south, while during the warmer months the region's countless streams and rivers attract anglers in canoes, rafters in kayaks, and hungover college students in inner tubes. The Shenandoah is also home to most of the state's commercial caves, led by Luray Caverns, the largest and most spectacular on the East Coast. You could easily take a week driving from Front Royal to the North Carolina border along the crest of the Blue Ridge, following the Skyline Drive—linchpin of Shenandoah National Park—and the Blue Ridge Parkway.

M

THE SHENANDOAH

CIVIL WAR IN THE SHENANDOAH

As the Civil War slowly tore through Virginia, the strategic value of the Shenandoah made it crucial to the strategies of both sides. The valley was not only the fertile breadbasket of the Confederacy, but it could also allow troops to march unseen practically to the steps of Washington, D.C.—or, in the other direction, to flank Richmond. "If the valley is lost," declared Stonewall Jackson, "Virginia is lost." And the Rebel commander would add his own legend to the two short but bloody years that transformed a pastoral landscape into a smoking wasteland.

Spring 1862: Jackson's Valley Campaign

Robert E. Lee's orders to Jackson were simple: defend the valley, and prevent Federal reinforcements from joining the attack on Richmond. With that in mind, Jackson pitted his 17,000 troops against heavy odds in an incredible display of cunning, endurance, and luck. In seven weeks, Jackson's famous "foot cavalry"—consisting of the 2nd, 4th, 5th, 27th, and 33rd Virginia infantry regiments and the elite Rockbridge Artillery—fought four battles and six skirmishes, marched more than 600 miles, and eventually immobilized and inflicted twice its casualties on some 60,000 Federals.

Jackson believed, "There are two things never to be lost sight of by a military commander: always mystify, mislead, and surprise the enemy if possible . . . [and] never fight against heavy odds, if by possible maneuvering you can hurl your own force on only a part, and the weakest part, of your enemy and crush it." Not surprisingly, he employed a strategy of surprise and deception that suited the uneven terrain perfectly and kept his dogged troops showing up whenever and wherever they were least expected.

Jackson had quickly realized that speed was of the essence and once led his troops 350 miles in 30 days. His tactics worked: as of 1864, the Stonewall Brigade had yet to be driven from a field that it defended.

At the First Battle of Kernstown, on March 23, Jackson attacked a force he thought to be only a few

General Philip Sheridan

© DOVER PUBLICATIONS, INC.

regiments strong, but which turned out to be Gen. James Shields' entire division. Both sides raced for the cover of a wall in the middle of an open field. The Confederates won, though they eventually had to retreat in the face of overwhelming numbers. The Rebels did, however, manage to keep Shields from joining McClellan's peninsular campaign.

On May 3, Jackson mystified even his own subordinates when he ordered half his army to march eastward out of the valley. Almost to Charlottesville, the troops suddenly found themselves herded onto railroad cars and shipped back to Staunton. There they disembarked and marched off for a surprise attack at McDowell on May 8, forcing Union troops under Gen. Robert Milroy to flee into West Virginia.

With help from the spirited spy Belle Boyd, the Confederates captured Front Royal on May 23 after joining with Jubal Early's command in a surprising move and passing through a gap in Massanutten Mountain. During this battle, members of the 1st Maryland Division from each side found themselves facing, greeting, and then fighting their own neighbors and relatives.

The First Battle of Winchester, on May 25, followed a race toward the important supply city lost by Union Maj. Gen. Nathaniel Banks. At sunset, Banks, believing the fighting ended, went upstairs to take a bath. Under Jackson, though, the Confederate attacks continued, sending the Union troops scurrying in retreat toward Washington, D.C. (When asked by Banks if he loved his country, one retreating soldier replied, "Yes sir, and I'm trying to get back to it as fast as I can.") Pursuit was eventually called off because Jackson's men were too worn out from marching the previous nights.

Two more victories in June near Port Republic secured the Confederate hold on the valley. On June 8, Gen. Richard S. Ewell sent a larger army under Gen. John C. Fremont packing, and the next day Jackson defeated Brig. Gen. Erasmus Tyler.

In a tragic irony, Jackson was killed by his own men following the Rebel triumph at Chancellorsville one year later.

Summer 1864: The Tide Turns

As the war dragged on, Lincoln and his Union commanders realized they would have to bring the South to its knees by any means possible to keep the war from dragging on indefinitely. Soon after the Battle of New Market on May 15, in which 10 VMI cadets were killed, Union Lt. Gen. Ulysses S. Grant began a massive statewide offensive intended to end the war once and for all. Lee sent Lt. Gen. Jubal Early to defend the valley. Early's Maryland Campaign, as it became known, began with successes at Cool Spring on July 19 and the Second Battle of Kernstown on July 24. By August, Early had his sights set on Washington, D.C., itself.

Embarrassed by the continued defeats and alarmed by the threat to the capital, Grant realized that the Union had to win the valley at all costs. He sent Maj. Gen. Philip Sheridan south with orders to raze the Shenandoah so completely "that a crow flying over it will have to carry his provender with him." Sheridan's Valley Campaign spelled doom for the area as surely as Jackson's had meant its temporary salvation. Early's 12,000 remaining troops found themselves facing 40,000 Union soldiers who advanced down the valley slaughtering countless livestock, ruining fields, and putting buildings to the torch. Scattered stone foundations still recall the frenzy of destruction remembered for generations simply as "The Burning."

The Battle of Opequon (Third Winchester), on September 19, was the largest in the valley, leaving 5,000 Federals and 3,500 Confederates dead in its wake. Despite the numbers, it was still considered a Union victory. Three more wins—Fishers Hill, on September 22, Toms Brook, on October 9, and Cedar Creek (near Strasburg), on October 18—marked the beginning of the end for the Confederate hold on the valley. At the Battle of Waynesboro, on March 2, 1865, Sheridan crushed Early's remaining forces and condemned the South to defeat.

CIVIL WAR IN THE SHENANDOAH

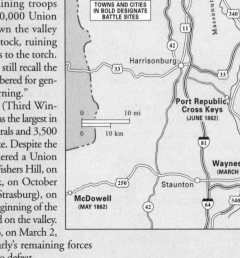

THE SHENANDOAH

ACCESS

I-81 runs the length of the valley along the well-worn route of the Old Valley Pike, once worn deep into the soil by native tribes, European settlers, and Civil War troops. That older, more scenic route (Old Valley Pike) lives on as US 11, worlds away from the interstate, though the two are often within sight and sound of each other. The Blue Ridge is pierced by one interstate (I-66, roughly paralleled by the Amtrak line from Charlottesville to West Virginia via Staunton) and several smaller roads (US 211 from Luray, US 33 from Harrisonburg, and US 60 from Lexington). Interstate 66 leads to Winchester and the mountains for the weekend hordes from Washington, D.C.

RESOURCES

The **Shenandoah Valley Travel Association,** P.O. Box 1040, 277 W. Old Cross Rd., New Market, VA 22844, 877/VISIT-SV (847-4878) or 540/740-3132, fax 540/740-3100, www.svta.org, can provide more information on touring the area. For detailed listings of local inns and B&Bs, try the **Blue Ridge Bed & Breakfast Reservation Service,** 2458 Castleman Rd., Berryville, VA 22611, 800/296-1246 or 540/955-1246, fax 540/955-4240, email: blurdgbb@shentel.net, www.blue ridgebb.com; or **Bed and Breakfasts of the Historic Shenandoah Valley,** www.bbhsv.org. **Visit the Valley,** www.visitthevalley.org, is another good information resource, organized by more than a dozen local foundations.

Winchester and Vicinity

Known for its apple blossoms and Civil War battles, Winchester (pop. 22,000) has alternately enjoyed and endured its position as the gateway to the northern Shenandoah Valley. The largest city in Virginia's apple heartland of Frederick and Clarke counties, Winchester is surrounded by acres and acres of orchards, filled with delicate buds in the spring and teams of migrant harvest workers in the fall. From padded shoulder buckets to wooden crates in the backs of rumbling trucks, the fruit eventually makes its way to dozens of processing plants near town that infuse the air with the sweet smell of cider, vinegar, apple butter, and applesauce in the making. More than half of each yearly crop of 200–300 million pounds is sold fresh across the country.

Several natives of this region have gone on to nationwide fame, including progressive 1920s Governor Harry Byrd and author Willa Cather (*Death Comes for the Archbishop*). Country singer Patsy Cline was born at 608 S. Kent Street in 1932, worked in Gaunt's Drug Store at the corner of S. Loudoun Street and Valley Avenue, and is buried on a boulevard named in her honor east of the interstate.

A quiet pedestrian mall in the center of downtown (Loudoun St. between Piccadilly and Cork)

is crowded with restaurants, bookstores, coffeeshops, and gift stores within a few blocks. Sadly, many empty windows and "For Rent" signs attest to competition from malls and gigantic depot-type stores farther out of town.

HISTORY

Virginia's oldest city west of the Blue Ridge, Winchester began as a Shawnee campground and was settled by Pennsylvania Quakers in 1732. Settlers soon arrived from all over Europe, including Scottish-Irish, Welsh, English, and French. Germans left their mark in trim houses set flush against sidewalks and with tidy gardens in back.

In 1748, an eager red-haired 16-year-old arrived to survey thousands of rolling acres belonging to Lord Fairfax. Within a decade, George Washington had set about building Fort Loudoun to protect the frontier town from Indian attacks and French encroachment. Soon he was elected to his first political office, in the House of Burgesses.

During the Civil War, Winchester saw as much action as any city in Virginia. On the cusp of the valley with Maryland, less than 50 miles to the north, Winchester changed hands 72 times during the course of the war—13 times in one day. Some

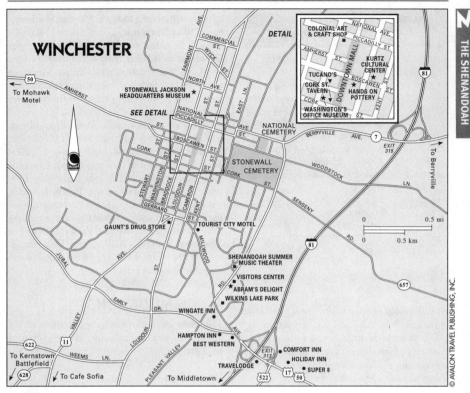

WINCHESTER

THE SHENANDOAH

of these capitulations were, of course, questionable—a single soldier left in town after the opposition retreated, for instance—but no fewer than five major battles were fought within the city limits. The Third Battle of Winchester (a.k.a. Opequon), on September 19, 1864, was the largest fought in the valley. Confederate forces under Lt. Gen. Jubal Early killed more than 5,000 of Sheridan's Federal troops, but the battle was still considered a Union victory. Thousands of wounded were brought here from Gettysburg and Antietam, helping fill close to 8,000 graves in two major cemeteries along Woodstock Lane—Stonewall for the Confederates, National for the Federals.

SIGHTS

Block tickets to Winchester's three main historical sights can be purchased at any of the three

($10 adults, $4 children 7–18, $20 family). Individual admission is also available, for $5 adults, $2.50 children, $12 families. Each location is open Apr.–Oct. Mon.–Sat. 10 A.M.–4 P.M., Sun. noon–4 P.M.

Abram's Delight, 1340 S. Pleasant Valley Rd., 540/662-6519, sits across from the visitors center and next to pleasant Wilkins Lake Park. The oldest home in the city, it began in 1734 as the log house of Quaker settler Abraham Hollingsworth, who called his 582 acres "a delight to behold." It originally stood downtown but was dismantled there, reassembled here, and filled with tools, a loom, and other well-worn artifacts.

The limestone main house next door was built in 1754 by Abraham's son Isaac and served as the city's first Quaker meeting house. Five generations of Hollingsworths used beautiful antiques including a melodeon (a small reed organ),

PATSY CLINE CHRONOLOGY

1932	Born Virginia Patterson Hensley in Winchester
1957	Breaks into show business by winning Arthur Godfrey's talent program with "Walkin' After Midnight"
1958	Joins Grand Ole Opry
1961–1962	#1 Female Recording Artist
1962	#1 song: "I Fall to Pieces"
1963	Dies in plane crash in Tennessee at age 30
1973	Inducted into Country Music Hall of Fame
1993	Commemorative stamp issued
1994	Inducted into Cowgirl Hall of Fame
1995	*Greatest Hits* album sells six million copies

a 1790 walnut plantation desk, and a solid cherry butler's desk with mahogany veneer dating to 1800. Rope beds upstairs had to be tightened every night with a special crank (hence the phrase "sleep tight"). Abraham's ghost is said to move things around when nobody's looking.

The 1854 Gothic Revival building that served as **Stonewall Jackson's Headquarters,** 415 N. Braddock St., 540/667-3242, originally belonged to Lt. Col. Lewis Moore, great-grandfather of Mary Tyler Moore (who donated the reproduction gilt wallpaper). The building was taken over by the Confederate general from late 1861 to the start of his Valley Campaign in 1862. Civil War–era furniture and relics include original Confederate flags, uniforms, and Jackson's prayer book and camp table. Heft an 1861 Springfield rifle and try to figure out whether *you* could have handled the percussion caps, minnie ball bullets, and ramrod quickly enough to load and fire it three times in one minute.

Between September 1755 and December 1756, future Founding Father George Washington, still a 23-year-old colonel in the Virginia militia, organized the frontier town's Revolutionary War defenses from a three-room

structure preserved today as **George Washington's Office Museum,** 32 W. Cork St., 540/662-4412. The oldest surviving structure in town, the museum is filled with Revolutionary War and Civil War memorabilia, antique surveying tools, and a model of Fort Loudoun. Bloodstains under one window bear witness to one of the city's many battles.

At the corner of Braddock and Piccadilly in front of Kimberly's Linens and Gifts sits the **World's Largest Apple,** built to top a 5,200-pound monument in rival apple town Cornelia, Georgia (actually a 1927 gift from Winchester). A few blocks over on the downtown mall, children can try their hand at a mock apple-packing center, one of the many interactive exhibits at the **Shenandoah Valley Discovery Museum,** 540/722-2020. Open Tues.–Sat. 9 A.M.–5 P.M., Sun. 1–5 P.M.; $4 pp. Browse the museum shop for free.

ACCOMMODATIONS

The most interesting lodgings in the area are outside the city, in Berryville, White Post, and Middletown.

Under $50

Both the **Tourist City Motel,** 214 Millwood Ave., 540/662-9011, and the **Howard Johnson Lodge,** 2649 Valley Ave., 540/662-2521, have rooms for $50 or less. The **Mohawk Motel,** 2754 Northwestern Pike, 540/667-1410, also offers budget quarters and has for close to 50 years. It's worth the drive out of town (three miles south on Rt. 37 from I-81 exit 317, then two miles west on US 50) for the views.

$50–100

Exit 313 onto US 50 off I-81 has most of Winchester's midpriced hotels, including the **Hampton Inn,** 1655 Apple Blossom Dr., 540/667-8011, fax 540/667-8033, and the **Best Western Lee-Jackson,** 711 Millwood Ave., 540/662-4154, fax 540/662-2618. In addition to its rooms, the **Travelodge of Winchester,** 160 Front Royal Pike, 540/665-0685, fax 540/665-0689, has a heated pool and eight efficiencies.

$100–150

The **Fuller House Inn,** 220 W. Boscawen St., 540/722-3976, email: stonsoup@shentel.net, www.stonesoupgallery.com, was Winchester's first B&B. The huge Greek Revival mansion, parts of which date to 1780, encloses 10 fireplaces, a circular two-floor staircase made of cherry, and two rooms ($125–150) and a suite ($175). Winchester's **Wingate Inn,** 150 Wingate Dr., 540/678-4283, fax 540/662-4439, is the most modern place in town, with a business center, conference center, and heated pool.

FOOD

Downtown Mall

Starting at the north end, the **Violino Restaurante Italiano,** 181 N. Loudoun St. at Piccadilly, 540/667-8006, serves creative Italian fare that earned four stars in one local review. Franco and Marcella Stocco from Turin offer classical Northern cuisine, graced by excellent sauces, in the $7–10 range, including many vegetarian plates. Lunch and dinner are served daily in the main dining room, decorated with instruments, or on the small patio facing the mall.

Half a block down is the **Snow White Grill,** 540/662-5955, a diner usually crammed with locals in for ice cream and cheap eats ($2–3). Closed Sunday. The **Olde Towne Cafe,** at Loudoun and Boscawen, 540/665-1805, does the diner tradition a bit more justice with generous lunch specials for $4–5 served Tues.–Sun.

At the same intersection, two coffee shops coexist peacefully side by side. The **Daily Grind,** 540/662-2115, offers java, light food, Internet access, and live music on Friday and Saturday nights. Open daily from 7 A.M.–10 or 11 P.M. (8:30 A.M.–6 P.M. Sundays). Readings, discussions groups, and acoustic jams are more the style at the **Satisfied Mind Books & Coffee,** 540/665-0855. Ginseng and ginkgo elixirs give a pot of tea extra zing.

Open daily at 6:30 A.M., the **Chelsea Bagel Bakery,** 24 S. Loudoun St., 540/678-4637, churns out fresh bagels, sandwiches, and great homemade soups for less than $5. Keep going to the southern end of the mall and take a right to the **Cork Street Tavern,** 8 W. Cork St., 540/667-3777. This snugly casual place serves burgers ($5), award-winning ribs, and other hearty entrées ($9–14) in front of a big stone fireplace and bar. The building itself has a history: some parts date to the 1830s; it was shelled during the Civil War; and as "The Rustic Tavern" it survived both the Depression and World War II.

Elsewhere in Town

Just a block off the mall sits **Tucano's,** 12 S. Braddock St., 540/722-4557. Delicious Brazilian dishes with a worldly flair, including *aves* (poultry), *paixes* (fish), and *pratos vegetarianos* (vegetarian plates) are $4–6 for lunch, Mon.–Fri., and $10–15 during dinner Mon.–Sat.

One of the few authentic Slavic restaurants in the country, **Cafe Sofia,** 2900 Valley Ave., 540/667-2950, is warmed by a log fireplace and filled with Eastern European weavings, baskets, dolls, and plates. Owner/chef Bozidar Janakiev has worked for the Russian Tea Room in New York City and the Watergate Complex in Washington, D.C., and this intimate place has been featured in *Bon Apétit* and the *Washington Post.* Servers in traditional Bulgarian dress serve entrées such as *pierogi* (a type of savory turnover) and goulash, accompanied by Bulgarian wine and Turkish coffee. Dishes range from $7–10 for lunch (Tues.–Fri.) and $18–20 for dinner (Tues.–Sat.). Don't forget to save room for apple strudel or *palachinka* (crepes) for dessert.

In the same direction is **Passage to India,** 2644 Valley Ave., 540/662-6488, where subcontinental appetizers are $3–5 and entrées $8–12 for lunch, $11–17 for dinner. As usual, there are many vegetarian options, including tandoori bread for $2. Open daily for lunch and dinner.

ENTERTAINMENT

From mid-June to early August, you can enjoy performances by the **Shenandoah Summer Music Festival,** 1460 University Dr., 877/580-8025 or 540/665-4509, the only professional theater of its kind in the valley. Tickets for productions such as *Annie, Fiddler on the Roof,* and *Oklahoma!* are $18–21.

Live music can be found at **Brewbaker's Restaurant,** 168 N. Loudoun St., 540/535-0111, and **Big D Saloon & Grill,** 1815 Millwood Pike, 540/665-3105, which also has pool tables and bluegrass on Sundays.

EVENTS

To usher in spring and its acres of blooming orchards, normally conservative Winchester erupts with pink and green clothing, parades, music, and parties. The first **Apple Blossom Festival** was organized in 1924, and except for a break during World War II, it's been going strong ever since. Five days of marching entertainment, food, and fun, including a circus and the coronation of the Apple Blossom Queen, take place every May the weekend before Mother's Day. For more information, call 800/230-2139, or try their website (www.apple-blossom.com).

May is also the month of the **Spring Fly-In** at the Winchester Regional Airport, featuring antique, home-built, and experimental planes. The end of the apple season in September is occasion for its own celebration: the **Apple Harvest Arts and Crafts Festival,** with square dancing and every kind of apple food imaginable the third weekend of the month. The **Old Town Farmer's Market** is held at the south end of the mall during growing season (roughly May–Oct.). Finally, Winchester's **Hot Air Balloon Festival,** 888/558-5567, www.hotairballoonfestival.com, takes place in mid-October at Historic Long Branch, an 1811 Greek Revival mansion in Millwood. Rides, launches, music, artisans, wine tasting are all part of the fun. Admission is $5 pp or $20 per car. To get there, take Rt. 624 (Red Gate Rd.) 10 miles east of White Post.

SHOPPING

At the north end of the mall, **Handworks,** 150 N. Loudoun St., 800/277-0184 or 540/662-3927, sells unusual and beautiful handicrafts from all over the world, including handcrafted wooden boxes from Poland, batik masks from Indonesia, and Peruvian carved gourds. World music and beads galore lead toward the Global Village tea-

room in back. Wrought iron decorates the porch of the **Colonial Art & Craft Shop,** 25 W. Piccadilly Street, 540/662-6513. This shop housed in an old mansion is the kind of place that comes to mind with the phrase "bull in a china shop," stocked from creaking floor to ceiling with porcelain, crystal, and other country gifts.

INFORMATION

The **Winchester/Frederick County Visitors Center,** 1360 S. Pleasant Valley Rd., Winchester, VA 22601, 800/662-1360 or 540/662-4135, fax 540/450-0099, email: cvb@winchesterva.org, www.winchesterva.org, occupies a former grist mill near a small park and lake. Open daily 9 A.M.–5 P.M., it has videos of the area and of Patsy Cline, a small shrine to the singer, and brochures of walking and driving tours. In the Kurtz Building near the downtown mall, the **Old Town Welcome Center,** Cameron and Boscawen, 540/722-6367, is more of a local museum, with exhibits on the valley's role in the Civil War and a gift shop. Open Mon.–Sat. 10 A.M.–5 P.M., Sun. noon–5 P.M.

NEAR WINCHESTER

Berryville

For a change of pace from the usual hotels, motels, and B&Bs, consider a spiritual stay at the **Holy Cross Abbey,** 901 Cool Spring Lane, 540/955-1425 or 540/955-3124, email: fruitcake@shen-tel.net, www.holycrossabbeybrryvlle.org, one of 17 working Trappist monasteries in the country. Members of the Cistercian Order of the Strict Observance, begun in France in 1098, live a quiet life on 1,200 acres in the rolling Blue Ridge foothills alongside the Shenandoah River. The monastery's main means of support is a bakery, where the monks find time, between their six daily services, to turn out 24,000 famous fruitcakes a year.

An elegant guesthouse located a short distance from the monastery can be rented by anyone interested in joining the monks in quietness and prayer. Retreats run Mon.–Fri. ($100–200 pp) or Fri.–Sun. ($75–100). Guests are welcome to join in the services, sung liturgy, and family-style meals. Reservations should be made as far in advance as possible. A gift shop and information center, open daily 8:30 A.M.–noon and 1:15–5 P.M., sells Cistercian publications and monastery products, including Trappist preserves, creamed honey, fudge, and bread.

To get there, follow Rt. 7 east from Berryville, turning left immediately before crossing the Shenandoah River onto Rt. 603, and watch for a sign on the right after one mile.

White Post

Eight miles south of Winchester at the intersection of US 522, US 340, and Rt. 277 looms **Dinosaur Land,** 540/869-2222, www.dinosaurland.com, a Jurassic-themed landmark that's been around for decades. Thirty-five dinosaur replicas, including all those tongue-tying names your kids know by heart—brontosaurus, stegosaurus, yaleosaurus, and saltoposuchus—stand next to a 60-foot shark, a 70-foot octopus, and a 20-foot cobra. Open daily Mar.–Dec. 9:30 A.M.–5 or 6:30 P.M.; $4 adults, $3 children 2–10.

In the same town but at the other end of the cultural spectrum is **L'Auberge Provençale,** P.O. Box 190, White Post, VA 22663, 800/638-1702 or 540/837-1375, fax 540/837-2004, email: cborel@shentel.net, www.laubergeprovencale.com. Innkeepers Alain and Celeste Borel have created a small, charming French country inn in the middle of the fields and pastures of the Shenandoah. Three buildings huddle near an expansive flower garden, full of tulips in the spring and sunflowers every fall. Both the *Washington Post* and *Discerning Traveler* have called it one of the most romantic inns in the country.

Alain, the French-born chef, draws regular visitors from as far as Washington, D.C., for a taste of his native Avignon in the dining rooms of the 18th-century stone manor house. Fresh ingredients from the gardens and local farmers add the final touch to five-course gourmet candlelight dinners featuring foie gras, smoked rabbit, and fresh Shenandoah trout—and that's just for appetizers. Breakfast is almost as much of a production: scones, salmon, poached eggs, and

© JULIAN SMITH

Dinosaur Land

croissants may all grace your plate. The four-diamond restaurant is open to visitors as well as guests for dinner Wed.–Sun., with a five-course meal including dessert for $67 pp.

Provençal fabrics, canopy beds, and fireplaces fill 10 guest rooms in the manor house, each with its own private garden view and entrance. Rooms with breakfast are $145–195 per night, with a suite available for $240. Three more rooms are available in the Villa La Campagnette, set on 18 wooded acres three miles from L'Auberge. This equally impressive spread, decorated like a Mediterranean villa, has a brick terrace next to a pool and outdoor Jacuzzi. Rooms here are $195–250.

Middletown

Antique stores and a curious mix of old and new houses line US 11, called Main Street as it passes through the center of Middletown. At number 7783 you'll find the **Wayside Inn,** 877/869-1797 or 540/869-1797, fax 540/869-6038, email: reservations@alongthewayside.com, www.alongthewayside.com, one of the oldest inns in the United States. It received its first guests in 1797, when it was Wilkerson's Tavern, and it later served as a stagecoach rest stop and waystation for soldiers from both sides of the Civil War. With the arrival of the automobile, it became America's first motor inn, regaining much of its antique charm during a restoration in the 1960s.

An antique parlor of a lobby welcomes guests with chiming clocks and brick-and-stone fireplaces. Antiques and books are everywhere, including a combination chess and cribbage board. The stately Colonial dining room of Larrick's Taverns dates to the 1720s, with lunch entrées for $8–10 and daily specials. Each of the 24 rooms has a distinct personality, and the hotel offers popular romantic escapes for honeymoons and anniversaries that include champagne, breakfast in bed, and a special late checkout. Rooms are $100–150.

Just south of the inn, the small, intimate **Wayside Theater,** 540/869-1776, email: info@waysidetheater.org, www.waysidetheater.org, began as a movie house in the 1940s before being converted with a stage in 1962. The second oldest professional theatre in Vir-

ginia, it's now under the management of a nonprofit community foundation, which has welcomed actors such as Susan Sarandon, Kathy Bates, and Stacy Keach. Tickets are $20–25 adults, $7.50–10 children under 17.

Housed in an old feed store, the **Route 11 Potato Chip Factory,** 7815 Main St., 800/294-7783 or 540/869-0104, is said to be the smallest of its kind in the country. Watch the spudmasters at work and sample the chips Fri. 10 A.M.–6 P.M., Sat. 9 A.M.–5 P.M.

Cedar Creek Battlefield

In the predawn mist of October 19, 1864, 21,000 Confederates under Lt. Gen. Jubal Early made a surprise attack on 32,000 sleeping Union troops. The Rebels soon had the larger force on the run to the north of Middletown, but Maj. Gen. Philip Sheridan, hearing the roar of cannons, managed to gallop from Winchester in time to rally his forces. The Federals pushed their opponents back to the south and eventually out of the valley altogether, signaling the end of Confederate military power in the Shenandoah. More than three times as many Confederate soldiers were killed or wounded as Union soldiers, whose ranks included Rutherford B. Hayes, William McKinley, and George Armstrong Custer. "Never since the world was created," wrote Capt. S.E. Howard of the 8th Vermont Infantry, "was such a crushing defeat turned into such a splendid victory as at Cedar Creek."

Today a **visitors center,** one mile south of Middletown, 888/628-1864 or 540/869-2064, www.cedarcreekbattlefield.org, is open Apr.–Oct. Mon.–Sat. 10 A.M.–4 P.M., Sun. 1–4 P.M.. It's run by a nonprofit organization, and a film on the battle is included in the $2 pp admission fee. The fields have changed little in the years since the battle, which is reenacted every year the weekend closest to October 19. More than 2,500 participants take part under the gaze of 15,000 spectators, who are allowed on the actual battlefield (prohibited in National Historical Parks).

Belle Grove Plantation, 540/869-2028, www.bellegrove.org, sits in the middle of the battlefield opposite the visitors center. Once one of the valley's most prestigious homes, it was built in 1794–1797 by Major Isaac Hite, Jr., with design help from Thomas Jefferson. Sheridan used the mansion as his headquarters for his devastating march down the valley and ended up burning many of the farm buildings. James and Dolley Madison later honeymooned here. A quilt and fabric shop fills the basement, and Colonial craft demonstrations are held in the smokehouse, icehouse, and blacksmith shops. Open Mar.–Oct. Mon.–Sat. 10 A.M.–3:15 P.M., Sun. 1–4:15 P.M.; $7 adults, $6 children 6–12.

The **Battle of Cedar Creek Campground,** 800/343-1562 or 540/869-1888, is 1.5 miles north of I-81 exit 298 on US 11. Sites costs $15–24 and include a pool, playground, recreation room, and laundry.

The Northern Valley

FRONT ROYAL

Called Hell Town during its frontier days, this riverside city is thought to have been unintentionally renamed by an exasperated colonial drill sergeant. His repeated orders for his troops to "front the royal oak" in the center of town (oaks were considered the royal tree of England) struck someone's fancy, and the name stuck. In the Civil War, Front Royal was captured in May 1862 by Stonewall Jackson with the help of spy Belle Boyd.

Today, a long bridge over the Shenandoah leads to tree-lined Royal Avenue (US 340). Turn left onto E. Main Street at the Warren County Courthouse to reach the Village Commons with its gazebo, big red caboose, and the town visitors center. Front Royal serves as the northern gateway to Shenandoah National Park and the Blue Ridge, which rises to the south of town.

Sights

A local chapter of the United Daughters of the Confederacy owns and operates the **Warren Rifles Confederate Museum,** 95 Chester St., 540/636-6982, containing a large collection of arms, uniforms, flags, pictures, and personal items that evoke the Civil War exploits of Stonewall Jackson, Mosby's Rangers, J.E.B. Stuart, and Robert E.

MATA HARI OF THE CONFEDERACY

B elle Boyd, the Confederacy's most colorful secret agent, was born in Martinsburg, Virginia in 1843 and reveled in attention from an early age. With the arrival of the Civil War, the vivacious young woman used her feminine charms and quick mind to coax military secrets from Union troops and pass them on to Confederate officers. By age 21, she had achieved a measure of infamy within Union forces: she had been reported 30 times, arrested six or seven, and thrown in jail twice. During one stay in Washington, D.C.'s Old Capital Prison, Boyd put intelligence messages in India rubber balls and threw them to an accomplice waiting outside her window.

Fellow Southern belles were shocked at Boyd's life of risk. She often traveled alone, meeting with officers from both sides in their private tents with little concern for decorum. Refusing to disguise her handwriting or encode her messages, the socialite spy found herself an international celebrity called "La Belle Rebelle" in France and "That Secesh Cleopatra" in New York.

Front Royal served as her main base of operations. When a Federal regiment under Gen. Nathaniel P. Banks occupied the city in May 1862, Boyd invited the officers to a ball and plied them for information. After her guests had fallen asleep, she reportedly rode 30 miles in the dead of night to pass the intelligence to Stonewall Jackson, who attacked the next morning and captured three-quarters of the Union forces.

After the war ended, Boyd tried her hand at acting and gave public lectures on her secretive adventures. In 1865, she published *Belle Boyd in Camp and Prison,* a dramatic tell-all of life as a female secret agent. She died in 1900 in Wisconsin.

Lee. Open Apr. 15–Oct. Mon.–Sat. 9 A.M.–4 P.M., Sun. noon–4 P.M.; $2 adults.

Learn more about life during the days of Belle Boyd, along with details about the spy herself, at the **Belle Boyd Cottage,** 101 Chester St., 540/636-1446. Open May–Oct. Mon.–Fri. 10 A.M.–3:30 P.M.; $2 adults, $1 children. There's an interesting **elephant mural** by nationally known artist Patricia Wondrow entitled *The Not So National Zoo* on the side of a barn at High and Jackson streets. To see more murals, head down High Street toward **Wondrow's gallery,** 540/636-8993, at the Main Street intersection, or take a peek inside Main Street Mill restaurant.

Accommodations

You can find rooms between $50–100 at the **Bluemont Inn,** 1525 N. Shenandoah Ave., 540/635-9447, fax 540/635-1991, and the **Scottish Inn,** 533 S. Royal Ave., 540/636-6168, fax 540/636-3120. The **Quality Inn,** 10 Commerce Ave., 540/635-3161, fax 540/635-6624, and the **Twi-Lite Motel,** 53 W. 14th St., 540/635-4148, are also in the same category, but offer outdoor pools as well.

Architecture is one highlight of the **Chester House B&B,** 43 Chester St., 800/621-0441, fax 540/636-8695, email: mail@chesterhouse.com, www.chesterhouse.com. The 1905 Georgian-style home sits amid two acres of lily ponds, garden mazes, and imported fountains and statuary. Three sitting rooms inside are warmed by fireplaces with marble mantels. The Carriage House out back has a kitchen, loft bedroom, and wide windows overlooking the gardens. Rooms are $95–125, and there's a suite for $135 and separate, two-story garden cottage built around 1905 for $210.

Innkeeper Susan O'Kelly runs the Edwardian mansion known as **Killahevlin,** 1401 North Royal Ave., 800/847-6132 or 540/636-7335, fax 540/636-8694, email: kllhvln@shentel.net, www.vairish.com, built by a local limestone baron on one of the highest perches in town. A strong Irish influence pervades, from the reproduction wallpaper to the private pub with oak bar and Irish beer on tap. The three "color" rooms (Green, White, and Raspberry) are $136–185, while

suites in the early-1900s Tower House out back, near the koi pool and gazebos, cost $235.

The Woodward House, 413 S. Royal Ave., 800/635-7011, fax 540/635-8217, email: woodhous@rma.edu, www.acountryhome.com, also boasts a pub, along with three rooms ($95) and five suites ($105–125).

Camping

Campers should head two miles south of town on US 340 to the **Front Royal/Washington D.C. West KOA,** 800/562-9114 or 540/635-2741, fax 540/635-4089, email: FrntRylKOA@aol.com. Campsites are $27 ($35 with full hookups), and 20 Kamping Kabins cost $47–56.

Food

Set in the old Proctor Biggs building next to the town park, the **Main Street Mill,** 500 E. Main St., 540/636-3123, serves sandwiches and burgers for around $5 and heartier entrées such as ribs, pork chops, and pastas for $8–13. Dine inside by the animal paintings or out on the porch. Open daily for lunch and dinner.

Schnitzel and wurst are the standbys of **Stadt Kaffe,** 300 E. Main St., 540/635-8300, run by local Teutonic transplant Elke Cafter. Vegetarians can enjoy delicious gulasch and Jaeger schnitzels, and there's plenty of German beer to go around. Open Mon.–Sat. for lunch ($4–10) and dinner ($10–15). The **14th Street Bistro,** 101 W. 14th St., 888/636-8414 or 540/636-8400, is a classy affair with a full bar and dancing. They serve lunch and dinner daily.

Next to the Royal Cinema sits **Sharon's Deli,** 117 E. Main St., 540/631-9171, a diner packed around noon for its great sandwiches. They offer breakfast and lunch in the $2–4 range Mon.–Sat. **Wynn's,** 219 E. Main St., 540/635-5956, is another popular breakfast and lunch spot open from 5 A.M. Tues.–Sat. **L Dee's Pancake House,** 522 E. Main St., 540/635-3791, offers "breakfast all day" starting at $2.

Recreation

Several local outfitters take advantage of the fact that one of Virginia's favorite rafting rivers flows practically through their backyard. Most operate campsites down the South Fork of the Shenandoah for overnight visitors during the floating season of March–November. Prices should include equipment, brief instruction, maps, and shuttle service.

The **Front Royal Canoe Co.,** 800/270-8808 or 540/635-5440, email: frcanoe@rma.edu, www.frontroyalcanoe.com, has day trips for $36–56 along with longer excursions of 2–3 days. Their full moon canoe trips ($28 pp) are popular, and they also rent canoes, kayaks, and rafts. In Bentonville, eight miles south on US 340, the **Downriver Canoe Company,** 884 Indian Hollow Rd., 800/338-1963 or 540/635-5526, fax 540/622-2656, email: somebody@downriver.com, www.downriver.com, has canoe trips for $37–44 pp on weekdays and $40–60 pp on weekends. Overnight trips start at $83.

Take a guided horseback ride with **Highlander Horses,** 5197 Reliance Rd., 540/636-4523, www.highlanderhorses.com, for $25–50 pp. They have year-round access to 200 acres of riding terrain. Reliance Rd. (Rt. 627) is off Rt. 532 north of town. A flight with **Blue Ridge Hot Air Balloons,** 5552 Milldale Hollow Rd., 877/RIDE-AIR (743-3247) or 540/622-6325 or 540/622-7800, email: balloon@rideair.com, www.rideair.com, will set you back $150 pp, but the views are wonderful (and the champagne toast afterward doesn't hurt).

Events

Front Royal is home to the **Virginia Wine and Mushroom Festival,** www.wineandmushroom.com, held the third Saturday of May. Contact the visitors center for more information. In early August, the **Warren County Fair,** 540/635-5827, brings a 4-H livestock auction, car show, music, rides, and pageants, and in late September the **Blue Ridge Oktoberfest & Chili Cookoff** welcomes in autumn.

Shopping

On summer weekends and holidays, the **Front Royal Antique and Flea Market,** 540/635-7336, is *the* place for assorted treasures, junk, and crafts spread among 100 booths. It's on the US 522 bypass between the Quality Inn and Rt.

55. Alternately, you can browse year-round through the antiques, pottery, crafts, and paintings in **Grandma Hazel's Attic,** 403 E. Main St., 540/622-2864, run by Hazel Van Wyen with a little help from Cricket the dog.

Information

The **Front Royal/Warren County Visitor Center,** 414 E. Main St., 800/338-2576 or 540/635-5788, fax 540/635-9758, email: visitfr@shentel.net, www.ci.front-royal.va.us, sits in the restored train station in the town park. They have a well-done walking-tour brochure and are open daily 9 A.M.–5 P.M.

Adventure Nearby

Opened to the public in 1939, **Skyline Caverns,** 800/296-4545 or 540/635-4545, www.skylinecaverns.com, were discovered a few years earlier by means of a giant sinkhole where the parking lot now sits. The highlight of these caves, otherwise overshadowed by their southern neighbors, are glittering calcite formations called anthodites. These delicate spikes are found in only one other cave in the United States (and there in much smaller quantities). They grow one inch every 7,000 years, either pure white or stained brown by iron oxide. Skyline Cavern's crop sprouted in a vacuum left by a receding underground pool.

Throughout the rest of the cave, high, smooth passages evoke slot canyons of the American southwest. Kids love the Skyline Arrow, an outdoor miniature train that crawls near the entrance. Open daily 9 A.M.–4 or 6:30 P.M., depending on season; $12 adults, $6 children 7–13. (Discount tickets are available at the Front Royal visitors center.)

One of the newest additions to Virginia's state park system, the **Raymond R. "Andy" Guest, Jr. Shenandoah River State Park,** 540/622-6840, email: shenandoahriver@dcr.state.va.us, www.dcr.state.va.us/parks/andygues.htm, encompasses 1,600 acres along the south fork of the river eight miles south of Front Royal, including 5.6 miles of river frontage. Open daily 8 A.M.–dusk, $2 per car ($3 on weekends).

Guided horseback rides are offered through

Indian Hollow Stables, 800/270-8808 or 540/635-5440, www.frontroyalcanoe.com/ horse.htm, starting at $14 pp for a half-hour ride ($18 on weekends). Their "Saddles & Paddles" package combines riding with canoeing.

STRASBURG

One of the earliest settlements in the valley, Strasburg has been a crafts center since being chartered in 1761. A tradition of earthen and stoneware pottery was once manifest in six shops going at once in a section called Pot Town. Antiques are now the main draw of the self-proclaimed "Antiques Capital of Virginia," with local ceramics running a close second.

Try any of the dozen or so shops in town for furniture, clothing, folk art, and rugs, including **Vilnis and Company Antiques,** 329 N. Massanutten St. (US 11 and US 55), 540/465-4405, **Green Acres Antiques,** 131 N. Massanutten St., 540/465-4702, and **Wayside Of Virginia,** 132 N. Massanutten St., 540/465-4650. For a larger-scale approach, stop by the 65,000-square foot **Great Strasburg Emporium,** 160 N. Massanutten St., 540/465-3711, one of the largest antiques centers in the state. It consists of 100 dealers sharing an old former silk mill, and it's open year-round.

WEST OF THE INTERSTATE

Bryce Resort

Only a few miles from the West Virginia border, this small resort features two lifts and eight ski slopes ranging from beginner to expert. Nearly 9,000 square feet were added to the lodge in 1997, where lift tickets sell for $28–38 pp per day, with half days for $18–30. The ski instruction program, developed by German National certified instructor Horst Locher, start with children as young as four. Night skiing ($15–20), ski rentals, and snowboarding are all options. In the summer, an 18-hole, par 71 golf course enjoys mountain views and all the amenities. Fuests can also choose from horseback riding, mountain biking, tennis, grass skiing, and boating in Lake Laura.

To get there, take I-81 exit 273 onto Rt. 263 and head 11 miles to the entrance on the right. For more information on the resort and lodging options, contact 800/821-1444 or 540/856-2121, fax 540/856-8567, email: bryce@bryceresort.com, www.bryceresort.com.

Orkney Springs

Five weekends between late May and the end of August are filled with symphony, big band, jazz, and folk music during the **Shenandoah Valley Music Festival** in this tiny town in the hills. A benefit ball kicks things off, and ice cream socials and special children's concerts are part of the program. Tickets are $15–18 for individual events for both reserved seating (on the lawn and in the open-air pavilion) and general admission, available at the gate or from the festival office in Woodstock, 102 N. Main St., 800/459-3396 or 540/459-3396, fax 540/459-3730, email: svmf@shentel.net, www.musicfest.org.

The concerts have been held since the early 1960s at the Shrine Mountain Retreat and Conference Center, a venerable mineral springs resort dating to the turn of the 20th century. The town is 15 miles west of I-81 exit 273 via Rt. 263.

NEW MARKET AND VICINITY

Two major Indian pathways gave this spot on the upper North Fork of the Shenandoah its first official name—Cross Roads. The first inhabitants, the Senedo tribe, were wiped out by the Catawbas from the south when their paths crossed around 1700. In 1796, the town of New Market was established, named after the city in England with the famous racetrack (mirrored in one that once stood here to the west of the settlement). A famous Civil War battle nearby left the town with memories of cannons in the rain and a three-inch shell hole in a post at the intersection of Breckinridge Lane and Congress Street (US 11 through town).

Accommodations

The **Blue Ridge Inn,** 2251 Old Valley Pike, 540/740-4136, fax 540/740-3148, has more character than most motels with rooms for around

$85 in high season. It's one mile north of I-81 exit 264, along with a **Budget Inn,** 2192 Old Valley Pike, 540/740-3105, fax 540/740-3108 ($50–70). At the same exit, you'll find a **Quality Inn Shenandoah Valley,** 162 W. Old Cross Rd., 800/228-5151 or 540/740-3141, fax 540/740-3250, offering a pool and miniature golf ($60–85).

Dating to the end of the 18th century, the **Red Shutter Farmhouse B&B,** 17917 Farmhouse Ln., 540/740-4281, fax 540/740-4661, email: geonita@shentel.net, sits on 20 acres off Rt. 793 on the way to Endless Caverns. Rooms and suites are $65–78, and there's a veranda with rocking chairs. The **Jacob Swartz House,** 574 Juggard Rd., 877/740-9208 or 540/740-9208, email: jshouse@shentel.net, www.shenwebworks.com/jshouse, can put up guests in a two-bedroom cottage with a living room, full kitchen, woodburning stove, and screened porch set along a river bluff. Rates start at $125 per night, including full breakfast. (Call for exact directions.)

The **Cross Roads Inn Bed & Breakfast,** 9222 John Sevier Rd., 540/740-4157, fax 540/740-4255, email: freisitz@shentel.net, www.crossroadsinnva.com, was built in 1925 for Claude Hoover, one of the driving forces behind Shenandoah National Park. The late Victorian home is run by an Austrian couple who serve afternoon tea with authentic homemade apple strudel. Six rooms range from inexpensive to expensive and include use of an outdoor Jacuzzi. Room prices range from $65 for the Hideaway to $100 for Miss Mamie's Room or the Rose Room. It's at the intersection of Rt. 211 to Luray and John Sevier Road, just east of Rt. 11 north.

Camping

Campsites at the **Harrisonburg-New Market KOA,** 3.3 miles east on Rt. 608 from I-81 exit 257, 540/896-8929, are $19–28 each, and Kabins are $36. The **Rancho Campground,** 2.1 miles south on US 11 from I-81 exit 264, 540/740-8313, has 65 sites for $19 each.

Food

The **Battlefield Restaurant,** 9403 S. Congress St., 540/740-9400, serves dependable, inexpensive fare, with homemade soups and sandwiches like Googy's Grilled Chicken around $3–5, and steaks and other entrées for $8–12. Open Mon.–Sat. 11 A.M.–9 P.M. Across the street sits **The Coffee Mouse,** 9428 S. Congress St., 540/740-2888, a cute espresso bar and Internet café.

With a real 1950s-diner feel, the **Southern Kitchen,** 9579 S. Congress St., 540/740-3514, has sandwiches for $3–6 and dinners for around $10 (open daily 7 A.M.–9 or 10 P.M. Fri. and Sat.). A statue of the man himself marks the **Johnny Appleseed Restaurant** of the Quality Inn Shenandoah Valley, serving homestyle food daily 6:30 A.M.–10 P.M., with complimentary apple fritters at every meal.

Shopping

A handful of antique stores lines Congress Street within a few blocks of the center of town at Old Cross Road, stocking everything from pottery to Civil War relics. **New Market Antiques,** 9298 S. Congress St., 540/740-4446; **Benny Long's Antiques,** 9386 S. Congress St., 540/740-3512; or **Packrat Willy's,** 9394 S. Congress St., 540/740-4300, are all chock full of collectibles, jewelry, coins, and Civil War relics.

Shenandoah Valley Crafts & Gifts, 9365 N. Congress St., 540/740-3899, sells quilts, baskets, and Virginia hams. Farther down the street is **Paper Treasures,** 9595 S. Congress St., 540/740-3135, a captivating place to spend hours browsing among thousands of used books, old comics, records, prints, and magazines dating to the 19th century. At the intersection of US 11 (Congress St.) and Rt. 793 toward Endless Carvens is **Art Studio Pottery,** 540/896-4400, chock full of the works of Joan Cordner and other regional ceramic artists.

Information

Just off I-81 exit 264, the **Shenadoah Valley Visitor Center,** 277 W. Old Cross Rd., 877/847-4878 or 540/740-3132, is open daily 9 A.M.–5 P.M.

New Market Battlefield Historical Park

On May 15, 1864, one of the last Confederate victories in the valley featured a famous charge by 257 VMI cadets against a line of Union artillery under Maj. Gen. Franz Sigel. The well-preserved

VMI Cadets Thomas G. Jefferson (left) and Moses Ezekiel (right) were among those killed at New Market Battlefield.

struction of the valley railroad and opened to the public in 1922. They're the only ones in the state with an elevator, and they feature tempting flowstone slabs called the Bacon Formations. Open daily 9 A.M.–5 P.M.; $13.50 adults, $6 children, 540/477-3115. **American Celebrations on Parade,** 540/477-4300, a 40,000-square-foot exhibit of 50 years worth of parade floats from around the country, can be visited for a separate admission ($8 adults, $6 children 6–14) or as part of a discounted package ($17.50 adults, $7 children).

battlefield is easily understood and absorbing, whether or not you think children in war is something worth celebrating.

Bypass the private museum on your left to reach the Hall of Valor, run by a nonprofit organization under the authority of VMI. Inside is a visitors center, 540/740-3101, and a museum dedicated to the cadets. Two short films give some background on Stonewall Jackson's Valley Campaign and the cadets themselves.

Pick up a walking-tour brochure and step outside to begin the mile-long loop trail. Imagine yourself as one of the students—as young as 15—your spirits high at being called to defend your home, then drenched by four days' march in the rain. A headlong charge takes you through the buildings of the Bushong farm, where the terrified family hides in the basement, and across the mud-clogged Field of Lost Shoes toward the deafening thunder of the Union guns.

A 200-foot vista over the peaceful Shenandoah River marks where the trail turns back. Ten cadets died in the process of capturing one cannon, an event honored in a formal ceremony every May 15 at VMI. The costumed reenactment of the battle and the cadets' charge is one of the oldest in the country, held around the same date. Open daily 9 A.M.–5 P.M.; $5 adults, $2 children 6–15.

Shenandoah Caverns

North of New Market (I-81 exit 269), these caverns were unearthed in 1884 during the con-

Endless Caverns

The largest billboard in the eastern United States points off I-81 toward this serpentine network of passages and tunnels discovered in 1879 by two boys hunting a rabbit. Five miles have been mapped so far, with no end in sight, giving Endless Caverns, 540/896-2283, the most untamed feel of Virginia's caves. Refreshments are available in the 1920s limestone lodge, and 100 campsites are available with full hookups. Open daily 9 A.M.–4 or 7 P.M., depending on season; $12 adults, $6 children 3–12.

LURAY

The seat of Page County is known for what it's near: the central entrance for Shenandoah National Park and the most impressive caverns in the east. The US 211 Bypass serves as Main Street, divided into east and west at Broad Street (US 340).

Luray Caverns

By far the most impressive of the valley's commercial caves, this U.S. Registered Natural Landmark encloses the most-visited caverns in the East. From the start, the ceilings bristle, the floors bulge, and the walls flow in a scale that makes you wish the tour lasted longer than an hour. Fifty-foot drapery is pulled so thin that some parts are translucent; near pure white calcite columns

SHENANDOAH AREA WINERIES

Deer Meadow Vineyard
540/877-1919 or 800/653-6632
Near Winchester; Rt. 629 off Rt. 608, 6.5 miles south of US 50/US 55 intersection

Guilford Ridge Vineyard
540/778-3853
Near Luray; Rt. 632 off 211 south of town

Landwirt Vineyard
540/833-6000
Near Harrisonburg; I-81 exit 257, US 11 south two miles, Rt. 806 west 3.3. miles

North Mountain Vineyard & Winery
540/436-9463
Near Maurertown; Rt. 655 south of Strasburg

Peaks of Otter Winery
540/586-3707
Near Bedford; Rt. 680 near Penick's Mill off Rt. 43
Known for fruit wines.

Shenandoah Vineyards
540/984-8699
Near Edinburg; I-81 exit 279 to Stoney Creek Rd. to Rt. 675 (S. Ox Rd.)

Rockbridge Vineyard
540/377-6204
Near Raphine; Rt. 606 off I-81 exit 205

and a 170-ton fallen stalactite the size of a school bus are other highlights. Dream Lake, 2,500 feet square, is only 1–6 inches deep.

The most famous feature of Luray Caverns, though, is only half natural: a "stalacpipe organ," which produces tones with electronically controlled rubber mallets striking stalactites to produce sounds oddly like those of a marimba. Covering 312 acres, the organ is listed in the Guinness Book of World Records as the largest natural instrument in the world.

Back out in the fresh air is an Antique Carriage and Car Museum, with 140 models as old as 1625 (included in admission). No cavern resort

complex would be complete without a garden maze ($5 adults, $4 children), gas station, airport, restaurant, golf course, and gift shop, selling everything from cheap pottery to handcuffs. Open daily 9 A.M.–4 to 7 P.M., depending on season; $14 adults, $6 children 7–13, 540/743-6551, www.luraycaverns.com.

Other Diversions and Recreation

The **Luray Reptile Center, Dinosaur Park and Petting Zoo,** 540/743-4113, is home to one of Virginia's largest scaly collections, both extinct and living. Cobras, alligators, and 20-foot pythons coexist with tropical birds and a monkey along Rt. 211 half a mile west of town, with a petting zoo for the children and herpetophobes. Open May–Oct. daily 10 A.M.–5 P.M. (weekends only Nov.–Apr.); $5.50 adults, $4.50 children 3–12. A carillon of 47 bells fills the **Luray Singing Tower** on West Main Street opposite the caverns. Free live concerts are given in the spring and fall Saturday and Sunday at 2 P.M. and during the summer on Tuesday, Thursday, Saturday, and Sunday at 8 P.M.

The South Fork of the Shenandoah from Luray to Front Royal is known for great bass fishing, packing the placid waters with canoes, tubes, and private boats on busy weekend afternoons from spring to fall. **Shenandoah River Outfitters, Inc.,** 6502 S. Page Valley Rd. (Rt. 684), 800/622-6632 or 540/843-0574, email: canoes@shenandoah-river.com, www.shenandoah-river.com, offers rentals and trips along the river 10 miles northwest of town. White-water canoe classes start at $48 for a one-day course for two people, or you can opt for an eight-mile flatwater float for the same price. Tube rentals and cookouts are only two of the other options. They also operate fully furnished cabins ($90–140 per night) and campgrounds ($6 pp) along the way.

Accommodations

Rooms at the nearly identical **Luray Caverns Motel East,** 831 W. Main St., 540/743-4531, and **Luray Caverns Motel West,** US 211 W, 540/743-4536, range from $62–72. **The Mimslyn,** 401 W. Main St., 800/296-5105 or

THE SHENANDOAH

540/743-5105, fax 540/743-2632, email: mimslyn@shentel.net, www.svta.org/mimslyn, opened in 1931 on top of a commanding hill just outside the center of town. The "Grand Old Inn of Virginia" sits amid 14 acres of lawns and gardens overlooked by a terrace and solarium. Through the front doors, a red carpet flows down the central staircase. An antique and art gallery houses works by Virginia artist P. Buckley Moss. Forty-nine rooms and suites are $96–107.

A long driveway leaves the bustle of the US 11/Broad Street intersection, passing horses grazing in fenced pastures, to reach **The Ruffner House B&B,** 440 Ruffner House Rd., 800/969-7855 or 540/743-7855, email: info@ruffner-house.com, www.ruffnerhouse.com. Built in 1840 to replace an original 1739 log cabin, the spacious house features high ceilings, wide hallways, and four gigantic guest rooms. Outside are gardens and a pool. Four rooms are $130, including afternoon tea and breakfast. Rooms in **The Cardinal Inn,** 1005 E. Main St., 540/743-5010, fax 540/743-3407, are $70–100, and the hotel has a porch area and a view of the mountains.

The **Woodruff Collection of Victorian Inns,** 540/743-1494, fax 540/743-1722, email: woodruffbnb@rica.net, www.woodruffinns.com, is headquartered in **The Victorian Inn,** 138 E. Main St., but the 1885 Fantasy Victorian building is only the beginning; there's also **The Woodruff House,** an 1882 Fairytale Victorian; **The Victorian Rose,** an 1890 French Country Victorian; and **The Shenandoah River,** a grouping of several riverfront cottages. Rates range from $100–300, and amenities include outdoor garden hot tubs, flower gardens, Jacuzzis, and private balconies.

Head five miles east on the US 211 bypass to reach **The Cabins at Brookside,** 2978 US 211E, 800/299-2655 or 540/743-5698, email: brookside@rica.net, www.brooksidecabins.com, in the heart of the rich farmlands of the Shenandoah foothills. Eight rooms fill private log cabins, formerly a 1940s-era filling station, set next to a rushing stream. The cabins range in price from $80–195 per night, and most have fireplaces and

kitchens but no phones or TVs (honeymoon cabins have hot tubs). The nearby **Brookside Restaurant** will do for guests who don't want to make the trek back into town.

Camping

Yogi Bear's Jellystone Park, 800/420-6679 or 540/743-4002, is off Rt. 211 three miles east of town. Campsites are $26–$35, and cabins range from $54 for "bear bones" to $105 for "comfort." On hand are a stocked fishing pond, pool, camp store, and laundromat. **The Country Waye RV Resort,** 3402 Kimball Rd., 888/765-7222, offers unfurnished cabins for $30–35 and 78 campsites for $19–27. All the amenities are included: pool, hot tub, game room, laundry, and even an Internet café. Maintained by the National Forest, **Camp Roosevelt** has 10 basic sites for $9 each, 8.5 miles northwest of Luray on Rt. 675.

Food

Virginia wines and a view of the Massanutten Mountains are two reasons to stop by the **Parkhurst Restaurant,** 540/743-6009, on Rt. 211 2.5 miles west of the caverns. The menu covers all the bases—chicken, pasta, fish, and beef—with a cozy Colonial flair, making reservations for dinner a good idea. Open daily for lunch and dinner.

Events

Luray's **Mayfest,** the third Saturday of May, fills the streets with pony and llama rides, antique dealers, and food vendors. A traditional maypole dance and historic home tours are also part of the festivities. Around Columbus Day in October, the **Page County Heritage Festival** has been known for arts and crafts since 1969.

Information

For information on either festival and any other activities in town, contact the **Luray-Page County Chamber of Commerce,** 46 E. Main St., 888/743-3915 or 540/743-3915/4530, email: pagecofc@shentel.net, www.luraypage.com. It also operates a visitors center, open daily 9 A.M.–5 P.M.

Shenandoah National Park

One of the country's most popular national parks protects nearly 300 square miles of the Appalachian Mountains, from some 60 rough-edged peaks to all the stream-filled nooks and wildflower crannies in between. Zipping it all together is the Skyline Drive, stretching for 105 miles along ridgetops from Front Royal to Waynesboro. Probably the most beautiful drive in the eastern United States, this meandering byway continues as the Blue Ridge Parkway south toward North Carolina and the Smoky Mountains.

Few visitors venture far off the road, either because they're content with the countless overlooks or because they're in a hurry to move on. Those who do leave their cars discover gushing spring waterfalls, quiet oak glades, and mountaintop views that beat anything available from the asphalt. It may take some effort to put the miles between you and the high-season crowds, but you won't be disappointed.

All mileposts are measured from 0 at Front Royal.

HISTORY

The idea of protecting a large swath of Virginia's mountains had been around since the turn of the 20th century, but it took Governor Harry Byrd's creations of a state conservation and development commission in 1926 to get the ball rolling. At the time, the region's soil and forests were suffering so much as the result of farming that many doubted whether the ecosystem (though the word had not yet been coined) could survive. Without federal money to buy land, the Virginia State legislature passed an act that required landowners to sell their plots within 10 years. The project received the enthusiastic support of President Hoover, who spent every moment he could spare at a fishing camp on the upper Rapidan River within the borders of the proposed park.

Ground was broken for the Skyline Drive in 1931, supposedly after Hoover got the idea during a horseback ride along the crest of the moun-

tains. Local farmers provided the labor in exchange for money from drought-relief funds, while Franklin Delano Roosevelt's Civilian Conservation Corps pitched in with the construction of scenic overlooks, picnic areas, and landscaping. Four thousand mountain residents had found somewhere else to live by the time the park was dedicated in 1936. When the road was finished three years later, the land was slowly allowed to return to its natural state—so much so that in 1976 Congress declared two-fifths of the park (more than 79,000 acres) wilderness.

HABITATS

Flora

With elevations ranging from 600 feet at the northern entrance to more than 4,000 feet on mountain peaks, Shenandoah National Park encloses mostly mature deciduous forest. Close to 100 tree species and 47 species of mosses and ferns blanket the slopes. A chestnut blight near the turn of the 20th century wiped out most of that native species, leaving oak and hickory the most common trees in the park. Pines and scrub oak grow on drier slopes, while ash and basswood line many streams. Rhododendrons and azaleas fill the understory.

At the right time of year, meadows sparkle with wildflowers and berries—especially Big Meadows, which are thought to have been burned clear by Native Americans looking to attract game and create more room for berry bushes. Higher elevations help the spring blossoms of violets, chickweeds, and bloodroots persist after summer heat has claimed the Piedmont. Periwinkles and columbines flower in April, followed by gaudy yellow cowslips in May and black-eyed Susans and Queen Anne's lace in August.

Fauna

Lucky hikers may spot a bobcat or wild turkey among the trees, while unlucky ones may have a too-close encounter with a timber rattler or copperhead. At dawn and dusk, white-tailed deer

THE APPALACHIAN TRAIL

North America's most famous footpath winds 2,155 miles from Maine to Georgia, connecting Appalachian ridges and river valleys, pristine wilderness and stoplight suburbia like an enormous green zipper. All but 3 percent of the greenway is protected by government-owned land or private rights-of-way; the U.S. Forest Service administers 850 miles, and 14 states oversee another 420 miles.

As classic as it is, the AT isn't a historic trail. The "impossible" idea began in 1921 as a proposal by Massachusetts regional planner Benton MacKaye, who envisioned it as an escape for residents of the increasingly populated east. (Even today, close to two-thirds of the population of the U.S. lives within 500 miles of the trail.) The Appalachian Trail Conference (ATC), a loose organization of local hiking clubs, was formed in 1925. Thanks to its unpaid efforts, the first continuous trail opened in 1937, but various highways, extreme weather, and the privations of World War II almost buried the project. In the early 1950s, the entire pathway was relocated, cleared, and marked, and in 1968 it was declared the nation's first National Scenic Trail (akin to a linear National Park, but without the funding).

At its northern end, the trail starts at the peak of Maine's Mt. Katahdin (5,267 feet), winding its most isolated miles through the Maine backwoods. From

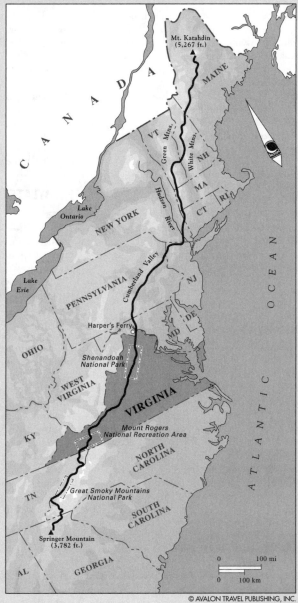

there it passes through the White Mountains of New Hampshire and the Green Mountains of Vermont before clipping off the western ends of Massachusetts and Connecticut. Southern New York state, where the trail crosses the Hudson River, marks the beginning of the trail's least rural section. Northern New Jersey is next, followed by the Cumberland Valley in eastern Pennsylvania. Soon the ATC headquarters in Harper's Ferry, West Virginia, comes into sight, where through-hikers sign a logbook and have their pictures taken, foot-weary but smiling.

Virginia contains one-quarter of the AT and some of its most breathtaking scenery. Winding down around the Skyline Drive through Shenandoah National Park, the trail then steers west to touch the West Virginia line. It crosses the Blue Ridge Parkway only twice on its way through some of the state's most beautiful wilderness, including the Mt. Rogers National Recreation Area. South of Virginia, the AT follows the state line between Tennessee and North Carolina on its way through the rugged undulations of the Great Smoky Mountains National Park. The finish line (or starting point, if you're heading north) comes at the peak of Springer Mountain (3,782 feet), in Georgia's Chattahoochee National Forest. White painted blazes mark the path the entire way, doubled at turns and junctions.

Through-hiking, as difficult and expensive as it is (4–6 months and thousands of dollars each way), has become a way of life for some people ever since Early Shaffer first hiked the entire length of the trail in 1948. Hikers ranging from a six-year-old to octogenarians have completed the journey, including a blind man led by his seeing-eye dog. Decades of experience in regulating the trail have resulted in a time-proven set of regulations and strong suggestions. No motorized traffic, horses, or pack animals are allowed on the trail, and dogs must be on a leash (they're prohibited in the Smokies, and discouraged in general). Stay on the trail,

since much of the surrounding land is private, and leave no trace; camp at established sites and build no campfires. Overnight camping permits are necessary in the two national parks. Try not to hike alone because solitary travelers have met with harassment and worse.

Information

Two organizations serve as information clearinghouses and administrative centers for the Appalachian Trail. The 5,500-member **Potomac Appalachian Trail Club,** 118 Park St. SE, Vienna, VA 22180, 703/242-0315 (242-0965 for a weekly recorded message on hikes and other activities), email: info@patc.net, www.patc.net, concentrates on the 200 miles of trail from Pennsylvania to Virginia. It maintains 80 percent of the trails in Shenandoah National Park, along with huts and cabins along the AT. Each primitive cabin in the park (Corbin, Doyle, Jones Mountain, Pocosin, Range View, Rock Spring, and Schairer) holds 8–14 people and costs $15–20 weeknights and $25–40 weekends and holidays. Membership is $30 per year for individuals, $35 per couple, and includes a subscription to the monthly newsletter, the *Potomac Appalachian*. Dozens of maps and guidebooks are also available.

The **Appalachian Trail Conference,** 799 Washington St., P.O. Box 807, Harpers Ferry, WV 25425, 304/535-6331, fax 304/535-2667, email: info@atconf.org, www.atconf.org, works to maintain the trail and to preserve the natural habitats and inhabitants of the surrounding buffer zone. Membership is $30 pp per year and comes with a year's subscription to *Appalachian Trailway News* and discounts in their Ultimate Trail Store. Its booklist includes guidebooks and maps for different sections of the trail, the *AT Thru-hikers' Companion,* and the *AT Data Book,* updated yearly. Other volumes cover natural history, hikers' memoirs, geology, and history of the trail.

congregate in open areas, particularly Big Meadows, browsing on tender plants until spooked by a car or breeze.

Shenandoah National Park has one of the highest densities of black bears of any park in the country—about one per square mile. It's rare to see more than paw prints or scat, though, unless you leave your empty tuna cans outside the tent at night. A few colonies of beavers live along the Thornton and Rapidan rivers.

Two hundred species of birds include permanent residents such as the barred owl and ruffed grouse. Migratory woodcocks arrive in the early spring, while warblers, thrushes, tanagers, and flycatchers move in during the summer. A hawk or six-foot turkey vulture circling the updrafts is a common sight along the Skyline Drive. Virginia's first breeding pair of peregrine falcons in 40 years was found nesting in the park in 1994.

ACCESS

Shenandoah National Park is divided into three sections by roads bisecting the Skyline Drive. The Northern District stretches from the entrance station at Front Royal (US 340, milepost 0) to Thornton Gap (mile 31.5), where US 221 connects Luray to the Piedmont. The Central District continues south to Swift Run Gap (mile 65.5), where US 33 crosses the park as it runs between Harrisonburg and Charlottesville. Rockfish Gap (mile 104.6) marks the boundary of the Southern District and the Skyline Drive, with access to I-64 and US 250.

Each entrance has an information booth where you can pay your admission fee and receive a map of the park and a copy of *Shenandoah Overlook* magazine. Various hiking trails enter the park from the base of the mountains on either side, often continuing as far as the crest and the Skyline Drive.

Fees

Shenandoah National Park's early years—when it cost 25 cents to enter and $1 for an annual pass—are long gone. In the mid-1990s, national park fees were raised throughout the country in an effort to make up for chronic underfunding and

to direct more dollars back into the parks. Today, a pass (good for seven consecutive days) costs $10 per car and $5 per pedestrian or bicyclist.

A year-long Shenandoah Passport is now $20, and a Golden Eagle Passport—good at any national park for a year—is $50. U.S. citizens over age 62 can buy a Golden Age Passport ($10) for lifetime access to any national park, and visitors with disabilities can receive free Golden Access Passports with similar privileges. Fees in all national parks are suspended on August 25 for Founders Day, celebrating the establishment of the National Park Service.

When To Go

Lying only 72 miles from Washington, D.C. can seem a curse on weekends and holidays in the summer and fall, when traffic on the Skyline Drive crawls along at well below the speed limit and RVs seem to jam every turnoff. This also happens to be the time when haze from power plants in the Ohio Valley can almost obscure the view. For the height of the fall foliage display, it may be necessary to make accommodation reservations as much as one year in advance.

The best time to avoid the two million people who visit per year, then, while still getting the view, vegetation, and wildlife you came for, is in the spring and on weekdays during the summer and fall. In the winter, most facilities shut down, staffing is reduced to a minimum, and parts of the Skyline Drive are often closed due to inclement weather. You'll have most of the park to yourself, which can be a magical experience if you're prepared. Bring a full tank of gas, tire chains or snow tires, water, and warm clothing—even for a drive.

HIKING

Close to 500 miles of trails crisscross the Shenandoah. City softies beware: they're usually uphill or downhill, and occasionally precipitous. More than a dozen waterfalls accessible only on foot are a highlight of any sweaty ramble. Remnants of early settlements are visible in crumbling walls and chimneys and mossy cemeteries hidden in the underbrush.

Each visitors center has free maps of each of the

112 trails, along with Potomac Appalacian Trail Club (PATC) topographical maps and a detailed one-sheet map of the entire park published by Trails Illustrated. Various trail guides are available at the bookstore in the park headquarters building near Luray. **Pets** are allowed on most trails, as long as they're on leashes (ask at the visitors centers which trails are off-limits). **Bicycles** are only allowed on Skyline Drive and other paved areas.

A 101-mile segment of the **Appalachian Trail** threads its way down the Skyline Drive, making it ideal for short hikes as it crosses and re-crosses the road. The trail to **Old Rag Mountain** leaves a parking lot off Rt. 231 between Sperryville and Madison, south of US 221 to the east of the park. The 7.2-mile (roundtrip) trail winds up, over, and around a huge jumble of granite boulders to the peak (3,291 feet), dotted with water-filled depressions called "buzzard baths." As you enjoy the view, think about the fact that the rock you're standing on is considered some of the oldest exposed rock on the East Coast—around 1.1 billion years old.

An easy self-guided nature walk called the **Traces Nature Trail** starts at mile 22.2, passing old settlements and mature oak forest for 1.7 miles roundtrip. Another short self-guided trail, the **Stony Man Nature Trail**, climbs the second-highest peak in the park from mile 41.7.

Just south of Skyland Lodge, you'll find the trail to **White Oak Canyon** (mile 42.6), a spectacular hike down a steep gorge past six waterfalls ranging from 35–85 feet. The 1,000-foot climb gets harder the farther down you go, but there are campsites at the bottom near the town of Syria. The 1.2-mile **Limberlost Trail** also leaves from Skyland, heading past centuries-old hemlocks and white oaks. A crushed-stone walkway makes it the first and only fully accessible trail in the park.

A steep path leaves from Hawksbill Gap (mile 45.6) to the top of **Hawksbill Mountain** (4,049 feet), the highest point in the park. Climbing 1,557 feet in less than one mile, the trail crosses a heavily logged area to reach an observation tower at the peak (a great spot to watch hawks). Sharing the same trailhead is the track to **Cedar Run Falls,** 3.5 miles roundtrip.

Near milepost 51 spreads **Big Meadows,** the largest treeless area in the park—150 acres of fields and wetlands thought to be the result of an ancient fire, either from lightning or the hand of man. This is one of the most popular destinations along the Skyline Drive, offering various visitor facilities and a good chance of spotting herds of deer unimpressed by cars or people. Three trails lead to different waterfalls, including the popular Dark Hollow Falls, a 70-foot flow over green volcanic stone (1.4 miles roundtrip). Alternately, head down a 1.8-mile self-guided nature trail or the half-mile path to Big Meadows Swamp, filled with wildflowers in the spring.

At mile 52.5, the **Mill Prong Trail** leads to Camp Hoover, the former president's unofficial weekend White House donated to the park in 1933. At the South River Picnic Area (mile 62.8), a trail leads to **South River Falls,** the third highest in the park at the head of a steep gorge. The moderate hike climbs 850 feet in 2.6 miles roundtrip. Near mile 90, the 10-mile **Riprap Hollow Trail** offers not only great views but also one of the park's largest swimming holes.

OTHER RECREATION

Park staff offer various interpretive programs throughout the spring, summer, and fall. Campfire talks on the park's cultural background, naturalist-led hikes, and wildflower identification walks are only a few of the possibilities for getting under the skin of the park. Schedules are posted in **Shenandoah Overlook** and on bulletin boards at visitor centers and lodges.

Visitors interested in fishing can pursue brook trout in dozens of short, steep streams running the length of the park. Only artificial lures are allowed, and some streams are under catch-and-release regulations. Pick up a fishing brochure and a list of streams at any visitors center or park headquarters. Skyland Stables at Skyland Lodge offers the only opportunity for horseback riding in the park—down a handful of yellow-blazed trails. Even if you don't get out of your car, 75 official scenic overlooks the length of the Skyline Drive are more than enough to fill an entire day.

the Blue Ridge mountains

© JULIAN SMITH

ACCOMMODATIONS, CAMPING, AND SERVICES

Information and reservations for Big Meadows Lodge, Skyland Lodge, and the Lewis Mountain Cabins can be had from **ARAMARK,** P.O. Box 727, Luray, VA 22835, 800/778-2851 or 540/743-5108, www.visitshenandoah.com. Prices are highest in October, and a few different packages are available; the Blue Ridge Package, for example, includes lodging, dinner, and breakfast for two people for two nights for $269. Gasoline, oil, air, water, groceries, and camping supplies are available at all three waysides (Elkwallow, Big Meadow, and Loft Mountain).

The park's four main campgrounds (Dundo at mile 83.7 is four groups only) are open spring through fall and feature roomy tent, trailer, and RV sites (no water or electric hookups) with picnic tables and grills for $12–14. The Potomac Appalachian Trail Club maintains six primitive cabins with mattresses and pit toilets along the Appalachian Trail; contact them at 118 Park St. SE, Vienna, VA 22180, 703/242-0315 or 703/242-0965, email: info@patc.net, www .patc.net, for more information. Backcountry

camping is free, but you'll need a permit from one of the visitors centers, entrance stations, or park headquarters (also available by mail). Most facilities are open from March or April to October or November, so call ahead if you plan to visit at either end of the season.

Starting from Front Royal, the **Matthews Arm Campground** at mile 22.1 has 179 sites and is near the trailhead for Overall Run Falls, the tallest waterfall in the park. **Elkwallow Wayside** (mile 24.1) has a restaurant, snack bar, grocery store, gas station, and gift shop. At **Thornton Gap** (mile 31.5), the Panorama Restaurant, serves breakfast and lunch daily. **Skyland Lodge** began as Stoneyman Camp in 1894. At 3,680 feet it's the highest point on Skyline Drive (mile 41.8), which means great views from most of the 117 rooms. "Rustic" cabin rooms are $52–105, motel-style rooms in the main lodge range from $79–122, and suites are $113–177. None have phones, but some have TVs. The glass-walled restaurant lets you enjoy steaks, trout, and other basic fare while looking out over the forest, and the Tap Room has live entertainment on summer nights. Guided horseback and pony rides are available from the stables.

Built in 1939, the **Big Meadows Lodge** has a cozier feel, thanks to stone walls paneled with native chestnut wood. The sitting room features a fireplace and outdoor deck with the requisite gorgeous vista; otherwise, the facilities are similar to those at Skyland. Rooms in the main lodge are $67–120, cabins are $75–87, and suites $107–142. At the same turnoff (mile 51.2) is the park's largest and most popular campground with 217 sites. This is the only place you can reserve sites in advance (between mid-May and November, you have to), by calling 800/365-2267. Next door are a coffee shop, gas station, camp store, and ranger station.

Lewis Mountain (mile 57.6) has cabins with one or two rooms, ranging from $61–94. All are heated and provide linens, but they don't have phones or TVs. Cooking is done outdoors on a grill. Tent cabins are also available for $17–22. Thirty-two campsites are first-come, first-served, right next to the information center, gift and food shop, showers, and laundry. At **Loft Mountain** (milepost 80), you'll find a wayside and campstore with showers, laundry, and a grill with a limited food selection. More than 200 campsites are available on a first-come, first-served basis.

INFORMATION

Maps

Probably the best map of the park is printed by **Trails Illustrated,** www.trailsillustrated.com (now owned by National Geographic). Their 1:100,000-scale map (number 228) is printed on tearproof plastic and is also available at visitor centers for $10. The PATC also sells three topographical maps (numbers 9, 10, and 11) covering the entire park. If you're absolutely determined not to get lost (or just a techno-junkie), a digital topographical map of the park is available on either of two TrailSmart CD-ROMs sold by Trails Illustrated for $30 each: "National Parks of the East Coast and Midwest" and "National Parks of the USA—15 Major National Parks." More detailed quadrangle maps drawn in 1969 (and thus somewhat out of date) are available from the U.S. Geological Survey (USGS), Information Services, P.O. Box 25286, Denver, CO 80225, 800/275-8747, fax 303/202-4693, email: ask@usgs.gov, mapping.usgs.gov. These maps are also available online at TopoZone (www.topozone.com).

Visitors Centers and Ranger Stations

The park has three visitor centers, one in each region. The **Dickey Ridge Visitors Center** is at mile 4.6; the **Harry F. Byrd, Sr. Visitors Center** is in Big Meadows at milepost 51; the **Loft Mountain Information Center** is at mile 79.5. Each is open Apr.–Oct. daily 9 A.M.–5 P.M., with reduced hours through the end of November, and all are stocked with information, exhibits, maps, and books. There are **ranger stations** at the Front Royal and Rockfish Gap entrance stations at either end of the park, and at Thornton Gap (mile 31.5) and Swift Run Gap (mile 65.5).

Park Headquarters, 540/999-3500, fax 540/999-3601, email: SHEN_Superintendent@ nps.gov, www.nps.gov/shen, are four miles east of Luray on US 211, open Mon.–Fri. 9 A.M.–5 P.M. The same building is home to the bookstore of the **Shenandoah Natural History Association,** 540/999-3581/3582, www.snpbooks.org, with a large selection of books on the flora, fauna, trails, and history of the park.

Harrisonburg and Vicinity

The urban center of the northern Blue Ridge is home to 40,000 people and some 20 major industries. Surrounding Rockingham County is first in the state in production of beef, dairy products, and poultry (only one county in the nation produces more turkeys annually) and leads four other Virginia counties and three in West Virginia who come to Harrisonburg to shop and invest. Thousands of local farmers come together in huge farmers' markets. At these, you might find yourself parked next to a black horse-drawn buggy carrying a family of Old Order Mennonites—about 1,000 live in the area in a severe, simple lifestyle similar to Pennsylvania's Amish, with whom they share a common Anabaptist religious heritage. Three of the Shenandoah's largest schools—James Madison University (JMU), Bridgewater College, and Eastern Mennonite University—have campuses in or near the city.

HISTORY

Harrisonburg was founded in the 1740s by Thomas Harrison near the intersection of the Spotswood Trail and the main Indian road down the valley. Strict Methodists started the city's first school in 1794, outlawing gaming and "instruments of music" and decreeing that no student be "permitted on any account whatever to wear Ruffles or powder his hair." The Battle of Harrisonburg, on June 6, 1862, saw the death of Gen. Turner Ashby, one of Stonewall Jackson's most trusted and respected officers.

SIGHTS

Court Square

The heart of downtown rings the limestone-faced Rockingham County Courthouse. Dating to the turn of the 20th century, the imposing building is the fifth to sit on the original 1.5-acre plot of land donated by Thomas Harrison in 1779. Look for the round copper dome of the **springhouse** at the southwest corner, an exact

replica, erected in 1995, of the original watering hole and meeting place.

Virginia Quilt Museum

Both traditional and modern masters of the art of quilting have works on display in the 1855 **Warren-Sipe House,** 301 S. Main St., 540/434-3818. People originally began making quilts—blanket covers made out of scraps—out of necessity, since new bedclothes were expensive, but quilting has since evolved into its own art form. Three rotating exhibits per year feature some wild, colorful examples edging toward fabric impressionism. Notice the one made from old Bull Durham tobacco pouches. Open Mon., Thur.–Sat. 10 A.M.–4 P.M., Sun. 1–4 P.M.; $4 adults, $2 children 6–12.

James Madison University

Twelve thousand students call this beautiful 472-acre campus home for as many years as it takes to complete a bachelor's or master's degree in the sciences, arts, business, health, or education. The well-rounded public university is consistently cited by national publications as one of the top regional public insitutions of higher learning. JMU also supports several successful sports teams that make regular appearances in the NCAA playoffs. Information is available by calling 540/568-6211.

The gently sloping, grassy **Quadrangle** is the perfect place for reading in the shade, Frisbee-throwing or sunbathing, or just taking a quiet stroll around this focal point of campus. The gracious red-roofed bluestone dormitory, classroom, and administration buildings, including the always reliable Wilson Hall clocktower, constitute the original campus of the State Normal School for Women, a teachers' college founded in 1908.

At the other end of the spectrum, the **College of Integrated Science and Technology (CISAT)**—the first and most challenging curriculum of its kind—on the other side of I-81 (connected to campus by a bridge) is a modern marvel that is now the highest point in town (students call it

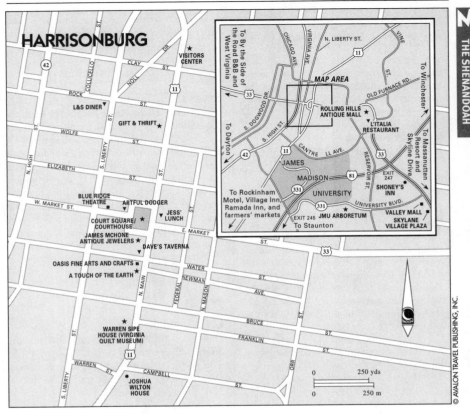

HARRISONBURG

VISITORS CENTER

CLAY ST.
COLLICELLO
NOLL
ROCK ST.
L&S DINER
GIFT & THRIFT
WOLFE ST.
ELIZABETH
S. LIBERTY
N. HIGH ST.
ST.
BLUE RIDGE THEATRE
W. MARKET ST.
ARTFUL DODGER
JESS' LUNCH
COURT SQUARE/ COURTHOUSE
JAMES MCHONE ANTIQUE JEWELERS
E. MARKET
DAVE'S TAVERNA
OASIS FINE ARTS AND CRAFTS
A TOUCH OF THE EARTH
WATER
NEWMAN
N. MAIN
FEDERAL
N. MASON
ST.
AVE.
BRUCE
WARREN SIPE HOUSE (VIRGINIA QUILT MUSEUM)
FRANKLIN
ST.
WARREN ST.
CAMPBELL
S. LIBERTY
JOSHUA WILTON HOUSE
ST.
ORR

To By the Side of the Road B&B and West Virginia

N. LIBERTY ST.
CHICAGO AVE.
VIRGINIA AVE.
VINE
11
MAP AREA
OLD FURNACE RD.
To Winchester
ROLLING HILLS ANTIQUE MALL
L'ITALIA RESTAURANT
To Dayton
S. DOGWOOD DR.
S. HIGH ST.
CANTRELL AVE.
RESERVOIR ST.
To Massanutten Resort and Skyline Drive
42
11
JAMES
MADISON
81
EXIT 247
33
SHONEY'S INN
To Rockingham Motel, Village Inn, Ramada Inn, and farmers' markets
331
UNIVERSITY
331
UNIVERSITY BLVD.
EXIT 245 JMU ARBORETUM
VALLEY MALL
SKYLINE VILLAGE PLAZA
To Staunton
33

0   250 yds
0   250 m

MOON

© AVALON TRAVEL PUBLISHING, INC.

the Emerald City). Sunset-watching is terrific from the parking lot outside the main building.

JMU administers the **Edith J. Carrier Arboretum,** 540/548-3194, www.jmu.edu/arboretum, on University Boulevard. One hundred twenty-five acres of mature natural forest surround ponds and landscaped plots of shrubs and flowers. Nature trails weave through the leaves and across little Monet bridges over a stream. It's open dawn to dusk for free, with occasional tours, lectures, and workshops.

ACCOMMODATIONS

Under $50

Head south past I-81 exit 243 into the countryside to reach the classic **Rockingham Motel,** 4035 S.

Main St. (US 11), 540/433-2538, fax 540/433-0832, with 20 rooms and views of the mountains.

$50–100

The Village Inn, 4979 South Valley Pike (US 11), tel./fax 540/434-7355, has been family owned and operated since 1936. **Shoney's Inn,** 45 Burgess Rd. (I-81 exit 247), 540/433-6089, fax 540/433-6485, offers a heated indoor pool, sauna, whirlpool, exercise room. The **Ramada Inn,** 1 Pleasant Valley Rd., 540/434-9981, fax 540/434-7088, is off I-81 exit 243, with an outdoor pool and restaurant.

$100–150

The Joshua Wilton House, 412 S. Main St., 540/434-4464, fax 540/435-9525, email: jwhouse@rica.net, www.home.rica.net/jwhouse,

GHOSTS OF HARRISONBURG

On December 1, 1900, an aunt was checking on a baby in an upstairs bedroom when she bent to blow out an oil lamp. Low on oil, the lamp suddenly exploded, igniting the woman's dress and burning her so badly that she died the next day. Local legend holds that glowing hand prints from the unlucky aunt appear on the wall of the old house, now part of the Willow Hill subdivision. Previous owners have witnessed the door to the master bedroom slamming shut on its own.

Residents of the Funk House on Mason Street—usually college students—tell of blasts of cold air gusting through rooms and doors closing without visible assistance. One person reported that in the early 1970s she woke up in the middle of the night feeling as if she were suffocating and couldn't get out of bed. As a possible explanation, folklore scholars point out the old English custom of "mattressing," in which poor families piled mattresses on sick or elderly people they couldn't afford to take care of and sat on them until they suffocated.

Harrisonburg's most famous specter is said to be Colonel Warren, of the Warren-Sipe House, killed during the Battle of the Wilderness by a bullet in the head. Several witnesses have spotted his ghost at the first landing of the stairway, standing in full uniform with its head wrapped in wide bandages.

vies for the titles of most elegant hotel and restaurant in the city. The Victorian mansion was built in 1888 by the owner of a hardware store on Court Square, who went on to start the local electric company. Wilton's residence, naturally, was the first in town with electricity— even before it had plumbing.

Much of the original materials and craftsmanship remain, including the leaded glass in the front door and the parquet floor and banister in the main hall, which even survived the house being used as a fraternity house for several years in the mid-1900s. Five bedrooms feature period antiques, four-poster beds, and faux-marble fireplaces. Enjoy the inn's award-winning cuisine in the two front rooms. More casual fare is served in

three back rooms and on an outdoor patio café, with smoked salmon and crayfish cakes appetizers and entrées such as Cornish game hen and shrimp and steak specials. Rates ($105–120) include gourmet breakfast in the sunroom.

$150–200

By the Side of the Road B&B, 491 Garber's Church Rd., 540/801-0430, email: bytheroad@ aol.com, www.by-the-side-road-bb.com, fills a Revolutionary-era Flemish bond building two acres to the east of downtown. It served as a hospital during the Civil War, during which Union soldiers tried to set fire to the foundation three times, unsuccessfully. Four suites in the main house all have two or three rooms, and the Fitzgerald Cottage next door has a spiral staircase leading to the whirlpool tub in front of the fireplace on the second floor. Rates are $120–175.

FOOD

Coffee and Snacks

Couches, a gift shop, a cybercafé, and local art on the walls make **The Artful Dodger,** 47 W. Court Square, 540/432-1179, a classic coffeehouse hip enough to make up for the lack of funk elsewhere in town. It also serves desserts and light food for lunch (Mon.–Fri.) and dinner (Mon.–Sat), and occasionally has live music at night.

Look for the 20-foot ice cream cone in front of **Kline's Dairy Bar,** 58 E. Wolfe St., 540/434-6980, serving soft-serve ice cream, sundaes, and shakes from the same Electro Freeze machine since 1943. It's open daily for lunch and dinner in season and is packed on weekend evenings in the summer.

Inexpensive Fare

Luigi's 1059 S. High St., 540/433-0077, is legendary among students and residents alike for its affordable and always delicious pizza, sandwiches, and calzones, as well as its extensive list of microbrew offerings. The menu and prices have been the same for almost 10 years—and no one's complaining! Check out the two huge bulletin boards in the back room displaying photos of former employees, friends, and regular customers wearing Luigi's shirts at famous spots all over the world. The joint is small and well-known, so expect to wait on a weekend night, but consider it well worth it.

Jess' Lunch, 22 S. Main St., 540/434-8282, is an old city standby with the best hot dogs in town for $1 (three college students once ate 53 at a sitting). Low-priced breakfast and lunch (hardly anything is more than $5) are served in diner booths and at the counter from 9 A.M.–midnight every day of the year. "Home cooking from scratch" is the calling card of the bright-red **L&S Diner,** 255 N. Liberty St., 540/434-5572. It was started in 1947 and has counter seating only for three meals Mon.–Sat. Gyros, souvlaki, and homemade soups and salads keep **Dave's Taverna,** 95 S. Main St., 540/564-1487, in business. Lunch specials are $4 and pizzas run $6.50–11.50. Open for lunch and dinner Mon.–Sat.

Finer Dining

Aside from The Joshua-Wilton House, Harrisonburg's other establishment of note is the **Olympic Room** at the Four Points Hotel Harrisonburg, 1400 E. Market St., 540/433-2521. Continental food is served in an elegantly relaxed setting for three meals daily, including a Sunday brunch. Entrées are $9–12 for lunch and $10–22 for dinner. **L'Italia Restaurant,** 815 E. Market St., 540/433-0961, is another local favorite, serving Italian fare among candles and romantic music for lunch and dinner Tues.–Sun.

ENTERTAINMENT

James Madison University's College of Arts and Letters supports various music and drama offerings throughout the year, from the Richmond Ballet and jazz to opera and touring Broadway musicals. There's a box office in Warren Hall, 540/568-7960, or call the main campus number, 540/568-6211, for information. Tickets to **JMU Dukes** football and basketball games can be ordered by calling 540/568-6777.

The **Blue Ridge Theatre,** 540/564-1998, puts on several performances throughout the year near Court Square.

SHOPPING

A Touch of the Earth, 163 S. Main St., 540/432-1894, stocks a little bit of everything from far-off corners of the planet. Afghani carpets, southwestern Indian pottery, Balinese carvings, and a roomful of drums are only the beginning. If you can't find it there, swing by **Gift & Thrift,** 227 N. Main St., 540/433-8844, covering the rest of the globe with Salvadoran painted boxes, Vietnamese ceramics, and Philippine shell ornaments. Half thrift shop and half international crafts store, this fascinating place is run by the Mennonites as a nonprofit organization.

James McHone Antique Jewelry, 75 S. Court Sq., 540/433-1833, specializes in estate jewelry both new and antique, with a great selection of pearls and Wedgewood cameos. **Oasis Fine Arts & Crafts,** at the corner of N. Main and Water Sts., 540/442-8185, stocks paintings, jewelry, furniture, photography and pottery. Fifty dealers fill the **Rolling Hills Antique Mall,** 779 E. Market St., 540/433-8988, stuffed to the rafters with everything from kitchen collectibles to "automobilia."

EVENTS

The Rockingham County Fairgrounds keep busy year-round, hosting the **Spring Arts and Crafts Show and Sale** in late March, and the **Shenandoah Valley Food & Business Fair** and **Annual Memorial Day Horse Fair & Auction** in May. The **Summer Feast** rolls into Court Square in June. Biggest of all is the **Rockingham Country Fair** in August, an agricultural expo rated as one of the top 10 in the country by the *Los Angeles Times*. Competitions in flowers, crops, livestock, and art compete with country music, tractor pulls, and demolition derbies for a week near the middle of the month. Call 540/434-0005 for information on these events.

INFORMATION

The Harrisonburg-Rockingham Convention and Visitors Bureau operates a **visitors center** at 10 East Gay St., 540/434-2319, fax 540/433-2293, email: hrcvbdirector@rica.net, www.harrisonburg.org/hrcvb, open daily 9 A.M.–5 P.M. and weekends May–December.

NEAR HARRISONBURG

Farmer's Markets

The flowing valley farmland surrounding Harrisonburg sets the stage for two examples of the original rural version of the shopping mall. Follow S. Main Street out of town as it turns into US 11 to reach the **Shenandoah Heritage Farmer's Market** between I-81 exits 240 and 243, where you can browse Civil War memorabilia, antique tractors, model trains, crafts, and furniture as well as produce. It's open year-round Mon.–Sat.; call 540/433-3929 for current hours. A few miles farther south on Rt. 42 between Bridgewater and Dayton is the **Dayton Farmer's Market**, 540/879-9885, open Thurs.–Sat. year-round. Homemade breads, cheese, and jellies fill about 20 booths next to country hams, jams, and toys.

Dayton

The centerpiece of the **Shenandoah Valley Folk Art and Heritage Center,** 382 High St. 540/879-2616, www.heritagecenter.com, is a huge electrified map tracing the comings, goings, and clashings of Stonewall Jackson's Shenandoah Valley Campaign. A 20-minute narrated tape explains things in dramatic tones. Regional ceramics, textiles, paintings, and sculptures fill the folk art section, close to a genealogy research library. Open Mon., Wed.–Sat. 10 A.M.–4 P.M., Sun. 1–4 P.M.; $4 adults, $1 children 5–18.

Green Valley Book Fair

Some 25 years ago Kathryn and Leighton Evans got the idea of selling surplus new and used books out of an old family barn. Today the idea has evolved into a huge affair filling three floors with half a million volumes on all subjects. New titles from most major publishers are 60–90 percent off

retail—enough to entice buyers from nearby states. The sale is held six weekends a year in Mt. Crawford off I-81 exit 240. Head east onto Rt. 682 for 1.5 miles, then take a left on Rt. 681 at the Green Valley sign. Contact the organizers at 800/385-0099 or 540/434-0309, email: info@gvbookfair.com, www.gvbookfair.com, for specific dates.

Massanutten Resort

Some of the state's best skiing waits east of Harrisonburg in a natural depression behind Massanutten Peak. With the longest vertical drop in Virginia, Pennsylvania, or Maryland (1,100 feet), Massanutten boasts 14 runs ranging from green to black, and five lifts including one quad. Other attractions include night skiing, a snowboard park, kids' programs, and NASTAR races. Lift tickets cost $30–44 adults, $25–35 children, with two hours at the state's first and only snow tubing park for $12. Equipment rentals are another $16–24.

During the rest of the year, Massanutten keeps busy with an 18-hole golf course, pool, tennis, in-line skating rink, and an indoor fitness complex. The mountain's trails are open for mountain bikes, but only to guests of the resort. The Massanutten Mountain Bike Hoo-Ha! is an annual competition in mid-August; call 540/289-4957 or stop by www.bikeva.com/Hooha.htm for more information.

The resort is 10 miles from Rt. 33 on Rt. 644. For information on activities and lodging, contact the resort at 800/207-6277 or 540/289-9441, email: skimass@shentel.net, www.massresort.com.

Natural Chimneys Regional Park

Seven limestone towers 65–120 feet tall form the nucleus of this small park near Mt. Solon (I-81 exit 240). The columns used to be part of the same block of limestone left from when Virginia was covered by an inland sea, but a layer of harder rock on top protected them from erosion. Natural Chimneys' other claim to fame is the jousting tournaments held the third Saturdays of June and August, making them some of the oldest continually held sporting events in the country. No one crashes to the ground in full armor here, though—the tournaments are based on accuracy, with contestants aiming their lances through small rings at full gallop. A campground has sites for $24–26 each, along with a pool, store, hot showers, and playground. The park is open daily 9 A.M.–dusk for $3 pp or $6 per car. For more information, call 888/430-2267 or 540/350-2510, or stop by their website (home.rica.net/uvrpa).

Grand Caverns Regional Park

Up there with Virginia's best, this network of caves includes huge Cathedral Hall, one of the largest underground rooms in the east, and the 5,000-square-foot Grand Ballroom, where dances were actually held in the early 1800s.

This one was discovered in 1804 by a 17-year-old looking for a raccoon trap, making it the oldest show cave in the country, and was once visited by Thomas Jefferson on horseback from Monticello. Signatures on the walls record the quartering of Stonewall Jackson's troops near here during the Valley Campaign. More than 200 formations called "shields" are a mystery to geologists.

The caverns, 540/249-5705, home.rica.net/uvrpa, are east of I-81 exit 235 and open Apr.–Oct. daily 9 A.M.–5 P.M., and some weekends in March. Admission is $13 adults, $6 children 3–12, and the park also encloses picnic shelters, hiking and biking trails, a pool, tennis courts, and a miniature golf course.

Staunton and Vicinity

One of the oldest cities in the Shenandoah Valley, Staunton (pop. 25,000) is a pretty, if hilly, town to amble through for an afternoon or two. Since it was spared from Civil War destruction, Staunton still claims historic architecture to rival that of any city in the state. Faded advertisements for feed, fertilizer, and hardware on brick buildings give the downtown a railroad-era look, while grand private homes fronted by sloping lawns line West Frederick Street. Intense restoration efforts have resurrected the train station and are now being focused on the warehouses of the adjacent Wharf area.

HISTORY

Originally homesteaded by Scottish-Irish immigrant John Lewis in 1732, Staunton ("STANton") first served as a waystation at the intersection of the old Valley Pike and the westbound Midland Trail, where travelers could rest themselves and their horses and stock up on supplies. Hundreds of hogs once churned the muddy streets as they were driven to markets east of the Blue Ridge. In 1787 it served briefly and unexpectedly as the capital of Virginia when the General Assembly fled Charlottesville ahead of the British.

A little more than 50 years after the town was chartered, in 1801, the Central & Ohio Railroad

arrived, beginning Staunton's transformation from a rural outpost to a thriving commercial city and transportation hub of western Virginia. Woodrow Wilson was born here to the wife of a local Presbyterian minister in 1856. Staunton served as a supply base during the Civil War.

SIGHTS

No less than five lovingly preserved National Historic Districts earned Staunton a spot on the

"MAD ANN" BAILEY

Indian attacks took a heavy toll in the early years of Augusta County. When one Richard Trotter fell to flying arrows, his wife went on the warpath herself. Ann, who had arrived in America as an indentured servant, quickly became one of the area's most renowned Indian fighters. Dressed in men's clothes and carrying a rifle, tomahawk, and knife, she did her best to even the score as a messenger, scout, and spy. According to one account she "halways carried a hax and a hauger and could chop as well as hany man" and was said to have "killed more than one person's share of Indians." She lived to 83.

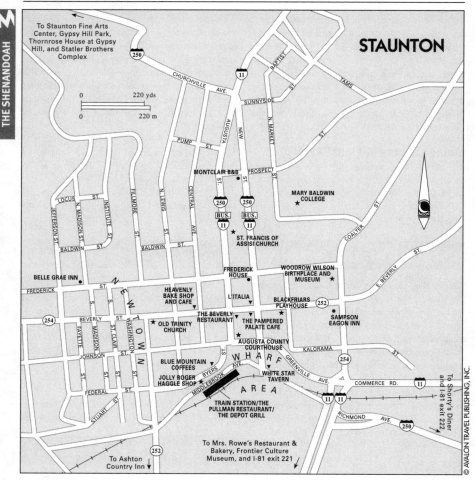

STAUNTON

To Staunton Fine Arts Center, Gypsy Hill Park, Thornrose House at Gypsy Hill, and Statler Brothers Complex

0   220 yds
0   220 m

CHURCHVILLE AVE.
SUNNYSIDE
PUMP ST.
MONTCLAIR B&B
PROSPECT ST.
MARY BALDWIN COLLEGE
ST. FRANCIS OF ASSISI CHURCH
LOCUST ST.
JEFFERSON ST.
N. MADISON ST.
INSTITUTE ST.
FILLMORE ST.
N. LEWIS ST.
CENTRAL AVE.
BALDWIN ST.
BELLE GRAE INN
FREDERICK
FREDERICK HOUSE
WOODROW WILSON BIRTHPLACE AND MUSEUM
HEAVENLY BAKE SHOP AND CAFE
L'ITALIA
BLACKFRIARS PLAYHOUSE
THE BEVERLY RESTAURANT
OLD TRINITY CHURCH
THE PAMPERED PALATE CAFE
SAMPSON EAGON INN
BEVERLY ST.
FAYETTE
MADISON ST.
ST. CLAIR ST.
WASHINGTON ST.
AUGUSTA COUNTY COURTHOUSE
KALORAMA
JOHNSON ST.
WHARF AREA
BLUE MOUNTAIN COFFEES
JOLLY ROGER HAGGLE SHOP
BYERS AVE.
MIDDLEBROOK
WHITE STAR TAVERN
GREENVILLE AVE.
COMMERCE RD.
FEDERAL ST.
TRAIN STATION/THE PULLMAN RESTAURANT/ THE DEPOT GRILL
STUART ST.
RICHMOND AVE.
To Shorty's Diner and I-81 exit 222
To Ashton Country Inn
To Mrs. Rowe's Restaurant & Bakery, Frontier Culture Museum, and I-81 exit 221
BAPTIST ST.
TAMS
AUGUSTA ST.
NEW ST.
N. MARKET ST.
COALTER ST.
E. BEVERLY ST.

© AVALON TRAVEL PUBLISHING, INC.

National Trust for Historic Preservation's 2001 list of "A Dozen Distinctive Destinations" nationwide. The cobble-lined **Wharf District** includes the early-1900s train depot (now an Amtrak station), with old cabooses at the end of a long platform that hummed with activity during the city's railroad heyday. Many of the nearby warehouses and mill buildings have been turned into galleries and antique shops.

Beautiful Victorian buildings from the boom years of 1860–1920 fill the **Beverly** district, along the street of the same name between Lewis and

Market streets. West of Lewis Street is **Newtown,** actually the city's oldest residential area, home to prominent citizens and their less wealthy neighbors who labored in local factories. **Stuart Addition** adjoins the campus of Mary Baldwin College, and **Gospel Hill,** filled with elegant residences, gets it names from religious meetings originally held in the late 18th century.

Woodrow Wilson Birthplace and Museum

Only a few original presidential birthplaces are

FRONTIER CULTURE MUSEUM

In the 1700s, three ethnic groups—English, German, and Scottish-Irish—dominated the small-scale farming settlements of the Shenandoah Valley frontier. Over the next two centuries, their distinctive traditions would blend into a uniquely American heritage brought back to life in this fascinating living-history center that focuses on the common man rather than the patrician. Ignore the traffic hum from I-81, and it's easy to be carried back in time by the smells of fresh-cut hay and open-hearth cooking and the sounds of cows lowing, pigs rooting, and the clank of hammer on anvil.

At the **visitors center,** 540/332-7850, email: info@frontiermuseum.state.va.us, www.frontiermuseum.org, films and a small museum tell you about the Colonial cultures you're about to experience. (The **Staunton/Augusta Travel Information Center,** 800/332-5219 or 540/332-3972, is in the same building.) Step outside to begin a five-eighths-mile self-guided walking loop through four distinct farms. All the buildings are original, disassembled where they stood, shipped here, and reassembled on site. Everything was re-created to be as authentic as possible, down to bringing in thatchers from Ulster to roof the Irish cottage.

Costumed interpreters keep each farm running, from planting and harvesting crops to tending rare, authentic breeds of cattle and making cast-iron implements by hand. They know all about what life for their antecedents was like and are happy to explain what they're doing. A long list of daily demonstrations varies throughout the year, including fabric weaving, sheep shearing, woodworking,

© JULIAN SMITH

The museum's four distinct settlements contain original buildings.

and cooking. Some of the more popular activities require special admission fees and preregistration.

The 18th-century German farm from the Rhineland-Palatinate region is first. A framework of thick posts and beams is covered with wattle and daub (woven sticks covered with a mixture of soil, water, sand, lime, and manure). This style became common in Colonial America, though wooden planks would eventually replace the twigs and fertilizer.

Twin walls of whitewashed stone separated by a layer of rubble make up the early 19th-century Scottish-Irish cottage and outbuildings, one of which encloses a working forge. A small field is planted every spring with flax to make linen, a common crop in northern Ireland at the time. The 18th-century English farmhouse from West Sussex is the most substantial so far, a two-story wooden building with an elaborate brick chimney. Furniture inside is carved from oak and walnut.

Last comes an entry from Botetourt County near Roanoke. The clapboard-covered log house features a full-length back porch and an open hearth that doubled as furnace and kitchen. Among the eight farm buildings you won't find an outhouse—chamber pots were still emptied outdoors in the 19th century.

The museum is on US 250 west of I-81 exit 222 (follow signs). It's open daily 9 A.M.–5 P.M.; $8 adults, $4 children 6–12. Most of the grounds and buildings are wheelchair accessible, and motorized scooters are available free of charge to mobility-impaired visitors.

still open to the public (that cabin in Kentucky probably isn't the one where Lincoln was born), and this modest city boasts one of them. The original home of the 28th president features period furniture, personal belongings, and Wilson's favorite 1919 Pierce-Arrow limousine. Boxwood gardens outside were restored in 1993 by the Garden Club of Virginia. Guided tours trace his life from here to Princeton and the White House. The museum is on Coalter St., 888/496-6376 or 540/885-0897, email: woodrow@cfw.com, www.woodrowwilson.org. Open Mar.–Nov. daily 9 A.M.–5 P.M., Dec.–Feb. daily 10 A.M.–4 P.M.; $6.50 adults, $2 children 6–12.

Statler Brothers Complex

The famous family of country singers has its offices and a miniature museum in the building where they once went to school, 501 Thornrose Ave. near Norfolk Ave., 540/885-7927, www.statlerbrothers.com. Gifts sent by fans fill one room, while another has been set up as it looked when the brothers were learning their ABCs. Free tours are given Mon.–Fri. at 2 P.M., and a gift shop is open Mon.–Fri. 10:30 A.M.–3:30 P.M.

Other Landmarks

The cream-brick **Augusta County Courthouse,** on the corner of Johnson and Augusta streets, is the fifth such structure on this particular site. Its classic design includes large stone columns supporting a dome topped by a weather-greened statue of Justice. Dating to 1855, the Gothic Revival **Old Trinity Church** replaced one that hosted the Virginia General Assembly in 1787. The lime-green **St. Francis of Assisi Catholic Church** sits on the highest hill in town.

   Mary Baldwin College was founded by the Rev. Rufous Bailey in 1842 as the Augusta Female Seminary, making it the oldest continually operating women's college in the South. The Greek Revival structure sits on Sycamore Street overlooking downtown. Tennis courts, playgrounds, a golf course, and a swimming pool fill **Gypsy Hill Park,** northwest of downtown along Churchville Avenue.

ACCOMMODATIONS

$50–100

Both the **Econo Lodge Staunton,** 1031 Richmond Ave., 540/885-5158, fax 540/885-5281, and the **Super 8 Motel,** 1015 Richmond Ave., 540/886-2888, fax 540/886-7432, are off I-81 exit 222 and have rooms for around $60. Fox hunt decor marks the **Montclaire B&B,** 320 N New St., 877/885-8832 or 540/885-8832, email: mebang@rica.net, www.bbonline.com/va/montclair/index.html. Sheri and Mark Bang run the Italianate home (c. 1880), which features a library, private sitting rooms, and four guest rooms for $90.

   Across the street from Gypsy Hill Park sits the stately Georgian **Thornrose House at Gypsy Hill,** 531 Thornrose Ave., 800/861-4338 or 540/885-7026, fax 540/885-6458, email: innkeeper@thornrosehouse.com, www.thornrosehouse.com. Fireplaces warm the dining room and a guest parlor decorated with family heirlooms and oriental rugs. Relax on a rocking chair on the wraparound veranda or stroll through the grounds and gardens or the park across the street. Rooms are $60–80.

$100–150

Frank and Laura Mattingly have garnered repeated awards and recommendations as one of the best inns in the state, if not the country, with **The Sampson Eagon Inn,** 238 E. Beverly St., 800/597-9722 or 540/886-8200, email: eagoninn@rica.net, www.eagoninn.com. A porch swing and period antiques enhance the 1840s inn, known for its gourmet "skip-lunch" breakfasts. Laura's delectable Grand Marnier pancakes and Belgian Kahlua waffles might make you want to skip that jog around town as well—or at least postpone it. Five rooms and suites decorated with period antiques range in price from $90–125.

   Up on the high western end of Frederick Street perches the **Belle Grae Inn,** 515 W. Frederick St., 888/541-5151 or 540/886-5151, email: bellegrae@sprynet.com, www.bellegrae.com. Originally part of a 200-acre farm on the edge of town, the "Old Inn" was opened to the public in 1983. A front veranda and 12-foot ceilings grace the first of three federal stories, and azaleas bloom in the garden in back. Fifteen rooms and suites are shared between the main building and the adjacent townhouse, both erected in the 1870s. The Belle Grae Inn offers several dining choices, along with rooms for $100–140 and suites for $140–170. A separate "Honeymoon Hideaway" cottage runs $200–240.

The **Ashton Country House,** 1205 Middlebrook Ave., 800/296-7819 or 540/885-7819, email: ashtonhouse@aol.com, www.bbhost.com/ ashtonbnb, sits one mile southwest of the center of town. Three verandas and a 40-foot central hall are only the beginning. Pine and maple floors, brick interior walls, high ceilings, and 25 bucolic acres complete with farm buildings and animals give a convincing taste of what this Greek Revival mansion must have been like in its heyday in the latter 19th century. Of the five bedrooms ($70–100), four have fireplaces and one is fully accessible to visitors with disabilities.

$150–200

Frederick House, 28 N. New St., 800/334-5575 or 540/885-4220, email: stay@frederickhouse.com, www.frederickhouse.com, is a small European-style inn with an attached tearoom (enter from the parking lot on New Street). The building, some parts of which date to 1810, features a Federal-style curving stairway. Eight rooms and six suites are spread between the main house and nearby cottages and townhouses. Prices range from $75–170.

FOOD
Beverly Street

Starting at the east end and working west, **The Pampered Palate Cafe,** 26-28 E. Beverly St., 540/886-9463, offers quiches, pita sandwiches, and New York–style bagels for $4–6. Many vegetarian and lowfat options are balanced by a gourmet goodie, coffee, and wine shop. Open Mon.–Sat. for breakfast and lunch. Regional dishes like veal Sorrentina and steak alla Pizziada are a specialty of **L'Italia Restaurant,** 23 E. Beverly St., 540/885-0102. Casual lunches ($7–11) and dinners ($10–15) served Tues.–Sun. are enlivened by occasional jazz on weekends.

The Beverly Restaurant, 12 E. Beverly St., 540/886-4317, serves homestyle Southern meals including chicken and dumplings, ham hocks and cabbage, and chipped-beef gravy breakfasts. Both their chocolate milkshakes and the homemade pecan pies are said to be "the best you'll ever eat" (let me know *your* verdict). Open Mon.–Sat. 6 A.M.–7 P.M., with afternoon tea Wed. and Fri. 3–5 P.M.

The **Heavenly Bake Shop and Cafe,** 101 W. Beverly St., 540/886-4455, offers sandwiches, salads, pastries, and libations under a cloud-filled sky painted on the ceiling. Open for lunch Tues.–Sat., and dinner on Fri., with live music during the "coffee house" hours (6:30–9:30 P.M.) on Fri. and Sat.

Elsewhere Downtown

Today, more people head to the old C&O depot to try one of the two restaurants there than to board a train. The centerpiece of **The Pullman Restaurant,** 540/885-6612, is an 1880s Victorian soda fountain and ice cream bar. Tiffany lampshades, marble counters, and antiques evoke an old-time railroad atmosphere. Cuisine is Cajun and Creole inspired, and entrées run $5–9 for lunch and $12–20 for dinner. Farther down the platform, **The Depot Grill,** 540/885-7332, boasts a marvelous 40-foot bar rescued from a luxury hotel demolished in Albany, New York. Seafood is also a favorite here, starting with shrimp, crab legs, and crawdads at the steamer bar. Sandwiches are $6–10, and entrées $10–17. Both restaurants are open daily for lunch and dinner.

Also in the Wharf district, **Blue Mountain Coffees,** 18A Byers St., 540/886-4506, serves muffin- and bagel-type fare for breakfast and lunch Mon.–Sat., with occasional musical and artistic events. No less than *Gourmet* magazine says that the owners of the **Belle Grae Inn,** 515 W. Frederick St., 888/541-5151 or 540/886-5151, "take the second 'B' in B&B seriously." They offer two dining options: fine dining in the Old Inn Wed.–Sun. means appetizers such as sweet potato and crawfish bisque ($6–8) and entrées for $18–22. Floor-to-ceiling windows in The Bistro make á la carte dining a sunny affair (entrées $10–15, sandwiches slightly less). In fine traditional style, tea is served every afternoon at 4 P.M. with cookies and cakes. Nonguests should call ahead.

Beyond Downtown

Mrs. Rowe's Restaurant & Bakery, US 250 just east of I-81 exit 222, 540/886-1833, has been serving three hearty meals daily since it opened in 1947 (and was *also* praised by *Gourmet* magazine, thank you very much). Bread, biscuits, and pies are all baked fresh from her original recipes, and the fried chicken is prepared to order, but well worth the wait. The gleaming metal exterior of **Shorty's Diner,** 1013 Richmond Rd., 540/885-8861, goes well with the retro-chic red vinyl seats and CD jukebox. An order of Your Mama's Chicken Soup or Three Alarm Chili might leave room—barely—for blue-plate specials (around $6) such as meatloaf and country-fried steak. Shakes, malts, and pies are also on the menu, of course. Open daily 7 A.M.–9 or 10 P.M., with breakfast served all day for $2 and up.

ENTERTAINMENT AND TOURS

Local artists are thankful for the **Staunton-Augusta Art Center,** 540/885-2028, at the intersection of Churchill and Thornrose avenues near Gypsy Hill Park. Crafts such as paintings, pottery, jewelry, and scarves are sold near the holidays. Open Mon.–Fri. 9 A.M.–5 P.M.; free. From late May to late October, free **guided walking tours** leave from the Woodrow Wilson Birthplace and Museum every Saturday at 10 A.M. Brochures are also available for self-guided rambles. Contact the Historic Staunton Foundation, 540/885-7676, or the Staunton/Augusta Travel Information Center for more information.

All the buzz in 2001 was the impending opening of the **Blackfriars Playhouse** of the internationally acclaimed Shenandoah Shakespeare theater company, 11 East Beverly St., Ste. 31, 540/885-5588, fax 540/885-4886, email: sse@shenandoahshakespeare.com, www.shenandoahshakespeare.com. This authentic, 300-seat indoor playhouse should make the group's boast to "blow the cobwebs out of Elizabethan drama" easier, allowing the productions to be staged as

they originally were: on a simple stage sharing the same light as the audience section, giving a communal feel to the performances. The world-class venue—eventually to be joined by a duplicate of London's 1614 Globe Theatre—will be open year-round for Shakespeare productions and other special musical and theatrical events.

EVENTS

The Stonewall Brigade Bandstand in Gypsy Hill Park is Staunton's music epicenter during the summer. The **Stonewall Brigade Band,** one of the nation's oldest continuous community bands, performs on Monday evenings Oct.–May, and the **Jazz in the Park** series brings more music on Thursday evenings, rain or shine (both are free). The **Staunton Music Festival,** 540/885-7873, www.stauntonmusicfestival.org, offers classical and family music concerts at various locations around the city for $6.50–8.50 pp (less or free for some shows).

SHOPPING

Shaunton's most interesting spot to browse is unquestionably the **Jolly Roger Haggle Shop,** 27 Middlebrooks Ave., 540/886-9527. Leave yourself an hour or more to do justice to roomfuls of old lunch boxes, turquoise jewelry, antique tools, militaria, books, and records piled to the ceiling. They boast "more than one million items," and it's easy to believe. Other craft/antique stores are clustered near Beverly and New streets, including **Warehouse Antiques & Collectibles,** 26 W. Beverly St., 540/885-0891, the city's largest antique store, and the **White Swan Gallery,** 107 E. Beverly St., 540/886-0522.

The **Staunton/Augusta Farmers' Market,** 540/332-3802, features locally grown fruits, veggies, and other edibles on Saturday mornings from Apr.–Oct in the Wharf parking lot at Johnson Street and Central Avenue.

INFORMATION AND TRANSPORTATION

Look for the **Staunton/Augusta Travel Information Center,** 800/332-5219 or 540/332-3972, in the Museum of Frontier Culture, and the **City Welcome Center,** 540/332-3971, in the Woodrow Wilson Birthplace. Both are open daily 9 A.M.–5 P.M. For information online, try the Staunton Convention and Visitors Bureau website www.stauntonva.org, or the city's website www.staunton.va.us.

Trains leave the **Amtrak** station for Charlottesville and Clifton Forge.

WAYNESBORO

Take exit 94 off I-81 to reach this industrial town just west of a major pass through the Blue Ridge. Accommodations await two blocks off Main Street at the **Belle Hearth B&B,** 320 S .Wayne Ave., 800/949-6993 or 540/943-1910, fax540/ 942-2443, email: bellehrth@aol.com, www.inngetaways.com/va/belle.html. Adorned with a gabled roof and wraparound porch, the early-1900s building is filled with Victorian furnishings and no fewer than seven fireplaces—hence the name. Three rooms and one suite range from $80–110.

The **P. Buckley Moss Museum,** 150 P. Buckley Moss Dr. (US 340), 800/343-8643 or 540/949-6473, www.p-buckley-moss.com, houses dozens of works by the well-known local artist. Her distinctive "Valley Style," inspired by the scenery and people of the Shenandoah, is marked by bare, wiry trees, sensuous horses, chunky Canadian geese, and elongated portraits of Amish

THE GREAT OIL HOAX OF 1895

In 1895, a sly group of entrepreneurs announced they had found oil near Waynesboro. They proceeded to sell stock and even made a convincing show of drilling. With every day that passed without producing any black gold, though, the townspeople grumbled more.

Sales of the stock picked up again when several barrels of oil were poured into the ground surreptitiously one night, prompting several investors to retire in anticipation of their newfound wealth. In time, the scam was unearthed, and the only thing that ever came out of the hole that wasn't dumped there was clean drinking water.

and Old Order Mennonite farmers. There's a gift shop downstairs, where prices for even small prints start in the hundreds. Open Mon.–Sat. 10 A.M.–6 P.M., Sun. 12:30–5:30 P.M.; free.

You can watch brass and iron pieces being sand-cast at the factory showroom of **Virginia Metalcrafters,** 1010 E. Main St., 540/949-9432. The rest of the building is filled with any and all kinds of metal accessories imaginable, from sundials and garden animals to lamps, trivets, and candlesticks. They also have an outlet store in Waynesboro Outlet Village (Building 16B) on Rosser Avenue (Rt. 340), 540/949-8190.

Allegheny Highlands

Encompassing Highland, Bath, and parts of Augusta and Allegheny counties, this wrinkled western spur is surprisingly accessible for such a wild area. Long, narrow peaks of the Allegheny Mountains ripple off into West Virginia, split by river valleys running arrow-straight southwest to northeast. With fewer than 3,000 people spread over 455 square miles, Highland County ("Virginia's Switzerland") doesn't lack for open space. Most of it is higher than 4,000 feet above sea level, giving it the highest average elevation of any county east of the Mississippi. Many residents live off the land as their ancestors did, still referring to locations as "three mountains over."

Bath County, in contrast, is one of the richest in Virginia, thanks to the fully realized resort possibilities of a series of thermal springs to which native tribes once ascribed healing powers. In 1750, a visiting doctor wrote, "The spring is very clear and warmer than new milk . . . The settlers would be better able to support travelers was it not for the great number of Indian warriors that frequently take what they want from them, greatly to their prejudice." Over the next few centuries, the wealthy residents of the Piedmont learned that the mountains and waters were the perfect escape from the unbearable summer mugginess of their own region. Thus began a tradition of lavish seasonal retreats, which is carried on today in The Homestead—possibly the grandest in the state.

OUTDOOR RECREATION

Fishing is one of the top draws in this part of the state, attracting anglers from hundreds of miles away in search of bass (largemouth, smallmouth, and rock), trout, catfish, crappie, and muskies. Several of Virginia's major rivers have their headwaters in these choppy hills. Almost any of the streams and rivers flowing southwest, including the Maury, Bullpasture, and Cowpasture, offer great casting. The Jackson River flows into Lake Moomaw, a 12-mile flood-control reservoir with some of the best fishing in the state (bass in the three- to four-pound range love the clear waters). The 60-acre Douthat Lake in Douthat State Park offers fee fishing for stocked trout.

Many wildlife management, recreation, and wilderness areas present endless opportunities for hiking and camping amid the spruce and northern hardwood forests. Pocahontas County, just over the border in West Virginia, is a nationally known destination for mountain biking, and this side of the border is almost identical, though largely unexplored by knobby-tire enthusiasts. Finding your own track should be a cinch, or take a look at one of the biking books in the "Booklist."

ACCESS

Possibly the prettiest road to the highlands—or anywhere in the state, for that matter—is Rt. 39, the "Avenue of Trees" from Lexington to Warm Springs via Goshen Pass. A 150-foot suspension bridge over the Maury River leads into

HUMPBACK COVERED BRIDGE

Virginia's oldest covered bridge spans Dunlap Creek, three miles west of Covington on US 60. Built in 1835, Humpback Covered Bridge was used until 1929. In 1953, it was restored for foot traffic, and the surrounding land was set aside as a park and picnic area. Ropes dangle underneath for (illicit) swings into the water, and the inside of the bridge, sadly, is defaced by graffiti. It's one of only eight covered bridges in Virginia, three of which are on private property.

© JULIAN SMITH

tens of thousands of acres administered by the state. Frequent pulloffs and swimming spots galore can easily turn this 42-mile drive into a half-day trip. US 250 from Staunton to Monterey comes in a close second, passing through the quaint burg of Churchville (with its church-lined Main Street and 40-cent soda machines) before becoming a rising corridor through the George Washington National Forest. A great view at the crest welcomes you to Highland County before the road inches its tortured way down the other side of the ridge, only to rise, and fall, again and again. Finally, no-nonsense I-64 heads from Lexington straight into West Virginia.

There's an **Amtrak** station, 400 Ridgeway St.

in Clifton Forge, with trains to Staunton and White Sulphur Springs, West Virginia, and through bus service to Roanoke. Call 800/872-7245 for information.

MONTEREY

Coming over the mountain at just the right time can make the Highland County seat seem like a vision, nestled as it is in a narrow, gently sloping valley. It's a small town, with about 250 people at last count and only one traffic light (a flashing one, at that). US 250 turns into Main Street as it runs through the center of town, lined with dozens of old buildings from the turn of the 20th century or before. The Landmark House, across from the courthouse, was built from logs in 1790 and renovated in 1977.

Accommodations

The pink stone **Montvallee Motel,** 540/468-2500, offers 1950s-style charm at the intersection of US 250 and US 220, with double rooms for less than $50. Farther on into town sits the Victorian **Highland Inn,** 888/466-4682 or 540/468-2143, fax 540/468-3143, www.highland-inn.com, built in 1904 as a vacation getaway. Gingerbread trim decorates the stacked front porches where rocking chairs sway in the breeze. Seventeen guest rooms range from $55–85. Inside are the Black Sheep Tavern and a dining room, both heated by wood burning stoves for cooler evenings.

Keep going up Main Street through town to reach the **Mountain Laurel Inn,** 800/510-0180 or 540/468-3401. Dark wood paneling, Victorian furnishings, and a clawfoot bathtub in the hall bathroom evoke the house's early-1900s origins. Rates ($85–110) include full breakfasts of fresh-baked goodies, seasonal fruits, and daily specials. Almost next door is the **Selby Inn,** 540/468-3234, another century-old place with rockers on the front porch, a resident Corgi, and rooms for $95–105. The **Cherry Hill Bed & Breakfast,** 540/468-1900, email: secrets@cfw.com, perches on Mill Alley one block off Main Street. Bay windows look out over a wraparound porch to a great view of the town and valley, and a hammock sways in the quiet flower garden out back. Room rates are $75–95.

Food

Look for the fish on the roof of the **Maple Restaurant,** 540/468-2684, on Spruce St. (behind the courthouse on the right). Specialties including rainbow trout, country ham, and fried chicken start at $5 for a full dinner plate, with sandwiches as low as $1. They're open the latest in town—until 9 P.M. **High's Restaurant,** 540/468-1600, across from the Highland Inn, is the oldest in town and even cheaper. Their homemade pies and fresh bread are worth a stop.

The dining room of the Highland Inn serves dinner Wed.–Sat. and brunch on Sunday. Sandwiches are around $5 and entrées around $10, with nightly specials for slightly more. Try **Royal Pizza & Subs,** 540/468-3333, for ice cream, sandwiches, and pizza, plus a look at a mural of the valley by local artist Anne Witschey. It's behind the Texaco station, open daily 11 A.M.–9 or 10 P.M., and includes the **Pour House Pub,** with live entertainment on the weekends.

Recreation

For guiding and instruction in caving, rock climbing, mountain biking, and camping, contact **Highland Adventures,** 540/468-2722. The **Lions Club city pool,** on US 250 past the Curry Alexander B&B, is fed by mountain streams. It's open daily during the during the summer for free.

Events

Fans of Virginia fairs know Monterey's **Highland Maple Festival** is one of the first major ones of the year. Held the second and third weekends in March, the festival centers on the fact that Highland is the only county in Virginia that produces maple syrup and all its tasty byproducts. Some 50,000 people eager to see the sun after being inside all winter make the trek to enjoy crafts and an all-you-can-eat pancake breakfast—topped with fresh maple syrup, of course.

Shopping

Opposite the courthouse sits the **H&H Cash Store,** 540/468-2570, an old-fashioned mercantile stocking maple sugar candy, buckwheat flower, tools, and clothing. **The Gallery of**

Mountain Secrets, 540/468-2020, offers jewelry, pottery, and photography, and **Evelyn's Pantry,** 540/468-3663, is full of edible treats such as jellies, spices, and deli meats. Used and rare books are bought, sold, and bound at **Field Books,** 540/468-3339. Their hours are "long but irregular," so call ahead to see if they're open.

Information

The **Highland County Chamber of Commerce,** 540/468-2550, fax 540/468-2551, www.highlandcounty.org, has an office in the Highland Center on Spruce Street.

Near Monterey

The 374-acre **Laurel Fork Preserve,** part of a 10,000-acre special management area, covers the tip of the point sticking into West Virginia. This pristine area shelters "relic communities" left over from cooler times, including rare species such as the endangered Virginia northern flying squirrels, which soar through the red spruce forests. Almost 30 miles of trails roam through the craggy hills, many following old railroad grades. Popular ones include the Laurel Fork, Buck Run, and Locust Springs Run trails. A campground has shelter for up to six people. To get there, take Rt. 642 east from Blue Grass. Contact the Warm Springs Ranger District of the George Washington National Forest, 540/839-2521, www.southernregion.fs.fed.us/gwj, for more information.

If even Monterey isn't far enough away for you, consider staying at the **Endless Mountain Retreat Center,** an environmentally focused lodge so far into the hinterlands you could throw a rock and hit West Virginia. The center welcomes everyone from individuals to groups of up to 25, who can stay in three simple, snug pine cabins with shared bathhouse ($65) or the larger log cabin ($75), which feels straight out of the Wyoming foothills. The latter has a large common room with a piano, cooking facilities, a hot tub, and spectacular views from the wide windows and wraparound porch. Seminars on flora, fauna, animal tracking, and edible plants are held year-round, and the owners can organize expeditions to go fly-fishing, horseback riding, mountain biking,

or snowshoeing through their hundreds of untouched acres. Relax in the evening in front of the wood-burning stove in the main room or in the sand-floored sauna. Guests can cook their own meals or pay another $5 pp for breakfast. For more information and detailed directions, contact the lodge at HC-2 Box 141, Hightown, VA 24465, 540/468-2700, email: endless@mountain-retreat.com. www.mountain-retreat.com.

RAMSEY'S DRAFT WILDERNESS AREA

Some of the most isolated and craggy territory in the George Washington National Forest fills this preserve, which you enter off US 250 about 21 miles east of Monterey. Thousands of acres of virgin forest—spared the axe thanks to their inaccessibility—include yellow poplar, white oaks, and hemlocks, making up one of the largest expanses of old-growth forest in the East. ("Draft" means creek, and you'll cross plenty while hiking here.) The seven-mile Ramsey's Draft Trail winds alongside a stream of the same name, and a National Forest campground sits nine miles north of US 250 on Rt. 715 (continue one mile northeast on Forest Road 95, then one mile southwest on Forest Road 95b). Call the Deerfield Ranger District of the U.S. Forest Service in Staunton, 540/885-8028, www.southernregion.fs.fed.us/gwj, for more information.

WARM SPRINGS

The Bath County seat nestles in a valley near a small set of natural thermal springs. Eighteenth-century buildings, many white with green trim, constitute the original town center known as "Old Germantown" off Rt. 39 just west of US 220.

Accommodations and Food

The **Warm Springs Inn,** 703/839-5351, fax 703/839-5352, email: poco007@tds.net, members.nbci.com/poco007/warmsprings.htm, occupies a hillside right at the intersection of US 220 and Rt. 39 across the street from the springs. The sprawling structure began as a log jail built in 1792 and a stone courthouse (1796), replaced with brick in 1842. It's been augmented over the years with other buildings and architectural styles, resulting in an interesting mix of Victorian inn and funky motel. Huge porcelain vases and other antiques fill the main foyer, which leads to the Courtroom Restaurant. A sunny glassed-in porch looks out over a swing bench in a tree out front. Rooms are $54 and suites are $95.

Take Old Germantown Road (Rt. 692) off Rt. 39 toward the center of Warm Springs to reach the **Anderson Cottage Bed & Breakfast,** 540/829-2975, email: JeanBruns@webtv.net, on your left. The two buildings are among Bath County's oldest, having served over the years as a tavern, a girl's school, and a summer inn. They've been in the present owner's family since the 1870s. Rates range from $70–110; the separate guest cottage, formerly an early-19th-century brick kitchen, is $125 for the first night and $90 per night thereafter.

To find **The Inn at Gristmill Square,** 540/839-2231, fax 540/839-5770, email: grist@va.tds.net, www.vainns.com/grist.htm, look for the waterwheel on Old Mill Rd. (Rt. 645) in the heart of Warm Springs. A mill has stood here since 1771, but the present buildings date to the 19th century. Janice and Jack McWilliams, who bought the place in 1981, have added tennis courts, a pool, and a sauna in the process of restoring four buildings: the Blacksmith Shop, the Miller House, the Steel House, and the Hardware Store. All 17 guest rooms have wood-burning fireplaces and are tastefully furnished with antiques and exotic curios. Rates ($110–155) include Continental breakfast. Fine food is served with a country flair in the adjacent **Waterwheel Restaurant.** Dinner, served daily, features expensive but savory dishes such as roast duck with apricots and veal picatta. Sunday brunch is also available.

Three campgrounds can be found west on Rt. 39 into the George Washington National Forest. Hidden Valley is 1.5 miles west and one mile north on Rt. 621, and Blowing Springs is nine miles west. The Bolar Mountain Campground is 13 miles west, then seven miles south on Rt. 600.

Recreation

A pair of oddly shaped buildings at the Rt. 39/US 220 intersection house the **Jefferson Pools,** owned by the Homestead (see following entry). These large stone pools of naturally warm water were built in the late 18th century, when the Virginia elite would make the round of different pools in the area. Thomas Jefferson may have lent his design flair to the structures: the men's pool house has eight sides and the women's has 22. As you relax in the 98°F water, be thankful fashions have changed—according to one account, the stylish bather of the 1830s had to don "a large cotton gown of a cashmere shawl pattern lined with crimson, a fancy Greek cap, Turkish slippers, and a pair of loose pantaloons." For a change of pace, try hydrotherapy, where part of the 1,200-gallon-per-minute flow is released on your back as you sit in a special chamber outside and below the pool. The pools are open daily 10 A.M.–6 P.M.; free to hotel guests or for a fee to the public.

At the foot of Courthouse Hill just off US 250, the **Warm Springs Gallery,** 540/839-2985, houses both permanent collections (don't miss Tom Ferguson's stoneware pottery) and rotating exhibits by regional artists ranging from paintings to metalwork.

ON THE ROAD TO HOT SPRINGS

Virginia novelist Mary Johnson (*To Have and To Hold*) built the central part of **Three Hills Inn & Cottages,** 540/839-5381, fax 540/839-5199, email: inn@3hills.com, www.3hills.com, in 1913. Today the hotel, which is reached by a winding driveway from US 220, commands an impressive view from 38 acres of hillside just south of the Rt. 39/US 220 intersection. Rooms in the main house are $70–100, suites are $120–180, and several cottages with kitchenettes can hold up to six people ($140–190). Duplex townhouses are being planned. Rates include breakfast (full on weekdays and Continental on weekends).

This neck of the woods also happens to be home to one of Virginia's most celebrated musical venues—the **Garth Newel Music Center,** 877/558-1689 or 540/839-5018, email: office@garthnewel.org, www.garthnewel.org. Classical concerts are held on Saturday and Sunday afternoons from July 4 through Labor Day. Call for current schedule and prices.

Three miles north of Hot Springs on Rt. 220, the **Roseloe Motel,** 540/839-5373, is a friendly place that's as nice as motels get. Rooms are $60, and some have kitchenettes for $80.

HOT SPRINGS

The Homestead

Virginia's premiere resort is more like a richly endowed university than a hotel. So big that US 220 curves around it and you need little arrows to navigate the hallways, this world-class spread covers 15,000 acres of Bath County with spotless grounds, stately brick buildings, and one of the finest mountain golf courses in the country.

The first lodge here was built in 1766 by Lt. Thomas Bullitt, a frontier militiaman. The facilities were improved to the status of "modern hotel" in the mid-19th century, just in time to serve as a field hospital during the Civil War. The first spa and golf and tennis courses were opened in 1892, but most of the buildings vanished in a fire in 1901 and were rebuilt.

Inside the main structure, the cavernous Great Hall is lined with fireplaces surrounded by cozy chairs. The opulent President's Lounge has a view of the inner courtyard, and the Jefferson Parlor features wall paintings of Thomas Jefferson and the Homestead itself. For meals, guests can choose between the formal main dining room and the more casual Casino Grill or one of two Cascades Clubs. The Café Albert, serving snacks in a deli setting, has an outdoor deck. Cottage Row off the Great Hall contains a small mall's worth of shops selling fine gifts, children's items, and gourmet foods. Golf, ski, and tennis shops elsewhere in the complex rent and sell sporting goods.

The Homestead offers more than enough activities to keep guests busy year-round, both indoors and out. Three golf courses—including the regular top-100 contender Cascades Course—draw the most visitors. One boasts the oldest first tee in the country, in use since 1890. Instruction and full equipment services are available for golfers and patrons of the hotel's nine

tennis courts. Canoeing, mountain biking, and 100 miles of hiking trails lure hikers into the hills, and there's a four-mile private trout stream and a shooting club for the sporting types. One of the first European-style spas in the country is an old standby, offering aromatherapy, hydrotherapy, massage therapy, facials, and an indoor springfed pool opened in 1903. Bowling alleys and a movie theater keep night owls busy, while the Homestead Kid's Club occupies the children. In the winter, a small ski area—the South's first—has nine slopes, a snowboard park, snowmaking equipment, and a full-service ski shop.

The hotel has more than 500 rooms and suites. Room rates range from $276 on an off-season weekday to $450 during the holiday season, and suites starts at $460 and climb from there. Various golf, spa, and romance packages are also available. Contact the hotel at US 220, Hot Springs, VA 24445, 800/838-1766 fax 540/839-7670, email: homestead.info@ourclub.com, www.thehomestead.com.

Also in Hot Springs

The **King's Victorian Inn,** 540/839-3134, occupies a Queen Victorian house surrounded by maple trees and full of antique furniture and carpets. Porch rockers and wicker chairs dot the first-floor veranda. Six rooms are $85–140 including a full breakfast.

DOUTHAT STATE PARK

Virginia's oldest state park has 40 miles of hiking trails winding through 4,493 rugged acres high in the Allegheny Mountains. Blustery ridges and deep forest surround 50-acre Douthat Lake, stocked twice a week with rainbow trout (as is Wilson Creek below the dam). Three miles of the creek have been designated children-only, giving budding anglers easy access and clearings to perfect their casts into well-stocked pools. Douthat is the only Virginia state park split by a road—Rt. 629, which leaves I-64 north from exit 27.

Campsites (open Mar.–Nov.) are $18 each with or without hookups, and reservations are essential on busy weekends from Memorial Day to Labor Day. One-room, one-bedroom, and two-bedroom cabins are priced from $80–120 (less on weekdays and in the off-season). Two five-bedroom lodges can be rented by the week or for a minimum of two nights: **Creasey Lodge** is $154 per night (less on weekdays and in the off-season), and rooms in the **Main Lodge** are $233 per night

(ditto). A restaurant overlooking the lake serves lunch and dinner Wed.–Sun., and there's also a camp store and gift shop. For more information and reservations, contact the park at Route 1, Box 212, Millboro, VA 24460, 540/862-8100, www.dcr.state.va.us/parks/douthat.htm.

Lexington

Take a smallish, mannerly town, steep it in Civil War history, overlay with a nationally recognized college or two, and you'll end up with something approaching this quiet community (pop. 7,100), close to both Natural Bridge and the Blue Ridge Parkway. Crewcut cadets stroll in full gray dress uniform down tree-shaded streets, while other students jog in red-and-yellow school colors past grand houses with names and stories going back a century or more. Within the town limits lie two of the most honored heroes of the Confederacy: Robert E. Lee and Stonewall Jackson.

Founded in 1777, Lexington was leveled by fire in 1796 and rebuilt with lottery proceeds. Less than 30 years after its founding, the Virginia Military Institute (VMI) was the target of Union

Gen. David Hunter's guns in June 1864. The barracks and much of town were left in ruins.

In the meantime, things have improved: in 2000 the city was included in The National Trust for Historic Preservation's list of a "Dozen Distinctive Destinations," representing some of the best preserved and unique communities in America.

SIGHTS
Washington & Lee University
Known as "W and L," this small private college enjoys a national reputation: 90 percent of students come from the top fifths of their high school classes. It was founded in 1749 and saved from

© JULIAN SMITH

Robert E. Lee once served as president of the historic Washington & Lee University.

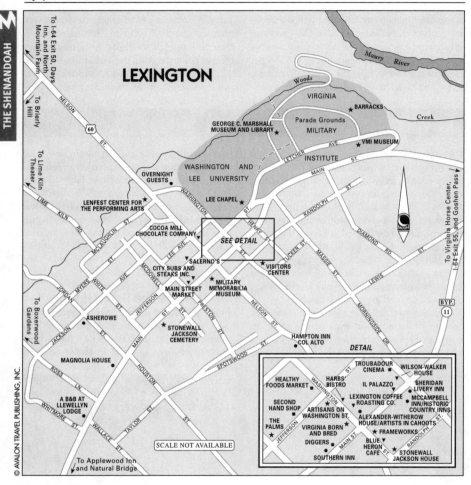

LEXINGTON

To I-64 Exit 50, Days Inn, and North Mountain Farm

To Brierly Hill

To Lime Kiln Theater

NELSON ST.

60

WASHINGTON ST.

LIME KILN RD.

LENFEST CENTER FOR THE PERFORMING ARTS

OVERNIGHT GUESTS

WASHINGTON AND LEE UNIVERSITY

LEE CHAPEL

GEORGE C. MARSHALL MUSEUM AND LIBRARY

VIRGINIA

BARRACKS

Parade Grounds
MILITARY

INSTITUTE

LETCHER AVE.

VMI MUSEUM

MAIN ST.

Woods

Maury River

Creek

To Virginia Horse Center, I-64 Exit 55, and Goshen Pass

COCOA MILL CHOCOLATE COMPANY

LEE AVE.

MCLAUGHLIN ST.

MCDOWELL ST.

SALERNO'S

CITY SUBS AND STEAKS INC.

MAIN STREET MARKET

MILITARY MEMORABILIA MUSEUM

VISITORS CENTER

SEE DETAIL

HENRY ST.

RANDOLPH ST.

TUCKER ST.

MASSIE ST.

LEWIS ST.

DIAMOND RD.

MORNINGSIDE DR.

MOON

BYP. 11

JORDAN ST.

MYERS ST.

WHITE ST.

JEFFERSON ST.

PRESTON ST.

NELSON ST.

To Boxerwood Gardens

ASHEROWE

JACKSON ST.

MAIN ST.

STONEWALL JACKSON CEMETERY

SPOTSWOOD ST.

HAMPTON INN COL ALTO

DETAIL

MAGNOLIA HOUSE

ROSS LN.

HOUSTON ST.

A B&B AT LLEWELLYN LODGE

WHITMORE ST.

WALLACE ST.

TAYLOR ST.

SCALE NOT AVAILABLE

To Applewood Inn and Natural Bridge

DETAIL

HEALTHY FOODS MARKET

WASHINGTON ST.

HARBS' BISTRO

TROUBADOUR CINEMA

IL PALAZZO

WILSON-WALKER HOUSE

SHERIDAN LIVERY INN

SECOND HAND SHOP

LEXINGTON COFFEE ROASTING CO.

MCCAMPBELL INN/HISTORIC COUNTRY INNS

THE PALMS

ARTISANS ON WASHINGTON ST.

VIRGINIA BORN AND BRED

ALEXANDER-WITHEROW HOUSE/ARTISTS IN CAHOOTS

FRAMEWORKS

JEFFERSON ST.

DIGGERS

MAIN ST.

BLUE HERON CAFE

SOUTHERN INN

STONEWALL JACKSON HOUSE

RANDOLPH ST.

bankruptcy in 1796 by a substantial gift from George Washington. Fresh from Appomattox, Robert E. Lee served as its president from 1865 to 1870. The college honored him in 1871 by renaming itself to join Lee's name to Washington's. Today, 2,000 students enjoy a beautiful central campus (declared a National Historic Landmark in 1972) made up of a row of dark red brick buildings fronted by bright white colonnades. The university's main information number is 540/463-8400, and its website is www.wlu.edu.

In the center of the campus stands the

Lee Chapel and Museum, 540/463-8768, leechapel.wlu.edu (not to be confused with the Robert E. Lee Episcopal Church, at Washington St. and Lee Ave.). The former Confederate commander supervised its construction in 1867–1868 and set up his offices in the lower level. The simple, pretty Romanesque chapel was actually never consecrated, serving instead as a hall for meetings and weddings. Inside is Charles Wilson Peale's portrait of George Washington—the first Washington ever sat for—in the incongruous uniform of a British colonel. A famous Edward Valentine statue of Lee in repose is surrounded by Confederate flags. Notice that Lee is represented not as dead, but resting: his feet are crossed and his hand rests on the hilt of his sword. Downstairs are the Lee family crypt and a small museum, which includes Lee's office just as he left it on September 28, 1870. Lee's horse, Traveler, is buried outside. Open Mon.–Sat. 9 A.M.–5 P.M., Sun. 1–5 P.M. (until 4 P.M. daily Nov.–Mar.); free.

Virginia Military Institute

The country's first state military college, 540/464-7452, www.vmi.edu, was founded in 1839 on the site of the Lexington Arsenal with a class of 23. Twenty-five years later, 1864 was a big year for VMI: in May, her cadets fought in the Battle of New Market, and in June the barracks were shelled to the ground by Federal forces. In 1983, female cadets were allowed to endure the infamous freshman "rat line"—which claims 25 percent of each incoming class—for the first time. The "cadettes" lived on the same floors as men under the ruling that any fooling around would result in the dismissal of both parties. New outdoor security lighting, emergency phones, and modified communal bathrooms made the adjustment slightly easier. In 1998, 23 of 30 made it through the rat line as part of the institute's first co-ed class without any major incidents to mar the transition.

Crenellations (battlements) top somber gray buildings around the huge central parade ground where cadets practice sports and military drills. (The Corps of Cadets gives a review parade most Friday afternoons.) At the southwest corner, the **George C. Marshall Museum and Library,** 540/463-7103, www.marshallfoundation.org, commemorates the 1901 graduate who went on to serve as general of the army, the highest military rank possible. While he was secretary of state, his Marshall Peace Plan for the rebuilding of Europe after World War II won him the Nobel Peace Prize. The museum, open daily 9 A.M.–5 P.M. ($3 adults, $1 children) contains army memorabilia, personal papers, and a narrated map of World War II.

The **Virginia Military Institute Museum,** 540/464-7232, www.vmi.edu/museum, occupies the basement of Jackson Memorial Hall at the opposite corner of the parade ground. Stonewall Jackson's field desk and a statue of his favorite horse, Little Sorrel, are both on display along with period clothes, weapons, and historical VMI artifacts. Open daily 9 A.M.–5 P.M.; free.

Stonewall Jackson House

The only home the Confederate commander ever owned stands in the heart of Lexington, at 8 E. Washington St., 540/463-2552, www.stonewall-jackson.org. Jackson occupied the modest brick town house for two years with his second wife, Anna Morrison, before riding off to war in April 1861, never to return. Restored in 1979, the brick building contains many of his possessions and other Civil War–era pieces, along with a gift shop. The kitchen garden has been replanted behind the house. Tours are given every half-hour. Open Mon.–Sat. 9 A.M.–5 P.M. (6 P.M. June–Aug.), Sun. 1–5 P.M. (6 P.M. June–Aug.); $5 adults, $2.50 children 6–18.

Stonewall Jackson Cemetery

After being accidentally killed by his own men at Chancellorsville, "Old Jack" was laid to rest in this burial ground at the south end of Main Street. An Edward Valentine statue marks his tomb in the center, surrounded by the graves of other Civil War notables and prominent local citizens. Open dawn–dusk.

Boxerwood Gardens

Local doctor Robert Munger began planting rare trees and shrubs around his house in 1952. After his death in 1988, his gardener bought the place and opened it to the public in 1997. More an arboretum than a flower garden, Boxerwood, 963 Ross Rd., 540/463-2697, www.boxerwood.com, encloses 15 rolling acres of exotic species like Japanese maples and dwarf conifers alongside local dogwoods, rhododendrons, and azaleas, all with a panoramic view of the Blue Ridge Mountains. Everything is labeled but left more raggedly natural than neatly pruned. Maps are available for self-guided tours, but half the fun is simply wandering and seeing what you find. Open Mar.–Nov. Tues.–Sun. 9 A.M.–4 P.M., $5 pp.

STONEWALL JACKSON

Born Thomas Jonathan Jackson on January 21, 1824, in Clarksburg, Virginia, the Civil War's most famous field commander found himself an orphan by age seven. He grew up in the house of an uncle, before squeaking into the U.S. Military Academy at West Point. (The first choice from the local congressional district, it seemed, had quit after his first day.) There he survived, in his own words, "by the skin of my teeth," graduating in 1846, 17th in a class of 59.

During the Mexican-American War, Jackson saw action in Cerro Gordo, Veracruz, and Chapultepec, and his outstanding conduct in the artillery earned him early promotions. In 1851, though, he left the rank of major to become a professor of military tactics and physics at the Virginia Military Institute (VMI). Students disliked and derided his dull teaching style and classroom quirks, starting with a shrill voice that belied his six-foot, 170-pound frame. Jackson lived in Lexington for the next decade, joining the Presbyterian Church and local Bible society. Two of those years were spent in the house on Washington Street that is now a museum.

Within weeks of the outbreak of the Civil War, Jackson was back in the ranks, assuming a post as infantry colonel on April 21, 1861. Quickly promoted to brigadier general, the former teacher marched a group of VMI cadets to Richmond to help train the budding Confederate Army. His famous nickname came at the First Battle of Bull Run, in July 1861, soon after Confederate forces had begun to flee the fight. Seeing Jackson's troops holding their ground, Brig. Gen. Barnard E. Bee cried, "There stands Jackson like a stone wall! Rally behind the Virginians!" Bee was killed minutes later, but the tide of battle turned, and the name stuck.

Shortly after being promoted to major general, Stonewall cemented his place in history with his famous Valley Campaign in the spring of 1862, often called one of the most brilliant in military history. He continued to shine through the battles of Antietam and Second Bull Run, where his unorthodox tactics and uncanny rapport with General Lee won him fight after fight. Stonewall worked best when he was free to march and attack at will, pushing his men to the limit and always appearing when and where his opponents least expected.

Through it all, "Old Jack" remained a strange bird, obsessed with secrecy and concealing his plans even from direct subordinates. (Maj. Gen. Richard Ewell eventually concluded that his superior was a few pecks short of a bushel.) At Chancellorsville in early May 1863, Jackson detached from General Lee's forces to flank the Federal XI Corps under Maj. Gen. Joseph Hooker. The risky but inspired maneuver routed the enemy troops in one of the most dramatic and decisive Confederate victories of the war. But Stonewall's finest hour was too soon followed by his final one: out riding the evening of May 2, he was fired on by mistake by Confederate guards. Two of his aides were killed, and Jackson was shot once in the right hand and twice in the left arm. In a nearby home that served as a field hospital, doctors decided to amputate the shattered limb. "He has lost his left arm," Lee said as Jackson lay dying, "but I have lost my right."

Jackson gave a good fight, but pneumonia set in and his condition deteriorated. On May 10, his doctors decided that he wouldn't last until sundown. The Confederacy's star commander died that afternoon after a final request: "Let us cross over the river and rest in the shade of the trees." His valiant Stonewall Brigade, hardened by dozens of battles, was never the same after losing its leader, though eight of its men went on to become generals.

Museum of Military Memorabilia

Uniforms, weapons, flags, and accouterments from France, Great Britain, Germany, and the United States, spanning wars from 1740 to the Gulf War, fill a small gallery at 122-1/2 S. Main St., 540/464-3041. Open May–Oct. Wed.–Fri. noon–5 P.M., Sat. 9 A.M.–5 P.M.; $3 adults, with guided tours.

Virginia Horse Center

On Rt. 39 just north of I-64 lies one of the most outstanding equine complexes in the country. Shows, clinics, and sales are held year-round, including the Virginia Horse Trials, the National Miniature Horse show, and the Southwest Virginia Hunter/Jumper Association. The **American Work Horse Museum** includes just about everything horse-powered, from farm equipment to rural postal wagons. It's open most weekends or whenever there is an equine event happening. Call 540/463-2194 or 540/463-4300 for current schedules, or stop by www.horsecenter.org on the Internet.

ACCOMMODATIONS

Befitting its role as one of Virginia's most popular getaway towns, Lexington and the surrounding area is positively rife with guesthouses.

In Town

Overnight Guests, 216 W. Washington St., 540/463-3075, is an old-style rooming house with six rooms and two shared baths. For $10 pp you have access to cable TV and the rocking chairs on the porch. The decor of **Asherowe,** 314 S. Jefferson St., 540/463-4219, reflects the owner's love of travel, books, cats, and gardening. The 1911 home has a two-story library and a front porch swing, as well as outdoor garden areas and two cats. Three rooms (two doubles and a single) are $55 each.

The **Magnolia House,** 501 S. Main St., 877/355-4664 or 540/463-2567, fax 540/463-4358, email: magnolia@rockbridge.net, www.magnoliahouseinn.com, dates to 1868 and boasts high ceilings and spacious rooms. Suites are $90–105. John Roberts, the owner of **A Bed & Breakfast at**

Llewellyn Lodge, 603 Main St., 800/882-1145 or 540/463-3235, fax 540/464-3122, email: LLL@rockbridge.net, www.Llodge.com, was born in the Stonewall Jackson house and knows Lexington and the area like the back of his hand, especially the outdoors. He's run the B&B with his wife Ellen for 13 years, making it the oldest in town. Six rooms are moderate to expensive, including a celebrated full gourmet breakfast. Room rates are $100–120.

Historic Country Inns of Lexington, 11 N. Main St., 877/463-2044 or 540/463-2044, fax 540/463-7262, email: mail@lexingtonhistoric inns.com, www.lexingtonhistoricinns.com, is based in the 1809 **McCampbell Inn.** They also rent out the **Alexander-Witherow House** (c. 1789) across the street, as well as the 1850 **Maple Hall Country Inn,** seven miles north of town. A total of 31 rooms and five suites range in price from $85–160, including expanded Continental breakfast. An 1827 manor home has been converted into the **Hampton Inn Col Alto,** 401 E. Nelson St., 800/426-7866 or 540/463-2223, fax 540/463-9707, graced by a Palladian porch and many antiques. Room rates are $150–300.

Out of Town

The **Best Western Inn at Hunt Ridge,** 25 Willow Springs Rd., tel./fax 540/464-1500, is a modern place with a colonial flair. Prices ($100) include a full breakfast in G. Willaker's Restaurant. On US 60 4.5 miles west of Lexington is the **Days Inn Keydet General Motel,** 325 W. Midland Trail, tel./fax 540/463-2143, with rooms for $60–75, and off I-64 exit 55 is an **Econo Lodge,** 540/463-7371, fax 540/463-6095 ($88).

The **Applewood Inn,** Buffalo Bend Rd., 800/463-1902 or 540/463-1962, fax 540/463-6996, email: applewd@cfw.com, www.applewoodbb.com, is an environmentally friendly B&B offering 36 acres of rustic comfort south of town. A California redwood hot tub sits on an enclosed porch that's part of the house's solar envelope construction, where a layer of heated air surrounding the entire building provides warmth well into the night. Guests are welcome to use the pool and kitchen, and the owners offer two-hour llama treks to a gourmet luncheon in the hills for guests and day visitors. To get there, take Rt. 11 for 4.5 miles south of town and make a right onto Buffalo Bend Road, following signs for the next two miles. Room rates are $100–135.

Most of the rooms at **Brierley Hill,** 985 Borden Rd., 800/422-4925 or 540/464-8421, fax 540/464-8925, email: brierly@cfw.com, www.brierlyhill.com, have verandahs or windows overlooking Shenandoah Valley and the Blue Ridge. Three rooms are $95–130, and two suites with fireplaces are $160. Hiking trails wind through the 113 wooded acres that surround the **North Mountain Farm,** 378 Paw Paw Rd., 800/500-6709, email: nmfarmva@aol.com, www.northmountainfarm.com. Choose from a three-bedroom cedar home with cathedral ceilings that sleeps eight ($150) or an original loft homestead that sleeps four ($100). Both are fully furnished and have satellite TVs, woodstoves, stereos, and porches. Take 60 W to Rt. 850 (Midland Trail), go three miles and take a left on Big Hill Road, then four miles and take a right on Rt. 647 (Unexpected Rd.) and another quick right on Paw Paw Road.

Autumn Ridge Cottages, 540/463-3387, www.autumnridgecottages.com, are two miles south downtown, set on 40 acres with fields and mountain views in every direction. The "old-style" cabins are fully modern inside, with Jacuzzis and fireplaces. Rates range from $125–175 per night, depending on length of stay.

Camping

Long's Campground, 540/463-7672, has sites for $11 (full hookup $18) along with a pool, game room, camp store, hot showers, and movie rentals. It's on Rt. 39 three miles west of the intersection of I-64 and US 11.

FOOD

Breakfast

Omelets, French toast, and waffles are all less than $3 at **City Subs and Steaks Inc.,** 159 S. Main St., 540/464-7827. The deli is open Mon.–Sat. 7:30 A.M.–9 or 10 P.M. (They also serve inexpensive soups, salads, steaks, and subs.) **Harbs' Bistro,** 19 W. Washington St., 540/464-

1900, offers full breakfast and lunch daily in a cheery atmosphere.

Sweets and Snacks

Although there may not be any sign for **Caroline's Sweets,** 8 N. Main St., 540/463-5691, it's still the best old-fashioned bakery in town. Open for breakfast and lunch Tues.–Sat. The **Cocoa Mill Chocolate Company,** 115 W. Nelson St., 800/464-8400, has shelves dripping with handmade fudge, truffles, and pecan, caramel, or chocolate "snappers"—and free samples to start you off. **Lexington Coffee Roasting Co.** 9 W. Washington St., 540/464-6586, serves a hearty cup of joe along with pastries and Italian sodas in cozy seats by the fireplace. Open Mon.–Sat. from 7:30 or 8 A.M. until 5 P.M. **Washington Street Purveyors,** 9 E. Washington St., 540/464-9463, offers regional and international wines, microbrews, cigars, and gourmet snacks. Wine tastings are held occasionally.

Moderately Priced

Near the top of Lexington's long list of Italian restaurants is **Il Palazzo,** 24 N. Main St., 540/464-5800. For dinner, pastas are $8–10 and veal, steak, and chicken entrées run $13–16 (up to $21 for seafood). The place also cooks up pizzas and subs, with lunch specials in the $5–6 range. Open daily for lunch and dinner. **Salerno's,** 115 S. Jefferson St., 540/463-5757, has an all-you-can-eat spaghetti special on Monday from 5–10 P.M. Open daily for lunch and dinner.

A big green neon sign lights the way to the **Southern Inn,** 37 S. Main St., 540/463-3612, a long, high-ceilinged place open since 1932. The food is well-prepared, whether it's the pan-fried catfish for lunch (entrées $9–13) or the baked salmon for dinner ($15–24). Sandwiches are around $6, and they have a wide selection of wines.

Owner/"food goddess" Jaurie Macrae says her **Blue Heron Café,** 4 E. Washington St., 540/463-2800, is the only completely vegetarian restaurant for miles around. Excellent, healthy plates such as spicy fried noodles topped with nasturtiums are around $5 for lunch served Mon.–Sat. (dinner Fri. and Sat.). More healthy eats, including smoothies and vegan pizza, can be found at the **Healthy Foods Market,** 110 W. Washington St., 540/463-6954, open for lunch Mon.–Sat. Meals to go ("like Mother makes") are prepared in the My Kitchen deli in the back of the **Main Street Market** grocery store, 167 S. Main St., 540/463-5004.

Fine Dining
Subdued lighting and antique etchings and paintings set the tone in the **Wilson-Walker House Restaurant,** 30 N. Main St., 540/463-3020, in a beautiful two-story classical revival house (c. 1820) with columns and balconies in front. Dinner features standbys including crab, pasta, and trout, along with daily specials and "Creative American" creations such as Tofu Wellington and pecan-crusted pork loin with ginger sauce. An extensive list of Virginia wines ensures that there's always something to pair with your entrée ($15–20). They offer a $5 lunch special and a $20 prix fixe four-course dinner special Tues.–Thurs. Open Tues.–Sat. for lunch and dinner.

ENTERTAINMENT AND RECREATION

Theaters
On the outskirts of Lexington, the ruins of a 19th-century kiln have been converted into one of the more unusual and enjoyable places to see a play in the entire Mid-Atlantic region. Founded in 1983, the **Lime Kiln Theater,** 540/463-3074, www.theateratlimekiln.com, seems to rise up out of the ground itself amid the vine-covered stones where workers once smelted lime and cut stones. Actors and musicians now perform on summer evenings on one of three stages—two open to the stars and one a tent in case of rain. The theater season runs May.–Sept. with performances Tues.–Sat., while the Coors Summer Concert Series brings folk and rock music from around the country. The theater can be reached from Lime Kiln Road off White and McLaughlin from Main Street, or via Border Road south off US 60 West.

Washington and Lee's **Lenfest Center for the Performing Arts,** US 60 W and Glasgow, 540/463-8000, also hosts plays and concerts by students and professionals. The W&L Film Soci-

ety also screens movies at the **Trubadour Cinema** at the corner of Main and Henry streets, often for free. Head north on Rt. 39 about five miles to reach the classic dinosaur called **Hull's Drive-In Theater,** 540/463-2621, one of only eight left in the state. It's the real thing, sno-cones and all.

Nightlife
Students name **The Palms,** 101 W. Nelson St., 540/463-7911, as the biggest and most popular bar in town. It's open from lunch (sandwiches and burgers) through dinner (light fare—chicken and pasta) until 1 or 2 A.M. Downstairs, the **Traveller's Bar & Grill,** 16 Lee Ave., 540/462-6014, also draws a crowd.

Tours
From late May to October, the **Ghost Tour of Lexington,** 540/348-1080, guarantees a scare—or at least a shiver—as it takes you on the candlelit rounds of haunted sites around town. The 75-minute tour leaves from the visitors center at 8:30 P.M., where tickets ($8 adults, $6 children 4–10) are available. A daytime option is a tour of Lexington's major historical sights by horse-drawn carriage with the **Lexington Carriage Company, Inc.,** 540/463-5647. Its 45-minute tours leave from Washington Street across from the visitors center, Apr.–Oct. 10 A.M.–4:30 P.M. (June–Aug. 9 A.M.–5 P.M.); $14 adults, $7 children 7–13.

Outdoors
Narrow but pretty **Woods Creek Park** follows the creek of the same name for two miles the length of Lexington. At the northern end where it reaches the Maury River, you can pick up the **Chessie Nature Trail,** a seven-mile stretch of the old Chesapeake and Ohio rail line through rural countryside to Buena Vista. Damage from Hurricane Camille in 1969 caused the line to be abandoned, allowing the Nature Conservancy to acquire it in 1978. Along the way you'll pass old canal locks and cross a 235-foot bridge over the South River near its confluence with the Maury River. To reach the starting point, cross US 11 near VMI Island using the foot bridge; the pedestrian trail begins near the north end of the US 11 bridge.

Reel Time Fly Fishing & Outfitter, 23 W. Washington St., 540/462-6100, www.reel-timeflyfishing.com, rents and sells equipment, 40,000 flies, guide service, local stream information, and fishing licenses. **Kelly's Corner,** 876 W. Midlothian Trail., 540/463-5452, offers hand-tied flies custom-designed for the area, along with fly-fishing equipment, snacks, fishing licenses, and advice. It's on Rt. 60, 2.5 miles west of Lexington.

Afternoon canoe and kayak trips on the Maury and James rivers can be arranged through the **James River Basin Canoe Livery, Ltd.,** 1870 E. Midland Trail, 540/261-7334, email: information@canoevirginia.com, www.canoe-virginia.com, for $35–60 pp. Longer trips are also possible. The **Wilderness Canoe Company,** 800/422-6634 or 540/291-2295, will send you off down the James River in a canoe or kayak, including shuttle service, maps, and equipment. Finally, there's a **U.S. Forest Service Information Center** in front of the Stonewall Inn at Natural Bridge.

EVENTS

On the third Monday in January, **Lee-Jackson Day,** commemorates the birthdays of Robert E. Lee (Jan. 19) and Stonewall Jackson (Jan. 21) with celebrations throughout the South, but particularly in Stonewall's hometown. Free tours of Jackson's home and other festivities honor the local hero. In March of election years, Lexington comes alive with Washington & Lee's famous **Mock Convention,** an outrageous parade and party that also happens to be one of the most accurate predictors of presidential politics in the country. Since William Jennings Bryan defeated John A. Johnson in 1908, the counterfeit caucus has correctly predicted presidential nominees 15 of 20 times. Despite the festive atmosphere, a year's worth of serious research goes into keeping up such a good track record (last broken in 1972, when Ted Kennedy was chosen for the Democratic nomination over George McGovern). The convention happens early in the actual races, giving it serious political sway that attracts national interest.

The Virginia Horse Center hosts the **Virginia Horse Festival** the third weekend in April, showcasing dozens of different breeds with demonstrations, seminars, and equestrian merchandise and art for sale.

SHOPPING

Local artists have formed a cooperative gallery in the Alexander Witherow House called **Artists in Cahoots,** 1 W. Washington St., 540/464-1147, showcasing beautiful crafts from photography and stained glass to hand-painted silks and delicate carved birds. Some artists also work here. **Virginia Born and Bred,** 16 W. Washington St., 540/463-1832, stocks Americana including hand-carved nutcrackers and folk art alongside jellies, hams, and wines.

Textiles and ceramics, both Virginian and from elsewhere, fill **Artisans on Washington Street,** 22 W. Washington St., 540/464-3625, while **Original Frameworks,** 1 N. Main St., 540/464-6464, is a frame shop with a back room full of Civil War relics, prints, and paintings. You'll find a little bit of everything—and then some—at **The Second Hand Shop,** 7 S. Jefferson St., 540/463-7559, from crates of records and old guitars to photographs, clothes, and antiques.

Lexington has too many antique stores to mention—practically one on every block—but for sheer volume you can't beat the **Lexington Antique and Craft Mall,** 540/463-9511, with 250 dealers spread over 40,000 square feet. It's in the College Square Shopping Center, southwest of the center of town on Rt. 672 (Enfield Rd.).

INFORMATION AND TRANSPORTATION

Lexington's well-organized **visitors center,** 106 E. Washington St., 540/463-3777, features a miniature museum, slide show, and helpful employees. It's open daily Sept.–May 9 A.M.–5 P.M., June–Aug. 8:30 A.M.–6 P.M.

There is a **Greyhound** bus terminal, 800/231-2222 or 540/261-5254, at 221 W. 21st St. in Buena Vista, six miles east of Lexington.

South of Lexington

THE SHENANDOAH

NATURAL BRIDGE

Rockbridge County derives its name from this 215-foot-tall limestone span—all that remains of a huge cavern carved out over thousands of years by tiny Cedar Creek. Thomas Jefferson, who once owned Natural Bridge, called it "so beautiful in archeology, so elevated, so light, and springing as it were up to Heaven, [that] the rapture of the spectator is really indescribable" (brochure literature names it as one of the dozen or so Seven Wonders of the World). Thousands of tourists make the pilgrimage annually.

Natural Bridge is spectacular, to be sure—one of Virginia's most impressive natural sights—but almost as fascinating is the spectacle that has evolved around it. Interstate billboards are stacked like dominoes for hundreds of miles in every direction, and even ticket sellers can't keep a straight face describing the nightly *Drama of Creation* colored-light show, complete with music and solemn narration intoning the origins of the universe. If you run out of money, there's an ATM; if you find religion, there's a Baptist church. In the end, the whole package, which has little to do with the bridge itself, gives a new shade of meaning to the slogan "The Wonder of It All."

History

According to native legend, the "Bridge of God" materialized to help a band of Monocan Indians in flight from raiding Shawnee and Powhatans. In 1749, British Lord Fairfax hired Col. Peter Jefferson—who, six years earlier, had fathered a son destined to become president—to survey the land around today's Rt. 11. One young assistant carved his initials on the stone wall; the faint "GW" is still visible, making George Washington the only president to have officially defaced a Virginia landmark. In 1773, Thomas Jefferson gained title to the bridge and 157 surrounding acres from King George III for 20 shillings ($2.40 today). Near the base he built a log cabin and installed a "sentiment" book in which prominent visitors could record their im-

pressions. During the Revolutionary War, soldiers made bullets by pouring molten lead from the bridge into the creek below and mined saltpeter from nearby caves for gunpowder.

The Bridge

All visits start at the main ticket building, which encloses a gargantuan gift shop, an indoor pool, a miniature golf course, an ATM, and a post office. Brochures in French, German, Spanish, Russian, Chinese, and Japanese describe what you're going to see as soon as you've decided which ticket package to buy. Options include the bridge only ($10 adults, $4.50 children 6–15); the bridge, cave, and wax museum ($17 adults, $8.50 children); any two ($14 and $7); or the cave or museum only ($7 and $3.50). Alternately, you can drive over the bridge for free—Rt. 11 heading east toward the Blue Ridge Parkway crosses right over it—but you can't see anything from above. Open daily 8 A.M.–10 P.M. (shorter hours

© JULIAN SMITH

the impressive limestone span for which Rockbridge County was named

Oct.–Apr.), 800/533-1410, email: info@naturalbridgeva.com, www.naturalbridgeva.com.

Walk downhill or take a shuttle bus to the beginning of the trail, where the **Summer House Cafe** offers light fare in an open patio alongside the creek. Children's voices echo up the deep, wooded gorge where you'll get your first glimpse of the sheer size of the thing. At 50–150 feet wide and 90 feet long, it's massive—but surprisingly graceful for 36,000 tons of stone. The trail continues along the creek, a pleasant walk when it's not too crowded. Past an open space where Easter sunrise services have been held since 1947 are an old saltpeter mine, picnic areas, and the Lace Waterfalls.

Other Sights

George Washington, Daniel Boone, and Robert E. Lee share quarters with some 175 others in the **Natural Bridge Wax Museum,** 540/291-2426. Narrated historic scenes include the Garden of Eden and a theatrical presentation of Leonardo da Vinci's *Last Supper.* An explanation of the making of wax figures is part of the tour. Open daily 9 A.M.–9 P.M. (shorter hours Oct.–Apr.) It's said that the ghost of a woman haunts the **Natural Bridge Caverns,** 540/291-2121, the deepest cave on the East Coast. Guided tours to spots including the Wishing Well Room, Colossal Dome Room, and Mirror Lake leave every half-hour. Open daily mid-Mar.–Nov. 10 A.M.–5 P.M.

Natural Bridge Zoo, 540/291-2420, harbors the usual—giraffes, camels, bears, and monkeys—along with rare and endangered species such as a white tiger born in 1997. It also boasts the largest petting zoo in the state. Don't let the kids hear about the elephants rides ($7 adults, $4 children 3–12), or you'll have no choice but to stop by. If you haven't had enough animals by now, stop by the **Virginia Safari Park,** 540/291-3205, a 180-acre drive-through zoo. A three-mile road takes you past bison, zebra, antelope, and ostriches roaming free (more or less), and there's also a petting zoo and a primate house. Guided wagon tours ($3 pp) run at 1 and 3 P.M. on weekends. Open Apr.–Oct. daily 9 A.M.–6 P.M. (Mar. and Nov. weekends only 9 A.M.–5 P.M.); $7 adults, $5 children 3–12.

Accommodations and Food

Next to the ticket building, the **Natural Bridge Hotel,** 800/533-1410, has rooms in the hotel itself for $50–90 and four- to six-room cottages across the road for $50–70. There's also an Olympic-sized pool and the restaurant serving all meals daily, with outdoor dining on the veranda and popular weekend buffets. Various packages include lodging, meals, and admission to the attractions; the Jefferson Packages is an example, including one night's lodging, breakfast and dinner, and admission to the bridge, caverns, and museum for $190 per couple.

Camping

The **Campground at Natural Bridge,** 540/291-2727, has full-hookup sites for $24, tent spots for $17–19, and cabins for $40–85 per night. They rent boats, canoes, and tubes to enjoy the nearby James River and charge a small fee for fishing in their stocked pond. To get there, take Rt. 130 east from I-81 exit 175 for 4.5 miles, take a right onto Rt. 759, then your first left onto Rt. 782. Tent sites at the **Natural Bridge/Lexington KOA Kampground,** 800/562-8514 or 540/291-2770, are $20, with RV campsites for $23–25 and Kamping Kabins for $35–40. They're just off I-81 exit 180 on Rt. 11. A short drive up into the Jefferson National Forest brings you to the **Cave Mountain Lake Recreation Area,** 540/291-2189, where 42 sites near the cold, clear lake are $10 each. Take Rt. 130 east from I-81 exit 175 or 180 for 3.2 miles, turn south onto Rt. 795 for another 3.2 miles, and turn right onto Rt. 781 for 1.6 miles to the recreation area's paved entrance road.

BLUE RIDGE PARKWAY

Like a vine connecting two ripe grapes, this scenic highway unites the Shenandoah and Great Smoky Mountains national parks in one long, lovely stretch of Appalachia. It was begun during the Great Depression as a federal public-works project and finished within a decade. Designers took liberties with the philosophy of the shortest distance between two points, choosing instead to follow the wandering 3,000-foot ridgeline wherever it chose to go. Of the parkway's 469 miles, 217 are in

Virginia, and the first 114, between Waynesboro and Roanoke along the crest of the Blue Ridge Mountains, are widely thought to be the most impressive. Miles of tranquil farm scenes are punctuated by crumbling graveyards and gaps, which open to grand panoramas in either direction.

Access

The parkway is open year-round, though few facilities outside Peaks of Otter are open beyond May–October, and parts of the road may be closed due to inclement weather. Entry is free. Between I-64 at Waynesboro and US 460 at Roanoke, drivers can reach the road via US 60 near Buena Vista, Rt. 30 and Rt. 501 east of Natural Bridge, and Rt. 43 east of Bucanan.

Flora and Fauna

Vegetation along the parkway is more southern (i.e., drier) than in Shenandoah National Park. Forests of white pine, hemlock, and hawthorn burst into color during an extended fall season, thanks to the wide range of altitudes along the road (649 to 6,047 feet). In the autumn spectrum, reds are probably maples or dogwoods, yellows hickory, and orange sassafras. Spruce, fir, and pine provide a green backdrop. Spectacular flame azalea blooms between Roanoke and the

Smokies in May and June, followed by purple Catawba rhododendron near Peaks of Otter. Many of the larger animals come out at dusk and are gone by dawn, leaving daytime to the groundhogs, squirrels, and chipmunks. White-tail deer, bobcats, raccoons, and black bears all make occasional appearances.

Camping

Of the four campgrounds along the Blue Ridge Parkway, two (Otter Creek and Peaks of Otter) are north of Roanoke. All are open roughly May–October, but call ahead during other months because they might keep a few sites going year-round. Campsites are first-come, first-served, $12 per site for two adults, and limited to a 21-day maximum stay from May–October. Some campsites are accessible to visitors with disabilities. Trailers up to 30 feet are permitted, and all campgrounds have dumpstations (but no water or electrical hookups). Pets must be on leashes. Off the parkway, backcountry camping is permitted in the George Washington National Forest.

Rockfish Gap to Roanoke

All locations along the parkway are measured in mileposts (milepost), from 0 at the southern terminus of Shenandoah National Park at Rockfish Gap to 218 at the North Carolina border. The speed limit along the entire parkway is 45 mph, but traffic can crawl during high season. In emergencies, call 800/PARK-WATCH (727-5928).

At the **Humpback Rocks Visitor Center,** mile 5.8, a self-guided trail leads through a reconstructed historic farmstead. Across the road, a steep three-quarter-mile trail climbs to the jagged top of Humpback Rocks for a 360-degree view of the Blue Ridge Mountains. Sunrise from the top of Humpback with a box of donuts and a steaming thermos of coffee is one of my personal favorites in the whole state. Past **Devil's Knob** (3,851 feet) is a turnoff to Rt. 664 toward Wintergreen Ski Resort. The **Sherando Lake Recreation Area** is next, centered on a pair of lakes created in the early 1900s by the Civilian Conservation Corps for recreation and flood control. The 25-acre lower lake is open to swimming and boating, while the seven-acre lake

THE DEVIL'S MARBLEYARD

An easy one-mile hike up the west side of the Blue Ridge leads to a hillside strewn with white quartzite boulders. Split by frost wedges during the last Ice Age, these boulders cover eight acres, leading to a great view of Arnold's Valley from the top. (Watch for spiders and biting insects in the summer, though.) To get there, take Rt. 130 south from Natural Bridge to Natural Bridge Station, then take a right on Rt. 759 (Arnold's Valley Rd.). Cross the James River and the Shenandoah Valley, pass a correctional center on the left, then head left on Petite's Gap Road at a three-way intersection. Parking is on the left, marked "Belfast Trail." You can access the Appalachian Trail from the top, and it's easiest to descend on the trail to the right of the rockslide.

above it is known for trout, bass, and bluegill fishing. Almost 20 miles of forest roads and single-track make up the Sherando Lake Loop, including a 1,000-foot climb from the lake through "Big Levels" to the Bald Mountain Overlook.

At **Tye River Gap** (2,969 feet), take Rt. 56 east to the head of the **Crabtree Falls Trail,** leading to the highest waterfall east of the Mississippi. Five cascades tumble more than 1,200 feet in all. (This is also a good spot to access two of the state's choicest wilderness areas: the **Priest Wilderness,** with eight peaks higher than 4,000 feet, and **Three Ridges Wilderness,** with more mountains and waterfalls. For more information on these hikes, contact the Glenwood-Pedlar Ranger District of the George Washington National Forest, 540/291-2188, www.southernregion.fs.fed.us/gwj.

Pass the **Whetstone Ridge Ranger Station** and a basic restaurant near milepost 29 to reach **Yankee Horse** at milepost 34.4, named for an unfortunate Union mount that had to be shot after it fell from exhaustion. Here an overlook trail leads along a remnant of an old logging railway from the 1920s to 30-foot Wigwam Falls in a shady grove. **Otter Creek** (mile 60.8) rolls down the hillside toward the James River, lined by blooming mountain laurel in May and June. A campground has 69 sites, a coffee shop, and a service station.

There is a visitors center at **James River Over-look,** mile 63.6, the lowest point on the parkway. A self-guiding trail leads over a footbridge and along the river bluff to restored locks along the Kanawha canal. The **Peaks of Otter Recreation Area,** milepost 86, encloses a visitors center, 151 campsites, and the **Peaks of Otter Lodge,** 800/542-5927 or 540/586-1081, fax 540/586-4420, www.peaksofotter.com, the only place on the parkway guaranteed to be open year-round. Sixty-three rooms overlooking Abbott Lake each have two double beds but no TVs or phones, with prices ranging from $59 for low-season weekdays to $89 for high-season weekends. The view from the dining room is justly famous, and the hotel has a coffee shop, lounge, and gift shop. Trails near the campground lead to the Old Johnson Farm, Harkening Hill, and Flat Top. Long thought to be the highest point in the state, Sharp Top (3,875 feet) can be reached by foot and sweat via a steep 1.5-mile trail, or on a tour bus from the hotel that drops you off near the peak.

Information

The Blue Ridge Parkway is administered by the National Park Service, which can be contacted at 199 Hemphill Knob Rd., Asheville, North Carolina 29901-3417, 828/271-4779, 828/298-0398 (recorded visitor information message), fax 828/271-4313, www.nps.gov/blri. Each visitors center sells excellent books detailing hikes, history, and wildlife along the road.

Northern Virginia

Northern Virginia is a study in contrasts. On one hand you have the half-paved expanses of Arlington and Fairfax counties: full of shopping malls, housing developments, and little else, this area once languished in the shadow of the Capitol. On the other hand are miles of undulating pastures dotted with mansions and farms housing purebred stallions. In one direction, suburbia; in the other, arcadia; in all, a region that's definitely worth a second glance.

Still, the two halves have more in common than may be evident at first. For one, money. Hunt Country is among the nation's wealthiest regions per capita, and dollars have been pouring into local coffers ever since the federal government built the Pentagon on the eve of World War II. Another commonality is the area's vicinity to Washington, D.C. District residents have always looked to places like Old Town Alexandria, Great Falls, and the parks south along the Potomac as refuges from the downside of urban life. Now they're looking even farther west and finding enchanting B&Bs, gourmet restaurants, and quiet, historic towns. Some like it so much they're buying land and relocating—bringing with them (some would

the George Washington Masonic Memorial in Alexandria

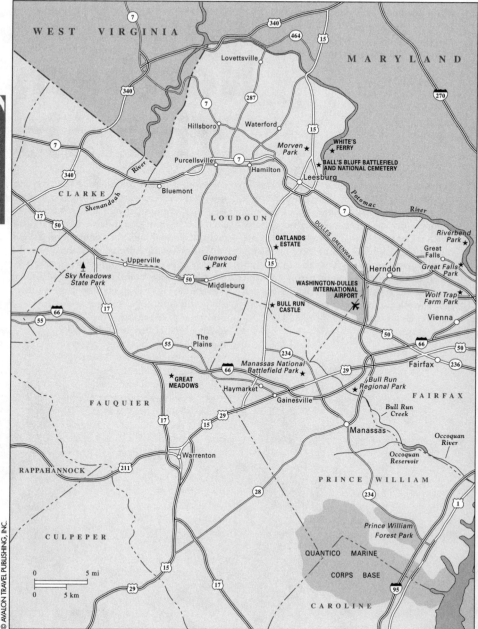

NORTHERN VIRGINIA

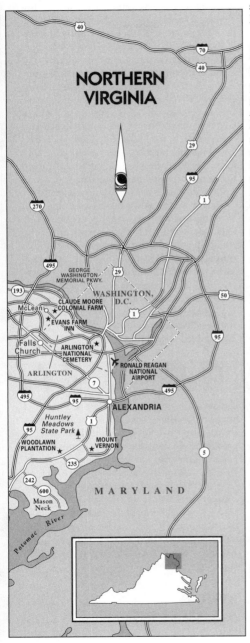

**NORTHERN
VIRGINIA**

say) a wave of development that inches along the Dulles Greenway one subdivision at a time.

HIGHLIGHTS

History fans will be surprised at the pockets of the past hidden among the highrises in northern Virginia. More than 2,000 buildings in Old Town Alexandria are listed in the National Register of Historic Places, while George Washington's home at Mt. Vernon retains most of its Revolutionary allure despite tourist crowds. Arlington National Cemetery and the Pentagon lie within sight of the capital skyline, and Robert E. Lee's mansion in Arlington National Cemetery overlooks waves of headstones, which are only a short drive from Manassas, site of two major Civil War battles. Travelers interested in things modern will enjoy Frank Lloyd Wright's Pope-Leighey House at Woodlawn and the cutting-edge Newseum in Arlington.

For outdoor recreation, there's the Washington & Old Dominion Trail running from Arlington to Purcellville, a scenic success of converting a former railroad bed into a multiuse trail. A visit to horse-happy Hunt Country, centered around Leesburg, will show you why the American foxhound is the Virginia state dog, while a sea-kayak paddle around Mason Neck might net you a bald eagle sighting.

ARRIVING AND GETTING AROUND

Northern Virginia does prove one sprawl theory true: driving can be a nightmare, especially on major highways during the weekday rush hours of 6–9 A.M. and 4:30–7 P.M. (One gate guard answered my directional question with a laugh: "*Quickest* way? Where are you from?") A maze of highways and swarms of traffic lights sometimes seem designed solely to slow things down, simply turning around can be a chore, and don't get caught driving alone in a high-occupancy vehicle (HOV) lane, marked with white diamonds, or you'll get a hefty fine.

Inside the Beltway (the loop of I-495 and I-95 around the nation's capital), the **Metrorail,** 202/637-7000, www.wmata.com, provides a clean, quiet, and quick way to get around. Three lines enter northern Virginia from Washington. The orange and blue lines cross the Potomac together into northern Arlington; from there the orange heads west as far as Vienna, while the blue turns south past Arlington National Cemetery to join with the yellow (spanning the river next to I-395) at the Pentagon. This pair continues south to the King Street Station before splitting for a final stop or two.

Trains run until midnight from 5:30 A.M. on weekdays and 8 A.M. on weekends. Fares depend on distance and whether you're traveling during rush hour (weekdays 5:30–9:30 A.M. and 3–8 P.M.). Passengers ages four and up have to buy magnetic paper fare cards, which you swipe through a machine on entering a station and again when you leave the system. The value of the trip ($1.10–3.25) is automatically deducted from your card; if you don't have enough value, you'll have to add more at machines near the exit. One-day passes are $5, and you can buy 7- and 28-day passes as well.

Metrobuses connect with Metrorail stations for travel to outlying areas. Fares are $1.10 per trip, but transfers from the Metrorail are free. One-day passes cost $2.50.

Washington National Airport, 703/417-8000, www.metwashairports.com/National, recently had Ronald Reagan's name officially attached to it, but most people ignore the Gipper and still just call it "National." The blue and yellow Metro lines both stop at the airport, located in Arlington.

Washington-Dulles International Airport, 703/572-2700, www.airwise.com/airports/us/IAD/IAD_01.html, is about a half-hour drive (depending on traffic) from Arlington National Cemetery along the Dulles Access Road. This runs parallel to the Dulles Toll Road, but is free. The Metro orange line ends at the West Falls Church station, where you can catch a transfer bus to the airport every half hour daily from 5:30 A.M.–midnight (8 A.M.–1 A.M. on weekends).

You can get from one airport to the other with **Washington Flyer Coach,** 703/417-8471, 888/WASH-FLY (927-4359), www.washfly.com, for $26 pp roundtrip ($16 one-way), which also runs between Dulles and the West Falls Church Metro station ($14/$8). To get to and from downtown D.C., call **Super Shuttle,** 800/258-3826, which runs taxis to Dulles for $32 for two people. **Greyhound/Trailways,** 703/998-6312, has a station at 3860 S. Four Mile Run Drive near Walter Reed Drive in South Arlington.

Arlington County and Vicinity

At just under 26 square miles, Arlington County is the third smallest in the United States. Still, almost 200,000 residents call it home, mostly in the north and west. Even with four bridges connecting it to the capital, Arlington has started to grow out of its role as a D.C. appendix, full of "bedroom communities" that lie empty during the day. Computer and communications industries have set up shop in neighborhoods (the county has no incorporated cities) such as Clarendon, Ballston, and Crystal City, sparking the birth of the Internet and sparing local employees the cross-river commute. Federal buildings and monuments still concentrate in the eastern portion, along with highrise condos and most of the county's 37 hotels.

Together with Fairfax County, Arlington is part of a region many Virginians consider almost another state. Closer in demeanor and skyline to the nation's capital than to most of the rest of Virginia, this part of the Old Dominion is one of the few areas that consistently votes Democratic in presidential elections. It *is* part of Virginia, though, and has more than a few spots that merit a visit.

Without any true urban centers, Arlington County hotels and restaurants are spread throughout the area. To find out what's going on here, as well as in D.C., pick up a copy of the *Washington Post*'s "Weekend" section (out on Friday), the *Washington City Paper,* a free weekly, or look at the "Calendar" section of *The Arlington Connection.*

HISTORY

Originally part of the arbitrary diamond of the District of Columbia, Arlington County was ig-

D.C.'S MISSING PIECE

The otherwise perfect diamond of the District of Columbia once extended as far south as Alexandria, donated by Virginia along with part of Fairfax County to form the newly organized Capital district in 1789. Residents welcomed the honor at first, but started to grumble when the government prohibited the construction of public buildings south of the Potomac and denied District residents congressional representation and the right to vote for president (the former grievance, amazingly, is still an issue). The threat of a ban on slavery in the District was the final straw. Several petitions later, in 1847, the region was given back to Virginia, leaving a ragged bite out of D.C.'s southern border.

nominiously trimmed in 1847 when District planners decided no territory was needed across the Potomac. Both the Custis (as in Martha Custis Washington) and Lee (Robert E.) families, which eventually merged, had extensive landholdings here in the 18th and 19th centuries. The Lee family mansion gave the county its name. By the 20th century, war offices and commuter homes for capital workers had started to replace farmlands, setting the stage for high-tech businesses and defense industries.

ARLINGTON NATIONAL CEMETERY

The country's most famous burial grounds embrace 612 acres of hills, grass, and endless, mesmerizing rows of white marble headstones. Almost 250,000 American veterans from every war are buried here, and the graves are visited by four million mourners and sightseers every year.

Even with the crowds and circling Tourmobiles, Arlington National Cemetery is a somber place. Most visitors heed the numerous signs for quiet and respect, leaving a silence punctuated only by birdcalls, the infrequent crack of a rifle salute, and the plaintive notes of "Taps" during the hundred or so services held every week.

History

The cemetery began as an estate surrounding Arlington House, built from 1802–1817 by George Washington Parke Custis, grandson of Martha Washington (née Custis). In 1831, the house and property changed owners when Mary Custis, George's granddaughter, married Robert E. Lee, who had often come to visit from his home in Alexandria. Robert and Mary lived in Arlington House for 30 years until, on April 22, 1861, Lee accepted the command of Virginia's forces in the war against the Union.

In 1864 the 1,100-acre estate was confiscated by the federal government when Martha couldn't appear in person to pay the property taxes. Quartermaster Gen. Montgomery Meigs, a Georgian who had remained loyal to the Union, considered Lee the worst kind of traitor and came up with a scathing revenge: the burial of Union dead, literally, in Lee's backyard. Meigs crossed the Potomac to personally oversee the interment of the first Union soldiers in Martha's rose garden. Eventually, 16,000 soldiers were buried in the fields around Arlington House, ensuring that Lee would never live there in peace again.

After the war, Lee's grandson, George Washington Custis Lee, sued the U.S. government for possession of the estate and won after taking the case to the Supreme Court. In 1883, he turned around and sold it back to the government for $150,000. Two hundred acres were set aside to start the cemetery.

Sights

At the main entrance gate, the **Women in Military Service for America Memorial,** 703/533-1155 or 800/222-2294, contains an education center and theater dedicated to all women serving in the armed forces in war and peace. It's open daily 8 A.M.–7 P.M. (5 P.M. Oct.–Mar.); free. A short uphill walk brings you to the eternal flame at the grave of former president **John F. Kennedy.** This is the most visited sight in Arlington. A low marble wall engraved with his "Ask not" speech faces a view of the Potomac and the Capitol. The resting places of **Jaqueline Kennedy Onassis** and her two infant sons lie nearby, as does that of **Robert F. Kennedy,** whose

NORTHERN VIRGINIA

grave, as requested in his will, is marked only by a single white wooden cross and excerpts from two of his speeches on civil rights.

On the hilltop above the Kennedys presides **Arlington House,** 703/557-0613, www.nps.gov/arho, the Greek Revival mansion that Robert E. Lee described as the spot "where my affection and attachments are more strongly placed than at any other place in the world." In 1933, the house was transferred to the care of the National Park Service and filled almost to its 12-foot ceilings with Lee-era antiques and reproductions. The Marquis de Lafayette called the view of the Potomac and the Capitol "the finest view in the world" in 1824. Today the Memorial Bridge heads straight from Arlington House toward the Lincoln Memorial in a symbolic link between the two former adversaries. Pierre Charles L'Enfant, Revolutionary War veteran and designer of the Capitol, was reburied in front in 1909. Behind the house stands one of the last wooded areas left in the cemetery, which puts it at the center of a debate over where to put more bodies as empty space runs out. Open daily Apr.–Sept., 9:30 A.M.–6 P.M., Oct.–March 9:30 A.M.–4:30 P.M.

Look for the white marble **Memorial Amphitheater** and pass behind it to reach the **Tomb of the Unknowns,** where unidentified bodies from World War I, World War II, the Korean War, and the Vietnam War are guarded around the clock by the U.S. Third Infantry in an amazing display of discipline and precision. Each guard paces back and forth in 21 unerring steps, snapping his or her heels at every turn, often under the gaze of hundreds of people. Three people take part in the changing of the guard (every 30 minutes Apr.–Sept., every hour otherwise), in which one gives the orders as two others march in step, inspect weapons, and transfer orders.

Dozens of other memorials are scattered about Arlington, including the **Mast of the Battleship *Maine,*** whose mysterious explosion on February 15, 1898, in Havana Harbor sparked the Spanish-American War; the **Tomb of the Unknown Dead of the Civil War,** guarding 2,111 bodies; and the **Challenger Memorial,** for the crew of the downed space shuttle.

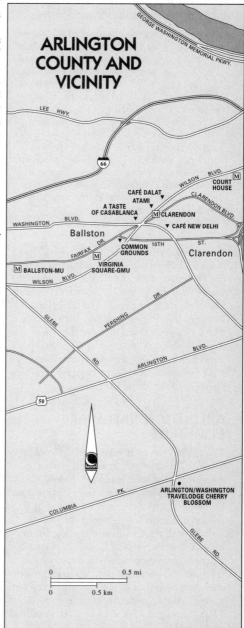

ARLINGTON COUNTY AND VICINITY

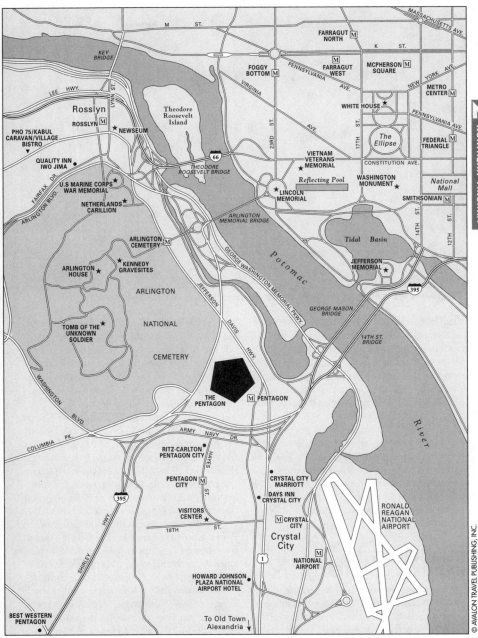

NORTHERN VIRGINIA

© JULIAN SMITH

The gravestones of Arlington National Cemetery attest to the lives lost in American wars.

Visiting Arlington National Cemetery

The **visitors center,** 703/697-2131, www.arlingtoncemetery.org, is open daily 8 A.M.–5 P.M., (7 P.M. Apr.–Sept.); free. It has its own Metro stop on the blue line, and paid parking is available on Memorial Drive (private vehicles may not enter the cemetery). Narrated shuttle tours aboard the **Tourmobile,** 202/554-5100, www.tourmobile.com, start from here and visit the John F. Kennedy gravesite, the Tomb of the Unknowns, and Arlington House for $5.25 for adults, $2.50 for children 3–11. Passengers can buy tickets from the driver and get on or off different buses all day. Call for information on optional extensions to Mt. Vernon and Washington, D.C.

NEAR ARLINGTON NATIONAL CEMETERY

On the cemetery's northern border stands the 50-bell **Netherlands Carillon,** www.nps.gov/gwmp/carillon.htm, given in 1960 from the people of Holland in gratitude for American help against the Nazis in World War II. Concerts are given by outstanding carillonneurs (there's one for the business card) on Saturdays and national holidays May–Sept. in the afternoons or evenings; call the U.S. Park Service's George Washington Memorial Parkway number, 703/289-2550, for a schedule.

Just to the north, the **U.S. Marine Corps War Memorial** depicts Joe Rosenthal's Pulitzer Prize–winning photograph of Marines raising the U.S. flag over Iwo Jima during the Battle for the Pacific in 1945. The memorial is the largest cast bronze statue in the world, erected in memory of all marines who have died serving their country since 1775. Open daily, 24 hours; free.

A footbridge connects the Virginia side of the Potomac with **Theodore Roosevelt Island,** www.nps.gov/gwmp/tri.htm, an 88-acre bird sanctuary dedicated to the 26th president. The island, crossed by the Theodore Roosevelt Bridge (I-66), is open daily 8 A.M.–dusk. Farther south along the George Washington Memorial Parkway, an abrupt exit (look carefully for the sign) leads to the peaceful, 15-acre **Lyndon B. Johnson**

Memorial Grove at the southern end of Lady Bird Johnson Park. Call the Park Service number for more information.

The Pentagon

The headquarters of the Department of Defense occupies the largest office building in the world, just to the south of Arlington National Cemetery. Designed in just one weekend in 1941 by the U.S. Army Corps of Engineers, it was built over a filled-in swamp after only 16 months, and came complete with a host of monolithic statistics. The building covers 6.5 million square feet spread over five floors. Each of the five sides is longer than the U.S. Capitol, and the whole thing is covered by 7.1 acres of glass. About 23,000 employees (half military and half civilian) tell time by 4,200 clocks, drink from 691 water fountains, and navigate 17.5 miles of corridors that were planned so well it supposedly takes them only seven minutes to walk between any two points in the building. Such classified employees are currently the only ones who will be walking the halls. Formerly open for public tours, this impressive structure was closed to visitors following the terrorist attacks on September 11, 2001. Current information is available through the Pentagon itself, 703/695-1776, www.defenselink.mil/pubs/pentagon.

Newseum

One of Virginia's newest museums presents a high-tech, interactive look at the media and its profound effect on our society. Funded by the nonpartisan Freedom Forum, an international foundation dedicated to "free press, free speech, and free spirit," the Newseum starts with a look at the history of news from Sophocles to satellites. Along the way, you'll learn about journalistic integrity, consider the effects of reporting accuracy, and behold mesmerizing images from this century's top stories.

Check out what's going on back home, wherever that may be, with the display of 70 daily newspaper front pages from around the world, and find out what the headlines were the day you were born. Peek in the working broadcast studio; it's near the 126-foot video news wall,

which faces a display of famous news photos, both beautiful and wrenching. Downstairs you can try your hand at playing anchor in front of the TelePrompTers in the mock newsroom and even buy a tape of yourself on camera.

The Newseum, 1101 Wilson Blvd., 703/284-3725 or 888/639-7386, www.newseum.org, is open Tues.–Sun. 10 A.M.–5 P.M.; free. Educational programs include talks with the Journalist of the Day. Refreshments are available in the (groan) News Byte Cafe.

ACCOMMODATIONS

Lodgings in Arlington are often a cheaper alternative to staying across the river, with the Metro providing a quick and easy link to the capital. A central toll-free reservation number, 888/743-8292, covers the whole county. **Bed & Breakfast Accommodations Ltd.,** 202/328-3510, fax 202/332-3885, email: bnbaccom@aol.com, www.bnbaccom.com, can arrange stays in about 10 private homes, guest houses, inns, and small hotels in northern Virginia (moderate and up). The **Alexandria and Arlington Bed & Breakfast Network,** 703/549-3415 or 888/549-3415, email: aabbn@erols.com, www.aabbn.com, also sets up accommodations.

$50–100

The **Arlington/Washington Travelodge Cherryblossom,** 3030 Columbia Pike, 703/521-5570 or 800/578-7878, fax 703/271-0081, has rooms for around $75.

$100–150

Convenient to Arlington National Cemetery is the **Quality Inn Iwo Jima,** 1501 Arlington Blvd., 703/524-5000 or 800/228-5151, fax 703/522-5484, and there's an **Econo Lodge—Metro Arlington,** 6800 Lee Hwy., 703/538-5300 or 800/785-6343, fax 703/538-2110, farther west on I-66 near its intersection with Lee Hwy./Rt. 29.

More accommodations are concentrated to the south in Crystal City and Pentagon City. All offer complimentary shuttle service to National Airport. The **Best Western Pentagon,** 2480 S.

SPRAWL

Urban sprawl is a little like pornography—offensive to many, hard to define exactly, but one of those things that you know when you see it. In city-planner jargon, it's large-lot residential subdivisions beyond the edge of service and employment areas. To those who experience it every day, it's a land-devouring invasion of single-use zones that separate homes from businesses, shopping areas, schools, and parks, resulting in cities delineated only by stoplights, endless strip-style commercial developments along indistinguishable highways, and a subtle social malaise that can make strangers out of neighbors and conglomerations out of communities. Virginia's worst-hit sprawl areas are inside the Beltway and in the Hampton Roads/Tidewater region. With populations in both expected to skyrocket over the next few decades, more people are starting to look around, look ahead, and worry.

Sprawl is the direct result of poor planning. Developers, looking to make a quick buck, steamroll their plans through local political systems, which are often willing to share in the profits as they sell community interests down the river. People moving to the suburbs to live in "the country" and to flee the (often-imagined) crime of urban centers leave inner cities with declining tax bases and crum-

bling infrastructure. Cities spread outward instead of upward, squelching farmland and empty acres under parking lots, bypasses, and office buildings.

As a result, everyone has to drive everywhere. People who thought they left urban gridlock behind find themselves trapped in their cars for more hours than before. Interstate freeway systems, designed to carry drivers in and out of downtown areas, become useless for suburb-to-suburb commuters (currently estimated at 39 million people, or 44 percent of all American commuters). Beltways become packed—in 1981 the average speed on I-495 was 47 mph; 10 years later it was 23 mph—and commuters looking for shortcuts through local roads get in more accidents. Billions of dollars in fuel and work time go up in a carbon monoxide haze.

The environmental costs are just as high. Sediment from building sites and fertilizers from acres of lawns overload local ecosystems with nutrients, which build up to toxic levels without the filtering and water-holding capacity of the wetlands and forests they replaced. One study in 1995 placed Virginia among the country's top 10 states in extreme danger of losing its native ecosystems, and named suburban sprawl as one of the major factors. All these people need to drink,

Glebe Rd., 703/979-4400 or 800/426-6886, fax 703/685-0051, sits near the intersection of S. Glebe Road and I-395 (Shirley Hwy.), almost across the street from the **Days Inn Crystal City,** 2000 Jefferson Davis Hwy., 703/920-8600, fax 703/920-2840.

More Than $250: At the **Crystal City Marriott,** 1999 Jefferson Davis Hwy., 703/413-5500, fax 703/413-0192, guests can enjoy a heated pool, saunas, and an exercise room. A short passage connects the hotel with a shopping mall and the Crystal City Metro stop. Tops in the area is the **Ritz-Carlton Pentagon City,** in the Fashion Centre complex, 1250 S. Hayes St., 703/415-5000, fax 703/415-5061, laden with antiques, paintings, and every amenity you could ask for. The elegant Grill restaurant gets four stars from AAA, and the Pentagon City Metro Station is minutes away. Rooms are in the high $300s.

FOOD

Connected by Wilson Boulevard, Rosslyn and Clarendon are both good places to take advantage of Arlington's increasing ethnic diversity. A little plaza off the 1700 block of Wilson Boulevard has no less than five options, all open daily for lunch and dinner. **Pho 75,** 703/525-7355, is a popular nook with low-priced, tasty Vietnamese food. Middle Eastern rugs and a huge samovar decorate **Kabul Caravan 1,** 703/522-8394, which offers Afghani fare heavy on the rice and lamb. Dinner entrées are in the $15 range, with lunch plates for around $9. Pasta, fish, and meat dishes are served next door at the **Village Bistro,** 703/522-0284, which has some outside seating.

More ethnic eateries follow in the livelier neighborhood of Clarendon. **Café Dalat,** 3143 Wilson Blvd., 703/276-0935, earns consistent awards

so huge reservoirs are created, in the process drowning thousands of more acres.

Sprawl almost always ends up costing more in the long run. Infrastructure must be extended to service outlying areas, so counties and towns have to shell out more money for new roads, water and sewage lines, fire and police services, libraries, schools, and parks. Even though people are pouring in, their tax dollars aren't enough to cover the costs, so municipalities have to keep raising taxes or go into debt. It's estimated that some $8.5 billion for roads alone may be required to service new suburbs in Tidewater and northern Virginia by 2020, and guess who's going to be footing *that* bill? Not the developers who got the ball rolling. Thanks to million-dollar incentive packages, they're often only liable for 12–15 percent of the new infrastructure costs their creations necessitate—often more than half the total price of development.

Sprawl's most insidious effect is also its most indirect. By spreading people so thinly over such a faceless space, it threatens the quality of community life. Impersonal corridors of glass and gray replace nature's browns and greens, and residents of impersonal tract houses find they often don't know who lives right next door.

The Alternative

Through the strategy of "smart growth"—basically, planning ahead—local governments can avoid the side effects of sprawl, protect their environment, and save money. If development is kept compact and close to existing social centers, infrastructure costs plummet as fewer sewer mains and electrical wires and less pavement are needed. Buffer zones can protect sensitive natural areas like shores, streams, and wetlands, both for the enjoyment of citizens and the preservation of the local ecological balance. By building a range of housing types near each other and near schools, offices, and shopping areas, builders can increase the odds of pedestrian neighborhoods where people actually bump into each other on the street.

Planners have their work cut out for them. Almost $50 billion worth of road projects are in the blueprint stages in Virginia in the coming decade, and currently established sprawl has to be addressed. Future transportation and water-supply issues must be solved, and somebody has to figure out, quite simply, where to put all these people. But with foresight and restraint, sprawl is anything but inevitable.

---

for both its value and its Vietnamese menu. It's plain inside, but don't let that fool you; everything from the $5 lunch buffet to the entrées such as spicy citronella chicken is carefully prepared. Open daily for lunch and dinner. Right next door is another good deal: **Atami,** 3155 Wilson, 703/522-4787, Japanese, has special *bento* lunch boxes for $4.50–6.50 with soup and salad (open daily for lunch and dinner). They also offer a dinner special with all the sushi you can pack down for $25. **Queen Bee,** 3181 Wilson Blvd., 703/527-3444, is yet another Vietnamese favorite that's packed as often as Pho 75. They have vegetarian dishes and a mouth-watering *pho* (noodle soup).

Keep going around the corner to **A Taste of Casablanca,** 3211 N. Washington Blvd., 703/527-7468, decorated with Moroccan fabrics and brass teaware. Four-course lunch specials are $8, served Tues.–Fri., with dishes such as couscous and chicken with lemon and olives served for dinner daily. A five-course Sunday brunch is $10, and there's belly dancing on weekend nights. Northern Indian cuisine is the specialty of the **Cafe New Delhi,** 1041 N. Highland St., 703/528-2511, served for lunch and dinner Tues.–Sun. Lunch specials run $6–8 and dinner specials are $8–13.

Filling a former funeral parlor (and town hall), **Common Grounds,** 3211 Wilson Blvd., 703/312-0427, is a comfy local spot with couches and board games. Sandwiches, served 11 A.M.–9 P.M., cost $5–6. They're open at 7 A.M. on weekdays and stay open until 2 A.M. on Friday and Saturday.

ENTERTAINMENT AND RECREATION
Nightlife
Galaxy Hut, 2711 Wilson Blvd., 703/525-8646,

has a long list of beer on tap and features live local bands. They charge a door admission, as does the **Iota Club and Café,** 2832 Wilson Blvd., 703/522-8340, which hosts everything from folk to alternative rock. For jazz and blues, try **Whitlow's on Wilson,** 2854 Wilson Blvd., 703/276-9693, while the **Rhodeside Grill,** 1836 Wilson Blvd., 703/243-0145, occasionally hosts world music and has a large basement bar with wide-screen TVs for sports watching. Improv comedy is on the bill on Saturdays at **The CG Café,** 1211 N. Glebe Rd., 703/486-4242, for $12 admission.

Outdoor Activities

Bikers, joggers, strollers, and stroller-pushers flock to the **Mt. Vernon Trail,** which runs for 18 miles along the George Washington Memorial Parkway and the Potomac River from Memorial Bridge south to Mt. Vernon. As you pass the Lyndon B. Johnson Memorial Grove and Old Town Alexandria, you can stop to watch jets taking off from National Airport, boaters sliding their crafts into the river, and lights as they start to sparkle in the evening.

To the north, the unpaved **Potomac Heritage Trail,** www.nps.gov/pohe, continues along the Virginia side of the river for 10 miles from the west end of the Theodore Roosevelt Island parking lot to the west end of the I-495 bridge. This path sees much less traffic, even though it passes through a riverside wilderness, along clifftops, and across countless streams gurgling toward the Potomac. It's blazed in blue, and you can reach it from eight access points including Potomac Overlook Park, Fort Marcy, and Turkey Run Park. The **Washington & Old Dominion Trail** begins in Shirlington off of I-395.

For maps and more information, contact the **Northern Virginia Regional Park Authority,** 703/352-5900, www.nvrpa.org, or the **Arlington County Department of Parks and Recreation,** 703/228-3323, www.co.arlington.va.us/prcr.

EVENTS

In May, the D.C. Blues Society co-sponsors the **Columbia Pike Blues Festival,** 703/892-2776, at the Patrick Henry Elementary School, 701 S. Highland St., north of the intersection of Columbia Pike and Walter Reed Street. The outdoor festival takes place from noon to 6 P.M., rain or shine.

August brings 60,000 people or more to enjoy the rides, music, crafts, and international food of the **Arlington County Fair,** 757/920-4556, at the Thomas Jefferson Center, 3501 S. 2nd St. and Old Glebe Rd. The **Rosslyn Jazz Festival,** 703/522-6629, swings through Gateway Park at the Virginia end of the Key Bridge in mid-September, followed by the **Marine Corps Marathon,** 800/786-8762, www.marine-marathon.com, in late October. Seventeen thousand runners huff through Arlington, Georgetown, and Washington, D.C., in the country's fourth-largest marathon, which begins and ends at the Iwo Jima Memorial.

INFORMATION

The **Arlington County visitors center,** 735 S. 18th St., 800/677-6267 or 703/228-5720, www.stayarlington.com, is open daily 9 A.M.–5 P.M. To find it, leave the Jefferson Davis Hwy. (US 1) in Crystal City onto 20th Street heading west, take a right on Eads Street, a left on 18th Street, and it's at the corner of a park where Hayes Street leaves 18th Street.

Old Town Alexandria

Less than one hour from downtown D.C., one of the country's oldest port cities (pop. 116,000) preserves a core that is little changed, at least cosmetically, from the days when George Washington and a young Robert E. Lee called it home. Tall, narrow houses in brick or pastel clapboard line cobblestone streets, embellished by ivy escaping over the walls of small front gardens. In all, almost 4,000 buildings from the 18th and 19th centuries have been preserved and restored to give Old Town a dignified Colonial aura, from the smallest "spite" or "mother-in-law" house to the red brick mansions of Captain's Row along Prince Street.

District residents escape to Old Town for more than a history lesson, though—scores of shops and restaurants keep the sidewalks crowded and the parking spaces filled on most weekend evenings. The restored waterfront area along the Potomac, which once echoed with the hammers of shipbuilders and the cries of tobacco auctioneers, now features the famous Torpedo Factory Arts Center, riverside parks, and the occasional America's Cup contender, paddle-wheeler, or old-style sailboat.

HISTORY

In 1669, British Gov. Sir William Berkeley granted 6,000 acres along the Potomac to English ship captain Robert Howsing, as a reward for bringing 120 settlers to the area. Less than one month later, Howsing sold the land to John Alexander, a Scottish captain, for "six thousand pounds of Tobacco and Cask." In 1748, the town of Alexandria, organized by Scottish merchants William Ramsay and John Carlyle, was named in his honor. One year later, the 60-acre plot was surveyed by John West, Jr., and, according to local tradition, a 17-year-old George Washington. Washington liked the location so much he returned to buy a house and a pew in Christ Church, and later he drilled troops in Market Square and served as worshipful master of the local Masonic Lodge.

Plantations flourished into the 18th century,

turning Indian trails into "rolling roads" on which horse and ox teams rolled hogsheads of tobacco to public warehouses along the water. As the last good anchorage before the falls upriver, Alexandria grew into an important shipping port complete with taverns, shipyards, and a public ferry. Soon hemp and wheat became exports as important as tobacco, drawing caravans of "flour wagons" from as far as Winchester for shipment to England. A French visitor in 1796 called Alexandria "beyond all comparison the handsomest town in Virginia—indeed . . . among the finest in the United States."

Harry "Light-horse" Lee, Robert E. Lee's father, brought his family to Alexandria in 1810. By the mid-19th century, so many of Robert E. Lee's relatives lived near the corner of Oronoco and Washington streets that it became known as "Lee Corners." The future general spent the first few decades of his life in his father's house in the heart of town.

Soon after receiving city status in 1852, Alexandria saw much of its oceangoing trade lured away by Baltimore and its clipper ships. The 20th century has seen an influx of out-of-towners (once called the "Foreign Legion") drawn by old houses just dying for renovation.

ORIENTATION

The George Washington Memorial Parkway becomes Washington Street as it passes through downtown, intersecting with the major east-west thoroughfare of King Street. Rt. 1 splits into one-way northbound (Patrick St.), and southbound (Henry St.) stretches a few blocks west. Traffic and parking can be tough, espcially at night, so it's usually best to park your car in a lot or on the street (the visitors center has free passes) and walk.

SIGHTS

Old Town

George Washington, Thomas Jefferson, and the Marquis de Lafayette were among the many patrons of **Gadsby's Tavern Museum,** 134 N.

NORTHERN VIRGINIA

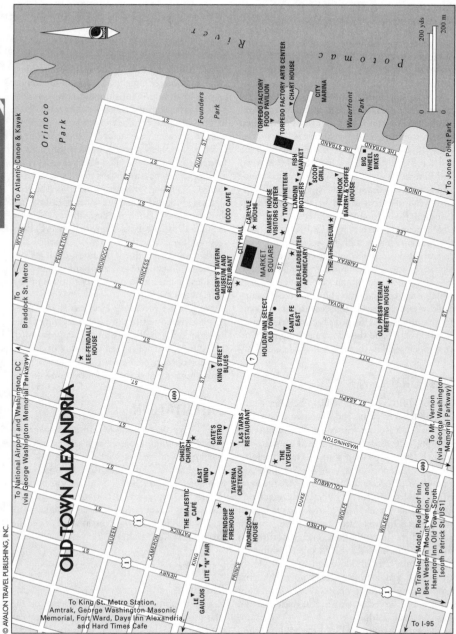

NORTHERN VIRGINIA

© AVALON TRAVEL PUBLISHING, INC.

OLD TOWN ALEXANDRIA

Potomac River

Orinoco Park

Founders Park

Waterfront Park

TORPEDO FACTORY FOOD PAVILION
TORPEDO FACTORY ARTS CENTER
CHART HOUSE
CITY MARINA

FISH MARKET
TWO-NINETEEN
LANDINI BROTHERS
SCOOP GRILL
FIREHOOK BAKERY & COFFEE HOUSE
BIG WHEEL BIKES

ECCO CAFE
CARLYLE HOUSE
RAMSEY HOUSE VISITORS CENTER
CITY HALL
MARKET SQUARE
GADSBY'S TAVERN MUSEUM AND RESTAURANT
STABLER-LEADBEATER APOTHECARY
THE ATHENAEUM
HOLIDAY INN SELECT OLD TOWN
SANTA FE EAST
OLD PRESBYTERIAN MEETING HOUSE

LEE-FENDALL HOUSE
KING STREET BLUES

CHRIST CHURCH
CATE'S BISTRO
LAS TAPAS RESTAURANT
THE LYCEUM
EAST WIND
TAVERNA CRETEKOU

THE MAJESTIC CAFE
FRIENDSHIP FIREHOUSE
MORRISON HOUSE
LITE "N" FAIR
LE GAULOIS

To Atlantic Canoe & Kayak
To Braddock St. Metro
To National Airport and Washington, DC (via George Washington Memorial Parkway)
To Jones Point Park
To Mt. Vernon (via George Washington Memorial Parkway)
To Travelers Motel, Red Roof Inn, Best Western Mount Vernon, and Hampton Inn Old Town South [south Patrick St/US1]
To I-95
To King St. Metro Station, Amtrak, George Washington Masonic Memorial, Fort Ward, Days Inn Alexandria, and Hard Times Cafe

UNION
THE STRAND
LEE
FAIRFAX
ROYAL
PITT
ST. ASAPH
WASHINGTON
COLUMBUS
ALFRED
WOLFE
WILKES

QUAY ST.
PENDLETON
ORONOCO
PRINCESS
WYTHE
QUEEN
CAMERON
KING
PRINCE
DUKE
HENRY
PATRICK

0 200 yds
0 200 m

Royal St., 703/838-4242, since it opened at the end of the 18th century. The tavern and the adjacent City Hotel have been restored and converted into a museum on dining, drinking, and dozing in the heart of Colonial America. While you're in the mood, stop by the Colonial restaurant of the same name next door. A lavish ball and banquet commemorating the first president's birthday has been held in the upstairs ballroom since 1797. Tours are given Tues.–Sat. 10 A.M.–5 P.M., Sun. 1–5 P.M. (until 4 P.M. Oct.–Mar.); $4 adults, $2 children 11–17.

Established in 1792, the **Stabler-Leadbeater Apothecary,** 105-107 S. Fairfax St., 703/836-3713, operated for almost 150 years, making it the second-oldest shop of its kind in the country. George and Martha Washington shopped here, as did Robert E. Lee, who bought paint for his house. A five-minute taped tour points out the finest collection of medicinal bottles in America, pill machines, original cash registers, and jars filled with native cures such as dandelion, sassafras, and snakeroot. Colored water fills a pair of two-foot show globes in the windows, which are said to have served as an early version of Open/Closed signs. Red indicated "stay away: plague," blue or green meant "all clear, come on in." Open Mon.–Sat. 10 A.M.–4 P.M., Sun. 1–5 P.M.; $2.50 adults, $2 children 11–17.

Scottish merchant John Carlyle built **Carlyle House,** 1212 N. Fairfax St., 703/549-2997, for his blushing bride Sarah Fairfax in 1753. Two years later, Maj. Gen. Edward Braddock met here with five Colonial governors to organize a tax on the colonies to pay for Britain's role in the French and Indian War. Local governments refused to pay, marking one of the first serious rifts between England and America. Today the property remains an outstanding 18th-century manor home, furnished with period furniture and sheltering a small but radiant garden out back. Tours are given every half hour until closing. Open Tues.–Sat. 10 A.M.–5 P.M., Sun. noon–5 P.M.; $3 adults, $2 children 10–17.

The Northern Virginia Fine Arts Association has found a home in the Greek Revival **Athenaeum,** 201 Prince St. at Lee St., 703/548-0035, built in 1850 as a banking house. National and local art exhibits are open to the public for free; call for hours.

Head toward the croak of gulls perched on riverfront pilings to find the **Torpedo Factory Arts Center,** 105 N. Union St., 703/838-4565, www.torpedofactory.org. The name is no hyperbole: shell casings for torpedoes were built here during the first part of the century. The factory was reopened in 1983 as one of Virginia's first and best artistic cooperatives. About 150 painters, potters, sculptors, glassmakers, photographers, and fiber artists turn out artwork both fine and fun. The artists occupy 84 studios and four galleries in exchange for opening their creative process and workspaces to the public. Colorful painted factory pipes add an artsy-industrial touch. Open daily 10 A.M.–5 P.M.; free. **Alexandria Archeology,** 703/838-4399, maintains a museum and research lab on the third floor dedicated to unearthing the town's long history. Open Tues.–Fri. 10 A.M.–3 P.M., Sat. 10 A.M.–5 P.M., Sun. 1–5 P.M.; free.

The **Old Presbyterian Meeting House,** 321 S. Fairfax St., 703/549-6670, has been in use for all but 60 years since it was built in 1774. George Washington attended services here in 1798, one year before ministers preached at his memorial service. Twin balconies bracket the plain, almost severe interior, and many of the stones in the graveyard behind it have weathered into near-illegibility. Several of Washington's friends and local luminaries, including William Ramsay and John Carlyle, are buried near the Tomb of the Unknown Soldier of the American Revolution. Open Mon.–Fri. 9 A.M.–3 P.M.; free.

Built in 1839 in the style of a Doric temple, the pale orange **Lyceum,** 201 S. Washington St., 703/838-4994, served as a hall for meetings, debates, and lectures on literature, history, and science. Today the imposing, two-story columns flank the entrance of a museum, which covers Alexandria's history from Native Americans to the 20th century. Open Mon.–Sat. 10 A.M.–5 P.M., Sun. 1–5 P.M.; free. One block west, the **Friendship Firehouse,** 107 S. Alfred St., 703/838-3891, commemorates the city's first organization to battle blazes, founded in 1774.

Washington's involvement is debated by historians, but around here it's taken for granted. Antique fire-fighting equipment, including an engine, is open to the public Fri. and Sat. 10 A.M.–4 P.M., Sun. 1–4 P.M.; free.

Historians do agree that the first president and his wife attended services beneath the distinctive octagonal tower of **Christ Church,** 118 N. Washington St. at Cameron St., 703/549-1450. Established in 1773, the church served as the place for Robert E. Lee's confirmation, and it still holds Episcopal services. Both the Washington and Lee family pews remain inside. Grave markers in the surrounding burial ground (the only one in town until 1805) don't necessarily mark actual gravesites; many were moved by Union soldiers during the Civil War to make room for campfires and grazing horses. The restored Old Parish Hall next door contains a gift shop and small historical museum. Open Mon.–Sat. 9 A.M.–4 P.M., Sun. 2–4:30 P.M.; free.

At the intersection of Orinoco and Washington streets stands the **Lee-Fendall House,** 614 Oronoco St., 703/548-1789, built in 1785 by a relative of Harry "Light-horse" Lee. It was renovated in 1850 in the Greek Revival style and remained in the Lee family until 1903. Free tours are given every hour until 3 P.M. Open Tues.–Sat. 10 A.M.–4 P.M., Sun. 1–4 P.M.; $4 adults, $2 children 10–17.

Beyond Old Town

Head west on King Street past the Metro stop to reach the monumental neoclassic spire of the **George Washington Masonic National Memorial,** 101 Callahan Dr., 703/683-2007, www.gwmemorial.org. Towering atop Shuter's Hill—considered as a potential site for the U.S. Capitol when Alexandria was part of the District of Columbia—the memorial encloses a 17-foot bronze statue of the first worshipful master of Alexandria Lodge No. 22 gazing over the city and the Potomac. Three-story marble columns and heroic murals on either side make this a monument on the D.C. scale. A museum on the fourth floor contains Washington memorabilia like the clock stopped by his physician at 10:20 P.M., the moment of his passing, along with the largest Oriental carpet in the world. Keep going to the ninth-floor observatory for a spectacular view

George Washington Masonic National Memorial

clear across the river. Guided tours are given about every 45 minutes. Open daily 9 A.M.–5 P.M.; free.

During the Civil War, Washington, D.C. was one of the most heavily defended locations in the nation. Thirty-six guns and 162 earthwork forts and batteries bristled from hillsides around the capital, all awaiting the all-out Confederate assault that never came. Today, part of those fortifications are preserved in the **Fort Ward Museum and Historic Site,** 4301 W. Braddock Rd., 703/838-4848 (museum) or 703/838-4831 (park), a 45-acre park enclosing restored earthwork bastions, six guns, and a Civil War–era museum. To get there, take King Street west, then bear left onto West Braddock, and it's on the right near I-395 exit 4. Open Tues.–Sat. 9 A.M.–5 P.M., Sun. noon–5 P.M.; free. (The park and its picnic facilities are open daily until sunset.)

ACCOMMODATIONS

Services

The **Alexandria and Arlington Bed & Breakfast Network,** 703/549-3415 or 888/549-3415, email: aabbn@erols.co, www.aabbn.com, can help with lodgings in Old Town, as can **Princely Bed & Breakfast,** 800/470-5588, which is based out of Roanoke. Alexandria has a main accommodations hotline: 800/296-1000, and you can make reservations through the Convention and Visitors Association's www.FunSide.com.

$50–100

Most of Alexandria's less expensive lodgings are outside of Old Town. A **Days Inn Alexandria,** 110 S. Bragg St., 703/354-4950, fax 703/642-2873, sits near the intersection of Duke St./Little River Tpk. and I-395 west of Old Town. Head south along Rt. 1 (first called the Jefferson Davis Hwy., then Richmond Hwy.) to find the **Travelers Motel,** 5916 Richmond Hwy., 800/368-7378 or 703/329-1310, near I-95 and US 1 South, and the **Red Roof Inn-Alexandria,** 5975 Richmond Hwy., 703/960-5200, fax 703/960-5209. Keep going for the **Best Western Mount Vernon,** 8751 Richmond Hwy., 703/360-1300, fax 703/799-7713, seven miles south of Old Town.

$100–150

The **Hampton Inn Old Town South,** 5821 Richmond Hwy., 703/329-1400 or 703/329-1424, is also south of town, on the border of Alexandria proper just south of the I-95/I-495 intersection. Back in town is the **Best Western Old Colony Inn,** 615 1st St., 703/739-2222, fax 703/549-2568, at the junction with Washington Street.

$150–250

There's a **Holiday Inn Hotels & Suites,** 625 First St., 703/548-6300, fax 703/548-8032, off the George Washington Memorial Parkway just east of the intersection of 1st and Washington streets.

The refined historic feel of the **Holiday Inn Select Old Town,** 480 King St., 703/549-6080, fax 703/684-6508, may be a surprise to guests expecting another off-the-rack hotel. Six floors of rooms smack in the middle of Old Town top a heated indoor pool, sauna, exercise room, restaurant, and cocktail lounge.

Over $250

The small but luxurious **Morrison House,** 116 S. Alfred St., 703/838-8000 or 800/367-0800, fax 703/684-6283, email: mhresrv@morrisonhouse.com, www.morrisonhouse.com, evokes a Colonial manor house—from the butler at the top of the curving entrance staircase to the Federal Period reproductions in its 45 rooms and suites. A pianist occasionally graces the first-floor lounge near the library and parlor. The outstanding Elysium Restaurant serves a sophisticated Mediterranean menu, while the Grill Bar offers more casual fare.

FOOD

Standards

The former chef of the Watergate Hotel moved here to open the unpretentious **Lite "N" Fair,** 1018 King St., 703/549-3717. It may not be much to look at, but the menu's mix of French, Italian, Asian, and German draws raves for quality and value. Open for lunch Mon.–Sat., dinner Tues.–Sat. Stained glass and a gigantic James Dean poster decorate the playful **Ecco Café,** 220

N. Lee St., 703/684-0321, a popular Italian place set in an 18th-century tobacco warehouse. Pick a wine from the daily board to go with your home-made pasta, gourmet pizzas, and fresh grilled seafood, all served in generous portions for moderate prices. Open daily for lunch and dinner, with a live jazz brunch on Sunday.

Catie Archuleta added German and French accents to an Italian bistro to come up with **Cate's Bistro,** 715 King St., 703/549-0533, perfect for a romantic date or a family dinner. Everything from the bread and pasta to soup and desserts is home-made, with dinner entrées in the $13–18 range. Steaks and seafood are staples of **The Chart House,** 1 Cameron St. on the waterfront, 703/684-5080. Diners can stay inside under the cavernous ceiling or opt for outside in nicer weather overlooking the Potomac. Dinner entrées run $17 and up. Open for dinner daily, plus Sunday brunch.

Head west a few blocks to reach the **Fish Market,** 105 King St., 703/836-5676, where big pots of chowder on the bar, checkered tablecloths, and an open, clattering kitchen are all clues to some of the best seafood in town. Prices range from $5 sandwiches to $15 platters. Open daily for lunch and dinner. One block west is **Two-Nineteen,** 219 King St., 703/549-1141, offering fine dining, Cajun-style. Catfish, Cajun fried oysters, jambalaya, and seafood gumbo are all served with Southern flair, ranging from $7–14 for lunch to around $20 for dinner. The Bayou Room downstairs serves less expensive meals, and the Basin St. Lounge whoops it up on weekends.

Snacks

The **Firehook Bakery & Coffee House,** 105 S. Union St., 703/519-8020, serves lunch plates along with breads and pastries you can watch being made at their plant at 214 N. Fayette Street. Enjoy homemade ice cream and frozen yogurt beneath stained-glass lampshades at **The Scoop Grill,** 110 King St., 703/549-4527, which also offers breakfast specials. A handful of inexpensive lunch options fill the glass-walled **Torpedo Factory Food Pavilion** by the river. Simple, effective Southwestern decor sets the stage for the chile rellenos and chipotle chicken at **Santa Fe East,** 110 Pitt St. S., 703/548-6900.

Speaking of out West, the chili at the **Hard Times Café,** 1404 King St., 703/837-0050, is said to be ambrosial, whether you pick the Texas, Cincinnati, or vegetarian version. Also on the menu are microbrewed beers, rootbeer floats, and an authentic Frito chili pie. Both are open daily for lunch and dinner.

Upscale and Unusual

Cross a roadhouse with a funhouse, add neon, and you'll end up with something like **King Street Blues,** 112 N. Asaph St., 703/836-8800. Voted the best BBQ, burger, and "cheap eats" in town, this art-bar serves up sammies, po' boys, and blue-plate specials amid riotous paintings and sculptures. Try the Eastern Shore Chicken Pie (baked with oysters). Open daily for lunch and dinner. **Gadsby's Tavern Restaurant,** 138 N. Royal St. at Cameron St., 703/548-1288, re-creates the 18th century in its pewter plates, creaking wood floor, and costumed waiters. The food is just as authentic, with strolling minstrels providing entertainment during dinner. Open daily for lunch and dinner.

The latest big news in the thriving Alexandria restaurant scene is the rebirth of **The Majestic Café,** 911 King St., 703/837-9117, which stood empty for more than two decades. It's been updated and refitted by retired artisans whose résumés include the National Gallery and the White House, so you know the owners are serious. The restored art deco exterior and chic inside scheme go well with chef Susan McCreight Lindeborg's cuisine: modern American with local Southern influences, served for lunch Tues.–Sat. and dinner Tues.–Sun., plus Sunday brunch. Lunch entrées such as black-eye pea cakes are $8–13, while dinner plates like braised rabbit leg are in the $14–20 range.

International

Look for the wooden Gallic heads outside **Le Gaulois,** 1106 King St., 703/739-9494, a southern French-style bistro with quiches, casseroles, and a Pot au Feu special. Open daily for lunch and dinner.

East Wind, 809 King St., 703/839-1515, offers that incomparable blend of Chinese, French, and Japanese influences known as Vietnamese cooking.

Open for lunch Mon.–Fri. and dinner daily, with inexpensive lunches ($6–8) and dinners ($10–14). For fine Italian, try **Landini Brothers,** 115 King St. between Lee and Union sts., 703/836-8404, a dark, quiet, cozy place with entrées in the $12 range and antipasti for $6–8. A menu full of K's marks the **Taverna Cretekou,** 818 King St., 703/548-8688, as the real thing. Greek specialties like mousakka, spanakopita, and baklava are $6 for lunch, $11–20 for dinner, both served daily.

More than 50 *tapas* (small dishes) grace the menu of **Las Tapas Restaurant,** 710 King St., 703/836-6900, most in the $4–6 range. Order enough and you can make a meal, from ceviche to stuffed clams—or order an entrée ($17–23) such as their famous seafood-rice paellas. Finish off with a glass of dry sherry and settle back for the music and entertainment offer almost every night. Open daily for lunch and dinner.

It's in a shopping strip a little ways out of town, but the **Bombay Curry Company,** 3110 Mount Vernon Ave., 703/836-6363, rewards those who venture this far with unusually tasty tandooris and curries for rock-bottom prices. Sunday afternoon buffets include a little of everything for $7–8. Open daily for lunch and dinner.

ENTERTAINMENT AND RECREATION
Nightlife
Two-Nineteen's **Basin Street Lounge,** 219 King St., 703/549-1141, hops with swing and big-band jazz on weekends, and **King St. Blues** hosts live music in its first-floor bar on Thursday evenings. **The Birchmere Music Hall,** 3701 Mt. Vernon Ave., 703/549-7500, www.birchmere.com, features nationally known bluegrass, folk, and country acts. To get there, head west on Pendleton to West Street, turn right, then quickly left onto Braddock, and finally right onto Mt. Vernon. It's just south of Glebe Road.

The **Virginia Beverage Company,** 605-607 King St., 703/684-5397, offers home-brewed beer and one of the largest collection of single-malt scotches and bourbons in northern Virginia, along with pasta, steaks, and burgers. Look for the copper brew machinery in the front windows. For a

pint of Old-Country stout, try **Murphy's Irish Pub,** 713 King St., 703/548-1717. The latter was voted one of the 50 best bars in the D.C. area, thanks to its roaring fireplace, generous pub fare, and nightly Irish and Welsh sing-alongs. This is what's known as a "happy bar" in technical parlance, meaning they've been known to go through 10 kegs of Guinness on a Saturday night.

Both the **Laughing Lizard Lounge Comedy Club,** 1322 King St., 703/548-2582, and the **Fun Factory,** 3112 Mt. Vernon Ave., 703/684-5212, are good for a laugh. For jazz, try the **Evening Star Café,** 2000 Mount Vernon Ave., 703/549-5051, or **St. Elmo's Coffee Pub,** 2300 Mount Vernon Ave., 703/739-9268; and for folk head to **Pat Troy's,** 111 N. Pitt St., 703/549-4535. The **Las Tapas Restaurant** offers flamenco performances on Tuesdays and Thursdays and salsa instruction with dancing on Sundays.

Tours
Daily walking tours of Old Town leave from the Ramsey House Visitors Center at 10:30 A.M., Mon.–Sat., and 2 P.M. on Sundays from Apr.–Nov. ($10 pp). **The Old Town Experience,** 703/836-0694, also offers daily guided walking tours of major sites in Old Town with tidbits of legends and folklore along the way. The tour leaves from Ramsay House from late Mar.–Nov.

With a spectral slant is **Doorways to Old Virginia,** 703/548-0100, which leads a lantern-lit Ghost & Graveyard Tours with guides in period costume. The one-hour walks leave from the visitors center on Fri.–Sun. nights, Mar.–Nov., and end up in a graveyard ($6 adults, $4 children 7–12). Candle-lantern tours of Alexandria are led by costumed guides from Gadsby's Tavern Museum on Friday nights, Mar.–Nov., for $5 adults, $2 children 11–17. You can even hire a six-person horse-drawn carriage, complete with coachman, from **Harmon's Carriages,** 703/327-6731.

The **Potomac Riverboat Company,** 703/684-0580 or 877/502-2628, www.potomacriverboatco.com, offers a variety of floating tours from the city marina near the Torpedo Factory from Apr.–Oct. A 40-minute narrated tour of Alexandria from the water aboard the **Admiral Tilp** is $8 adults, $5 children. They also send boats to the

NORTHERN VIRGINIA

Washington, D.C. monuments, ($16/8) and Mt. Vernon ($26/13). The *Dandy*, 757/683-6076, www.dandydinnerboat.com, is a 100-ton restaurant cruise ship that leaves from Waterfront Park at the end of Prince Street. Three-course lunches ($33–38) and five-course dinners ($68–80) compete with the D.C. monuments for your attention on three-hour cruises up to the capital.

Outdoors

With the **Mt. Vernon Trail** ending just to the north, Alexandria sees plenty of foot and bike traffic in the sunny months. **Big Wheel Bikes,** 2 Prince St., 703/739-2300, rents hybrid bicycles;

and **Bike the Sites,** 202/966-8662, runs guided bike tours to Mount Vernon.

Judy Lathrop's **Atlantic Canoe & Kayak Company,** 1201 North Royal St., 800/297-0066 or 703/838-9072, email: kayak@erols.com, www.atlantickayak.com, leads well-praised sea kayak classes and tours ranging from day trips up both sides of the Potomac to overnights on the Eastern Shore. Their tours, including sunset and full-moon excursions, start at $80 per day and are open to paddlers of all experience levels. Shorter trips to nearby marshes and monuments start at $40 pp. They also offer gear rentals, sales, demonstrations, and classes.

WASHINGTON & OLD DOMINION TRAIL

The Washington & Old Dominion Trail (technically the W&OD Railroad Regional Park) links northern Virginia's split personalities in a 45-mile stretch from the suburbs of Arlington County to Loudoun County's rural reaches. A train ran this route from 1859–1968, but today all you'll encounter on the way from condos to meadows, or vice versa, are other walkers, bikers, and riders on horseback.

The asphalt path begins at the intersection of Shirlington Road and Four Mile Run Drive in Arlington County, two blocks north of I-395 exit 6. From here it noses west through Falls Church in Fairfax County. A parallel bridle path joins in Vienna, and the double trail continues through Reston, Herndon, and Leesburg before ending at Purcellville west of Leesburg, on 21st Street (Rt. 690) one block off Main Street (Rt. 7).

Camping isn't allowed along the trail, but plenty of hotels and motels on the way make it possible to spend a few days making the whole trip. For more information, contact the **Friends of the W&OD Trail,** 21293 Smiths Switch Rd., Ashburn, VA 22011, 703/729-0596, www.wodfriends.org. The group also sells a 56-page guide and REI map. The trail itself is owned and operated by the Northern Virginia Regional Park Authority, 5400 Ox Rd., Fairfax Station, VA 22039, 703/352-5900, email: info@nvrpa.org, www.nvpra.org.

EVENTS

For details on any of the following events, contact the Alexandria Convention and Visitors Association's **Special Events Hotline** at 703/838-4200, ext. 1. Most charge a small admission fee.

Both Harry "Light-horse" Lee and his son Robert are honored during the **Lee Birthday Celebrations** the third Sunday in January with special tours, refreshments, and period music at the Lee-Fendall House and The Boyhood Home of Robert E. Lee. The third weekend in February brings another party, this time for **George Washington's Birthday.** On Saturday, a black-tie/Colonial-costume Birthnight Banquet & Ball at Gadsby's Tavern commemorates George and Martha's attendance there in 1798 and 1799. A Revolutionary War encampment at Fort Ward follows on Sunday, including a mock skirmish between British and Revolutionary troops. On Monday, a gigantic parade snakes through honoring Alexandria's favorite son with Colonial drums and bugle musters.

At the end of May, the **Memorial Day Jazz Festival** arrives in town (call the events line for location), and in June the **Alexandria Red Cross Waterfront Festival** arrives along with tall ships, live music, living history, and amusement rides. The fourth weekend of July brings the **Virginia Scottish Games,** one of the premiere Celtic events in the United States. Two days of fiddling, bagpiping, Scottish food, and a national-level heptathlon all happen at the Episcopal High School.

Alexandria also enjoys several **ethnic festivals** throughout the year, including the Armenian Festival in mid-May; the African-American Heritage & Cultural Festival in late July; the Irish Festival in early August; the American Indian Festival in late August; and the Italian Festival in early September.

The Scottish theme continues with the **Scottish Christmas Walk** the first Saturday in December, with a parade through Old Town and traditional Highland dancers. Then the holiday spirit rolls right into the **Historic Alexandria Candlelight Tour** the next weekend, passing through three museums and Gadsby's Tavern.

SHOPPING

Alexandria abounds with places to shop, so serious browsers will simply want to start at the **Torpedo Factory** and work their way west. Inside the Carriage House, 215 S. Union St. between Prince and Duke sts., you'll find **Rocky Road to Kansas,** 703/683-0116, a quilt shop with antiques, rugs, and bags. Jewelry, furniture, and vintage clothing fill **Bird in the Cage Antiques,** above the Scoop Grill at 110 King St., 703/549-5114. **The Sil-**ver **Parrot,** 113 King St., 703/549-8530, stocks silver and jewelry from around the world. **Khasa Jewelers,** 101 N. Union St., 703/838-0588, also has an international selection of fine jewelry.

You'll find everything from handcarved decoys to historic reproduction brass, linens, and porcelain at **The Pineapple, Inc.,** 106 N. Lee St., 703/836-8180, which also serves afternoon tea Wed.–Sun. from 2–4 P.M. **Gallery West,** 205 S. Union St., 703/549-7359, is the oldest artist-owned and operated gallery in northern Virginia, and displays paintings, photography, and sculpture works that are constantly rotating.

The southern section of Market Square is home to the Alexandria Saturday-morning **farmer's market,** 703/838-4770. It's been going since 1753, making it one of the oldest continuously operating markets in the country. Early morning is the best time to go, and on cold days it's moved inside the lobby of city hall. Keep going to **Boxwood Antiques & Fine Art,** 303 Cameron St., 703/518-4444, for Colonial and Federal items from the 19th and 20th centuries, along with porcelain and sterling.

Glass, crystal, and pottery fill **Creative Classics,** 111 S. Alfred St., 703/518-4663, while

NORTHERN VIRGINIA

© JULIAN SMITH

a street in historic Old Town

Elder Crafters of Alexandria, Inc., 405 Cameron St., 703/683-4338, is a nonprofit store that sells handcrafted quilts, clothes, toys, jewelry, and pottery all made by the elderly. **Funk & Junk,** 106-1/2 N. Columbus St., 703/836-0749, offers "Cool stuff for cool people at cool prices," which includes vintage clothes, TV and cartoon items, and art deco knickknacks. Crafts from the developing world are the specialty of **Ten Thousand Villages,** 824 King St., 703/684-1435, which also has a gourmet coffee shop.

TRANSPORTATION

The yellow and blue Metro lines converge at the **King Street station,** west on King Street just before the George Washington Masonic Memorial. From here you can hop a free **Dash About** bus, 703/370-DASH (370-3274), www.dashbus.com, down King Street to Market Square, which runs every 15 minutes on Fri. 7 P.M.–midnight, Sat. 10 A.M.–midnight, and Sun. 11 A.M.–10 P.M. Across the street is the Alexandria **Amtrak** station, 703/836-4339. There's another yellow/blue Metro stop at **Braddock Rd.;** to reach it, head west on Wythe Street, jig right on West Street and then left on Braddock Road. For tips on navigating Old Town, see "Orientation."

INFORMATION

Alexandria's Convention and Visitors Association runs a **visitors center** in the Ramsay House, 221 King St. at Fairfax St., 703/838-5005 or 800/388-9119, email: acva@FunSide.com, www.FunSide.com. The building itself, the oldest in town, was built in 1749 by Scottish merchant William Ramsay, a friend of George Washington and one of the founders of Alexandria. Over the years it served as a tavern, grocery store, cigar factory, and rooming house and is thought to have been brought here on a barge from its original location some 30 miles downriver.

Along with brochures, walking-tour maps, and lists of hotels, restaurants, and shops, the visitors center hands out free 24-hour parking permits for two-hour metered street zones, which can be renewed each day. They also sell discounted block tickets to Gadsby's, Stabler-Leadbeater and Carlyle for $9 adults, $5 children 11–17, along with the summertime VIP Pass that includes Gadsby's, Carlyle House, Stabler-Leadbeater Apothecary, and the Lee-Fendall House, along with a guided walking tour and a cruise on the Potomac, for $26 adults, $14 children.

Near the Beltway

McLEAN
Claude Moore Colonial Farm

The homestead of a family of poor tenant farmers circa 1771 is brought to life inside the Beltway at this small but respectable living-history enclave. A one-room log farmhouse anchors the 100-acre site, surrounded by a barn and fields of tobacco, wheat, flax, corn, and rye. Split-rail "worm fencing" keeps the turkeys, hogs, and chickens out of the kitchen gardens and the quarterhorse out of the orchard. Costumed historical interpreters are on hand to explain the care and feeding of the Devon cattle and the use of 18th-century tools and clothing.

The best times to stop by are during **market** **fairs** in May, July, and October, when visitors can buy homegrown produce, bob for apples, taste period food, and see a puppet show. Other special events include the **wheat harvest** in June, the **tobacco harvest** in August, **threshing day** in November, and **wassail** near the winter solstice in late December. Eighteenth-century skills are taught in workshops throughout the year.

The farm, 6310 Georgetown Pike, 703/442-7557, www.1776.org, is open Apr.–Dec. Wed.–Sun. 10 A.M.–4:30 P.M.; $2 adults, $1 children 5–12. To get there, take Rt. 738 off Old Dominion Drive (Rt. 309) into McLean, turn north onto Chain Bridge Road for half a mile, then east on Dolley Madison Boulevard (Rt. 123). After two miles, turn north on Georgetown Pike (Rt. 193), and make an immediate right on Colonial Farm Road. It's on the left.

GREAT FALLS PARK

The Potomac would have been the perfect transport route for goods between the ocean and the heart of the colonies, except for one small detail: a 77-foot drop in just one-quarter mile as the river seethes over the unyielding shelf of the fall line. Now this source of historical headaches is one of the most natural places within an hour of the capital (traffic permitting), combining trails, historic ruins, rugged rocks, and white water.

History

Great Falls stood as a barrier between the open water and important Maryland ports until 1802, when a firm founded by George Washington (is there anything he *didn't* do?) opened the Patowmack Canal parallel to the river on the Virginia side. Elevator locks were hewn from solid rock, and a small settlement sprang up around the steady trade. In 1828, the Chesapeake & Ohio (C&O) Canal took over on the opposite bank from downtown D.C. to Cumberland, Maryland. By the mid-19th century, one million tons of goods per year flowed through the C&O's 75 locks, but the opening of the Baltimore & Ohio Railroad in 1924 spelled the end of water transport on both sides.

Visiting Great Falls

Start at the **visitors center,** 703/285-2965 or 703/285-2966, which has exhibits on the geology and human and natural history of the area. There's a snack bar downstairs and picnic table nearby. Many trails wind along the edge of the steep cliffs above the river. Be careful on the slippery rocks near the edge because fatal falls happen with frightening regularity. Notice the posts indicating high-water marks of floods that cover the falls completely about once a decade, occasionally reaching as high as the visitors center. It's possible to hike a 5.1-mile loop, passing the ruins of the canal locks and the original trade village of Matildaville. Along the way you'll pass skunk cabbage and jewelweed in the swampy former riverbed,

and upstream you might spot a red-shouldered hawk, osprey, or great blue heron.

Fishing and cross-country skiing are other seasonal possibilities. Great Falls is the most popular spot in the state for rock climbing, with more than 100 climbs up to 5.12 in difficulty. Needless to say, swimming and boating are prohibited in the falls, though of course a few suicidal thrill-seekers have snuck in and done it. On the Maryland bank, the **C&O Canal National Historical Park** contains the historic Great Falls Tavern and a footbridge to an island in the middle of the torrent. Mule-drawn barge trips run Apr.–Oct. Call 301/722-8226 for more information.

The park, www.nps.gov/grfa, is open daily dawn to dusk, with visitors facilities open 10 A.M.–5 P.M. (6 P.M. on weekends in season; 4 P.M. in winter). Three-day admission passes are $4 per car, $2 per pedestrian or cyclist May–Oct. To get there, take I-495 exit 13 to Georgetown Pike (Rt. 193). Follow this four miles west to Rt. 738, and take a right into the park.

RIVERBEND PARK

Adjoining Great Falls to the north, this small reserve encloses a calmer section of river inhabited by animals rare for the area, such as foxes, minks, river otters, and the infrequent bald eagle. Ten miles of hiking, biking, and equestrian trails explore the park's 400 acres of meadows and forest, including two miles along the river and a short paved trail for disabled visitors. Huge beech, elm, birch, and poplars grow along the 1.7-mile Potomac Heritage Trail (which shares its name with one farther south).

To reach the park, keep going west past the Great Falls entrance to Riverbend Road, take a right, and another right on Jeffrey Road. Another right after two miles brings you to the riverbank and the **visitors center,** 703/759-9018, with small museum displays, trail maps, and brochures (open Wed.–Mon. 9 A.M.–5 P.M.). Outside are picnic areas, fishing spots, and a boat ramp, and a **Nature Center** is just down Jeffrey Road. Kayak tours are given from June–Sept. for $20–25 pp. An entrance fee of $4 per car is charged on summer weekends and holidays; otherwise entrance is free.

GREAT FALLS TOWN

Two special eateries make this otherwise unassuming town, centered at the intersection of Georgetown Pike (Rt. 193) and Walker Road (Rt. 681), an appetizing place to stop before or after visiting the falls. The **Serbian Crown Restaurant,** 1141 Walker Rd., 703/759-4150, serves authentic Serbian and Russian fare along with a wide selection of iced vodka to top things off. Start with beluga caviar and some borscht, then move on to Sole Vladimir or *kulibiaka* (Russian salmon with lobster sauce). They're open daily for dinner and for lunch on Friday and Sunday; reservations are recommended on weekends. Take Walker Road south from Georgetown Pike for two miles to find it.

Jacques Haeringer's **L'Auberge Chez Francois,** 332 Springvale Rd., 703/759-3800, holds a special place in the heart of Washingtonians, who vie for reservations weeks ahead of time. An *auberge* is a small local restaurant traditionally run by a chef/owner and his family, and this Alsace-meets-Virginia version measures up well. Copious four-course dinners in the $40 range include entrées like salmon in pastry crust with crab and lobster, real Dover sole with wild mushrooms, pheasant, and Alsatian specialties like *matelote* and choucroute. Outdoor tables under the trees are first-come, first-served, and the wine list draws, naturally, from France and Virginia. Open for dinner Tues.–Sat., and Sun. 1:30–8 P.M. To get there, head west of the main intersection about one mile to Springvale Road, turn right, and it is on the left after 2.5 miles.

WOLF TRAP FARM PARK

The country's only national park dedicated to the performing arts offers a wide array of performances throughout the year, both indoors and under the stars, on 130 acres of hills and woodlands. Jazz, opera, folk, country, and popular music concerts are held in the **Filene Center,** 703/255-1860, a partially outdoor amphitheater, during the summer, and inside at **The Barns at Wolf Trap,** 703/938-2404, Oct.–May. The two 18th-century barns, relocated from upstate New York, are half a mile down Trap Road from the Filene Center. The **Wolf Trap Opera Company,** 703/255-1935, performs in both venues. Children's programs, from mime to storytelling, happen in the **Theater-in-the-Woods,** 703/255-1800, in July and August, and an International Children's Festival spans three days over Labor Day weekend.

Dining options include **Ovations Restaurant,** 703/255-4017, serving á la carte or buffet meals nightly two hours before evening performances (make reservations online at www.maisonculinaire.com), or The Barns' drink and snack bar. You're welcome to bring your own picnic to the Filene Center, or you can order one ahead of time from **Catering by Windows,** 703/519-3505, www.catering.com/wolftrap, and have it waiting the night of the performance.

Tickets are available at the park box office, through the park's website or from various outlets of Tickets.com, 800/955-5566 or 703/218-6500, www.tickets.com. Prices range from $8 for lawn space to $70 for orchestra seats. Children's shows are $3. The park is on Trap Road between Rt. 7 and the Dulles Toll Road, north of Tysons Corner. Parking is free. For Filene Center performances (except operas), the **Wolf Trap Metro Shuttle Bus Express** runs to and from the West Falls Church Metro station (on the orange line) for $3.50 pp roundtrip. For more information, contact the **Wolf Trap Foundation,** 703/255-1900 (ticket information 703/255-1860), email: wolftrap@wolf-trap.org, www.wolf-trap.org or www.nps.gov/wotr.

Hunt Country

Some of Virginia's choicest acres pick up where the Beltway sprawl ends, stretching all the way to the Shenandoah. From the banks of the upper Potomac—one of the wildest urban rivers in the East—to the foothills of the Blue Ridge, Hunt Country is a mix of tiny villages and huge estates, with a few modest farms still holding on in between. Old stone walls crawling with honeysuckle curve into neat lines of black and white fences along dirt lanes sunken with centuries of use. Cows and horses speckle emerald fields among silver silos, red barns, and white farmhouses.

Ever since Lord Fairfax first rode off behind a braying pack of hounds, both Loudoun (LOUD-un) and Faquier (fah-KEER) counties have been known as Virginia's Hunt Country. Presidents from Washington to Kennedy have fled the bustle of the capital to chase foxes through the early-morning tranquillity of the countryside. Some of the richest people in the world breed, show, train, and race thoroughbreds on multimillion-dollar estates, popping into towns like Middleburg and Upperville to repair a harness or pick up a quart of oil for the Mercedes.

The development juggernaut, though, rolls slowly nearer. High-tech industries moving west from Arlington and Fairfax have made Loudoun one of the fastest-developing counties in the country. Huge tracts of land not yet swallowed up by office parks and housing developments stand on the brink, not yet urbanized but no longer rural. Hunt Country holds its future in its hands, and if its performance with Disney is any indication, it will be awhile before these farmlands are paved. The Mouse (a.k.a. the Walt Disney Co.) wanted to build a $650 million-dollar history theme park on 3,000 acres of Fairfax and Loudoun counties. Concerns surfaced over visitor impact—the complex would have been only four miles from the Manassas Civil War battlefields—and good taste (how would Disney portray slavery?). Despite Governor George Allen's support, the plan fell to an organized opposition led by an unlikely coalition of Ralph Nader and Old Money.

MANASSAS NATIONAL BATTLEFIELD PARK

The gently rippled hills north of Manassas, still almost as rural as they were 150 years ago, saw two major Civil War battles. The first opened the war with a horrific bang, and the second set the stage for Lee's invasion of the North three years later.

NORTHERN VIRGINIA

HUNT COUNTRY FUN

Perhaps the best way to get a sense of the pastoral sweep of the land here is from above, with only the occasional roar of the gas burner to keep you moving with the wind. **United Balloon Ventures,** 540/439-8621, email: kingjd@juno.com, sends hot-air balloons aloft at sunrise and sunset from their farm between Warrenton and Bealeton in Faquier County. One-hour flights are $350 for two people. **Balloons Unlimited,** 540/281-2300, www.balloonsunlimited.com, is based in the Hunter Mill Shopping Center in Oakton. It operates in the Middleburg area as well as the Shenandoah Valley. Sunrise and sunset flights are $150 pp.

Get a taste of the equine world during the **Hunt Country Stable Tour** on Memorial Day weekend. During the self-driven auto tour, you can visit barns, stables, and training facilities on exquisite country estates where thoroughbreds are raised and ridden. Chat with a re-enactor along the way and become familiar with various breeds of horses, foxhounds, and livestock in hands-on demonstrations at the historic estate of the late Mr. Jack Kent Cooke. Tickets are $15 pp ($8 more for the catered luncheon served daily at Trinity Church Parish Hall), and all proceeds go to charity. Order them ahead of time from the Trinity Episcopal Church in Upperville, 540/592-3711, www.middleburgonline.com/stabletour.

First Battle of Bull Run (First Manassas)

In 1861, Manassas was a vital railroad junction only 30 miles from Washington, D.C. Union Gen. Irvin McDowell found himself under pressure from a populace flush with patriotism and the romance of a clean, quick war to send his inexperienced troops against the equally untried Confederate army. On July 18, McDowell led 35,000 Federals against 22,000 Confederates under Brig. Gen. P.G.T. Beauregard, his West Point classmate. Ten thousand more Rebels fresh from the Shenandoah Valley under Gen. Joseph E. Johnston joined the fray, which climaxed on Henry House Hill, where 85-year-old Judith Henry refused to leave her home despite Confederate sharpshooters firing from her windows.

Union gunfire killed Ms. Henry and began to crumble the Rebel lines when Gen. Thomas Jackson incited his men to hold the hill, earning him the nickname "Stonewall" and turning the tide of battle. Reinforcements arrived, and the Confederate army was able to send the Federals into retreat even though they were too exhausted to pursue. Three-fifths of the 4,900 casualties were members of the Union Army, which by July 22 was back in Washington, D.C. George McClellan soon replaced McDowell as general, and the war had begun in earnest.

A statue in the park commemorates Jackson's stand.

Second Battle of Bull Run (Second Manassas)

A little more than a year later, Robert E. Lee, having pushed McClellan back from the gates of Richmond, attacked 62,000 Union soldiers under Gen. John Pope in hopes of crushing the Federals before McClellan could arrive with reinforcements. Together with Stonewall Jackson and Gen. James Longstreet, Lee had 55,000 men, plus the advantage of Pope's poor judgment. On August 30,

the Union general ordered a pursuit when the Rebels weren't retreating and watched his line crumble under Longstreet's counterattack. During hand-to-hand fighting in an unfinished railroad bed, Confederate soldiers threw rocks when they ran out of ammunition. A nighttime retreat avoided a complete Union rout, but the army still again lost half as many as the Confederates. Pope, blaming his officers for conspiring against him, was relieved of command, and Lee rode the momentum of victory as far north as Antietam, Maryland.

Visiting the Park

The **Henry Hill Visitors Center,** 6511 Sudley Rd., 703/361-1339, is on Rt. 234 south of its intersection with Rt. 29. It's open daily 8:30 A.M.–5 P.M. ($2 pp), with slide programs every half hour and tour maps of the battlefields. You can walk the loop trail of First Manassas in about 45 minutes, passing reconstructed houses and a muscular statue of Jackson commemorating his bold stand. Nine sites of Second Manassas are linked by a driving tour. Visit the park on the Internet at www.nps.gov/mana.

© JULIAN SMITH

BULL RUN REGIONAL PARK

One thousand wooded acres along Bull Run Creek include the northern end of the **Bull Run-Occoquan Trail,** which traverses four regional parks in 17.5 rural miles along the river and Occoquan Reservoir. Wood thrushes, scarlet tanagers, hooded warblers, and red-eyed vireos all make an appearance along the blue-blazed trail. It's moderately strenuous and open to hikers and horses. Inside the park, the 1.5-mile **Bluebell Nature Loop** erupts with countless Virginia bluebells in mid-April.

The park, 703/631-0550, www.nvrps.org/bullrunpark.html, has a camp store, pool, miniature golf course, playground, and 11 picnic areas open Mar.–Dec. Entrance is $5.50 per vehicle. There are also 150 campsites for $14.50–18. If these are full, try the **Haymarket Farm Family Campground,** 14004 Shelter Ln. in Haymarket, 703/754-7944, for $20–24.

A MAN'S HOME IS . . . SOMETHING ELSE ENTIRELY

Part antique shop, part military surplus store, part Second-Amendment stronghold, **Bull Run Castle,** 703/327-4113, is the kind of place that once again proves that anyone with enough vision, time, and money (in that order) can do just about anything. This isn't just a townhouse with a cute little tower stuck on. This is an honest-to-God, four-story, cement-and-iron castle, complete with dungeon, portcullis, armory, and enough crenellations to repel a Mongol horde.

It's all the work of John Roswell Miller, former Army officer, civilian contractor, and handyman supreme. Step inside his world on the $2 tour (he'll give you back $10 if you don't like it) and learn how he spent his 71st birthday skydiving, and how he's been working on this place since 1986. Sometimes it's lonely work, and finding ingredients is touch and go—a steel staircase here, a shipment of Enfields there—but things have definitely progressed since the days he was living on-site in a tent with his family.

The tour takes you from the workshop basement, with its coal stoves and blastproof ceiling (Dulles airport, a major target, is only seven miles away), through the oak-beamed main hall and up into the keep, which can be sealed and defended almost indefinitely—should the need arise. Along the way you'll learn how he acquired a chandelier from John F. Kennedy's townhouse, how to cool a building with underground air (just ask Thomas Jefferson), and why God is a Republican. Huge stone hearths, Hummel figurines, and half-sized Confederate caskets (for legless burials): it's almost too much to absorb in one go. Almost everything in the jam-packed place is for sale, and he plans to open four upstairs rooms as a bed-and-breakfast, as soon as they're complete, for $60 a night and "any breakfast you want" in the morning.

From the five-inch iron-shod front door to the solar collectors on the roof, Bull Run Castle is a monument to self-sufficiency and singlemindedness. Before you let yourself get too creeped out, look carefully for the twinkle in Miller's eye when he talks about throwing lawyers and liberals in the dungeon. It's a crazy dream, and he knows it, but he keeps plowing ahead regardless—and as of 2001, he was most of the way there. The fact that a group of local vampires has stayed the night only adds to the whacked-out charm.

The castle is on US 15 in Aldie, two miles south of the intersection with US 50 (Gilberts Corner); open Mon.–Fri. 8 A.M.–7 P.M., Sat. and Sun. 8 A.M.–9 P.M., or frankly, whenever he's around and not digging a tunnel or something.

© JULIAN SMITH

NORTHERN VIRGINIA

NORTHERN VIRGINIA

NORTHERN VIRGINIA WINERIES

Breaux Vineyards
36888 Breaux Vineyard Ln.
540/668-6299
Near Leesburg; Rt. 7 west three miles to Rt. 9 west, through Hillsboro to right on Rt. 671 north, one mile

Chrysalis Vineyards
23876 Champe Ford Rd.
800/235-8804 or 540/687-8222
Near Middleburg; one mile south of US 50 between Aldie and Middleburg

Farfelu Vineyard
13058 Crest Hill Rd.
703/364-2930
Near Flint Hill; Rt. 6 exit 27, 12.5 miles west on Rt. 647

Glenway Winery
14437 Hume Rd.
540/635-9398
Near Front Royal; six miles south on Rt. 522 to intersection with Hume Rd.

Grey Ghost Vineyards
14706 Lee Hwy.
540/937-4869
Near Amissville; 11 miles west of Warrenton on Rt. 211

Hartwood Winery
345 Hartwood Rd.
703/752-4893
Near Fredericksburg

Linden Vineyards
3708 Harrels Corner Rd.
540/364-1997
Near Linden; I-66 exit 13 at Linden, one mile east on Rt. 55, right onto Rt. 638 for two miles

Loudoun Valley Vineyard
540/882-3375
Near Waterford; from Leesburg Rt. 7 west two miles to Rt. 9 west, five miles

Naked Mountain Vineyard
540/364-1609
Near Markham; I-66 exit 18N, 1.5 miles on Rt. 688

The Oasis Winery
800/304-7656 or 540/635-7627
Near Hume; I-66 exit 27 at Marshall, four miles on Rt. 647, right onto Rt. 635 for 10 miles

Piedmont Vineyards
540/687-5528
Near Middleburg; three miles south on Rt. 626

Shaddwell-Windham Winery
14727 Mountain Rd.
540/668-6464
Near Hillsboro; Rt. 690

Spotted Tavern Winery and Dodd's Cider Mill
540/752-4453
Near Hartwood; from Rt. 17/I-95 intersection, five miles north on Rt. 17, right onto Rt. 612 for four miles

Swedenburg Estate Vineyard
Winery Ln.
540/687-5219
Near Middleburg; one mile east on US 50 south

Tarara Vineyard & Winery
13648 Tarara Ln.
703/771-7100 or 703/438-8168
Near Leesburg; Rt. 15 north eight miles to Lucketts, right on Rt. 662, three miles

Willowcroft Farm Vineyards
38906 Mt. Gilead Rd.
703/777-8161
Near Leesburg; south on Rt. 15, right onto Rt. 704, left onto Rt. 797, three miles

LEESBURG

Poised between the weight of the past and modern development pushing from the east, the largest city in Hunt Country noses up against the Potomac at the far horizon of D.C.'s suburban spread. One of northern Virginia's oldest cities, it began as a cluster of log houses at the intersection of two settler's roads. It served as an outfitting post during the French and Indian War and was eventually named for Robert E. Lee's ancestors. During the War of 1812, 22 wagonloads of government documents, including the Declaration of Independence and the Constitution, were brought here for safekeeping as the British put D.C. to the torch.

Leesburg's Historic District, enclosed by the original 1878 boundaries, is chock full of antique stores and rows of narrow 18th- and 19th-century buildings, usually with one or two residential levels over a ground-floor shop or apartment. Freestanding houses with picket fences, small lawns, and Victorian-style architecture line narrow, quiet streets, many of which are one-way.

Sights

The **Market Station** complex, at Loudoun and Harrison streets on the site of Leesburg's former "waterless wharf," consists of nine historic buildings including a freight depot, an 18th-century mill, and a log cabin dating to the mid-19th century. Among and inside these are various shops, offices, the visitors center, and one of the town's most popular restaurants. Parking at the garage at Market and Wirt streets is free for the first three hours.

Stop by the **Loudoun Museum,** 16 W. Loudoun St., 703/777-7427, www.Loudoun-museum.org, for a walking-tour brochure. While you're there, look over the collection of artifacts spanning Leesburg's three centuries of history; $1 adults, 50 cents children 5–18. A restored 1767 log cabin across the street houses a gift shop. Both are open Mon.–Sat. 10 A.M.–5 P.M., Sun. 1–5 P.M.

Other notable buildings include the Classical revival **Thomas Balch Library,** 208 Market St., 703/779-1328, built in 1922, and the

Loudoun County Courthouse at the corner of Market and King streets, dating to 1894. The courthouse, topped by an octagonal tower, was the third built on this site. General George C. Marshall's late 19th-century Federal-style **Dodona Manor,** 217 Edward's Ferry Rd. (Rt. 7), was undergoing restoration in 2001. It may be open by appointment; ask at the visitors center.

Follow Rt. 15 south of town a few miles to find the **Leesburg Animal Park,** 703/433-0002, www.zoo-to-you.com, a petting zoo with animals ranging from the mundane (sheep, donkeys) to the exotic (ring-tailed lemurs, giant tortoises). Open Tues.–Thurs. 10 A.M.–3 P.M., Fri. 10 A.M.–5 P.M.; $7 adults, $5 children. Call for off-season hours and information on their Pumpkinville fall celebration.

Accommodations

The **Best Western Leesburg-Dulles,** 726 E. Market St., 703/777-9400, fax 703/777-5537, is a short way east of the town center on Rt. 7 ($130). Keep going to reach the **Holiday Inn at Carradoc Hall,** 1500 E. Market St., 703/771-9200, fax 703/771-1575, www.leesburgvaholidayinn.com, with 126 rooms and four mansion suites in the 18th-century structure surrounded by rolling lawns. Room rates are around $150.

Once described as the finest tavern in town, the **Laurel Brigade Inn,** 20 W. Market St., 866/777-1020 or 703/777-1010, email: laurelbrigadeinn.@aol.com, www.laurelbrigade.com, was built in stone in the early 1800s to replace an older version dating to 1759. Period antiques and French marble mantelpieces decorate the modest house, which has six guest rooms ($95–145). The Laurel Brigade Restaurant, open for lunch and dinner Tues.–Sun., overlooks a graceful garden and gazebo in back. Contemporary Southern appetizers are $6–10 and entrées like pan-seared trout range from $17–25, open for lunch and dinner Tues.–Sun.

The **Tarara Vinery Bed & Breakfast,** 13648 Tarara Ln., 703/771-7100, ext. 4, fax 703/771-8443, email; tararabb.erols.com, www.tarara.com/bednbreak.html, occupies a stone and glass house set on 475 acres on a bluff over the Potomac River. Inside are a baby grand piano, stone

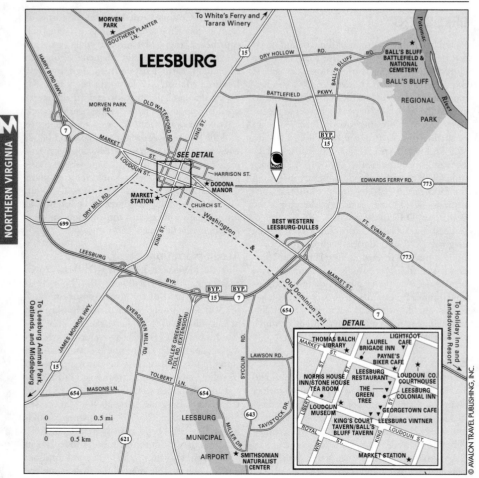

fireplaces, a bar, and three bedrooms and a suite. Prices ($120–135) include use of the walking trails, tennis court, and a stocked fishing lake—and, of course, a complimentary bottle of wine. To get there, take Rt. 1 north from Leesburg for eight miles, then take a right on Rt. 662 in Lucketts for three more miles.

Persian cats claim the sunny upstairs sitting room of **The Norris House Inn,** 108 Loudoun St. SW, 800/644-1806 or 703/777-1806, fax 703/771-8051, email: inn@norrishouse.com, www.norrishouse.com. Rooms in the 1760 Fed-eral home have brass and feather beds and the occasional fireplace ($100–145 with full country breakfast), and the Stone House Tea Room across the garden serves afternoon tea (call for schedule). Pam and Don McMurray also offer a guide to B&Bs and bike trails in Virginia, West Virginia, and Maryland on their website.

Four miles east of Leesburg on Rt. 7, the **Landsdowne Resort,** 44050 Woodridge Pkwy., 800/541-4801 or 703/729-8400, fax 703/729-4096, www.landsdowneresort.com, has 305 deluxe guest rooms and 14 suites styled after

Frank Lloyd Wright overlooking the Potomac River valley. Amenities include a Robert Trent Jones, Jr., championship golf course, a full-service spa and salon, a health club, tennis courts, and indoor and outdoor pools. For dining there's the Potomac Riverside Hearth, serving all meals with a view of Sugarloaf Mountain; the Potomac Grill and Fairways on the golf course; and Stonewalls Tavern off the lobby. Prices are $220 and up.

Food

For Colonial food aficionados, it doesn't get much more authentic than **The Green Tree**, 15 S. King St., 703/777-7246. Months of research in the Library of Congress unearthed a menu's worth of 18th-century recipes that are prepared to the letter for lunch and dinner daily. Choose from salmagundi salad once served at Monticello, Welsh rarebit, calf's liver, and green herb soup with 21 herbs and spices. Finish things off with a real hot buttered rum in the cherrywood-paneled pub, a bread pudding, or brandied peaches over ice cream. Solid oak tables and pewter candlesticks seem like they came with the 200-year-old building.

Another popular option is the **Tuscarora Mill Restaurant**, 703/771-9300, housed in an 1899 mill building in Market Station. Moved here and restored in 1985, the structure still feels like an antique with its bare wood beams adorned with plants and quilts. Delicious, varied entrées like Portuguese seafood pasta are $8–11 for lunch and $15–20 for dinner, served in the café and dining room. Open daily.

The **King's Court Tavern**, 2D Loudoun St., 703/777-7747, continues the Colonial tradition with a short menu of entrées for $15–20. Head downstairs and forward a century or so to the **Ball's Bluff Tavern** with its Civil War recipes and relics. Both are open daily for lunch and dinner. The **Lightfoot Restaurant**, 2 W. Market St., 703/771-2233, serves a light, healthy menu with plenty of salads in a spare, elegant setting. Open daily for lunch and dinner.

No-nonsense breakfasts ($5), sandwiches ($4–5), and dinner plates ($8–11) can be found at the **Leesburg Restaurant**, 9 S. King St., 703/777-3292. The **Leesburg Vintner**, King and Loudoun sts., 703/777-3322, combines a

wine shop with a gourmet deli serving sandwiches and bagels. In Market Station, **For Goodness' Sake**, 703/771-7146, is a natural food store with sandwiches, books, and gifts; and **South Street Under**, 703/771-9610, combines a coffeehouse, bakery, wine bar, and bistro, with soups for $3 and panini sandwiches for $5–6.

Entertainment and Recreation

Both **King's Court Tavern** and **Ball's Bluff Tavern** host live music nightly (Ball's Bluff has been voted best live entertainment in the county), and the **Americana Stage** at the Leesburg Restaurant presents original acoustic music. Having survived a fire in 1998, **Payne's Biker Cafe** is as real a biker bar as you're likely to find in Loudoun County. It faces the courthouse (a neon sign reads, Better off here than across the street), and has pool tables, a jukebox, and a bar menu—look for it on the wall next to the beer posters.

Budding zoologists, along with anyone interested in the natural world, should stop by the **Smithsonian Naturalist Center,** in the Leesburg Airpark Business Center at 741 Miller Dr. SE, Suite G-2, 800/729-7725 or 703/779-9712, email: natcenter@aol.com. It's a small branch of the National Museum of Natural History and houses a great study collection of 30,000 items from mounted bugs to a horse skeleton and the biggest polar bear you've ever seen. Lab equipment and a reference library are also available. Open Tues.–Sat. 10:30 A.M.–4 P.M.; free.

Events

On the first Friday of every month except January, galleries and shops in the city offer wine and cheese open houses in the evenings during the **First Friday Gallery Walk** series. The **Leesburg Flower and Garden Show** blooms in late April, and June–August, the **Bluemont Concert Series** brings everything from big bands to folk music to the courthouse lawn. Concerts are held Sundays at 7 P.M., so bring a blanket or chair and a picnic. Ask at the Loudoun Museum or visitors center for details on these and the **L.A.U.G.H.S** (Loudoun's Annual Unforgettable Gigantic Hilarious Story Festival) in June. A costumed street fair, Revolutionary War encampment, and 18th-century crafts and music are all part of **Court Days,** held the third weekend in August. See **Vicinity of Leesburg** for more annual happenings in the area.

Shopping

With more than 100 shops in town—and most of these sell antiques—Leesburg has plenty of options for browsing and buying. **Glenfiddich Farm Pottery,** 17642 Canby Rd., 703/771-3329, sells Richard Busch's handmade, salt-fired stoneware out of a 160-year-old dairy barn to the west of town on Catoctin Mountain. Americana and folk art is the specialty of **Country Collections,** 9 Loudoun St. SW, 800/390-3026 or 703/737-7740.

Antique stores have taken over Leesburg's historic center like an occupying army. Start at the **Leesburg Antique Gallery of Shoppes,** 19487 James Monroe Hwy., 703/777-7799. The **Black Shutter Antique Shoppes,** 1 Loudoun St., 703/443-9579, also has a large selection spread throughout more than 20 rooms. After that, if you still have time and energy, you might try **Barnes Trading Co.,** 312A E. Market St., 703/777-0022, or **Magnolia Marketplace,** 217 E. Market St., 703/771-9337.

Information

The **Loudoun Convention and Visitors Association** has a visitors center in the lower level of Market Station, 800/752-6118, ext. 11, www.visitLoudoun.org. It's open daily 9 A.M.–6 P.M.

VICINITY OF LEESBURG

Ball's Bluff Battlefield and National Cemetery

On the evening of October 20, 1861, a Union reconnaissance force of 1,000 mistook a row a haystacks for Confederate tents, exposing themselves to an actual enemy force in their confusion. The next day, the Federals crossed the Potomac into disaster, finding themselves trapped between the water and a row of high bluffs as Confederate rifle fire mowed them down from above. Nine hundred Union troops died in the skirmish, including their commander, Gen. Edward Baker, a

U.S. senator and friend of Lincoln. Bodies floating downriver to Washington galvanized the U.S. government into organizing its forces in earnest.

A three-quarter-mile self-guided interpretive trail loops to the top of the bluff and back, passing a tiny cemetery ringed by Virginia bluebells and white trout lilies in the spring. Open daily dawn–dusk. The adjacent **Ball's Bluff Regional Park,** 703/737-7800, www.nvrps.org/ballsbluff.html, claims a mile-long stretch of riverbank. Guided tours of the battlefield are given on weekends from May–October.

White's Ferry

The only cable-guided ferry on the East Coast has been hauling people and cargo across the Potomac since the 1820s. Today the *General Jubal Early* carries cars and bicycles across the quarter-mile stretch from Rt. 655 to Maryland. On the opposite bank, the C&O Towpath runs downriver toward the capital, and a snack bar/souvenir store has fishing supplies and boats for rent. The ferry runs daily 5 A.M.–11 P.M., weather permitting, but is occasionally closed due to flooding. Call 301/349-5200 for information.

Morven Park

The 1,200-acre estate of Governor Westmoreland Davis, who was elected in 1918, centers on a Greek Revival mansion where lavish parties once filled the Renaissance Great Hall with laughter, music, and candlelight. Paintings, tapestries, and sculptures acquired by Mrs. Davis in her travels through Asia and Europe adorn the Jacobean dining room and French drawing room.

In the north wing, a **Museum of Hounds and Hunting** displays art, photos, clothes, and artifacts from centuries of fox chasing, including a 1731 hunting horn carried by a Colonial governor. The estate's **Winmill Carriage Collection** contains more than 100 antique coaches, one of the largest personal collections in the world. Wrought-iron gates and a reflecting pool set off the impressive boxwood gardens surrounded by the original brick walls.

Morven's International Equestrian Center has a full calendar of events, including horse shows, trials, competitions, schools, and steeplechase races throughout the year. The third weekend in June the **Potomac Celtic Festival,** one of the country's best, brings Highland games, music, artisans, and a historical reenactment of life in 200 B.C. Kids' activities include storytelling and games, and for the adults there's single-malt whiskey tastings and the caber toss. Call the Loudoun Tourism Council for more information. Morven's **Christmas Open House** lights the mansion with roaring fireplaces and a 12-foot tree in the great hall the entire month of December.

Morven Park, 703/777-2414, www.morvenpark.com, is northwest of Leesburg. Take Rt. 7 west one mile from the town center, make a right onto Morven Park Road, then a left onto Old Waterford Road. Open Apr.–Oct. Thurs.–Mon. until 6 P.M. (weekends only otherwise), with guided tours given in the afternoons. Admission is $7 adults, $1 children 6–12.

Waterford

A gorgeous drive along Rt. 662 deposits you in this village on the bank of Catoctin Creek. Most of the town has been declared a National Historic Landmark. Almost painfully pretty, Waterford is a diametric opposite to the soulless suburbs near the capital. Mossy stone walls, gravel lanes, big trees, and sloping lawns set off dozens of 18th- and 19th-century homes in a smorgasbord of architectural styles. Granted, there aren't any video stores or McDonald's, but that's the point.

Bluemont

Previously (and unenviably) known as Pumpkintown and Snickersville, Bluemont is home to the **Bear's Den Hostel,** 540/554-8708, email: bearden@crosslink.net, half a mile south of Rt. 7 on Rt. 601. The snug stone building, only minutes from the Appalachian Trail, has dorm rooms ($12 pp for Hostelling International members, $15 otherwise), a full kitchen, dining room, laundry facilities, and camp store. Camping spots are also available.

The **Bluemont Fair** the third weekend of September features plenty of old-fashioned fun such as stagecoach rides, farmer's markets, crafts, food, and music. Call 540/554-2367 for more information.

Oatlands Plantation

George Carter, the great-grandson of planter baron Robert "King" Carter, built a boxy Greek Revival mansion here in 1803. Refugees, both black and white, sought shelter on the 3,000-acre plantation during the Civil War, which was later operated as a guest retreat until mounting debt forced its sale in 1897. William Corcoran and Edith Morton, a pair of affluent Washingtonians, bought the place and restored it as an English country house to entertain weekend guests from the capital. The formal gardens, designed by Carter, are so lavish that Morton was said to have bought the place after one look without even seeing the house. Don't miss the 1920s tea house, reflecting pool, and boxwood bowling allée.

Oatlands, 703/777-3174, email; oatlands@erols.com, www.oatlands.org, is six miles south of Leesburg on Rt. 15, open Apr.–Dec. Mon.–Sat. 10 A.M.–4:30 P.M., Sun. 1–4:30 P.M. Oatlands hosts **Hunt Country Antique Fairs** in April, and September, the **Middleburg All Breed Dog Show** in Oct., and in May the **Sheepdog Trials** includes border collie demonstrations.

MIDDLEBURG AND VICINITY

Leesburg may be the commercial center of Hunt Country, but Middleburg captures its essence. Established in 1787, it began as a local commercial center halfway along the stagecoach route from Alexandria to Winchester (hence the name). Today Middleburg is still a one-stoplight place with fewer than 1,000 residents, but it's sure worth more than the original $2.50 an acre. This is barn jacket and Range Rover territory, surrounded by huge estates whose owners pay well to live in one of northern Virginia's quaintest small towns. Upscale shops sell fine cigars, antique jewelry, and everything horse-related right next to the big incongruous Safeway stuck in the center of town.

Accommodations

The **Red Fox Inn,** 2 E. Washington St. at Madison St., 800/223-1728 or 540/687-6301, fax 540/687-6053, email: innkeeper@redfox.com,

THE GRAY GHOST OF LOUDOUN COUNTY

Born on December 6, 1833, in Edgemont, Virginia, John Singleton Mosby was raised near Charlottesville and entered the University of Virginia in 1849. During his stay he shot and wounded a few other students, for which he had to serve a short jail term before graduating in 1852. His imprisonment sparked an interest in the law; three years later, he was admitted to the bar and practiced law in Bristol until the start of the Civil War.

Mosby saw action as a scout with J.E.B. Stuart's Confederate cavalry in First Bull Run and the Seven Days Campaign, where it was his idea to ride completely around McClellan's Union Army. In January 1863, with nine men, he began the guerrilla attacks that would make him famous. Under the Partisan Ranger Law, Mosby's Rangers began to attack isolated Union posts in Maryland and northern Virginia. Dressed in his

© DOVER PUBLICATIONS, INC.

trademark ostrich-plumed hat and red-lined cape, the dashing horseman led lightning-quick cavalry strikes to disrupt communication and supply lines. Anywhere from 20 to 80 volunteers, convalescents, and civilians made up the Rangers, whose officers were chosen by merit and dismissed when ineffective. Men furnished their own uniforms, weapons, food, and horses and divided captured goods evenly among themselves. When danger threatened, they melted into the night, staying with private families or living in the hills near Middleburg. At any moment, bragged Mosby, he could gather his band at a predetermined time and place "like Children of the Mist," ready for their next raid.

As a result, Mosby estimated that he kept at least 30,000 Union soldiers on his tail instead of at the front. Loudoun County became known as Mosby's Confederacy, and Union generals were livid at the guerrillas' audacious exploits and rising fame. Ulysses S Grant ordered all supplies and forage in Loudoun County destroyed and all men younger than age 50 arrested to prevent them from joining the Rangers. Federal officials regarded the cavaliers as criminals rather than soldiers—for their habit of keeping cap-

---

www.fedfox.com, began as Mr. Chinn's Ordinary in 1728 (making it the second-oldest tavern in the country). A young George Washington stopped by on a surveying trip, and on June 17, 1863, John Mosby met here with J.E.B. Stuart to discuss the upcoming Gettysburg campaign. The latter left his name on a room where JFK occasionally held press conferences. It's been known as the Red Fox since 1937 and houses 20 rooms in four buildings. A restaurant on the first floor, open daily, offers a short but high-powered menu in a fox-hunt ambiance. Rates are $150–175.

An old carriage stands in front of the **Middleburg Country Inn,** 209 E. Washington St., 800/262-6082 or 540/687-6082, fax 540/687-5603, www.midcountryinn.com, where a night in one of eight period rooms comes with the outdoor hot tub in back, full country breakfasts,

and five-course gourmet dinners on weekends. Fireplaces and four-poster beds are included, too. Rates are $125–145 (up to $265 on weekends).

Food

Tutti Perricone's **Back Street Café,** 4 E. Federal St., 540/687-3122, is a local favorite for its zesty cooking and live jazz on weekend evenings. Pizzas, salads, sandwiches, and pasta are served inside and on the outdoor deck. Open for lunch and dinner Mon.–Sat. One block away, the **Hidden Horse Tavern,** 7 W. Washington St., 540/687-3828, occupies a 200-year-old building. Seafood and other Hunt Country standbys are offered daily for lunch and dinner. **The Coach Stop,** 9 E. Washington St., 540/687-5515, is popular with celebrity spotters (was that Sam Shepard?). For breakfast or a midday snack, try the **Black Cof-**

tured spoils—and put a price on their heads. (When the Rangers also started hanging prisoners without trial, though, the order was rescinded.) Grant even considered taking the families of known Rangers hostage.

On March 9, 1863, Mosby led 29 men through the Federal lines at Fairfax Court House, where corpulent Union Brig. Gen. Edwin Stoughton sat surrounded by mountains of food and wine. The Confederates captured Stoughton, 33 men, and 58 horses ("For that I am sorry," Lincoln said, "for I can make brigadier generals, but I can't make horses"). They also made off with a canvas sack holding $350,000 worth of gold and silver coins and jewelry, which Mosby and a companion were forced to bury during hot pursuit by Union troops. Mosby was never able to return for the loot, which by his recall was stashed somewhere between Haymarket and New Baltimore in a shallow hole between two tall pine trees. His partner was eventually captured and hung, and the treasure has never been found.

The "leather-bed soldiers" were mustered into the regular army on June 10, 1863, where the "Gray Ghost" continued to attract followers and earn praise from Stuart and Robert E. Lee. In late 1864, Maj. Gen. Philip Sheridan sent Capt. Richard Blazer and 100 men armed with Spencer repeating rifles to hunt down the marauding band at all costs. The Rangers suffered 18 casualties before killing or wounding all but two of Blazer's party and capturing their rifles. By April 1865, Mosby had been promoted to colonel, wounded seven times, and sat in command of eight well-trained companies. His last raid came on April 10, the day after Robert E. Lee surrendered at Appomattox. He disbanded his men soon after, urging them to turn themselves in and seek individual pardons as he did himself two months later.

After the war, Mosby returned to practicing private law in Warrenton. His legendary status followed, dimmed only slightly by his support of Republican candidate Ulysses S Grant, who had become an admirer himself, for president. Mosby wrote two books during terms as U.S. Consul to Hong Kong and assistant attorney in the Justice Department: *Mosby's War Reminiscences and Stuart's Cavalry Campaigns* (1887), and *Stuart's Cavalry in the Gettysburg Campaign* (1908). He died in Washington, D.C. on May 30, 1916.

fee **Bistro,** S. Madison and E. Federal sts. 540/687-3632, or **Dank's Deli,** 2 N. Liberty St., 540/687-3456, with hot and cold sandwiches and outdoor seating. The **Upper Crust Bakery,** 2 N. Pendleton St., 540/687-5666, is a local favorite named without a trace of irony and offering cookies and sandwiches among the usual array of baked goods.

Events

Several **Point-to-Point** horse races gallop through town in March, April, and May, followed by the **Virginia Hunt Country Stable Tour** with wine tastings, food, and crafts on the second weekend in May. The **Middleburg Garden Tour** happens in May, **polo** is played June–August, and more races, trials, and horse shows occur in September and October.

Shopping

Middleburg has to have one of the highest antique store-to-resident ratios in the state. **The Shaggy Ram,** 3 E. Washington St., 540/687-3546, sells English and French antiques, while **Wickets Garden Style,** 17 S. Madison St., 540/687-5505, specializes in European garden antiques. For gifts and general goods, visit **The Fun Shop,** 117 W. Washington St., 540/687-6590, a two-story department store. Outfit your filly at **The Tack Box,** 7 W. Federal St., 540/687-3231, with riding equipment, clothing, and gifts.

Information

For details on events and anything else about the area, pop in the **Pink Box Visitors Information Center,** 12 Madison St., 540/687-8888, www.middleburgonline.com. It really is a pink-hued stone building, surrounded by a white picket fence and open Mon.–Fri. 11 A.M.–3 P.M., Sat. and Sun. 11 A.M.–4 P.M.

Glenwood Park

A long list of annual equestrian events at this track, a few miles north of Middleburg off Foxcroft Rd. (Rt. 626), is capped by the Middleburg Spring Races, the state's oldest steeplechase event. On the third Saturday in April, thousands of race fans watch riders compete for a purse totaling $140,000. Call 540/687-5593 for details.

Great Meadows

Hunt Country's premiere horse-racing venue, 540/253-5001, lies in the opposite direction near a village called The Plains. Everyone puts on their best and packs the tailgate with gourmet munchies for the **Virginia Gold Cup Races,** held the first Saturday in May. Seven races, held since 1925, draw more than 40,000 spectators, including most of Capitol Hill. Order your ticket well ahead of time and arrive early.

The **Virginia Wine Festival** brings dozens of wineries and hundreds of vendors for the state's oldest celebration of the grape. Food, rides, and music of all kinds round out the fun, held in June. The **Middleburg Classic Horse Show** arrives in mid-September, followed by the **International Gold Cup,** another steeplechase, near the end of October.

SKY MEADOWS STATE PARK

Almost 2,000 acres of clover-dotted fields and wildflower pastures were once part of a 7,883-acre tract purchased from Lord Fairfax in 1713. A bridle trail and five foot paths, including 3.6 miles of the Appalachian Trail, head across open meadows ringing with bird calls and into the forested hills beyond. Take the Gap Run Trail to a primitive campground with 12 sites ($8 per night). The **Mount Bleak visitors center,** 703/592-3556, occupies an early-19th-century farmhouse on a hilltop near a picnic area and fishing pond.

To get there, take US 17 south from US 50 for 1.2 miles to the park entrance on Rt. 710. You can also reach US 17 from I-66 exit 18. Open daily 8 A.M.–dusk, $1 per car ($1 pp on weekends).

Down the Potomac

HUNTLEY MEADOWS PARK

Fairfax County's Hyble Valley hides 1,425 acres of wetlands, meadows, and forests. The Potomac flowed here long ago, leaving behind freshwater marshes dotted by beaver ponds and teeming with birdlife. Local birdwatchers know the wildlife viewing tower is one of the best places in the Washington area to spot yellow-crowned night herons, woodpeckers, and any one of 200 other resident species.

In the spring, park naturalists lead an evening hike along a half-mile interpretive boardwalk trail to the sounds of a frog chorus. Bicycles are allowed on another two-mile trail. The park entrance and visitors center, 3701 Lockheed Blvd., 703/768-2525, is reached from US 1. Open dawn–dusk; free.

MOUNT VERNON

Close to one million people visit the home of America's first president every year, making it second only in popularity to the current president's house. If you can avoid or ignore the crowds, though, it's still possible to glimpse those things that made Mount Vernon so dear to George Washington's heart—the view of the Potomac on a misty morning, the wind through the fig trees in the evening, and all the smells and sounds of a practical, prosperous farm estate far from the public eye.

History

In 1726, George's father Augustine Washington obtained half of a 5,000-acre property called Hunting Creek. Nine years later, he moved his family, including three-year-old George, into a cottage he had built on a bluff overlooking the Potomac, but the Washingtons soon moved away again. George returned at age 16 when his half-brother Lawrence inherited the property in 1743. Washington assumed ownership in 1761 after the death of Lawrence's daughter Sarah, the original inheritor.

The current mansion was begun two years later. Washington continually added to the house and property until he owned 8,000 acres surrounding one of Virginia's finest plantations. George's vision of a quiet farming life had to wait through a few interruptions—the Revolutionary War, the Philadelphia Constitutional Convention, becoming the first president of the United States—but by 1797 he was finally able to retire to Mount Vernon for two quiet years, which he spent with his wife Martha until his death from a throat infection on December 14, 1799, at age 67. By the dictates of his will, he was buried in a mausoleum on his beloved estate and was joined there by his wife in 1802. In 1858, the newly formed Mount Vernon Ladies' Association of the Union raised enough money to purchase the crumbling building and begin to restore it to its former glory.

Visiting Mount Vernon

A wide bowling green leads to the main house, which is flanked by two curved colonnades of outbuildings. The 19-room mansion mixes the original Georgian style with the feel of an English Palladian villa, thanks to its owner's later remodelings. As they were in Washington's time, the outer pine boards have been painted and beveled to resemble masonry, with sand mixed in the paint to simulate stone. The view from the columned riverfront facade, 126 feet over the Potomac, rivals even hilltop Monticello's view.

Many original pieces have been tracked down and returned to rooms painted their original eye-catching shades of Prussian blue and bright green. Lafayette sent Washington the key to the Bastille displayed in the main reception room, and the English harpsichord once played by Martha's granddaughter Nelly Custis sits silent in the "little parlor." Notice the agricul-

tural motifs—wheat, shovel, and scythe—carved into the ceiling plaster in the two-story dining room, and the globe in the study that's missing the yet-unknown continent of Antarctica. Upstairs are the bedroom where French diplomat Lafayette slept on three visits and Washington's bedroom, containing the bed in which he died (possibly because of overbleeding by his doctors).

The half-moon of outbuildings includes a kitchen, smokehouse, slaves' quarters, stable, and archaeological museum. Don't miss the recycling outhouses (known in George's day as "necessaries") and the rebuilt eight-sided barn. Mount Vernon is still a working farm as it was when Washington kept detailed records of his experiments with crop rotation and different strains of plants. A squad of hard-working employees tends flourishing herb and vegetable gardens and a barnyard of horses, sheep, and chickens. Imported English deer mingle with native species in a cleared space by the river. George and Martha's tombs are found south of the vineyard, marked with simple inscriptions: "Washington," and "Martha, consort of Washington."

Mount Vernon, 703/780-2000, www.mount vernon.org, is eight miles south of Old Town Alexandria via US 1 or the George Washington Memorial Parkway (Rt. 235). It's open daily 8 A.M.–5 P.M. (Apr.–Aug.), 9 A.M.–5 P.M. (March, September, and October), and 9 A.M.–4 P.M. (Nov.–Feb.). Admission is $9 adults and $4.50 children 6–11, but on Washington's Birthday (also a national holiday) visits are free and a wreath-laying ceremony takes place at his tomb. Tours are self-guided, but interpreters are ready to explain details of the house and grounds. For more information, you can rent an audio tour or buy a guidebook at the gift shop, in front of the gate near the snack bar, post office, and ATM. Costumed waiters serve Colonial food and Virginia wine by the glass at the elegant **Mount Vernon Inn**, 703/780-0011, which has five dining rooms and three fireplaces. Open daily for lunch and candlelit dinners. Special annual events include garden tours, craft demonstrations, and children's activities (call for a schedule).

Transportation, Tours, and Trails

If you can't drive to Mount Vernon, don't worry—there are plenty of other ways to get there. One option is to take the **Metro** blue or yellow lines to Huntington and catch the Fairfax Connector bus (#101), 703/339-7200, to the estate for another 50 cents.

The **Spirit Cruise Line,** 202/554-8000, www.spiritcruises.com, offers three-hour cruises on the *Potomac Spirit* from Mar–Sept. Tues.–Sun. It leaves Pier 4 at 6th and Water streets SW in Washington D.C. at 9 A.M., arriving in Mount Vernon at 10:30 for a 2.5-hour stay ($30 adults, $20 children roundtrip, including admission). From King and Union streets in Old Town Alexandria, the **Potomac Riverboat Company,** 703/548-9000, runs the *Miss Christin* to Mount Vernon at 12:15 P.M. Tues.–Sun. Mar.–Oct. (weekends only in April, September, and October) for $26 adults, $13 children roundtrip, including admission and a narrated tour. Finally, the **Accokeek Dory,** 301/283-2113, runs between Mount Vernon and Colonial Farm, Maryland, across the river three times a day on weekends June.–Sept ($26/13 roundtrip).

Grey Line Tours, 202/289-1995, sends buses from Union Station in Washington at 8:30 A.M. daily for a four-hour tour of Mount Vernon ($28 adults, $14 children including admission). Free pickups at major hotels are possible. **Tour Mobile Sightseeing,** 202/554-7950, offers a similar service leaving three times a day from the Washington Monument, the Lincoln Memorial, or Arlington National Cemetery from late Mar.–Nov. ($22/11 including admission). **All About Town,** 202/393-3696, sends a four-hour tour to Old Town Alexandria and Mount Vernon on Monday, Wednesday, Friday, and Sunday for $32/$16; call for details.

The **Mount Vernon Trail** parallels the George Washington Memorial Parkway from here to north of Alexandria. See **Near D.C.: Arlington County and Vicinity** for more on the trail.

WOODLAWN PLANTATION

A pair of homes reflecting very different eras share a part of the original Mount Vernon estate grounds

to the west. **Woodlawn Mansion** was presented to Washington's nephew Lawrence Lewis on his marriage to Eleanor Parke Custis, Martha's granddaughter by her first marriage. Built 1800–1805, the brick building was designed in part by William Thornton, one of the architects of the U.S. Capitol. Period antiques set off carved marble mantels and the walnut rail lining the winding central staircase. The gardens include an exceptional collection of 19th-century roses.

Frank Lloyd Wright designed the low, angular **Pope-Leighey House,** in 1914 as an example of his Usonian style, meant to be an affordable, tasteful home for middle-income families. Originally near Falls Church, the L-shaped building was rescued from destruction in 1964, dismantled, and rebuilt here. Inside it's snug but comfortable thanks to high ceilings, warm cypress walls, and strategically placed windows.

Both buildings, at the intersection of the Mount Vernon Memorial Parkway (Rt. 235) and US 1, are open daily Mar.–Dec. 10 A.M.–5 P.M. Separate admission is $6 adults, $4 for children under 12, or a combination ticket is $10 adults, $7 children. Tours of both homes are included. The mansion hosts the country's oldest **Needlework Show** in March, along with a **Quilt Exhibition** in the fall. Call 703/780-4000 for details.

MASON NECK

Pohick Bay Regional Park

The first stop on this stubby peninsula is named for the Algonquin word for "water place" and offers a huge pool, a campground with hookups ($14.50–18), a camp store, boat access, a golf course, picnic areas, and nature trails. The park, 703/339-6104, www.nvrpa.org/pohickbay.html, is open year-round daily 8 A.M.–sunset for $4 per car. Sailboats, jon boats, and paddleboats are for rent, and the pool is open Memorial Day–Labor Day for separate admission. Take Rt. 242 from US 1, and the entrance is on the left.

Gunston Hall Plantation

A short distance farther sits an 18th-century plantation built for George Mason, one of the nation's undersung founding fathers. Mason was a friend of George Washington and the author of the Virginia Declaration of Rights, whose words Thomas Jefferson borrowed for the Declaration of Independence. Even though he helped write the U.S. Constitution, Mason refused to sign the document because it didn't abolish slavery or include a bill of rights.

A certain serenity pervades the Georgian mansion and 550 acres of grounds, all that's left of the original 5,500-acre tobacco and wheat plantation. Stop by the **visitors center** to see a short film on Mason before taking a tour of the house, built 1755–1760. Many of the furnishings are original, as are the remarkable decorative woodcarvings done by a young British indentured servant named William Buckland. Mason designed the formal boxwood gardens. Visitors can follow the nature trail through the wooded deer park to the Potomac and visit the grave of Mason and his wife Ann.

Gunston Hall, 800/811-6966 or 703/550-9220, email: Historic@GunstonHall.org, www.GunstonHall.org, is open daily 9:30 A.M.–5 P.M.; $7 adults, $3 children under 17. A museum holds a gift shop and a cafeteria serving an inexpensive lunch. Call ahead for information on interpretive activities such as cooking and harvest demonstrations, and the Kite Festival in March.

Mason Neck National Wildlife Refuge

Six miles of shoreline, 2,000 acres of hardwood forest, and northern Virginia's largest marsh fall within the first national wildlife refuge created specifically to protect the habitat of bald eagles. Along with the Occoquan Bay and Featherstone refuges, it's part of the Potomac River National Wildlife Refuge Complex, encompassing a sizable chunk of the Chesapeake Bay/Susquehanna River ecosystem. The majestic raptors feed in the 245-acre Great Marsh alongside a 1,000-pair colony of great blue herons, ducks, and 200 varieties of songbirds. Trails lead through fern-filled glades and over streams to the marsh edge. Open year-round, dawn–dusk, free. Call 703/490-4979 for more information.

Mason Neck State Park

In 1969, the state of Virginia purchased 1,800 acres from The Nature Conservancy, leaving the na-

tional wildlife refuge split into two sections on either side of Belmont Bay. The Dogue Indian tribe once hunted and fished here among the oak, ash, and maples. Today you can view ospreys, great blue herons, and one-quarter of the Chesapeake Bay's 250 nesting pairs of bald eagles from several short trails and walkways over marshy areas. A **visitors center,** 703/550-0362, operates a museum and can provide information on guided activities such as beachcombing, canoe trips, bird watching, and night hikes. Guided eagle-spotting walks leave on Saturday at 4 P.M. The park, 703/550-0960, www.dcr.state.va.us/parks/masonnec.htm, is open year-round, dawn–dusk, with an entrance fee of $1 per car ($2 on weekends and holidays).

PRINCE WILLIAM FOREST PARK

Inhabited as early as 4,500 B.C., the watershed of Quantico Creek was home to Potomac Indian villages from A.D. 700 until the arrival of English colonists. After centuries of severe erosion from overfarming, it was turned over to the National Park Service in 1948 to become a wooded oasis between the Quantico Marine Base and metropolitan northern Virginia.

Hardwoods and pines dominate 18,500 acres straddling a transition between cooler northern and warmer southern climates. A wide variety of plants (95 species) and birds (152 species) include great horned owls and the rare whorled pogonia orchid.

Start at the **Pine Grove visitors center,** 703/221-7181, www.nps.gov/prwi, on Rt. 619 from I-95 exit 150. Ask here for directions to the fishing ponds and picnic areas and for information on interpretive programs and the 35 miles of trails. Open year-round, daily 8:30 A.M.–5 P.M.; $2 pp/$4 per car for three days.

Campers have several choices. The Oak Ridge tent campground charges $10 per night for up to six people. The Chopawamsic Backcountry Camp, three miles west of the town of Triangle on Rt. 619, is basic but free with a permit from the visitors center. For hookups, steer toward the **Travel Trailer Village,** 703/221-2474, off Rt. 234 a few miles west of I-95 exit 152, where sites run $20–25.

Side Trip to D.C.

History

On June 20, 1783, hordes of unpaid soldiers descended on Philadelphia, demanding back pay from the War of Independence. A nervous Congress was quickly convinced that the fledgling United States needed a federal city where its lawmakers could govern in relative peace. Creating one would be no easy task: the 13 colonies were united in freedom but divergent in interests; there was no president yet; and the war had left the national coffers nearly empty.

Nonetheless, the location for the country's new capital was decided by a combination of political compromise and pragmatism. Southern states, who helped bail out their northern brethren after the war, insisted in return that the city be located to the south. Newly elected president George Washington decided on a spot near where the Anacostia River meets the Potomac, for its economic potential near the tobacco market of Georgetown and a planned canal across the Cumberland Gap to the western frontier.

French engineer and revolutionary volunteer Pierre L'Enfant was given the task of designing the nation's capital, which he planned on a grand scale in the spirit of his beloved Paris. A bold grid pattern, anchored by great parks and monumental squares, was overlaid with diagonal avenues named for the states and radiating outward from the White House and the

Washington D.C.

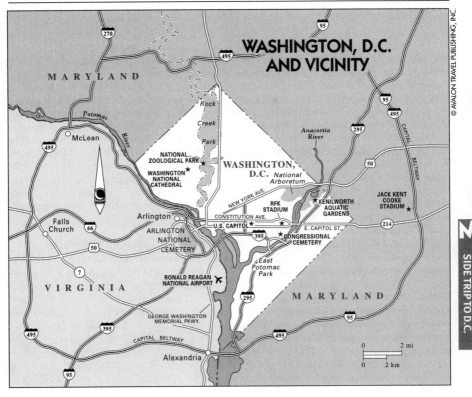

WASHINGTON, D.C. AND VICINITY

MARYLAND

Potomac River

McLean

Rock Creek Park

Anacostia River

NATIONAL ZOOLOGICAL PARK ★

WASHINGTON NATIONAL CATHEDRAL ★

WASHINGTON, D.C.

National Arboretum

NEW YORK AVE.

RFK STADIUM

★ KENILWORTH AQUATIC GARDENS

JACK KENT COOKE STADIUM ★

Falls Church

Arlington

CONSTITUTION AVE.

U.S. CAPITOL ★

E. CAPITOL ST.

ARLINGTON NATIONAL CEMETERY

★ CONGRESSIONAL CEMETERY

East Potomac Park

RONALD REAGAN NATIONAL AIRPORT ✈

VIRGINIA

MARYLAND

GEORGE WASHINGTON MEMORIAL PKWY.

CAPITAL BELTWAY

Alexandria

0   2 mi

0   2 km

SIDE TRIP TO D.C.

Capitol building, both of which were begun in 1793. In October 1800, the governmental archives and general offices were shifted to Washington from Philadelphia; President John Adams moved into the White House; and Congress met for the first time in the Capitol.

Critics soon began to attack D.C.'s seemingly arbitrary location. What was conceived as a "city of magnificent distances" was derided as the "Capitol of Miserable Huts," and members of both Congress and the national press tried to have the capital moved to a more accessible location. National outrage over the British invasion in 1814, however, firmly seated Washington, D.C. as America's capital in the minds of her

citizens. The city's key role in the Civil War, as the heart and brain of the victorious Union, further solidified its symbolic image.

A sudden influx of 40,000 freed slaves more than doubled D.C.'s population and set it on a course of racial diversity that eventually would embrace immigrants from every country in the world. Into the 20th century, the capital's identity continues to evolve and mutate, as wealthy neighborhoods stand next to slums, and homeless people sleep in the shadows of the country's greatest monuments. Our most monumental, symbolic, and international city serves as a reminder of all that is desirable—and much that is not—in the country it embodies.

The Mall Sights

The area between Constitution Avenue NW and Independence Avenue SW is truly America's backyard. The grassy expanse, wide as a football field, stretches 2.5 miles from the Capitol at the east end to the Lincoln Memorial at the west. Along both sides stand many of the Smithsonian museums, and just north is the White House. The Mall itself encloses monuments to George Washington and Vietnam veterans, outstanding national gardens, the Reflecting Pool, and even a charming merry-go-round.

For information on any of the free attractions on the Mall, call or write Superintendent, National Capital Parks Central, 900 Ohio Dr. SW, Washington, DC 20242, 202/485-9880. Be aware that access to many sites in the D.C. area may be limited due to security concerns.

Constitution Gardens

The last of the unsightly "temporary" buildings marring the Mall was finally removed in the mid-1970s and replaced by this tranquil oasis of landscaped gardens, meandering footpaths, and a duck pond. A willow-shrouded island at the center of the pond contains a roster of the signers of the Declaration of Independence, inscribed on a granite-and-gold plate.

Lincoln Memorial

While more than a century elapsed before the Washington Monument moved from contemplation to completion, the Lincoln Memorial was built in 60 years. Henry Bacon's white marble temple is another D.C. testimonial to the Greeks, while the 19-foot statue of Lincoln by Daniel French that sits inside the temple bears signs of Roman influence, especially in the chair arms bearing *fasces,* symbols of Roman imperial power. Although the 1922 unveiling ceremonies were segregated, the site began a long association with the civil rights movement 17 years later when Marian Anderson sang from the steps after she was barred from performing at nearby Constitution Hall. Ms. Anderson ascended the steps again in 1963, preceding the Reverend

Martin Luther King, Jr.'s momentous "I Have a Dream" speech.

During World War II, the Lincoln Memorial was the only edifice in D.C. to come under friendly fire: a nervous trooper manning the big guns atop the Department of the Interior building managed to blow off bits of the marble rooftop. Located at the west end of the Mall, the memorial is best visited at night, when the spirit of the place is most alive. Like other Mall attractions, the Lincoln Memorial is open all day every day. Rangers are on duty 8 A.M.–midnight daily except Christmas Day.

Korean War Veterans Memorial

Washington's newest memorial, dedicated in 1995, honors veterans of the Korean War. The centerpiece is the triangular "field of service," depicting a wedge of soldiers slogging through the countryside. This symbolic patrol of 19 stainless-steel

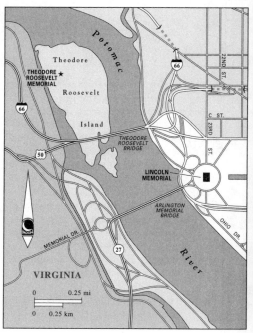

figures is made up of members from each of the four main branches of the armed services. The memorial is most haunting when the seven-foot-tall soldiers are softly illuminated at night. Staffed by park rangers 8 A.M.–midnight every day except Christmas, the memorial is located just south of the Reflecting Pool near FDR Memorial Park.

Vietnam Veterans Memorial

The revolutionary work that designer Maya Lin described simply as "a rift in the earth" doesn't trumpet the glory of struggle or the legacy of some lauded general. Instead it lists, in neat, simple, endless columns, the name of every person killed in America's longest war. More than 58,000 names are carved into the 492-foot wall of black granite, the polished surface of which reflects the faces of those who visit to pay homage. The names are listed chronologically in the order of death, and at each end of the memorial are paperback registers listing the names alphabetically with a key to their location on the wall.

Vietnam veteran Jan Scruggs raised the funds to construct the memorial through a nonprofit organization, and today it is America's most potent shrine, a place of grief and cleansing where every year tens of thousands of people bring offerings of poems and rings, harmonicas and sardines for lost friends, lost sons, or for the parent they never knew. Some leave only their thoughts for future generations, such as, "Understand that if the time comes when you must kill, it will destroy you for all of this life."

Vietnam Women's Memorial

This bronze sculpture portraying three women and an injured soldier was dedicated on November 11, 1993. Artist Glenna Goodacre honors the women who served in Vietnam with a solid, uncomplicated piece that communicates the emotional bond that formed between the male soldiers and women who served primarily as nurses and support staff.

Washington Monument

According to federal law, no structure in the

SIDE TRIP TO D.C.

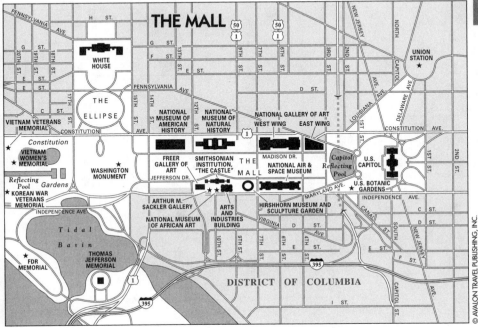

USING THE METRO IN D.C.

Location	Metro Station/Line
Botanical Gardens	
Botanical Gardens Federal Center	SW/Blue or Orange
FBI Building	
Archives-Navy Memorial	Yellow, Green, or Red
Federal TriangleFederal Triangle	Blue or Green
Folger Shakespeare Library Capitol South	Blue or Green
Ford's Theater	
Metro Center	Blue, Orange, or Red
Kennedy Center/Watergate	Foggy Bottom/Blue or Orange (walk south along New Hampshire Ave.)
Library of Congress	
Capitol South	Blue or Green
or Union Station	Red Line
MCI Center Gallery Place	Green, Red, or Yellow
National Aquarium Federal Triangle	Blue or Green
National Archives Archives-Navy Memorial	Yellow or Green
National Building Museum Judiciary Square	Red
National Mall Smithsonian	Orange or Blue
National Museum of American Art Gallery Place	Green, Red, or Yellow
National Portrait Gallery Gallery Place	Green, Red, or Yellow
Rosslyn Rosslyn	Blue or Orange (walk north across Francis Scott Key Bridge)
Shakespeare Theatre Archives	Green or Yellow
Union Station Union Station	Red
Washington National Cathedral Woodley Park-Zoo	Red (walk west along Woodley Rd.)
White House Metro Center	Blue, Orange, or Red
Zoological Park	
Woodley Park-Zoo	Red

Metro Transfer Stations include Federal Center SW, Gallery Place, King Street, Metro Center, Pentagon, Rosslyn, and Stadium-Armory.

System Map

Legend

- Red Line • Glenmont to Shady Grove
- Orange Line • New Carrollton to Vienna/Fairfax-GMU
- Blue Line • Franconia-Springfield to Largo Town Center
- Green Line • Branch Avenue to Greenbelt
- Yellow Line • Huntington to Mt Vernon Sq/ 7th St-Convention Center

Station in Service
Planned Station
Transfer Station

Virginia Railway Express
AMTRAK MARC

Commuter Rail

Parking

SIDE TRIP TO D.C.

*7th St. Convention Center scheduled to open March 2003. Existing Convention Center at 9th & H Sts. served by Metro Center and Gallery Pl-Chinatown stations.

© COPYRIGHT 2000
WASHINGTON METROPOLITAN
AREA TRANSIT AUTHORITY

No Smoking

No Eating or Drinking

No Animals (except service animals)

No Audio or Video Devices (without earphones)

No Litter or Spitting

No Dangerous or Flammable Items

capital can be built higher than the 555-foot tapered shaft of the Washington Monument. In 1783, the Continental Congress first suggested a monument honoring the nation's inaugural president, but more than a century passed before the idea became reality; from cornerstone to completion took 40 years. During one embarrassing interlude from 1854 to 1876, the obelisk languished as an unsightly stump of 150 feet, described by Mark Twain as "a factory chimney with the top broken off."

When work began again, the marble originally drawn from a Maryland quarry had been exhausted; thus the noticeable change in shade of the remaining 400 feet. The monument finally opened in 1888 with women and children dutifully trudging up the 898 steps (the elevator designed by Mr. Elisha G. Otis was considered patently dangerous, braved only by men). Today everyone rides the elevator, ascending to 360-degree views of the capital's historic heart through narrow windows.

The monument is open daily 9 A.M.–5 P.M., every day except Christmas, with extended summer hours for nighttime viewing. Tickets are required. Depending on the availability of staff, summer weekend walking tours down the steps are also offered. For more information, call 202/426-6841, or write Superintendent, The Washington Monument, 1100 Ohio Dr. SW, Washington, DC 20242 or visit the website at www.nps.gov/wamo.

National Gallery of Art

In the 1930s, this museum's west wing sprang full-grown from the wallet of rapacious banker Andrew Mellon, who wisely declined to append his name to the edifice. I.M. Pei designed the angular east wing, which was built in 1978. Both wings are constructed of pink Tennessee marble, but there the similarity ends: the east displays 20th-century works by the likes of Miró, Magritte, and Matisse, while the homier, more crowded west wing is the domain of classic art by the likes of Raphael, Rembrandt, and Renoir. Historians of the presidency are invariably drawn to the west wing, which sits over the bones of the old B&P Railroad Station where, in 1881, President James A. Garfield was shot twice in the back by Charles Guiteau. The gallery, 600 Constitution Ave. NW,

202/737-4215, www.nga.gov, is open Mon.–Sat. 10 A.M.–5 P.M., Sun. 11 A.M.–6 P.M. Closed New Year's Day and Christmas Day; free.

Mall Merry-Go-Round

On the grounds of the south side of the Mall, a small carousel offers a pleasant respite from the solemnity of its monumental surroundings. A circular journey or two aboard gaily painted horses, serenaded by cheery carnival tunes, can serve as a bracing antidote to historic dates and endless museum rounds. The carousel spins just east of the Smithsonian Castle and is open daily 9 A.M.–5 P.M., depending on the weather, closed major holidays. General admission is $1.

SMITHSONIAN INSTITUTION

Smithsonian Castle

In 1829, eccentric English chemist James Smithson passed on, leaving to the United States—a country he had never seen—105 bags of gold sovereigns "to found an establishment for the increase and diffusion of knowledge." After no small amount of puzzlement and a fair amount of wrangling, Congress decided in 1846 to spend Smithson's largesse on an institute of scientific research. In 1855, James Renwick completed the fairytale red sandstone structure popularly known as the Castle.

The institution quickly outgrew these grand confines, and today the building serves simply as an information center guiding visitors to the Smithsonian's scattered holdings. Smithson's dusty remains rest in a crypt beneath the castle, his corpse having gained these shores at last in 1904. Most Smithsonian attractions are on the Mall. The National Museum of American Art, the National Portrait Gallery, the Anacostia Museum, and the National Zoological Park are elsewhere in the city. The Castle sits at 1000 Jefferson Dr. SW, Washington, DC 20560, 202/357-2700, and is open daily 10 A.M.–5:30 P.M. Closed Christmas Day.

National Air and Space Museum

Year after year, this is the most visited attraction in the city. People just can't get enough of the model

the Castle, c. 1862

or write Office of Public Affairs, Arthur M. Sackler Gallery, MRC 707, Smithsonian Institution, Washington, DC 20560, or call 202/357-3200 for information.

Arts and Industries Building

At the conclusion of the 1876 U.S. International Exposition in Philadelphia, most exhibiting nations and many U.S. states craftily donated their exhibits to the U.S. government, thus saving the costs of shipping them home. It took 60 trains to transport all these objects to the Smithsonian, increasing its holdings fourfold and requiring the construction of this Victorian edifice to house it all. Today, the Arts and Industries Building (202/357-1300, fax 202/357-2700) features a reproduction of that 1876 Exposition, with an appealing hodgepodge of artifacts ranging from Kansas wheat to California wines, and some terrifying 19th-century medical and dental tools. The Smithsonian can never bear to throw anything away, hence nothing is too big—witness the full-size elevators, steam engines, and locomotives—or too numerous, as evidenced by the 100 nosegay posy holders. Located at 900 Jefferson Dr. SW, the museum is open daily 10 A.M.–5:30 P.M. Closed Christmas Day. Admission is free. For more information, visit the Castle or the website web1.si.edu/ai.

Freer Gallery of Art

Charles Lang Freer raked in millions designing railroad cars, then began to spend his accumulated wealth on fine art. Freer first became enamored of the prints, pastels, oils, and watercolors of James Whistler, then, at the artist's urging, began accumulating Asian art. When Freer died in 1919, his entire collection went to the Smithsonian; this gallery opened four years later. Today the Freer houses more than 26,000 objects, including

of Sputnik, the 1903 Wright Brothers *Flyer,* Charles Lindbergh's *Spirit of St. Louis,* a knockoff of the Hubble space telescope, and a walk through a full-scale reproduction of the Skylab space station. Perhaps the most popular item on display is the four-billion-year-old shard of lunar rock brought back by the astronauts of Apollo 17; hardly anyone can resist running fingers over this chunk of another world. The museum is open daily 10 A.M.–5:30 P.M. with extended summer hours determined annually; closed Christmas Day. Admission is free, though a fee of $2–7 is charged to view IMAX films in the museum's Albert Einstein Planetarium and Samuel P. Langley Theater. Visit the Castle, call 202/357-1400, or check their website (www.nasm.edu.nasm/visit/visit.htm) for more information.

Arthur M. Sackler Gallery

This eye-boggling three-tiered subterranean museum at 1050 Independence Avenue SW houses 5,000 years of Asian art. Highlights of the Sackler's unequaled permanent collection include Chinese bronze, jade, and lacquerware; delicate Persian paintings; Near Eastern works in silver, gold, bronze, and clay; and a pantheon of Buddhist and Hindu deities executed in stone and bronze. Open daily 10 A.M.–5:30 P.M., closed Christmas Day. Tours begin at 11 A.M. except Wednesday. Admission is free. Visit the website at www.asia.si.edu

more than 1,200 works by Whistler, the largest collection of the artist's work found anywhere. On Jefferson Dr. SW, 202/357-4880, the gallery is open daily 10 A.M.–5:30 P.M. Closed Christmas Day. Admission is free. Visit the Smithsonian Castle or website web1.si.edu/ai for more information or write Office of Public Affairs, Freer Gallery-MRC 707, Washington, DC 20560.

Hirshhorn Museum and Sculpture Garden

Created to quiet critics who complained that the Smithsonian cared only for classic art, the Hirshhorn is built around the extensive 11,000-piece modern art collection of uranium tycoon Joseph Hirshhorn. The museum's revolving exhibitions are dedicated to promulgating appreciation for "the art of our time." The museum, located on Independence Ave. and Seventh St. SW, is open daily 10 A.M.–5:30 P.M. (the garden is open 7:30 A.M.–dusk). Closed Christmas Day. Admission is free. Call 202/357-2700 or visit the website at hirshhorn.si.edu for more information.

National Museum of African Art

Founded as a private institution in 1964 and absorbed by the Smithsonian in 1979, this underground museum focuses primarily on the traditional arts of sub-Saharan Africa. Permanent exhibits include pieces from the royal court of the kingdom of Benin as it was before British colonial rule; traditional and modern ceramic works from varying regions of the continent; a display of utilitarian objects, each an example of the aesthetics found in daily African life; and a small collection of objects from the ancient city of Kerma, the oldest known African city south of Egypt, on loan from Boston's Museum of Fine Arts. Located on 950 Independence Ave. SW, the museum is open daily 10 A.M.–5:30 P.M. Closed Christmas Day. Admission is free. For more information, call 202/357-4600, visit the Castle, or go to website www.si.edu/nmafa.

National Museum of American History

Living up to the nickname "America's attic,"

this museum is as big, rich, and sprawling as the country from which it collects. The sheer quantity of material is staggering; it would require several hours to appreciate the intricate, painstaking, exhaustively informative lightbulb display alone. Nothing is too big for the museum's curatorial staff, who have hauled in a full-size gunboat and an entire post office, among other things. See Foucault's pendulum, proof the earth still turns; and the tattered fabric Francis Scott Key immortalized as *The Star-Spangled Banner*, proof the flag *is* still there. Discover the charge in a kiss in the Hall of Electricity, and on the 3rd floor review the heartbreaking collection of effects left at the Vietnam Veterans Memorial. It's located at 14th St. and Constitution Ave. NW, and is open daily 10 A.M.–5:30 P.M. with extended summer hours determined annually. Closed Christmas Day. For more information, call or visit the Castle, or go to www.si.edu/nmah on the Internet.

National Museum of Natural History

Here you'll find an endless amalgamation of artifacts—animal, vegetable, and mineral—from the jaws of a prehistoric shark large enough to swallow entire automobiles to the Hope diamond. A 13-foot-tall stuffed African elephant and a great stone head from Easter Island round out the collection. An extensive exhibit on Native Americans inspired Rudyard Kipling to ponder "the wonder of a people who, having extirpated the aboriginals of their continent more completely than any other modern race had ever done, honestly believed that they were a Godly little New England community, setting examples to brutal mankind." Hands-on displays in the Discovery Room (open afternoons by ticket only) are geared toward children. The museum, located on Constitution Ave. NW, is open daily 10 A.M.–5:30 P.M., with extended summer hours. Closed Christmas Day. For more information, go to www.mnh.si.edu, call 202/357-2700, or write National Museum of Natural History, Smithsonian Institution-MRC 106, Washington, DC 20560, or call or visit the Castle.

More Capital Sights

TIDAL BASIN

Separating West Potomac Park from East Potomac Park, the Tidal Basin was originally dredged as a reservoir but soon proved popular as a recreational area. From 1917–1925, white Washingtonians flocked to a segregated beach located where the Jefferson Memorial now stands. Today the basin is famous worldwide for the 1,300 cherry trees along its banks. The first batch, a peace offering from Japan, arrived in 1909, but the trees were contaminated with insects and were immediately destroyed. In 1912, a second shipment fared better and thrived through World War II, notwithstanding occasional efforts by enraged citizens to fell them. These days it is possible to cruise the basin on rented paddleboats (two-seaters for $7 and four-seaters for $14, picture ID required), available Mon.–Fri. 10 A.M.–5 P.M. and Sat.–Sun. 10 A.M.–6 P.M.; for information, call 202/479-2426. A public area, there is no admission to the Tidal Basin, which is officially open 8 A.M.–midnight daily. For more information, write Information—Superintendent, National Capital Parks Central, 900 Ohio Dr. SW, Washington, DC 20242, or call 202/485-9880. Be aware that access to many sites in the D.C. area may be limited due to security concerns.

FDR Memorial

Composed of four outdoor rooms, one for each of Franklin Delano Roosevelt's terms in office, this granite structure spreads along the banks of the Tidal Basin in West Potomac Park. Visitors to the memorial enter past an inscribed FDR quote—"This generation of Americans has a rendezvous with destiny"—and a bronze bas-relief of the presidential seal as it appeared at FDR's first inauguration in 1933. The interiors of each room include waterfalls, plants, shrubs, and trees, as well as sculpture and inscriptions highlighting FDR's accomplishments as president, from bringing the nation out of the Great Depression to leading the United States during World War II. The fourth room includes FDR's "four freedoms:" Freedom of Speech, Freedom of Worship, Freedom from Want, Freedom from Fear—symbolizing what the United States was fighting for during the war. It also presents the contributions of First Lady Eleanor Roosevelt as U.N. ambassador after her husband's death.

There was some controversy over the memorial at its unveiling. Initially the memorial completely neglected the fact that Roosevelt used a wheelchair for most of his life because of the polio he contracted as a child. After protests by historians and the disabled community, the memorial's designers agreed to include images of FDR in his wheelchair. Park staff are on duty 8 A.M.–midnight every day but Christmas. Admission is free. For more information, write Information—Superintendent, National Capital Parks Central, 900 Ohio Dr. SW, Washington, DC 20242, or call 202/426-6841, or visit the website at www.nps.gov/fdrm/home.htm.

Jefferson Memorial

Though the Jefferson Memorial has stood only since 1942, it is today under almost constant repair, its columns cracked by the effects of auto exhaust and acid rain. Nevertheless, the 19-foot-tall hollow bronze of Thomas Jefferson in furs is undeniably impressive, centered in an open-air rotunda surrounded by massive ionic columns, an architectural copy of Jefferson's own rejected plans for the White House. The interior walls are crammed with quotes from Jefferson's voluminous writings, although not all are accurate: there are more than a dozen errors in the excerpt from the Declaration of Independence alone. Located on the south shore of the Tidal Basin, the memorial is open all day, every day. Park staff are on duty 8 A.M.–midnight. Closed Christmas Day. Admission is free. For more information, write Information—Superintendent, National Capital Parks Central, 900 Ohio Dr. SW, Washington, DC 20242, or call 202/426-6821, or visit the website at www.nps.gov/thje/home.htm.

"The Awakening"

Brave the gauntlet of joggers and golfers in East Potomac Park to arrive at J. Seward Johnson's bold,

SIDE TRIP TO D.C.

boisterous sculpture of a great bearded giant angrily erupting from the chains of the earth. Only the head and portions of each naked limb have broken through the grass at the tip of Hains Point, but the wild look in his eyes promises a great awakening indeed. Children can't resist reaching inside the great shouting mouth. Located at Hains Point in East Potomac Park at the southernmost point of Ohio Drive SW, "The Awakening" is viewable all day, every day. For more information, write Superintendent, East Potomac Park, Ohio Dr. SW, Washington, DC 20024, or call 202/485-9880.

Theodore Roosevelt Island

Those proposing a memorial for the nation's 26th

president decided nothing less than an entire island would do, choosing 88 wilderness acres in the middle of the Potomac. Three miles of flat, easy trails wander through the swampy, wooded expanse of willow and ash, mud and muskrat. Rocky beaches with D.C. city views compete for visitors' attention with Paul Manship's 17-foot-tall bronze statue of the conservation-minded Roosevelt. There is only one way to get to the island: drive from D.C. into Virginia across the Theodore Roosevelt Bridge, veer right onto the northbound lanes of George Washington Parkway, pull into the poorly signed Roosevelt Island lot, and walk across the pedestrian footbridge that provides the only access to the island. The island memorial to the Bull

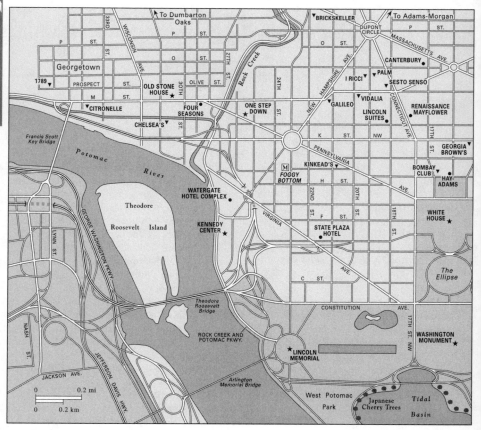

Moose candidate is open 7 A.M.–dusk daily. Closed New Year's Day and Christmas Day. Admission is free. For nature/historical tours, call 703/285-2600 at least seven days in advance; no winter tours are offered. For more information, write Information—District Ranger, Theodore Roosevelt Island, George Washington Memorial Pkwy., c/o Turkey Run Park, McLean, VA 22101, or call 703/285-1925, or visit the website at www.nps.gov/this.

Bureau of Engraving and Printing

Here some 2,300 people labor around the clock to produce more than $100 billion in paper currency each year. Through plates of thick glass, visitors can watch workers inking, stacking, cutting, and

examining millions of dollars a day. There's also an interesting exhibit on the curious history of money, and yes, bags of shredded bills are for sale in the gift shop (*everyone* considers trying to glue them back together, but it's futile). The Bureau, located at 14th and C sts. SW, 202/874-3188, is open Mon.–Fri. 9 A.M.–2 P.M. Closed federal holidays. Admission is always free, though tickets, available inside the building, are required from Easter to Labor Day. For more information, visit the website at www.moneyfactory.com.

United States Holocaust Memorial Museum

A truly wrenching experience, the Holocaust

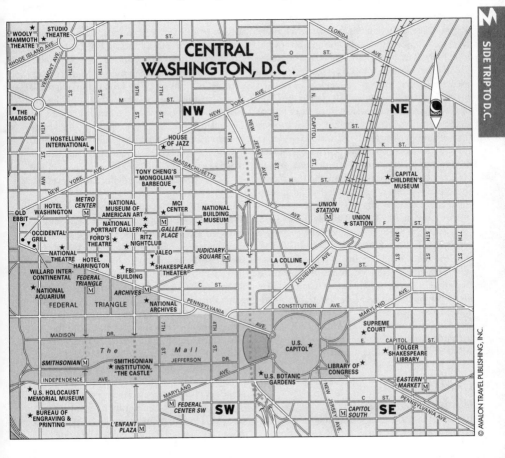

CENTRAL WASHINGTON, D.C.

SIDE TRIP TO D.C.

THE LIFE SPAN OF MONEY

U.S. currency is ubiquitous—the dollar bill is one of the best-known images in the world, right up there with Mickey Mouse and Bugs Bunny. But just how long, literally, does a U.S. bill last? According to the U.S. Treasury, it depends on how often it changes hands, which in turn depends on how big it is. Hundred-dollar bills usually last around nine years, twenties four years, tens three, and fives two. The lowly but ever-useful one-dollar bill has an average life span of just 18 months.

Museum is one of the most moving exhibits in this or any other city. From the outside, the building intentionally resembles the high brick ovens used to dispose of the bodies of millions of European Jews; inside, exhibits methodically trace the rise of Nazi Germany and its systematic implementation of its policy of genocide. The displays make clear that government officials in the United States and elsewhere were well aware of Hitler's implementation of the final solution, but chose to do nothing. Visitors will witness many depictions of horrific atrocities, but perhaps the most affecting items are the heaps of personal effects collected by the Nazis from those they murdered: mute piles of shoes, brushes, hair. Not recommended for children under age 11.

It's located at 100 Raoul Wallenberg Place SW (formerly 15th St.) at Independence Avenue right off the Mall, 202/488-0400, www.ushmm.org. The museum is open daily 10 A.M.–5:30 P.M., with occasional extended hours. Admission is free, though you must have tickets to enter. There are two ways to get tickets: reserve tickets in advance from Ticketmaster, which charges a service charge; from D.C. call 800/400-9373, or get same-day tickets at the museum box office. Allow at least 4–5 hours to visit.

CAPITOL HILL
Library of Congress
In 1800, the nation's legislators allocated a modest $5,000 "for the purchase of such books as

may be necessary for the use of Congress." The collection was contained in a single room and was consulted as much to settle bets as to divine fine points of law. In 1814 the British put the entire nascent library to the torch. Fortunately for the nation, Thomas Jefferson was suffering through one of his periodic spasms of acute financial distress around the same time and sold to Congress his entire personal library of 6,500 volumes to rebuild the collection after the fire.

Today "Mr. Jefferson's Library" consists of more than 28 million books, with an additional 80 million holdings of film, photographs, music, other media, and splendid exhibitions. The library complex consists of three structures and 532 miles of shelves; start at the stunning Jefferson Building, completed in 1897 and offering a feast of mosaics and murals, sculptures and bas-reliefs. The Main Reading Room, with 236 desks arranged in an elegant circular pattern beneath a 160-foot dome, is one of the most beautiful sights in the city. The Library of Congress is not a lending library—materials must be perused on site. Located on 1st St. SE between Independence Ave. and East Capitol St., the library is open Mon.–Fri. 8:30 A.M.–9:30 P.M., Sat. 8:30 A.M.–6 P.M. Closed New Year's Day and Christmas Day. Call 202/707-5000 or 202/707-8000 or check www.lcweb.loc.gov for library events.

Union Station
When it was completed in 1907, Union Station, modeled after the Baths of Caracalla in Rome, was the largest train station in the world. For the next 50 years, most visitors to the city first set foot in D.C. upon the station's elegant marble floors. By the 1970s, however, the place had become a national embarrassment: the floors buckled, torrential rains caved in portions of the roof, and a runaway train had slammed into the station, scattering spiraling shards of cars.

In 1981, Union Station was shut and sealed, until a business/government consortium invested $160 million to restore it to its former grandeur. Today visitors revel in acres of white marble floorings, bronze grills, coffered ceilings, gold leaf, Honduran mahogany, and a plethora of stone carvings and statues. Being a working train station, Union Station is open all day, every day, and there is no admission. Visit Union Station at 40 Massachusetts Ave. NE, 202/371-9441.

U.S. Capitol

Any first-time visitor to D.C. should take advantage of the opportunity to peek at our elected congressional officials at work. The small but well-appointed Senate chamber offers each senator a private desk separate from the rest, whereas House representatives are jammed together in long curved pews. The rest of the building presents its own peculiar charms: halls and rotundas stuffed with statues, and the frenzied frescoes of Constantino Brumidi, whose work was incisively described by Mark Twain as "the delirium tremens of art." A word of warning: much of the Capitol is off-limits to nonofficeholders, and visitors must heed the guidance of Capitol police.

To observe the House and Senate in session, U.S. citizens must obtain passes from the office of their senator or representative. International tickets are available in the Capitol for visitors from foreign countries (picture ID is required for visits to the House gallery). Another option is simply to cruise through the congressional office buildings across from the Capitol, where you're often more likely to experience the hustle and bustle of the political scene. The Senate buildings are to the north, on Constitution Avenue, and the House buildings are south of the Capitol on Independence Avenue. The Capitol is open to visitors daily 9 A.M.–4:30 P.M. Closed New Year's Day, Thanksgiving Day, and Christmas Day. Free guided tours depart every 10–20 minutes from the information desk beneath the rotunda. Reservations are recommended. For more information, write Information—United States Senate/House of Representatives, U.S. Capitol Building, Washington, DC 20510 (20515 for the House), 202/224-3121. Be aware that, as with all D.C. sights, access to the Capitol building may sometimes be limited due to security concerns.

Capital Children's Museum

The guiding principle of this elaborate, realistic educational experience is encapsulated in the Chinese proverb, "What I hear, I forget; what I see, I remember; what I do, I understand." From learning how to make animated cartoons to sliding down a fire pole, children learn how the world works by taking the controls. Luckily, there's enough here to keep most grown-ups interested, too. Climb inside a soap bubble (adults welcome), visit Mexico, and tour the Ice Age in a collection of exhibits that change almost daily. The museum is open daily 10 A.M.–6 P.M.; until 5 P.M. Labor Day through Easter. Admission is $6 adults, $4 seniors. Kids under two are admitted free. Located at 800 3rd Street NW, right at the Union Station Metro stop on the red line, the Capital Children's Museum fits easily into a tour of the Capitol Hill area. Call 202/675-4120 or visit www.ccm.org for more information.

Folger Shakespeare Library

The bard lives on at this combination research library, museum, and theater, brimming with art, music, and literature. Inside is an eerie and delightful working reconstruction of an Elizabethan theatre, where family events are held and the Shenandoah Shakespeare Express (based in Staunton, see "Shenandoah" chapter) performs Shakespeare's finest. Poetry readings attract the likes of Robert Haas, Czeslaw Milosz, Octavio Paz, and John Updike. The Folger Consort, a chamber music ensemble, performs works from the 12th through the 18th centuries. The marmoreal facade of this great museum fits neatly between the imposing Library of Congress and the august Supreme Court building. The Folger is open Mon.–Sat. 10 A.M.–4 P.M. at 201 E. Capitol St. SE; Free. Call 202/544-4600 for more information, or visit www.folger.edu on the Internet.

U.S. Supreme Court

Completed in 1935, this structure is undeniably opulent, with lush curtains, grandiose statues, and portentous inscriptions at every turn. The main chamber is particularly impressive, with the seats of the nine justices placed high above the rest of the court.

From October–April, the Court hears oral arguments twice a month on Monday, Tuesday, and Wednesday 10 A.M.–3 P.M., and in May and June the justices read opinions from the bench each Monday at 10 A.M. The public is welcome to attend, but there is limited seating, allocated on a first-come, first-served basis to those willing to line up outside the building. When the Court is not in session, visitors can attend courtroom lectures on the half-hour 9:30 A.M.–3:30 P.M. Check schedule in advance. The Supreme Court Building, at One 1st St. NE, Washington, DC 20543, 202/479-3030, is open Mon.–Fri. 9 A.M.–4:30 P.M. Closed on federal holidays. Admission is free.

Congressional Cemetery

In the early 19th century, D.C. was a remote, pestilential city, which sometimes proved fatal to those sent to govern from it. Congressional corpses faced weeks of daunting travel on slow roads and primitive waterways to reach hometown interment, so it was much easier to bury them in the city itself. In 1812, Congress purchased 100 plots in a five-year-old cemetery, which eventually held 14 senators and 60 representatives.

A peaceful, rarely visited, and ultimately desolate place, the cemetery is mostly full of children because of the high infant mortality rate in the 19th century. Others among the 60,000 souls laid to rest here include FBI director J. Edgar Hoover and his longtime companion Clyde Tolson; Taza and Push-ma-ta-ha, two native chiefs felled by disease while visiting D.C.; and David Herold, hung for his role in the assassination of Lincoln and quietly buried in a grave unmarked to this day. Dozens of cenotaphs honor members of Congress actually buried elsewhere. In this working cemetery, someone can usually be found around the small gatehouse just inside the E Street entrance; ask for the walking-tour brochure. The cemetery grounds are open daily 6:45 A.M.–dusk. For more information, write Information—Association for the Preservation of Historic Congressional Cemetery, 1801 E St. SE, Washington, DC 20003, or call 202/543-0539.

U.S. Botanic Garden

Another lovely idea of Thomas Jefferson's, this humid haven has enchanted visitors since 1820. Wander amidst a wealth of tropical, subtropical, and desert plants; guide dinosaur-entranced young ones to the garden of the Jurassic; or picnic on a flowery terrace overlooking the Capitol reflecting pool. The conservatory is closed for renovation, but the outer gardens are open to the public. Located at 100 Maryland Ave. SW, 202/225-8333, near the east end of the Mall, the gardens are open daily 9 A.M.–5 P.M. Closed Christmas Day. For more information, write Information—United States Botanic Garden, 100 Maryland Ave. SW, Washington, DC 20024, or visit the website http://www.aoc .gov/usbg/overview.htm.

THE WHITE HOUSE

First occupied by John Adams, the mansion at 1600 Pennsylvania Avenue NW was known as the President's House until it was whitewashed to cover smoke damage from the 1814 British burning of the city. It's not nearly as accessible today as it was during Jefferson's time, when enthusiastic dairymen would bustle in to deposit huge cheeses in the East Room. Nevertheless, it's the only chief executive's abode in the world that opens itself to tourists five days a week. When visiting the White House, don't step across the boundary ropes or make other foolish moves—those friendly men patrolling the halls can turn serious suddenly.

Tours of the White House are free, though tickets are required in spring and summer. Calling first is recommended. Tickets are available at the White House visitors center at the corner of 15th and E streets, 202/456-7041, open 7:30 A.M.–4 P.M. Arrive early if you plan on touring the mansion the same day; there are usually no more tickets available after 8:30 A.M. The White House is open Tues.–Sat. 10 A.M.–noon. Closed major holidays and for official functions. No public restrooms or telephones are available. No photograph taking or videotaping are allowed. For more information, write Information—White House Historical Association, 740 Jackson Pl. NW, Washington, DC 20560, or call 202/737-8292, or visit the website www.whitehouse.gov. Be aware that access to the White House is sometimes limited due to security concerns.

OLD DOWNTOWN AND THE FEDERAL TRIANGLE

The area enclosed by Pennsylvania Avenue, Constitution Avenue, and 15th Street is home to such stern, solemn edifices as the IRS and Justice Department buildings. For many years, the area was the most notorious neighborhood in D.C., popularly known as "Murder Bay." During the Civil War, the region was redubbed "Hooker's Division" in honor of the prostitutes encamped there. The place didn't get straight until the U.S. government bought up the land in the 1930s, razing the shacks and replacing them with grim granite.

The area north of Federal Triangle, between the White House and the Capitol Building, and bordered to the north by New York and Massachusetts avenues, was the city's original downtown area. Popular restaurants and theaters, fashionable tailors' shops, and other, more practical business kept those in office from having to stray too far from their seats of power for dining, entertainment, and life's necessities. Between the time that the buildings of the Federal Triangle were built and the late '60s, the area became quite rundown, gaining the name "Old Downtown" to separate it from "New Downtown"—the area north of the White House, where new businesses opened shop next door to vendors fleeing rundown Old Downtown. The entire Old Downtown area, especially Pennsylvania Avenue, gained a major facelift in the '80s. Today, the area again boasts popular restaurants and galleries, as well as landscaped plazas and memorials.

National Building Museum

In 1885, the general-cum-architect Montgomery Meigs erected the Pension Building. Damned at its dedication as an "unsightly monstrosity," the structure is recognized today as a masterpiece. Built of more than 15 million bricks, it features a 1,200-foot-long terra cotta frieze of Union soldiers forever filing for pensions. Eight central Corinthian columns, the largest in the world, dominate a great hall large enough to contain a 15-story building.

Today the eccentric old edifice is home to the National Building Museum, the only institution in the United States dedicated to architec-

tural achievements. On permanent display are exhibits dedicated to D.C. and the Pension Building itself. Recent temporary shows covered the humble, classic American barn and the aftermath of the April 1995 bombing of the federal building in Oklahoma City. Located at 401 F St. NW, the museum is open Mon.–Sat. 10 A.M.–5 P.M., Sun. noon–5 P.M. Closed New Year's Day, Thanksgiving Day, and Christmas Day. Call 202/272-2448 or fax 202/272-2564, or go to www.nbm.org on the Internet.

National Museum of American Art

Housed in an imposing edifice Philip Johnson once adjudged "the greatest building in the world," this eclectic collection of two centuries of American art includes truly marvelous works in the folk and ethnic traditions. (The building is under renovation and will not reopen until 2003. Programs take place at other sites. See website www.nmaa .si.edu for more information.) See especially D.C. janitor James Hampton's *The Throne of the Third Heaven of the Nations' Millennium General*, the fruit of some 15 years of cementing together found objects such as light bulbs, electrical cables, and aluminum foil; and the spirit-rich *Man on Fire* by Luis Jiminez, sprung from a legend of an unlucky Aztec man put to the torch by 16th-century conquistadores. Additional offerings include giraffes constructed solely of bottle caps and the psychedelic stain paintings of Morris Louis.

At 8th and G streets NW, the museum is open daily 10 A.M.–5:30 P.M. Closed Christmas Day. Admission is free. For more information, write Information—Smithsonian Information Center, 1000 Jefferson Dr. SW, Washington, DC 20560, or call 202/357-2700.

National Portrait Gallery

On the site where D.C. designer Pierre L'Enfant once wished to build a national cathedral stands this fascinating gallery of America's heroes and villains portrayed in sculptures, paintings, and photographs. (The building is under renovation and will not reopen until 2003. Programs take place at other sites. See website www.npg.si.edu for more information.) See especially the serious and sardonic self-portraits, the dizzying diversity of the Gallery of Notable Americans, and the treasury of 19th-century black-and-white photography. At 8th and F streets NW, the gallery is open daily 10 A.M.–5:30 P.M. Closed Christmas Day. For information, write Information—Smithsonian Information Center, 1000 Jefferson Dr. SW, Washington, DC 20560, or call 202/357-2700.

The National Aquarium

Besides the usual collection of fish tank fare, the nation's oldest public aquarium offers belligerent fiddler crabs banging on the glass, sleepy sloe-eyed alligators, gape-mouthed eels exuding yellow slime, and pale moist axolotl salamanders. A touch pool allows young ones to gently maul the likes of horseshoe crabs, while a small sign puts the whole shark business in perspective: people kill and consume 4.5 million sharks each year, while sharks rarely kill humans. The aquarium holds shark feedings Monday, Wednesday, and Saturday at 2 P.M., and piranha feedings Tuesday, Thursday, and Sunday. Regular hours are 9 A.M.–5 P.M. daily. Admission is $2 adults, $.75 children (ages 2–10) and seniors. The entrance to the aquarium, which is located in the basement of the Commerce Building, is on 14th Street. There is no street address, but you can write to U.S. Department of Commerce Building, Room B-037, Washington, DC 20230, or call 202/482-2825 for more information.

J. Edgar Hoover FBI Building

The free one-hour tour of FBI headquarters, 935 Pennsylvania Ave. NW, offers an extremely selective history of the bureau, including Dillinger, drugs, and a firearms demonstration by an FBI sharpshooter. Guided tours (mandatory) depart eight times a day Mon.–Fri. 8:45 A.M.–4:25 P.M. The tour entrance is on E St. NW, and reservations are recommended during peak seasons. Plan well ahead; this is a popular attraction. Arrange your visit by phoning the bureau or through your congressional representative. Admission is free. For more information, call 202/324-3447 or visit www.fbi.gov. Closed federal holidays.

District of Columbia Courthouse

This Greek Revival edifice at 500 Indiana Avenue NW originally served as Washington's first

city hall; it also saw duty as a hospital, patent office, and slave market. For more than 100 years, it's been the D.C. courthouse, the place where accused local lawbreakers are processed through the criminal justice system. In 1881, Charles Guiteau, the lunatic assassin of President James Garfield, babbled and bellowed through his trial in these rooms, then ascended the gallows reciting poetry until he was stopped by the rope. There are information pamphlets at the Public Information Desk to the left of the entrance. Stop here, after passing through the metal detector, for the lowdown on the juicy trials of the day. The courthouse is open Mon.–Fri. 8 A.M.–5 P.M. Closed all federal holidays. Admission is free; call 202/879-1010 for more information.

Old Post Office

When it was completed in 1899, this former home of the U.S. Postal Service was denounced as a monstrosity, "a cross between a cathedral and a cotton mill." These days, surrounded by the abominations of modern architecture, the old joint looks pretty good, housing federal workers for such agencies as the National Endowment for the Arts (NEA) and the National Endowment for the Humanities (NEH). Take the glass elevator to the clock tower; at 315 vertical feet, it offers one of the finest aerial views in the city. It's located at 1100 Pennsylvania Ave. NW, 202/289-4224, www.nps.gov/opot/index2.htm; admission to the building is free. The tower is open daily Apr.–Oct. 8 A.M.–11 P.M., Nov.–Mar. 9 A.M.–5 P.M.; the shops are open Mon.–Sat. 10 A.M.–8 P.M., Sun. noon–6 P.M. Closed Christmas Day.

National Archives

Preservationists of "the nation's memory," archivists here determine the worth of billions of documents generated annually by the world's busiest government. Pride of place goes to the Declaration of Independence, the Constitution, and the Bill of Rights, which are displayed daily, then mechanically lowered into a 50-ton vault to shield them from vandals and nuclear attack. Famous primarily as a center of genealogical research, the Archives have in recent years become a pilgrimage site for those wishing to listen to Nixon's Watergate tapes.

At 8th St. and Constitution Ave. NW, the Archives are open daily 10 A.M.–5:30 P.M., sometimes extended during summer. Closed Christmas Day. Reservations are required and are available by appointment only. Call 202/501-5205 for details. For more general information, write to the archives (zip code 20408), or call 202/501-5400 or visit the website www.nara.gov.

Ford's Theatre National Historic Site

In one of history's tragic ironies, President Abraham Lincoln was shot in Ford's Theatre just five days after Confederate General Robert E. Lee surrendered at Appomattox. Today the basement of the theater is a shrine to the martyred president, while upstairs the show goes on. See the bronze of a slumping, exhausted Lincoln; the simple contents of his pockets at the time of his death, from an Irish linen handkerchief to Confederate money; and the .44 single-shot derringer used by assassin John Wilkes Booth. Located at 511 10th St. NW, the theater is closed to visitors during rehearsals and matinees (usually Thursdays and weekends), but the museum is always open. Admission to the museum is free. For theater box office information, call 202/347-4833. The box office is open daily 9 A.M.–5 P.M. Closed Christmas Day. For more information, write Information—Su-perintendent, National Capital Parks Central, Washington, DC 20242, or call 202/485-9880, or visit the website www.nps.gov/foth.

Petersen House

After his shooting by John Wilkes Booth, Abraham Lincoln was carried from his box in Ford's Theatre across 10th Street to the boardinghouse of William Petersen, a German-born tailor. Today, three rooms of the Petersen domicile are preserved as they were that night in April 1865; the front bedroom that Secretary of War Edwin Stanton turned into a temporary White House; the parlor where Mary Lincoln waited and prayed; and the room where Lincoln died, which had been commandeered from William T. Carl, a young man out on the town that night celebrating the end of the war. The house is open daily 9 A.M.–5 P.M. Closed Christmas Day. Admission is free. For more information, write Information—Superintendent, National Capital Parks Central, 900 Ohio Dr. SW, Washington, DC 20242, or call 202/426-6830.

ADAMS-MORGAN

Adams-Morgan is D.C.'s version of New York City's East Village, only smaller. Most of this teeming quarter's nightlife takes place along two main drags: Columbia Road and 18th Street, joined together in a V at their northern apex. A little bit tony, a little bit tawdry, Adams-Morgan is a place where Washingtonians feel free to step outside the bars of their pinstriped suits.

Where yankee-doodle Washington is built on a monumental scale, Adams-Morgan is a concrete redoubt, an urban refuge. The streets actually become more crowded after 6 P.M., while the rest of D.C. rolls up its sidewalks. Here it's safe

Ford's Theatre, c. 1865

SIDE TRIP TO D.C.

to be neurotic, to be gay, to be straight, to stay up late, to drink too much, to pretend.

Once a row of tired Ethiopian restaurants scrunched cheek-by-jowl into red brick townhouses, Adams-Morgan has hip-hopped into its own over the last decade, as Washington discovered that there was life after legislation. This is an immigrant neighborhood, a largely Hispanic enclave that is also home to wealthy Anglos and a veritable United Nations of other ethnicities.

When the world starts getting you down, there's room enough for two (and plenty more) on Adams-Morgan's roofs; rooftop partying is de rigueur. There's **Perry's,** 1811 Columbia Rd., 202/234-6218, that offers sashimi by starlight. There's also **Roxanne's,** 2319 18th St., where you can enjoy eclectic Cajun cuisine under the stars.

One way to get your bearings in Adams-Morgan is by zigging and zagging. Best to zig down to 18th Street and to zag up to Columbia Road. Such an erratic route will take you up and down (mostly up, for Adams-Morgan is hilly) delightfully leafy lanes lined with elegant townhouses, many of which come with huge picture windows.

A big problem is that there are no convenient Metro stops near Adams-Morgan. It's a long walk from the nearest station, DuPont Circle, to the heart of the quarter. It's best to pay for taxis or, better yet, let a friend drive: finding a parking spot in Adams-Morgan has been known to reduce would-be visitors to tears. There is one convenient 200-space parking lot at 2419 18th Street.

Club Heaven, 2327 18th St. NW, 202/667-4355, provides an antidote for the fiendish parking. Appropriately, Club Heaven shares its townhouse venue with—you guessed it—Club Hell, downstairs. (Just in case you're wondering about the afterlife, Club Hell has the trendier crowd—and a larger dance floor.)

In addition, Adams-Morgan offers a wide variety of good restaurants and entertainment. This is the only area of town apart from Georgetown where it's possible to shop, relax over drinks, then walk down the street to find dinner. Afterward, you can stroll up the block to a club to close the night, unwind with some dancing, or just relax and listen to good music.

UPPER NORTHWEST

A series of residential neighborhoods, arranged in a succession of rings, gives the Upper Northwest its own distinct character and allure. Arguably, **DuPont Circle** marks the center of the area that fills the district's borders between Adams-Morgan and the Maryland state line. On one side of the circle sits some of the city's great think tanks, such as the **Brookings Institution,** 1775 Massachusetts Ave., established in 1927. Near the circle along Connecticut Avenue, you'll find good restaurants in a variety of price ranges. To the north, **Kramerbooks & Afterwords,** 1517 Connecticut Ave. NW, 202/387-1462, is a D.C. institution. The bookstore offers a café in back, where, after browsing the aisles you can hear live music Wed.–Sat. On Friday and Saturday, Kramerbooks stays open 24 hours for late-night literary binges.

One ripple out from DuPont Circle is **Woodley Park,** known principally for the National Zoo. The area also claims to be home to more international restaurants than anywhere in D.C., which in this international metropolis is saying a lot.

Beyond Woodley Park is exclusive **Cleveland Park,** where former President Grover Cleveland built his "summer White House," and consequently lent his name to the neighborhood. Today, the area is home to former Senator Bill Bradley, Jim Lehrer of the "News Hour," and satirist Mark Russell. If you're here at lunchtime, try the local Irish pub **Ireland's Four Provinces,** 3412 Connecticut Ave. NW, 202/244-0860, serving shepherd's pie and Irish brew.

Heading farther north, the campus of **American University,** alma mater of Willard Scott and novelist Anne Beattie, covers 84 acres in the area known as Tenleytown. The final reaches of the Upper Northwest extend out to Friendship Heights and Chevy Chase at the border of Maryland. **Friendship Heights** is a busy entertainment/shopping district offering the tony urban mall known as Mazza Gallery, and **Chevy Chase** is an exclusive address where you'll find one of the best movie palaces in Washington: the **Cineplex Odeon Avalon 2,** built in 1925, with 679 seats in the main theater.

Washington National Cathedral

Medieval cathedrals often required centuries to complete, so perhaps it's not so embarrassing that 199 years passed before this one was considered finished. In 1791, D.C. designer Pierre L'Enfant envisioned a "church intended for national purposes, and assigned to the special use of no particular Sect or denomination, but equally open to all." In 1893 Congress finally allocated funds for the edifice, and in 1990 the last stone was placed atop a west front pinnacle.

The cathedral is a truly magnificent structure, and its stone and wood carvings, stained glass, and metalwork are unsurpassed on these shores. The Gothic wonderment is constructed of Indiana limestone, with all details carved from the walls by hand. High above dwell angels, gargoyles, and grotesques; outside, visitors to the 57-acre grounds can stroll a medieval walled garden of roses and herbs. The cathedral is located at Massachusetts and Wisconsin streets NW, 202/537-6207, www.cathedral.org/cathedral. There is no admission fee to the cathedral, which is open Mon.–Sat. 10 A.M.–4:30 P.M., Sun. 7:30 A.M.–4:30 P.M. Services are held at 7:30 A.M. every day, and the Chapel of the Good Shepherd is always open.

National Zoological Park

Under the auspices of the Smithsonian Institution, the National Zoo is one of the nation's more humane animal parks. More than three miles of trails wander past 5,000 animals caged on 163 hilly acres at the edge of Rock Creek. Visitors will find no class hierarchy here: paramecia and leaf-cutter ants are displayed as proudly as lions, tigers, and bears. An enclave of naked mole rats even get exposure via the Internet with the zoo's live naked mole rat Web-cam (http://natzoo.si.edu/hi-lights/webcams/molerat1/nmcam.htm).

Visitors can "ooh" and "aah" over such rarities as Komodo dragons, watch the cuttlefish transform from a mass of transparent jelly into a voracious predator, or ponder the ways animals use their brains, described in the Think Tank exhibit. The rainforest environment of the Amazonia exhibit approaches D.C.'s own August heat and humidity. Admission to the zoo, at 3001 Connecticut Ave. NW, is free, though there is a some-

what steep charge for on-site parking (maximum $10.50); 202/673-4800, http://natzoo.si.edu. The zoo grounds are open daily May 1–Sept. 15, 6 A.M.–8 P.M., Sept. 16–Apr. 30, 6 A.M.–6 P.M. Closed Christmas Day. Zoo buildings are open May 1–Sept. 15, 10 A.M.–6 P.M., Sept. 16–Apr. 30, 10 A.M.–4:30 P.M. Closed Christmas Day.

Rock Creek Park

These 1,750 acres were purchased in 1890 by Congress for the "pleasant valleys and ravines, primeval forests and open fields, its running waters, its rocks clothed with rich ferns and mosses, its repose and tranquility, its light and shade, its ever-varying shrubbery, its beautiful and extensive views." Rock Creek Park still offers all that, as well as more than one million wildflowers.

Bordering the Upper Northwest to the east, the city's largest park comprises a magical ribbon of green. Here hikers, horseback riders, and joggers have the right of way, and on Sunday, with long sections of the park's roads closed to cars, they take control. Rock Creek Park offers some 15 miles of hiking trails, from toddler-friendly to quite rugged. Trail maps are available at both the park headquarters and the nature center. An 11-mile bike path from the Lincoln Memorial to the Maryland border runs the full length of the park; it's paved the entire distance and closed to vehicular traffic on weekends and holidays. Numerous access points make visiting the park on bike or on foot an easy day's outing. Trail rides ($25) are available at the **Rock Creek Park Horse Center,** 5115 Glover Rd. NW, 202/362-0118.

The cemetery in Rock Creek Park is the oldest in the city and home to one of the most arresting statues in D.C. In 1883, Marian Adams, wife of historian Henry Adams, downed enough photographic chemicals to end her life. Her husband interred her in Rock Creek Cemetery, then commissioned sculptor Augustus Saint-Gaudens to create a monument in bronze, adding "no attempt is to be made to make it intelligible to the average mind." When the work was ready the grave-keepers were horrified, saying they wanted no part of it. But Adams persisted, and the cloaked, hooded lady was set among holly and ivy in section E. Adams called it *The Peace of*

SIDE TRIP TO D.C.

God, the sculptor *The Mystery of the Hereafter,* but most visitors agree with Mark Twain that the most appropriate designation is simply *Grief.*

The cemetery is located on Rock Creek Church Rd. NW and open daily 7:30 A.M.–dusk. Admission is free. The nature center is open Tues.–Sun. 9 A.M.–5 P.M. Pierce Mill (202/426-6908), a working cornmeal and wheat flour gristmill, is open Wed.–Sun. 9 A.M.–5 P.M. Here visitors can purchase the mill's products, make the flour and meal themselves in small handheld grinders, or just come in and watch. Both the nature center and mill are closed on major holidays. For more information, write Rock Creek Park Superintendent, 3545 Williamsburg Ln., NW, Washington, DC 20008, or call 202/282-1063, or visit the website www.nps.gov/rocr.

Society of the Cincinnati

Established in 1783 by George Washington and the officers in his Continental Army, the Society still limits membership to only one direct descendant per original officer. For 15 hours each week (Tues.–Sat. 1–4 P.M.; closed federal holidays), the society's beautiful beaux arts mansion is thrown open to the public, and visitors may walk among elegant furnishings and priceless artwork, or peruse the excellent Revolutionary-era reference library. Admission to Anderson House, 2118 Massachusetts Ave. NW, 202/785-2040, is free.

GEORGETOWN

President Kennedy lived in Georgetown 1957–1961 during his pre-presidential term as a U.S. senator and before becoming president. Syndicated columnist George Will keeps his office here. The latter was a New Deal Democrat, then later a staunch Republican. Still, they hailed from the same place, a neighborhood sandwiched between Rock Creek and the Potomac River known as Georgetown. No one is certain who named the quarter: some say it was named after one of the King Georges or one or another of the area's founders. Georgetown didn't become part of the District of Columbia until after the Civil War.

Since then, it has had ups and downs, good times and bad, but the present moment is decidedly up. Between the peaceful towpaths of the old C&O Canal to the south and what has come to be known as "the most civilized square mile in America" to the north abides some of the most expensive real estate on earth. An average-sized, even smallish house in Georgetown runs into the millions of dollars. Like Beverly Hills in Los Angeles, the homes in Georgetown are pedigreed, known by their former famous owners, like the house at 3017 N Street where Jacqueline Kennedy lived for a time.

History and personality blend in Georgetown's streets. Many great authors, such as Katherine Anne Porter and Sinclair Lewis, have called the neighborhood home. Herman Wouk still lives here, as does celebrity biographer Kitty Kelly. Historical figures such as Alexander Graham Bell called Georgetown home, as did Dr. Walter Reed, the American Army surgeon who proved yellow fever was carried by mosquitoes.

Georgetown's main crossroads are M Street and Wisconsin Avenue, a bustling area of boutiques, jazz clubs, and good restaurants. Just south of Wisconsin on M Street, **Canal Square,** built in 1842, was first used as a grain warehouse, then as a cooperage, and finally as home to a census bureau contractor known as the Tabulating Machine Company. Though its headquarters are currently in Armonk, New York, you'll recognize the company's more recent acronym: IBM.

From Canal Square, a block south of M Street toward the Potomac you'll find lock number 4 of the **Chesapeake & Ohio Canal.** Operated by National Park Service rangers dressed in 19th-century costumes, a working barge takes visitors under the bridge and through the locks on a half-mile mule-towed journey through the past. A bit farther south is **Washington Harbor,** known by some as "Baghdad on the Potomac." This terraced extravaganza is a riverfront development of condominiums, shops, and restaurants. Once something of a joke, the Harbor has grown into a delightful and popular setting of nightspots. With lots of fun restaurants, gushing fountains, bright lights, fluttering flags, fabulous river views, and a romantic promenade, the harbor makes for great people-watching.

Despite being 20 minutes by foot from the nearest Metro station, Georgetown definitely deserves, and can easily consume, a day or more of touring. Walk the historic homes, idle at Dumbarton Oaks, and dine in town.

Dumbarton Oaks

The crown jewel of Georgetown is Dumbarton Oaks, 1703 32nd St. NW, a former estate that is now a museum and 43-acre garden spot. In 1944, as World War II moved into its final climactic phase, the leaders of the United States, Britain, China, and the Soviet Union met here to lay the groundwork for what was to become the United Nations.

For visitors to Dumbarton Oaks, it's easiest to think of the estate in three parts. The first is the 16-acre compound owned by Harvard University and known as the Dumbarton Oaks Research Library and Collection. Here you'll find the estate's renowned collection of some 1,500 eastern Mediterranean artifacts dating from 330 to 1453 A.D. The library holds more than 12,000 Byzantine coins, one of the most complete collections in the world. Next comes the 27-acre Dumbarton Oaks Park, 202/339-6410 (open daily until dusk). Ten acres of the park are given over to one of the finest examples of European-styled formal gardens in America, with nearly 1,000 rose bushes, 10 pools, and nine fountains. The entrance is on R Street, and it's open Apr.–Oct. 2 P.M.–6 P.M. and Nov.–Mar. 2 P.M.–5 P.M.; $5 adults, $3 seniors and children. The remaining 17 acres of the Dumbarton Oaks estate are covered by well-groomed parkland. Call 202/342-3200 or visit www.doaks.org for more information.

Georgetown University

Another cornerstone of the community is the 104-acre main campus of Georgetown University, one of the nation's pre-mier schools for law and international affairs, and the oldest Catholic university in the nation. Free maps and brochures on the campus and environs are available at the main gate, 37th and O sts. NW. Be sure to visit the Gaston Hall collections of Victorian dolls and Indian artifacts. For more information on the university, check out www.georgetown.edu or call 202/687-0100.

Old Stone House

The oldest standing structure in the city, the house was built in 1765 by a cabinetmaker named Christopher Layman in what was then the Town of George. Over the years, the dwelling also served as boardinghouse, tavern, bordello, and artists' studio. Today its low doorways and lumpy beds are preserved as a relic of working-class life in pre-Revolutionary times. Rumor that Pierre L'Enfant worked here while designing D.C. helped secure congressional protection for the structure in the 1950s. It is said that children are those most likely to encounter the many ghosts inhabiting the structure. The house, 3051 M St. NW, 202/426-6851, is open Wed.–Sun. 10 A.M.–4 P.M., winter hours noon–5 P.M. Closed Christmas and New Year's Day; free.

Old Stone House

SIDE TRIP TO D.C.

© WASHINGTON DIVISION, D.C. PUBLIC LIBRARY

EAST OF THE CAPITOL

Kenilworth Aquatic Gardens

This 12-acre haven along the Anacostia River is the only U.S. national park devoted exclusively to water plants. Beginning in 1880, one-armed Civil War veteran Walter Shaw and his industrious daughter methodically dredged a series of ponds here, growing lilies and lotuses that they marketed to plant-happy Washingtonians. The government acquired the property in 1938, and today a network of trails crisscrosses levees separating dozens of bright marshy ponds.

Don't miss the lotus, once thought to be extinct, which was grown from 900-year-old seeds unearthed in a dry Tibetan riverbed; be on the lookout too for frogs, salamanders, snakes, mallards, and turtles. Admission to the gardens, located at 1900 Anacostia Dr. NE, 202/426-6905, is free. The entrance is just off Anacostia Avenue near Quarles and Douglas streets. Kenilworth Aquatic Gardens is open daily 7 A.M.–4 P.M.

Closed Christmas and New Year's Day. Tours and walks can be made by arrangement. Visit their website at www.nps.gov/nace/keaq.

U.S. National Arboretum

Along the Anacostia River lies this 444-acre natural jewel, featuring stunning collections of bonsai, dwarf conifer, dogwood, and azalea. There are nine miles of paved roads, but it's more enjoyable to park somewhere and get out and walk. At the center of the arboretum are 22 ghostly Corinthian columns rising from a grassy knoll; for 125 years they supported the east portico of the Capitol. Other highlights of the arboretum include the National Herb Garden, containing more than 800 useful herbs from around the world, and the National Grove of State Trees, a perfect place for picnicking. The arboretum staff is currently attempting to reintroduce bald eagles to the nation's capital. Admission to the arboretum is free; 3501 New York Ave. NE, 202/245-2726, fax 202/245-4575, www.ars-grin.gov/ars/Beltsville/na/. Hours are daily 8 A.M.–5 P.M. Closed Christmas Day.

Accommodations

For the most part, accommodations in the District are pricey. There are exceptions to that rule, though, and your options increase dramatically if you consider staying outside of D.C. in Maryland or Virginia. Some D.C. hotels offer discounts when you make reservations through Capitol Reservations, www.capitolreservations.com.

UNDER $50

The **Washington, DC Hostel** is centrally located downtown at 11th and K streets NW, near the Smithsonian Museums, the White House, and other attractions. Only a three-block walk from Metro Center station, the renovated eight-story hotel offers 250 beds, a kitchen and laundry facilities, lockers/baggage storage area, and wheelchair accessibility. For night owls, the hostel offers 24-hour access; there are also tours, movies, and other special programs. Rates run approximately $18–21. The DC Hostel is open year-round

and private rooms are available on a limited basis. Groups are also welcome, but reservations are required, 202/737-2333, fax 202/737-1508, or email DChostel@erols.com. Reservations are accepted by phone or fax with 24-hour advance notice and credit card confirmation and can also be made using the Hostelling International toll-free number (within the U.S. only); have your credit card ready and dial 800/909-4776, then enter the DC Hostel two-digit access code (04) to be connected.

At another low-cost option, the rooms are spartan, the beds sometimes lumpy, the plumbing occasionally scaldingly unpredictable, and the wooden central staircase groans loudly at the lightest tread. Nevertheless, the willfully eccentric proprietors of the four-story ex-senator's home at **2005 Columbia Rd.,** 202/265-4006, offer what may be the best rates in the city. A favorite of students, conferees, and Bohemians from overseas, 2005 Columbia has nine air-conditioned rooms when the air-conditioning works (non-smoking available) for $30 s, $40 d.

$50–100

The **Adams Inn,** 1744 Lanier Place NW, 800/758-6807 or 202/745-3600, fax 202/319-7958, email adamsinn@adamsinn.com, www.adamsinn.com, consists of three brick townhouses and a carriage house hidden away on a leafy residential street two blocks from the heart of the Adams-Morgan district. Built around 1913, the inn has a definite Victorian feel, from the furnishings to the parlors to the rules: no phones, no TVs, and no smoking. Guests will find plenty of books and games, though, and the lavish Continental breakfast included in the price of your stay features truly heaping portions. A total of 27 rooms ($55 s, $75 d) are available with private or shared baths (the latter on average about $10 less per person). As elsewhere in Adams-Morgan, parking is limited.

The charming, inexpensive **Kalorama Guest House,** 1854 Mintwood Place NW, 202/667-6369, fax 202/319-1262, consists of six Victorian townhouses filled with creative antique furnishings, like brass beds and Oriental rugs, set off by fresh flowers. Enjoy a sherry in front of the fire or lemonade on the patio, then take the short walk to many of the finest restaurants in the city. Really two venues, one at this location in Adams-Morgan and another in Washington's pleasant Woodley Park neighborhood, the guest house offers 30 air-conditioned rooms ($65 s, $75 d), all nonsmoking. Reservations with full payment are required.

Located a few blocks from the White House, the **Center City Hotel,** 1201 13th St. and M St. NW, 202/682-5300, fax 202/371-9624, offers 100 traditional-style guest rooms at decent rates ($89 s, $125 d). There are free movies in all the rooms, refrigerators in some, and a restaurant on the premises. Nonsmoking rooms are available. In regard to pets, the front desk says, "We take small animals, but no snakes!"

The venerable, friendly **Hotel Harrington,** 436 11th St. NW, 800/424-8532 or 202/628-8140, fax 202/347-3924, www.hotel-harring-ton.com, is located downtown, only two blocks from the Smithsonian. The excellent location makes the Harrington a particular favorite of international travelers. The Harrington also offers a restaurant and pool, and is wheelchair accessible. The 265 rooms and 25 suites must be booked in advance. Parking is available at a lot next door. The large rooms ($70) are clean and comfortable.

The Savoy Suites Georgetown, 2505 Wisconsin Ave. NW, 800/944-5377 or 202/337-9700, fax 202/337-3644, features fine, large rooms. The 150 suites, some with excellent views of the D.C. skyline, run $79 s, $89 d. The hotel restaurant, a favorite of locals, offers outdoor dining in season and serves as gallery space for area artists. Area transportation services are available at the Savoy, including a D.C. Metro shuttle.

International visitors feel welcome at the **Swiss Inn,** 1204 Massachusetts Ave. NW, 800/955-7947 or 202/371-1816, with managers who speak a plethora of European languages. The inn's seven air-conditioned apartments ($79 s, $119 d) have bathrooms and kitchenettes with refrigerators. During the off-season (November 15 through the end of February), the apartments rent for $420 per week. If you need a ride from the airport or bus stop, just give the place a call, and a staff member will come pick you up.

The friendly, 10-story **Hampshire Hotel,** 1310 New Hampshire Ave. NW, 202/296-7600, fax 202/293-2476, has 82 spacious rooms, most with two double beds ($99 s, $109 d). This DuPont Circle hotel also features a health club, free in-room movies, and "smart phones" offering access to a bewildering variety of services. All of the rooms allow you to eat in privacy in the kitchen units, which include coffeemakers, refrigerators, and microwaves.

$100–150

Located close to DuPont Circle, the cozy **Tabard Inn,** 1739 N St. NW, 202/331-8528, fax 202/785-6173, is an unspoiled mark of good taste. This country inn in the heart of Washington offers doubles with baths for $115–170, but don't be fooled by the bargain. The Tabard's indoor-outdoor restaurant is without peer in its business-class price range.

Located by the Lincoln Memorial, the Mall, and George Washington University, the **State Plaza Hotel,** 2117 E St. NW, 800/424-2859 or 202/861-8200, fax 202/659-8601, is a favorite among those Kennedy Center performers who aren't staying at the posh and expensive Watergate. The 223 suites ($135 and up) are pleasant and spacious, with full kitchens. The State Plaza also offers a restaurant on premises, a fitness center, and coin-operated washing machines for those taking a longer stay. For those needing to get out of the city or wishing to visit Arlington Cemetery, the State Plaza is conveniently located just blocks from Memorial Bridge.

D.C.'s only waterfront hotel, the **Channel Inn,** 650 Water St. SW, 800/368-5668 or 202/554-2400, fax 202/863-1164, peers out over Washington Channel toward the island of East Potomac Park. Each of the 100 rooms ($98 s, $140 d) offers a balcony, and some provide fine views of the boats in the harbor. Try the raw bar at the hotel restaurant, the Engine Room.

$150–250

The **Henley Park Hotel,** 26 Massachusetts Ave. NW, 800/222-8474 or 202/638-5200, fax 202/638-6740, is a converted 1918 seven-story Tudor structure featuring faux 18th-century furnishings, a facade bristling with 119 gargoyles, and a telephone in every bathroom. The 90 air-conditioned rooms run $165 s, $185 d. Ask if there's a four-poster bed available, and be sure to take afternoon tea in the Wilkes Room.

The **Carlyle Suites,** 1731 New Hampshire Ave. NW, 800/964-5377 or 202/234-3200, fax 202/387-0085, is a wonder. The bold exterior and accompanying interior frills are pure art deco, a motif abandoned only in the suites, which are washed in pastels splashed with charcoal and gray. The on-site Neon Café is stuck firmly in the 1940s: here you can dig into a large steak while swinging to the sounds of live weekend jazz. Located on a pleasant residential street near DuPont Circle, the eight-story Carlyle features 170 guest suites ($159 s, $169 d) with sitting areas, kitchenettes, and limited complimentary parking.

The Gaelic place in DC—the **Phoenix Park Hotel,** 520 N. Capitol St. NW, 800/824-5419 or 202/638-6900, fax 202/393-3236—is nine stories of Irish linen, hospitality, finery, and food. The Phoenix Park features 84 rooms ($150) and regular live entertainment, both scheduled and unscheduled. AAA members can secure drastic rate reductions.

The **Washington Courtyard,** 900 Connecticut Ave. NW, 800/321-2211 or 202/332-9300, fax 202/328-7039, is surprisingly affordable for all that it offers: chandeliers in the lobby, mahogany armoires, and phones with modems, for starters. The hotel is also host to the pricey **Claret's** for eats and the clublike **Bailey's** for drinks. Children under 18 sleep with their parents for free. Prices at this 170-room hotel range from $125–280 depending on the season and availability. Located in Kalorama, an upscale residential neighborhood near Embassy Row, the hotel hosts many foreign diplomats, who undoubtedly enjoy the marble baths and fax machines of the executive rooms. All guests can enjoy the outdoor pool and the fitness room.

Situated only five blocks west of the White House, the **Hotel Lombardy,** 2019 I St. NW, 800/424-5486 or 202/828-2600, fax 202/872-0503, www.hotellombardy.com, provides sumptuous accommodations including cherry-wood furnishings, dusty rose carpeting, and fine art on the walls. Most of the 129 rooms ($115 s, $130 d) offer fully equipped kitchens, but the Lombardy features a fine restaurant as well. Rates are reduced sharply in the off-season.

Located just two blocks from DuPont Circle, the **Canterbury Hotel,** 1733 N St. NW, 800/424-5920 or 202/393-3000, fax 202/785-9581, occupies a site where Theodore Roosevelt once lived with his large family. The lobby is lined with hunting prints, and you can heave darts in the homey English pub, which serves appropriate dinners of fish and chips and finger sandwiches. The 10-story edifice features 99 suites ($140 s, $245 d), breakfast included. Junior suites with kitchenettes are also available; children aged 12 and under stay free. In a town where parking is at a premium, this snug hotel has its own lot.

The 10-story **Washington Suites,** 2500 Pennsylvania Ave. NW, 800/222-8733 or 202/333-

8060, fax 202/338-3818, offers 124 spacious one- and two-bedroom suites ($119 s, $219 d), with kitchens. If you're absolutely determined not to get away from it all, this is the place: some rooms offer two telephones and two TVs.

The **Radisson Barcelo Hotel DC,** 2121 P St. NW, 800/333-3333 or 202/293-3100, fax 202/331-9719, is the first D.C. joint venture of the Mallorca-based Barcelo chain, offering European service at decent American prices. The 301 marble and mahogany decorated rooms run $119 s, $200+ d. The hotel restaurant, **Gabriel,** is excellent, and the hotel bar is popular with locals. Enjoy swimming in the rooftop pool while watching the stars.

When it's time to inaugurate a president, no hotel offers better views of the parade than the 80-year-old **Hotel Washington.** With 344 rooms, you couldn't get much closer to the Treasury Building and the White House. Located at 15th Street and Pennsylvania Avenue, it offers two top-floor restaurants, the informal Sky Terrace and the more formal Sky Room, that offer spectacular vistas of the White House, the Ellipse, and the Washington Monument. It was from here Woodrow Wilson reviewed U.S. troops marching off to war. Rooms range upwards from $185 to the $680 suites. For reservations, call 800/424-9540 or 202/638-5900, or visit the website at www.hotelwashington.com.

OVER $250

Built by D.C. hotel magnate Harry Wardman, **The Jefferson,** 1200 16th St. NW, 800/368-5966 or 202/347-2200, fax 202/331-7982, www.thejeffersonhotel.com/jefferson_home.html, offers 100 air-conditioned rooms ($309 d, $329 suite). Hailed by some as one of the top 10 hotels in the world, it's the sort of place where, even after a single visit, the staff will recall every detail of your preferences and peculiarities. A favorite since 1923 of arty types such as Vivien Leigh, Van Cliburn, and Leonard Bernstein, the hotel's legendary discretion also made it a favorite of reporters such as Edward R. Murrow and H.L. Mencken.

The 150-year-old **Willard Intercontinental Hotel,** 1401 Pennsylvania Ave. NW, 800/327-

0200 or 202/628-9100, fax 202/637-7326, http://washington.interconti.com, is the grand dame of Pennsylvania Avenue, located just around the corner from the White House. Its architect, H.J. Hardenberg, designed New York's prestigious Plaza, but did his best work in Washington. The hotel also features the locally popular Occidental Grill. Special weekend rates are as low as $198 per night, but prices go much higher during the week. Prices for suites like the 1,550-square-foot "Oval Room" with marbled foyer aren't even listed.

The aristocratic edifice of the **Hay-Adams,** One Lafayette Square NW, 800/853-6807 or 202/638-6600, fax 202/638-2716, www.hayadams.com, was erected in 1927, the work of tireless D.C. hotel builder Harry Wardman, who intended it "to provide for the socially elite as well as men who loom large in the country's life." It was named for the structures it replaced, the homes of McKinley cabinet member John Hay and historian Henry Adams. Years before, Confederate arch-spy Rose Greenhow plied her duplicitous trade on this site. Each of the 143 rooms ($199–345) offers luxurious antiques, ornaments, and amenities.

The venerable **Stouffer Renaissance Mayflower Hotel,** 1127 Connecticut Ave. NW, 800/468-3571 or 202/347-3000, fax 202/466-9082, www.renaissancehotels.com, was snapped up by the Stouffer chain in 1991 for a cool $100 million. Formerly the haunt of political stalwarts such as Huey P. Long and J. Edgar Hoover, the stately Mayflower is Washington's answer to New York City's Waldorf-Astoria. Lines of black limos parked around the hotel signal that government dignitaries have dropped by for a meal or are staying for the night in one of 660 air-conditioned rooms ($235–275). Hoover arrived at the Mayflower Grille Room every day of the last 20 years of his life for his regular meal of chicken soup, grapefruit, and cottage cheese. Franklin Delano Roosevelt wrote "the only thing we have to fear is fear itself" in suite 776.

For a price, you can stay in the ritzy hotel wing of the complex that brought down a president. On June 17, 1972, Watergate security guard Frank Wills surprised five men burgling the offices of the Democratic National Committee;

a little more than two years later the burglars' employer, Richard Nixon, was a disgraced ex-president on his way home to San Clemente. The **Watergate Hotel,** 2650 Virginia Ave. NW, 800/424-2736 or 202/965-2300, fax 202/337-7915, www.swissotel.com/html/brochure.html, has long been a favorite of the high and mighty— Attorney General John Mitchell, who authorized the Watergate break-in, maintained an apartment here, as did would-be chief executive Robert Dole. Monica Lewinsky, too. Many of the actors, dancers, and musicians who appear at the Kennedy Center across the street enjoy shorter stays in one of the hotel's 250 rooms ($275 s, $295 d). On the weekend, singles and doubles start at $155.

Food

POLITICALLY CORRECT

Washington's answer to New York's Sardi's, **The Palm,** 1225 19th St. NW, 202/293-9091, fax 202/775-1468, www.thepalm.com, features an earnest menu that only occasionally misses the mark. Steaks are another matter—get one. Enjoy the brilliant waiters and see what it feels like to be treated as a powerbroker. Reservations are recommended, and make sure you ask for the main dining room.

In French, **La Colline,** 400 N. Capitol St. NW, 202/737-0400, means "The Hill," as in Capitol Hill. The food is good, the service is solid, but the restaurant itself sometimes suffers from a slight case of the conventional. There always seems to be enough room, so reservations are not usually necessary.

Relaxed but stately, the **Old Ebbitt Grill,** 675 15th St. NW, 202/347-4801, www.clydes.com/current/oldebbitt.html, offers wonderful service and very good food. The bar is long on character and the Kumamoto oysters are magnificent. Call for reservations and ask for the main room to catch the power-lunch scene. Try breakfast; it's a pleasant surprise.

When White House staff members take a break to celebrate a political victory, the courtly **Occidental Grill,** 4th and Pennsylvania sts. (part of the Willard Hotel complex), 202/783-1475, known locally as the "Oxie," is their destination. Straighten your tie, make your reservations, and admire the century-old trophy wall of 1,800 photographs portraying Washington's famous faces. Don't miss out on the martini with quail eggs.

Bullfeathers, 410 1st St. SW, 202/543-5005, is beery, a bit overpriced (but still cheap by D.C. standards), and loud, so have a drink at the bar if there's room. It's hamburgers for lunch and happy hour for those in the nearby House office buildings who need to change their mood.

Georgia Brown's, 950 15th St. NW, 202/393-4499, is unique in Washington for its soul-food version of haute cuisine—collard greens and black-eyed peas never looked this fancy. Enjoy the handsome crowds, smashing ambience, and tantalizing menu descriptions.

EXPENSIVE

D.C. Coast, 1401 K St. NW, 202/216-5988, is one of the city's hot new eateries—boldly designed, on two levels, its decor is matched only by its cuisine. Chef Jeff Tunks's specialty is seafood, and he describes his cuisine as "tri-coastal," meaning the Atlantic, the Pacific, and the Gulf. Pay special attention to his Louisiana-style fare. The place is pricey, with entrées in the upper twenties, but the evening is its own reward.

Roberto Donna is one of D.C.'s culinary kings. Elegantly Italian with an outdoor terrace to enjoy summer, Donna's flagship restaurant, **Galileo,** 1110 21st St. NW, 202/293-7191, www.robertodonna.com, is a showcase of Piedmontian cuisine. Make reservations for the chef's table and watch a great kitchen at work.

Kinkead's, 2000 Pennsylvania Ave. NW, 202/296-7700, www.kinkead.com, is a gleaming red-white-and-blue answer to a French bistro. Seafood is Chef Bob Kinkead's specialty—try the tapas or the Carolina shrimp with corn pudding and Virginia ham.

L.T. Bridwell's Saloon and Oyster Bar, c. 1890

Makoto, 4822 MacArthur Blvd., 202/298-6866, could well be among the top five Japanese restaurants in the United States. There are only four tables, with just 10 seats at the sushi bar. Try the "kaiseki" fixed-price (i.e., very expensive) dinner.

The setting at **I Ricchi,** 1220 19th St. NW, 202/835-0459, www.iricchi.net, is romantic, the service is personable and relaxed (and very professional), and the food would make a Florentine jealous. This is hands down one of the finest and most consistent restaurants in the city.

Vidalia, 1990 M St. NW, 202/659-1990, is a southern belle of a restaurant known for its roasted Vidalia onion appetizer and manicured Southern cooking. But don't be misled: the food here is elegant, imaginative, and the menu is a palette for the palate. All this and valet parking, too.

With a glass-enclosed wine "cellar" surrounding the newly renovated dining room, **Citronelle,** 3000 M St. NW, in the Latham Hotel, 202/625-2150, www.citronelledc.com, is one of Washington's finest restaurants. If you consider how French wines were reborn in the Napa Valley, then you might imagine how French cuisine would fare when transplanted and ripened to perfection here in Washington.

The setting for **1789,** 1226 36th St. NW,

202/965-1789, www.clydes.com, is a Federal-style townhouse overlooking Georgetown. The oak-walled bar serves perfect silver bullets, while Chef Ris Lacoste conspires to fuse East and West with soys, peanut flavors, and lime marinades.

The **Bombay Club Restaurant,** 815 Connecticut Ave. NW, 202/659-3727, prepares the best Indian food in Washington, served in a setting as elegant as the best of India's famed Hill Stations. The service is magnificent and courtly, a relief from the earnest and overly eager professionalism in most city restaurants.

Morton's of Chicago is now in Washington, 1050 Connecticut Ave. NW, 202/955-5997, fax 202/338-8033. Situated in one of the city's prime business corridors across from the Mayflower Hotel, this is a classic martini and steak house. Waiters are part of the entertainment, as they present the day's fresh vegetables, meats, and treats (the lobsters don't bite). This is a place for power lunch and power dinner, and don't be afraid to remind your attentive waiter about the pet you left back at the hotel—no one can eat Morton's proportions.

FUN

Ah, beer! Miles of beer. The **Brickskeller,** 1523 22nd St. NW, 202/293-1885, is Washington's monument to the mighty brew, packing more than 800 varieties from 50 countries, including 400 from the United States alone. The owners claim to have served 5,000 different styles of suds since opening in 1957. Enjoy the upstairs game room and buckets of mussels at good prices.

The cuisine at **Jaleo,** 480 7th St. NW, 202/628-7949, is Spanish and the tapas are terrific. Heft a jug of sangria and settle in at this exuberant restaurant in the renewed area near downtown known as Penn Quarter.

If a restaurant can be sexy and reasonably priced, **Sesto Senso,** 1214 18th St. NW, 202/785-9525, certainly qualifies. The people-watching is excellent, even at lunch: Mick Jagger eats here when in town. The menu ranges from fair to very fine, and the service is as good as you make it, so take advantage of it.

Kids love **Tony Cheng's Seafood Restaurant,** 619 H St. NW, 202/842-8669, the home of kung fu cooking. Patrons circle the huge round griddle that dominates the restaurant, selecting foods from surrounding trays. Chefs then fry up the selections and swipe the finished dinners onto small round plates without dropping so much as a soybean.

Washington has many good Ethiopian restaurants, and **Red Sea,** 2463 18th St. NW, 202/483-5000, is one of the city's classics—outdoor dining in summer and great prices all year round. But remember, in Ethiopia, there's nothing between you and dinner, not even utensils. Every dish is finger-food, sopped up with yeasty *injera* bread.

If your imagination runs to the great backroom dives of Tijuana, **Cactus Cantina,** 3300 Wisconsin Ave. NW, 202/686-7222, manages the atmosphere without any of the grit. A fun place for Sunday brunch or a relaxed dinner.

Chef and owner Elizabeth Bright has managed to create a "real" restaurant in a neighborhood setting. **Coppi's Vigorelli,** 3421 Connecticut Ave. NW, 202/244-6437, is a local eatery that just happens to serve exquisite food—baby artichokes and sheep's milk cheese. This is serious dining, but casual too.

Entertainment and Nightlife

CLUBS

The classy **Habana Village,** 1834 Columbia Rd. NW, 202/462-6310, seemingly offers one activity for each of its four rooms: food, entertainment, dance, and a singles scene. The restaurant ambience is wicker and white wine. The cigars are allowed. Upstairs it's dance and the singles set, and above that two heavenly lounges (with Latin music, of course).

The eclectic heart of the late-night **Ritz Nightclub,** 919 E St. NW, 202/638-2582, beats to the sound of R&B. Five separate dance floors rock to reggae, go-go, hip-hop, R&B, salsa, soul, funk, and world music. Upstairs is a good lounge for singles, though the bar menu is pedestrian. Covers range up to $10, but big-time acts can raise the range—call ahead.

The timeless **One Step Down Jazz Club,** 2517 Pennsylvania Ave. NW, 202/955-7141, features live music six nights a week. The club, known locally as "The Step," holds the honor of being America's second-oldest surviving jazz club, and seating is limited to 75. The club hosts big-name performers on the weekends and first-rate local talent during the week.

A Georgetown landmark (assuming you can find it), **Blues Alley,** 1703 Wisconsin Ave. NW, 202/337-4141, www.bluesalley.com, is a side-street success. The 130-seat club attracts top acts to the town that gave birth to Duke Ellington. Covers are high, from $13 to more than $40. Usually, you get what you pay for.

The **9:30 Club,** 815 V St. NW, 202/393-0930, hosts the likes of Sean Lennon and Ziggy Marley. This pantheon of punk can hold up to 1,000 dancing, drinking guests within its walls. Parking is secure. Check out the downstairs bar to escape the crush. Visit the club's website www.930.com for concert information and to view the beer list and bar menu.

Looking like nothing so much as a below-ground Paris jazz cave, tiny **U-topia,** 1418 U St. NW, 202/483-7669, has become a part of the city's U Street scene. U-topia offers a bit of everything, from take-out food to jazz and blues.

Decorated with Kremlin leftovers, **State of the Union,** 1357 U St. NW, 202/588-8810, caters primarily to a younger crowd. The music is loud and there's lots of it. Jazz on Monday, reggae on Wednesday, and no two days are the same, so call ahead.

THEATER AND CONCERTS

John F. Kennedy Center for the Performing Arts

This D.C. landmark, New Hampshire Ave. and Rock Creek Pkwy. NW, 202/467-4600, www.kennedy-center.org, is home to the **National**

Symphony Orchestra (NSO) and the **Washington Opera.** Founded in 1931, the National Symphony Orchestra has enjoyed a succession of brilliant musical directors—Antal Dorati, Mstislav Rostropvoich and, today, Leonard Slatkin. The NSO has promised to visit all 50 states, but don't miss them while in Washington.

Artistic Director Placido Domingo gives the 42-year-old Washington Opera Company the sex appeal and gravitas it so much deserves, making D.C. one of the nation's centers for song. The Kennedy Center Opera House and the center's Eisenhower Theatre offer a prolific 74 performances of about eight operas annually.

The Kennedy Center also presents Broadway shows, repertory theater, jazz, Shakespeare, and more. Free performances are held every day at 6 P.M. on the Millennium Stage featuring performers from the local area and around the world. Tours of the center's main theaters and selected art holdings are offered 10 A.M.–5 P.M. during the week, and 10 A.M.–1 P.M. on weekends.

Other Venues

The **National Theatre,** 1321 Pennsylvania Ave. NW, 202/628-6161, www.nationaltheatre.org, is Washington's only Broadway-style theater and the city's oldest cultural institution. "West Side Story" had its world premiere here, as did "Hello Dolly." The theater's acoustics are excellent, but watch out for the distant seats in Balcony Two. The Helen Hayes Gallery (a workshop-sized auditorium) hosts free events weekly.

The classical and Shakespearean adaptations for which the **Shakespeare Theatre,** 450 7th St. NW, 202/547-1122, www.shakespearedc.org, is known are vivid and nontraditional productions, attracting big-name actors and actresses. The company regularly returns to more traditional presentations, such as Tennessee Williams's "Sweet Bird of Youth."

The **Folger Elizabethan Theatre,** 201 East Capitol St. SE, 202/544-7077, inside the Folger Library, is a full-scale recreation of a 250-seat Elizabethan theater. Here one can experience life as a "groundling," as well as allowing its children to discover something of the life of Elizabethans, including William Shakespeare.

From repertory classics to musicals, the three stages at the **Arena Stage,** 1101 6th St. NW, 202/488-3300, www.arenastage.org, have pulled down 54 prestigious Helen Hayes theater awards. The Arena was the first theater outside New York to capture a coveted Tony Award. James Earl Jones, Dianne Wiest, Kevin Kline, James Woods, and many other notable actors and actresses have graced its stages.

The **Woolly Mammoth Theatre,** 1401 Church St. NW, 202/234-6130, is Washington's off-Broadway-style venue for experimental cutting-edge works. Productions are first-rate, and free parking is just across the street. Be careful when buying seats because the quality of the views ranges widely.

The **Studio Theatre,** 14 and P sts. NW, 202/332-3300, www.studiotheatre.org, has grown

National Theatre, c. 1890

more ambitious each year and recently renovated its two theaters, the Mead and the Milton, to allow longer show runs. The productions are contemporary and first quality.

COMEDY

People say Washington's a funny town, and when they're talking about humor, they're probably referring to the **D.C. Improv** at 1140 Connecticut Ave. NW, 202/296-7008. Open Tues.–Sun., show time is usually 8:30 P.M. but sometimes varies, so call or check www.dcimprov.com. Tickets are usually $15 but can range up to $20. Lunches and dinners are reasonable, around $10 for entreés, and diners get the best seats for the shows. Try the "57 Chevy" for a cocktail—vodka, amaretto, and lots of vitamin C.

The Capitol Steps, one of the nation's leading singing and performing satirical companies, perform at **Petitbon's American Grill and Bar,** 1911 N. Ft. Myer Dr., Rosslyn (across the Key Bridge from Georgetown, next to the Rosslyn Metro), 703/527-7501, www.petitbons.com. The Steps are the main attraction, performing (most) Friday and Saturday nights, and reservations are highly recommended. Call ahead for schedules and information on other performances.

Free jazz, blues (Friday and Saturday nights), and beer, **Mr. Henry's Adams Morgan,** 1836 Columbia Rd. NW, 202/797-8882, has only one drawback: it closes at midnight. The burgers are good, and Mr. Henry's patio is a perfect place for a bite.

MORE EVENTS AND ENTERTAINMENT

Located in the heart of Chinatown, the **MCI Center,** 601 F St. NW, 202/628-3200, www.mcicenter.com, is not your typical sports venue. Home to the NHL's Washington Capitals, NBA's Wizards, and WNBA's Mystics, the center features a video center showcasing historic moments in athletics, a sportscasters hall of fame, a sporting goods store, and the Discovery Channel's three-story, 25,000-square-foot interactive store.

Robert F. Kennedy Memorial Stadium, 2400 East Capitol St. SE, 202/547-9077, was once home to the Washington Redskins, but now hosts the city's pro soccer team, D.C. United, as well as rock concerts and the occasional outdoor convention. (The Redskins moved out of the city in 1996 and now play at **Jack Kent Cooke Stadium** in Landover, Maryland.) There are numerous ticket outlets in the D.C. area—check the local yellow pages or www.redskins.com or call 800/551-7328 or 202/432-7328. Parking at the stadium may cost $20 (the Redskins are fighting a parking war with fans), but extra Metro buses and trains make the journey to Maryland much more convenient. Contact WMATA headquarters, 202/637-7000, TDD 202/638-3780, www.wmata.com, for information.

The 4,200-seat **Carter Barron Amphitheatre,** 4850 Colorado Ave. NW, 202/426-6837, could host a major tennis tournament but more often offers free concerts during the summer. Located along the 16th Street corridor, it is also easily accessible. **Ford's Theatre,** 511 10th St. NW, 202/347-4833, the site of President Lincoln's last act and still a working theater, produces plays and musicals aimed at portraying the eclectic character of American life.

Washington is a monumental city, a city of lights. A fine way to capture the capital's dramatic sights is by cruising its feisty boundary, the Potomac River. **Odyssey Cruises,** 600 Water St. SW, 202/488-6000, www.odysseycruises.com, offers river tours, serving lunch, brunch, or dinner on board. **The Wharf,** 900 Water St. SW, offers another way to look at the Potomac, through its floating seafood stalls, shelling out everything from octopus to Carolina crabs. The river complex offers historic sites, quality restaurants, and fresh seafood.

Transportation

GETTING THERE

By Air

The Washington area is served by three major airports: Dulles International Airport receives both international and domestic arrivals; National Airport primarily takes domestic arrivals; and Baltimore-Washington International Airport (BWI) also receives international and domestic flights. Expect between 20 and 45 minutes driving time to reach downtown from any of the airports, longer at rush hour. Taxis downtown from Dulles (26 miles west in Virginia) and BWI (25 miles northeast in Maryland) will run $40–50, from National (four miles south of downtown) about $15.

Shuttle service is also available from all three airports. The Washington Flyer Express bus (888/927-4359) runs every 30–60 minutes from National (daily 6 A.M.–9 P.M.; $8 one-way, $14 round-trip) and from Dulles (daily 5 A.M.–10 P.M.; $16 one-way, $26 round-trip) to its city terminal at 1517 K St. NW. There is another Washington Flyer Express bus from Dulles to the West Falls Church Metro Station every 20–30 minutes (Mon.–Fri. 6:30 A.M.–10:30 P.M., Sat.–Sun. 7:30 A.M.–10:30 P.M.; $8 one-way, $14 round-trip). Trains run from this station to Metro Center station and on to downtown. Courtesy shuttles are available at the Washington Flyer terminal at Dulles to various downtown hotels. The BWI Super Shuttle offers hourly departures (daily 6 A.M.–1 A.M.; $19 one-way, $29 round-trip) to the 1517 K St. NW terminal.

National is the only airport with direct Metrorail service. The station is across from North Concourse and links directly with Metro Center and other stops along the Yellow Line. From BWI, the Maryland Rail Commuter Service (MARC) offers peak-hour service (Mon.–Fri. only, 5:30 A.M.–8 A.M. and 3:45 P.M.–6:45 P.M.; $5 one-way, $8.75 round-trip) to Union Station. Amtrak offers daily service ($12 one-way, $24 round-trip) from BWI to Union Station. Both MARC and Amtrak take about 45 minutes to reach the city.

GETTING AROUND

Most of the major sightseeing highlights in central Washington—the Mall, the White House, the Tidal Basin area—are within walking distance of each other, so using public transportation is only an option. If you want to see anything away from these areas or need to travel to any of the outlying neighborhoods, Washington has one of the best subway systems of any major city in the world. The related bus service is quite reliable, and there are always plenty of taxis and rental car options. Driving around downtown should always be your last choice: besides the confusing layout of the streets and the accompanying confusion of trying to read a map, parking fees are astronomical.

By Subway

The Washington Metropolitan Area Transit Authority (WMATA) operates the Metrorail, the D.C. subway system that's known by residents simply as "the Metro." It covers the downtown area and the suburbs (except Georgetown), but expansion is almost constant and new stations are scheduled to open in the next decade. Metro stations are identified by a large letter "M" atop a brown pylon.

You can purchase magnetic **fare cards** from vending machines at your departure station. Simply insert the card into the turnstile, and when you get where you're going use the card to exit. The turnstile will magnetically record the remaining value on your fare card. Cards can be purchased for the base fare of $1.10, or for as much as $45. Should your card not have enough credit for you to exit the station, use one of the special exit-fare machines and try the turnstile again. **Children** under the age of four ride free when accompanied by a paying adult, up to a limit of two children.

On average, expect to pay between $1.10 and $3.25 during peak times (5:30–9:30 A.M. and 3–8 P.M.) and between $1.10 and $2.10 at other times. Metro trains run Mon.–Fri. 5:30 A.M.–midnight, and Sat. and Sun. 8:30 A.M.–midnight, and most public holidays. The trains arrive/depart every 5–6 minutes during peak times and every 10–15 minutes at other times.

The Metro also offers a variety of useful **train passes.** For $5 you can purchase a one-day pass valid from the time of purchase until closing (but not before 9:30 A.M. on weekdays). If you plan on being in the capital for an extended stay, you might consider purchasing the $50 Fast Pass, good for 14 consecutive days of unlimited rail travel. For even longer stays, WMATA offers the $100 28-Day Pass, good for unlimited rail travel for almost a month. Another good option, especially if you plan on riding the Metro buses in addition to the trains, is the $65 Bus/Rail SUPER Pass, good for 14 consecutive days of unlimited bus and rail travel. If you don't want to spend the money or don't plan on staying for two weeks, rail-to-bus transfers are available on the train platform for only $.25.

Passes are available at the WMATA headquarters, 600 5th St. NW, Washington DC 20001, 202/637-7000, TDD 202/638-3780, www.wmata.com; and at the Metro Center station sales office at 12th and F sts. NW. Some banks, liquor stores, and some Safeway and Giant grocery stores also sell rail and bus passes. Metro **route maps** are available for $2 from the marketing office at WMATA headquarters.

By Bus

Like the subway, the **Metrobus** base fare is $1.10, and buses run at the same times as the trains, although some operate until 2 A.M. Rail-to-bus transfers are available, and so are bus-to-bus transfers (only $.10)—simply hand your bus-transfer pass, which you must purchase for each transfer, to the driver of the second bus. Bus fare is acceptable either as cash or in the form of tokens worth $1.10 and available in rolls of 10 or 20. You can also purchase a $25 Flash Pass, good for 14 consecutive days of unlimited bus travel.

By Taxi

Because not every D.C. neighborhood is served by the Metro (most notably Georgetown and Adams-Morgan), the capital's taxicabs are a nice complement to the subway and bus systems. A few reliable taxi companies include **Super Shuttle,** 800/258-3826, **Capitol Taxi,** 202/546-2400, and **Yellow Cab,** 202/544-1212. For information on cabs and fares in Washington, call the Taxicab Commission at 202/767-8319.

Rental Car

Most rental car agencies have offices at Dulles International Airport, National Airport, and Union Station, although you probably won't need a car if you're planning on staying within the city limits.

Resources

Suggested Reading

Background

General History

Barbour, Philip, and Tate, Thad, eds. *The Complete Works of Captain John Smith, 1580-1631.* Chapel Hill: University of North Carolina Press, 1986. Three volumes, including *A True Relation of Such Occurrences and Accidents of Note as Hath Happened in Virginia* (1608), and *A Generall Historie of Virginia* (1624).

Dabney, Virginius. *Virginia: The New Dominion.* Charlottesville, VA: University of Virginia Press, 1989. The consummate state history.

Dabney, Virginius. *Richmond: Story of a City.* Charlottesville, VA: University Press of Virginia, 1990. The story of the state capitol.

Jefferson, Thomas. *Notes on the State of Virginia.* Chapel Hill: University of North Carolina Press, 1996. Jefferson's only full-length book, an American classic, opens a vivid window into the author's personality and life in the 18th century.

McGraw, Mary Tyler. *At the Falls: Richmond, Virginia, and Its People.* Chapel Hill: University of North Carolina Press, 1994. Beautiful photos, prints, and engravings enhance this comprehensive history of the state capital.

Civil War History

Catton, Bruce. *America Goes to War: The Civil War and Its Meaning in American Culture.* Middletown, CT: Wesleyan University Press, 1992. Catton also wrote a compelling three-volume account of the war, consisting of *The Coming Fury, Terrible Swift Sword,* and *Never Call Retreat.*

McPherson, James. *Battle Cry of Freedom: The Civil War Era.* New york: Ballantine Books,

1988. Dense (900 pages), but probably the best single-volume history of the war.

Ward, Geoffrey C., Ric Burns, and Ken Burns. *The Civil War: An Illustrated History.* New York: Alfred A. Knopf, 1990. The lavishly illustrated companion volume to Ken Burns' award-winning PBS series.

Recreation

Civil War Touring

Braselton, Susan, ed. *Official Guide to the Civil War Discovery Trail.* New York: Hungry Minds, Inc., 1998. A handy guide that covers the entire theater.

Lawliss, Chuck. *The Civil War Sourcebook: A Traveler's Guide.* Out of Print (1991). Excellent background and touring information.

Hiking

Adkins, Leonard. *50 Hikes in Northern Virginia.* Woodstock, VT: The Countryman Press, 2000. For rambles near D.C., from the mountains to the bay.

Adkins, Leonard. *Walking the Blue Ridge.* Chapel Hill, NC: University of North Carolina Press, 1996. Details every trail that touches the Blue Ridge Parkway, 122 in all. Plus descriptions of flora, fauna, history, and geology, and a roadside bloom calendar.

Clauson-Wicker, Su. *Inn to Inn Walking Guide: Virginia and West Virginia.* Birmingham, AL: Menasha Ridge Press, 2001. Details 20 day hikes from one B&B to another.

de Hart, Allen. *The Trails of Virginia: Hiking the Old Dominion.* Chapel Hill, NC: University of North Carolina Press, 1995. The authoritative work, covering every trail in the state from Civil War battlefields to back-country.

Gildart, Bert & Jane. *Best Easy Day Hikes Shenandoah*. Helena, MT: Falcon Press, 1998. Pocket-sized version of the Gildarts' larger guide to the park (below). Twenty-six hikes with maps and pertinent details.

Gildart, Bert & Jane. *Hiking Shenandoah National Park*. Helena, MT: Falcon Press, 2000. Fifty-nine hikes from one end of the park to the other, from easy day hikes with children to overnight ventures. Detailed descriptions and maps.

Johnson, Randy. *Hiking Virginia*. Helena, MT: Falcon Press, 1992. A slim but functional guide to a selection (52) of the state's trails, including history hikes, beach rambles, and Shenandoah National Park.

Manning, Russ. *75 Hikes in Virginia's Shenandoah National Park*. Seattle, WA: The Mountaineers Books, 2000. Includes maps, photos, and information on history, plants, animals, and geology.

Bicycling

Adams, Scott. *Mountain Bike America: Virginia*. Guilford, CT: The Globe Pequot Press, 2000. With close to fifty choice trails (and 19 more "honorable mentions") described in detail, this guidebook also throws in GPS-quality topo maps, elevation profiles, and plenty of other tidbits. Highly recommended.

Porter, Randy. *Mountain Bike! Virginia*. Birmingham, AL: Menasha Ridge Press, 2001. Exhaustive guide to 91 bike trails from the coast to the Blue Ridge. Maps and detailed descriptions provided for each one.

Skinner, Elizabeth & Charlie. *Bicycling the Blue Ridge*. Birmingham, AL: Menasha Ridge Press, 1990. Point-by-point description of both Skyline Drive in Shenandoah National Park and the Blue Ridge Parkway in Virginia and North Carolina. Includes elevation profile, maps, and info on restaurants, accommodations, and stores along the way.

Rafting

Sehlinger, Bob, Dave Denner, and Ed Grove. *Appalachian Whitewater: The Southern States*. Birmingham, AL: Menasha Ridge Press, 2000. Covers class I-IV whitewater in Alabama, Georgia, South Carolina, North Carolina, Tennessee, Kentucky, Virginia, Maryland and West Virginia

Fishing

Camuto, Christopher. *A Fly Fisherman's Blue Ridge*. New York: Holt & Co., 1992. The author, an angler and naturalist, traces one year of fly fishing in the Blue Ridge. A good read for anyone interested in fishing or the natural history of streams.

Gooch, Bob. *Virginia Fishing Guide*. Charlottesville: University Press of Virginia, 1992. Revised edition.

Ingram, Bruce. *The James River Guide*. Corvallis, OR: Ecopress, 2000. An intimate portrait of the James above Richmond, useful to floaters, anglers, and naturalists.

Miller, Skip. *Tidewater Fishing; The Complete Guide to Eastern Virginia Waters*. Out of Press. Focuses on the shore and the Chesapeake Bay.

Murray, Harry. *Virginia Blue Ribbon Fly Fishing Guide*. Portland, OR: Frank Amato Publications, 2000. Fly-fishing spots and advice for streams and rivers statewide.

Slone, Harry. *Trout Streams of Virginia: An Angler's Guide to the Blue Ridge Watershed*. Woodstock, VT: The Countryman Press, Inc., 1999. Third edition, revised and expanded.

Climbing

Watson, Jeff. *Virginia Climber's Guide*. Mechanicsburg, PA: Stackpole Books, 1998. The most comprehensive guide to rock climbing throughout the state.

Hörst, Eric. *Rock Climbing Virginia, West Virginia, and Maryland.* Helena, MT: Falcon Press, 2001.

Natural History

Badger, Curtis. *A Naturalist's Guide to the Virginia Coast.* Mechanicsburg, PA: Stackpole Books, 1996. Great beach reading, split between background and visiting information. Heavy on birding.

Duda, Mark Damian. *Virginia Wildlife Viewing Guide.* Helena, MT: Falcon Press, 1994. Produced in partnership with a host of state and federal resource agencies and private organizations, this guide points the way to 80 of the state's best viewing areas, with information on who and what you'll see. Color maps and photos.

Frye, Keith. *Roadside Geology of Virginia.* Missoula, MT: Mountain Press, 1986. Includes general information on the state's geologic history, plus guides to those parts visible along major highways throughout the sate.

Gupton, Oscar. *Wildflowers of the Shenandoah Valley and Blue Ridge Mountains.* Out of Print. Gupton also wrote *Trees and Shrubs of Virginia* (UPV, 1989), *Wildflowers of Tidewater Virginia* (UPV, 1989), *Wild Orchids of the Middle Atlantic States* (American Orchid Society, 1987), *Fall Wildflowers of the Blue Ridge and Great Smoky Mountains* (out of print), and *Wildflowers of the Shenandoah Valley and Blue Ridge Mountains* (out of print).

Nock, Anne. *Child of the Bay: Past, Present, and Future.* Charlottesville: Hampton Roads Publishing Co., 1993. Natural history of the Eastern Shore.

Williams, John Page Jr. *Chesapeake Almanac: Following the Bay Through the Seasons.* Centreville, MD: Tidewater, 1993. A collection of the author's columns from "Chesapeake Bay Magazine" that trace the life in, and around the Bay for a year.

Experienced naturalists know it's hard to beat the illustrated *Peterson Field Guides* series, published by Houghton Mifflin (Boston), the straightforward standard for amateur and professional alike. Covering the mid-Atlantic are *A Field Guide to the Mammals* (William H. Burt, 1998), *A Field Guide to Animal Tracks* (J. Murie, 1998), *A Field Guide to the Birds* (Roger Tory Peterson, 1998), and *A Field Guide to Reptiles & Amphibians: Eastern & Central North America* (Roger Conant and Joseph Collins, 1998).

Other Recreation

Noe, Barabara. *The Official Rails-to-Trails Conservancy Guidebook: Maryland, Delaware, Virginia, and West Virginia.* Guilford, CT: Globe Pequot, 2000. A state-by-state guide to walking, jogging, biking, and skiing 32 of the area's rail-trails.

Sloane, Bruce. *Scenic Driving Virginia.* Helena, MT: Falcon Press, 1999. A former park ranger details 22 day-long drives across the state, from Mount Rogers to the Potomac, including information on history and geology.

Fiction

Crane, Stephen. *Red Badge of Courage.* New York: HarperCollins, 1996. The battle of Chancellorsville as seen by an idealistic, frightened young Union recruit. A classroom classic for a reason.

Styron, William. *The Confessions of Nat Turner.* New York: Random House, 1993. Pulitzerprizewinning account of the abortive 1831 slave uprising in Southampton County.

Folklore

Barden, Thomas, ed. *Virginia Folk Legends*. Charlottesville: University of Virginia Press, 1991.

Garrison, Webb. *A Treasury of Virginia Tales.* Nashville, TN: Rutledge Hill Press, 1996. Subtitled "Unusual, Interesting, and Little-Known Stories of Virginia."

Jameson, W.C. *Buried Treasures of the Appalachians: Legends of Homestead Caches, Indian Mines and Loot from Civil War Raids.* Little Rock, AR: August House, 1991. Subtitled. Forty tales of lost wealth, gathered from interviews with those who have searched for it. Even includes maps.

Jameson, W.C. *Buried Treasures of the South: Legends of Lost, Buried, and Forgotten Treasures-From Tidewater Virginia and Coastal Carolina to Cajun Louisiana.* Little Rock, AR: August House Publishers, 1992.

Nonfiction

Blake, Allison. *The Chesapeake Bay Book: A Complete Guide* Lee, MA: Berkshire House Publishers, 1999. A great book for those interested in exploring the bay up into Maryland.

Dillard, Annie. *Pilgrim at Tinker Creek.* Hightstown, NJ: McGraw Hill, 2000. Metaphysical, beautifully written observations on life and the universe set in the Roanoke valley.

Lautman, Robert. *Thomas Jefferson's Monticello: A Photographic Portrait.* New York: The Monacelli Press, 1997. Gorgeous, atmospheric black-and-white photos.

Mariner, Kirk. *Off 13: The Eastern Shore of Virginia Guidebook.* New Church, VA: Miona Publications, 2000. Available locally and full of native nuggets.

Warner, William. *Beautiful Swimmers: Watermen, Crabs and the Chesapeake Bay.* New York: Little, Brown & Co., 1994. Pulitzer-prizewinning account of life on the bay.

Washington, Booker T. *Up From Slavery.* New York: Signet Classic, 2000. A vivid account of the struggle faced by African-Americans at the turn of the century.

Whitehead, John Hurt, III. *The Watermen of the Chesapeake Bay.* Centerville, MD: Tidewater Publishing, 1987. Photographic account of watermen in the 1980s, interspersed with colorful quotations.

Whitman, William. *The Wines of Virginia: A Complete Guide.* Warrenton, VA: Virginia Heritage Publishers, 1997.

Internet Resources

A quick—or long—look at the Internet before you travel in Virginia can make your journey both easier and more rewarding. You can do practically anything online except actually set foot on Old Dominion soil, from booking hotel reservations and reserving theater tickets to finding out when the fall colors are their brightest.

Yahoo Virginia (dir.yahoo.com/Regional/ U_S__States/Virginia/)
The Yahoo web directory's Virginia portal is the best place to start if you're browsing or don't know exactly what you're trying to find.

The Official Commonwealth of Virginia Home Page (www.state.va.us)
Virginia's state government home page offers links to information on government, education, business, and other practical matters.

Virginia is For Lovers (www.virginia.org)
Virginia Tourism Corporation's main website provides a wide variety of resources, including information on wineries, outdoor sports, and seasonal events.

Virginia.com (www.virginia.com)
This general state travel website includes city guides, white and yellow pages, and a hotel reservation service.

HomeTownFreePress (www.hometownfree press.com/va.htm)
A list of local Virginia newspapers.

Virginia Department of Conservation and Recreation (www.dcr.state.va.us)
Everything you ever wanted to know about Virginia's natural world, including parks and recreation areas.

Great Outdoor Resource Page (GORP): Virginia (www.gorp.com/gorp/location/va/va.htm)
Details on all the state's outdoor glory, from hiking and camping to mountain biking and winery tours.

Civil War Traveler: Virginia (www.civilwar-va.com/Virginia)
This great resource for planning Civil War-based sightseeing trips throughout the state includes information on regional attractions and events, with maps and more details available by mail.

The Mountain Laurel (www.mtnlaurel.com)
This "journal of mountain life" focuses on Virginia's Blue Ridge. Online issues include interviews with old timers, tall tales, crafts, recipes, backroad tours, and genealogy.

Cybercafés (www.cybercafes.com, www.netcafeguide.com)
Virginia's list of Internet cafes is constantly changing, but these are both good sites for recent lists.

Acknowledgments

Writing guidebooks can be as fun and frustrating as herding cats, equal parts I-get-paid-for-this? and I'm-not-getting-paid-enough-for-this. This edition would not have been possible without the help of many people across Virginia and beyond, including Lorraine Brooks (Colonial Williamsburg), Janene Charbeneau (Richmond), Jean Clark (Lexington), Catherine Fox (Roanoke), Sam Martinette (Norfolk), Robin Magrisi (Virginia Beach), Margaret McMann (Danville), Merrie Morris (Alexandria), Debby Padgett (Jamestown-Yorktown), Suzanne Pearson (Newport News), Amy Proctor (Shenandoah Valley), Rose Rulon (Eastern Shore), Sherly Stanley (Lexington), Susan Thrash (Norfolk), Sergei Troubetzkoy (Staunton), and Cathy Wiliams (Blacksburg).

Likewise, Deborah Chandler, Rosemarie Fiore, Virginia Gabriele, Rhonda Howdyshell, Sylvia New Strawn, Mark Riddell, Allison Sharp, Beverly Shelton, Karin Sherbin, Diane Stalling, Victor Wagher, Sarah Walls, and Catherine Wooley each lent a unique helping hand.

Special thanks go to Jeff Baker and Corey Firestone for the home-away-from-home in Washington, DC.

Index

A

Abby Aldrich Rockefeller Folk Art Museum: 149
Abingdon: 237–242
Abingdon Vineyard & Winery: 221
Abram's Delight: 255–256
Accomack: 203
accommodations: general discussion: 45–48; *see also specific place*
acid rain: 8
A Colonial Christmas: 156
Adams, John: 14
Adams-Morgan district: 361–362
Adam Thoroughgood House: 185, 187
Afton Mountain Vineyards: 80
Agecroft Hall: 74
Air Power Park: 168
airports: Charlottesville-Albemarle Airport 112; Lynchburg Regional Airport 125; Newport News-Williamsburg International Airport 154, 166, 170; Norfolk International Airport 180; Roanoke Regional Airport 224; Washington-Dulles International Airport 308, 375; Washington National Airport 308, 375
air travel: 54, 55; *see also* airports; *specific place*
Albemarle County Courthouse: 105
Alexandria Archaeology: 319
Alexandria Red Cross Waterfront Festival: 324
Allegheny Highlands: 287–293
Alliance for the Chesapeake Bay: 6
Amazement Square: 122
American Armoured Foundation: 131–132
American Celebrations on Parade: 266
American Indian Heritage Celebration: 11
American Music Festival: 43, 194
American University: 362
American Work Horse Museum: 297
Amrhein's Wine Cellar: 221
amusement parks: Busch Gardens Williamsburg 154–155; Dinosaur Land 259; Ocean Breeze Waterpark 192–193; Paramount Kings Dominion 87; Water Country USA 155
Anheuser-Busch Brewery: 155
Anne Spencer House and Garden: 121–122
Annual Memorial Day Horse Fair & Auction: 279
Antique & Classic Boat Show: 170

Antique and Classic Boat Show and Rally: 129
Antique Carriage and Car Museum: 267
antiques: general discussion 44; Abingdon 242; Cape Charles 200; Fredericksburg 98; Front Royal 263; Harrisonburg 279; Leesburg 336; Lexington 300; Lynchburg 124; New Market 265; Norfolk 179; Old Town Alexandria 325; Petersburg 92; Richmond 84; Roanoke 222; Staunton 286; Strasburg 264; Virginia Beach 193; Wytheville 232
Appalachian Trail: 235, 270–271
Applaud the Sun Harbor Party: 200
Apple Blossom Festival: 258
Apple Harvest Arts and Crafts Festival: 258
Appomattox Court House National Historic Park: 126–127
Appomattox Iron Works: 88
Arena Stage: 373
Arlington County: 308–316
Arlington County Fair: 316
Arlington House: 310
Arlington National Cemetery: 309–310, 312
Artfest: 92
Arthur M. Sackler Gallery: 351
Art Museum of Western Virginia: 218
Arts and Sciences Building: 351
Arts Council of the Blue Ridge: 218
Arts Deport, The: 237
Ashe, Jr., Arthur: 69
Ashland-Highland: 115, 118
ashram: 128
Assateague Coastal Trust: 209
Assateague Island and Chincoteague National Wildlife Refuge: 207–209
Assateague Island National Seashore: 209
Assateague Island Waterfowl Week: 209
Assateague State Park (Maryland): 208
Association for Research and Enlightenment (ARE): 185
Astor, Lady: 131
Athenaeum: 319
Atlantic Wildfowl Heritage Museum: 185
ATMs: 57
attitudes: 27–28
Auctioneers Park: 131
Augusta County Courthouse: 284

Autumn Hill Vineyards/Blue Ridge Winery: 80
"Awakening, The": 353–354

B
babysitting agencies: 58
Back Bay National Wildlife Refuge: 195
Bacon's Rebellion: 157
ballet: Concert Ballet of Richmond 83; Rich-
mond Ballet 83; Roanoke Ballet Theatre 222;
Virginia Ballet Theatre 178; Virginia Beach
Ballet 193
Ball's Bluff Battlefield and National Cemetery: 336
Ball's Bluff Regional Park: 336
Barboursville Vineyards and Historic Ruins: 80,
112
Barns at Wolf Trap, The: 328
Barter Theatre: 238, 241
baseball: Norfolk Tides 178; Richmond Braves 84
basketball: James Madison University (Dukes)
279; University of Virginia (Cavaliers) 110;
Washington Mystics 374; Washington Wiz-

ards 374
Bassett Hall: 148
Battle of Bull Run (Manassas): 330
Battle of Chancellorsville: 20–21, 100–101
Battle of Fredericksburg: 20, 100
Battle of Gettysburg: 21
Battle of Spotsylvania Court House: 22, 101
Battle of the Wilderness: 21–22, 101
Bayly Art Museum: 104
Bayou Boogaloo and Cajun Food Festival: 179
Beachevents: 193
Beach Music Weekend: 193–194
Beach Street USA: 194
Beale, Thomas Jefferson: 122
bed-and-breakfasts: general discussion: 45, 46;
see also specific place
Bedford: 126
Belle Boyd Cottage: 262
Belle Grove Plantation: 260–261
Belle Isle: 73
Belmont: 99

Battles, Battlefields, and Monuments

general discussion: 40
Ball's Bluff Battlefield and National Cemetery:
336
Battle of Bull Run (Manassas): 330
Battle of Chancellorsville: 20–21, 100–101
Battle of Fredericksburg: 20, 100
Battle of Gettysburg: 21
Battle of Spotsylvania Court House: 22, 101
Battle of the Wilderness: 21–22, 101
Booker T. Washington National Monument:
129–130
Cape Henry Memorial: 187
Cedar Creek Battlefield: 260–261
Challenger Memorial: 310
Cornwallis' Cave: 158
Douglas MacArthur Memorial: 173
Five Forks Battlefield: 89
Fort Monroe: 168–169
Fredericksburg and Spotsylvania National Mili-
tary Park: 100–102
George Washington Birthplace National Mon-
ument: 135, 137
George Washington Masonic National Memor-
ial: 320–321
Korean War Veterans Memorial: 346–347

Manassas National Battlefield Park: 329–330
"March to the Sea": 22
Mast of the Battleship *Maine:* 310
Memorial Amphitheater: 310
Monument Avenue: 69, 72
National D-Day Memorial: 126
Netherlands Carillon: 312
New Market Battlefield Historic Park:
265–266
Pamplin Park: 89
Petersburg National Battlefield Park: 89
Richmond Battlefield National Park: 72
Saltville Massacre: 237
Second Battle of Manassas: 20
Seven Days' Battles: 20, 67
Stonewall Jackson Shrine: 101–102
Tomb of the Unknown Dead of the Civil War:
310
Tomb of the Unknowns: 310
U.S. Marine Corps War Memorial: 312
Victory Monument: 158
Vietnam Women's Memorial: 347
Women in Military Service for America Memo-
rial: 309
World War II and Korean War Memorial: 74

Birdwatching

general discussion: 37
Assateague Island and Chincoteague National
  Wildlife Refuge: 207–209
Back Bay National Wildlife Refuge: 195
Chincoteague: 206
Eastern Shore Birding Festival: 198
Eastern Shore of Virginia National Wildlife
  Refuge: 196, 198
Great Dismal Swamp National Wildlife
  Refuge: 181–182
Huntley Meadows Park: 340
International Migratory Bird Celebration: 209
Mason Neck National Wildlife Refuge: 343
Theodore Roosevelt Island: 312

Berkeley Plantation: 160–161
Berryville: 258–259
Big Gig, The: 86
Big Meadows: 273
Big Pencil: 231
Big Stone Gap: 244–247
Big Walker Lookout: 232
Bike Virginia: 31
biking: general discussion 30–3l; Allegheny High-
  lands 287–293; Bike Virginia 31; Chincoteague:
  206; clubs 32–33; Colonial Williamsburg 153;
  cycling clubs 30–31; 32–33; Eastern Virginia
  Mountainbike Association 30–31; Galax 234;
  Grand Caverns Regional Park 281; International
  Biking Association 31; Mt. Vernon Trail 316;
  Mt. Rogers National Recreation Area 235–236;
  Old Town Alexandria 323; Richmond 85; River-
  bend Park 327 ; road rules 31; Rock Creek Park
  363; Shenandoah National Park 273; Tangier Is-
  land 212; Virginia Cycling Association 31; Vir-
  ginia State Bicycle Coordinator 31; York River
  State Park 154
Birchmere Music Hall: 323
black bears: 272, 303
Blackfriars Playhouse: 286
Black History Museum and Cultural Center of
  Virginia: 69
Blacksburg: 226–231
Blacksburg Electronic Village: 227
Blackwater Creek Natural Area: 122
black widow spiders:
Blessing of the Fleet: 207

Block Parties: 170
Bluebell Nature Loop: 330
Bluefish Derby: 139
Bluemont: 337
Bluemont Concert Series: 335
Bluemont Fair: 337
Blue Ridge Folklife Festival: 225
Blue Ridge Oktoberfest & Chili Cookoff: 263
Blue Ridge Parkway: 302–304
Blue Ridge Theatre: 279
Blues and Brews: 194
Boardwalk Art Show and Festival: 194
Boardwalk Trail: 182
boating: general discussion 35; Great Falls Park
  327; Norfolk 178; Reedville 139; Smith
  Mountain Lake 128; Tangier Island 212; York
  River State Park 154
"Bonny Barbara Allen": 186
Booker T. Washington National Monument:
  129–130
Boone, Daniel: 247
Boxerwood Gardens: 295
Boyd, Belle: 261
Brafferton: 148
Breaks Interstate Park: 243–244
Breaux Vineyards: 332
breweries: Anheuser-Busch Brewery 155; Rich-
  brau Brewing Company 79; Virginia Beverage
  Company 323
Brookings Institution: 362
Brown's Island: 74
Brush-Everard House: 147
Bruton Parish Church: 147
Bryce Resort: 264
Buckroe Beach: 169
Bull Run Castle: 331
Bull Run-Occoquan Trail: 330
Bull Run Regional Park: 330
Bureau of Engraving and Printing: 355
Burke's Garden: 246
Burnley Vineyards & Daniel Cellars: 80
Busch Gardens Williamsburg: 154–155
business hours: 58
bus travel: 42, 53; *see also specific place*
Byrd Park: 72
Byrd Theater: 83

C

Cabbage Festival: 226
Camberley's Martha Washington Inn: 238,

239–240

camping: general discussion 30, 46–47; Abingdon 240; Assateague State Park (Maryland) 208; Back Bay National Wildlife Refuge 195; Bull Run Regional Park 330; Chincoteague 205; Colonial Williamsburg 151; Cumberland Gap National Historical Park 249; Douthat State Park 292–293; Floyd 226; Galax 234; Hampton 169; Jamestown 157; Lexington 298; Luray 268; Middletown 261; Mt. Rogers National Recreation Area 236; Natural Bridge 302; Natural Chimneys Regional Park 280–281; Natural Tunnel State Park 246–247; Petersburg 91; Prince William Forest Park 343; Richmond 77–78; Shenandoah National Park 274–275; Smith Mountain Lake State Park 129; Virginia Beach 189–190; Westmoreland State Park 137; Wytheville 232

Canal Square: 364

Canal Turning Basin: 86

Canal Walk: 74

C & O Canal National Historical Park: 327

canoeing: general discussion 34–35; Front Royal 263; Galax 234; Lexington 300; Luray 267; Mason Neck State Park 343; Old Town Alexandria 323; Scottsville 118; Tangier Island 212; see also specific place

Colleges and Universities

American University: 362

Association for Research and Enlightenment (ARE): 185

College of Integrated Science and Technology: 276–277

College of William and Mary: 148

Georgetown University: 365

Hampton University: 168

James Madison University: 276–277, 279

Lynchburg College: 124

Mary Baldwin College: 284

Medical College of Virginia: 64

University of Richmond: 85

University of Virginia: 104–105, 110

Virginia Commonwealth University: 64, 85

Virginia Military Institute: 295

Virginia Tech: 227–228

Virginia Union University: 62

Washington & Lee University: 293–295

Cape Charles: 198–200

Cape Charles Day: 200

Cape Charles Museum and Welcome Center: 199

Cape Henry Memorial: 187

Capital Children's Museum: 357

Capitol Hill: 356–358

Capitol, The: 146

Carlyle House: 319

Carpenter Center for the Performing Arts: 83

carriage rides: 99, 153, 299, 323

Carter, A. P.: 248–249

Carter Barron Amphitheatre: 374

Carter Family Memorial Festival: 43, 249

Carter Family Museum: 249

Carter's Grove Plantation: 149

car travel: 51–53; hazards 52; rental 52–53

Carytown: 73–74

Carytown Watermelon Festival: 86

Cascades Recreational Area: 230, 231

Casemate Museum: 168–169

caves/caving: general discussion 37–38; Dixie Caverns 224; Endless Caverns 266; Grand Caverns Regional Park 281; Luray Caverns 266–267; Natural Bridge Caverns 302; safety 38; Shenandoah Caverns 266; Skyline Caverns 263; spelunking clubs: 36–37

Cayce, Edgar: 185

Cedar Creek Battlefield: 260–261

Celtic Festival: 124

cemeteries: Arlington National Cemetery 309–310, 312; Ball's Bluff Battlefield and National Cemetery 336; Congressional Cemetery 358; Fredericksburg National Cemetery 100; Glendale Cemetery 72; Hollywood Cemetery 73; Old City Cemetery 121; Popular Grove National Cemetery 89; Rock Creek Park Cemetery 363–364; Stonewall Jackson Cemetery 295

Centre Hill Mansion: 88

Challenger Memorial: 310

Champagne and Candlelight Tour: 118

Charlottesville: 102–112

Charlottesville-Albemarle Airport: 112

Charlottesville and University Symphony Orchestra: 110

charter boats: 35; see also specific place

Chateau Morrisette: 221

Cherokee: 243

Chesapeake & Ohio Canal: 364

Chesapeake Bay: 5

Chesapeake Bay Bridge-Tunnel: 199

Index

Chesapeake Bay Center: 188
Chesapeake Bay Foundation: 6
Chessie Nature Trail: 299
Chickahominy: 11
Chick Charter Club Annual Tuna Tournament: 201
Children's Museum of Virginia: 181
children, traveling with: 58
Chimborazo Medical Museum: 75
Chincoteague: 203–207
Christ Church (Irvington): 139
Christ Church (Old Town Alexandria): 320
Christmas Open House: 337
Chrysalis Vineyards: 332
Chrysler Hall: 177–178
Chrysler Museum of Art: 174–175
churches: Bruton Parish Church 147; Christ Church (Irvington) 139; Christ Church (Old Town Alexandria) 320; First Baptist Church 89; Holy Cross Abbey 258–259; Little England Chapel 168; Old Trinity Church 284; Presbyterian Church 97; South River Meeting House 122; St. Francis of Assisi Catholic Church 284; St. George's Episcopal Church 97; St. James Episcopal Church 203; St. John's Church 168; St. John's Episcopal Church 75; St. Paul's Episcopal Church 173–174; Washington National Cathedral 363
Church Hill: 75
Cinco de Mayo: 179
City Market Building: 217
City Point: 89
Civil War Trails: 41
Civil War Visitors Center: 72
Civil War Weekend: 158
clams: 49, 200, 208
Classic Amphitheater: 83
Claude Moore Colonial Farm: 326
Cleveland Park: 362
climate: 5–6
Cline, Patsy: 256
Clogging Classic: 179
coal mining: 243. 244–245
Cockram's General Store: 225
Cold Harbor: 72
College of Integrated Science and Technology: 276–277
College of William and Mary: 148
Colonial Christmas: 158
Colonial Downs: 85

Colonial National Historical Park: 157
Colonial Williamsburg: 141–162
Columbia Pike Blues Festival: 316
Commodore Theater: 181
Concert Ballet of Richmond: 83
Congressional Cemetery: 358
conservation: general discussion 6–9; Assateague Island and Chincoteague National Wildlife Refuge 207–209; Assateague Island National Seashore 209; Back Bay National Wildlife Refuge 195; Blackwater Creek Natural Area 122; Crooked Creek Wildlife Management Area 234; Eastern Shore of Virginia National Wildlife Refuge 196, 198; First Landing State Park 188; Great Dismal Swamp National Wildlife Refuge 181–182; Ivy Creek Natural Area 111; Laurel Fork Preserve 290; Mason Neck National Wildlife Refuge 343; organizations 6–7; Peters Mountain Wilderness 231; Ramsey's Draft Wilderness Area 290; Riverbend Park 327; Ruskin Freer Nature Preserve 122; Theodore Roosevelt Island 312, 354–355; Virginia Coast Reserve 201
Conservation Fund's Civil War Battlefield Campaign, The: 6
Constitution Gardens: 346
Contemporary Art Center of Virginia: 187
Cooper Vineyards: 80
copperhead snakes: 56
Cornwallis' Cave: 158
cottonmouth moccasin snakes: 56
country inns: general discussion: 45–46
Court Days: 336
Courthouse Galleries: 181
Court House Hill: 120
Courthouse of 1770: 146
Cove Ridge Center: 247
Crab Orchard Museum and Pioneer Park of Southwestern Virginia: 242–243
crabs/crabbing: 49, 178, 208, 210
Crabtree Falls: 304
crafts: 44
credit cards: 56–57
crime: 56, 64
Crooked Creek Wildlife Management Area: 234
Crozet: 114
cruises: general discussion 35; Chincoteague 206; Mount Vernon 342; Norfolk 178; Reedville 139; Tangier Island 212; Washington, D.C.

374; *see also specific place*
Cumberland Gap National Historical Park: 247, 249
currency: 56–57
cybercafés: 382; *see also specific place*
cycling clubs: 30–31; 32–33; *see also biking*

D
Dan Daniel Park: 131
Daniel's Hill: 121
Danville: 130–133
Danville Museum of Fine Arts and History: 130
Danville Science Center: 131
d'Art Center: 179
Davis, Jefferson: 130
Davis, Westmoreland: 336
D.C. United: 374
Debtor's Prison: 203
Decoy Factory, The: 207
Deer Meadow Vineyard: 267

Devil's Knob: 303
Devil's Marbleyard: 303
DeWitt Wallace Decorative Arts Museum: 148–149
Diamond Hill: 120
Dinosaur Land: 259
disabled travelers: 57
District of Columbia: *see* Washington, D.C.
District of Columbia Courthouse: 360
Dixie Caverns: 224
Dodona Manor: 333
Dog Mart: 99
Dog Mouth Fountain: 217
Dogwood Dell: 83
Dogwood Festival: 111
Dominion Wine Cellars: 80
Douglas MacArthur Memorial: 173
Douthat Lake: 288
Douthat State Park: 292–293
Down Home Family Reunion: 86

Washington D.C. Highlights

Arthur M. Sackler Gallery: 351
Arts and Sciences Building: 351
Bureau of Engraving and Printing: 355
Capital Children's Museum: 357
Congressional Cemetery: 358
Constitution Gardens: 346
District of Columbia Courthouse: 360
FDR Memorial: 353
Folger Shakespeare Library: 357
Ford's Theatre National Historic Site: 361, 375
Freer Gallery of Art: 351–352
Hirshhorn Museum and Sculpture Garden: 352
J. Edgar Hoover FBI Building: 360
Jefferson Memorial: 353
John F. Kennedy Center for the Performing Arts: 372–373
Kenilworth Aquatic Gardens: 366
Korean War Veterans Memorial: 346–347
Library of Congress: 356
Lincoln Memorial: 346
MCI Center: 374
Metrorail: 348–349, 375–376
National Air and Space Museum: 350–351
National Aquarium: 360

National Archives: 360–361
National Building Museum: 359
National Gallery of Art: 350
National Museum of African Art: 352
National Museum of American Art: 359
National Museum of American History: 352
National Museum of Natural History: 352
National Portrait Gallery: 359–360
National Zoological Park: 363
Old Post Office: 360
Old Stone House: 365
Pentagon, The: 313
Rock Creek Park: 363–364
Smithsonian Institution: 350–352
U.S. Botanic Garden: 358
U.S. Capitol: 356
U.S. National Arboretum: 366
U.S. Supreme Court: 357–358
Union Station: 356
United States Holocaust Memorial Museum: 355–356
Vietnam Women's Memorial: 347
Washington Monument: 347, 350
Washington National Cathedral: 363
White House, The: 358

Downtown Presents: 83
Dragon's Tooth: 224–225
Dr. Pepper: 232
Duke of Floucester Street: 148
Dumbarton Oaks: 365
DuPont Circle: 362
Dye's Vineyard: 221

E
East Coast Surfing Championship: 194
Easter Decoy and Art Festival: 207
Eastern Shore: 196–212
Eastern Shore Birding Festival: 198
Eastern Shore of Virginia Blue Crab Music Festival: 200
Eastern Shore of Virginia National Wildlife Refuge: 196, 198
Eastern Shore Railroad Museum: 203
Easter on Parade: 86
Eastville: 200–201
economy: 25
Edgar Allan Poe Museum: 74–75
Edgewood Plantation: 161
email: 382; *see also specific place*
Empire Theater, The: 83
Endless Caverns: 266
Endless Mountain Retreat Center: 290
Endview Plantation: 163
E.S. Marlin Club Fall One Day Marlin Tournament: 201
E.S. Marlin Club's Billfish Release Tournament: 201
Evelynton Plantation: 161
Executive Mansion: 68

F
Fall Festival & Halloween at the Crossing: 133
False Cape State Park: 195–196
Fan, The: 69, 72
Farfelu Vineyard: 332
fauna: 4, 269, 272, 303
FDR Memorial: 353
Federal Hill: 121
Federal Triangle: 359–361
Ferrum: 225
Ferry Farm: 99–100
Festevents: 179
Festival & Guitar Competition: 236
Festival in the Park (Danville): 133
Festival in the Park (Roanoke): 223–224

festivals and events: general discussion 42–43; A
Colonial Christmas 156; Alexandria Red
Cross Waterfront Festival 324; American Indian Heritage Celebration 11; American Music
Festival 43, 194; Annual Memorial Day Horse
Fair & Auction 279; Antique & Classic Boat
Show 170; Antique and Classic Boat Show
and Rally 129; Applaud the Sun Harbor Party
200; Apple Blossom Festival 258; Apple Harvest Arts and Crafts Festival 258; Arlington
County Fair 316; Artfest 92; Assateague Island
Waterfowl Week 209; Bacon's Rebellion 157;
Bayou Boogaloo and Cajun Food Festival 179;
Beach Music Weekend 193–194; Beach Street
USA 194; Beachevents 193; Big Gig, The 86;
Bike Virginia 31; Blessing of the Fleet 207;
Block Parties 170; Blue Ridge Folklife Festival
225; Blue Ridge Oktoberfest & Chili Cookoff
263; Bluefish Derby 139; Bluemont Concert
Series 335; Bluemont Fair 337; Blues and
Brews 194; Boardwalk Art Show and Festival
194; Cabbage Festival 226; Cape Charles Day
200; Carter Family Memorial Festival 43, 249;
Carytown Watermelon Festival 86; Celtic Festival 124; Champagne and Candlelight Tour
118; Chick Charter Club Annual Tuna Tournament 201; Christmas Open House 337;
Cinco de Mayo 179; Civil War Weekend 158;
Clogging Classic 179; Colonial Christmas
158; Columbia Pike Blues Festival 316; Court
Days 336; Dog Mart 99; Dogwood Festival
111; Down Home Family Reunion 86;
Downtown Presents 83; E.S. Marlin Club Fall
One Day Marlin Tournament 201; East Coast
Surfing Championship 194; Easter Decoy and
Art Festival 207; Easter on Parade 86; Eastern
Shore Birding Festival 198; Eastern Shore of
Virginia Blue Crab Music Festival 200; Fall
Festival & Halloween at the Crossing 133;
Festevents 179; Festival & Guitar Competition 236; Festival in the Park (Danville) 133;
Festival in the Park (Roanoke) 223–224; First
Assembly Day Commemoration 157; First
Friday Gallery Walk 335; First Night Norfolk
180; Flatfood Jamboree 225; Fleet Week
179–180; Floyd Flatfoot Jamboree 43; Foods
& Feasts of Colonial Virginia 156, 158; Friday
Cheers 124; Friday Concerts at The Point
179; Fridays at the Crossing 133; First
Thanksgiving Festival 161; Galax Farmer's

Market 234; George Washington's Birthday 324; Grand Illumination 154; Grand Illumination 86; Grayson Highlands Fall Harvest Festival 236; Great Peanut Bicycle Tour 92; Great Rappahannock Whitewater Canoe Race 99; Green Valley Book Fair 280; Hallows Eve tours 92; Hampton Bay Days 170; Hampton Cup Regatta 170; Hampton Jazz Festival 43, 169–170; Harborfest 179; Henry Street African-American Heritage Festival 224; Heritage Festival 99; Highland Maple Festival 289; Historic Alexandria Candlelight Tour 325; Holiday House Tours 86; Holiday Lights at the Beach 194; Hot Air Balloon Festival 258; Hunt Country Antique Fairs 337; Indian Heritage Festival and Pow Wow 11; International Azalea Festival 179; International Gold Cup 340; International Migratory Bird Celebration 209; James River Bateaux Festival 124–125; James River Blues Festival 125; James River Parade of Lights 86; Jamestown Day 157; Jamestown Landing Day 156; Jazz in the Park 286; June, July & Jazz 170; Kaleidoscope 125; L.A.U.G.H.S. 335; Lee Birthday Celebrations 324; Lee-Jackson Day 300; Leesburg Flower and Garden Show 335; M.S.S.A. Maryland Saltwater Sportfishermen's Association 201; Mainstreet Moments Festival 242; Marine Corps Marathon 316; Masquerade in Ghent 180; Mattaponi Pow Wow 11; Mayfest 268; Memorial Day Jazz Festival 324; Memorial Day Parade 181; Middleburg All Breed Dog Show 337; Middleburg Classic Horse Show 340; Middleburg Garden Tour 339; Middleburg Spring Races 340; Mock Convention 300; Molasses Festival 235; Monacan Pow-Wow 11; Monticello Wine and Food Festival 111; Montpelier Hunt Races 114; Musical Mondays 86; Nansemond Indian Tribe Association Pow Wow and Festival 11; National Miniature Horse Show 297; National Wildlife Refuge Week 209; Needlework Show 342; Neptune Festival 194; North American Sand Soccer Championships 194; Old Time Fiddler's Convention and Fiddlefest 43, 233; Old Town Farmer's Market 258; Oyster Roast and Bluegrass on the Lawn 139; Page County Heritage Festival 268; Pigs in the Park 133; Point-to Point Races 339; Pony Roundup and Swim 207; Potomac Celtic Festival 337; Quilt Exhibition 342; Railroad Festival 127; Ramp Festival 235; Red, White, and Blue Billfish Tournament 194; Reggae on the River 179; Revolutionary War Weekend 158; Richmond Children's Festival 86; River Rib Fest 179; Roanoke Antique and Collectable Expo 222; Roanoke Symphony Polo Cup 224; Rockingham Country Fair 279; Rosslyn Jazz Festival 316; Round Robin Softball Tournament 86; Scottish Christmas Walk 325; Seafood Festival 207; Seafood Fling 170; Second Street Festival 86; 17th Street Farmers' Market 74; Sheepdog Trials 337; Shenandoah Fall Foliage Bike Festival 31; Shenandoah Valley Food & Business Fair 279; Shenandoah Valley Music Festival 264; Smith Mountain Lake Wine Festival 129; Spring Arts and Crafts Show and Sale 279; Spring Fly-In 258; Starvation Ball 92; State Fair of Virginia 86; Staunton Music Festival 286; Strawberry Festival 224; Strawberry Hill Races 86; Suffolk Peanut Fest 92; Summer Breeze Jazz Concert 179; Summer Feast 279; Summer Festival 118; Tackiest Christmas Decorations Tour 86; Taste of the Blue Ridge Blues & Jazz Festival 224; Thomas Jefferson Tomatoe Faire 124; Tour de Chesapeake 31; Tour DuPont 86; Town Point Jazz and Blues Festival 43, 179; Town Point Virginia Wine Festival 179; Traditional Small Boat Show 139; Vinton Old-Time Bluegrass Festival and Competition 224; Virginia Beach Saltwater Fishing Tournament 194; Virginia Cantaloupe Festival 133; Virginia Children's Festival and Halloween Spooktacular 179; Virginia Film Festival 111–112; Virginia Garlic Festival 118; Virginia Gold Cup Races 340; Virginia Highlands Festival 241–242; Virginia Horse Festival 300; Virginia Horse Trials 297; Virginia Hunt Country Stable Tour 339; Virginia Indian Heritage Festival 11, 156; Virginia Mountain Peach Festival 224; Virginia Peanut Festival 92; Virginia Pork Festival 92; Virginia Scottish Games 324; Virginia State Championship Chili Cook-Off 224; Virginia Waterfront International Arts Festival 179, 194; Virginia Wine and Mushroom Festival 263; Virginia Wine Festival 340; Viva Elvis Festival 194; Volunteer Fireman's Carnival 201; Warren County Fair 263; Washington County Fair

and Burley Tobacco Festival 242; Waterman's Festival and Blessing of the Fleet 139; Wayne C. Henderson Music ; Whitetop Mountain Maple Festival 235; Williamburg Scottish Festival and Celtic Celebration 154; World Striped Bass Championships 194; X-Crab-A-Ganza 170
Fields-Penn House: 238
Filene Center: 328
First Assembly Day Commemoration: 157
First Baptist Church: 89
First Battle of Bull Run: 19
First Friday Gallery Walk: 335
First Landing State Park: 188
First Night Norfolk: 180
First Thanksgiving Festival: 161
Fisherman's Museum: 138
fishing: general discussion 36; Allegheny Highlands 288; Back Bay National Wildlife Refuge 195; Beartree Lake 235; Cascades Recreation Area 231; Chincoteague 205–206; Edith J. Carrier Arboretum 277; Galax 234; Great Falls Park 327; Hale Lake 235; Hot Springs 292; Lexington 300; license 36; Mt. Rogers National Recreation Area 235; Norfolk 178; Pandapas Pond 230; Reedville 139; Shenandoah National Park 273; Smith Mountain Lake 128; Virginia Beach 191; Wachapreague 201; York River State Park 154; see also specific place
Five Forks Battlefield: 89
Flatfood Jamboree: 225
Fleet Week: 179–180
flora: 3–4, 5, 269, 303

Gardens

Anne Spencer House and Garden: 121–122
Boxerwood Gardens: 295
Burke's Garden: 246
Constitution Gardens: 346
Hirshhorn Museum and Sculpture Garden: 352
Kenilworth Aquatic Gardens: 366
Kenmore Plantation and Gardens: 96–97
Lewis Ginter Botanical Garden: 76
Middleburg Garden Tour: 339
Norfolk Botanical Gardens: 174
Peace Gardens: 163
U.S. Botanic Garden: 358
U.S. National Arboretum: 366

Floyd: 225–226
Floyd Flatfoot Jamboree: 43
Folger Elizabethan Theatre: 373
Folger Shakespeare Library: 357
food: 48–49; see also specific place
Foods & Feasts of Colonial Virginia: 156, 158
football: James Madison University (Dukes) 279; University of Virginia (Cavaliers) 110; Virginia Tech 229; Washington Redskins 374
Ford's Theatre National Historic Site: 361, 375
Fort Harrison: 72
Fort Monroe: 168–169
Fort Story: 187–188
Fort Ward Museum and Historic Site: 321
Foxfield: 110
fox hunts: 33–34
Francis Land House: 187
Fredericksburg: 93–102
Fredericksburg and Spotsylvania National Military Park: 100–102
Fredericksburg Area Museum and Cultural Center: 96
Fredericksburg National Cemetery: 100
Freedom Forum: 313
Freer Gallery of Art: 351–352
Friday Cheers: 124
Friday Concerts at The Point: 179
Fridays at the Crossing: 133
Friendship Firehouse: 319–320
Friends of the North Fork of the Shenandoah: 6
Friends of the Shenandoah River: 6
Frontier Culture Museum: 283
Front Royal: 261–264
fruit picking: 38
Fun Fort: 165

G
Gadsby's Tavern Museum: 317, 319
Galax: 233–234
Galax Farmer's Market: 234
galleries: Arts Deport, The 237; Courthouse Galleries 181; d'Art Center 179; McGuffey Art Center 105; Staunton-Augusta Art Center 286; Torpedo Factory Arts Center 319; Turner Sculpture 203; Warm Springs Gallery 291; William King Regional Art Center 238
Garland Hill: 121
Garth Newel Music Center: 291–292
gay and lesbian travelers: 57
geology: 2–3, 4

Historic Homes and Buildings

Abram's Delight: 255–256
Adam Thoroughgood House: 185, 187
Agecroft Hall: 74
Albemarle County Courthouse: 105
Anne Spencer House and Garden: 121–122
Appomattox Court House National Historic Park: 126–127
Appomattox Iron Works: 88
Arlington House: 310
Ashland-Highland: 115, 118
Athenaeum: 319
Augusta County Courthouse: 284
Bassett Hall: 148
Belle Boyd Cottage: 262
Brafferton: 148
Brush-Everard House: 147
Camberley's Martha Washington Inn: 238, 239–240
Capitol, The: 146
Carlyle House: 319
Centre Hill Mansion: 88
City Market Building: 217
Colonial Williamsburg: 145–149
Courthouse of 1770: 146
Debtor's Prison: 203
District of Columbia Courthouse: 360
Dodona Manor: 333
Executive Mansion: 68
Ferry Farm: 99–100
Fields-Penn House: 238
Francis Land House: 187
Friendship Firehouse: 319–320
George Wythe House: 147
Governor's Palace: 146
Grayson County Courthouse: 233
Hopkins & Bro. Store: 202
Hugh Mercer Apothecary Shop: 95–96
Inn at Little Washington: 113
James Fort: 156
Jamestown Glasshouse of 1608: 157
Jefferson Hotel: 77
John Marshall House: 68
Kenmore Plantation and Gardens: 96–97
Kerr Place: 202
Lee Hall Mansion: 163
Lee-Fendall House: 320
Little England Chapel: 168
Loudoun County Courthouse: 333

Lyceum: 319
Lynnhaven House: 187
Magazine and Guardhouse: 146
Maggie L. Walker National Historic Site: 69
Market Station: 333
Mary Washington House: 96
Masonic Lodge No. 4: 97
Maymont: 72–73
Michie Tavern: 114
Montpelier: 112–114
Moore House: 158
Moses Myers House: 175
Nelson House: 158
Old Cape Henry Lighthouse: 187–188
Old Courthouse (Eastville): 200
Old Presbyterian Meeting House: 319
Old Stone House: 365
Old Trinity Church: 284
Pest House Medical Museum: 121
Petersen House: 361
Peyton Randolph House: 147
Point of Honor: 121
Pope-Leighey House: 342
Popular Forest: 125
Presbyterian Church: 97
Printing Office: 148
Public Gaol: 147
Public Hospital of 1773: 147
Raleigh Tavern: 146–147
Rising Sun Tavern: 94–95
Robertson's Windmill: 148
R.S. Bristow Store: 140
Sherwood Forest: 161
South River Meeting House: 122
Stabler-Leadbeater Apothecary: 319
St. John's Episcopal Church: 75
Stonewall Jackson House: 295
Stonewall Jackson's Headquarters: 256
Tavern: The: 240–241
Virginia State Capitol: 68
Washington County Courthouse: 238
Wedding Cake House: 130
White House (Washington, D.C.): 358
White's Mill: 238
Willoughby-Baylor House: 175
Woodlawn Mansion: 342
Wren Building: 148

George C. Marshall and Museum and Library: 295
Georgetown: 364–365
Georgetown University: 365
George Washington Birthplace National Monument: 135, 137
George Washington Masonic National Memorial: 320–321
George Washington's Birthday: 324
George Washington's Office Museum: 256
George Wythe House: 147
ghosts: 278, 299, 323, 365
giardia: 55
Glendale Cemetery: 72
Glenway Winery: 332
golf: general discussion 38; Colonial Williamsburg 151; Hot Springs 292; Newport News 163; Scottsville 119; *see also specific place*
government: 25–26
Governor's Palace: 146
Grand Caverns Regional Park: 281
Grand Illumination: 86, 154
Grant, General Ulysses S.: 91, 101, 253
gratuity: 58–59
Graves Mountain Lodge: 114
Grayhaven Winery: 80
Grayson County Courthouse: 233
Grayson Highlands Fall Harvest Festival: 236
Grayson Highlands State Park: 235, 236
Great Dismal Swamp National Wildlife Refuge: 181–182
Great Falls Park: 327
Great Falls Town: 328
Great Peanut Bicycle Tour: 92
Great Rappahannock Whitewater Canoe Race: 99
Green Valley Book Fair: 280
Grey Ghost Vineyards: 332
Guilford Ridge Vineyard: 267
Gunston Hall Plantation: 342–343
Gypsy Hill Park: 284

H
Haller-Gibboney Rock House Museum: 231
Hallows Eve tours: 92
Hampton: 166–170
Hampton Bay Days: 170
Hampton Coliseum: 169
Hampton Cup Regatta: 170
Hampton Jazz Festival: 43, 169–170
Hampton Roads Admirals: 178

Hampton Roads History Center: 167
Hampton Roads Naval Museum: 173
Hamptons Carousel: 167
Hampton University: 168
Hampton University Museum: 168
Harborfest: 179
Harper's Ferry: 16
Harrisonburg: 276–281
Harrison Museum of African-American Culture: 219
Hartwood Winery: 332
Hawksbill Mountain: 273
health and safety: general discussion 55–56; black widow spiders 55; crime 56, 64; giardia 55; hiking 55; hypothermia 56; jellyfish 56; lightening 56; Lyme disease 55; mosquitoes 55; poison ivy 56; poisonous snakes 56; stinging insects 55
Henry, Patrick: 144
Henry Street African-American Heritage Festival: 224
Heritage Festival: 99
Heritage Repertory Theatre: 110
Hermitage Foundation Museum: 173
Hewick Plantation: 140
Highland Maple Festival: 289
hiking: general discussion 30; Back Bay National Wildlife Refuge 195; Breaks Interstate Park 244; Bull Run Regional Park 330; Cascades Recreational Area 230, 231; Chessie Nature Trail 299; Cumberland Gap National Historical Park 247, 249; Douthat State Park 292; Dragon's Tooth 224–225; False Cape State Park 195–196; Grand Caverns Regional Park 281; Great Dismal Swamp National Wildlife Refuge 181–182; Great Falls Park 327; Hot Springs 292; Laurel Fork Preserve 290; Mason Neck State Park 343; Mt. Rogers National Recreation Area 235; Mt. Vernon Trail 316; Natural Tunnel State Park 246–247; Riverbend Park 327; Rock Creek Park 363; Shenandoah National Park 272–273; *see also specific place*
Hill Top Berry Farm & Winery: 80
Hirshhorn Museum and Sculpture Garden: 352
Historic Alexandria Candlelight Tour: 325
history: general discussion 9–25; Abingdon 237; Arlington County 308–309; Blacksburg 226–227; Charlottesville 102; Charlottesville 114–115; Chincoteague 203–204; Civil War

18–23; colonial 10–14; Colonial Williams-burg 141, 144, 145–159; Danville 130; First Battle of Bull Run 19; Fredericksburg 93–94, 100–102; Great Dismal Swamp National Wildlife Refuge 181–182; Great Falls Park 327; Hampton 167; Harrisonburg 276; Hunt Country 329–340; key dates 24; Lexington 293–294; Lynchburg 119, 122, 125; Middle-town 260–261; modern 23–25; Mount Ver-non 340–342; New Market 265–266; Norfolk 170–173; Old Town Alexandria 317; Peters-burg 88, 90, 91; Portsmouth 180; precolonial 9–10; Revolutionary War 14–15; Richmond 62–63, 67; Roanoke 215, 217; settlement 26; Shenandoah 250–253; Shenandoah National Park 269; slavery 15–16; Staunton 281–282; Tangier Island 209–210; Winchester 254–255; Washington, D.C. 344–345
History Museum of Western Virginia: 218
hockey: Hampton Roads Admirals 178; Rich-mond Renegades 84; Washington Capitals 374
Holiday House Tours: 86
Holiday Lake State Park: 127
Holiday Lights at the Beach: 194
Hollywood Cemetery: 73
Holy Cross Abbey: 258–259
Holy Land USA: 126
home exchanges/stays: 47–48; *see also specific place*
Homestead, The: 292
Hopkins & Bro. Store: 202
horseback riding: general discussion 32–34; Abingdon 241; Front Royal 263; Grayson Highlands State Park 235; Mt. Rogers Nation-al Recreation Area 235; Raymond R. "Andy" Guest, Jr. Shenandoah River State Park 263–264; Riverbend Park 327; Rock Creek Park 363; Scottsville 119; Virginia Highlands Horse Trail 235; Virginia Horse Center 297; Virginia Horse Council 33; Westmoreland State Park 137
horse racing: general discussion 34; Char-lottesville 110; Glenwood Park 340; Great Meadows: 340; International Gold Cup: 340; Middleburg Classic Horse Show: 340; Mid-dleburg Spring Races: 340; Richmond 85; Virginia Gold Cup Races: 340
Horton Cellars Winery/Montdomaine Cellars: 80
hostels: 47; *see also specific place*
Hot Air Balloon Festival: 258
hot air balloons: general discussion 39; Char-

lottesville 111; Front Royal: 263; Hunt Coun-try 329
hotels: 45, 46; *see also specific place*
hot mineral springs: 290, 291, 292
Hot Springs: 292
Hugh Mercer Apothecary Shop: 95–96
Huguenot Woods: 73
Humpback Covered Bridge: 288
Humpback Rocks: 303
Hunt Country: 329–340
Hunt Country Antique Fairs: 337
hunting: 36–37; *see also specific place*
Huntington Park: 165
Huntington Tugboat Museum: 174
Huntley Meadows Park: 340
H.W. Meador Coal Museum: 246
hypothermia: 56

I
Indian Heritage Festival and Pow Wow: 11
Ingleside Plantation Vineyards: 144
Ingles, Mary Draper: 229
Inn at Little Washington: 113
International Azalea Festival: 179
International Gold Cup: 340
International Migratory Bird Celebration: 209
Internet resources: 382; *see also specific place*
Irvington: 139–140
Island Aquarium: 204
Ivy Creek Natural Area: 111

J
Jack Kent Cooke Stadium: 374
Jackson, Stonewall: 69, 100, 101–102, 105, 252, 256, 266, 295, 296, 330
Jackson Ward: 68–69
James Cittie townsite: 157
James Fort: 156
James Madison University: 276–277; sports 279
James Monroe Museum and Memorial Library: 96
James River Bateaux Festival: 124–125
James River Blues Festival: 125
James River Overlook: 304
James River Parade of Lights: 86
James River Park: 73
James River Plantations: 159–161
Jamestown: 10–11, 155–157
Jamestown Day: 157
Jamestown Glasshouse of 1608: 157
Jamestown Island: 157

Jamestown Landing Day: 156
Jamestown Settlement: 156
Jamestown Yacht Basin: 156–157
Jazz in the Park: 286
J. Edgar Hoover FBI Building: 360
Jefferson Hotel: 77
Jefferson Memorial: 353
Jefferson National Forest: 229–230
Jefferson Pools: 291
Jefferson Theater: 110
Jefferson, Thomas: 15, 60–61, 102, 104, 114–115, 116–117, 125, 148, 301, 353
Jefferson Vineyards: 80
jellyfish: 56
John F. Kennedy Center for the Performing Arts: 372–373
John Fox, Jr. Museum: 246
John Marshall House: 68
June, July & Jazz: 170
June Tollivar Playhouse: 245

K
Kaleidoscope: 125
kayaking: general discussion 34–35; Breaks Interstate Park 244; Cape Charles 200; Chincoteague 206; Galax 234; Norfolk 178; Reedville 139; Richmond 85; Tangier Island 212; Virginia Beach 192; Westmoreland State Park 137
Kenilworth Aquatic Gardens: 366
Kenmore Plantation and Gardens: 96–97
Kennedy, John F.: 309–310, 364, 372–373
Kennedy, Robert F.: 309
Kerr Place: 202
Kiptopeke State Park: 198
Klockner Stadium: 110
Klugs Estate Winery and Vineyard, The: 80
Korean War Veterans Memorial: 346–347

L
Lake Anna Winery: 80
Lake Moomaw: 288
land: 2–9
Landwirt Vineyard: 267
L.A.U.G.H.S.: 335
Laurel Fork Preserve: 290
Lawn, The: 104
Lee Birthday Celebrations: 324
Lee Chapel and Museum: 294
Lee-Fendall House: 320

Lee Hall Mansion: 163
Lee-Jackson Day: 300
Lee, Robert E.: 67, 69, 105, 252, 261–262, 309, 310, 320, 330, 361
Leesburg: 333–336
Leesburg Animal Park: 333
Leesburg Flower and Garden Show: 335
L'Enfant, Pierre: 344
Lenfest Center for the Performing Arts: 299
Lewis and Clark/105
Lewis Ginter Botanical Garden: 76
Lexington: 293–300
Library of Congress: 356
lightening: 56
Lightship Museum: 181
Limberlost Trail: 273
Lime Kiln Theater: 299
Lincoln, Abraham: 252, 253, 346, 361
Lincoln Memorial: 346
Linden Vineyards: 332
Little England Chapel: 168
Little Theater of Virginia Beach: 193
Live Arts: 109–110
llama trekking: 236
Loudoun County Courthouse: 333
Loudoun Museum: 333
Loudoun Valley Vineyard: 332
Luray: 266–268
Luray Caverns: 266–267
Luray Reptile Center, Dinosaur Park and Petting Zoo: 267
Luray Singing Tower: 267
Lyceum: 319
Lyme disease: 55
Lynchburg: 119–130
Lynchburg College: 124
Lynchburg Fine Arts Center: 124
Lynchburg Regional Airport: 125
Lynchburg Symphony Orchestra: 124
Lyndon B. Johnson Memorial Grove: 312–313
Lynnhaven House: 187

M
Mabry Mill: 226
Madison, James: 112–114, 115–116, 118
Magazine and Guardhouse: 146
Maggie L. Walker National Historic Site: 69
Maier Museum of Art: 121
Mainstreet Moments Festival: 242
Main Street Station: 74

Mall: 346–347, 348–352
Mall Merry-Go-Round: 350
Manassas National Battlefield Park: 329–330
maps: 56, 275
"March to the Sea": 22
Marine Corps Marathon: 316
Mariners' Museum: 162
Market Square: 217
Market Station: 333
Mary Baldwin College: 284
Mary Washington House: 96
Masonic Lodge No. 4: 97
Mason Neck: 342–343
Mason Neck National Wildlife Refuge: 343
Mason Neck State Park: 343
Masquerade in Ghent: 180
Massanutten Resort: 280
Mast of the Battleship *Maine:* 310
Mattaponi: 11, 141
Mattaponi Pow Wow: 11
Mattaponi Reservation: 141
Matthews Museum: 233
Maury, Matthew Fontaine: 69
Mayfest: 268
Maymont: 72–73
McGuffey Art Center: 105
MCI Center: 374
McIntire Department of Music: 110
McLean: 326–327
McLean, Wilmer: 127
Meadows of Dan: 226
Medical College of Virginia: 64
Melchers, Gary: 99
Memorial Amphitheater: 310
Memorial Day Jazz Festival: 324
Memorial Day Parade: 181
Merrimac: 19–20
Metro Richmond Zoo: 87
Metrorail: 348–349, 375–376
Michie Tavern: 114
Middleburg:337–340
Middleburg All Breed Dog Show: 337
Middleburg Classic Horse Show: 340
Middleburg Garden Tour: 339
Middleburg Spring Races: 340
Middleneck: 140–141
Middletown: 260
Military Through the Ages: 156
Mill Mountain: 219
Mill Mountain Theater: 218

Mill Mountain Zoo: 219
Mill Prong Trail: 273
Millward Theatre: 231
mineral springs: 264
Misty Mountain Vineyards & Winery: 80
Mock Convention: 300
Molasses Festival: 235
Monacan: 11
Monacan Pow-Wow: 11
monasteries: 258–259
money: 56–57
Monitor: 20
Monterey: 289–290
Monticello: 114–115, 116–117
Monticello Wine and Food Festival: 111
Montpelier: 112–114
Montpelier Hunt Races: 114
Monument Avenue: 69, 72
Monument Terrace: 120
Moore House: 158
Morven Park: 336–337
Morven's International Equestrian Center: 336–337
Mosby, John Singleton: 338–339
Moses Myers House: 175
mosquitoes: 55
motels: 45, 46; *see also specific place*
motorcycle rentals: 194
mountain biking: *see* biking; cycling clubs
Mountain Cove Vineyards and Winegarden: 80
Mountain Dew: 232
Mountain Lake: 230–231
Mountain Lake Resort: 229–231
Mountain Lake Wilderness: 231
mountains: 3
Mount Vernon: 340–342
M.S.S.A. Maryland Saltwater Sportfishermen's Association: 201
Mt. Rogers National Recreation Area: 235
Mt. Trashmore Park: 187
Mt. Vernon Trail: 316, 324
Muscarelle Museum of Art: 148
Museum of Geological Sciences: 228
Museum of Hounds and Hunting: 336
Museum of Military Memorabilia: 297
Museum of Natural History: 228
Museum of 19th Century Mourning Customs: 121
museums: Abby Aldrich Rockefeller Folk Art Museum 149; Air Power Park 168; Alexandria

Archaeology 319; Amazement Square 122; American Armoured Foundation 131–132; American Celebrations on Parade 266; American Work Horse Museum 297; Antique Carriage and Car Museum 267; Art Museum of Western Virginia 218; Arthur M. Sackler Gallery 351; Arts and Sciences Building 351; Association for Research and Enlightenment 185; Atlantic Wildfowl Heritage Museum 185; Bayly Art Museum 104; Belmont 99; Black History Museum and Cultural Center of Virginia 69; Cape Charles Museum and Welcome Center 199; Capital Children's Museum 357; Carter Family Museum 249; Casemate Museum 168–169; Chesapeake Bay Center 188; Children's Museum of Virginia 181; Chimborazo Medical Museum 75; Chrysler Museum of Art 174–175; Civil War Visitors Center 72; Contemporary Art Center of Virginia 187; Crab Orchard Museum and Pioneer Park of Southwestern Virginia 242–243; Danville Museum of Fine Arts and History 130; Danville Science Center 131; DeWitt Wallace Decorative Arts Museum 148–149; Dumbarton Oaks 365; Eastern Shore Railroad Museum 203; Edgar Allan Poe Museum 74–75; Fisherman's Museum 138; Fort Ward Museum and Historic Site 321; Fredericksburg Area Museum and Cultural Center 96; Freer Gallery of Art 351–352; Friendship Firehouse 319–320; Frontier Culture Museum 283; Gadsby's Tavern Museum 317, 319; George C. Marshall and Museum and Library 295; George Washington Masonic National Memorial 320–321; George Washington's Office Museum 256; Hampton University Museum 168; Haller-Gibboney Rock House Museum 231; Hampton Roads History Center 167; Hampton Roads Naval Museum 173; Harrison Museum of African-American Culture 219; Hermitage Foundation Museum 173; Hirshhorn Museum and Sculpture Garden 352; History Museum of Western Virginia 218; Huntington Tugboat Museum 174; H.W. Meador Coal Museum 246; James Monroe Museum and Memorial Library 96; John Fox, Jr. Museum 246; Lee Chapel and Museum 294; Lightship Museum 181; Loudoun Museum 333; Maier Museum of Art 121; Mariners' Museum 162;

Matthews Museum 233; Muscarelle Museum of Art 148; Museum of Geological Sciences 228; Museum of Hounds and Hunting 336; Museum of Military Memorabilia 297; Museum of Natural History 228; Museum of 19th Century Mourning Customs 121; NASA 207; National Air and Space Museum 350–351; National Building Museum 359; National Gallery of Art 350; National Museum of African Art 352; National Museum of American Art 359; National Museum of American History 352; National Museum of Natural History 352; National Portrait Gallery 359–360; Natural Bridge Wax Museum 302; Naval Shipyard Museum 181; Newseum 313; Old City Court House Museum 120; Old Coast Guard Station 185; Oyster and Maritime Museum 204; P. Buckley Moss Museum 287; Peninsula Fine Arts Center 162; Pest House Medical Museum 121; Pocahontas Exhibition Coal Mine 243; Quartermaster Museum 88–89; Refuge Waterfowl Museum 204; Richmond Children's Museum 75–76; Science Museum of Virginia 75; Science Museum of Western Virginia 218; Shenandoah Valley Discovery Museum 256; Shenandoah Valley Folk Art and Heritage Center 280; Shockoe Bottom Arts Center 74; Siege Museum 88; Softball Hall of Fame 88; Southwest Virginia Museum 246; Statler Brothers Complex 284; Thomas J. Boyd Museum 231; To The Rescue Museum 219; United States Holocaust Memorial Museum 355–356; U.S. Army Transportation Museum 165; Valentine Museum, The 68; Virginia Air and Space Center 167–168; Virginia Aviation Museum 76; Virginia Discovery Museum 105; Virginia Historical Society Center for Virginia History 73; Virginia Holocaust Museum 75; Virginia Living Museum 163, 165; Virginia Marine Science Museum 183, 185, 192; Virginia Military Institute Museum 295; Virginia Museum of Fine Arts 73; Virginia Museum of Transportation 218–219; Virginia Quilt Museum 276; Virginia Sports Hall of Fame & Museum 181; Virginia War Museum 165; Walton's Mountain Museum 118; Warren Rifles Confederate Museum 261–262; Watermen's Museum 158; White House and Museum of the Confederacy 64, 66; Winmill Carriage Collection 336; Winthrop Rockefeller Archeology Museum 149; Woodrow Wilson Birthplace and Museum 282, 284; Yorktown Victory Center 158–159

Musical Mondays: 86

Music Theatre of Williamsburg: 163

N

Naked Mountain Vineyard: 332

Nansemond: 11

Nansemond Indian Tribe Association Pow Wow and Festival: 11

NASA: 207

National Air and Space Museum: 350–351

National Aquarium: 360

National Archives: 360–361

National Building Museum: 359

National D-Day Memorial: 126

National Gallery of Art: 350

National Miniature Horse Show: 297

National Museum of African Art: 352

National Museum of American Art: 359

National Museum of American History: 352

National Museum of Natural History: 352

National Park Service: 157

National Portrait Gallery: 359–360

National Symphony Orchestra: 372–373

National Theatre: 373

National Wildlife Refuge Week: 209

National Zoological Park: 363

Native Americans: general discussion 9–11, 13; American Indian Heritage Celebration 11; Cherokee 243; Chickahominy 11; Indian Heritage Festival and Pow Wow 11; Mattaponi 11, 141; Mattaponi Pow Wow 11; Mattaponi Reservation 141; Monacan 11; Monacan Pow-Wow 11; Nansemond 11; Nansemond Indian Tribe Association Pow Wow and Festival 11; Pamunkey 11, 141; Pamunkey Indian Reservation 141; Powhaten Indian village 156; United Rappahannock 11; Virginia Indian Heritage Festival 11

Natural Bridge: 301–302

Natural Bridge Caverns: 302

Natural Bridge Wax Museum: 302

Natural Bridge Zoo: 302

Natural Chimneys Regional Park: 280–281

Natural Tunnel State Park: 246–247

Nature Conservancy, The: 7, 201

Nauticus: 173

Naval Shipyard Museum: 181

Needlework Show: 342

Nelson House: 158

Neptune Festival: 194

Netherlands Carillon: 312

New Market: 264–266

New Market Battlefield Historic Park: 265–266

New River Trail State Park: 234

Newport News: 162–166

Newport News Park: 162–163

Newport News-Williamsburg International Airport: 154, 166, 170

Newseum: 313

Nina Abady Festival Park: 86

Norfolk: 170–182

Norfolk Botanical Gardens: 174

Norfolk International Airport: 180

Norfolk Naval Base: 174

Norfolk Tides: 178

North American Sand Soccer Championships: 194

North Bend Plantation: 162

Northern Neck: 135–140

North Mountain Vineyard & Winery: 267

Norwegian Lady: 183

O

Oakencroft Vineyard & Winery: 80

Oasis Winery, The: 332

Oatlands Plantation: 337

Ocean Breeze Waterpark: 192–193

offbeat highlights: 42

Old Cape Henry Lighthouse: 187–188

Old City Cemetery: 121

Old City Court House Museum: 120

Old City Hall: 68

Old Coast Guard Station: 185

Old Courthouse: 200

Olde Towne: 88

Olde Towne Lantern Tours: 181

Old Post Office: 360

Old Presbyterian Meeting House: 319

Old Rag Mountain: 273

Old Stone House: 365

Old Time Fiddler's Convention and Fiddlefest: 43, 233

Old Town Alexandria: 317–326

Old Town Farmer's Market: 258

Old Trinity Church: 284

Onancock: 201–203

opera: Music Theatre of Williamsburg 163;

Opera Roanoke 222; Virginia Opera (Norfolk) 178; Virginia Opera (Richmond) 83; Washington Opera 373; Wolf Trap Opera Company 328
Opera Roanoke: 222
organized tours: 41–42; *see also specific place*
Orkney Springs: 264
Otter Creek: 304
Oyster and Maritime Museum: 204
Oyster Roast and Bluegrass on the Lawn: 139
oysters: 7–8, 49

P, Q
Page County Heritage Festival: 268
Pamplin Park: 89
Pamunkey 11, 141
Pamunkey Indian Reservation: 141
Paramount Kings Dominion: 87

park fees: 272; *see also* parks
Parksley: 203
Pasteur and Galt Apothecary Shop: 148
P. Buckley Moss Museum: 287
Peace Gardens: 163
Peaks of Otter Recreation Area: 304
Peaks of Otter Winery: 267
Peninsula Fine Arts Center: 162
Peninsula SPCA Petting Zoo: 165
Pentagon, The: 313
performing arts: Barns at Wolf Trap, The 328; Canal Turning Basin 86; Carpenter Center for the Performing Arts 83; Carter Barron Amphitheatre 374; Chrysler Hall 177–178; Classic Amphitheater 83; Dogwood Dell 83; Filene Center 328; Hampton Coliseum 169; John F. Kennedy Center for the Performing Arts 372–373; Lenfest Center for the Per-

Parks and Recreation Areas

Assateague State Park (Maryland): 208
Ball's Bluff Regional Park: 336
Breaks Interstate Park: 243–244
Bull Run Regional Park: 330
Byrd Park: 72
C & O Canal National Historical Park: 327
Cascades Recreational Area: 230, 231
Cleveland Park: 362
Cumberland Gap National Historical Park: 247, 249
Dan Daniel Park: 131
Douthat State Park: 292–293
False Cape State Park: 195–196
First Landing State Park: 188
Grand Caverns Regional Park: 281
Grayson Highlands State Park: 235, 236
Great Falls Park: 327
Gypsy Hill Park: 284
Holiday Lake State Park: 127
Huntington Park: 165
Huntley Meadows Park: 340
James River Park: 73
Jefferson National Forest: 229–230
Kiptopeke State Park: 198
Mariners/ Museum Park: 162
Mason Neck State Park: 343
Morven Park: 336–337
Mountain Lake Wilderness: 231

Mt. Rogers National Recreation Area: 235
Natural Chimneys Regional Park: 280–281
Natural Tunnel State Park: 246–247
Newport News Park: 162–163
New River Trail State Park: 234
Peaks of Otter Recreation Area: 304
Peters Mountain Wilderness: 231
Pohick Bay Regional Park: 342
Priest Wilderness: 304
Prince William Forest Park: 343
Raymond R. "Andy" Guest, Jr. Shenandoah River State Park: 263–264
Riverbend Park: 327
Riverside Park: 122
Riverview Park: 111
Rock Creek Park: 363–364
Shenandoah National Park: 269–275
Sherando Lake Recreation Area: 303–304
Shot Tower Historical State Park: 234
Sky Meadows State Park: 340
Three Ridges Wilderness: 304
Westmoreland State Park: 137
White Rocks Recreation Area: 231
Wolf Trap Farm Park: 328
Woodley Park: 362
Woods Creek Park: 299
York River State Park: 154

Plantations

Belle Grove Plantation: 260–261
Berkeley Plantation: 160–161
Carter's Grove Plantation: 149
Edgewood Plantation: 161
Endview Plantation: 163
Evelynton Plantation: 161
Gunston Hall Plantation: 342–343
Hewick Plantation: 140
Kenmore Plantation and Gardens: 96–97
Mount Vernon: 340–342
North Bend Plantation: 162
Oatlands Plantation: 337
Shirley Plantation: 160
Stratford Hall Plantation: 137–138
Westover Plantation: 161
Woodlawn Plantation: 342

forming Arts 299; Live Arts 109–110; Lynchburg Fine Arts Center 124; Nina Abady Festival Park 86; Phi Beta Kappa Hall 153; Richmond Coliseum 84–85; Riverfront 86; Roanoke Civic Center 222–223; SCOPE Center 177; Virginia Beach Amphitheater 193; William and Mary Hall 153; Wolf Trap Farm Park 328
permits: fishing 36, 37; hunting 37
Pest House Medical Museum: 121
Petersburg: 88–93
Petersburg National Battlefield Park: 89
Petersen House: 361
Peters Mountain Wilderness: 231
pets, traveling with: 48
Peyton Randolph House: 147
Phi Beta Kappa Hall: 153
Piedmont Vineyards: 332
Pigs in the Park: 133
planetarium: 165
Pocahontas: 10
Pocahontas Exhibition Coal Mine: 243
Pohick Bay Regional Park: 342
Point of Honor: 121
Point-to Point Races: 339
poison ivy: 56
poisonous snakes: 56
pollution: 7–9; air 8–9; water 7–8
polo matches: 34
Pony Pasture: 73

Pony Roundup and Swim: 207
Pope-Leighey House: 342
Popular Forest: 125
Popular Grove National Cemetery: 89
Portsmouth: 180–181
Potomac Appalachian Trail Club: 30
Potomac Celtic Festival: 337
Potomac Heritage Trail: 316
Powhatans : 10–13, 156, 301
precipitation: 5–6
prehistory: 2–3
Presbyterian Church: 97
presidents: 17
Priest Wilderness: 304
Prince Michel & Rapidan River Vineyards: 80
Prince William Forest Park: 343
Printing Office: 148
psychic phenomenon: 185
Public Gaol: 147
Public Hospital of 1773: 147
Quartermaster Museum: 88–89
Quilt Exhibition: 342

R

race relations: 23–24
racing/Langley Speedway: 169
Railroad Festival: 127
Rails-to-Trails Conservancy: 30
Raleigh Tavern: 146–147
Ramp Festival: 235
Ramsey's Draft Wilderness Area: 290
rattlesnakes: 56
Raymond R. "Andy" Guest, Jr. Shenandoah River State Park: 263–264
Rebec Vineyards: 80, 118
Red, White, and Blue Billfish Tournament: 194
Reedville: 138
re-enactments: general discussion 40–41; Appomattox Court House National Historic Park 126–127; Claude Moore Colonial Farm 326; Colonial National Historical Park 157; Frontier Culture Museum 283; George Washington Birthplace National Monument 135, 137; Jamestown Settlement 156; Military Through the Ages 156; Olde Towne Lantern Tours 181; Virginia's Explore Park 219; Yorktown Victory Center 158; Yorktown Visitors Center 157–158
Refuge Waterfowl Museum: 204
Reggae on the River: 179

religion: 28
Renaissance Theatre Festival and Virginia Western Theatre: 223
restaurants: *see* food; *specific place*
Revolutionary War Weekend: 158
Richmond: 62–87; accommodations 76–78; entertainment 82–86; food 78, 81–82; history 62–63; sights 64–76; transportation 86–87
Richmond Ballet: 83
Richmond Battlefield National Park: 72
Richmond Braves: 84
Richmond Children's Festival: 86
Richmond Children's Museum: 75–76
Richmond Coliseum: 84–85
Richmond International Raceway: 85
Richmond Kickers: 84
Richmond Renegades: 84
Richmond's Landmark Theater: 83
Richmond Symphony: 83
Riprap Hollow Trail: 273
Rising Sun Tavern: 94–95
Riverbend Park: 327
Riverfront: 74, 86
River Rib Fest: 179
Riverside Park: 122
Riverview Park: 111
Roanoke: 215–226
Roanoke Antique and Collectable Expo: 222
Roanoke Ballet Theatre: 222
Roanoke Civic Center: 222–223
Roanoke Regional Airport: 224
Roanoke Star: 219
Roanoke Symphony Orchestra: 222
Roanoke Symphony Polo Cup: 224
Robert F. Kennedy Memorial Stadium: 374
Robertson's Windmill: 148
Robinson, Bill "Bojangles": 69
rock and roll: 166
Rockbridge Vineyard: 80, 267
rock climbing: 34, 327
Rock Creek Park: 363–364
Rockfish Gap: 303–304
Rockingham Country Fair: 279
Rolfe, John: 10–11
romantic getaways: 47
Roosevelt, Elinor: 353
Roosevelt, Franklin Delano: 353
Rose Bower Vineyard & Winery: 81
Rose River Vineyards & Trout Farm: 81
Rosslyn Jazz Festival: 316

Round Robin Softball Tournament: 86
Route 11 Potato Chip Factory: 260
R.S. Bristow Store: 140
Ruskin Freer Nature Preserve: 122

S
sales tax: 44
Saltville Massacre: 237
Satchidananda Ashram: 128
Science Museum of Virginia: 75
Science Museum of Western Virginia: 218
SCOPE Center: 177
Scottish Christmas Walk: 325
Scottsville: 118
scuba diving: 192
seafood: 49*see also specific place*
Seafood Festival: 207
Seafood Fling: 170
sea turtles: 195
Second Battle of Manassas: 20
Second Street Festival: 86
seniors: 58
Seven Days' Battles: 20, 67
Shaddwell-Windham Winery: 332
Shakespeare Theatre: 373
Sharp Rock Vineyards: 81
Sheepdog Trials: 337
Shenandoah Caverns: 266
Shenandoah Fall Foliage Bike Festival: 31
Shenandoah National Park: 269–275
Shenandoah Overlook: 273
Shenandoah Summer Music Festival: 257
Shenandoah Valley Discovery Museum: 256
Shenandoah Valley Folk Art and Heritage Center: 280
Shenandoah Valley Food & Business Fair: 279
Shenandoah Valley Music Festival: 264
Shenandoah Vineyards: 267
Sherando Lake Recreation Area: 303–304
Sherwood Forest: 161
Shirley Plantation: 160
Shockoe Bottom: 74
Shockoe Bottom Arts Center: 74
Shockoe Slip: 74
shopping: 44
Shot Tower Historical State Park: 234
Showtimers: 223
Siege Museum: 88
Sierra Club: 7
sika deer: 208

skiing: general discussion 38; Abingdon 241; Blacksburg 230; Bryce Resort 264; Great Falls Park 327; Hot Springs 292; Massanutten Resort 280; Scottsville 118
skydiving: 38; *see also specific place*
Skyline Caverns: 263
Sky Meadows State Park: 340
slavery: 15–16
Smith, Captain John: 12
Smith Mountain Dam: 128
Smith Mountain Lake: 128–129
Smith Mountain Lake State Park: 129
Smith Mountain Lake Wine Festival: 129
Smithsonian Castle: 350
Smithsonian Institution: 350–352
Smithson, James: 350
Smokehouse Winery: 81
snow geese: 195
soccer: D.C. United 374; Richmond Kickers 84; University of Virginia (Cavaliers) 110
Society of the Cincinnati: 364
Softball Hall of Fame: 88
South River Meeting House: 122
Southwest Virginia Museum: 246
space technology: 167–168
spelunking clubs: 36–37; *see also* caves/caving
sports: Carter Barron Amphitheatre 374; Charlottesville 110; Jack Kent Cooke Stadium 374; James Madison University 279; Klockner Stadium 110; MCI Center 374; Norfolk 178; Richmond 84–85; Robert F. Kennedy Memorial Stadium 374; Virginia International Raceway 132; Virginia Sports Hall of Fame & Museum 181; Virginia Tech 229; Washington, D.C. 374; *see also* specific sports; teams
Spotted Tavern Winery and Dodd's Cider Mill: 332
Spring Arts and Crafts Show and Sale: 279
Spring Fly-In: 258
Stabler-Leadbeater Apothecary: 319
stalacpipe organ: 267
stalactites: 267
stalagmites: 247, 249
Starvation Ball: 92
State Fairgrounds at Strawberry Hill: 83
State Fair of Virginia: 86
statistics: 26–27
Statler Brothers Complex: 284
Staunton: 281–287
Staunton-Augusta Art Center: 286
Staunton Music Festival: 286

St. Francis of Assisi Catholic Church: 284
St. George's Episcopal Church: 97
stinging insects: 55
St. James Episcopal Church: 203
St. John's Church: 168
St. John's Episcopal Church: 75
Stone Mountain Vineyards: 81
Stonewall Brigade Band: 286
Stonewall Jackson Cemetery: 295
Stonewall Jackson House: 295
Stonewall Jackson's Headquarters: 256
Stonewall Jackson Shrine: 101–102
Stonewall Vineyards & Winery: 81
Stony Man Nature Trail: 273
St. Paul's Episcopal Church: 173–174
Strasburg: 264
Stratford Hall Plantation: 137–138
Strawberry Festival: 224
Strawberry Hill Fairgrounds: 85
Strawberry Hill Races: 86
Stuart, J.E.B.: 66, 69
student travel: 57
Studio Theatre: 373–374
subway: *see* Metrorail
Suffolk Peanut Fest: 92
Summer Breeze Jazz Concert: 179
Summer Feast: 279
Summer Festival: 118
surfing: 35, 192
Swedenburg Estate Vineyard: 332
symphony orchestras/classical music: Birchmere Music Hall 323; Charlottesville and University Symphony Orchestra 110; Garth Newel Music Center 291–292; Lynchburg Symphony Orchestra 124; McIntire Department of Music 110; National Symphony Orchestra 372–373; Richmond Symphony 83; Roanoke Symphony Orchestra 222; Stonewall Brigade Band 286; Virginia Beach Symphony Orchestra 193; Virginia Symphony 178

T

Tackiest Christmas Decorations Tour: 86
Tangier Island: 209–212
Tarara Vineyard & Winery: 332
Taste of the Blue Ridge Blues & Jazz Festival: 224
Tavern, The: 240–241
taxes: 44
taxis: *see specific place*
Tazewell: 242–247

M

Index

Trails

Appalachian Trail: 235, 270–271
Bluebell Nature Loop: 330
Boardwalk Trail: 182
Bull Run-Occoquan Trail: 330
Chessie Nature Trail: 299
Civil War Trails: 41
Crabtree Falls: 304
Limberlost Trail: 273
Mill Prong Trail: 273
Mt. Vernon Trail: 316, 324
Potomac Appalachian Trail Club: 30
Potomac Heritage Trail: 316
Rails-to-Trails Conservancy: 30
Riprap Hollow Trail: 273
Stony Man Nature Trail: 273
Traces Nature Trail: 273
Virginia Creeper National Recreation Trail: 235, 241
Washington & Old Dominion Trail: 316

temperature: 5–6
terminology: 163
Theater-in-the-Woods: 328
theaters: Arena Stage 373; Barter Theatre 238, 241; Blackfriars Playhouse 286; Blue Ridge Theatre 279; Byrd Theater 83; Carpenter Center for the Performing Arts 83; Empire Theater, The 83; Folger Elizabethan Theatre 373; Ford's Theatre National Historic Site 361; Heritage Repertory Theatre 110; Jefferson Theater 110; June Tolliver Playhouse 245; Lime Kiln Theater 299; Little Theater of Virginia Beach 193; Mill Mountain Theater 218; Millward Theatre 231; National Theatre 373; Renaissance Theatre Festival and Virginia Western Theatre 223; Richmond's Landmark Theater 83; Shakespeare Theatre 373; Shenandoah Summer Music Festival 257; Showtimers 223; Studio Theatre 373–374; Theater-in-the-Woods 328; Theatre-Virginia 83; Vineyard Hill Theater 110; Virginia Stage Company 178; Wayside Theater 260; Woolly Mammoth Theatre 373
TheatreVirginia: 83
Theodore Roosevelt Island: 312, 354–355
Thomas J. Boyd Museum: 231
Thomas Jefferson Tomatoe Faire: 124
Three Ridges Wilderness: 304

Tidal Basin: 353
time zones: 58
tipping: 58–59
tobacco: 74, 119, 125, 132–133
Tobacco Row: 74
Tomahawk Mill Winery: 81, 221
Tomb of the Unknown Dead of the Civil War: 310
Tomb of the Unknowns: 310
Torpedo Factory Arts Center: 319
To The Rescue Museum: 219
Tour de Chesapeake: 31
Tour DuPont: 86
tourism information: 56
tours: *see specific place*
Town Point Jazz and Blues Festival: 43, 179
Town Point Virginia Wine Festival: 179
Traces Nature Trail: 273
Traditional Small Boat Show: 139
train travel: 54; *see also specific place*
transportation: general discussion 51–55; air 54, 55; bus 53; car 51–53; hazards 52; insurance 53; rentals 52–53; train 54; *see also specific place*
travelers: disabled 57; gay and lesbian 57; seniors 58; students 57; with children 58
travel insurance: 53, 58
trolleys: 99, 181
Turner Sculpture: 203
Tye River Gap: 304

U
Union Station: 356
United Rappahannock: 11
United States Holocaust Memorial Museum: 355–356
University of Richmond: 85
University of Virginia: 104–105; sports (Cavaliers) 110
Urbanna: 140–141
urban sprawl: 314–315
U.S. Army Transportation Museum: 165
U.S. Botanic Garden: 358
U.S. Capitol: 356
U.S. Marine Corps War Memorial: 312
U.S. National Arboretum: 366
U.S. Supreme Court: 357–358

V
Valentine Museum, The: 68
Victory Monument: 158
Vietnam Women's Memorial: 347

Villa Appalaccia: 221
Vineyard Hill Theater: 110
Vinton Old-Time Bluegrass Festival and Competition: 224
Virginia: 20
Virginia Air and Space Center: 167–168
Virginia Aviation Museum: 76
Virginia Ballet Theatre: 178
Virginia Beach: 183–196
Virginia Beach Amphitheater: 193
Virginia Beach Ballet: 193
Virginia Beach Saltwater Fishing Tournament: 194
Virginia Beach Symphony Orchestra: 193
Virginia Cantaloupe Festival: 133
Virginia Children's Festival and Halloween Spooktacular: 179
Virginia Coast Reserve: 201
Virginia Commonwealth University: 64, 85
Virginia Conservation Network: 7
Virginia Creeper National Recreation Trail: 235, 241
Virginia Cycling Association: 31
Virginia Department of Conservation and Recreation: 7, 29
Virginia Department of Environmental Quality: 7
Virginia Department of Game and Inland Fisheries: 36, 37
Virginia Discovery Museum: 105
Virginia Film Festival: 111–112
Virginia Garlic Festival: 118
Virginia Gold Cup Races: 340
Virginia Highlands Festival: 241–242
Virginia Highlands Horse Trail: 235
Virginia Historical Society Center for Virginia History: 73
Virginia Holocaust Museum: 75
Virginia Horse Center: 297
Virginia Horse Council: 33
Virginia Horse Festival: 300
Virginia Horse Trials: 297
Virginia Hunt Country Stable Tour: 339
Virginia Indian Heritage Festival: 11, 156
Virginia International Raceway: 132
Virginia Living Museum: 163, 165
Virginia Marine Science Museum: 183, 185, 192
Virginia Metalcrafters: 287
Virginia Military Institute: 295
Virginia Mountain Peach Festival: 224
Virginia Museum of Fine Arts: 73
Virginia Museum of Transportation: 218–219

Virginia Natural Heritage Program: 6–7
Virginia Opera (Norfolk): 178
Virginia Opera (Richmond): 83
Virginia Peanut Festival: 92
Virginia Pork Festival: 92
Virginia Quilt Museum: 276
Virginia Safari Park: 302
Virginia Scottish Games: 324
Virginia's Explore Park: 219
Virginia Sports Hall of Fame & Museum: 181
Virginia Stage Company: 178
Virginia State Capitol: 68
Virginia State Championship Chili Cook-Off: 224
Virginia Statute of Religious Freedom: 93
Virginia Steeplechase Association: 34
Virginia Symphony: 178
Virginia Tech: 227–228; sports 229
Virginia Union University: 62
Virginia War Museum: 165
Virginia Waterfront International Arts Festival: 179, 194
Virginia Wine and Mushroom Festival: 263
Virginia Wine Festival: 340
Virginia Zoological Park: 174
Viva Elvis Festival: 194
Volunteer Fireman's Carnival: 201

W

Wachapreague: 201
walking tours: Appomattox Court House Town 128; Ball's Bluff Regional Park 336; Big Stone Gap 246; Charlottesville 111; Fredericksburg 98–99; Jamestown Island 157; Leesburg 333; Lexington 299; Mount Vernon 341; New Market Battlefield Historic Park 266; Old Town Alexandria 323; Portsmouth 181; Staunton 286
Walton's Mountain Museum: 118
Warm Springs: 290–292
Warm Springs Gallery: 291
Warren County Fair: 263
Warren Rifles Confederate Museum: 261–262
Washington & Lee University: 293–295
Washington & Old Dominion Trail: 316
Washington, Booker T.: 129–130
Washington Capitals: 374
Washington County Courthouse: 238
Washington County Fair and Burley Tobacco Festival: 242
Washington. D.C.: 344–376; accommodations 366–370; entertainment 372–374; food

Wineries

Index

general discussion: 49–50
Abingdon Vineyard & Winery: 221
Afton Mountain Vineyards: 80
Amrhein's Wine Cellar: 221
Autumn Hill Vineyards/Blue Ridge Winery: 80
Barboursville Vineyards and Historic Ruins: 80, 112
Breaux Vineyards: 332
Burnley Vineyards & Daniel Cellars: 80
Chateau Morrisette: 221
Chrysalis Vineyards: 332
Cooper Vineyards: 80
Deer Meadow Vineyard: 267
Dominion Wine Cellars: 80
Dye's Vineyard: 221
Farfelu Vineyard: 332
Glenway Winery: 332
Grayhaven Winery: 80
Grey Ghost Vineyards: 332
Guilford Ridge Vineyard: 267
Hartwood Winery: 332
Hill Top Berry Farm & Winery: 80
Horton Cellars Winery/Montdomaine Cellars: 80
Ingleside Plantation Vineyards: 144
Jefferson Vineyards: 80
Klugs Estate Winery and Vineyard, The: 80
Lake Anna Winery: 80
Landwirt Vineyard: 267
Linden Vineyards: 332
Loudoun Valley Vineyard: 332

Misty Mountain Vineyards & Winery: 80
Mountain Cove Vineyards and Winegarden: 80
Naked Mountain Vineyard: 332
North Mountain Vineyard & Winery: 267
Oakencroft Vineyard & Winery: 80
Oasis Winery, The: 332
Peaks of Otter Winery: 267
Piedmont Vineyards: 332
Prince Michel & Rapidan River Vineyards: 80
Rebec Vineyards: 80, 118
Rockbridge Vineyard: 80, 267
Rose Bower Vineyard & Winery: 81
Rose River Vineyards & Trout Farm: 81
Shaddwell-Windham Winery: 332
Sharp Rock Vineyards: 81
Shenandoah Vineyards: 267
Smokehouse Winery: 81
Spotted Tavern Winery and Dodd's Cider Mill: 332
Stone Mountain Vineyards: 81
Stonewall Vineyards & Winery: 81
Swedenburg Estate Vineyard: 332
Tarara Vineyard & Winery: 332
Tomahawk Mill Winery: 81, 221
Villa Appalaccia: 221
White Hall Wineyards: 81
Williamsburg Winery, Ltd.: 144
Willowcroft Farm: 332
Windy River Winery: 144
Wintergreen Winery: 81

370–372; history 344–345; Mall 346–347, 348–352; Metrorail 348–349; sights 353–366; transportation 375–376
Washington-Dulles International Airport: 308, 375
Washington, George: 14, 90, 99–100, 157–158, 182, 256, 301, 309, 320, 327, 340–342, 344, 364
Washington Harbor: 364
Washington Monument: 347, 350
Washington Mystics: 374
Washington National Airport: 308, 375
Washington National Cathedral: 363
Washington Opera: 373
Washington Redskins: 374
Washington Wizards: 374

Water Country USA: 155
waterfalls: Cedar Run Falls 273; Great Falls 327; South River Falls 273; Wigwam Falls 304
Waterford: 337
Waterman's Festival and Blessing of the Fleet: 139
Watermen's Museum: 158
Waterside Festival Marketplace: 179
Wayne C. Henderson Music
Waynesboro: 287
Wayside Theater: 260
websites: *seespecific place*
Wedding Cake House: 130
Westmoreland Berry Farm and Orchard: 138
Westmoreland State Park: 137
Westover Plantation: 161

whale-watching: 169
Whetstone Ridge Ranger Station: 304
White Hall Wineyards: 81
White House and Museum of the Confederacy: 64, 66
White House, The: 358
White Oak Canyon Trail: 273
White Post: 259–260
White Rocks Recreation Area: 231
White's Ferry: 336
White's Mill: 238
Whitetop Mountain Maple Festival: 235
wildlife sculptures: 203
wild ponies: 208–209
William and Mary Hall: 153
William King Regional Art Center: 238
Williamsburg Pottery Factory: 153–154
Williamsburg Scottish Festival and Celtic Celebration: 154
Williamsburg Winery, Ltd.: 144
Willoughby-Baylor House: 175
Willowcroft Farm: 332
Wilson, Woodrow: 23
Winchester: 254–261
Windy River Winery: 144
wine: see specific place; wineries
Winmill Carriage Collection: 336
Wintergreen Resort: 118–119
Wintergreen Winery: 81
Winthrop Rockefeller Archeology Museum: 149
Wolf Trap Farm Park: 328
Wolf Trap Opera Company: 328
Wolstenholme Towne: 149

Women in Military Service for America Memorial: 309
Woodlawn Mansion: 342
Woodlawn Plantation: 342
Woodley Park: 362
Woodrow Wilson Birthplace and Museum: 282, 284
Woods Creek Park: 299
Woolly Mammoth Theatre: 373
World's Largest Apple: 256
World Striped Bass Championships: 194
World War II and Korean War Memorial: 74
Wren Building: 148
Wren, Christopher: 148
Wytheville: 231–232

X, Y, Z
X-Crab-A-Ganza: 170
Yankee Horse: 304
Yogaville: 128
York River State Park: 154
Yorktown: 157–159
Yorktown Victory Center: 158–159
Yorktown Visitors Center: 157–158
zoos: Island Aquarium 204; Leesburg Animal Park 333; Luray Reptile Center, Dinosaur Park and Petting Zoo 267; Metro Richmond Zoo 87; Mill Mountain Zoo 219; National Aquarium 360; National Zoological Park 363; Natural Bridge Zoo 302; Peninsula SPCA Petting Zoo 165; Virginia Living Museum 163, 165; Virginia Safari Park 302; Virginia Zoological Park 174

MOON HANDBOOKS provide comprehensive

coverage of a region's arts, history, land, people, and social issues in addition to detailed practical listings for accommodations, food, outdoor recreation, and entertainment. Moon Handbooks allow complete immersion in a region's culture—ideal for travelers who want to combine sightseeing with insight for an extraordinary travel experience in destinations throughout North America, Hawaii, Latin America, the Caribbean, Asia, and the Pacific.

WWW.MOON.COM

Rick Steves shows you where to travel and how to travel— all while getting the most value for your dollar. His Back Door travel philosophy is about making friends, having fun, and avoiding tourist rip-offs.

Rick has been traveling to Europe for more than 25 years and is the author of 22 guidebooks, which have sold more than a million copies. He also hosts the award-winning public television series *Rick Steves' Europe*.

WWW.RICKSTEVES.COM

ROAD TRIP USA

Getting there is half the fun, and Road Trip USA guides are your ticket to driving adventure. Taking you off the interstates and onto less-traveled, two-lane highways, each guide is filled with fascinating trivia, historical information, photographs, facts about regional writers, and details on where to sleep and eat— all contributing to your exploration of the American road.

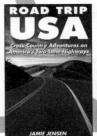

"[Books] so full of the pleasures of the American road, you can smell the upholstery."
>BBC radio

WWW.ROADTRIPUSA.COM

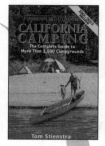